John Bannister

A Glossary of Cornish Names

John Bannister

A Glossary of Cornish Names

ISBN/EAN: 9783337296162

Printed in Europe, USA, Canada, Australia, Japan

Cover: Foto ©Thomas Meinert / pixelio.de

More available books at **www.hansebooks.com**

A

¡LOSSARY OF CORNISH NAMES,

ANCIENT AND MODERN, LOCAL, FAMILY, PERSONAL, &c.:

0,000 CELTIC AND OTHER NAMES,

NOW OR FORMERLY IN USE IN

CORNWALL:

With derivations and significations, for the most part conjectural, suggestive and tentative of many, and lists of unexplained names about which information is solicited.

BY THE

REV. JOHN BANNISTER, LL.D., VICAR OF ST. DAY.

———◆———

"Si quid novisti rectius istis
Candidus imperti ; si non, his utere mecum."

———◆———

WILLIAMS & NORGATE,

14, Henrietta Street, Covent Garden, London; and 20, South Frederick Street,
Edinburgh;

J. R. NETHERTON, 7, Lemon Street, Truro.

Price in Cloth, Twelve Shillings.

NETHERTON, PRINTER, TRURO.

Entered at Stationers' Hall.

TO

AUGUSTUS SMITH, ESQ.,

OF TRESCO ABBEY, ISLES OF SCILLY,

R.W.G. MASTER OF

THE PROVINCIAL GRAND LODGE

OF

ANCIENT, FREE, AND ACCEPTED MASONS

OF

CORNWALL,

This attempt to illustrate the Nomenclature of the

"FIRST, LAST, AND BEST COUNTY IN ENGLAND,"

and to shew how much of the old and but recently extinct Vernacular is still
preserved in

ITS LOCAL NAMES,

Those of Towns, Villages, Hamlets, Hundreds, Parishes, Manors, Estates, Farms,
Tenements, Fields, Moors, Mines, Hills, Headlands, Rocks, Rivers, Streams,
Coves, Camps, Tinbounds, Fishermen's-marks, &c. ;

ITS FAMILY NAMES,

Both ancient and modern, native and foreign, territorial, local and official,
patronymics, sobriquets, &c. ;

AND PERSONAL NAMES,

Those found on the ancient Inscribed Stones of the County ; the Patron Saints of the
several Parishes and extinct Chapelries ; manumitted Celtic Serfs in the
Bodmin Gospels, their Saxon Manumitters and Witnesses ;
Tenants in Domesday, &c., &c.;

by giving
the various meanings that have been assigned to many of these, and the authorities
for the same ; conjectural derivations and tentative renderings of
others ; lists of unexplained names, &c., &c. ;

A WORK OF MANY YEARS LABOUR,

BUT A LABOUR OF LOVE,

IS BY PERMISSION DEDICATED BY HIS OBEDIENT AND OBLIGED SERVANT AND BROTHER,

JOHN BANNISTER, P.M. Tregullow, 1006,
P.P.G. CHAPLAIN OF CORNWALL.

Vicarage, St. Day, Cornwall, Feb. 25, 1871.

IN PREPARATION,

Introductory and Supplementary to

The Glossary of Cornish Names,

By the same Author,

THE

NOMENCLATURE OF CORNWALL:

IN WHICH WILL BE GIVEN

ADDITIONS TO, AND CORRECTIONS OF, MISTAKES AND MISFITS IN

THE GLOSSARY.

———

Hints and Helps Solicited.

PREFACE.

THE close of the 18th century witnessed the final extinction, as a spoken language, of the old Celtic vernacular of Cornwall. Dolly Pentreath, who died in 1788, has had the credit of being the last person who could talk and scold in this tongue; but William Bodenner, who died about the year 1794, at a very advanced age (102, the same as Dolly Pentreath's), could "converse with old Dolly," and "talked with her for hours together in Cornish"; so says the historian, Polwhele [*]; and further he says [†] of Tomson, "a native of Truro, an engineer or maker of engines for the use of mines," who, as well as he knew, might be alive when he wrote, "he knows more, I believe, of the Cornish language than the old lady, whom he celebrated, ever knew." "I met him at Plymouth Dock" (now Devonport) "in 1789; the old man, hearing my name announced, saluted me instantly with the motto of my family," *Karenza whelas karenza,* love worketh love.

The only known literary remains of the old language are very meagre. They are the following [‡]: "Mount Calvary," a poem of little more than 2000 lines, of the 15th century; five miracle plays (*Guaremirs*) or dramas—three, "The Origin of the World," "The Passion of our Lord Jesus Christ," and "The Resurrection, with the Death of Pilate," of about the same date—one dated 1611, "The Creation of the World, with Noah's Flood,"—and another dated 1504, "The Life of St. Mereadocus, Bishop and Confessor," discovered in 1869, by Mr. Wynne, among his manuscripts in the Peniarth library; a Vocabulary of the language as it was spoken about the 10th or 11th century [‖]; another Vocabulary, [§] with the corresponding Welsh, Armoric and Irish words, collected by the learned Edward Lhuyd, at the beginning of the last century, when the language was fast dying out; a Grammar by the same with a Preface in Cornish, of the language as it was spoken in his day; he also gives us an old "Tale"; and, "An Elegy on the death of William the Third," of his own composing. There are also two or three versions of the first chapter of Genesis, the Creed, the

---

[*] "Language, Literature, and Literary Characters of Cornwall," p. 19.   [†] ib., p. 43.
[‡] "The Ancient Cornish Drama, edited and translated by Mr. Edwin Norris," v. 2, p. 437; Preface to "Lexicon Cornu-Britannicum, a Dictionary of the ancient Celtic language of Cornwall, in which the words are elucidated by copious examples from the Cornish works now remaining, with translations in English, and synonyms from the cognate dialects of Welsh, Armoric, Gaelic, and Manx," by the Rev. R. Williams, of Rhydycroesau; "Chips from a German Workshop," by Professor Max Müller, v. 3, p. 268.
[‖] "Vocabularium Latino-Cambricum," British Museum, Bibl. Cotton., Vespasian. A 14. printed as it is written, by Zeuss in his "Grammatica Celtica," p. 1100; and by Mr. Norris arranged alphabetically, &c., in his "Drama," v. 2, p. 319.
[§] "A comparative Vocabulary of the Original Languages of Britain and Ireland," Title II of his Archæologia. In Title I, "Comparative Etymology," there are also long lists of Cornish words.

Lord's Prayer, and the Ten Commandments; * a pastoral song; another on the curing of pilchards; many proverbs, wise saws, and riddles; some colloquies and colloquial phrases; a few mottoes on the coats of arms of the old families, and epitaphs; a letter written in 1776 by William Bodenner; and a few other small trifles.†

But though these are the only known literary remains, they are not the only remnants of the old tongue. Scawen, writing about two centuries ago, says, "The Cornish tongue hath mostly resided for some ages past in the names of the people, the gentry chiefly (?), and in the names of places observed to be significant mostly as to the site &c., or for something eminent about them."‡ The discovery of a meaning of these names in the old language, which would fit the places, has long been a favourite pursuit with the antiquary; Camden in his Britannia, Carew in his Survey, Norden in his Speculum, (i.e. Mirror), Scawen in his Dissertation, Hals, Tonkin, Polwhele, Hitchin and Drew, Davies Gilbert, Sir John Maclean, and others, in their Parochial and Family Histories, Baxter in his Glossarium, Lhuyd and Pryce in their Archæologia, Borlase in his Antiquities and Natural History, Whitaker in his Cathedral, Blight, Murray, Black, Besley, &c., in their Guides or Handbooks, and many others in various works and papers on the peculiarities of the county, have thus given translations of many hundreds of these names, some good, some bad; some right, but perhaps more wrong.

The first aim of the compiler of the following work was to collect together as many as possible of the names which had thus been translated. He then saw that the analogy of these, assistance that he might expect ‖ from various parts of the County, a knowledge of the old language, and some acquaintance with its kindred dialects would enable him to give fair and reasonable explanations of many other names. He proceeded to collect these names from the histories, gazeteers, and directories of the county; from old deeds and other documents; from maps § and plans; from newspapers

* To be found at the end of Davies Gilbert's "Mount Calvary" and "Creation," and of Williams's Lexicon.

† Most of these minor pieces may be seen at the end of Pryce's "Archæologia"; Davies Gilbert "Mount Calvary," &c.; and in the Journal of the Royal Institution of Cornwall, No 5, p. 7. Among others Mr. Davies Gilbert gives "A protestation of the Bishops in Britain to Augustine the monk, the Pope's legate in the year 600 after Christ" ! a piece of not twenty words. Bodenner's letter is given in "Archæologia," v. 5, p. 83, and an extract in Mr Sandys' "Specimens of Cornish Provincial Dialect." Boson's song on the curing of pilchards is in the Journal R.I.C., No 5. p. 14. Mr. Williams gives a corrected version of the Creed, Lord's Prayer, Ten Commandments, and First Chapter of Genesis at the end of his Lexicon. He is also preparing for publication the "Life of St. Mereadocus."

‡ Davies Gilbert's "Parochial History," v. 4, p. 209.

‖ That the compiler was right in his expectations, the list of authorities, references, abbreviations, &c., p. 207, will prove; and he desires to express his best thanks, not only to those whose names are there given, but also to the many others who have rendered him assistance, some of whom have desired that their names might not be published, and as a consequence, when he has agreed with their views, he has not distinguished their renderings from his own, except it may be by the omission of a †, the mark of uncertainty. Among his helpers he can reckon dignitaries of the church, and members of both houses of parliament, learned professors at the universities. parsons, and methodist preachers, both rounders and local; doctors and lawyers, and land surveyors; officers of the army and navy, and members of the society of friends; national schoolmasters. and registrars of births and deaths; mine agents and miners; master mariners and fishermen. The following notice of the Glossary in the Western Daily Mercury, almost too flattering to be republished by the compiler, shews well how these and others can help. "To criticise adequately such a work as this would demand an acquaintance with its subject-matter as great as Dr. Bannister himself possesses, and to this not even the omniscience of a journalist would pretend. But to make suggestions as to the correct rendering of special words is within the province of any native of the district, and we can hardly recommend Cornishmen with a little leisure a more graceful employment, than thus helping Dr. Bannister in his illustration of their county's history." By such help, in some cases, crude guesses at the meaning of the names have been turned into correct renderings.

§ More especially Martyns', 1748, &c. In these, and the Index he published, which was afterwards republished by the late Rev. W. Wallis of Bodmin, the names are most accurately spelt; and a reference to these will generally shew in what parish in the county the more important places, the names of which are given in the Glossary, are found.

and bills of sale; and lastly from the Tithe Apportionments of the several parishes. These last have proved a most prolific source, but at the same time a very puzzling one. Here, in many parishes, every field has its distinctive name; and, more particularly in the western parts of the county, many of these are decidedly Celtic; some so correctly spelt that it can{at once be said what the derivation is (*i.e.* what words enter into their composition), and what is the plain meaning of the names. But in a far greater number of cases it requires a familiarity with the general Celtic nomenclature of the county to enable one to see in the badly spelt name, resemblance to any known words; and often they have been so distorted from the fair, simple, rational meaning that they bore in the Celtic, that they appear to be common English names with a frivolous, foolish, absurd meaning. In giving these and other names in his Glossary, the compiler has not attempted to correct the spelling,* so as to make the meaning he supposes the names ought to bear more evident. In every case, as often as seemed necessary, he has given in *italics* (*within parenthesis*) the Celtic words, generally in their primary form, which he supposes have entered into the composition of the name. Very often, in consequence of the grammatical laws of initial mutation,† common to all Celtic languages, and still oftener, from there being no fixed orthography for the Cornish branch, and the utter ignorance of the language by the surveyors, who wrote down the names of the fields, and the labourers and farmers who told them the names,‖ names that perhaps had never been written or spelt before, there may seem to be little resemblance between the supposed roots and the name; and hence it has often been said, by a little manipulation you can make a name mean anything you like: vowels go for nothing, and the consonants † may be changed for any other. But this is not the case; as, notwithstanding a great amount of latitude that is allowed, there are certain fixed canons, which must be attended to, and which limit the range of conjecture.

What has just been said with regard to field names, given in comparatively recent times, and which, to those who gave the fields the names by which they are called in the Tithe Apportionments, were scarcely proper names at all, but common appelatives, descriptive, in their vernacular, of "their scite on high or low ground, their relative situations," ‡ their shape, particular trees growing in them, their produce—wheat, barley, &c., or derived from the animals feeding in them, or birds frequenting them, some event that happened in them, or some former owner or occupier, is true of other names. Those who first wrote them down were probably ignorant of the language in which they were significant; and those who pronounced the names commonly had no idea of their etymology,‖ and could neither write nor spell; so that the scribes had to

---

* It is possible that the spelling, though bad, may lead another to a better derivation and meaning than the compiler has been able to discover.

† In all languages letters of the same organs are liable to be mutually interchanged, often according to the caprice of individual pronunciation; but in the Celtic languages this is done by fixed grammatical rule, *e.g. tre*, a dwelling, becomes in certain cases *dre, drea*, but could not become, as Dr Charnock in the preface to his Patronymica Cornu-Britannica, p. xii, says it does, *fra, fre, free, frea*, &c.; *d* is a dental, *f* a labial, and they are not thus interchanged; but *b* in *brea, bre*, a hill, is a labial, and therefore this word assumes these latter forms in certain cases when entering into the composition of proper names.

‡ Polwhele's "History of Cornwall," vol 1, p. 166.

‖ Tonkin, writing to Gwavas, 1736, a sort of dedication to his Cornish Vocabulary, the manuscript of which came into Dr. Pryce's hands, and, as he acknowledges, was largely used by him, says, "I may add too, that very few of those who speak the language, can give any tolerable account of the orthography, much less of the etymology or derivation of those words which they make use of, and are many times apt to write and spell according to their several ideas of propriety, or individual fancy or caprice, as well as they could catch the names from their ignorant informers, who also might differ among themselves in their pronunciation of the same names or words, thus introducing another element of discord and difficulty.

Some may say, such being the case, where is the good of attempting to recover the meaning of a host of "uncouth," "barbarous " * names of places, &c., of which very few persons ever heard, and still fewer care. With much to encourage him in his long and arduous task, the compiler has had many discouragements; and his endeavours have been spoken of as hopeless and useless. He himself thinks otherwise. Within the last one hundred years, a language or dialect believed by some once "to have been spoken throughout the central and southern divisions of England by the original in-habitants,"† has died a natural death, and every effort ought to be made to preserve what little remains of it. Even with regard to proper names, permanent as they may seem, they are liable to be changed or lost. Within two miles of the place where this is written are villages now known as Higher and Lower Cusgarne. Not a hundred years ago they were Cusgarne Wartha and Wollas; the meaning of *Wartha* and *Wollas* is now unknown to everyone in the two villages. In the same way, many of the field-names in the Tithe Apportionments, made forty years ago, have been changed; though in some cases the English name, substituted for the old Celtic one, has much the same signification as the latter, the tenant having been guided by the same peculiarities of the field as his predecessor; but ask him about the field by its old name, and he will not know which it is. Hence the importance of at once collecting together these old names, while some of those still live who made the surveys for the Tithe Apportion-ments, or who gave these persons the names they entered on their plans, &c.

In the opinion of the compiler, old personal names, the names of individuals,

---

jumble two or three words together, making but one of them all, tho' they pronounce them rightly enough. Of this you were pleased to give me lately some instances, as in *merastadu*, which they thus pronounce in one breath, as if it had been one word, whereas it is a contraction of four, *meor 'ras tha Dew*, much thanks to God, and anciently written, *maur gras tha Deu* ; and *merastawhy*, much thanks to you, a contraction of *meor 'ras tha why.*"—*Cambrian Journal*, 1861, to which it was sent by Prince Louis Lucien Bonaparte, in proof of Dr. Pryce's plagiarism.

* The compiler has heard these terms applied to the old names, by Cornishmen, who preferred the "more euphonious" (?) English names. But what can be more melodious than the following string of names put into a sort of song, nonsense verse, though every name is significant, by old Mr. Le Grice, copied as here given, excepting the punctuation, from a very old manuscript :—

" Karn e quiden, pol pen henna ;	Praes an bygle, vellan vrane.
Wheal eu druckia, barle wenna ;	Pous a nooth, bos traze, tre tane.
Treg a varnh ; treeu, chi kembra,	Amal veer, drul as, tre neere.
Tol peden penwith, pen drea hendra,	Skil e wadden, boughe heere.
Karn kie nudjack ; garle diunin,	Peden a vounder ; gwills, carn jue
Mene darva ; vellan hoggan,	Tre reef, pedn pons, gnon gumpas, treu.
Morther uny, tre ga minion ;	Pedn a venton, treu je venn,
Amal veor ; pol goon, Bos ahau ;	Chi un, carne gwavas, usk a jean.
Trego nebris ; begil tuhan,	Em la, chi pons : gwal an crane
Hally widden ; wal crous woola ;	Pous an dain ; tren gwainton carne.
Tre In warren : park in skeba,	Drin. be jowa ; crouse en vra
Clies, tre gerthen ; ambe juah,	Kille ankar, boen, trem bah."

Professor Max Müller speaking of the language says ("Chips," v. 3, p. 257), "It seems to have been a melodious and yet by no means an effeminate language, and Scawen places it in this respect above most of the other Celtic dialects :—' Cornish,' he says, ' is not to be gutturally pronounced, as the Welsh for the most part is, nor mutteringly, as the Armorick, nor whiningly, as the Irish (which two latter qualities seem to have been contracted from their servitude), but must be lively and manly spoken, like other primitive tongues '."

† Advertisement of a "Gerlevar Cernewac," i.e Cornish Word-Book, in 1842, by the Rev. Robert Williams of Rhydycroesau, which he published or rather completed, having previously published part, in 1865, as the "Lexicon Cornu-Britannicum" ; see p. v, Note ‡.

enter largely into the composition of Cornish local names. In all ages and countries, persons have been in the habit of calling their lands and their houses after their own names, or others have so called them. There are not many ancient purely Cornish personal names extant as such, but there are very many Welsh, Armoric, and Gaelic ones. The reason of the difference is plain; while these languages have very ancient records, poems, legends, histories,* &c., there are no very ancient Cornish writings, no ancient history of Cornwall, and not many references to it in the histories of other countries. In Domesday Survey we have the names of tenants, both in the Conqueror's own time, and in the time of Edward the Confessor; but nearly all these are plainly Teutonic, and, with a recognized meaning in the Anglo-Saxon tongue, which will be generally found given in the following pages; and these names, Teutonic though they are, very often are found suffixed to the Celtic Tre-, Ros-, Pol-, Lan-, Caer-, and Pen-, as well as prefixed to the Teuton -ford, -ley, -ham, and -ton, in names of places in Cornwall. Older than Domesday are the records of manumissions in the Bodmin Gospels.† In these, while the manumitters and witnesses bore for the most part Teutonic names of the same character as those in Domesday, and used in like manner, many of the serfs manumitted have names, so peculiar, that they are at once seen to have their origin from another, and altogether different, language. Some of these are very similar to those found in the genuine ancient Welsh genealogies and other writings, and they are, without any doubt, pure Celtic, though badly spelt by Anglo-Saxon scribes. But while there are a few here, that may be possibly thus identified, very numerous are the instances in which the suffixes in local names are the same, or nearly the same, as those old Welsh and other Celtic personal names; and the compiler has not hesitated to use them in explaining the Cornish names of places. Many of the ancient inscribed stones of the county also bear similar names; and the saints, whose names enter into the composition of the names of parishes, have names closely resembling those found in Wales, Brittany, and Ireland. What the meaning of many of these is, the compiler cannot say; others may be able to suggest a meaning, and so trace out remnants of the language that have escaped him. Doubtless many of these names are not indigenous, but adopted, with certain variations, from the nomenclature of other people, introduced by foreign merchants and immigrants, Christian missionaries, or Roman and other conquerors; but where they are indigenous, taking their rise in the land, given by the people themselves from their native language, they will commonly be found significant in the vernacular, as the others are in the tongues whence they are derived.

* Contrast the meagre remains of Cornish literature, enumerated on page v., with the account Mr. M. Arnold gives in his essays "On the study of Celtic literature," in the "Cornhill Magazine" for 1866.— The Myrvyrian manuscripts (Welsh) in the British Museum amount to 47 volumes of poetry, containing 4,700 pieces, in 1,600 pages, besides 2,000 Englynion, or epigrammatic stanzas; and 53 volumes of prose, in about 15,300 pages. In the library of Trinity College, Dublin, and in that of the Irish Academy, there is, according to Professor O'Curry, even a greater number of Irish manuscripts. There are the Book of the Dun Cow, the Book of Leinster, the Book of Ballymote, the Speckled Book, the Book of Lenin, &c., &c. The Annals of the Four Masters give the years of the foundations and destructions of churches and castles, the obituaries of remarkable personages, the inaugurations of kings, the battles of chiefs, the contests of clans, the ages of bards, abbots, bishops, &c. There are books of pedigrees and genealogies, martyrologies, and festologies, and topographical tracts, in which we touch the most ancient traditions, traditions which were committed to writing, when the ancient customs of the people were unbroken. We get the origin and history of the countless monuments of Ireland, of the ruined church and tower, the sculptured cross, the holy well, and the commemorative name of almost every townland and parish in the whole island. Such materials are invaluable in the study of nomenclature, and they have been made good use of by Mr Joyce in his excellent work on "The Origin and History of Irish Names of Places." Such helps, alas! are altogether wanting in Cornwall.
† See *B.m.* on page 207.

A greater variety of family names or surnames exists in Cornwall than in any other county; for, in addition to the common ones found in all parts of England, especially patronymics, there are many names that are peculiarly Cornish. Some of these are the Celtic equivalents of common English ones, which are found in Cornwall side by side with them, and are derived from that infinite variety of sources that have given rise to surnames, such as trade, occupation, rank, profession. natural temperament, bodily peculiarity, animals, birds, trees, &c. But others, and these more easily recognized as Cornish, are the local names beginning with the well-known prefixes "Tre, Ros, Pol, Lan, Caer, and Pen," by which, as Camden says, "You may know the *most* Cornish men." Not that persons bearing such family names are the most numerous in Cornwall, they are far outnumbered by those who have simple patronymics; but these are the most distinctly and peculiarly Cornish names; and persons bearing such names, wherever found, may, as a rule, but not without many exceptions, be considered as from Cornwall, *i.e.*, taking their name from some place in Cornwall, whether their ancestors, who first had the name, were originally Cornish, or only Anglo-Saxon, Norman, or other settlers, connected with the place whence the name was taken, by ownership or otherwise. Many however of these local family names have been so altered, through ignorance, or caprice in spelling, that one cannot say positively, in the absence of documentary evidence, whence they were originally derived, and they may be referred to several places as their possible source.

In conclusion, the compiler would apologize for the many irregularities and inaccuracies, mistakes and misfits that he knows exist in the Glossary He must plead in extenuation of these, want of experience in the art of book-making; the nature of his undertaking, something like a first attempt to recover a lost language; and the length of time the work has been passing through the press.* It is more than six years since it was announced as shortly to be published, and subscriptions solicited to enable him to bring out his book, a work of immense labour, but one, in which, from its nature, but few could be expected to take any interest. He has at intervals published parts of the book, to show the progress he was making, excite and keep up an interest in the subject, and obtain hints and help. He has never wished it to be supposed that he considers himself to have succeeded in discovering or recovering the original, and therefore the correct, rendering of all, or even most of the names† he has attempted to

---

* It might be thought that the length of time the work has been in hand ought to have made the result more perfect. The compiler has constantly been adding to his materials, and seeking fresh information, by communication with persons in all parts of the county, correspondence in the public papers, and lecturing in various towns He has again and again had to modify his views as to the meaning of words and names; and now after being so long occupied with this, he feels less inclined to speak confidently with regard to many of the names, than he did when he began to publish nearly three years ago. He has been blamed for giving so many and so different meanings to the same names; but where authorities are given he thought it best that each writer should be heard, and where no authority is mentioned, the names seemed to him fairly to admit of these varied renderings; and he would say, as E. Lhuyd formerly said, "Eligat lector quod maxime placet." It is possible, too, that as the same names occur over and over again, in various parts of the county, the different derivations and meanings may fit different places. It is the same with proper names, as Professor Müller says it is with other words, while one word may, by a varied process of corruption, assume different forms, widely different words may, by the same means, assume the same form

† Many of the names in the Glossary, to which a conjectural derivation, often little better than a guess, has been given, might rather have been relegated to the Lists of Unexplained Names; and the compiler thinks, if he had to do his work over again, he should now so do; but at the time he was influenced by the feeling that led Lhuyd to write his Cornish Grammar. In his preface he says, "I know very well that the inhabitants could have done this work much better than is done by me. But yet I considered, that *it was better to give some sort of help, than no help at all*, and likewise that this poor work of mine might induce another to begin a good one."

xplain. The number of notes of interrogation (??), marks of doubt, and also the various renderings he has given of the same names, shew this. It would require a much better acquaintance with the history, traditions, and peculiarities of so many families and places than is attainable, to speak with certainty of their true derivation and real original meaning. He wishes his renderings, &c to be considered for the most part as conjectural—tentative, and suggestive. He courts correction, and would be obliged by anyone pointing out *mistakes* and *misfits* with regard to their own names, or the names of places in their own neighbourhood; and to scholars living in other countries, where not only a Celtic nomenclature prevails, but also a Celtic language is still spoken, if, from the analogy of their own nomenclature, they would point out what may seem to them more probable meanings of these names in Cornwall. It is possible that these latter persons may see in the many names found in Cornwall, which are in the Glossary characterized as Teutonic, a Celtic derivation;* and also that the general philologist may detect in many of the names, especially in those in the lists of Unexplained Names, traces of other languages, and proofs of various theories that have been propounded as to a Semitic or Turanian element. The compiler does not at present enter into a discussion on these points. Whilst giving the best explanation he could of the apparently non-Celtic names, referring them to what appeared to him their proper languages, his chief aim has been to shew how much of the old Celtic vernacular appears to be still preserved in the current nomenclature of the county.

---

* Dr. Stratton, in his interesting little work on the "Celtic Origin of Greek and Latin," gives the Celtic roots of many classical proper names; but, W. Obermüller in his "Deutsch-Keltisches Geschichtlich Geographisches Wörterbuch," goes much beyond this; reversing the plan followed by the Rev. W. Lysons in his "British Ancestors" and holding that the Celt was the precursor of civilization everywhere, and the universal nomenclator of the world, he gives Celtic derivations not only for the names of rivers, cities, provinces, peoples and persons belonging to the Aryan family in Europe and Asia, but also to the Turanian in China, and the Semitic in North Africa and Palestine; and has a Celtic derivation even for the
sacred, incommunicable and ineffable name
of the incomprehensible, self-existent, all-creative, omnipotent, omnipresent,
eternal and immortal Most High God,

THE TETRAGRAMMETON,

יהוה

POSTSCRIPT.—UNEXPLAINED NAMES.—Page 193.—It was intended, as is intimated at the foot of page 192, to have had inserted after the Glossary, the third and fourth pages of the wrappers of Parts 1 to IV, on which were given the names the compiler had met in his researches, but for which he could not at the time give a reasonable conjectural rendering. He has, however, been persuaded to reprint these names, and has added many others which he has since found in the Tithe Apportionments of the parishes referred to in the number put after the name, the key to which will be found in the LIST, page xii. He solicits assistance from persons connected with the places, to enable him, if possible, to get at the true derivation and meaning of these names, and to trace in them any relics of the old vernacular. To some of these persons many of the names may seem to require no explanation; but, it may be otherwise with those who have not the knowledge they themselves possess of local history, traditions, peculiarities, usages, idioms, &c., and therefore it may be desirable that explanations should be given. Some of the names, doubtless, are plain English, "meaning what they say;" and either, given with some definite reason, or are mere "fancy names," or, "called after some other place." But, on the other hand, some of these apparently English names may be modifications of good old Celtic words, disguised by *bad ortho-graphy*, or changed by the "metamorphic process" common in all "countries where two languages come in contact with each other, and where, in the end, one is superseded by the other." (Max M., *Chips*, v. iii., p. 300). Some again may be the result of mistakes, either from the imperfect pronunciation of those who gave the names to the surveyors, or from the difficulty these found in catching the sound, or in spelling names that never before had been spelt; or they may have arisen from their own mistakes in copying from "rough notes," or are misprints. As a consequence many may be of little value. However, it has been thought desirable to give all. They will serve to illustrate the nomenclature of the county in a way that has never before been attempted, and those who may follow the compiler, in the same field of philological research, will be saved the immense labour he has had in amassing and arranging them. The names explained in the Glossary will enable any one to see a probable, possibly the correct, meaning of many of these Unexplained names.

A LIST *of the* 208 ANCIENT PARISHES *wholly or in part in the* COUNTY OF ARCHDEACONRY *of* CORNWALL, Arranged and numbered so as to shew their relative situation, east and west, beginning with the Isles of Scilly and going from the Land's End towards Devonshire :—1-12 are as far west as Penzance ; 13-68 as far west as Truro ; 26-35 in the Meneage or Lizard district ; 69-114 as far west as Bodmin ; and 137-208 are beyond the limit laid down by Mr. Herman Merivale, in his Historical Studies, as the boundary between Celt and Saxon.

1 Isles of Scilly, (S. Mary's ; Tresco ; S. Martins ; Bryher ; S. Agnes). 2 Sennen. 3 S. Levan. 4 S. Just in Penwith, (Pendeen). 5 Buryan. 6 Morvah. 7 Sancreed. 8 Madron, (Penzance, S. Mary's *and* S. Paul). 9 Paul, (Newlyn East). 10 Zennor. 11 *Gulval.* 12 Towednack. 13 S. Ives, (Halsetown). 14 Uny Lelant. 15 *Ludgvan.* 16 S. Hilary, (Marazion ; S. Michael's Mount). 17 *Perranuthnoe.* 18 Breage, (Godolphin). 19 Sithney, (Porthleven). 20 Germoe. 21 St. Erth. 22 Phillack, (S. Elwyn, Hayle). 23 *Gwythian.* 24 Camborne, (Treslothan ; Penponds). 25 *Gwinear.* 26 Crowan. 27 Wendron, (Helston ; Carnmenellis). 28 Gunwalloe. 29 Mullion. 30 *Landewednack.* 31 Grade. 32 Ruan Minor. 33 *Ruan Major.* 34 Cury. 35 Mawgan in Meneage. 36 S. Martin's in Meneage. 37 S. Keverne. 38 Manaccan. 39 S. Anthony in Meneage. 40 Constantine. 41 *Mawnan.* 42 Budock. 43 Falmouth, (Penwerris). 44 Mabe. 45 Stithians. 46 S. Uny, Redruth, (Treleigh). 47 Illogan, (Tuckingmill ; Trevenson *or* Pool ; Portreath). 48 S. Agnes, (Mount Hawke). 49 Gwennap, (S. Day ; Lannarth). 50 Kenwyn, (Chacewater ; S. Johns *and* S. Georges, Truro ; Tregavethan). 51 Kea, (Baldhu). 52 *Perranworthal.* 53 Gluvias, (Penryn). 54 *Mylor,* (Flushing). 55 Feock, (Devoran). 56 *S. Anthony in Roseland.* 57 S. Just in Roseland, (S. Mawes). 58 Gerrans. 59 *Philleigh.* 60 *S. Michael Penkivel.* 61 *Lamorran.* 62 *Merther.* 63 S. Clements, (S Paul's, Truro) 64 S. Mary's, Truro. 65 *S. Erme.* 66 S. Allen. 67 Perranzabuloe, (Mithian ; Perranporth). 68 Cubert. 69 Crantock. 70 *Newlyn East.* 71 Ladock. 72 Probus. 73 *Cornelly.* 74 Ruan Lanihorne. 75 Veryan. 76 *S. Michael Carhayes.* 77 *Cuby,* (Tregony, S. James). 78 Goran. 79 *Mevagissey.* 80 *S. Ewe.* 81 *Creed,* (Grampound). 82 *S. Stephens in Brannell.* 83 S. Enoder, (Michell). 84 Colan. 85 S. Columb Minor, (Newquay). 86 S. Columb Major. 87 Mawgan in Pydar. 88 S. Eval. 89 *S. Ervan.* 90 S. Merryn. 91 Padstow. 92 *Little Petherick.* 93 S. Issey. 94 S. Breock, (Wadebridge). 95 S. Wenn. 96 *Withiel.* 97 *S. Dennis.* 98 *Roche.* 99 *S. Mewan.* 100 S. Austell, (Pentewan ; Charlestown ; Treverbyn). 101 S. Blazey. 102 *Luxulyan.* 103 Tywardreath ; (Par ; Tregaminion). 104 Fowey. 105 S. Sampson *or* Golant 106 *Lanlivery.* 107 Lostwithiel. 108 *Lanivet.* 109 Lanhydrock. 110 Bodmin. 111 Egloshayle. 112 S. Minver, (S. Enoder ; Porthilly). 113 Endellion. 114 S. Kew. 115 S. Mabyn. 116 S. Tudy. 117 Helland. 118 Cardinham. 119 S. Winnow, (S. Nighton's). 120 S. Veep. 121 Lanteglos by Fowey. 122 Lansallos, (Polperro). 123 Talland. 124 *Pelynt.* 125 Lanreath. 126 Duloe. 127 *Boconnoc.* 128 *Broadoak.* 129 S. Pinnock. 130 *Warleggan.* 131 Temple. 132 Blisland. 133 S. Breward *or* Simonward. 134 Michaelstow. 135 S. Teath. 136 Tintagel. 137 Trevalga. 138 Forrabury. 139 Minster. 140 Lanteglos by Camelford. 141 Advent. 142 Lesnewith. 143 Davidstow. 144 S. Clether. 145 Alternon, (Bolventor). 146 S. Neot's. 147 S. Cleer. 148 Liskeard, (Dobwalls). 149 S. Keyn. 150 Menheniot. 151 Morval. 152 S. Martin's, (East *and* West Looe). 153 S. Germans, (Tideford ; Hessenford). 154 Sheviock. 155 S. Erney. 156 Landrake. 157 Quethiock. 158 S. Ive. 159 Linkinhorne. 160 Northill. 161 Lewannick. 162 *Trewen.* 163 Laneast. 164 Treneglos. 165 Warbstow. 166 Otterham. 167 S. Juliot. 168 *S. Gennys.* 169 Poundstock. 170 *Marhamchurch.* 171 Stratton, (Bude). 172 Poughill. 173 *Kilkampton.* 174 Morwenstow. 175 Launcells. 176 §Bridgerule. 177 Jacobstow. 178 Week S. Mary. 179 Whitstone. 180 N. Tamerton. 181 Tresmere. 182 Tremaine. 183 Egloskerry. 184 *N. Petherwin. 185 Boyton. 186 *Werrington. 187 S. Stephens by Launceston, (Newport). 188 S. Thomas the Apostle, Launceston. 189 S. Mary Magdalene, Launceston. 190 South Petherwin. 191 Lawhitton. 192 Lezant. 193 Stoke Climsland. 194 *Southill.* 195 Callington. 196 Calstock, (Gunnislake). 197 S. Mellion. 198 Pillaton. 199 S. Dominick. 200 Botusfleming. 201 *Landulph.* 202 S. Stephens by (Saltash). 203 Antony East, (Torpoint). 204 S. John. 205 *Rame,* (Eddystone). 206 †*Maker.* 207 §S. Budeaux. 208 *S Giles in the Heath.

* Marks the parishes in the County of Devon but Archdeaconry of Cornwall ; † a parish partly in Devonshire but wholly in the Archdeaconry of Cornwall ; § parishes partly in the County but not in the Archdeaconry of Cornwall. *See also* p. 207.—The Tithe Apportionments of the Parishes *in italics* have not yet been examined ; the loan of these is solicited. The places within parenthesis are towns new parishes, or chapelries, now or formerly, wholly or in part, dependant on the ancient parish with which they are here joined.

UNEXPLAINED NAMES.

Continued from Page 200.

TENEMENTS, ESTATES, &c.—Coose Mr. 163, Cope H. 114, Copper Thorn 160, Copple Stone Heath 139, Corgorland 151, Corks 110, Cothouse 10, Cotislost 92, Cottys Point 67, Couches Folly 114, Counse 1, Courlands 119, Court Place 111, -Toll 40, Cowbridge 106, -ders 202, -dery Bridge 184, -land 65, -lisborough 169, -Sutton 167, Cox 67, -Burrow 100, Crabbe Walls 197, Crabtree 110, Cracketton 168, Craft 102, Crastis 119, Cray- or Creathorn 169, Crebinack 101, Creeken 71, Creeps 202, Crefle 153, Cresars 8, Creva 18, Cribbrick 75, Cribinnick 1, Criffle 150, Crig-murrian 59, -toll 91, Crill 42, Crimble Passage 206, Cripples Ease 14, Croft-a 95, -hole 154, Croswolla 27, Crowbridge 106, Crowders House in the Ball 20, Crowns 33, -Zawn 4, Crow-pound 144, -snest 147, Crumple Horn 122, Crylla 148, Cuddle Rock 1, Cullendraft 75, Culver-hole 1, -lake 190, Cumbletor 202, Cur-gell 102, -gotha 82, Cusveorth 51, Cyprus P. 189, Dalson 159, Dark Lane 86, Darleyford 159, Dassell 174, Daws-Hugo *Lizard*, -lands 192, Daycombe 75, Deacons 132, Deary 80, Deep Hatches 145, Deers 193, Delank *river*, Demains 74, Demeans or Dimeans 106, Dengle 87, Dennabowl 160, Deright 147, Diddis 171, Diddy Lake 144, Dighouse 193, Dilland 179, Dimma 177, Dimson 196, Dinnerdake 158, Dipper 179, Dobriggo 67, Dolgas *t.b.* 48, Dollys 37, Donniton *o.* Durreton 131, Downathan 112, -Rose 136, Dranna Point 37, Dregennes Common 144, Dribbles 132, Drillaville 135, Drissels Rock 67, Drocombe 189, Drugletts 132, Drump 46, Ducks Pool 200, Dussard 185, Dutchmans Carne 1, Dymlank 133, Dysart 168, Eanes-manen & -triven 7, East-coombe 122, -Cott 180, -Hay 175, -Heal 177, -Lawns 160, -ros 133, Egens Warra 175, Elldown 174, Elmgate 202, Empacombe 206, Endsleighs 100, Enescaven 97, Enquire the way 157, Ex-mill 190, -well 159, Faby 28, Farewell Lane 132, Fellamore 158, Fellover 133, Feltrick 47, Fine Apple 200, Fishes 171, Flanders 168, Fleahill 173, -trap 49, Folly 114, Fox-Holt Cliff 113, -Tor 145, -Water 173, Frallan 8, Franchise *Lizard*, Freewater 72, Frel 27, Frightens 16, Frogapit 183, Frosswell 184, Frost P. 187, Frowder 29, Furland 125, Fursnap 158, Fuzlow 157, Fuzzoe Clizow *t.b.* 11, Gamper Rock 3. Gan-nick *or* enick 1, Ganniornick 1, Ganoak 193, Garlidinnia 27, Gazza 57, Geen Mill 72, Gew Skerton Bottom *Kynance*, Gibraltar 176, Gilly Bold 203, Gillhay 191, Gilstone 1, Gimble Porth 1, Gimbletts 164, Gists 171, Glubhole 160, Gnatham 193, Godarick Wood 178, Golden Ball 1, Gonighter 74, Gonowrias 82, Goodman's Farthing 191, The Goose *rock* 69, Goreggan 1, Gravelings 114, Gregland 98, Grent Torfrey 105, Greystone 157, Gribbes Mill 45, Grinnaw, *rocks Mount's Bay*, Guethens Brass *rocks* 2, Gulcellars 4, Gutterages *rocks* 1, Gwallanmayn 36, Gwarthandrea 35, Hadys 157. Halgineck 185, Hallworthy 143, Hammetts 171, Handoran 88, Hardenf-as, -ast 193, Hardow Downs 180, Hard to come by 85, Har-dlewis, -lewis *rocks* 1, Harll 186, Harrowbridge H. 144, Harsdon 153, Hatches 196, Hats 1, Haycommons 189, Hayda 178, Haycrock 94, Haygomme 28, Haywell 153, Hella *point*, 3, Hellacanoe 24, Hellgelders 111, Hellweathers 1, Helstone Water 51, Hemmick 78, Hendergulling 123, Hendrifton 148, Hengeys 28, Hennard 136, Hensall Cove 30, Hensvissen 82, Herdstand 173, Hether Butts 113, Hervon 32, Hitherlands 193, Hodgland 145, Hoe Ditch 19, Hogs Cross 187, Holdavit, 184, Holecoombe 148, Holestrow *Kynance*, Hollabury 172, Hollaccombe 150, Holla-, Horle-french 180, Holland 125, Hollyvage 161, Hopewell *t.b.* 48, Hopwell 157, Horn Hill 136, Hot Point 30, House-l, -hole 30, Howard 171, Huas 80, Hurlas Rock 37, Inasidgen 1, Indian Queens ?, Industry 160, Innisvouls 1, Inow 40, Ivyleuf 172, Jackford 189. The Jay *rock* 37, Jericho 21, Jews-Piece 1, -Watering *Truro River*, Jilling the Tinker 168, Jollows 138, Joppa 21, Joy Rocks 37, Jump 141, Justing Place 202, Jutsworth 202, Kamplo 34, Kaun-ap -or -ep 27, Kanes Thorn 179, Keeper Corner 1, Kellan Head 113, Kellecough 111, Kelsters 51, Kensey *river*, Kerpit 95, Kerriack Cove 47, Kesworthy 184, Kewberr -ie, -is 51, Killednan 35, Killewad-den 12, Kilsome 178. Kinsom 119, Kingbath 120, King-lets 135, -ole 120, -sand 205, -ford Bridge 184, -sland 206, -smill 201, -s Palace 100, -swood 118, Kistle Morris 37, Kittern 1, Kitter Vale 71, Kit Worm 132, Knagat 119, Knaggery 119, Knaland Point 100, Knap *rock Plymouth Sound*, Knapmelake 165, Kurkinowan 46, Lady Vale 118, Laerenton 149, Lamelgate 147, Lan-agath, -egarth 50, Land-avissick 132, -house 58, Lane-end 98, -head 140, Lanet 108, Lan-, Lar-, Las-senwith 45, Lanvons 51, Lape 50, Lark-Bill 144, -Holes 147, Lawley 18, Lay-hayes 118, -Mill H. 159, Lazingey 8, Lea Zawn 4, Lead Pool

DOMESDAY.—Arganlis, Argentel, Bentewoin, Betnecote, Bewintone, Bochenod *or*
Botchenod, Borge, Botcinii, Botchatuuo, Brocclesbeorge, Cabulian, Cariahoil,
Dovenot, Egloshos, Elent, Elil, Ermenheu (*e*), Ghivaile, Gloeret, Heli, Herminhen
(*e.*), Karsalau, Lancharet, Lanchehoc, Landelech, Landicle, Lanehoc, Lantloha,
Lavredoch, Lisnestoch, Melledham, Nanchert, Nantnat (*e.* Namteciat), Odenol, Pen-
nadelwan, Peret (*e.* Pedret).— *For continuation see* Page 205.

DOMESDAY TENANTS.—Aluiet, Chitel, Dorgeret, Edzi, Haemar, Haeche, Merken.

INSCRIBED STONES.—Alroron 101, Clotuali 22, Icdinus 8, Isnioc 63, Morgratti 22 —
For continuation see Page 205.

BODMIN MANUMISSIONS.—Aedoc (*s.*), Adoyre (*w.*), Artaca (*w*), Cili-sri *or* -fri, Dinset
(*s.*), Glowmoed (*s.*), Gluiucen (*s.*), Gun-dret, -ithrit (*w.*), Guenguin (*s.*), Guennercen (*s.*),
Guenneret (*s.*), Guentunet (*s.*), Gurcantcest (*s.*), Gurcenor (*s.*), Gurheter (*s*), Gurient
(*s.*), Gurnaret (*s.*), Heneriat (*s.*), Hincomhal, Hresmen (*w.*), Iliuth (*s.*), Inaprost (*s.*),
Inisian (*s.*), Judhent, Lecem (*w.*), Lethelt, Loc *or* Loi (*s.*), Macoss (*w.*), Macurth (*w.*),
Mailloc (*s.*), Madsuth (*s.*), Medgnistil (*f.s.*), Medhuil (*f.s.*), Methwiustel (*s.*), Meore
(*f.s.*), Milian (*w.*), Modred, Morh-atho, -æththo, -ædo, -aytho, -ith (*w.*), Moriw, Ogurcen
(*s.*), Osian (*w.*), Ousduythal (*s*).—*For continuation see* Page 205.

FAMILY NAMES.*—Addi-cat, -cot, -son; Agnew, Ailes, Aitken, Akenhead, Alban, Aldridge, A'Lee, Alford, Alger, Allanson, Allicott, Allig, Allin, Allport, Alms, Alsyn, Amerdyther, Amice, Amory, Amwelle, Amy, Anevay, Angel, An-gelly, -giloy; Angle-en, Ancar, Anson, Anterson, Anthony, Appleton, Arcedekne, Ardelle, Arewood, Armstrong, Arnes, Arnontin, Arundell, Ash-born, -ford; Atkins, Aty, Audley, Anger, Aumarle, Auney, Aure, Aust-in, -yn; Axworthy, Aylworth, Aymand. Ayshton, Babbage, Badyng, Bagh, Bail-ey, -ie, -y, -lisbury; Bakes, Bale, Ball, Bal-aham, -san, -som, -sdon; Ban-bury, -dry, -dyn, -field, -om; Banks, Bankart, Bant, Barclay, Bard, Barentin, Bari-oat, Bark-ell, -la, -ley; Barlow, Baruby, Bar-on, -ron, -ons; Barrabill, Barry, Barsow, Barter, Bart-le, -ley; Bast-ard, -in, -ian, -ion; Baswednack, Bat-ershill, -eshull, -teshull, tison, -ton; Bather, Batting, Bawdry, Bayb-ey, -is; Baynard, Bayth, Bazeley, Beaden, Beamish, Bealmeis, Beanbulk, Bed-dard, -doe, -dow, -egree, -ford; Begech, Behanna, Behaven, Bel-champ, -etede; Bell, Bell-amy, -ingham, -man, -ringer, -ot, -ton; Ben-ose, Ben-ne, -ney, -nett, -netts, -oy, -son; Bern-ard, -bury; Berri-ball, -man; Berson, Bessake, Bestall, Bet-ard, -enson; Bett-any, -esworth, -ie, -ies, -ison, -ons, -ringer; Bevant, Bevetto, Beueli, Bevil, Beyle, Bickerleg, Biddick, Bigglestone, Bilkey, Bin-den, es; Birch, Birkhead, Bisc-oe, -ow; Bissicks, Bisthop, Black-er, -ler, -pole, -ney, -well; Blamey, Blanchminster, Blanning, Blasinpain, Blatch-ford, -ley; Blitch-ford, -ley; Blekennock, Blenkiusop, Bletsho, Blew-ett, -etts; Bloom-er, -field; Blowey, Blu-at, ett; Blundell, Bloy-e, -on, -owe, -ye; Blunt, Boa-s, -z; Bobb-et, -ot; Bocunyan, Bod-carme, -cuike, -dey, -dy, -ecastle, -elsgate, -enck, -gener, -inel, -kin, -leat, -mer, righam, rugon, -ymel; Bogg-an, -ans, -ons, -as, -is; Bohay, Boileaux, Boisragon, Bol-and, -land, eigh, -igh, -len, -t, -ytho; Bond, Bon-etto, -ifant, -ithan, -man, -ny, -nyman, -ser, thron, -ythorn; Boon, Boot, Booth, Bor-aston, -den, -deny, -dinner, -chard, -ehard, las, -mas, -row, -rough, -thy; Bos-anker, -cathnoe, -euse, -inney, -kea, -metherick, -per, varthick, -veal, -warthick, -waydel, -wellick; Bothell, Botr-all, -eux; Bott, Boucher, Bouges, Bouhard, Boul-den, -der, -derson, -dry, -ger, -t; Boun-d, -dy, -sall; Bourchier, Bov-ey, -ill; Bow-cher, -er, -les, -man, -se; Box, Boyeer, Boyle, Boyne, Boynes, Brad in, -yn; Bracey, Brad-hurst, -shaw, -y; Bragg, Bra-imer, -mer; Brak-gysh, -kish; Bram-ble, -well; Branch, Bran-dreth, -ton, -tons, -well; Braun-d, -tou; Brealey, Bree, Bree-kin, -n; Bregnan, Brentyngham, Brereton, Brestow, Brew-eter, -ster; Brice, Bricknell, Briddon, Bridg-es, -man; Brigh-t, -ton; Brim-acombe, -macombe, -macorn; Brinton, Brit-nall, -ton; Broad, -lick, -ley; Brock, -hill, -man; Brodrigan, Brogden, Broke, Brokenshar, Brokenshaw, Brokenshir, Brokenshire, Brokenshow, Bromell, Brom-ley, -ond; Bron, Brood, Brook-ings, -s, -sbank; Brooming, Bros, Brougham, Broun, Brown, -field, -ing; Browse, Bru-ere, -er; Brun-sham, -ton; Bru-res, -yn; Brush; Bryan; Buck, -ett, -ingham, -nam, -nall, -nell, -ston, -thought, -well; Bucton, Budd, el; Budenuxhead, Budok, Builder, Buglehole, Bulford, Bull, -cock, -ivan, -un; Bunk ing, -um; Bunney, Bunster, Bunt, Burchell, Bur-den, -eil, -gan, -gon, -wood; Burgh, Burke, Burn-and, -ard, -bury, -er, -erd, -ett, -ey; Burr-al, -idge, -ow, -ows; Burt, -on; Bus-combe, kay, -kin, -sall, -scowen, -ustow, -vargus, -well; Bush, -ell; But-cher, -ler, lin, -son, -ters, -terworth, -ton; Buxton, Buzon, Buzza, Byampre, Byestecolomp, Byle, Jad-dy, -y, -well; Caeron, Caesar, Calf, Call-agan, -ard, -away, -ey, -ick, -mady; Cal-way, woodley; Camul, Cann-iford, -ing, -on; Canter, Cantik, Capelayn, Caprust, Car-ah, ahayes, -bery, -berry, -bines, -binis, -burra, -byon, -d, -dell, -devile, -geege, -inthen, leton, -lian, -na, -nall, -nbal, -rah, -rel, -rew, -rey, rio, -rivick, -row, -ru, -ry, -ruthers, slegh, -swell, -ter, -vall, -vill, -y, -yhaes; Casabom, Case, -bourne, -ley; Cash, Cas-ley, sell, -tine; Catch-er, -preist; Cater, Cattell, Cannter, Caurie, Caus-e, -se; Cauthern, Jav-al, -all, -anagh, -ill; Cawadley, Cawdell, Cawrse, Cawse, Caynges, Cayzer, Cecely, Jeeley, Cennick, Cerbis, Cerisenux, Cernick, Chacepore, Chadwick. Chaintley, Chal-ers, ey, -law, -m, -mers, -on; Chamb erlain, -ers, -ron; Cham-ond, -pernoon, -pernon, -pion; Jhan, Chanceaux, Channing, -on; Chap-ell, -lin, -man, -pell, -pelayne; Chard, Charke,

* The names in Italics have not been found in, or connected with Cornwall, by the compiler; they are given on the authority of Dr. Charnock's "Patronymica Cornu-Britannica," in which there are some 1,600 names. A review of this book in the "West Briton" of July 7th, 1870, says "Many of these names are altogether new to us, and we do not believe they were ever in use in the county." The compiler would not speak so positively. Many a Cornishman has wondered where he has picked up his 20,000 names. Doubtless some of his, as well as Dr. Charnock's, are the result of bad spelling, affected orthography, arbitrary change, or even misprints; and persons bearing some of the names may have been only officially, or accidentally, connected with the county.

Charles, Charlton, Chasepore, Chatten, Chaumond, Che-ffers, -gin, -gwidder, -mhall
-mall, -nhalls, -nnell, -nock, -nnock, -noweth, -rlew, -verton, -ynalls; Ches-ter, -well
Chi-dley, -gwidden, -lcott, -lds, -n, -ng, -ner, -nery, -noweth, -pman, -sley, -ttock, -val
lier, -valliers, -vel, -vell; Cho-lwill, -ne, -unens,-wne, -owne; Christ-oe, -opher; Chubb
Chudleigh, Church, Churke, Chygwyn, -ke, -mmowe, -nk, -noweth, -vals; Cithared
Clackworthy, Clamo, Clar-ges, -idge, -k, -ke; Clatworthy, Clay, -pole, -ton; Clegg
Clem-ence, -mow, -o, -oes, -oor; Clen-ick, -soe; Cleverton, Clift, Climo, Clin-ch
-nack; Cloake, Cloen, Clogg, Cloke, Clouter, Clo-wberry, -berry; Clushbecke, Clyes
Clym-a, -o; Conk-er, -es; Coant, Coast, Cobbeldick, Cobham, Cobon, Cock, -ing
-worthy, -s; Codd, Code, Cog-worthy, Cok-er, -yn; Col-a, -burn, -eford, -ense, -enso
-ensoe, -es, -eshill, -lan, -lard, -lect, -leton, -lick, -lier, -ling, -lings, -lins, -liver, -man
-mer, -nay, -pit, -well, -will, -yn; Comb-ellack, -rigg; Com-erford, -merford, -ming
-mins, -mon, -mons, -plin; Con-dor, -derow, -dray, -dura, -gdon, -ner, -ning, -ock
-norton, -or, -way; Coo-e, -ch, -che, -k, -ke, -kworthy; Coo-m,-mbe, -me, -pe, -per, -t, -ze
Cop-elin, -p, -pen, -pin, -plestone; Cor-am, -ant, -by, -c, -clew, -field, -en, -in, -ington
-ton, -k, -khill, -lyer, -lyon, -nburgh, -nelius, -nellow, -nish, -now, -rah, -rdy, -teis.
-vyens, -y, -yton, -yn; Cos-bey, -by, -grave, -sa, -sentine, -tine, -way, -worth; Cou-l
-lam, -mbe, -rtice, -rts, -sins; Cov-en, -in, -er, -erdale, -erthorne; Cow-ard, -d, -l, -lin.
-ling, -lins, -lstock; Coy-nte, -sgarne, -thmore; Cox, Crabb, Cracherode, Crad-dock, -ick:
Crag-e, -o, -gs; Crahart, Craise, Crake, Crang, Crart, Crashdoor, Cravarth, Craveigh,
Crawling, Cre-agh, -ak, -ba, -bo, -ber, -eper, -ckledene, -ech, -eke, -gan, -geen, -goe,
-llis, -per, -sa, -stowe, -ws; Crid-dle, -land, Crigan, Cripps, Croc-hard, -kard, -ken;
Crogg-in, -on; Crofts, Croker, Cromwell, Crook, Croome, Cropp, Cross, -antine, -man;
Crothers, Crou-ch, -gey, -th; Crow-e, -l, -ley, -nem; Cruse, Crutchley, Cruves, Cryffle,
Cryol, Cudlipp, Cuer, Culling, Cum-bellac, -ing, -mins; Cun-dor, -nick, Cur-ganven,
-genwen, -le, -ra, -rah, -ry, -ris, -teis, -teys, -ties, -tis, -toys, -y; Cus-den, -din, -wath, -wyn;
Cut-tel, -ecliffe, -till, -tofre; Cyrson, Dabern-oun, -on; Dacon, Dadd-a, -ow; Dag-ell,
-g, -worthy; Dal-by, -ly, -phin, -ton; Dale, D'Alneto, D'Alton, Dame, Dan, -caster, -gar,
-iell, -iels, -nan, -ny, -t, -vers; Dar-by, -ell, -rant, -t, -ton; Dash, Daubuz, Daunt,
Dav-ey, -ie, -y, -ies, -is; Daw-barn, -ning, -son; Day, -man, -men, Dea-con, -ly, -son;
Debett, De Cant, Decoy, Deeker, Deimans, Dell, -ridge; Demble, Denn, Den-band, -bigh,
-ham; -ithorne, -ison, -isel, -isly, -nis, -ny, -nyngton, -ton, -zil; Derneford, Derrick,
Deson, Dev-any, -onshire; Devyock, Dewrant, Dick, -son; Dighton, Dillen, Dimond,
Din-ch, -ely, -gley, -gleys, -ner, -nes, -nis, Dir-a, -daunt; Ditton, Dixon, Dobree,
Dobson, Doc-at, -ton, -kton, -kin; Dodge, Dogge-t, -tt; Dol-ben, -lman, -man; Dom-
mett, Don-ald, -es, -ey, -ney, -nithorne, -y; Doogood, Dor-mar, -mer, -rington, -wick;
Dow-ding, -er, -erick, -laing, -rick; Down, -e, -ey, -ing, -hault; Doyle, Doyloy, Doyn
-ell, -gell; Drain, Drewry, Driscoll, Drown, Dryden, Duance, Duckham, Dudley, Duff,
Dug-dale, -gar; Dunn, Dun-calf, -gay, -kin, -ning; Duppen, Dure, Durham, Durnford,
Dust-ing, -ow; Dy-ala, -mond, -nrust, -nstone, -sart, -son; Ead, Earle, Earnell, East
-brook, -cott, -lake, -man, -mead; Eathorne, Ebbott, Eccless, Ede, -n, -vean, -veain, -y;
Edge-cumbe, -rs; Edmonds, Edsall, Edwards, Edy, -vane, -veain; Egar, Egbert, Eggins,
Eggo, Eglington, Eihrid, Eldridge, Elford, Elias, Ellary, Ellio-t, -tt; Elson, Elvins,
Elwin, Ely, Emans, Emidy, Eng-land, -lish; Ercedekne, Erskine, Eryngton, Escndi-
fer, Espi-akelin, Estorun, Euren, Eusti-ce, -s; Eva, Evel-combe, -eighs, -yn; Ever ett,
-son, -y; Evil, Ex-elby, -ton; Eykyn, Eyres, Eyst, Eyte, Fac-ey, -y; Fair-child,
-weather; Fal-cke, -k; Fan-ce, -ning, -shawe, -stone; Fare, Farr, Far-ley, -mer,
-naby, -quharson, -rell, -thing; Fatta, Fauckner, Faull, Favihild, Fawlyns, Fawn-hop,
-hope; Fayrer, Faz-an, -on; Fell, -enoweth; Fenwick, Fermack, Ferrill, Fes-ant, -tas,
-ting; Fid-dian, -ick, -ock; Field, Finch, -er; Finter, Finn-amore, -emore; Firrel, Fish,
-er; Fissacre, Fithian, Fitz-e, -Gerald, -Richard, -Rogonis, -Smith; Flavell, Fled, Flete,
Fletcher, Fliggard, Flindell, Flynn, Foard, Foggit, Fol-ey, -ly; Fonerau, Fookes, Foote,
For-esight, -rester, -far, -saith, -sett, -ster; Fouyer, Fow-ler, -nes; Fox-well, -worthy;
Franc-es, -is, -h; Fra-ser, -zer, -zier, -than, -wne; Fre-athy, -derick, -eman, -ethy, -they,
-ize, mewan, -wartha; French, Frend, Frere, Fricker, Fridge, Friend, -ship; Frig-en,
-gens, -nis; Fruren, Fugler, Fulford, Fur-long, -medge, -neaux, -ye, Furse, -brook;
Fynneux, Gadgcumbe, Gal-dsworthy, -sworthy, -gey; Gale, Galy, Gandi, Gar-ry, -tarell,
-trell, -y; Gashry, Gav-ed, -id; Gawman, Gayry, Geady, Gechard, Geddey, Gedge,
Geer, -e; Geffrie, Gentil, George, Ger-amandy, -man, -nigan, -ningham, -veys; Gevers,
Gew-en, -ett, Geyre, Gibson, Gichard, Giles, Gillet, Gimblett, Gist, Glading, Glasson,

Glaze, Glemham, Glissan, Glu·as, ·gas; God·man, Gogay, Gold·ney, smith, ·son; Goley, Gomersale, Good·fellow, ·land; Gouch, Goude, Gove, ·ley, lly; Gowf·yd, ·man; Goyn·e, ·es, ·s; Gran·ger, ·gey; Graves. Gray, Green ·wood; Greeves, Grenge, Gren·ell, Grew, Grey, ·nfelde; Grieve, Gribb·en, ·ens, ·le; Grig. ·er; Grills, Grimaldi, Grimes, Groub, Grove, Groves, Growdon, Grub, Gryke, Grundry, Gryllo, Guavas, Gubs, Guillez, Gullick, Gum, Gumm·a, ·oe; Gunn, Guppy, Gur ney, ·tyboys; Gushry, Gutheridge, Gwa·irnick, ·rnack, ·vis; Gwe·ator, ·rick; Gwi·n, ·nn; Gwy·n, ·nn, ·nne, ther; Gyans, Hage, ·n; Hai, ·le, ·mes; Hall·ep, ·op; Hal my, ·uwick, ·y; Ham·bly, blen, ·blyn, ·elye, ·ley, ·ilton, ·min, ·pden; Hand, ·ley, ·on, ·ra; Hankey, Harbord, Hard·eshull, ·way; Herepath, Har·pendene, ·ris, ·t, ·top, ·topp, ·wood; Haweish, Hawk, ·e, ·er, ·ins; Hawton, Hayden, Head, Heath, ·cote, ·erington; Heckens, Hedge land, ·s; Hedsore, Heeldon, Heither. Helens, Hell·ear, ·ier, ·yar, ·ins; Hend, ·eman, erson; Henn a, ·essy; Hens haw, ·leigh; Her·bert, ·goe, ·epath, ·naman, ·nes, ·ring, tland; Hewis, Hey·den, ·gsham, ·le, ·nes, ·wood; Hichens, Hicks, Higg·ans, ·ens, ·ins; Highman, Hin·der, ·dom, ·ds, ·gaston, ·gston; Hitch ens, ·ins; Hoar, ·e; Hob·house, lah, ·ling, ·son; Hockbridge, Hod·ges, ·son; Hoggaton, Hoige, Hold, Hol·dan, ·land, ley, ·lole; Holly·combe, ·wood; Holt, Honey·wood, ·chuch; Honicomb, Honor, Honyland, Hop·good. pen. ·per. ·y; Horde. Hor·man, ·nby, ·ndon, ·nington; Hors eking, ·ford, ·well; Hor·top, ·skin. ·wood, ·well, ·will; Hosk·en, ·ing, ·ins; Hotton, Houghton, House, Howar·d, ·th; Hoy, ·ge, ·te, ·ten; Hugh. es, ·son; Hugill, Hull, ah; Hume, Hungate, Humph·ery, rey, ·reys, ·ries; Hunken, Hunt, ·ford, ·ingdon; Hurd, Hus·band, ·sey; Hutching, Hutton, Idless, Illingworth, Ingham, Inness, Ir·by, ving, ·wine; Isaacs, Isseham. Ivell, Ivey, Ivimey, Jaca. Jackson, Jagoe, Jaen, James, on; J'Ans. Janys, Jaques, Jasper, Jeeves, Jelbert, Jemmat, Jenk·ens, ·ins, ·yns; Jentle, Jer·dan, myn, ·und; Jilbert, Jonchim. Job, Joel, John, ·son; Jolly, Jone, Jope, Jorey, Joubley, Jul·eff, ·iffe; Julian, Kali·nkiss, ·ynuck; Kaymerllmarth, Ke·am, ·em; Keand, Kearnzew, Keckwitch, Keels, Kelby, Kellock, Kellyow, Kelynack, Kembre, Ke·miel, Ken·alle, ·bond. ·dale, ·sham, ·shom, ·way. ·yon; Kepper, Ker·akosse, geek, kin, nahan, ·nock, ·swill, ·yell; Keve·ar, ·rand; Key·me, ·mer; Kibwinmith. Kidd, Killi·ck, grew, ·rington; Kil·vard, ·vert, ·warby; Kim ber, ·iell, ·ywith; Kindly, King, ·dom, ·ston; Kirby, Kirk, ·ness, ·wood; Kitson, Kitt, Kittow, Knapp, ·er; Kniverton, Knive·t, ·tt; Kuo kell, ·llis, ·wlys; Krabbe, Kruckenburge; Kyvera, Laas, Labatt, Ladd, Lad·ner, Laffere, Lait. Lake·man, ·y; Lam·b, ·be, ·hadarn, ·born, ·brey, ·brick, ·ergh, ·peck, ·peer, ·penc; Lan·caster, ·dary, ·den, ·dey, ·dry, ·uzelle; Lane, Lang, ·ford, ·ler, ·maid, ·man, ·sford, ·worthy; Lan·hadern, ·hedrar, ·herch, ·hidrock, ·horgy, ·igan, ·ksbury, ·nergy, ·ning, ·sdell, ·tegles, ·thuis, ·worduby; Lap·ham, ·idge, ·on; Larmer, Lasky, Late, Lath·an, ·ean, ·on, ·rope; Lauelis, Laun·drey, ·tyan; Lavedwen, Law·er, ·hyer, ·nce, ·rake, ·rance, ·rence, ·rie; Le·athan, ·gue, ·lean, ·min, ·Neve; Len deryow, ·drick, ·orgy; Leonardin, Les·birel, ·cas, ·nestock, ·ter, ·twithiel; Leukost, Le·vela, ·velis, ·vis, ·vy, ·warn, ·Warn; Lew·is, ·kenor; Leycock, Lezard, Liardett, Libbey, Liddicost, Light ·foot, ·ly; Lillathew, Lim·brick, ·bury, ·met; Lin·ford, ·ton, ·tern; Lissant; Little, ·cot, ·john, ·ton; Livins. Loan, Lochard, Lock, ·yer; Lo·doung, ·haryng; Long, ·bound, ·lands, ·man; Lonsdale. Looks, Loose, Lor·d, ·ing, ·nock, ·y; Lou·arn, ·ndes; Lov·ell, ·eport. ·ibond. ·ing, ·y; Lowe. Lowrey. Luby, Lucas, Lu·ce, ·cy; Lud·dington, ·low; Luer, Lug·ans, ·un, Luk·es, ·ie, ·ies; Lun et, ·ey, ·y, ·yon; Lusk·ey, ·y; Lutay, Lye, Lyn·n, ·am, ·om, Lyones. Lyths, Lyttleton, Mably Mac·Adam, ·Alister. ·armick, ·Car·thie, ·coll, ·cooey, ·cormick, Crachan, ·Donald, ·Dougall, ·Dowall, ·Ewan, ·ey, ·Fadycan, ·Farland, ·Ghee, ·chin, ·k, ·alkin, ·elkine, ·Keand, ·kenzie, ·kinnon. ·kworth, ·lean, ·leod, ·manus, ·Millan, ·Mullin, ·querd, ·y; Maddwis. Madge, Mact. Maffatt, Mahun, Mail, Mainprice, Maiowe, Maj endie, ·oloue; Mal·herbe, ·yon; Man·chester, ·daville, ·eton, ·ners, ·ning, ·scomb, ·sell, ·uell, ·ute, ·waring, ·weryng, xel; Mapowder, Mur ·chant, ·com, ·es, ·hus, ·kis, ·ks, ·ley, ·ney, ·rat, ·riott, ·sden, ·shley, ·ston, ·tin, ·tina, ·tyn; Mas·ery, ·selegh, ·selyn, ·sey, ·ters; Mathadarda, Mathew·mans, ·s; Matters, Matthew, ·s; Maule, Maxwell, May·ell, ·hope, ·how; Manser, Meadway, Mea ger, gor, ·ker; Meal, Meanwell, Mease, Meathre·l, ·ll; Med·hope, ·lin; Meech. Mees, Megra. Meh ieux, ·uish; Mella·dew, ·odew, ·ow, ·ows; Melyngissy, Mena·dawa, ·due, ·ndue, ·gwins, Men ·ear, ·adue, ·edew, ·henhick, ·hinack, ·hinnick. ·weneck, ·wenick, ·zaut; Mer·efield, ·iton, ·rin, ·sey, ·ton; Mewsam, Meyn, Meyrick, Mich·ael, ·amp; Middleton, Mil·dum, ·es, ·eton. ·iton. ·liton, ·ford, ·roy, ·wain; Mill, ·e. ·an; Mimpriss, Min·ar, ·ard. ·as, ·chin, ·nerd, ·ors, ·taye, ·ty; Miron, Moderet, Moffett, Moger, Molenneck, Mon·aghan, ·day,

-eron, -hure, -ton, Mont-acute, -ague, -gomery; Moor. -man; Mor-phew, -rish. -khead
.timer; Moss, Mottie, Mount Edgcumbe, -Stephens, -Steven, Mowne, Moyses, Moytt
Mudge, -on; Mugfor, -d; Mules, Mur-ray, ry, -rice, -rish, -t; Mushell, Myn e. -on, -w
.ors, -taye; Mythian, Nan-collins, -garthen, -julian, -kevill, -keville, -phant, -savallen
.scawen, -scorus, -scnke, -sevallen, -skevall; Napleton, Nause, -nell; Neaine, Neal. -es
Neilder, Neloude, Nett-ing, -el, -le; Nevel, Nev-etton, -oll; New-man, -son; Nina
Niblett, Nichol, -l, -as, -ls; Nick-ell. -els, -ett, -s; Nicols, Night, Nile, -s; Nin-iss
-niss; No-all, -ble, -ell, -le; Nor-man. -way; North, -am, -cott, -y; Nostunell, Not-hey
-well; Noy, Nu-bal, Nute. Nye, Nyvott, Nywelling; Oakes, -ton, Okeustone. Ovat-es
-ten. Obbs, Obern, Octanell, Odgers, O'Dogherty, Offill, Old-brook, -ham, -s; Olford
Olive, -r; Olliver. O'Niell, Onslow, Or-ven, -well; Os-berne, -ler; Ough, Owens, Ox
enberry, -ford; Pa-ige, -get, Pal-eologus, -mer, -ms; Panks, Panter, Pappin, Paris, -h
Park-inge, -ings, -s; Par-miter, -row, -sons; Pase, Pashley, Pas more, -singham; Pate
fond, Pat-erson, -herick, -riern, -ten, -terson, teson; Fau-coc. ll, -lett, -ling; Paver
Pawl-ey, -ing, -yn; Payton, Peake, Pear-den, -don, -n. -son; Pease. Peckard, Ped-der
-igree, -lar, -ler, -rick, -roncelli, -yfar; Peel, Peern, Peg-geh, -o, Pel-amountain, -ena
-lamounter, -low, -lowe, -mear, -mounter, -niddon; Pem-ber, -bridge, -ewan; Pen alurick
-bery, -bethy, -carow, -cavel, -dene, -deray, -dered, dred, -dry, eligan, -estone, -eystone, -fers
-fowne, -gursick, -gelley, -gillay, -gold, -gree, -guick, -gully, -halurick, -haluwick, -ikett
-ket, -keth, -kett, -kethley, -kethman, -kevil, -kivil, -kerviel, -lease, -lez, -lerick, ley, -ligan
-lirick, -nalyky, -nerkes, -nikett, -phraise, -price, -rhyn, -rin, -ruddock; -ruddocks, -tecost
-tine, -tquit, -ularick, -warn, -warverell, worverell, ystone; Per-cival, -cy, -er, -rer, -nall
-ken, -kin, -kins, -s, -son, -ue, -yes, Pet-aaleway, -er, -ers, -et, -ite, -yt, -ty, -tygrew
-igrew; Petheick, Peure, Peyntour, Peyton, Pheasant, Phillip, -s; Phythian, Pick-e
-ford; Pidwell, Piers, Pig-got, -ot; Pike. Pile, Pill-amontayne, -ivant, -ow; Piltenam
Pine, Pin-cerna, -found, -kerviel, -ney, -nick, -nock; Pleming, Plenderle-ath, -ith; Plomer
Plum-ber, -mer; Plymm, -in; Po-e, -er, -her, -heden; Pol-amonter, -amountain, -ard
-cvarne, -egreen, -ganhorn, -glose, -kearne, -kenhorn, -kinhorne, -korn, -lamountain, -lo
mounter, -omounter, -low, -lcowe, -len, -ley, -litn, -lybland, -lyn, -mere, -porth, -und
-warne, -wart, -warth, -wel, -well, -wheile, -whyll, -whyle, -wyl, -ybland; Pomeroy, Ponna
Popplestone, Port, -el, -eous, -er; Porthkellompen, Pothlony, Potter, Powerman, Pown-e
-ing, -re; Poydas, Poyle, Poynter, Praise, Pread, Precheur. Preen, Prest-on, -wood
Prethowan, Prewbody, Prin, -ce, -dle; Pris, -k, -ke; Proc-ter, -kter; Pro-fett, -fit, -phet
-wer, -use; Prydiaux, Prye, Pryn, -ne; Punnett, Purling, Pye, Pyp-ard, -er; Quin-s
-tral; Rad-cliffe, -dall, -dle; Raleigh, Ramback, Ran-dall, -dle, -k; Ras-coilen, -oiben
-pey, -saunt; Ratty, Rawling, Reburn, Redding, Relton, Rem-mick, -pbry; Ren-dall
-dell, -fry, -phry; Repp-er, -uke; Res-cassa, -corlia, -kelly, -kruge, -preme, -prynne, -s
-tallock; Retollock, Rhead, Rhyderarch, Rich, -ardson; Rid-del, -dle; Rilstone, Ring
wood, Rise, Riston, Ritson, Rivers, Rob-b, -bins, -yns, -inson; Rock-s, -wood; Rodd, -s
Rodeney, Roe, Rogger, Roll-e, -ing, -s; Ronalds, Rooper, Roper, Ros-carrack, -cos
-corlia, -craw, -crowe, -crowgie; Rose-monde, -wharm, Ros-ken, -killy, -killey, -se, -veare
-vere; Rothern, Rous, Rowly-n, -ngs; Runnalls, Rus-coe, -cow, -crowe, -sell; Ry-al, -all
-an, -ce, -se; Salts, Sam-mals, -psons, -uels; Sand-elands, -ers, -erson, -ford, -ilands
-oz; San-gar, -sbury, -to, -ty, Sar-gent, Satterley, Saunder-cock, -s; Savage, Saw, -dy
Saygemoor, Scaberius, Scawin, Scho-bell, -lar, -ler, -oles; Scorse, Scort, Scott, Scovern
Scown, Screech, Scriven-s, -er; Scudamore, Seal, -ey; Sedg-emoor, -more; Sedman
Seeleg, Sel-ke, -ioke, -lek, -lick; Sell-er, -ars, -ors; Selwood, Semple, Senior, Ser-eos
-geaux, -jeant, -jeaux; Shadford, Shakelok, Shapton, Sharp, -e; Shaw, Shell-ibear
-y; Shentelbury, Shep-hard, -heard, -herd, -pard; Sherris, Sherston, Shillebear, Shop
cott, Shovel, Shugg, Shuldham, Shute, Shuttleworth, Sickler, Silk, Silvest-er, -on
Sim-cock, -pson; Skelton, Skerreston, Skewys, Skeynock, Skinnfield, Skuse, Skyburlow
Skyrme, Slaughton, Slegh, Slight, Sloan, Slo-eman, -oman; Slugg, Slurbridge, Sly
Smart, Smedley, Smith, -am, -em, -eram, -ram, rem; Smyth, Sob-ey, -y; Somerset
Sondry, South-cot, -well, -wood; Spar-e, -goe, -nall, -nel; Spear, -man; Speck, Spink
Spoure, Spra-ke, -gge; Sprid al, -dle; Spur, -rier; Stan-naway, -tan, -way; Start
Steer, Stenlake, Stewart, Sticker, Stirrup, Stoddern, Stonnard, Stokes, Stone, Strangan
Strathon, Strick, Strood, Stroute, Stuart, Stubbs, Sturt-on, -ridge; Stuttaford, Sullivan
Summerfield, Sumpter, Sutherland, Symon, -ds, -s; Tadd, Tagert, Taleen, Tall, -ard, -ai
-ent, -ick; Tan-cock, -k, -gye, -nahill, -ner; Tape, Tap-perell, -rell; Tat-am, -ham;
Taunton, Taufield, Tavernor, Tayldor, Teazer, Tell-am, -an; Tencreek, Tevisden,

hackworth, Thauck, Thom-as, -pson; Thorn, -e; Thurnay, Tice, Tickell, Tilbury,
ill ey, -ie; Timewell, Timmins, Tin-cock, -ner, -ney, -ton; Tink, Todd, *Tol-cearne,*
rman, -er, *-lervey,* *-nie,* *-putt,* *-verne*; Tomlinson, Tong, Ton-kyn, -sen; Torley, Towey,
Townsend, *Tra-go,* *-hern,* *-in,* *-ynor,* *-nmer,* -then, *-veller,* -vil, -yhearne; Tre-ago, *-agus,*
ais, -ays, *-asure,* -barfoote, *-derrick,* -dethy, -eves, -fay, -felens, *-fethen,* *-fey,* *-ffey,* *-gaga,*
garrek, -gassan, -glidwith, -glissan. *-gloaa,* -gonel, -gonnell, -gonwell, -goz, *-gulla,* -hair,
harne, -havarike, -hearne. -hern, -herne, *-ingu,* *-ineer,* *-kellern,* -lago, -lawnay, -lawnee,
lawney, -lawnye, *-leaven,* -lego, -lewan, *-living,* -loer, -lowick. -ludro, -ludrow, -man-
eere, -marne. -mayn, -mbaut, -mbarth, *-mblant,* -mellan, -mellen, -milling, -menheere,
mewan, -mle, -mlett, *-naco,* *-nanall,* -naran, -ncer, -ncrow, *-ndinnick,* -neman, -ner,
nery, *-nessy,* *-ngone,* *-ngore,* -ngreene, -nhail, -nheale. -nner, -pess, *-rellevar,* *-ry,* *-saga,*
scothick, -sider, -sidder, -silian, -sonna, -ssider, *-tgothnau,* *-thawan,* *-thearth,* *-therde,*
therfe, -theway, -thinick, -thoau, *-thcwoan,* -thurf, -thurffe, -thyrfe, -uagnian, -uanian,
uilian, -uisa, -vages, *-vailor,* *-vollion,* *-valyan,* -vannance, *-var,* -varrick, *-varrow,* -vars,
vaskiss, -vaze, *-velle,* *-vel,,n,* -vennard, -verdern, *-verlyn,* -ves, *-vethnick,* -vihen, -villinion,
villizik, -vronck, -vylian, -vyllian, *-warverrell,* *-waves,* -wby, -weeke, -wern, -wethy,
whele, -widdle, -winard, -winn, *-winwick,* -wissan, -woofe, -worthike, -wrin, *-zecuet,*
zeguet, *-zevant,* -ziddar, -zidder, -ziese; *Tri-bhel,* -gge, -gwell, -mby, -vellian; Troane,
Trownson, Trudgian, Tru-body, *-cman,* *-man*; Turffrey, *Ty-ors,* *-ers,* -hiddy, -hyddy;
Jddy, Uglow, Umfry, Umfraville, Ust-eck, -icke; Vacy, Vage, Vale, Van-derheyden,
nar, -stort; Vell-enoweth, -huish, Velnowarth, Venn, Verrant, Viant. Vickary, Vicount,
'igo, *-e;* Vine, Vin-icombe, -sam, *-ter;* Vinian, Viv-an, -en; Vodd-en, -on; *Voss,*
Waade, Wal-degrave, -estbren, -key, -ker, -kyngdon, -per, -stenholme, -ters, -ton;
Wandsworth, Ward, -ham, -our; War-n, -rick, -wick, -yn; Wasek, Wat-erman, -ers,
kin, -kins, -kinson, -son, -ters; *Wuvis,* Waymouth, *Weaks,* *Week-es,* -s; Weale,
Weather-all, -ley; Webb, Well-esby, -s; Wemyss, Wen-moth, -sent; West, Wett-er,
on; Weymcuth, Whear, -e; Wheatley; Wheel, Whele, Whit-aker, -by, -church, -ford,
ing, -tam; Why-att, -te, -tefen; Wegram, Wild-bore, -man; Wilkin, -s, -son; Will
cock, -cocks, -ey, -imott; Wil-mot, -shaw, -son; Windham, Win-*inckett,* *ninckett*; -nin,
wick, Wisdum, Withell, *With-erick,* -ey, -y; Wolrington, Wolstemholme, Won-acott,
nacott; Wood-gate, -house, -ley, -ville, -wards, -yard; Wool-combe, -f; Wor-gan,
lidge, -ral; Wriford, Wright, -ington; Wul-coke, -ff; Wyatt, Wymhall, Wynn, -hall,
inck, -ter; Wyvill, Yeamon, Yeat-es, -s; Yelland, Yeoldon, Yew-ens, -ins; *Yoe,* York,
Young, Yurle, *Zelley.* *See also* Page 205.

ADDENDA, CORRIGENDA, ET DELENDA.

ÆTHOC, *for* "rich oak, *t.,Y.*," *read* "fiery."

ALSHIR, high (*hir,* long) cliff (*als*), *Cu.*

ALVERN, *add* "*i.q.* ALVERTON."

APPLEDORE, *add* "? = *apulder,* an apple tree, *s.*"

ARALLAS, *add* "83, ? = *ar-gollas,* bottom *or* low land, *B.M.*"

ARROW = *garrow,* rough, *E.G.H.*

ARGANTEILEN, ? silver harp (*telyn, w.*)

BACCHUS PARK, ? bush (*bagas*) close (*parc*).

BAGH BARRACK, *for* "stubble," *read* "fallow."

BAIN PARK ? *i.e.* PARK BEAN.

BEHENNA, *for* "little," *read* "Littler, *n.f.*"

BARGAINS, ? *i.q.* PARK EANES.

BEQUEST, ? *i.q.* PARK QUEST.

BINDON, little down, *C.*

BISCOVEY, = *pisgwydd,* lime *or* linden trees, *w., C.*; ? bishop's (*escop*) place (*ma, va*), *G.H.*

BLOOD PARK, ? *i.q.* PARK PLUD.

BODBRANE, the rookery, *C.*

BODELLIS, ? Ellis's house, *R.W.*

BODINALGAN, house (*bod*) by the (*a'n*) tin (*alcan, w.*) works, *C.*

BODINNICK, abode by the fortress (*din, -ic,* adjectival), *C.*

BOIA, ? = *bui,* yellow, *i.*

BOIETONE, *d.d.,* ? "Boia's enclosure, *t.*

For BOLANKEN, *read* BOLANKAN.

BONNY, *n.f.,* ? = *bonne haie,* good enclosure, *f.; i.q.* Fairfield.

BOSAVERN, *for* "tree," *read* "trees."

BOTHOG, ? = *bothoc,* a cottage.

BOWDEN, hill (*din*) house, *W.H.*

BRAND-ICE, -IZE, -YS, ? three cornered [field], *t.*

BRODEHOC, *d.d.*, ? from *bro*, a country, and *tioc*, a farmer, *W.S.*

BUCHENT, d.d. ? cow *(buch)* path *(hent, w.)*, *W.S.*

BULLOCK, *n.f.* ? = *a.* BALCH, haughty.

BURCOM, *i.q.* BERRYCOMBE.

BUSVEAL, ?? Beal's, *or* Veal's house *(bos)*; or *bus (i.e.* calf, *m.c.) field.*

BUSVIGO, ? Vigor's *(n.f.)* house.

CABEL CUT, ? wood *(coed)* chapel *(capel) T.C.*

CALLIBUDGIA, ? fold *(boudghi)* field *(gweal)*, or grove *(celli)*.

CALLINGTON, ? *i.q.* COLLENTON.

CALLM-ADY, -UDU, ? Madoc's field, *T.C.*

CANCER, *i.q.* CANSFORD, ? the ford causeway *or* path *(caunse, m.c.)*

CARBILLY, *after* "castle," add "*or* town *(caer)*, ?"

CAREWRGE, *add* "EWRGE goats, *pl. o iorch, W.S.*"

CARIORGEL, *dd,* IORGEL = *iyrchell,* young roe, *w.*, *W.S.*

CARN GOLEUA, rock of adoration *(gol)* of the moon *(leua)*, *C.*

CARNKIEF, rock basin, *C.;* rock o castle of hiding *(cuddva)*, *Ev.*

CARNHOAR, ? boundary *(or)* rock, *M*

CARNEDJACK, *add* "*hynadzha,* t groan, sigh."

CHILLCOTT, back of the wood, *W.S.*

CRINNIS, ? = *gorennys,* a peninsula

FEOCK, ? = *fiuch,* a raven, *e.*, *Cu.*

GARVEROT, *d.d.*, ? rough *(garo)* acre *(eru,* pl. *erot, w.)*, *W.S.*

HUEL BAGS, ? = *gweal bagas,* bush-field.

For "HYTHANCER," *read* "HYTHA-NEER."

KERR PARK, ? oat *(cerh, w.)* field.

PARK PAW, dirty *(buw)* close, *M.*

BALDHU, black hill. *Spelter* is a name in commerce for the impure metal, but no one would speak of a spelter mine. *R.H.*

BELLYACHE, the vulgar or slang name for a place, where smuggled brandy (a cur for the complaint) was formerly to be got, *A.A.V.*

BOLVENTOR, *m.*, = *Bol vên tor,* mountain of (china) clay stone, *or,* little *(vean)* cla *(bol)* hill *(tor)*, *F.R.*

BODMIN, in note *strike out* "monk's house, B." and add "B" after "Wh."

BUDOCK, in line 2 from bottom of foot-note, *for* "S. Budeaux, partly situated wes of the Tamar," read "partly in Cornwall though wholly east of the Tamar."

CASTEL AN DINAS, the earth-fort with a stone citadel, *C.*

COBBLETY CUT, COBLIDGICE, &c., names derived from a boy's game with nuts.

CONIUM, *m.*, given from supposing that Truro river was the Kenion of Ptolemy.

COPARCENARY, *to be struck out;* (a legal term that has crept into the Tithe Appor-tionment, and means property in undivided shares, *T.C.*)

GOONGLAZE, *add,* the sea, or green *(glas)* plain *(gwon)*, *B.*

HELLMOUTH, *m,* derived from a black gloomy gap in the cliffs: there is no water it is not the HEGELMITHE of Malmesbury.

KNIGHTONS KIEVE, the vat *(cyf, s.)*, or, retreat *(cuddva, w.)* of S. Nectan.

LAUGHER, *n.f.*, pronounced LAFFER, *T.C.;* = *lan vear,* great enclosure.

MORWENSTOW, place *(stow, s.)* of S. Morwenna, *R.S.H.*, of S. Wenna by the sea, *C*

MYENDU, "blak *(du)* mouth *(min)* or chimne," *Le.*

PARK OLVIN, ? sparrow *(golfin, w.)*, or bench *(colfin, w.)* close, *M.*

On Page 209 under *Nord.*, for "written 1584," *read* "the survey is supposed to have been made in 1584, but it must have been written much later as he makes fre-quent references to Carew's Survey and Camden's Britannia.

On Page 210 for "Ta" read "T.a.;" and *instead of* "Wanted, &c." read *See* LIST OF PARISHES, &c., Preface, Page xii.

For more ADDENDA, CORRIGENDA, ET DELENDA *see* Wrappers of Parts i., iii., and iv.; *also,* Page 206 where strike out in line 34 from bottom, "see also Page 200," and the whole of the last line.

For AUTHORITIES, REFERENCES, ABBREVIATIONS, &c., *see* Page 207.

For UNEXPLAINED NAMES, *See* Preface, Page xii., and 193.

GLOSSARY OF CORNISH NAMES.

ABBOT'S HENDRA, Abbot's old-town (*hendra*).

ABLES FIELD, *from* personal name ABEL, *w.B.m.*, diminutive of *abo*, a man, *t.*, F. (?) ; *or*, colts' (*ebol*) field.

ACCASINNY, ? Acca's manor-house (*inne, s.*).

ACHYM, *n.f.*, a descendant, issue, offspring, *H.* (*uch, R.W.*)—?=*s.* ac-*ham*, oak home, *or* boundary.

ACKEY'S FIELD, Hercules' * field.

ACKLAND, *n.f.*, oak (*uc, s.*) land, *t.*

ACRE CROFT, ? daisy (*egr*) croft.

ACTON, oak town *or* enclosure (*ton, s.*), *or* hill (*dun*).

ACTSWORTHY, ? Acca's field *or* farm (*worthig, s.*).

ADALBERD, *presbiter, B.m.*, noble bright, *t.*

ADDALBURG, *s.B.m.*, noble protection, *t.*

ADDICROFT, Addy's (?=Adam's *or* Eddy's) croft.

ADDIS, *n.f.*,=Addison.

ADDIT *or* ADIT FIELD, the mine conduit *or* water-course field.

ADELCES, *presbiter, B.m.*, noble pledge, *t.*

ADGEVEOR, ?=*an chy veor*, the great house.

ADGEWEDNACK, ?=*an chy wednack*, the (*an*) white house.

ADGEWELLA, ?=*an chy uhella*, the higher house.

ADJELS, ? low (*isal*) [fields].

ADLGUN, *f.s.B.m.*, ? noble war, *t.*

ADNIS, ? = ST. AGNES.

ADVENT, (*parish*), *from* patron saint *Adwen*, (*O.*).†

ÆDOC, *f.s.B.m.*, ? rich oak, *t.*, *Y.*

ÆLCHON, ÆULCEN, *s.B.m.*, ? *i.q.* ADLGUN.

ÆLFGYTH, *f.s.B.m.*, elf gift, *t.*

ÆLFRIC, *B.m.*, elf ruler, *t.*

ÆLFWERD, *B.m.*, elf protection, *t.*

ÆLFWINE, *B.m.*, elf friend, *t.*

ÆLGER, *w.B.m.*, formidable (*egel*) spear, *t.*

---

* Hercules is a not uncommon *fore*name in the County, sometimes represented by the equally *un*christian name Archelaus.

† S. Adwen, given by Leland as one of the twenty-four sainted children of King Brechan (*5th cent.*), is not found in the Welsh lists, though they give him twenty-four sons and twenty-four daughters, all saints. The *Inquisitiones Nonarum*, according to Dr. Oliver, calls the saint *Sca. Athewenna.*

ÆLSIG, ÆLFSIE, ÆILSIG, *w.B.m.*, ? elf, *or* formidable, conquest, *t.*

ÆLWOLD, *B.m.*, elf power, *t.*

ÆTHÆSTAN, *w.B.m.*, = *Athelstane*, noble, *or* precious, stone, *t.*

ÆTHAN, *s.B.m.*, fire, *k.*, *Y.*

ÆTHELFLÆD, *B.m.*, noble increase, *t.*

ÆTHELGAR, *B.m.*, noble spear, *t.*

ÆTHELHIDE, *B.m.*, noble cheer, *t.*

ÆTHELRÆD, *B.m.*, noble counsel, *t.*

ÆTHELWERD, *B.m.*, noble protection, *t.*

ÆTHELWINE, *B.m.*, noble friend, *t.*

AGAR, *n.f.*, = *Egiheri*, formidable warrior, *t.*; *or*,=*Œgir*, the god of the sea, *Y.*

AILBRIC, AILBRIHT, *t.d.d.*, noble bright, *t.*

AILM, *t.d.d.*, ? formidable (*ag*) helmet (*helm*), *t.*

AIRE, back, behind, the poop *or* stern, *Pr.* (*aeros*, *R.IV.*).

AISSETONE, *d.d.*, = Ashton; *or*, Saltash, "Esse his towne," *Car.*

AIULF, *t.d.d.*, = *Agilulf*, formidable wolf, *t.*

ALAN,=*all aon*, white river, *ga.*, *I.T.*

ALBALANDA, *i.q.* Blanchland, Whiteland, *lat.*

ALBASTON, ? Alva's (*Alueua*) town, *t.*

ALBURY, ? moor (*hal*) by the hill (*bre*); *or*, old (*ald*) fort (*bury*), *t.*

ALDERCOMBE, alder vale, *or*=Algar's coombe, *t.*

ALDERMYLLE, *corruption of* Algar's mill.

ALDESTOWE, the old (*ald*, *s.*), *or*, Athelstane's place (*stow*), *t.*

ALDON, = *hal dun*, hill moor; *or*, *aldton*, old town, *s.*

ALDREN, ? thorn (*dren*) moor (*hal*), *or*, hill (*alt*).

ALDWINNICK, ? the marshy (*gwinnick*) height (*alt*).

ALE AND CAKES, ?=*hal an cegas*, hemlock moor.

ALESDON, open (*ales*) height, *or*, hill (*dun*), *Pr.* (?). *See* ALSTON.

ALESTAN, *t.d.d.*, ? *i.q.* ALSTAN.

ALFEG, *t.d.d.*, = *Æfhæg*, high as an elf, *t.*

ALGAR, *t.d.d.*, hall, *or* noble, spear, *t.*

ALICE VEAN, little (*vean*) broad (*las*), *or* green (*las*) moor (*hal*).

ALLAN GUE, ?=*hal an gew*, moor by the gew, *or*, best field.

ALLEN, *n.f.*, *from* ALAN *or* ST. ALLEN.

ALLEN CROFT, *for* hurling croft.

ALLERCOMBE, alder-tree-vale, *t.*

ALLERTON, alder town *or* enclosure (*ton*), *t.*

ALLET, ALET, ALLIOT, ?=*hal yet*, moor gate.

ALLE WYDN, ?=*hal y widn*, white-moor.

ALLEYS, ALICE, ?=*hal les*, broad moor; *or*, green (*las*) moor.

ALLGATE, ?= *hal goed*, the wood moor, *or* Moorgate.

ALLOWS, ALOES, *for hallow*, moors.

ALMAR, *t.d.d.*, hall, *or* noble, fame, *t.*

ALNOD, *t.d.d.*, hall, *or* noble, compulsion, *t.*

ALRIC, *t.d.d.*, noble (*adel*) ruler, *t.*

ALS, ALSA, HALSE, cliff.

ALSEPHRAN, ALSIFARN, the hellish cliff, *i.e.*, deep as hell, *B.*

ALSI, *t.d.d.*, ? *i.q.* ÆLSIG.

ALSTAN, *t.d.d.*, hall, *or* old, stone, *t.*

ALSTON, high-cliff hill (*dun*), *Po.* ? the town of Alsi, *d.d.*

ALSVEAR, great (*veor*) cliff.

ALTARNUN, ALTERNON, the altar of the nun, *or*, of St. Nonna (the patron saint of the parish).

ALTERWEN, ? the oak (*derwyn*) moor (*hal*).

ALTON,=*ald ton*, old town (*s.*).

ALUREDUS, *t.d.d.*, elf peace, *t.*, *Y.*

ALURIC, *t.d.d.*, *i.q.* ÆLFRIC.

ALUUOLD, *t.d.d.*, hall power, *t.*

ALVACOT, (*d.d.* ALVEVACOTE), the cottage (*cot*) of Alva, (*Alueua*, *d.d.*). Howling (*olva*) cot, *Pr.*

ALVARDUS, ALWARD, *t.d.d.*, hall guard, *t.*

ALVER, *n.f.*, ?=*hal veor*, great moor.

ALVERN, alder (*gwern*) moor (*hal*).

ALVERTON, the town, or enclosure, (*ton*) of Aluuard (*d.d.*). — High green hill, *Pr.* (!)

ALVIGGAN, little (*bichan*) moor (*hal*).

ALWIN, *t.d.d.*, hall, noble, or, elf friend, *t.*

AMAL, AMEL, AMYLLE, ??=*ymyl*, *w.*, a boundary.

AMALIBRIA, hill (*bre*) Amal.

AMALVEOR, great (*veor*) Amal.

AMALVEAN, AMALWIDDEN, little Amal.

AMANETH, ?=*an menedh*, the mountain.

AMBERS HILL, Ambrose's hill.

AMBLE, AMMEL, ? *from* St. Adhelm, or, *i.q.* AMAL.

ANAGUISTL, *s.B.m.*, ? Ana (? *ph.* = Grace) the hostage (*guistl*, *w.*).

ANAOC, *w.B.m.*, ? Ana, or Grace, the younger (*og*, *i.*).

ANAU, priest *B.m.*, ? Grace.

ANAUDAT, *s.B.m.*, Ana, or Grace, the wise (*doeth*, *w.*).

ANCHOR, the hermitage, *Pr.* (*Ancar*, a hermit); ? the corner (*cor*).

ANDARDON, ANDERTON, the (*an*) oak (*dar*) hill (*dun*), *Pr.*

ANDENNIS, the fortification (*dinas*).

ANDERS FIELD, Andrew's field.

AN DINAS HILL, the fortification hill.

ANDRE, the town or dwelling (*tre*).

ANDREAS, *t.d.d.*, = Andrew.

ANDREW, *n.f.*, ?=*handeru*, a cousin german; or,=*an derow*, the oaks.

ANDREWARTHA, ANDWARTHA, *n.f.*, the higher town.

ANERAY, *o.n.f.*, ?=*an hir hay*, the long enclosure.

ANGARRACK, the rock (*carrac*), *Pr.*

ANGER, *n.f.*, ?=*an gaer*, the camp.

ANGEVAL, the horse (*cevil*).*

ANGEW, the support, *Pr.*

ANGEWNACK, ?=*an chy wednack*, the white house.

ANGLE DITCH, earthworm (*angle-twitch*, *m.c.*) [field].

ANGOLLA, the bottom (*goles*).

ANGOOSE CROFT, the wood (*coos*) croft.

ANGOVE, *n.f.*, the smith (*gof*).

ANGROUSE, the cross (*crows*).

ANGUIDAL DOWNS, the Irishman's (*gwyddel*, *w.*) downs; or from *gwyddwal*, a place full of thorns, brambles, bushes, *w.*

ANGWIN, *n.f.*, the white.

ANHAY, ANHEY, the enclosure (*hay*).

ANHELL, the hall (*hel*), *H.*

ANJARDEN, ?=*an chy ar dun*, the house on the hill.

ANJEWINJACK, ? *i.q.* ANGEWNACK; or=*an chy win issack*, the lower white house.

ANKERBURY, the camp hill (*bre*); or a reduplication, *bury* = castle, *t.*

ANKERVIS, ?=*an gaer ves*, the camp outside.

AN MAROGETH ARVOWED, the armed knight, *H.*

ANNEAL, *n.f.*, ?= *an hal*, the moor; or, *heyl*, river.

ANNEAR, ANAER, *n.f.*, ?=*an hir*, the, long.

ANNERSEY FIELD, ? the long dry (*an hir sich*) field.

ANNETT,=*Agnette*, little Agnes.

ANSTEY, ANSTIS, *n.f.*=Anastasius.

ANTERTAVES, *i.q.* HANTERTAVES.

ANTONY, (*parish*; *d.d.* ANTONE), ? *from* former patron, SAINT ANTHONY, (*now* Saint James, *O.*).

ANTICOOSE, ?=*hanter coos*, half the wood.

ANTRON, the (*an*) promontory, nose, tongue, or projection of land, *Pr.* —?=*hanter oon*, half, or middle, of the down.

AN TYER DEWETH, the Land's-end, *H.*

APLIN, *n.f.*, son (*ap*) of the king, (*belin*); or=*aplyn*, apples, *s.*

---

* *Gavel, w.*, is a fork or pass in a mountain; *Angeval* might be " the mountain pass," (*R.W.*).

APPLEDORE, apple, or colt's (cbol), land, (dor).

APPLEDORFORD, Appledore road (fordh), or passage.

APPLE PARK, ? colt (ebol) field.

APPS, n.f., ?=w., happus, happy; or, heps, m.c., a half door.—Son of Appe, from apr, fierce, t., F.

ARALLAS, upon (ar) the cliff (als), Pr.

ARAWAN, upon the down (oon), or, rivulet (avon), Pr.

ARCHDEKNE, o.n.f., archdeacon.

ARDEVORA,=ar devra, upon the lap, or bosom, or lake; or, upon the haven, Wh.

ARGALL, ARGLE, ARGOLL, ? on the ridge, promontory, or point (col); or, in front (arag) of the moor (hal); or,=w. argel, a concealing, hiding.

ARGALLACK, ? ? upon the rock (clog).

ARGALLAS, on the bottom (goles).

ARGANBRI, s.B.m., ? silver (argant) honour (bri), w.

ARGANTEILEN, f.s.B.m., ? silver forehead (talcen), w.

ARGANTINOET, s.B.m.,? silver fortune (tynged), w.

ARGENTEL, d.d., = TREGANTLE.

ARGUE, o.n.f., on the best field (gew); or, high (ard) gew.

ARISH PARK, stubble (arish, m.c.) field.

ARLYN, on (ar) the lake (lyn), or grove (llwyn, w.).

ARNALL, ARNOLD, n.f., eagle (arn) power (ald=vald), t.

ARRISH CROFT, stubble croft.

ARRY or ARRA VENTON, spring (fenton) field (eru).

ARSCOT, n.f., ? boundary (hars) wood (coed, w.), or cottage (cot, t.).

ARSON BEON, = arish an bean, the little stubble [field].

ARSON BROAZE, the great stubble.

ARTACA, w.B.m., ?=Arthgal, high courage, i.

ARTH, high (ard, arth); or,=ardd, ploughed land, w.

ARTHUR, high (ard) land (dour).*

ARVOSE, upon the ditch or entreuch-ment (fos), Pr.

ARWENNACK, upon the marshy place, Pr.—? From arwyn, w., blissful, happy, N.

ARWOTHAL, upon (arworth) the salt river (heyl), Pedler.—See PERRAN ARWORTHAL.

ASGAR, t.d.d., divine spear, t.

ASHLEY, the ash pasture (lea), t.

ASHTON, the ash enclosure (ton, s.), or = isa ton, lower lay.

ATHALBERTH, presbiter, B.m., noble brightness, t.

ATHILL, ATTLE, by the hill, t.

ATHWART PIECE, the cross-piece.

ATLEYS, by the pastures, t.

ATWELL, ATWILL, by the well, t.

ATWOOD, by the wood, t.

AUDIT FIELD, = ADIT FIELD.

AUSTIN, AUSTYN, n.f., = Agustinus, B.m.; Agustin, s.B.m.; Austius, w.B.m.

AVALDE, d.d., ? apple (aval) land (tir), = ALBALANDA.

AVARD, n.f., summer (haf) height (ard).

AVER, n.f.,=eaver, a kind of grass.

AVERACK, the fallow (havrec, a.).

AVERY, n.f., ?= haf vre, summer hill.

AVOH BICKEN, the signal, beacon, or proclamation, house, H. (?).

AWSCOTT, i.q. ARSCOT.

AXFORD, Acca's ford, t.

AXLE CLOSE, ? the low (isal) close.

---

* The name of King Arthur is derived from arth, a bear, w., (R.W.); or from ardrigh, ardheer, the highest chief, i., (Y.). Some of the Cornish Arthurs are corruptions of ANDREWARTHA. Arddwr, w. is a husbandman; ardwywr, a governor.

AYLMER, *n.f.* (*t.d.d.*AILMER), = *Athel-mar, or, Egelmar,* noble, *or,* formidable fame, *t.*

AYSLAND, waterfall (*eas, ga.*) land, *Beal.* ? *eas* = *hays,* enclosures, *t.*

AZZEL PARK, the low (*isal*) close (*parc*) ; *or,* hazel field.

BAAL FIELD, the mine (*bal*) field.

BAB, *n.f.,* ? = *papar,* an anchoret father, *o.n.*

BABER, Bab's land (*ar*).

BABBINGTON, the enclosure (*ton*) of the descendants (*ing*) of Bab, *t.*

BACCHUS PARK, field (*parc*) at the *back* of the *house.*

BACH, BACHE, BAGGE, BAGH, *n.f.,* = *w. Baugh* = little, *R. W.*

BACK BEAN, ? little (*byan*) back [field] ; *or i.q.* PARK BEAN.

BACKWELL, *n.f.,* ? = *parc uchel,* high field.

BACK WIDOW, ? ? = trees close, (*widow* = *gwydhow*), *R. W.*

BACON PARK, the beacon, *or* the little (*bichan*), close.

BADAFORD, ? house (*bod*) by the ford *or* road (*fordh*).

BADCOCK, *n.f.,* ? red (*coch*) house.

BADDON, BAD DOWN, ? house (*bod*), *or* peat (*beat*), down.

BADGE, BADGEY, *n.f.,* ? = *boudzhi,* cowhouse.

BADGER PARK, ? long (*hir*) cowhouse close.

BADGERY, *n.f.,* ? cowhouse (*boudzhi*), *or* the badger's field (*cru*).

BADHAM, ? Adam's house, (*bo* = *bod*).

BADHARLICK, ? house by the battle (*heir*) stone (*lech*).

BADWANNICK, ? house in the downy place (*gwonnick*).

BAGA PARK, ? little (*bach*) close.

BAGGANS, ? = *parc eanes,* lambs' close.

BAGH BARRACK, ? = *parc havrec,* stubble close.

BAGNEL FIELD, *i.q.* PARC AN HAL.

BAGSTON, bush (*bagas*) hill (*dun*), *Pr.*—? Bagge's enclosure (*ton*), *t.*

BAGWELL, *n.f., i.q.* BACKWELL.

BAHON, BAIN, *n.f.,* = *byhan, byan,* little.

BAINCOAT, *n.f.,* little wood.

BAKE, the beak, point, *or* promontory, *Pr.* (*pyg,* a projection, *w., R. W.*).

BAKE RINGS, small (*bach*) circular entrenchment, *M'L.*

BAL AN DREATH, mine (*bal*) on the sand (*traith*).

BAL, BALL, a mine ; *also,* a place, a spot ; a field, *Halliwell.*

BALCOATH, the wood (*coat*), *or* old (*coth*), mine.

BALCOMBE, ? ? field (*ball*) in the coombe.

BALCOUTHY, ? woods' (*coitau*) mine.

BALDEES, ? the people's (*dees*) mine.

BAL DOWNS, Baal's, *or* the mine, downs.

BALDUE, BALDHU, David's, *or* the black (*du*), mine or place.*

BALHATCHET, *n.f.,* ? the mine, *or* field, with the hatch-gate (*yet*).

BALINS, ? lambs' (*eanes*) field (*ball*).

BALKIN, ? mine on the ridge (*cein*).

BALKWELL, *n.f.,* the boundary-ridge (*balk*) well, *Halliwell.*

BALLANCE, ? lambs' (*eanes*) field (*ball*).

BALLARD, ? the high (*ard*) place.

BALLESWHIDDEN, the mine by the white (*gwidn*) court (*les*).

BALLET, *n.f.,* ? mine gate (*yet*).

BAL LODE ZAWN, mine lode cave, *or* cove (*zawn*).

BALL-LUHOL, (*Nord.*) = *bal uhal,* high mine.

BALLYACK DOWNS, ? hedge-hog (*bal-lawg, w.*) downs.

---

* *Baldhu,* a new vicarage in Kenwyn, is "black mine," from the spelter, zinc, or *black jack* mines there. The church is dedicated to Saint Michael.

BALMANEAR, long stone (*maen hir*) mine.

BALNOON, mine on the down (*an oon*).

BALROSE, the heath, *or* moor (*ros*), mine.

BALSCAT, the stopped, bankrupt, *or*, knacked (*scat*), mine.

BAMFIELD, BANFIELD, *n.f.*, tree (*beam*) field, *t.*

BAMPUSH, ? = *parc an bos*, the bush close.

BANNEL CROFT, broom (*banal*) croft.

BANKEY FIELD, the field with banks in it, *or* = *parc an ce*, the hedge field.

BANS, *ban*, a mountain, hill, high ground, *Pr.*

BARAGWANATH, *n.f.*, wheat (*gwaneth*) bread (*bara*).

BARALLAN, corn (*bara*) enclosure (*lan*), *Pr.* ? *i.q.* BORALLAN.

BARANWOON, top (*bar*) of the down (*an woon*).

BARAPILL, corn harbour (*pill*), *Pr.* (?)

BARBALINGY, ? field (*parc*) by the house pool (*pol an chy*).

BARBARY, BARBERRY, *n.f.*, ? top (*bar*) of the hill (*bre*).

BAREPPA, BARREPPA, BARRIPPA, BARREPER, &c., ? = *Parc haf maur*, the great summer close; *or*, = *Beaurepaire*, fair retreat, *f.*

BARGUS, top of the wood (*cuz*); *or*, wood close (*parc*).

BARGWANNA, *i.q.* BARAGWANATH; *or*, wheat field (*parc*).

BARHAM, *n.f.*, the bear's home, *t.*, *F.B.*

BARLANDEW, "God's acre" (*landhu*) summit; *or*, top (*bar*) of David's enclosure. ? Black orchard (*perlan, w.*), *R.W.*

BARLANZY, top (*bar*) of the dry (*serh*) enclosure (*lan*).

BARLOWENA, Mount (*bar*) Joy (*lowene*), *or* Mount Pleasant.

BARNACOT, ? barn by the wood (*coit*); *or*, the barn cot, *Pr.*

BARNCOOS, top of the wood.

BARNETT, ? barn gate (*yet*); *or*, little bear, *t.*

BARNICOAT, *n.f.*, *i.q.* BARNACOT.

BARNOON, BARON, BARANOON, THE BARROON, *i.q.* BARANWOON.

BAROGLAZE, *nickname*, grey beard, *Gw.* = *barv glas*, *R.W.*

BAROKE, over (*bar*) the oak, *Pr.* (?)

BARRABALL, BARRABLE, *n.f.*, ? barrow field (*ball*); *or*, *i.q.* BARAPILL.

BARRAS NOSE, ? cod-fish (*barvas*) headland (*ness, t.*).

BARRATON, ? barrow enclosure, *t.*

BARRETT, *n.f.*, little bear, *t.*

BARSHEBA, = *parc scaber*, barn close.

THE BARTERESS, ? *i.q.* PARK DARAS.

BARTH, BARD, BATH, *n.f.*, a mimic, bard, poet, *Pr.*

BARTILEVER, ? great (*veor*) Bartholomew's (*Bartle*) meadow (*lea, t.*).

BARTINE, BARTINNEY, hill (*bar*) of fire (*tan, c., teine, i.*); fiery top, *B.*

BARTON, the demesne lands of a manor.—The enclosure for the *bear* or crop, *T.*

BARWELL, ? = *bar-uchel*, high summit.

BARWICK, ? = *beor-wic*, barley village, *t.*; *or*, over (*war*) the creek (*gwic*).

BARWIS, *n.f.*, = *o.h.g.* Berwis, Bearbold, *F.*; *or* = *parc ves*, outside close.

BASCOMBE, *n.f.*, *i.q.* BOSCOMBE.

BASELEY, BAZELEY, *n.f.*, ? birch (*bezo*) pasture (*lea, t.*); *or* bees', *or* bays' pasture.

BASHER, *n.f.*, ? = *bashdour*, low water, *Pr.*, a ford, *B.*

BASIL, a herb, a palace, *T.* ? = *boshal*, moor house.

BASKAFULL, *n.f.*, *i.q.* Baskerville, *f.*; *or* = BOSCA FIELD, cottage field.

BASSETT, *n.f.*, diminutive of *bassi*, a bear, *o. norse*, *F.*

BASSOW, ? = *bissoe*, birches.

BASTAIN, BASTIN, BASTION, *n.f.*, ? tin (*stean*) house (*bos*), *or* mine (*bal*).

BAT, BATE, BATH, BATT, *n.f.*, *i.q.* BARTH, *or* = Bartholomew; *or*, *bat*, a dormouse; *or*, *bath*, a coin, money.

BATAVELLAN, mill (*melin*) house (*bod*).

BATTEN, BATTIN, BATTON, *n.f.*, diminutive of BAT; *or* = BAWDEN, *or* BATTERN.

BATTERN, fire (*bat, ga.*) place (*ern, s.*), *Beal.*

BATTERSHILL, BATTESHULL, *o.n.f.*, ? *i.q.* BOTESHALL.

BATTISON, BATSON, *n.f.*, Bat's son.

BAWDEN, castle *or* hill (*dun*), house (*bod*).

BAYSCABERRY, ? = *bosca bre*, the cottage on the hill.

BAZONE, ? house (*bos*) on the down (*oon*).

BEACON, BEAKEN, an eminence, a token, a look out, *Pr.*

BEADEN, *n.f.*, ? peat (*beat, m.c.*) down (*oon*).

BEADS PARK, ? outer (*ves*) close, *T.C.*

BEAGLEHOE, *n.f.*, ? corruption of BEAGLEHOLE, *n.f.*, ? = HAL AN BEAGLE.

BEAGLE MOOR, shepherd's (*bigel*) moor.

BEAGLE ROSE, shepherd's heath *or* moor.

BEAGLE-TODDEN *or* -TON, shepherd's pasture (*ton*), *or* hill (*dun*).

BEAK, ? *i.q.* BAKE.

BEAL, BEALE, BEEL, *n.f.*, ? *i.q.* BELI; *or* = BAAL; *or*, BAL.

BEALBURY, ? Baal's hill (*bre*); *or*, Beli's castle (*bury, t.*).

BEANCHY, *n.f.*, ? little (*byhan*) house (*chy*).

BEAN PARK, little (*byhan*) close.

BEAN STITCH, little long narrow strip.

BEARD, *n.f.*, ? *i.q.* BARTH, *or*, BIRT.

BEARDON, ? the farm (*bere, t.*) on the hill (*dun*); *or*, barley (*bere, s.*) hill.

BEARE, *n.f.* ? = *veor*, great; *or*, *bere, s.*, a farm.

BEAR FIELD, great (*veor*), *or* barley, field.

BEARFORD, *n.f.* ? = *Barfut*, barefoot, *or* bearfoot, *t.*

BEARLAND, ? barley (*bere, s.*) land, *t.*

BEARRAH, BEARA, ? the farm, *or*, the barley enclosure (*hay*), *t.*

BEATLEY, the peat (*beat, m.c.*) pasture.

BEATON, *n.f.*, ? peat down (*oon*).

BEAT PARK, peat field.

BEAUCHAMP, *n.f.*, = *de bello campo*, of Fairfield, *f.*

BEAUCOMBE, BEAUCAMP, *n.f.*, *the same*; *or* = *Bod combe*, vale-house.

BEAUFORD, *n.f.*, = *bod-fordh*, house by the road; *or* = *Beaufort*, fair castle, *f.*

BEAUREPER, (15 cent.), *i.q.* BAREPPA.

BEAUPRE, *n.f.*, = *de bello pruto*, of the fair meadow, *f.*

BECHAN, little [field].

BECKERLEG, *n.f.*, ? *i.q.* BEKELEGE.

BECKET, *n.f.*, ? little (*bech*) gate (*yet*); *or*, little (*beck*) brook, *t.*

BECKON HILL, beacon hill.

BECONNION, *i.q.* BOCONNION.

BECOVEN, ? *i.q.* BOSCOVEAN.

BEDACK, ? the place of birches.

BEDEUE, ? = *bedho*, birches.

BEDLAKE, ? willow (*helic*) house (*bod*).

BEDMAN- *or* PEDMAN-DOWE, *Nord.*, for PEDN-MEAN-DU.

BEDRAWEL, ? the house (*bod*), *or* grave (*bedh*), of Riowal.

BEDREWTHAN, BEDRUTHAN, = *beth-ru-haun*, the graves on the sloping haven, *M'L.*;— ? red (*rudh*) cove (*haun*) grave *or* house.

BEDRICK, ? = *parc dourick*, watery field.

BEDROGE, ? Rioc's grave.

BEDRONA, ? long (*hir*) grave (*bedh*) on the downs (*oonou*).

BEDRUGGAN, *i.q.* BODRUGAN.

BEDWIN, the aspen; *or*, *i.q.* BODWIN.

BEDYER, long (*hir*), *or* battle (*heir*), house (*bod*), *or* grave (*bedh*).

BEDZANGAVAR, ? cowhouse (*boudzhi*) for the goat (*gavar*).

BEEF PARK, BEE PARK, ? cow, *or* beeve (*beuch*), close.

BEENY, ? ? the lesser (*byhenna*) [field].

BEER, ? the farm (*bere, s.*).

BEERSHEBA, *i.q.* BARSHEBA.

BEESTON, ? the bees', or the cattle (best) enclosure (ton, t.).

BEFARNEL, moorfield (parc an hall) house (bod).

BEFILLICK, i.q. BOFILLICK.

BEG MEADOW, ? little (bech) meadow.

BEHAN PARK, little (byhan) field.

BEHEATHLAND, BOHELLAND, = bo-hel-lan, the dwelling by the water nigh the church, Pr. — ? Heath-land, or, moor (hal) house (bod), or field (parc).

BEHENNA, n.f., ? a comparative of byhan, = "Little" (le, less).

THE BEHEURY, ? i.q. PARK WHERRY, or BOHURRA.

BEIRAH, ? i.q. BEARRAH.

BEJOSAH, BEJAWSA, Jose's house (bod) or field (parc); see IOSA.

BEJOWAN, = BOD JOWAN, the lonely dwelling, or John's house.

BEJUTHNO, i.q. BOJUDNO.

BEKELEGE, (14th cent.), ? little (bich) pasture.

BEL, BELL, fair, or far off, Pr.

BELATHERICK, i.q. BOLATHERICK.

BELERION, the Land's-end of Diodorus Sic., (BOLERION, Ptolemy), = bol e rhin, head of the promontory, Bax.

BELHAY, the fair enclosure, Pr.

BELI, s.B.m., a giant, from belian, to bellow, o. norse, F.* ? from ph. Baal.

BELINGEY, the mill (melin) house (chy), Pr.

BELINNIS, fair, or distant, island (ynys), Pr.

BELITHO, n.f., i.q. BOLITHO.

BELKEY, ? far (pel) hedge (ce).

BELLASIZE, ? lower (isa) pillas [field].

BELLESDONE, d.d. ? Beli's hill, (dun).

BELLING, n.f., ? the descendant (ing) of BELI, t.

BELLOOAN, BELLOWAN, ? distant down.

BELL RICK FIELD, distant (pel) stack field.

BELLS DOWNS, ? pillas, or Baal's, downs.

BELLS GWIDDEN, ? little (vidn = vean) pillas field.

BELLURIAN COVE ? i.q. BELERION.

BELLYACHE, BELLY HAKE, ? = bolec, calves' house; or, i.q. BALLYACK.

BELOITHA, BOLOYTHA, BELOWDY, BELOWDA, ? house (bod) by the dairy (laity); or = PARK LAITA.

BELOVER, ? chimney (lwfer, w.) house; or, the great (veor) calf's (loch) house.

BENALLOCK, BENNALLACK, BENAL-LECK, broomfield, or, the broomy place, (banal, broom).

BENATHLACK, n.f., the same.

BENBOLE, BENBOUL, ? i.q. PENPOL.

BENBOW, n.f., ? = PARK AN BEU, or PENPOL.

BENEDIC, s.B.m., blessed, lat.

BENETHIC, ? = parc en ethic, the great close.

BENEVAL, ? i.q. PARK EN ABLE.

BENFIELD, n.f., ? little (byan) field.

BENHORE, ? i.q. PARK EN HOAR.

BENIAMEN, w.B.m., = Benjamin.

BENISKEY, ? = parc en is ge, close be-low the hedge.

BENITHEN, ? i.q. PARK NITHAN.

BENMER, nickname, great head = Pen-mer, Gw.

BENNERTON, (? d.d. BENNARTONE), ? Bernard's town, t.; or, long (hir) hill (pen) enclosure (ton, t.).

BENNICKE, o.n.f., ? = pinnick, the wry-neck, Po.

BENNY, ? the same; or = BEHENNA.

BENNYON, ? i.q. BENITHEN.

BENOCK, BENOKE, n.f., ? i.q. BEN-NICKE.

BENORTH, ? = parc en arth, the high

---

* This and other names of serfs in the records of manumissions in the Bodmin Gospels, referred by Mr. Ferguson to the Teuton, belong rather to the Celtic or Phœ-nician. "BELI was a great prince of the ancient Britons. See Williams's Eminent Welshmen." (R.W.).

field ; *or* high, *or* bear's (*arth*, *w.*), hill (*pen*).

BENTEWOIN, *d.d.*, ? *i.q.* PENTUAN.

BENTLEY, *n.f.*, ? couch grass (*bent*) meadow, *t.*

BENVETH, *n.f.*, ? *i.q.* PENWITH.

BEORLAF, *w.B.m.*, bear relic, *t.*

BEOW, ? cow (*beuch*) [field].

BEPHILLICK, *i.q.* BOFILLICK.

BEPOLVEA, *i.q.* BESPALFAN.

BERCLE, *n.f.*, *Car.*, the birch (*beorce,s.*) lea, *t.*

BERCOE, *n.f.*, ? = *parc cio*, snipe close.

BERDINNICK, ? = *bar dinnick*, the fortified hill, *T.C.* ; *or*, = *parc dinnick*, hilly field.

BERE, the farm, *t.* ; *or*, = *veor*, great.

BERE PARK, ? barley (*bere*, *s.*) close.

BERGES, ? *i.q.* BARGUS.

BERIES, BERRIES, ? *i.q.* PRAISE.

BERIOW, BERRIOWE, ? *pl.* of *bar*, the hills.

BERIPPER, BERREPPA, BERRIPPER, BERRUPPA, *i.q.* BAREPPA.

BERNARD, *t.d.d.*, firm bear, *t.*, *Y.*

BERNEL, *d.d.*, ? *i.q.* BRANNEL.

BERNER, *t.d.d.*, bear warrior, *t.*, *Y.*

BERNERH, *d.d.*, ? long (*hir*) hill (*bron*).

BERRAS, BERRYAS, ? *i.q.* PRAISE.

BERRICOT, *n.f.*, ? castle, *or*, hill cottage *or* wood (*coat*).

BERRIMAN, *n.f.*, castle, *or*, hill man, *or*, stone (*maen*).

BERRY, = *bre*, a hill ; *or*, *bury*, a castle, *t.*

BERRYCOMBE, the castle vale, *t.*

BERRY HILL, the castle hill.

BERRY PARK, the castle close.

BERSEY, *n.f.*, = BIRHSI.

BERTHEY BRUNE, *Cur.*, ? Beort's enclosure (*hay*), Brune's part.

BERWINNEY, ? = *parc winnic*, marshy close.

BESANKO, *n.f.*, *i.q.* BOSANKO.

BESAWN, cove *or* cave (*zawn*) house (*bos*) ; *or*, house on the down (*oon*).

BESCARN, rock (*carn*) house (*bos*).

BESCASSA, house (*bos*) by the woods (*cosow*).

BESCOLLA, school house, *Pr.*

BESCOLLIN, ? holly (*celin*) house.

BESCOWES, ? outside (*ves*) elder-trees (*scaw*) field (*parc*).

BESIDER, ? = *besidar*, a window.

BESLOW, ? = *parc isala*, lower close.

BESOAR, BESORE, the clomb, mud, *or* earthenware (*oar*) house, *Pr.* ? *i.q.* BASHER.

BESOWSA, *i.q.* BOSAWSA.

BESPALFAN, prayer on the palm of the hand, *H.* (!). *i.q.* BOSPOLVAN.

BESSOE, BESSOW, the birches.

BESSY OON, ? birch, *or*, cowhouse (*boudzhi*) down (*oon*).

BESTALL, *n.f.*, ? = *pistyll*, waterfall, *w.*

BEST PARK, ? cattle (*best*) close.

BESTRASE, ? the tailor *or* cutter's (*trahes*) house. House in the meadow (*pras*), *Pr.*

BESURREL, = ? *bos ar hal*, house on the moor ; *or*, Seiriol's (*w.*) house.

BESWARICK, BESWETHERICK, *n.f.*, *i.q.* BOSWETHERICK.

BESWIDDLE, *i.q.* BOSWIDDLE.

BESWORM, *T.A.*, ? for bee-swarm field.

BETALLICK, *i.q.* BOTALLACK.

BETHANEL, ? the grave (*beth*) on the moor (*hal*) ; *or*, = *benathel*, broom.

BETHAW HALL, ? = *bethow hal*, graves' moor.

BETHEDNICK, the lonely (*idnic*) grave.

BETHEGO, ? Iago's grave.

BETWEEN, ? *i.q.* BEDWIN.

BEUTY BILL, *T.A.*, ? field (*gweal*) by the cow (*beuch*) house (*ti*), (*w.beudy*).

BEVAN, *n.f.*, = *ab-Evan*, = John's son.

BEVERLY, *n.f.*, beaver pasture, *t.*

BE VES, = *parc ves*, outside close.

BEVESHOC, *d.d.*, ? Bevis's oak.

BEWES, BEWS, *n.f.*, ? *i.q.* Bevis, *f.* = *boge*, *Y.* See BOIA.

BEYLE, *n.f.*, *i.q.* BEAL.

BEZACK, *i.q.*, BEDACK.

BEZOAN, = *bos oon*, down house.

BEZUEN, *i.q.* BOSWEN.

BICE, *n.f.*, ? = *bais*, a ford, passage, *w.* ; *or*, *bois*, a wood, *f.*

BICKE, *n.f.* ? = *bich*, = *w.*, *bach*, little.

BICKEL, *n.f.*, ? = *bigal*, a shepherd.

BICKERLEIGH, BICKERLEY, BICKER-LY, *n.f.*, = BEKELEGE.

BICKFORD, *n.f.*, little (*bich*) passage (*fordh*).

BICKLEY, *n.f.*, little pasture (*lea*, *t.*).

BICTON, (*d.d.* BICHETONE), little town or enclosure.

BIDICK, *n.f.*, ? = *buddic*, an axe; or, *i.q.* BUDIC.

BIDIGO, ? *i.q.* BETHEGO.

BIGGAL, little islet *or* rocklet, *A.S.*; shepherd, *N.*

BIGLETUBBEN, shepherd's bank.

BIGLOUN, *o.n.f.*, ? shepherd's down, (*oon*).

BILCROOK, ? barrow (*cruc*) field (*gweal*).

BILGARS, BILGORS, ? fen (*cors*) field.

BILKUM, the coombe field.

BILL, *n.f.*, ? *i.q.* BELI. An axe, gentleness, *t.*, *F.*

BILLACOT, ? Beli's cottage.

BILLET, *n.f.*, ? *i.q.* BLIGHT, *or*, BLEW-ETT.

BILLIN CROFT, ? ball (*pellen*) croft.

BILLING, *n.f.*, *i.q.* BELLING.

BILLOWS, pillas [field].

BILLY BOUNDER, ? lane field (*gweal*).

BILSON, *n.f.*, ? pillas down (*oon*).

BINDON BEACON, top (*pen*) of the hill (*dun*) beacon.

BIN DOWN HILL, ? *a triplication of* hill; *or*, little down hill.

THE BINN, ? the little (*bihan*) [field].

BINNER, ? long (*hir*) hill (*pen*).

BINNER VEAN, little BINNER.

BIRCHINHAY, *n.f.*, birchen enclosure, *t.*

BIRHSI, BRYHSIGE, BYREHTSIGE, &c. *w.B.m.*, bright victory, *t.*

BIRT, *n.f.*, = Bright (*beort*, *s.*).

BISCAVILLET, ? the cottage (*bosca*) in the quillet *or* little field.

BISCAW WOUNE, *Cam.*, the cottage on the downs (*gwon*).

BISCOVALLACK, lower (*wollach*) cottage.

BISCOVEY, ? little (*bich*) cottage.

BISCOW, *Nord.*, the cottage.

BISHOPS BALLS, ? Bishop's fields.

BISKEY BROOM, ? pixey, *or* fairy, broom [field].

BISSA, BISSOE, BISSOW, BIZZA, birches.

BISSICK, the birch (*bezo*, *a.*) place.

BLA LAND, ? plain (*ble*, *w.*) land.

BLACALER, *n.f.*, ? cleared land (*clar*, *i.*) by the calves' house (*bolec*, *Po.*).

BLACKADOWN, ? calves' house down.

BLACKAMOOR, ? calves' house moor.

BLACKATON, ? black hill, *or* town.

BLACK HAY, ? calves' house close.

BLACK PARK, ? calves' house close.

BLACKUM, ? calves' house coombe.

BLADDER PARK, ? dog-stones (*baldar*, *w.*) close.

BLAGDON, ? calves' house hill (*dun*).

BLAKE, *n.f.*, ? = *bolec*, calves' house, *Po.*

BLARICK, BLARY, ? the place abounding with water cress (*beler*).

BLASS, *n.f.*, ? *i.q.* PELLAS; *or* = *plas*, a palace.

BLAYBLE, BLABLE, ? = *pol ebol*, the colt's pool.

BLEDERIC, *Duke*, ? BELI, the red (*dearg*, *ga.*).

BLEE, *n.f.*, ? *i.q.* BOLEIGH *or* BLIGH.

BLEIDIUD, *s.B.m.*, ? from *blaidd*, a wolf, *w.*

BLE-KENNOK, *W. Worc.*, ? parish (*plu*) of Caenog (*w.s.* 5 *cent.*); ? BOCONNOC.

BLENCOWE, *n.f.*, ? the mound (*how*) of the Billings, *t.*

BLENVILLE, ? ball (*pellen*) field (*gweal*).

BLERRAKE, a place of content, *Sc.*

BLETHCUF, *w.B.m.*, ? wolf belly (*kof*, *a.*).

BLETHROS, *w.B.m.*, ? wolf warrior (*rhys*, *w.*).

BLETHU, *t.d.d.*, ? black (*du*) wolf.

BLEU BRIDGE, parish (*plu*) bridge, *Bl.*

BLEWITT, BLUETT, *n.f.*, hair (*bleo*, *a.*) corn (*et*, *id*), *i.e.* barley, *W.N.*

BLIGHT, *n.f.*, ? *i.q.* BOLEIT; *or*, *blaidh*, a wolf.

BLISLAND, *parish* (*o.* BLISTON), ? BELI'S

land or enclosure, (c.d. St. Protasius, O.; St. Protus, v. Pratt, J.M.).

BLISS, BLISS PARK, pillas field.

BLITHE, n.f., ? i.q. BLIGHT.

BLOHIN, t.d.d., ? = blaen, w., head, point, chief, R.W.

BLOWSE HAY, Bloyse's or pillas close.

BLUE PARK, ? parish (plu) close.

BLUNG CLOSE, = belein, priest's, or, blueun, hairy field, B., (T.C.). (?).

BLUNTA, B.m., sleepy, t., F.

BOADEN, BODEN, n.f., i.q. BAWDEN.

BOAL FIELD, mine (bal) field.

BOASE, BOAYS, n.f., ? = bos, meat; a house, a dwelling; a bush.

BOCADDON, ? the house by the wood (coat) on the down (oon).

BOCARNE, = bod carn, rock house.

BOCHYM, cow or cattle (beuch) house (ham), H. (?).

BOCONNION, ? cold (ian) down (gon) house.

BOCONNOC, parish, ? Caennoc's house (bod), or, parish (plu). (p.s. not known, A.T.). See BLE-KENNOK.

BODANNAN, ? bod an oon, down house.

BODARDLE, BODARLE, o. BOCARDEL, ? the exiles' (gwr deol, w.), or, Gwrthwl's (w.s.) house.

BODBRANE, the crow (bran), or, Bran's house.

BODBREAN, hill (bryn), or, tree (pren) house.

BODDENNAR, BODINAR, ? high (arth) fort (din) house.

BODEAN, ? John's (ean = Evan) house.

BODEEVE, ? Ive's, or, summer (haf), house.

BODEGGO, the smith's (go) house, R.W.

BODELLAN, ? fir tree (aidhlan) house.

BODELLICK, ? Alexander's (Allick), or, willow (helic) house.

BODELLIS, step-son's (els), or, green moor (hal las) house.

BODELVA, ? Alva's, or, moor place (halva) house.

BODENNA, i.q. BODDENNAR.

BODENNICK, bod an ick, house by the water, H.; solitary (unic) house R.W.

BODER-LOGAN, -LUGGAN, -LUDVAN, ? long house by the grey stone (llwyd van, w.).

BODERWENNACK, ? the monk's (manach) long house (bod hir).

BODEWORGOIN, d.d. ? WURCON'S house; or, house on the down.

BODEWORGY, (d.d. BODEWORWEI), house on (war) the water (gwy).

BODGATE, ? the serf's (caid) house.

BODGURY, BODGARA, the further (gwarra) house.

BODIGA, ? Iago or James's house.

BODILGATE, Elchut's (w.) house; or, i.q. BODULGATE.

BODILLAN, ? church (lan) moor or hill (hal) house.

BODILLICK, i.q. BODELLICK.

BODILLY, house by the church (illy = eglos), T. ? i.q. BODILLICK.

BODINALGAN, O., ? ÆLCHON'S hill (dun) house (bod).

BODINAR, a habitation on a hill, Gw. (? bod an arth). i.q. BODDENNAR.

BODINIEL, the house by the river (heyl, T.Q.C.), or, on the hill (hal).

BODINNOCK, BODIOCK, i.q. BODEN-NICK.

BODITHIEL, ? Ithel's (w.) dwelling.

BODIVIAL, ? Eval's (c.s.) dwelling.

BODLAY, lay or pasture house.

BODLEIT, ? milk (lait), or Elaeth's (w.s.) house.

BODLEVAN, LEVAN'S (c.s.) house.

BODMAN, BODYMAN, O., the monk's (manach), or, stone (maen), house.

BODMIN, parish, (d.d. BODMINE), the monks' (menech) house; (c.d. St. Petrock).*

---

* " Bod-men, stone-house; bod-myn, the kid's abode; also, the dwellings on the ridge, or, edge of a hill. Lh." Pr.; "monk's house," B.; "mansion of the monks," Le., Cam., Car., Wh., &c.; "preacher (bode) man or men," T. (!)

BODOWAL, Howel's (*w.*), *or*, high (*uchal*), house.

BOD-, BOS-PROWEL, ? Riowal's (*a.*) son's (*ap*) house.

BODRANE, BODREAN, the thorny (*druen*) dwelling (*bod*, Pr.), *or* close (*parc*).

BODREGAN, Regan's house.

BODRIFTY, ? the house by (*ar*) the summer shed (*hafty*).

BODRIGY, house by the sea side, *or* tide place (*trigva*), Pr.

BODROLE, Raoul's house.

BODROGAN, BODRUGAN, *i.q.* BOD-REGAN.*

BODUELL, *i.q.* BODOWAL; *or*, = *w.* Bodvel, house of honey (*mel*), R.IV.

BODULLA, elm tree (*elau*), *or*, owl's (*ula*) house, Gw.; (? *wollach*, lower).

BODULGATE, ? = *bod hal coat*, Morewood House; *or*, Moorgate House; *or*, moor house gate.

BODVALGAN, (BODULCAN, Le.), ? ÆL-CHON'S house.

BODVILLE, *n.f.*, ? *i.q.* BODUELL.

BODWAIN, BODWAN, ? *i.q.* BODWIN.

BODWANNICK, down (*gwon*) house.

BODWAY, house by the river (*gwy*).

BODWEEN, BODWEN, house near the poplars *or* aspen trees (*bedewen*), Pr.

BODWIN, white house, *or*, house on the marsh (*win*), Pr.

BODWITHGY, (*d.d.* BODEWITGHI), ? house near the trees (*gwith*) by the river (*gwy*).

BODWITHIEL, WITHIEL'S house.

BODY, BODDY, *n.f.*, ? = *parc ty*, field house; *or*, *bodi*, a messenger, *o.n.*

BODYFORD, *n.f.*, *i.q.* BADAFORD.

BOFARNELL, *i.q.* BEFARNEL.

BOFILLICK, Phillack's house.

BOFINDLE, ? Gwendal's (*w.*), *or*, little (*bihan*) dale (*dol*) house (*bod*).

BOGAN, *n.f.*, ? = *bochan*, little; *i.q.* VAUGHAN.

BOGEE, BOJEA, = *boudzhi*, cowhouse.

BOGER, *n.f.*, ? = Bouchier, *or* Bourchier, (*f.*); *or* Bowyer, *see* BOIA.

BOGIEF, ?? summer (*haf*) cowhouse.

BOGULLAS, lower (*gullas*) house.

BOHAGUE, ? IAGO *or* James's house.

BOHELLAND, BOHELLAN, *i.q.* BE-HEATHLAND.

BOHENNA, *n.f.*, = BEHENNA, *or*, BO-KENNA.

BOHETHERICK, ? Ydroc's (*w.*) house.

BOHURRA, BOHURTHA, higher *ar* further (*urra, urtha*, = *gwartha*) house.

BOIA, *w.B.m.*, BOIE, *t.d.d.*, ? = *boge*, a bow, *s.*, whence *n.f.* Bowyer.

BOJEWYAN, ? *i.q.* BOJOWAN. Abode of the Jews (*edzhewon*, B.), *A. Esquiros.*

BOJIL, ? the moor *or* hill (*hal*) cowhouse (*boudzhi*); *or*, low (*isal*) house.

BOJOWAN, ? John's (*Dzhuan*), *or*, the lone (*jowan*) house.

BOJUDNO, ?? cowhouse (*boudzhi*) on the high naked exposure (*uthno*, Pr.).

BOKELLY, Grove (*celli*) House.†

BOKENNA, ? Caenog's (*w.s.*) house.

BOKENVER, ? Cynvor's (*w.*), *or*, the great (*veor*) ridge (*cein*) house.

BOKIDDICK, Cedig's (*w.*) house.

BOLANKEN, LUNCEN'S house (*bod*); *or*, the pool (*pol*) on the ridge (*an cein*).

BOLASE, *n.f.*, *i.q.* BORLASE.

BOLATHAN, ? ox (*lodn*) pool.‡

---

* Druid's house, B.; = "*Bo daro gun*, the house on the oak downs," Pr. and Po.; ? " = *Bod ru goon*, the house on the sloping down," M'L., (or on the slope of the downs); "the king's (*dragon*) house," W'h.; "the cows' (*bo*) sea side *or* tide (*trig*) habitation (*ham*); *or* the (*an*) cows' (*bo*) sea-shore *or* tide (*trig*)," H.

† Carew derives the family name from *Boch*, "a goat," and *Kelly*, "to lose,' "The lost goat," and adds "a goate he beareth for his coate."

‡ The *Chronic. Alexandrin.*, as quoted by Mr. Lysons in *Our British Ancestors*, says, "The Phœnicians and Syrians call Cronos" (*Saturn*) "El, and Bel, and BOLATHAN."

BOLATHERICK, *i.q.* POLLADRICK.

BOLEGH, BOLEIGH, *i.q.* BOLEIT. Baal's, *or,* the long (*pell*) grave-stone (*lech*), *W.N.*

BOLEIT, the dairy *or* milk (*lait*) cottage (*bod*), *Pr.*; the place of slaughter (*ladh*), *Bl.*;—? house of the clan (*leid*).

BOLENNA, BOLENNOW, house by the lakes (*lynnow*) *M'L.*

BOLHAM, *o.n.f.,* ?? field (*ball*) dwelling (*ham, s.*).

BOLINGY, *i.q.* BELINGY.

BOLITHO, ? great (*itho*), *or,* most distant (*eithaw, w.*) hill (*bol*), *or,* pit *or* pool (*pol*); *or, i.q.* BOLEIT *or* BELOITHA. A huge belly (*bol*), *Pr.*

BOLLOWAL, high (*uchel*) pit *or* pool.

BOLOGGAS, mice *or* rats' (*loggas*) house, *Pr.*; (*locus,* toffic, *m.c.*).

BOLOTHAS, BOLOWTHAS, house near the tumuli *or* barrows (*low, t.*), *M'L.*

BOLOYTHA, *i.q.* BOLITHO.

BOLSTER, the entrenchment (*bolla*), *or* clay (*bol*) ground (*tir*), *Pr.* ? Pillas ground.

BOLVENTOR, *new parish, &c.* (*c.d.* Holy Trinity); = *bol*[*d ad*]*venture, J.T.*

BOLY, *n.f., i.q.* Bodilly.

BONADY, *n.f.,* ? EDDY's house on the down (*bo-oon*).

BONAFORD, *n.f.,* ? down house by the ford, *or,* road (*fordh*).

BONALLACK, *i.q.* BANALLACK.

BONALVA, BONEALVA, BONY ALVA, ? Alva's down house.

BONE, BOON, *n.f.,* down house.

BONEAR, *n.f.,* long (*hir*) down house.

BONITHON, BONYTHON, the furzy dwelling, *Pr.* (*bod an eithen*).

BONNAL, the house on the cliff (*an alt*), *Pr.*

BONY, *n.f.,* ? = *bo an hay,* house in the enclosure.

BOOSEY, ? *i.q.* BOUDZHI.

BOO TOWN, BOVE TOWN, [field] *above* the *town* place *or* farm buildings.

BORALLAN, the house (*bod*), *or* hill

(*bar*), opposite (*rag*) the lake (*lyn*), *T.C.*

BORDEW, ? black (*du*) summit (*bar*).

BOREASE, ? lower (*isa*) summit.

BOREW, the bleak dwelling, *T.,* (*rew,* frost, ice).

BORGWITHA, ? higher *or* farther (*gwartha*) summit.

BORLASE, the green (*glas*) summit *or* top, *Pr.*

BORLASE VATH, high (*warth*) green summit.

BORNUICK, the dwelling (*bod*) by the (*a'n*) harbour *or* village (*gwic*), *Pr.*

BOROPARK, BOROUGH, BORROW, the barrow, *or,* mine-heap close.

BORSNEEUAS, (*a barrow*), "*in English* cheapfull," *Car.*; ? *i.q.* BOSNIEVES.

BORT HAY, ? broad, *or,* Beort's (*s.*) enclosure (*hay*), *t.*

BOSADON, ? the house (*bos*) on the hill (*dun*); *or,* Sadwrn's (*w.*) house.

BOSAHAN, BOSHAN, the summer (*han*) house, *Pr.*; *or = bos-haun,* house on the haven, *Po.*

BOSANKEN, a disquiet house, *or,* house of trouble (*anken, a.*), *Gw.*

BOSANKETH, *the same, Pr.* (16 *cent.* BUSSANGUITHE, wood house).

BOSANKO, house of death, (*ancow*).

BOSANNETH, dwelling house, *N.*; house of rest, *R.W.*; (*annedh,* a dwelling).

BOSANQUET, *n.f., i.q.* BOSANKETH.

BO-SAUSACK, -SAWSEN, the Saxon's (*saws*) house.

BOS-AVA, -SAVA, apple-tree (*aval,* apples) house, *T.C.*

BOSAVERN, alder-tree (*gwern*) house.

BOSAWNA, haven (*hauen*) house, *W'h.*

BOS-CAGELL, -CADZHELL, -CASWELL, castle house.

BOSCARNE, rock (*carn*) house.

BOSCARNON, ? down (*oon*) rock house.

BOSCASTLE = BOTREAUX's castle.

BOSCATHO, the boats' (*scatha*) house.

BOSCAVERRAN, marsh (*gwern*) cottage (*bosca*); *or,* alder (*gwern*) thicket (*bosc, o.n., I.T.*).

BOSCAWEN, *n.f.*, elder-tree (*scauan*) house, *Pr.* ; = *bosca woon*, the cottage on the down, *Gw.*

BOSCAWEN NOON, the dwelling (*bos*) on the down (*an oon*) of elders (*scaw*), *Pr.* ; ? down elder house.

BOSCAWEN ROSE, the house in the valley of elder trees, *Pr.* ; ? moor (*ros*) elder tree house.

BOSCEAN, BOSCEHAN, ? house on the ridge (*cein*), *R.W.*

BOSCOBBO, BOSCOPPER, house by the barn (*scaber*).

BOSCOLLA, school house, *Pr.*

BOSCOMBE, Vale House.

BOSCOSWYN, *O.*, white (*wyn*) wood (*cos*) house.

BOSCO-VEAN, -VEN, -VEY, the little (*vyhan, vich*) cottage.

BOSCORLA, the house by the sheepfold (*corla*).

BOSCREEGE, barrow (*creeg*) house.

BOSCREGAN, ? little (*an*) barrow, *or*, rock (*carrag*) house.

BOSCROWAN, ? house by the hovel (*crow*) on the down (*oon*).

BOSCUBBEN, little (*en*) coombe house.

BOSCUDDEN, ? wood-pigeon (*cudon*) house.

BOSCUNDLE, ? family (*cenedl, w.*) house, *R.W.*

BOSENCE, BOSENSE, holy residence, *M'L.* ; (*syns*, saints).

BOSENT, ? the saint's (*sant*) house.

BOSENVER, ? house by the road (*vor*).

BOSFRANCAN, the beaver (*francon, w.*) house ; *or*, great (*veor*) house on the down (*an goon*).

BOSSIGAN, BOSSIGANS, twenty (*igans*) houses, *Pr.* ; (? *i.q.* BOSIGRAN).

BOSIGRAN, house of sand (*grean*), *T.C.* ; ? Eigron's (*w.*) house.

BOSILLIACK, BOSULGIACK, ? SULLEISOC's house.

BOSIRON, ? *i.q.* BOSIGRAN ; *or*, long (*hir*) house (*bos*) on the down (*oon*).

BOSISSEL, ? lower (*isala*) house.

BOSISTOW, BOSSUSTOW, ? the advocate's (*sistwr, w.*) house ; *or, i.q.* BOSUSTICK.

BOSITHNEY, ? SITHANEY's house.

BOS-ITHY, -ITHOW, ? ivy (*idhio*), *or*, great (*ithic*) house.

BOSKEAR, castle (*caer*) house ; (*cear*, lovely, *Pr.*).

BOS-KEDNAN, -KENNA, the house on the ascent (*ascen*), *Pr.* ; *or*, on the ridge (*cein*).

BOSKELL, ? house by the hazels, *R.W.*

BOSKENNAL, ? the house on the ascent (*ascen*) of the cliff (*alt*), *or*, of Seachnall (*w.*).

BOSKENSO, BOSKINSOW, the first (*censa*), *or*, CHENISI's house.

BOSKENWYN, KENWYN's house.

BOSKERR-AS, -IS, the dwelling on the summit (*gwarhas*), *Pr.*

BOSKEVELLICK, Cyfelac's (*w.*), *or* the woodcock's (*cyvelac*), house.

BOSKINNING, Cyniu's (*w.*), *or*, leek (*cennin, w.*) cottage (*boscu*).

BOSLAMAN, SALAMAN's house.

BOSLEAKE, Helig's (*w.s.*), *or*, willow house.

BOS-, BUS-LEVAN, ? ST. LEVAN's house.

BOSLOGGAS, *i.q.* BOLOGGAS.

BOSLOVER, ? *i.q.* BELOVER.

BOSLOW, ? *i.q.* BOSWALLACK. House near the water (*l'eau, f.*), *Pr.*

BOSLOWACK, *i.q.* BOSWALLACK.

BOSMAWGAN, ? ST. MAWGAN's house.

BOSNANARTH, ? high (*arth*) down (*an oon*) house.

BOSNIEVES, Nywys's (*w.*) house.

BOSOLLAN, ? SALENN's, *or*, Allwn's (*w.*) house ; *or* house by the church (*lan*).

BOSORE, *i.q.* BESORE *or* BOSOUR.

BOSORN, ? corner (*orn = corn*) house.

BOSOUR, sisters' (*hoer*) house ; *or*, house by the water (*dour*), *R.W.* ; *or, i.q.* BASHER.

BOSOWSA, *i.q.* BOSAUSACK ; *or*, healthy (*sawsac*) house.

BOSPARVA, ? marsh (*morva*) house.

BOSPEBO, BOSPIBO, ? Pabo's (*w.s.*), *or*,

the baker's (*peber*) house.

BOSPIDNICK, ? *i.q.* PROSPIDNICK.

BOSPOLVAN, house by the little (*veun*) pool. *See* BESPALFAN.

BOSPRENNY, ? the wooden (*prennyer*), *or*, crows' (*bryny*) house.

BOSPRENNIS, the prince's (*prennis*) house, *B.* (*o.* BOSPORTHENNIS, ? castle (*dinas*) gate (*porth*) house.

BOSSEAN, *i.q.* BOSCEAN.

BOSSINEY, BOSYNEY, (*d.d.* BOTCINII), ? ISNIOC'S *or* Esne's house. ? = *Bos an ick*, house near the stream, *M·L.*

BOSSORROW, *i.q.* BOHURRA.

BOSSOON, house on the down (*oon*).

BOSSOW, BUSSOW, ? = *bussow*, shallows ; *or*, *i.q.* BISSOE.

BOSSULIAN, BOSULIAN, SULENN'S, *or*, Sulian's (*w.s.*) house.

BOSSULVAL, ? GULVAL'S house, *T.C.*

BOSTOCK, *n.f.*, Doc's (*w.*), *or*, the leader's (*doc, w.*), house ; *or*, = *bustach*, *w.*, a steer.

BOSTOWDA, ? Dodo's (*t.*) house.

BOSUE, black house (*bos du*), *Pr.*

BOS-UEN, -WEN, white (*wen*) house, *Pr.*

BOSURREL, *i.q.* BESURREL.

BOSUSTICK, Usteg's (*w.s.*) house.

BOS-, BUS-VARGUS, house on the top (*bar*) of the wood (*cuz*), *Pr.* *Bargus*, a kite.

BOS-VARREN, -VERRAN, ? alder *or* marsh (*gwern*) house.

BOSVATH-ICK, -OCK, Maedhog's (*w.*), *or*, the fugitives' (*fadic*), house.

BOS-VELLICK, -WELLOCK, house by the mill stream (*ick*), *T.*

BOS -VENNEN, -VENNING, the woman's (*benen*) house, *Pr.*

BOSVIGO, ? house by the little (*go*) stream (*gwy*), *II.M.W.* ; *or*, Wiga's, *or*, the warrior's (*wiga, s.*) house.

BOS-, BUS-VINE, little (*byhan*) house.

BOSVISACK, ? outer (*vesach*) house.

BOSVISICK, house by the river's (*gwy*) creek (*ick*), *Pr.* ? House by the birches (*bizzo*).

BOSWALL-OCK, -OW, ? lower (*wallack*) house.

BOSWARTH, high (*gwarth*) house.

BOSWARTHA, higher *or* further house.

BOSWARTH-AN, -EN, house on (*war*) the hill (*dun*), *T.C.*

BOS-, BUS-WARVA, ? *i.q.* BOSWARTHA.

BOSWASE, ? outside (*ves*) house.

BOSWATHICK, ? *i.q.* BOSWARTHA.

BOSWAVAS, ? outside (*ves*) winter (*gwaf*) house ; *or*, Gwavas's house.

BOSWEDD-AN, -EN, *i.q.* BOSWEN.

BOSWEDDREN, ? Medron's (*w.*) house.

BOSWEDNACK, ? Wednoc's house. White (*gwidn*) house by the water (*ack*), *T.C.*

BOS-WEN, -WIN, -WYN, white house.

BOSWENNEN, *i.q.* Bosvennen. Bees' (*guenen*) house, *T.C.*

BOSWENS, windy house, *B.* (*gwens*, wind).

BOSWETHERICK, ? PETHERICK'S house

BOSWHARTON, ? *i.q.* BOSWARTHEN.

BOSWIDDLE, ? Irishman's (*gwidhal*) house. House in open place, *or* one easily seen from, *T.* ; (*guydh*, conspicuous, high, *B.*).

BOSWINGRAN, ? white sand (WIN GRAN) house, *R.W.*

BOSWINGY, white (*gwin*) house by the rivulet (*gwy*), *Pr.*

BOSWOR-DY, -GY, -THA, -THY, ? house on (*war*) the river (*gwy*) ; *or*, *i.q.* BOSWARTHA.

BOSWORLAS, ? lower (*wollas*) house ; *or*, house on the green (*war las*), *R.W.*

BOSWORLAS LEHAU, ? Bosworlas flat stones (*lechau*).

BOSWYLLICK, ? Meilig's (*w.*), *or*, the priest's (*belec, a.*) house.

BOTAD-EN, -ON, ? *i.q.* BOSADON.

BOTALL-ACK, -ICK, -OCK, = *bod talog*, house on a promontory, *R.W.* ; high (*tallick*) house, *Pr.* ; house of the serpent (*hac*) god (*al, ph.*), *Buller.*

BOTARDELL, *i.q.* BODARDLE.

BOTATHAN, *i.q.* BOTADEN. The pope's, *or* father's (*tad, tat*) house, *Pr.*

BOTCONOAN, *d.d.*, *i.q.* Bocconion.

BOTELETT, BOTLETT, (*d.d.* BOTILED),

? *i.q.* BODULGATE ; *or*, BOLEIT.

BOTEN, *d.d.*, ? *i.q.* BOWDEN.

BOTENDLE, ? house in the vale (*dol*).

BUTERELL, BOTTRELL, *n.f.*, ? = *bod ar hal*, house on the moor ; *or*, *botterol*, a toad, *f.*, *W.N.* ; *or*, *potrael*, shepherd, *f.* ; *or*, *i.q.* BOTREAUX, *or*, PUTRAEL.

BOTERNELL, fire (*bot*) land (*tir*) hill, *ga.*, *Beal.*

BOTISHALL, *o.n.f.*, ? house (*bod*) under (*is*) the hill *or* moor (*hal*).

BOTHARDER, *d.d.*, ? long (*hir*) hill (*ard*) hut (*both*).

BOTHERAS, *n.f.*, ? = BOTREAUX, *or*, PORTHERAS.

BOTIVAL, *d.d.*, ? high (*iuhal*) house.

BOTOWN, BOVETOWN, *i.q.* BOOTOWN.

BOTREA, ? = *bod tra*, house beyond.

BOTREATH, ? red (*ridh*) house ; *or*, house on the sand (*treath*).

BOTREAUX, BOTTERAUX, *n.f.*, *from* Les Botteraux, in Normandy, *Lo.* ; castle on the sea *or* waters (*eaux*, *f.*), *Pr.*

BOTREVA, ? the tax-gatherer's (*refa*, *s.*) house (*bod*).

BOTTERS, ? Botreaux's [farm].

BOTTERTON, (*d.d.* BOTTHATUNO), ? cottage (*both*) on the hill (*dun*).

BOTUSFLEMING, (*parish*), ? Fleming's parish, (*plu*, *H.*), *or* station (*betws*, *w.*). (*c.d.* St. Mary, *W.E.V.*).

BOU-DGIE, -DZIII, -JEY, cow (*beuch*) house (*chy*) *or* fold.

BOUDZHI PARK YET, gate (*yet*) close (*parc*) with the cow-house.

BOUNDA PARK, ? lane (*bounder*), *or*, boundary close.

BOUNDANYET, the boundary by the gate.

BOVEHAY, *above* the enclosure, *t.*

BOWDEN, *n.f.*, *i.q.* BAWDEN. A sorry fellow, a bad man, a nasty place, *Pr.* (*Boden*, a grove, thicket, *a.*).

BOW-GEHEER, -GYHERE, long (*hir*) cow-house (*boudzhi*) ; *or*, long (*hir*) house (*bo*) by the water (*gwy*), *Pr.*

BOWHAY, cow (*beuch*) close.

BOWIDOC, *d.d.*, ? QUITHIOCK'S, *or* the wild-sow's (*gwyddhwch*, *w.*) house.

BOWITHICK, ? *the same* ; *or*, BUDIC'S house ; *or*, house in the woody place (*gwithic*).

BOWJEY BEAGLE, ? shepherds' (*begel*) cow-house.

BOWJEY REEN, hill (*rhyn*) [field] with the cow-house.

BOWKENNA, ? *i.q.* BOCONNOC.

BOWLAND, ? cow field ; *or* house (*bod*) in the enclosure (*lan*).

BOWZY FIELD, cow-house field.

BOYER, *n.f.*, ? *i.q.* BOWGEHEER, *or* BOGER, *or*, BOIA.

BOY-LAND, -PARK, ? cow field.

BOYTON, *parish*, (*d.d.* BOIETONE), BOIA'S enclosure, *t.* Ox (*biu*), *or*, wood (*bois*, *f.*) town, *T.* ; Colony of the Boii, *H.* (*p.s. not known*, *J.G.D.*).

BOZACON, ? cow-house (*boudzhi*) on the down (*goon*).

BRACKBERRY, ? brake, *or*, badger (*broch*, *w.*) hill (*bre*).

BRADDON, ? *i.q.* BRANDON.

BRADFORD, broad ford, *t.*

BRADINGHAM, ? dwelling (*ham*) in the broad meadow (*ing*), *t.*

BRADOCK, = BROADOAK, *parish*, (*p.s. St. Mary*, *O.*) ? place of treachery (*brad*, *w.*), *R.W.*

BRADRIDGE, broad ridge, *t.*

BRADSWORTHY, ? Beort's farm (*weorthig*, *s.*).

BRAES, ? Bray's [farm] ; *or*, lower (*isa*) hill (*bre*) ; *or*, hills.

BRA-HAN, -HANE, ? summer (*han*) hill (*bre*) ; cow brannel, *Pr.*

BRAKESDON, ? the brakes' hill (*dun*).

BRAN-DISE, -DIS, -DISH, ? *i.q.* PARK AN DISE. (*brandys*, *m.c.*, a tripod used in cooking, *T.Q.C.*).

BRAN-DON, -TON, ? crow hill.

BRANDY, ? crow (*bran*) house (*ty*) ; *or*, *i.q.* PARK AN TYE.

BRANNEL, ? = *bar an hal*, top of the moor *or* hill.

BRANSON, ? Bran's (*w.*) town.

BRASACOT, ?? meadow cottage.

BRASMORE, BRAZENMORE, ? the great (*maur*) meadow (*pras*).

BRASS WELL, ? high (*uchel*) meadow.

BRAVERY, ? further (*guarra*) hill.

BRAY, BREA = *bre*, mountain, hill.

BREACK PARK, ? *brake* close.

BREAGE, *parish, from p.s.* St. Breaca, *O.*

BREANICK, *i.q.* BRYANNICK.

BREAS, ? *i.q.* BRAES, *or*, PRAISE.

BREA VEAN, little (*bihan*) hill.

BRE-GA, -JA, -EDGA, ? lower (*isa*) hill.

BREMAN, ? hill with the stone (*muen*).

BRENCI, *s.B.m.*, ? king (*bren*) dog (*ci*).

BREN-DON, -TON, ?king's hill. Crow's (*brahan*) hill (*dun*), *Pr.*

BRENN, BRENT, BRENTA, the hill, *J.C.*

BRENTOR, hill (*tor*) of burning (*brenning, s.*), *T.Q.C.*

BRET, ? corn (*ed, et*) hill (*bre*).

BRETEL, *t.d.d.*, ? bright helmet (*helm*), *t.* ; *or, i.q.* BRITAIL.

BRETHA TOR, hill of judgment (*breath, ga.*), *Beal.*

BRETHEI, *d.d., i.q.* BURTHY.

BRETHOC, *s.B.m.*, ? = *bradawg*, traitor, *w.*

BREW, ? high (*uch*) hill (*bre*).

BREWE-R, -RS, ? from *bruyere*, heath, *f., T.*

BREWINNEY, ? = *bruinic*, rushy place.

BREY DOWN, hill (*bre*) down.

BRICTRIC, *t.d.d.*, bright rule (*ric*), *t.*

BRIDGERULE, *parish*, Raoul *or* Reginald's bridge, *t.* ; (*p.s.* St. Michael, *O.*)

BRIDGEVINE, stones (*myin*) of judgment (*brys*), *T.C.*

BRIEN-D, -SIUS, *t.d.d., i.q.* BRYANT = BRIAN, strong, *i.* ; *or, bruyant*, noisy, *f., Y.*

BRIGGERNOK, *cent.* 14, Cornish bridge.

BRIGHTOR, little (*biggan*) hill (*tor*), *Pr.* (?)

BRIGHTON, ? clay (*pry*) hill (*dun*).

BRIHFERD, *t.d.d.*, bright peace (*frid*), *t.*

BRILL, ?? moor (*hal*) hill (*bre*).

BRIMBOIT, *i.q.* BROMBOIT.

BRIMMELL, ? broom *or* bramble hill.

BRIN, BRINN, = *bren*, a tree, *Pr.* ? Hill, *bryn, w.*

BRIS-MAR, -MER, bear (*bersi, o.n.*) fame (*mar, s.*).

BRISONS, the prisons, *Bl.*

BRISTON, ? Brice's, *or,* BIRHSI'S town or farm, *t.*

BRISTUAL, *t.d.d.*, ? bright (*bricht*) power (*wald*), *t.*

BRIT, BRITA, *o.n.f.*, ? the Briton.

BRITAIL, *w.B.m.*, ? Brit the generous (*hael*) ; *or, i.q.* BRETEL.

BRITNOD, *t.d.d.*, ? bright (*bricht*) compulsion (*not*), *t.*

BRITTON, BRIDDON, *n.f.*, ? *i.q.* BRAY DOWN ; *or, reduplication of* Hill.

BRIXI, *t.d.d., i.q.* BIRHSI.

BROADA PARK, the broad close.

BROADOAK, *parish*, (*d.d.* BRODEHOC), see BRADOCK.

BROCKA BARROW, badger's barrow.

BROCKLE, ? badger's (*broch*) hill.

BRODE, *o.n.f.*, ? = *Beort*, bright, *s.*

BROKEN PARK, the badger's close.

BRODRE, *t.d.d.*, ? = *Beohrtric*, bright rule, *s.* ; (*brodre*, brothers, *d.*).

BROMBOIT, the boor's (*bromun*) hut (*both*), *ga., Beal.* ? = Broomwood.

BROMHILL, broom hill.

BRONEYR, *cent.* 14, ? battle (*heir*) hill.

BRONSEHAN, the dry (*sech*) round hill (*bron*), *R.W.*

BROTHECK, *Car., i.q.* BRADOCK.

BROWNDEEP, ? = *bron dubh*, black hill.

BROWNGELLY, ? grove (*celli*) hill.

BROWN QUEEN, BROWNQUIN, white (*gwin*) hill.

BROWNSUE, ? black hill.

BROWNWILLY, = *w.* Bronwylva, hill of watching, *R.W.* ; highest (*uhella*) hill, *J.B.* ; female (*brun*) attendant (*giolla*), *ga., Beal.*

BROWNWITHAN, tree (*gwidhen*) hill.

BRUIN CLOSE, rushes close.

BRUN, *B.m.*, brown ; *or*, impetuous, *t., F.*

BRUNE, *n.f.*, ? the same.

BRUNNION, ? = *brunnen*, a rush.

BRYANNICK, ? = *bruinic*, a rushy

place; the place under the hill; *rather*, = *pryan ick*, the place of clay, Pr.; the hill (*bre*) by the (*u'n*) water (*ick*), *M'L.*

BRYANT, *n.f.*, ? *i.q.* BRIEND.

BRYDON, clay (*pry*) hill (*dun*), Pr.

BRYHER, *o.* BREHER, long (*hir*), or, eagle (*er*) hill (*bre*), *N.*

BRYN, *i.q.* BRIN.

BRYTTHAEL, *w.B.m.*, ? *i.q.* BRITAIL.

BUCCAS MEADOW, scarecrows' meadow.

BUCHY, *i.q.* BOUDZIE.

BUCK, *n.f.*, = *boch*, a he goat.

BUCKA, ? cow (*beuch*) field (*hay*).

BUCKA BORROW, ? scarecrow barrow.

BUCKENVER, ? great (*vcor*) ridge (*cein*) house (*bod*).

BUCKLESOME, ? BUGGLE's home.

BUCKERNE, *Nord.*, *i.q.* BOCARNE.

BUCKLAWREN, ? fox (*lowern*) hole (*voug*).

BUCTON, *n.f.*, ? cow (*beuch*) enclosure.

BUDDA, *w.B.m.*, a messenger, *t.*, F.

BUDDLE, *n.f.*, ? = *budel*, a beadle, *t.*, Lo.*

BUDE, a haven, Pr. (?)

BUDEAUXHEAD, *n.f.*, St. Budeaux Point.

BUDGE, BUDGELL, *n.f.*, dim. of *boda*, a messenger, *t.*, F.

BUDGET, ? cow-house (*boudzhi*) gate (*yet*) [field].

BUDIC, *s.B.m.*, victorious (*buddic, w.*).

BUDLA, ? house (*bod*) by the enclosure (*lan*).

BUDNICK FIELD, ? bunchy (*bothan, B.*) field.

BUDOCK,† *v.* BIDDICK, parish, from *p.s.* St. Budocus, *i.q.* BUDIC.

BUDOCK VEAN WARTHA, higher little Budock.

BUDY BARN, cow-house (*beudy, w.*) barn [field].

BUFTON, ? ox close; or, *i.q.* BOO TOWN.

BUGGEL, *o.n.f.*, ? = *bugel*, a shepherd or herdsman.

BUGGIN, *n.f.*, = Bacon, *H.*; ? *i.q.* BOGAN.

BUGLE, ? cow (*beuch*) hill.

BULLAND, BULLEN, clay (*pol*) enclosure (*lan*), Pr.

BULLAPIT, ? the bulls' or clay pit.

BULLER, *n.f.*, a deceiver, *f.*, Lo.; ? = *belour*, a combatant, *a.*

BULLMORE, *n.f.*, ? great (*mawr*) pool (*pol*).

BULLOCK, *n.f.*, ? = *blouc'h*, without hair, *a.*

BULLREATH, ? red (*rydh*) pool.

BULSE, ? = PILLAS.

BULSEBEAR, ? pillas or poor farm (*bear*).

BULSWORTHY, ? bulls' field (*weorthi, s.*); or, *i.q.* BUSWORGY.

BUMBLE, rock, ? from *pwmpl*, a bubble, *w.*

BUNERDAKE, ? = *pen eru tec*, fair field end.

BUNNY, BUNY, ? *i.q.* BONY.

BUNGAYS, BUNGS PARK, ? cooper's (*bynciur*) close.

BUNKERSHILL, ? cooper's hill.

BUNT, *n.f.*, a swelling in a sail, &c., *o.e.*; or, *i.q.* Bennet.

BURCOMBE, ? birch (*beore, s.*) vale.

BURDOWN, *o.* BURDON, ? top (*bar*) of the down, or hill (*dun*).

BURGERED, *t.d.d.*, ? city council (*red, s.*)

BUR-GESS, -GOIS, -GOSS, -GUS, *i.q.* BARGUS.

BURGET, ? = *parc yet*, gate field.

BURGHGEAR, *reduplication of* castle.

---

* Rather = *Buddle-boy*, he who attends to the washing away of the impurities from the tin ore that has been crushed in the stamping mill.

† BUDOCK, *byth'ick*, oak haven, or, the border or skirt of the harbour, Pr.; from *birth*, a hut, cottage, or booth (*w.*), and *ick*, adjectival, or a creek, Ped. St. Budeaux, partly situated west of the Tamar, is also dedicated to St. Budocus, and is one of the very few parishes in Devonshire called after the patron saint.

BURGWALLANS, ? lower (*gwalla*) lambs' (*eanes*) field (*parc*).

BURINS, ? = *parc eanes*, lambs' close.

BURITON, (*now* Penzance), castle town, *Po.*

BURKEHAM, ? birch (*beorc*) border (*ham*), *t.*

BURKENHALL, ? birch moor *or* hill (*hal*).

BURLAND, ? top (*bar*) of the enclosure (*lan*); *or* barley (*bere*) land, *t.*

BURLACE, BURLASE, *i.q.* BORLASE.

BUR-LAWN, -LORNE, ? fox (*lewarn*) hill (*bar*).

B. EGLOS, Burlawn by the church.

B. PELLOW, ? further (*pella*) Burlawn.

BURLEY, ? burdock pasture, *t.*

BURLOWENA, *i.q.* BARLOWENA.

BURMSDON, ?? *Abraham's* hill.

BURN, BURNA, BURNE, ? = *burne*, a stream, *s.*; *or*, *bron*, a hill.

BURNAWITHAN, *i.q.* BROWNWITHAN.

BURNCOON, ? down (*goon*) hill.

BURNCOOSE, the high *or* hill (*bron*) wood (*cos*), *Pr.*; ? wood hill.

BURNERE, ? *i.q.* BERNERH, *d.d.*

BURNGULL-A, -OE, -OW, ? lower (*gwolla*) hill.

BURN-ON, -OON, -DOWNS, the high downs, *Pr.*; ? top of the (*bar an*) downs.

BURN-UHALL, -EWHALL, well (*burne*, *s.*) in *or* above (*yu*) the moor (*hal*), *Pr.*; ? high (*uchal*) hill (*bron*).

BURNWELL, *the same.*

BURRACOT, ? barrow cottage.

BURRATON, ? barrow hill (*dun*).

BURROW BELLES, the far (*pel*), broad, *or* large (*les*), burrow *or* sepulchre, *H.*

BURROW GAVES, ? barrow outside (*ves*) the fence (*ce*).

BURR-ELL, -ILL, ? *bar hal*, top of the moor *or* hill.

BURRIDGE, ?? = *broad ridge, t.*

BURRUPPA, *i.q.* BAREPPA.

BURSUE, the black (*zu*) top, *Pr.*

BURSWILLICK, *i.q.* BOSVELLOCK.

BURT-HAY, -HY, ? *i.q.* BORT HAY; *or*, bush (*perth*) enclosure.

BUR-THOG, -THOGGE, *n.f.*, ?? *the same.*

BURTHY BREWING, *i.q.* BERTHEY BRUNE.

BURTHY ROW, ? Rowe's, *or*, rough Burthy.

BURWELL, ? *i.q.* BURNUHALL.

BURWIN, white (*gwin*) top (*bar*), *Pr.*

BURYAS, ? *i.q.* PRAISE.

BURY, *i.q.* BERRY. The tumulus, *C.*

BURY CAMP, castle *or* hill camp, *t.*

BURY PARK, castle close.

BUSALLOW, *i.q.* BOSWALLOCK.

BUSAVEAN, ? little house (*bos*).

BUSCADJACK, ? dirty (*cassic*) house.

BUSCAVERRAN, *i.q.* BOSCAVERRAN; old house, *Pr.*

BUSCAREN, ? *the same*; *or*, *i.q.* BOSCARNE.

BUSCOLL, ? *i.q.* BOSCOLLA; *or*, house by the hazels (*coll*).

BUSCREEGE, *i.q.* BOSCREEGE; the dwelling by the cross *or* barrow, *Pr.*

BUSCRIGGAN, *i.q.* BOSCREGAN.

BUSHORNE, ? *i.q.* BOSORN.

BUSKEYS, ? shade (*sces*) close (*parc*).

BUS-LOW, -ELLA, -SULLOW, -WALLOW, *i.q.* BOSLOW.

BUSS MEADOW, calf (*buss*, *m.c.*) meadow.

BUSSAS HILL, ? hill where the urns (*bussa*, *m.c.*) were found.

BUSSAWSICK, *i.q.* BOSAUSACK.

BUSSILLIAN, *i.q.* BOSSULIAN.

BUSSOW, ? *i.q.* BOSSOW.

BUSSY, ? *i.q.* BOUDGIE.

BUSTICK, ? *i.q.* BOSUSTICK.

BUSTOW, ? *i.q.* BOSISTOW.

BUSVEAL, the calves' house, *Pr.*; ? house on the bare hill, (= *w. Bod y voel*), *R.W.*

BUSVEAN, *i.q.* BOSVINE.

BUSWAGE, ? *i.q.* BOSWASE.

BUSWARRA, *i.q.* BOSWARTHA.

BUSWASBER, ? VOSPER'S house

BUSWEDEN, *i.q.* BOSWEDDEN.

BUSWEEGA, ? *i.q.* BOSVISACK, *or,* BOSVIGO.

BUSWORLAS, *i.q.* BOSWORLAS ; house on the high (*warth*) green (*glas*), *Pr.*

BUSWORGY, *i.q.* BOSWORGY ; house above the river, *Pr.*

BUT-, BUTT-PARK, archery close.

BUTRIS, ? *i.q.* BARTERESS.

BUTSAVA, *i.q.* BOSAVA.

BUTCHER'S FIELD, ? *i.q.* BOUDGIE.

BUTS-BER, -PUR, ? Butt's farm (*bere*).

BUTTERAVILLE, Butter's house ; *or,* place where there is a view (*willy*), *E.*

BUTTERDON, *i.q.* BOTTERTON ; *or,* long (*hir*) house (*bod*) hill (*dun*).

BUTTERN, ? *i.q.* BATTERN.

BUTTERWELL, ? *i.q.* BUTTERAVILL.

BUTTON, *i.q.* BUFTON ; *or,* = *bod oon,* down house.

THE BUTTRESS, *i.q.* BUTRIS.

THE BUTTS, the place where archery was practised, *J.M.*

BUTTY, ? *i.q.* BUDY.

BUZMAUGAN, *i.q.* BOSMAWGAN.

BUZZA, *n.f.*, = BUSSA, *or,* BOUDGIE.

BUZZARAL, *i.q.* BOSURREL.

BYERLEE, *n.f.*, ? *i.q.* BURLEY.

BYHSTAN, *s.B.m.*, ? = *Brychstan,* bright stone, *t.*

BYRCHTYLYM, *s.B.m.*, ? *i.q.* BRETEL.

BYRHTFLOED, *B.m.*, bright influence,*t.*

BYRHTGYVO, *B.m.*, bright gift, *t.*

CAASE, ? lower (*isa*) enclosure (*ce*) ; *or,* the wood (*cois*).

THE CABE, ? = *cape,* promontory.

CABILLA, *i.q.* CARBALLA.

CABLAN, = *Cabm Alan,* the crooked (*cam*) ALAN ; *Po.*, (*now the* CAMEL).

CADAPIT, ? battle pit.

CADD, *n.f.*, ? battle (*cad, w.*).

CADES, ? = *caites,* a bondwoman.

CADGE-, CAGE-WITH, battle tree, *H.* ; ? = *scedgwith,* privet.

CADMADOC, ? Madog's battle-field (*cad, w.*).

CADOCK, *Duke,* = *cadwg,* warlike, *w.*

CADON BARROW, ? battle hill (*dun*) tumulus.

CADOR, *Earl,* warrior (*cadwr, w.*).

CADSON, ? bondwoman's down.

CADSON BURY, Cadson Castle.

CADUUALANT, *t.d.d.*, ? = *Cadwallon,* war lord, *Y.*

CADUSCOT, ? battle-field (*cad, w.*) be-low (*is*) the wood (*coat*) ; *or,* bondwoman's cot.

CADWIN, *pr. Cuden,* soldiers' hill,*M'L.*

CAER AN KLEDH, the camp with the ditch *or* trench, *M'L.* ; (*cledh,* left, north).

CAER BRAN, crow village, *Gw.* ; Brennus's Castle, *Po.*

CAERFOS, -FOSSOU, -FOZA, -VOZA, camp with the foss *or* dyke, *B.*

CAER GONIN, Conon's castle *or* camp.

CAERGUIDN, white castle, *B.*

CAERHEIZ, barley village, *Gw.*

CAER KIEF, companion castle, *Wh.* ; castle with ditch, *M'L.*

CAER KYNOCK, ? Caenog's (*w.*) castle.

CAER LADDON, ? broad (*ledan*), *or* bank (*ladn*) field (*cae, w.*).

CAERLEON, Lleon's (*w.*) castle. Castra legionis, *R.IV.* ; ? *i.q.* CALLEAN.

CAERNGREY, the *grey* rock (*carn*).

CAERTHILLIAN, ? the owl's (*dylluan*) carn.

CAFFIL MEADOW, ? horse (*cevil*) meadow.

CAIR, = *caer,* a camp, castle, city, village ; *or, care,* the mountain ash.

CAIRNE HAY, carn *or* rock close.

CAIRO, ? = *cacrau,* the camps.

CAKEVAL, ? horse (*cevil*) close (*cae, w.*)

CALADDRICK, ? Edrick's field (*gweal*) ; *or* watery (*douric*) fields (*gwealow*).

CALAMANSACK, the hard (*cal*) stony place, *or,* the stony grove, (*celli*), *Pr.*

CALA-MERE, -MEER, ? great (*mear*) field.

CALARTH, ? high (*arth*) field.

CAL-ARTHA, -ATHA, ? higher field.

CALCUFF, ? the smith's (*gof*) field.

CALDOWN, ? = *cold down.*

CAL-EDNA, -IDNA, -ENDO, -ENNO, ? *i.q.* GWEALEDNACK.

CALEN-DRA, -DRY, old house (*hendra*) field ; *or* = *celin dre*, holly house, *R.W.*

CALENICK, holly (*celin*) place ; *or*, moist (*lynnic*) enclosure (*cae*).

CALL, *n.f.*, hard, flinty, obdurate, *H.*

CALLASE, ? green (*glas*) field.

CALLE-AN, -ON, ? lamb (*ean*) field.

CALL-EEVAN, -EVAN, ? smooth (*levan*) field.

CALLENGIA, ? = *gweal an chy*, field by the house.

CALLESTOCK, hard (*cal*) broad (*les*) oak, *T.* ; ? broad field (*gweal*) with the dead stock of a tree (*stoc*).

CALLIBARRET, ? BARRETT'S grove.

CALLIBUDGIA, cowhouse (*boudzhi*) grove (*celli*), or field (*gweal*).

CALLILOND, ? grove land.

CALLIMAY POINT, *from* the Breton festival Kalamae, on the *calends* of *May*, *N.* ; ± *w. Calanmai, R.W.*

CALLINGTON, *v.* KELLITON, *d.d.* CAL-WETONE, (*p.s.* St. Mary), chapel (*cil, H.*), *or*, grove (*celli, T.*) town.

CALLIWITH. ? = *w. Collwith*, hazel grove, *R.W.*

CALSTOCK, *d.d.* CALESTOCK, (*p.s.* St. Andrew, *O.*), hard stock *or* oak, *Pr.*

CALVADNACK, *i.q.* GOLWEDNACK.

CALVENOR, ? slaughter (*ar*) stone (*maen*) field.

CALVER MEADOW, ? great field (*gweal veor*), *or*, pigeon-house (*culver*) meadow.

CALVORRY, ? further (*warra*) field.

CAMBEAK, crooked (*cam*) point (*pyg*).

CAMBERDENEY, CAMPERDENEY, Welshman's fortification (*dinas*),*N.*

CAMBERDOWN, Welshman's hill *or* down.

CAMBLAN, CAMB ALAN, *Cam.*, for CABM ALAN.

CAMBORNE, *o.* CAMBRON, (*c.d.* St. Meriadocus, *O.*), crooked hill (*bron*). The crooked *or* arched *burne* or

well, *H.* ; crooked river (*burne, s.*), *Nord.*

C. VEAN, little Camborne.

C. VEOR, great Camborne.

CAMBRIDGE, crooked bridge, *Pr.* ; ? bridge over the crooked [river] ; *o.* CAMBROSE, ? = *carn bras*, great carn, *T.C.*

CAMEL, crooked river, *Nord.*, (= *cam heyl, T.Q.C.*).

CAMEL FIELD, = *camomile* field.

CAMELFORD, the passage over the river CAMEL.

CAMERRANCE, *i.q.* CARMERRANCE.

CAMOEN, ? crooked down (*oon*).

CAMPASSUCK, *i.q.* CARNPESSUCK.

CAMPBELL, CAMEL, *n.f.*, ? from the river, *C.S.G.*

CANAKEY, *i.q.* CARNAKEY.

CANAL-IDGEY, -ISSEY, -EGIE, St. Issey Creek, *B.* ? carn on St. Issey moor (*hal*).

CANA PARK, ? = Corner close.

CANARTHEN, *i.q.* CARNARTHEN.

CANDRA, ? white *or* singing town.

CANDROW, ? down (*goon*) of oaks (*deru*).

CANE PARK, ? ridge (*cein*) close.

CANEAN, ? lamb (*ean*) rock (*carn*).

CANEDON, *i.q.* CARNEDON.

CANENV-OR, -ER, ? rock (*carn*) by the road (*en vor*).

CAN-ERA, -ARA, field (*eru*) ridge (*cein*), *Ped.*

CANHALLACK, *i.q.* CARNHALLACK.

CAN-HEWAS, -VASS, *i.q.* CARNHEWAS.

CANHILLY, ? *i.q.* GOONHILLY.

CANN, *n.f.*, ? = *can*, white ; a song ; a hundred ; the full moon, *Po.*

CANN-ELLAS, -ILLS, *i.q.* CARNELLAS.

CANNER PARK, ? = *corner* close.

CANNICK PARK, ? rocky (*carnic*) close.

CANNICOOSE, ? rock (*carn*) by the wood (*cuz*).

CANNYGLAZE, ? *i.q.* CARNGLASE.

CANODGEON, ? ox (*udzheon*) carn.

CAN ORCHARD, ? Orchard's down (*goon*), *or*, carn.

CANRETHEO, deacon, *w.B.m.*, ? singer (*cantor*) of merit (*reth*), *F.B.*

CANTGUEITHEN, CANTGETHEN, CAN-
GUEDEN, *deacon, w.B.m.,* ? singer
of prayer (*gweddi, w.*), *F.B.*

CANWORTHY, *i.q.* CARNWORTHY.

CARA, *n.f.,* ? = *carrag,* a rock, a stone ;
or, *carow,* a stag.

CARAC DIU, black (*du*) rock.

CARA-CLOSE,-CLOUSE,-CLOWZE,-CLUZ,
-GLOOSE, -GLOZE, -GLUZ, the grey
(*ludzh, Lh.*) rock.

CARA CLOWSE EN COWSE, "the hoare
rock in the wood" (*cuz*), *Car.**

CARA CROAK, = *carrac, i.e. the rock,*
a reduplication.

CARADJER, ? = *caer-, carn-,* or *cue issa,*
lower castle *or* town, carn, *or* close.†

CARADOCUS, *king, w.Caradwg* beloved.

CARADON, ?? castle on the hill (*dun*).
Sheep (*caor, ga.*) hill, *Beal.* (*o.* CAR-
NADON).

CARALLA, ? lower (*gwolla*) close.

CARALVA, ? Alva's c.

CARB-ALLA, -ELLA, -ILLA, ? lower c. ;
or, *i.q.* CARBILLY.

CARB-ARROW,-URROW,-ORRO, ? higher
(*gwarra*) c.

CARBEAN, *d.d.* CARBIHAN, little c.

CAR-BEELE, -BILLY, a rock *mentulæ
formæ, Sc.* ; ? rock of Bel *or* the sun.

CARBIGLETT, ? shepherd's (*bigel*) gate
(*yet*) close (*cae*).

CARBILLY, ? BELI's castle, *i.q.* BLIS-
TON.

CAR-BIS, -BOS, -BUS, rocky wood
(*bois, f.*), *or,* house *or* castle (*bos*)
of stone, *Pr.*

CARBLAKE, ? priest's (*belec, a.*) town.

CARBONENELLIS, *i.q.* CARNBONELES.

CARBOULING, ? Peulyn's (*w.*) c.

CARBOWL, ? the pool (*pol*) c.

CARC, ? = *currac,* a rock.

CARCARICK, ? rock c.

CARCLAZE, grey (*glas*) rock (*Pr.*), *or*
castle, *Po.*

CARCLEW, *o.* CRUCGLEW, the barrow
(*cruc*) with the ditch *or* fence,
(*cluth*), *Po.* ; the enclosure (? *clew*)
of barrows, *H.* ; the rocky-land
(*carrak*) of the creek (*loo*), *Ped.*

CARC-OW, -OE, ? barrows (*cregow*).
Camp of the warrior *or* dog (*cu,
ga.*), *Beal.*

CAR-DEW, -DU, black rock *or* castle,
Pr.

CARDI-EST, -EAST, ? c. of the witness
(*test*).

CARDIGGAN, ? sack (*tigan, B.*) close.

CARDINAN, *n.f.,* DINAN's c.

CARDINHAM, Dinan's *or* DINHAM's
town ; (*p.s.* St. Meubredus, *O.*).

CARDINNEY, ? hilly (*dinnick*) c.

CARDODDAN, ? the c. below (*dodn*).

CARDREAVY, ? the c. of the house
(*tre*) by the stream (*gwy*).

CARDREW, oak (*deru*), *or* Druids' c.

CARDWEN, ? = *gard wen,* white garden,
R.W.

CARE, *i.q.* CAER.

CAREG-LOOSE, -LOOZ, *i.q.* CARAG-
LOOSE.

CAREGROYNE, the seal (*groyne*) rock,
Po.

CAREG TOL, the holed rock, *Bl.*

CARENICK, ? the rocky place.

CAREW, *n.f.,* = *caerau,* pl. of *caer,* a
camp, castle, &c., *R.W.‡*

---

* *Cara Cowz* in *Clowze,* given in "Carew's Survey" (fol. 154), is either a misprint,
or a corruption, of *Cara clowse in Cowse,* "the ancient name of Saint Michael's Mount,"
(fol. 8.).

† In the following names, when from want of sufficient knowledge with regard to
the several places, it is doubtful whether CAR stands for *caer, carn,* or *cae* (the Welsh
equivalent of *ce,* "a hedge, enclosure," &c.), the abbreviation "c." is used.

‡ The name is pronounced Car'-ew in Ireland ; Ca-rew' in Devonshire ; Ca'-rey in
Cornwall and Wales. The old historian gives his patronymic a Norman origin,

"*Carew* of ancient *Carru* was, And Carru is a plowe,
"Romanes the trade, Frenchmen the word, I doe the name auowe."

CAREWR-GE, -GA, *d.d.*, the c. on the water; ? *i.q.* TREWORGY.

CAREY, *river*, ? = *carow*, a stag, *or*, *garw*, rough.

CARFURY, ?the camp on the hill (*bre*).

CARG-AAL, -AUL, -OL, the holy castle, *Pr.* (*d.d.* CARGAV).

CARG-ALLON, -OLLON, ? the enemies' (*galon, w.*) c.

CARGEASE, ?lower (*isa*) barrow (*crug*); *or, i.q.* CARKEASE, *or*, CARNKEZ.

CARGELLY, grove (*celli*) c.

CARGELLYO, the groves c.

CARGENTLE, ? family (*cenedel*) barrow (*crug*).

CARGENWEN, ? Kenwyn's c.

CARGERRACK, ? rocky *or* higher (*gwarrach*) c.

CARGIBBET,? the miser's(*cybydd, w.*) c.

CARGLOTH, the veiled *or* concealed castle *or* town, *ga., Beal*; ? trench (*clawdh, w.*), *or*, glutton's (*glwth, w.*) c.

CARGREAN, rock in the gravel (*grean*), *Sc.*; sun (*grian, ga.*) rock, *Beal.*

CARGURREL, court (*cur*) castle (*caer*) wall (*gual*), *Wh.*

CARHALL-ACK, -ICK, -OCK, moor (*hal*) castle port (*ock*), *or*, the rocky moor of oaks, *Pr.*; ? *i.q.* CARALLACK.

CARHANGIVES, ? ?castle of the gyves *or* fetters; *or, i.q.* CARNHANGIVES.

CARHARRACK, the long (*hir*) rocky dwelling, *Pr.* ? further (*gwarrach*) c.; *or, i.q.* CARCARICK.

CARHART, ? high (*arth*) c.

CARHAYES, the enclosed castle, *Pr.*; the barley (*heiz*) village, *Gw.*

CARICK ROADS, rock roadstead.

CARICK STARNE, saddle (*ysdarn, w.*) rock, *N.*

CARIC-ON, -ONE, ? rock (*carrac*) on the down (*gwon*).

CARIN CROFT, ? carn croft.

CARINES, ? lambs' (*eanes*) c.

CARINNA, ??castle on the promontory (*rhyn*).

CARJEWAY, ? David's (*Dewi*) close.

CARKEASE, ?lower (*isa*) rock (*carrag*).

CARKEEK, ? look out c. (*geek*, to peep, *m.c.*).

CARKEEL, "*i.q.* CARBEELE," *Sc.*; ? leech (*gel*) c.

CARKEEN, ? St. Keyne's c.; *or*, lamb's (*ean*) rock.

CARK-EET, -EIT, *n.f.*, ? *i.q.* GRUGGITH. (*carcath*, a ray fish; *gurcaeth*, a prisoner).

CARKEVAL, ? horse (*cevil*) c.; *or*, St. Eval's rock.

CARKEW, ? *i.q.* CARCOW.

CARLAND,?the c.of the enclosure(*lan*).

CARL-ANICK, -INNICK, *i.q.* CALENICK, *or*, = *kea linec*, a field of flax, *Pr.*

CARL-EAN, -EEN, -INE, -ION, ? *i.q.* CAERLEON; *or*, = *celyn*, holly.

CARLENNOW, ? linen clothes (*lennow*) field; ? the c. of the learned (*llen*, learning), *R.IV.*

CARLERRICK, ? the c. of the lunatic (*loerig, w.*), *or*, of Lleurwg, *w.*

CARLESCAS, ? the burnt (*leskys*) c.

CAR-LIDDEN, -LEDDON, the broad (*ledan*) carn.

CARLIGGA, ? *i.q.* CLIGHAR.

CARLOW ROCKS, ? the martin (*carlo, o.n.*) rocks.

CARLOGGAS, ? mice or rats' (*loggas*) c.

CARLOOSE, grey (*ludzh*) rock, *Pr.*

CARLYON, *o.* CAER LYGHON, the camp (*caer*) place (*le*) on the downs (*on = gwon*), *M'L.*

CARMAILOC, *cent.* 11, Mailoc's c.

CARMEAL BALL, "a honey (*mel*) hill of the beneficiall workes," *Nord.*

CARMELLOW ROCK, ? *i.q.* CARMAILOC.

CARMELOR, ? Meilyr's (*w.*) c.

CARMERRANCE, ? the c. of death (*mernans*).

CARMINNIS, *i.q.* CARNMINNISS.

CARM-INNOW, -ENNOW, little (*minow*) city, *Pr.*; the monks' (*menech*) castle, *T.Q.C.*; the rock hill (*menedh*), *H.*; a rock immoveable, *Sc.*

CARN, CARNE, rock, rocky place, natural pile of rocks.

CARN-ABEGGAS, -BEGGAS, bush (*bagas*) carn.

CARNACANOW, ? Caenog's (w.) carn.

CARNADNES, *St. Agnes* carn, *or* carn of warning, protection (*adnes, w.*), *N.*

CARNADON, ? rocky hill (*dun*).

CARNA-GWIDDEN,-GUIDDEN, the white (*gwidn*) carn. (KARNAWETHAN, the tree carn, *B.*).

CARN AIRE, the inner point, *or* cairn of slaughter, *Bl.* ; ? long (*hir*) carn.

CARNAKEY, ? carn by the hedge (*ce*), *or*, of the spirit (*nuggy*).

CARNAMINA, ? *i.q.* CARMINNOW.

CARN AN PEAL, the spire rock, *B.*

CARNANS, ? lambs' (*eanes*) carn.

CARNANTON, rock (*carn*) valley (*nans*) town, *H.* ; ? *i.q.* CARNADON.

CARNARTHEN, ? carn on the hill (*ar dun*) ; *or*, Arthen's (*w.*) carn.

CARNBANGAS, ? carn at the end (*pen*) of the wood (*cus*).

CARNBARGAS, kite's (*bargus*) carn.

CARN BARRA, ? loaf (*bara*), *or*, higher (*gwarra*) carn.

CARNBEAK, ? carn promontory (*pyg, w.*).

CARNBIN, ? little (*bihan*) carn.

CARN-BONELES, -BONELLES, -BONELS, ? the son-in-law's (*els*), *or*, green moor (*hal las*) down-house (*bo oon*) carn.

CARN BRANE, the crow (*bran*) carn.

C. BRAS, -BROSE, big (*bras*) carn.

CARNBREA, *Le.* CARNBRAY, the mountain (*bre*) rock, *Po.* ; ? = *caer an bre*, the castle on the hill ; *or*, *i.q.* Macpherson's "cairn-crowned hill."

CARNBURYANACK, the still, quiet (*anach*) spar stone (*carn*) grave *or* burying place, *H.* (*See* BRYANNICK).

CARN CAVAS, ? carn outside (*ves*) the hedge (*ce*) ; *or*, dirty (*cawys*) carn.

CARNCLEW, ? carn of light (*golcu, w.*).

CARN-CLOG, -CLOUGY, the cairn of hard rock, *Bl.*

CARNCRAVAH, ? carn of the banshea (*craevagh, i.*).

CARN CREAGLE, the crying cairn, *Bl.*

C. CREIZ, the middle (*crez*) carn.

C. CROUSE, ? the cross (*croes*) carn.

CARNDEAW, ? south (*dehau*) carn.

CARN-DEW, -DU, black (*du*) carn.

CARNDROSE, ? carn of the boast (*terros*).

CARNEBIN, little (*bihan*) carn.

CARNEBONE, ? down-house (*bo oon*) carn.

CARNEDON, the rocky hill, *T.*

CARNEGG-AN, -ON, ? carn on the downs (*goon*).

CARNEGGO, ? the smith's (*gof*) carn.

CARNE-GGY, -GIE, ? the inside (*agy*) carn.

CARNEGLOS, the grey (*glas*), *or* church (*eglos*) carn.

CARNEGOES, ? carn of blood (*goys*).

CARNEGUIDDEN, *i.q.* CARNAGUIDDEN.

CARNE HALLOW, ? rock moors (*hallow*).

CARNELLAN, ? elm tree (*ellan, Pr.*) carn.

CARNELL-A, ? -OW, ? carn by the moors.

CARNELLAS, ? green-moor (*hal las*), *or*, church (*eglos*) carn.

CARNELS, *the same* ; *or*, son-in-law's (*els*) carn.

CARNEMOGH, the pigs' (*moch*) carn.

CARNEMTRAL, ? the carn in the middle (*hanter*) of the moor (*hal*).

CARN ENYS, island (*enys*) carn ; *or*, lambs' (*eanes*) c.

CARN-ETHEN, -ITHIN, the birds' (*edhen*) carn.

CARNETON, *i.q.* CARNADON.

CARNERVAS, ? outside (*ves*) the long (*hir*) carn.

CARN EVALL, ? St. Eval's, *or*, the bald (*y voel, w.*) carn.

CARNE WARRA CARNE, the rocky waste about the higher carn.

CARNE WARTHA, the higher carn.

CARN EWAS, ? the carn of desire (*yeues*).

C. FRANKAS, the crow (*bran*) carn in the wood (*cus*), *T.C.*

C. GLA-SE, -ZE, the green *or* blue stone, *or*, grey rock, *Pr.*

C. GOLEUA, rock of lights, *B.*

C. GOLLA, ? lower (*gwolla*) carn.

CARNGREAN, the rock *or* altar of the sun (*grian, ga.*), *Beal.*

CARN-GREEB, -GRIBBA, the rock like a bird's crest *or* comb (*crib*), *Bl.*

CARN-GRESS, -CREASE, *i.q.* C. CREIZ.

CARN GREY ROCK, grey rock carn.

CARNGURTHA, higher (*gwartha*) carn.

CARN-HALE, -HALL, -HILL, the carn on the moor *or* hill (*hal*); *or,* carn by the river (*heyl*), *C.*; *or,* white moor (*can hal*).

CARNHANGIVES, ? carn of the house (*an chy*) outside (*ves*).

CARNHAUT, ? sea shore (*aut, B.*), *or,* duck (*hoet*) carn.

CARN HERMEN, long (*hir*) stone (*maen*) cairn, *Bl.*

CARN-HIMBRA, -KIMBRA, the Welshman's carn. Associated rocks, *C.*

CARNHINGEY, ?? carn by the house (*an chy*).

CARNHOAR, the sister's (*hoar*) carn.

CARNICK, the rocky place.

CARNIDDRIS, ? Idris's (*w.*) carn; (*edris*, learned).

CARNIDJACK,* (*Nord.,* CARNUIACK), the hooting (*idzhek*) carn, *B.*

CARNIFRIARS, the monks' carn, *N.*

CARNINNEY, ? *i.q.* CARNHINGEY.

CARNINOUS, ? lambs' (*eanes*) carn.

CARN IRISHMAN, ? Irishman's carn.

CARNITHIN, the birds' (*edhen*) carn.

CARN-KEE, -KEY, the stony hedge (*ce*), *Po.*; ? *i.q.* CARNKIE.

CARNKEZ, cheese (*ces*) carn.

CARN-KIE, -KYE, the dog (*ci*) carn.

CARNKIEFS, *i.q.* CAER KIEF.

CARN -LEA, -LEH, the group of flat

rocks, *North.* ? lesser (*le*) carn.

C. LEHAU, flat rocks (*lechau*) carn.

CARNLESBOEL, ? ? the broad (*les*) carn by the ox-cliff (*buallt, w.*).

CARNLESKYS, the rock of burnings, *B.*

CARNLOGE, the calf's (*loeh*) carn.

CARNLUSACK, ? *i.q.* CARNLESKYS.

CARNMANNAL, ? *i.q.* CARVANNAL.

CARN-MARTH,† open rock, *C.*

CARNMEAL, honey (*mel*), *or,* Michael's carn.

CARN-MEAR, -MEOR, great carn.

CARNMEASURE, ? ? the moon (*misor, Mur.*) carn.

CARNMELLYN, yellow (*melyn*), *or,* mill (*melin*) carn.

CARNMEN, ? kids' (*min*) carn.

CARNMENELLIS, ? green (*glas*), *or,* broad (*les*) moor (*hal*) stone enclosure (*maen hay*) carn. Manal yz, a sheaf of corn, *Lh.*; (*c.d.* Holy Trinity, *Du B.*).

CARNMINNIS, ? the small (*minys*) carn.

CARNMOAN, ? the maimed man's (*moun, a.*) carn.

CARNMORVAL, whale (*morvil*) carn, *N.*

CARN MURR, the rock frequented by the sea bird "murr," *Woodley.*

C. NEAR, = carn hir, long carn.

C. NIEGAN, twenty (*ugain, w.*) rocks, *C.*

C. OLVA, carn at the head of the beach, *Bl.* (*olva,* lamentation).

CARNON, ? carn on the downs (*oon*); *or,* rock downs.

CARNORU, ? rough (*harow*) carn; *or,* carn on the slope (*rhiw, w.*).

CARNPAREE, ? *i.q.* CARNBRE. A quantity *or* heap of rocks, (*parri, w.,* a flock), *C.*

---

* CARN KENI-DZHEK, -JACK, according to some; rendered "the head indented, notched, *or* jagged (*kenneagach, ga.*) cairn," *Beal*; "the ridge *or* head (*kean*) of the flying (*niedga*) serpent (*hac*)," *Buller.* An old west-countryman, whose family (including himself) always prided itself on keeping up the meaning of Cornish names, makes it "the carn of the nineteen (*nawnzac*) dogs (*cei*)," *T.C.*

† ? *i.q.* CHENMERCH, *d.d.*; Norden has "KERN-MARGH BEACON *or* CARN MARIGH, signifyinge *rocke wher horses* (*merch*) *shelter*"; Whitaker, "the knight's (*marheg*) cairn *or* barrow"; Polwhele, "the carn at the boundary (*mearc, s., mars, w.*). *Merch* is also "daughter," *c.*

CARN-PASSACK, -PESSACK, ? Easter (*pasc*) carn. (*Pesach*, rotten).

CARN POPE, Pope's carn ; *pob*, to bake.

C. PRIOR, the prior's carn.

C. RAW, Ralph's, *or*, the rough carn.

C. ROS, the carn of heath *or* moss, *Bl.*

C. SCATHE, the boat carn, *Bl.*

CARNSEW, black *or* bream rock, *Pr.* ; the dry (*sew, m.c.*) carn, *Bot.*

CARNSMERRY, ? ? St. Mary's carn ; *or*, Carne's miry hay *or* close.

CARN SPER-N, -NAC, bramble carn, *C.*

CARN-SULLAN, -SULAN, ? Sulcan's (*s.B.m.*), *or*, Sulien's (*w.s.*) carn ; = Bellevue, prospect rock, *C.*

CARNSWORTH, ? Carn's farm, *t.*

CARNTISCOE, ? elder-tree house (*ty scow*) carn.

CARN TOMMEN, the little hill (*tommen*) with the heap of rocks, *Heath.*

C. TORK, loaf-like (*torth, w.*) carn, *Bl.* (*twrch*, a hog, *w.* ; *torch*, a collar, *w.*).

C. TYER, ? thatcher's carn. Spar stone (*carn*) land (*tir*), *H.*

C. UNY, St. Uny's carn.

CARNVASSACK, outside rock, *Bl.*

CARNVENTON, well (*fenton*) carn.

CARNVESILEN, the carn outside (*ves*) the enclosure (*lan*), *T.C.* (*meslan*, a mastiff).

CARNVIEW, ? cow (*beuch*), *or*, look-out carn.

CARNVOEL, *i.q.* CARN EVALL.

CARN-VORTH, -Y VORTH, ship (*aorth, ga.*) carn, *Beal.*

CARNVRES, rock of judgment (*bres*), *Buller.*

C. WATCH, ? look-out carn.

CARN-WEATHER, -WORTHY, ? further (*wartha*) carn.

CARN-WHIDDEN, -WYTHAN, -Y WITH-AN, the tree (*gwedhen*), *or*, white (*gwidn*) carn.

CARNWINN-ECK, -ICK, ? boggy carn.

CARNWYNNEN, Gwynen's (*w.s.*) carn.

CARNYORTH, *i.q.* CARNVORTH ; carn of the bear (*orth*), *Buller.*

CARN Y VELLAN, *i.q.* CARN MELLYN.

CARN Y VERTH, ? hawthorn (*frith*) carn.

CAROE, *i.q.* CAIRO *or* CARA.

CARON MEADOW, ? rock meadow.

CARPALLOE, ? calf's house (*bod loch*), *or*, further (*pella*) c.

CARPENTER, ? the c. on the headland, (*pen tyr*).

CARPUAN, little (*bihan*) c.

CARRACK AN LOAR, ? moon (*loer*) rock.

CARRACKDUES, ? sheep *or* tongue (*devas*) rock. Black rocks, *C.*

CARRACK GLADDEN, ? broad (*ledan*), *or* brink *or* edge (*glan*) rock, *C.*

CARRACKS, rocks, *Bl.*

CARRA GROUND, rock (*carag*) land.

CARRAN CARRAW, ? stag (*carow*) carn.

CARRATON, ? *i.q.* CARADON.

CARRAW, ? brook (*currog*) [field].

CARREAN, ? lamb's (*ean*) c.

CARR-EAS, -IES, lower (*isa*) c. ; *or*, *i.q.* CARINES.

CARRELLOWE, ? c. on the moors (*hallow*) ; *or*, *i.q.* CARALLA.

CARRENACK, ? rocky [piece].

CARRENVER, ? c. by the road (*an vor*).

CARRICK CALYS, ? the submerged *or* lost (*collys*) rock ; (*calys*, hard).

C. -DEW, -DHEW, *i.q.* CARAC DIU.

C. GLOOSE, *i.q.* CARAGLOSE.

C. HOWELL, -OWL, high (*uhal*), *or*, Howel's rock.

CARRICKNATH, bare (*noth*) rock.

CARRIG GONNYON, white stones, *B.*

CARR-INE, -ION, *i.q.* CARREAN.

CARRINES, rock island (*enys*) ; *or*, island city *or* castle, *Pr.* ; ? *i.q.* CARNINOUS.

CARRIVICK, ? Herwig's (*t.*) c.

CARROCK GOAL, ? moor (*hal*) rock ; *or*, *i.q.* CARGAUL.

CARROGET, ? Argwedd's (*w.*) c.

CARRUAN, rocky river, *or*, castle on the river (*aun*), *Pr.* Ruan, = Roman, *Po.* ; St. Rumon, *C.*

CARRYGLOOSE, *i.q.* CARACLOSE.

CARSAWSEN, the Saxons' camp.

CARSCAIN, sedge (*hesken*) moor (*cors*), *or* c.

CARSELLA, *d.d.* KARSALAN, ? moor of the sun (*haul*) enclosure (*lan*), *M'L.* Stone of the view, (*sulw, w.*), *C.*

CARSEWES, ? outside (*ves*) the dry (*sech*) c.

CARSILGEY, rocky (*carn*) river (*gwy*) *or* house (*chy*) in open view (*sul*), *Pr.* ; ? rocking (*siglu*) stone, *C.*

CARSIZE, ? Saxon's (*sais*) camp.

CARSKILLING, ? holly (*kelinick*) moor (*cors*) ; secluded rock, *C.*

CARSLEWYE, rock reflecting light, *or,* very bright, *C.*

CARSULLAN, ? *i.q.* CARSELLA.

CARTARTHA, ? higher (*artha*) enclosure (*garth, w.*).

CARTHAMARTHA, rock over the TAMAR river, *C.*

CARTHEW, black (*dhu*) rock, *Gw.*

CARTHION, ? John's enclosure.

CARTHVEAN, little (*bihan*) enclosure.

CARTOWL, ? the devil's (*diawl*) c.

CARTREEVE, ? rock of dwelling, *C.*

CARTUTHER, ? Tudor's c.

CARVABIN, ? Mabin's (*w.*) c.

CARVAEN, stone (*maen*) fort ; *or, i.q.* CARWEN, white castle, *T.Q.C.*

CAR-VALLACK, *o.* -VALGHE, -VOLGHE, the castle with the deep trench, *Po.* ; (? *wollach*, lower).

CARVANNAL, broom (*banal*) c. Broomy place among the rocks, *Pr.*

CAR-VARTH, -VATH, the high (*warth*) castle, *Pr.* ; *varth*, splendour, *C.*

CAR-VEAN, *o.* -VIGHAN, *d.d.* -BIHAN, little camp ; (*or* marsh, *Wh.*).

CAR-VEDRAS, -WEDRAS, ? wether sheep (*gwedhar-es*) c.

CAR-VEER, -VEOR, great marsh *or* c.

CARVELDRA, ? castle of cunning *or* subtlety (*feldra*), *C.*

CARVENNER, ? long-stone (*menhir*) croft.

CARVERTH, the green (*verth*) place, *Pr.* ; flat *or* sunk-in rock, *C.*

CARVERY, *i.q.* CARFURY.

CARVETH, city (*caer*) grave (*beth*), *or,* castle burying place, *Pr.*

CARVIN-ICK, -ACK, stony (*maenick*) town, *R.W.**

CARVOLTH, ? Walloth's (*w.B.m.*) town. *Molletha*, to curse ; *emladhe,* to kill one's self.

CARVORRY, ? stone of direction ; (*forry*, to shew the way), *C.*

CAR-VOSSA, -VOSSOW, -VOWSA, -VOZA, the intrenched castle, *Pr.*

CARWALSICK, ? Wulsige's (*B.m.*) c.

CARWARTHEN, the c. on (*war*) the hill (*dun*).

CARWEDRAS, *i.q.* CARVEDRAS.

CAR-WEN, -WIN, -WYN, white, fair, good, *or* advantageously situated camp, *T.Q.C.* White rocks, *C.*

CARWICK, ? creek (*gwic*) c. ; *or, i.q.* CARWYTHENICK, *or,* CARWINNICK.

CARWINE, *i.q.* CARVEAN, *or* CARWEN.

CARWIN-EN, -IAN, -IN, -ION, *i.q.* CARWEN ; *or,* white (*gwyn*) c. on the downs (*oon*).

CARWINNICK, the dwelling on the marsh, *Pr.* ; ? *i.q.* CARVINICK.

CARWITHEN, the c. by the tree (*gwedhen*).

CARWITHER, ? Uther's c.

CARWOLL-EN, -ON, ? the high (*uhal*) c. on the downs (*oon*).

CARWORGY, *i.q.* CAREWRGE.

CARWYTHENICK, the castle in a woody place, *Pr.*

CARYBULLOCK, = *caer bulach*, prince's town *or* enclosure, *T.†*

CARYQUOITA, quoit-shaped rocks ;

* The city, dwelling (*caer*), *or* stony (*carn*) marsh (*winnick*), *Pr.* ; the rock (*carn*) spring, *or* fountain (*fenton*), leat, *or* rivulet of water (*ike*), *H.* Sharp-edged rock, *C.*

† Tonkin adopted this from Baxter, having previously rendered the name "the entrenched (*boll*) enclosure (*caer*) on the river (*ick*). Carew, *fol.* 115, tells us this was once a deer-park of the dukes ; but "now it hath lost its qualitie through exchanging *Deere* for BULLOCKE." *See D.G.*, iv, 8.—BULLOCK=*bwlch, w.*, a pass, a ravine, *C.*

or = *car y coedau*, *w.*, the rock in the woods, *C.*

CARZANTICK, sacred (*santic*) rock, *C.*

CASPARD, ? wood part (*parth*).

CASSACA-DDEN, -WEN, ? elder tree (*scawen*) wood (*cus*). The trench (*cwys, w.*) of the battle-field (*cadva*), *C.*

CASSLAKE, willow. (*helak*) wood (*cus*) or marsh (*cors*).

CASTALLACK, castle place.

CASTEL AN DINAS, *a reduplication.**

CASTERIL-LS, -LIS, ? wood (*cus*) land (*tir*) by the green-moor (*hal las*).

CASTICK, ? Usteg's enclosure (*cae*).

CASTILLEY, ? TILLEY'S wood *or* marsh.

CASTLE ANOWTHAN, the new (*noweth*) castle.

C. BEAN, little (*bihan*) castle.

C. BROSE, great (*bras*) castle.

C. BURY, *a reduplication;* or, hill (*bre*) castle.

C. CAERTH, ? high (*arth*) enclosure (*cae*) castle.

C. CARNUIACK, see CARNIDZHEK.

C. CAYLE, ? *see* CAYLE.

C. COFFER, ? rivulet (*gover*) or goat (*gavar*) castle.

C. COMBRIA, ? hill (*bre*) combe castle.

C. DOOR, -DORE, -DOAR, castle by the water (*dour*).

C. FUST, club *or* mace (*fust*) castle.

C. GOFF, -GOUGH, the smith's (*gof*) castle.

C. GOTHA, -GOTHEA, castle surrounded by woods (*coedau*), *M'L.*

C. HAY, castle close.

C. HEWES, ? outside (*ves*) castle close.

C. HORNECK, the iron (*haiarn*) castle, *Pr.*; corner (*horn*) castle, *Wh.*

C. KAER KIEF, *i.q.* CAER KIEF.

C. KEYNOCK, KINNICK, CANYKE,

CANOCK, &c., king's castle, *H.*; ? Cynoc's castle.

C. -KILLY BIRY, -KELLY BURY, grove (*celli*) castle, (*redup.*).

C. MAWGAN, MAWGAN'S castle.

C. MENN-ACK, -ECK, the castle on the hill (*pen*) near the water (*ick*), *M'L.*; ? monks' *or* stony castle, *R.W.*

C. PENCAYRE, ? head (*pen*) camp. (*caer*) castle.

C. SCUDZICK, = LESCUDJACK castle.

C. TERRIBLE, *treble* walled castle.

C. VEAN, *i.q.* CASTLE BEAN.

C. WARY, -WERRY, -WHARRY, castle on (*war*) the river (*gwy*), *M'L.*

CASTLEWITCH, ? *i.q.* CASTLE HEWES.

CASTLEZANCE, holy (*sans*) castle.

CATA-CLEW, -CLUSE, *corruption of* CARACLOWSE.

CATACOMBE, ? wood (*coat*) vale.

CATCH, ? ? = *cae issa*, lower close.

CATCHER, ? long (*hir*) CATCH; *or* daisy (*gajah, B.*) [field].

CATCHFRENCH, = *cadge fryns*, the prince's enclosure, *Wh.*; = *f. chasse franche*, free chase *or* warren, *E.*

CATGUSTEL, ? *s.B.m.*, war (*cad*) pledge (*guistel*).

CATIN, *m.s. Worthyvale*, ? = *Cadvan*, war horn, *Y.*

CATSTON BURY, *i.q.* CADSON; ? war hill castle. Camp down barrow, *C.*

CATTEBEDREN, *w., cad y bedren*, battle burying place, *C.*

CATTICOOMBE, *i.q.* CATACOMBE.

CATUUTIC, *s.B.m.* ? *i.q.* QUETHIOCK; *or* victorious (*budic*) battle (*cad*).

CAUNCE, CAUNSE, the causeway.

CAUSELAND, ? moor (*cors*) land.

CAUSEWELL, ? well by the causeway.

CAUTRELL, ? wood (*coat*) on (*ar*) the moor (*hal*).

---

* CASTELLAN DENIS *or* DANIS, the camp of the Danes, *Car., Cam.*; Tonkin has CASTLE CAER DANE; Whitaker suggests Castle on the hill (*dun*); Norden, the isolated castle, made by its ditch like an island (*Castle en Inis*). DINAS might be *din enys*, island fortress. Some make *Castle* to be a fortification of stone, *dinas* of earth.

CAVARAH, ? higher (*gwarra*) close (*ce*).

CAVELDRA, *i.q.* CARVELDRA.

CAVERLO, ? close (*ce*) over (*war*) the pool (*lo*).

CAVEWEDNACK, ? = *ce wednac*, white close.

CAVIL CLOSE, ? horse (*cevil*) close.

CAVINACK, *i.q.* CARVINACK.

CAWDERY, ? = *w.*, *coed deru*, oakwood.

CAWESPARK, ? causeway (*coanse, m.c.*) close.

CAWETII, ? *i.q.* CARVERTH ; *or*, CARVETH, (? stone grave, *C.*).

CAWJ-GORTHA, ? higher (*gwartha*) wood (*cuz*).

CAWSAWN, *i.q.* COSWINSAWSEN.

CAYLE, ? castle (*caer*) on the HAYLE.

CAYSE, *i.q.* CAASE.

CAZEHILL, ? wood (*cois*) hill.

CEENGULED, *s.B.m.*, ? feast (*guledh*) supper (*cean*).

CENGAR, *s.B.m.*, ? jewel (*cein*) of a friend (*car*).

CENHUIDEL, *s.B.m.*, ? whelp (*cyn*) of scent (*huadl*), *C.*

CENMENOC, *B.m.*, ? chief (*cyn*) monk (*manach*).

CENMYN, *presbiter B.m.*, ? jewel of a mouth (*meyn, w.*).

CENT-RY. -URY, *i.q.* SANCTUARY.

CHACEWATER, ? hunting ground by the stream ; (*c.d.* St. Paul.)

CHAIR LADDER, ? *redup.* of cliff (*scar, t.* ; *ladr, k.*).

CHALLACOMBE, the valley of jawbones (*challa*), *Pr.*

CHALL-ACOT, -COT, the cottage near the shed where kine are housed (*chall, T.Q.C.*).

CHALL PARK, ? kine house close.

CHAMPERNOWNE, *n.f.*, = Arnulph's field (*champ, f.*).

CHANNEL CROFT, moor house (*chy an hal*) croft.

CHAPEL AMBLE, the dull, blockish, or ignorant chapel, *H. See* AMBLE.

C. AN CROUSE, chapel of the cross.

C.-AN GADAR, -ENGARDER, ? the pirate's (*ancredour*) chapel.

C. ANJEW, the ruined (*andwy*) chapel, *C.*

C. AUNGER, hermit's (*ancar*) chapel.

C. CARNE BRAY, CARNE BREA with the chapel on it.

C. HAYES, chapel fields.

C.-IDNE,-JANE, the narrow chapel, *H.*

C. UNY, St. Ewinus' chapel.

C. WIDDEN, ? little (*vidn* = *vean*) chapel. Whitechapel, *C.*

CHARATON, CHARITON, = *car y don*, rocky down, *C.* ; *or*, play (*choary*) hill.

CHARK, ? cinder ; *or*, *i.q.* CHORK.

CHARLACK CROFT, wild mustard croft.

CHARLETON, *i.q.* CHARLESTOWN, *or*, the churl's (*ceorl, s.*) enclosure.

CHAUMOND, *n.f.*, = *De calvo monte*, of the bare hill, *Car.*

CHAYPOLE, ? house (*chy*) by the pool (*pol*) ; *or* = chapel.

CHEATER, ? house by the *tor*.

CHECOOSE, wood (*cuz*) house.

CHECOUCH, house of blood (*gudzh*).

CHEDDEN, ? *i.q.* CHYTANE.

CHEDODDEN, house in the lay field.

CHEESEWRING, pile of rocks like a cheese- (*or* cider-, *C.*) press ; (*choarion*, games), *B.*

CHEFRYE, house on the hill (*vre*).

CHEGARDER,?higher (*gwartha*) house ; garden (*gardda*) house, *C.*

CHEGENTER, ? nail (*center*) house.

CHE-GWIDDEN, -GWIN, white house.

CHEI, *d.d.*, ? enclosure (*hay*) house.

CHELEAN, linen (*lin*) house.

CHELENOCH, *d.d.*, ? *i.q.* CALENICK.

CHELLEW, house in the *lew* or shelter, *Bot.*

CHELTAN, under (*tan*) moor (*hal*) house.

CHEN-ALL, -HALE, -HALL, house by the moor (*an hal*) ; (*heyle*, river, *C.*).

CHENDUIT, ? David's old (*hen*) house.

CHENEATHRO, ?? house on the rough (*raw*) heath (*heyth*).

CHENEY, ? = *Chy an hay*, house in the enclosure.

CHENGWERTH, ? house in the green (*gwyrdh*) [field].

CHENISI, *t.d.d.*, ? = *censa*, the first.

CHE-NOWATH, -NOWAH, -NOWTH, *i.q.* CHYNOWETH.

CHENOWEN, house on the downs (*an oon*); new (*nowen*) house, *C.*

CHENGWENS, = *chy an gwens*, the windy house.

CHENRET, *t.d.d.*, ? bold counsel, *t.*

CHENTON, hill (*dun*) house; or, house on the lay.

CHEQUE-, CHEQUER-PARK, ? = PARK SKEBER.

CHEREASE, middle (*crez*) house.

CHEREEN, house on the hill (*rhyn*).

CHER-GWIDDEN, -GWIN, ? white long (*hir*) house; or = CHEGWIDDEN.

CHESEWARN, lower (*isa*) house by the marsh (*gwern*).

CHES-TEWAY, -TEWI, ? David's (*Dewi*) lower (*isa*) house.

CHETAN, ? *i.q.* CHYTANE.

CHE-TOADN, -TODDEN, ? *i.q.* CHENTON. Toad's house, or h. on the hill, *Pr.*

CHEVA FIELD, *i.q.* PARK SKEBER.

CHEVELAH, = *chy vaela*, house of trade, *i.e.* the shop, *C.*

CHEVYTODDEN, ? barn (*skeber*) lay or unploughed field (*todn*).

CHEYNEY, ? *i.q.* CHENEY.

CHEYNOY, ? nephews' (*noi*) house; or, *i.q.* CHENOWETH.

CHIB FIELD, ? = *sheep* field.

CHIBRAGGED, house of metheglin (*braggaud*), *T.C.*

CHICKEMBRA, CHIKEMBRA, = *chy cam bre*, house of crooked hillock, *C.*

CHIDA, *t.d.d.*, ? = *Ceadda*, war.

CHIDOW, ? house by the water (*dour*).

CHIELOW, cell, or house, by the lake (*lo*), *Po.* ? *i.q.* CHELLEW.

CHIENGWEAL, CHINGWEAL, house in the field (*gweal*).

CHIGOOLIN, ? house in the little field (*gweal vean*).

CHILBROOK, ? grove (*cilli*) by the brook

CHILCHETONE, *d.d.*, ? *i.q.* KILK-HAMPTON.

CHILCOT, *n.f.*, ? *i.q.* CHILCOIT, *d.d.*; ? = COLQUITE.

CHILDENNY, ? house on the hilly (*dennick*) moor (*hal*).

CHILIWORGY, ? grove (*celli*) on (*war*) the river (*gwy*).

CHILLIEN, ? linen (*lin*) house.

CHILLOWBETT, ? CHIELOW by the pit or grave (*beth*).

CHILL PARK, ? moor house (*chyhal*) close.

CHILLY WILLY WATTLE BOROUGH, *t.b.*, ? ? grove (*cilli*) field (*gweal*) refuse (*attle*) heap (*burrow*), *T.C.*

CHILORGORET, *d.d.*, ? *i.q.* KILLIGO-RICK.

CHILS-WORTH, -WORTHY, ? children's settlements, or, homestead for the husbandmen (*ceorles, s.*), *Beal.*

CHIMDER, ? reaper's (*meder*) house.

CHINESTAN, *t.d.d.*, ? ? jewel (*cein*) stone, *t.* Tin (*ystean*) house, *C.*

CHING PARK, white house (*chy wyn*) close, *C.*

CHINGWITH, house by the trees (*gwedh*).

CHINHALE, house by the river (*heyl*), *C.*, or, on the moor or hill (*hal*).

CHIN-HALS, -ALS, house on the cliff (*als*).

CHINOAN, ? *i.q.* CHENOWEN.

CHINVY, ? house by the river (*gwy*).

CHIOWNE, CHOON, = *chygwoon*, down house.

CHIP PARK, sheep close.

CHIPPER CLOSE, *i.q.* PARK SKEBER.

CHIPPONDS, ? house by the bridge (*pons*).

CHIPYE, ? magpie (*pia, w.*) house.

CHIR-GWIDDEN, -GWIN, -GWYN, white long (*hir*) house; or, *chir = chi.*

CHIRON WARTHA, higher long down house; or = *chy an wartha*, the higher house.

CHISEL PARK, low (*isal*) house close.

CHITODDEN, *i.q.* CHETOADN.

CHITOL, house by the hole (*tol*), *C.*

CHIVERTON, house upon (*war*) the hill (*dun*), *Pr.*; green (*gwyrdh, w.*)

lay (*ton*), *Gw.* ; (*ton* = down, *C.*).

CHIVILAS, ? house in the green field (*gweal las*).

CHIVORLOE, house over (*war*) the pool (*lo*), *or*, by the great (*veor*) pool, *Pr.*

CHOL, ? house on the moor *or* hill (*hal*) ; *or*, kine house (*chall*).

CHOLLOW, house by the moors (*hallow*).

CHOLWATER, higher (*wartha*) CHOL ; *or*, CHOL stream.

CHOONS, ? lower (*isa*) down house.

CHORI, *d.d.*, ? = *choary*, a game.

CHORK, ? roebuck's (*iorch*) house.

CHORLEY, *n.f.*, ?darnel (*jure,Po.*) field.

CHOSE FIELD, ? *Joe's* field.

CHOUGH ROCK, daw *or* Cornish *chough* rock.

CHRISTANE, ? middle (*creis*) under (*tan*) [field].

CHUBACOMBE, Chub's vale.

CHUBB, *n.f.*, ? house in the opening (*hop, m.c.*).

CHUDLEY, *n.f.*, ?? war (*chad*) pasture.

CHUNE, *i.q.* CHIOWNE.

CHURCH HAY, church-yard *or* close.

CHURCHTOWN, village by the church.

CHUREEN, ? games (*choarion*) ; *or*, house on the hill side (*rhyn*).

CHURN PARK, ?games' close.

CHYANCHY, house by the house,*R.H.*

CHYANDAUNCE, ? dance *or* castle (*dinas*) house.

CHYANDOUR, house by the waterside (*dour*), *Po.*

CHYANGWENS, ?windy (*gwens*) house.

CHY-ANHALL, -ENHALL, house on the moor (*hal*).

CHYAN NANCE, ? house in the vale (*nans*).

CHYANNOR, the ram's (*hor*) house,*Lh.*

CHYANWHEAL, house by the work *or* mine (*whel*).

CHYBARLEES, house on the high (*warth*) green (*las*), *Pr.*

CHYBARRAT, ? BARRAT'S house.

CHYBILLY, ? BELI'S, *or*, the colts' (*ebilli*) house.

CHYBUCKA, the cows' cot, *Pr.* ; ?the haunted house (*bucca*, a spirit).

CHYCAN-DRA, -DRIA, house of the singing (*can*) town (*tre*), *Po.* ; *candre*, white *or* bright village, *C.*

CHYCARNE, the stone house, *or*, on a rock, *Pr.* Rock House.

CHYCARRADRE, *i.q.* CHYCANDRA, *Po.*

CHYCOLL, house by the hazels (*coll,w.*)

CHY-COOSE, -COISE, -NCOOSE, wood (*cuz*) house.

CHYDOW, ?house by the water (*dour*) ; house of the scold (*dow*), *T.C.*

CHYENDOUR WEETHS, CHYANDOUR border fields *or* trees ; (? *gwydd*, wild, untilled, *w.*).

CHYFONS, ? bridge (*pons*) house.

CHYGAJOWAN, ? John's down (*goon*) house ; *i.q.* TREGAJORAN, *J. Ca.*

CHYGARDER, ? fiddler's (*crowder*) house.

CHYGARKIE, house by the low hedge (*gurgey, m.c.*) ; *or*, Gwrgi's (*w.*) house.

CHYGROUS, cross (*crous*) house.

CHYGWIDDEN, white house.

CHYHEIRA, battle field (*heirua*) house.

CHYJAH, lower (*isa*) house.

CHY-KEMBO, -KEMBRA, house of the Briton, *B.* ; *i.q.* CHICKEMBRA.

CHYLAN, enclosure (*lan*) house.

CHYLAS-ON, -SON, house on the green downs (*glas oon*).

CHYMBLO, ? Embla's (*t.*) house.

CHYMDER, *i.q.* CHIMDER.

CHYMOW, the hogs' (*mogh*) house.

CHYN-ALE, -HALE, *i.q.* CHINHALE.

CHYNANCE, *i.q.* CHY AN NANCE.

CHYNEEDY, ? the great (*ethy*) house.

CHYOISTER, *i.q.* CHYSAUSTER.

CHYOON, *i.q.* CHIOWNE.

CHYPIT, pit *or* grave (*beth*) house.

CHYPONS, bridge house.

CHYPRASE, meadow (*pras*) house.

CHYRANCHY, the place of the breach, the house by, *or rather*, over against (*ar*), the house, *R.H.*

CHY-RASE, -REASE, the middle house, *Gw.*

CHYREENE WARRA, higher (*wartha*) house on the hill (*rhyn*).

CHYROSE, heath (*ros*) house.

CHYS-AUSTER, -OISTER, heap- (*sawch, w.*) shaped (*i.e.* bee hive) houses, *C.*; dwellings on the south, *Bl.*; house of lodging (*ostia*), *B.*

CHYSHORE, ? sister's (*hoar*) lower (*isa*) house.

CHYTANE, lower house, *Pr.* (*tan,* under). ? Fire (*tan*) house, *R.W.*

CHYTRYAN, a house of cob *or* clay (*pryan*) walls, *Po.*; (*tryan,* a third part, *R.W.*) ; ? house of homestead, *C.*

CHYVARTON, *i.q.* CHIVERTON.

CHYVAVIAN, ? Peiban's (*w.*) house.

CHYVELIN, mill (*melin*) house.

CHYVERANS, ? crows' (*branes, w.*) house.

CHYVOAGE, -VOGUE, house in the hollow *or* by the cave (*vug*).

CHYVOUNDER, house in the lane (*bounder*).

CHYWEDNACK, white (*gwednack*) house.

CHYWH-ELA, -EELA, house in the fields (*gwealou*).

CHYWITTA, ? the widow's (*gwedho*) house.

CHYWOON, down (*gwon*) house.

CIRUSUIS, *m.s. Fowey,* = *Kerus,* beloved, *Ped.*

CLAH-AR, -AIR, ? = *i.q.* CLARE.

CLAM-, CLAMP-, CLAN-PARK, ? close with the foot bridge ; ? = *llam, w.,* a leap, a stride.

CLAMPITS, ? the holes near the foot bridge.

CLAN, CLAUN, ? = *w. llan,* an enclosure ; *or, glan,* a bank. A foot bridge, *T.Q.C.*

CLANDICE CLOSE, ? stack (*disc, B.*) close (*llan, w.*).

CLAPER PARK, ?? mire (*clabar*) close (*parc*).

CLAPPER ROCKS, humpy rocks, *C.*; (*clapier,* to speak, *Pr.*).

CLARE, ? *i.q.* CLEGHAR.

CLARKENWATER, CLERKANWATER, ? the parson's stream, *t.*

CLEASE, CLEESE, ? lower (*isa*) field (*gweal*).

CLEATHER, *n.f.,* from ST. CLEATHER.

CLEAVE, CLEEVE, the cliff.

THE CLEDE, ? the trench (*cledh*).

CLEEST, ? east (*est*) field (*gweal*).

CLEGHAR, = *clegar,* a rock, cliff.

CLELAR, Ilar's (*w.*) field.

CLEMOWE, *n.f.,* = Clement.

CLENCH ZAWN, ? cave (*zawn*) into which the tide flows, (*clench,* to flow in), *C.*

CLEN-ICK, -NICK, *i.q.* CALENNICK.

CLENICOME, CLINCOMBE, holly (*celinic*) vale.

CLEVENNER,?long-stone (*menhir*)field

CLEW, ? grey (*llwyd, w.*) [rock].

CLEWIS FIELD, ? GLUIS's field.

CLIAS, CLIES, CLYES, CLIJAH, a wattled fence, *Bot.*

CLIDDERN, ? thorn (*draen*) field.

CLIDGEY, *i.q.* CLIAS *or* CLODGY.

CLIFTON, the cliff enclosure, *t.*

CLIGGA, *i.q.* CLEGHAR.

CLIKE, ? Isaac's (*Ike*) field.

CLIMS-LAND, -TON, Clement's enclosure (*lan, c., ton, s.*).

CLINICK, CLINK, *i.q.* CLENICK.

CLINTON, ? holly (*celin*) hill (*dun*).

CLISEY, ? *i.q.* CLIDGEY ; *or,* lower (*isa*) field.

CLIVER, ? great (*veor*) field.

CLOBERY, CLOWBERRY, ? echo (*clow*) hill (*bre*) *or* barrow.

CLODE, *n.f.,* ? = *clod,* praise, fame.

CLODGY, CLOWGEA, CLOWGGY, miry, sticky [field], *Bot.*

CLOGDON, *i.q.* CLIGGER DOWNS, *M'L.*

CLOPPE COMBE, Clapa's (*d.*) vale.

CLOQUE, ? = *clog,* a steep rock.

CLOWANCE, = *clownance,* the hearing, *or* valley of echoes, *Pr.*; the valley of moorstones, *T.*; ?many (*llawer*) dingles (*nans*), *C.*

CLOWN, ? down (*oon*) field (*gweal*).

CLUBBERLEY, ? clover, *or,* dove-cot (*culver*) meadow.

CLUCKA MILL, ? rock (*clog*) mill.

CLUMYER FIELD, dove-cot field.

CLUNEWIC, *d.d.*, ? *i.q.* CALENIC.

CLUNK, ? *i.q.* CALENIC.

CLUSION, = *w.*, *clues y on*, encampment on the down, *or*, by the ash trees, *C.*

CNEGUMI, *m s. Mawgan*, ? = *w. Cnecus*, wrangling, jarring, *C.*

COAD, COAT, CODE, *n.f.*, wood.

COADDAH, ? wood enclosure (*hay*).

COAL PARK, ? cabbage (*caol*) close.

COANSE, the causeway.

COARSE HECKER, *i.q.* COOSE HECCA.

COARSE MOOR, ? *a reduplication.*

COATH, the wood (*coed, w.*).

COAT HILL, wood hill, *or* moor (*hal*) wood.

COAVER FIELD, field with the rivulet (*gover*).

COBALAND, ? rivulet land. Graves (*cobra*) of the temple (*lann*), *ga., Beal*

COBB, (*n.f.*) ? from *cob*, to break; *or*, *cob*, mud *or* earth for building.

COBBET THORN, *i.q.* COPPET.

COBBLEDICK, *n.f.*, = Cobbler Dick, *S.P.A.* ? *i.q.* CUBLIDOICE.

COBBLETY CUT, ? smithy (*govail*) house (*ty*) wood (*coat*).

COBBSHORNE, ? Cobb's corner (*horn*).

COBER, (*river*) the stream.

COBHAM, ? dwelling (*ham*) on the summit (*cop*), *t.*

COBMOOR, ? top of the moor.

COBNAS, *i.q.* GABNAS.

COCKALORUM, ? ? ram's (*hor*) dung (*cagal*) low-field (*ham*).

COCK CRIGATE, ? ? heron (*crychydd*) down (*goon*).

COCKFORD, ? red (*coch*) passage.

COCKINGTON, ? ? the enclosure (*tun*) of the descendants of Cocc (*t.*).

COCKLAKE, ? boat (*cwch, w.*) lake; *or* willow (*helak*) down (*goon*).

COCKLEMOOR, the moor where the weed *Cockle* grows; *or, Cuckold* moor. *See* COGLAND.

COCK MOYLE, ? the mule's (*moyle*) basin (*cawg, w.*).

COCK PULMARY, ? red (*coch*) pool of Mary, (*C.*), *or* Meore, *s.B.m.*

COCKWELL, ? ? = red (*coch*) well.

CODIFORD, the passage (*fordh*) by the wood; *or*, wood by the road.

CODNA COOS, neck (*codna*) of the wood (*cuz*).

CODNA PORTH, neck of the bay, *T.C.*

CODNAWILL-Y, -AN, lapwing (*codna-hwilan*) [field].

CODNEREETH, ? = *coed an rydh*, Redwood, *T.C.* (*ryd*, a ford).

CODNIDNE, the narrow (*edn*) neck, *Pr.*; ? fowler's (*idne*) wood, *T.C.*

COD PARK, ? wood (*coed, w.*) close.

COFFEN OWLA, ? lower (*golla*) excavation *or* open working.

COGEGOES, *v.* JIGGAS, ? ? mallow (*hocys, w.*) wood (*cuz*).

COGGAN ROCK, ? ? the red (*coch*) rock.

COGLAND, ? red land. (? from *gogelu*, *w.*, to conceal or shelter, *C.*).

COISFALA, *o.* COYTFALA, wood on the FAL.

COISPENHAILE, wood at the river's (*heyl, Pr.*) or moor's (*hal, R.IV.*) head (*pen*).

COITE, = *coed*, the wood, *w.*

COLAN, from *p.s.* St. Colanus, *O.*; from *glan*, bank; *or, clone*, a cave, *B.*

COL-, COLD-BIGGAN, the little (*bichan*) neck *or* ridge of the hill, *Pr.*

COLBORNE, the dry well, *Pr.* (?)

COL-COIT, -QUITE, neck *or* ridge of the wood, *Pr.*; Wood-hill, *C.*; *or*, = *w. Calcoed*, thistles (*call*) wood, *R.IV.*

COLCURROW, ? deer (*carrow*) ridge.

COLD-, COLE-BROOK, ? cold stream.

COLDCADE, ? *i.q.* COLCOIT; *or*, battle (*cad*) ridge.

COLDGARE, ? snipe (*giach, w.*) hill (*col*), *C.* Castle (*caer*) hill, *R.IV.*

COLDGOWREY, play (*guare*) ridge, *T.C.* ? rock (*carrag*) field (*gweal*).

COLD HARBOUR, ? cold shelter, *I.T.*; the narrow neck (*col*) over (*ar*) the camp (*burg*), *M'L.*; ? soldiers' (*arfwr, w.*) hill.

I

C. HERNICK, ? *i.q.* COLDRINNECK.

C. NORTH, ? north ridge.

C. QUAG, ? hollow or empty (*uag*) ridge.

COLDRIGGEN, ? king's (*dragon*) ridge.

COLDRINNECK, sharp-pointed (*rynick*) ridge, *Wh.*; thorny (*draenick*) hill (*col*), *C.*

COLD ROSE, ? ridge of the heath (*ros*).

COLDRUGLAR, ? heathy (*grugla*) hillock, *C.*

COLD-, COL-SLOGGET, ? Sloggett's ridge.

COLD-, COLE-VAZE, hillock (*col*) of open field (*maes*), *C.*

COLDVERTH, ? green (*gwyrdd*) ridge.

COLDWEST, hill of lodging *or* entertainment (*gwest*), *C.*

COLD-WIN, -WIND, ? white (*gwyn*) hill, *C.*

COLDWORTHY, ? = *gweal wartha*, higher field.

COLE, *n.f.*, ? = *coll*, the hazels.

COLEAN, lamb's (*ean*) field.

COLEBROOK, ? hill near the stream; or, *i.q.* COLDBROOK.

COLENZO, *o.* Kalenso, ? nettly (*lenzac*) enclosure (*cae*).

COLE PARK, ? cabbage (*caol*) close.

COLEZENT, ? holy (*sant*) hill, *C.*

COL-GARE, -GEAR, *i.q.* COLDGARE.

COLGREASE, middle (*creiz*) field (*gweal*) or ridge (*col*).

COLHAY, ? ridge enclosure (*hay*).

COLHENDER, ? field by the old house (*hendra*).

COLLACOT, ? lower (*golla*) cot.

COLLAND, ? hazel (*coll, w.*) land.

COLLATON, ? lower town *or* hill.

COLLEDROY, ? oak (*deru*) field.

COLLEGREEN, ? granite (*grouan*) hill, *C.*; ? gravel (*grean*) field.

COLLENTON, ? hazels on the hill.

COLLERY, ? hazel field (*eru*).

COLLET, ? = *gweal yet*, gate field.

COLLEVOR, ? great (*veor*) field (*gweal*).

COLLEY PARK, ? hazel close.

COLLFRETH, *i.q.* KILLIVERTH.

COLLING, ? = *w.* collen, a hazel.

COLLON, ? = *collen*, the hazel, *w., C.*

COLLURION, ? boundary (*yrhian*) ridge *or* field.

COLLY, ? = *celli*, a grove.

COLLYVEAN, ? little grove (*celli*).

COLLYVEAS, ? *i.q.* COLDVASE.

COLMETTYN, ? stone (*maiden = maen*) field (*gweal*).

COLPERREL, ? orchard (*perllan, w.*) hill, *C.*; ? rose (*breilu*) field.

COLQUITE, *i.q.* COLCOIT.

COLROSE, *i.q.* COLD ROSE.

COLSHILL, *n.f.*, neck (*col*) shields, *H.*; ? = Cole's hill.

COLSLUICK, ? Solveig's (*t.*) ridge, *or* ridge of prospect (*sulra, w.*).

COLVANNICK, stony (*maenic*) ridge; speckled (*manog, w.*) with boulder stones, *C.*

COL-VASE, -VAZE, *i.q.* COLDVAZE.

COLVENOR, *i.q.* CALVENOR.

COLVERNES, ? alder (*gwern*) fields.

COLWITH, ? hazel (*coll*) wood.

COLWOOD, ? *the same*; or wood on the ridge (*col*).

COM, COMBE, COOMBE, = *w.* cwm, a bottom, a vale, a place between two hills, a dingle.

COMBE KEAL, ? the concealed ravine, (*celu*, to hide, *w.*), *J.W.M.*

COMBELAND, ? valley enclosure (*lan*).

COMBEROW, ? valley of pear trees (*perwydd, w.*), *J.W.M.*

COMBULLOCK, *n.f.*, ? calves'-house (*bolec, Po.*) valley.

COME TO GOOD, = *cwm ty goed*, wood house valley, *Bellows.*

COM-FORD, -FORT, the great road *or* pass (*fordh*) between the hills, *Pr.* The combe with a road in it.

COMMENDS, ? fields at the *end* of the combe.

COMMERANS, *i.q.* CAMERRANCE.

COMMOW, ? pigs' (*mogh*) valley. Dark *or* close place, *Pr.*

COM-OERE, -UYRE, *w.B.m.*, ? *i.q.* Conmor, strength great, *Y.*

COMPASS, ? shallow (*bas*) valley.

COMPRIGNEY, ? fertile (*brygain, w.*)

valley, *J.W.M.*; ? down (*goon*) by the wood (*bryccini*, *T.R.*)

CONAGON, ? *corner* of the down (*goon*).

CONAN, *n.f.*, speech, *i.e.* orator, *w.*, *R.W.*

CONANDERS, ? Andreas's (*t.d.d.*) down.

CONARD, ? high (*ard*) down.

CONCE, CONES, *i.q.* CAUNCE.

CONDER QUOIT TOR, ? Condor's (*c.*) quoit peak.

CONDOLDEN, ? Gundulf's woody pasture (*den*, *s.*).

CONDORA, ? the head (*cean*, *ga.*) between the two waters (*dourau*), *M⸳L.*

CONDURR-A, -OW, druids' down, *B.*; the neck of water, *Pr.*; ? oak (*deru*) down (*goon*).

CONETOCUS, *m.s.* Cubert, ? = *gonidec*, victorious, *a.*

CONEY EAR, ? = *goon y hir*, the long down.

CONGDON, ? king's (*konge*, *d.*) hill.

CONGIER, ? camp (*caer*) down.

CONGWINIAN, ? bees' (*gwenyn*) down.

CONIUM, ? *coney* or rabbit border (*hem*) [field].

CONLY PARK, ? down pasture (*lea*, *t.*) close.

CONNAMANNING, ? butter (*manen*) down.

CONNA-, CONNER-PARK, ? = *corner* close.

CONNERIES, ? dream (*henrus*) down.

CONNERTON,* the scolding (*conner*) place, *Pr.*

CONNINGS WOOD, ? king's wood, *t.*

CONNIRON, ? the down at the boundary (*yrhian*).

CONNOCK, *n.f.*, rich, prosperous, *H.*

CON-NOR, -ORE, ? sister's (*hoar*) down.

CONQUER DOWNS, ? Congar's downs.

CONQUIDNO, ? Gwyddno's (*w.*) downs.

CONSTANTINE, from *p.s.* King Constantinus; (*v.* CUSTENTON).

CONVENE, ? little (*bihan*) down.

CONVENNA, lesser (*behenna*) down.

CONVENON, ? butter (*menan*) down.

CONYCOMBE, rabbit valley.

CONZION, *i.q.* GOONZION.

COOD, COODE, *n.f.*, *i.q.* COAD.

COOF, ? summer (*haf*) down.

COOMFORD, *i.q.* COMFORD.

COON, ? = *gwon*, *goon*, a down.

COOS, COOSE, the wood (*cuz*).

COOSEBEAN, little (*bihan*) wood.

COOSEHAY, wood close (*hay*).

COOSEHECCA, Dickie's (*Hecca*) wood.

COOSPOST, ? pillar (*post*) wood.

COOSVEA, COOZVEAN, little wood, *Pr.*

COOSWORTH, high (*gwarth*) wood.

COOZWARRA, higher (*wartha*) wood.

COPARCENARY, ? the stream (*cober*) near field ridge (*kein ery*, *Ped.*).

COPE HILL, ? top of the hill.

COPPET THORN, tufted (*coppog*, *w.*) thorn.

COQUARNELL, ? ? = *ogo gwar an hal*, the cave on the moor.

CORALLACK, ? *i.q.* CARALLA.

CORAN, COREN, ? *i.q.* CARN.

CORDEW, ? *i.q.* CARDEW.

CORG-A, -AY, -EE, ? = *gurgy*, a low hedge, *m.c.*

CORGARAH, ? further (*gwarra*) moor.

CORGELLY, ? the moor (*cors*) grove; *or*, *i.q.* CARGELLY.

CORGERRICK, ? *i.q.* CARGARRACK.

COR-LAIN, -LEAN, ? = *corlan*, a sheepfold.

CORLONEN, ? nettle (*linhaden*) close (*cae*); ? joyous (*llon*, *w.*) circle (*cor*), *J.W.M.*

CORMIGAS, ? Maccos's (*B.m.*) close.

CORN-AGY, -IGGY, ? *i.q.* CARNAKEY.

CORN-AIL, -ALL, -EAL, ? corner (*corn*) of the moor; *or*, *i.q.* CORNHILL.

CORNEGOES, ? carn of blood (*gois*).

CORNELLOE, ? corner of the moors (*hallow*).

CORNELLY, from *p.s.* St. Cornelius, *O.*

---

* *o.* CONNAWRTON, the town of the great (*mor*) hundred (*cant*), *or*, the great hundred town, *C.S.G.*; ? *d.d.* CONARDITONE, the town of Conard.

CORNHILL, *i.q.* CARNHALE.

CORN-, COR-PESACK, *i.q.* CARN PES-SACK (*pasgaid*, rich, *w.*, *M.*).

CORNWALL, the horn (*corn*) shaped land of the foreigner.*

CORSULLAN, *i.q.* CARSULLAN.

CORSULT, *Le.*, the conspicuous (*sull*) moors (*cors*), *Wh.*

CORUGAN, ? Eorcon's court (*cor*).

CORVA, ? the court, camp, moor, *or* circle place (*va*).

CORVISSACK, ? ivy (*idzhio*) croft.

CORVODE, ? rich (*roeth*) moor.

CORWENNA, ? white (*wennack*) rock.

CORY, *n.f.*, ? *i.q.* CAREY.

CORWENS, windy (*gwens*) moor.

COSAW-ES, -IS, the woods, *Pr.*; *i.q.* COSWINSAWSEN.

COS-EN, -SEN, *n.f.*, ? *i.q.* COSAWSAN.

COSGARNE, rocky (*carn*) wood, *Pr.*; ? crane's (*garan*) wood.

COSHAN, ? summer (*han*, *a.*) wood.

COSMEAL, Michael's *or* honey (*mel*) wood.

COSPOST, scratching post, *w.*, *J.W.M.*

COSSAWSIN, the Saxon's wood, *Po.*

COSTA LOSS, *T.a.*, = *Cost is lost*, *i.e.* Good for nothing [field].

COSWALL, ? wall (*gwal*) wood.

COS-, COSO-WARTH, high (*gwarth*) wood (*cuz*) *or* woods (*cuzow*).

COSW-IN, -YN, white (*gwyn*) wood.

COSWINSAWSEN, Saxon's white (*gwin*) wood. (*sawch*, a heap, *w.*, *C.*).

COTFORD, *i.q.* CODIFORD.

COTHELE, the river (*heyl*) wood (*coat*); = *cotele*, a wood, *R.W.*

COTTAPIT, ? cottage by the *pit.*

COT-TEL, -TLE, *n.f.*, *i.q.* COTHELE.

COTTERELL, *n.f.*, ? wood on (*ar*) the river. (*coterellus*, a cottager, *lat.*).

COTTEY, *n.f.*, ? wood *hay*, *or* close.

COTTON, *n.f.*, ? = down (*oon*) wood.

COTTON WEITH ZAWN, ? neck (*codna*) of the waste (*gwydd*, *w.*) ZAWN.

COTWYNE, *n.f.*, ? white wood.

COUCH, *n.f.*, = *w.* Coch, red, *R.W.* ? = *gudzh*, blood.

COULHENDERS, ? old house (*hendra*) fields (*gweal-s*).

COULSON, *n.f.*, son of Cole (*d.*).

COURLANDS, ? coarse lands, *or*, *i.q.* CORLEAN.

COURTENAY, *n.f.*, ? = *f.* Court nez, short nose, *Lo.*

COURTEYS, CURTEIS, CURTIS, *from lat.* cors, cortis, a pen, cattle yard, *Max M.*

COURAGE, *n.f.*, *i.q.* CROWDGIE.

COURT PELLES, ? distant court.

COVE BEAN, little (*bihan*) cove.

COV-EN, -IN, *n.f.*, ? = *cefn*, a ridge.

COVERACK, ? stream (*cober*), *or* goat (*gaver*), place; *or*, = COBER *rock*.

COWAN PARK, ? down (*gwon*) close.

COW HEELS, ? *i.q.* GWEAL GULLAS.

COWINAC, ? *i.q.* CAVEWEDNACK.

COW-ISSACK, -YJACK, lower (*issach*) enclosure (*cau*, *w.*).

COWLING, *n.f.*, ? = *collen*, a hazel.

COWLOE, ? = *cowlas*, the bay with the building, *Bl.*

COWNANCE, ? enclosure in the valley.

COYSPENHILEK, 14 *cent.*, ? broomy (*benalac*) wood. (*coys* = *coed*).

COYTMOR, *n.f.*, great (*mor*) wood.

CRABBINS PARK, ? lambs' (*eanes*) summer (*haf*) rock (*carn*) close.

CRAB ROCK, ? = *creeb*, a crest.

CRACADILLOCK, ? Dillic's barrow (*crug*) *or* rock.

CRACK, = *carac*, a rock.

C. AN GODNA, ? rock of the neck (*codna*).

CRACKER, ? long (*hir*) rock.

CRACK-HAMPTON, -INGTON, ? rock on the hill (*an dun*); ? *d.d.* CRACH-ENWE, rock by the river (*gwy*).

---

* *d.d.* CORNVALIA, CORNVALGIE; *o.* Kernow, *Cerniw*, the horns *or* promontories, *B.*; *Sammes* derives it from *ph.* *Cheren*, a horn; *Bp. Gibson* from *carn*, a rock; others from *Corineus*, Companion to Brutus; *Whitaker* makes it "Wales" (from *wealhas*, *s.*, the Welsh *or* foreigners) "in the corner" (*corn*).

Pr., CRACKETTON, a place (*ton*) where are shells (*cregyn*).

CRACKLAND, rock field.

CRADGY CRACK, ? CROWGEY barrow (*crug*), or rock (*carrag*).

CRADOCK, *n.f.*, = *w. caradog*, beloved.

CRAFTHOLE, ? hill (*hal*) croft.

CRAGANTALLAN, the high (*tal*) barrow (*crug*).

CRAGGY TOR, rocky peak.

CRAGOE, *n.f.*, ? = CREGO.

CRAKE DEW, black (*du*) rock.

CRAMS, ? outside (*ames*) rocks.

CRANE, ? *i.q.* CARN; or = *garan*, a crane, *H.*

CRANEY HAY, ? frog (*cranec*) close.

CRANIS, ? lambs' (*eunes*) rock.

CRANKAN, ? white (*can*) spring (*cren*), *B.*; ? rock (*carn*) of song (*can*).

CRANKUM, ? crane's valley (*cwm*).

CRANNOCK PARK, frog (*cranog*) close.

CRANNOW, ? *the same*.

CRAN-SEA, -SECK, -JACK, ? dry (*sech*), or, lower (*issach*) rock (*carn*).

CRANSON, ? the charm (*swyn, w.*) rock.

CRANSWORTH, ? crane's field, (*worth-ig, s.*); or, *i.q.* CARNSWORTH.

CRANTOCK, *from p.s.* St. Carantocus, *O.*; (*d.d.* St. Carentoch).

CRANYDON, ? frog (*cranec*) hill.

CRAPP, *n.f.*, ? = *gwrab*, an ape, *w.*

CRASKEN, ? *i.q.* CARSKAIN.

THE CRASSES, the middle (*cres*) [fields].

CRATHEN, CREATHEN, ? the birds' (*edhen*) rock; or = *certhen*, the mountain ash.

CRAVA, ? wild garlic (*crav*) close (*hay*).

CRAWLE, ? close (*ce*) on (*ar*) the hill (*hal*); or, hovel place (*le*).

CRAW PARK, ? hovel (*crow*) close.

CRAZE, *n.f.*, ? *i.q.* CARHAYES.

CREADLE-, CRADLE-FIELD, ? = *w. cardail*, manured land.

CREAN, ? = *grean*, gravel.

CREANY, ? = *greanic*, gravelly.

CREBAR, ? mountain ash (*care*) summit (*bar*), or close (*parc*).

CREBAWETHAN, the crest (*crib*) [rock] with a tree (*gwedhen*).

CRE-, CREG-BILLIOW, the round (*pel*) barrow (*redup. crug, k., low, t.*), *M^cL.*

CREEB, the crest- or combe-like rock.

CREDACOT, ? Cerdic's (*t.*) or Ceredig's (*w.*) cot.

CREED, *from p.s.* St. Crida.

CREEDIS, ? St. Crida's [cell].

CREEG CARROW, the deer's (*carow*) barrow (*creeg*), *Pr.*; or Roman (*row*) castle (*caer*) barrow, *Po.*

C. BROAZ, the great (*bras*) barrow, *Pr.*

C. GLAZE, the green (*glas*) barrow, *Po.*

C. LOGAS, the mice (*logas*) barrow.

C. MEAR, -MEER, the great (*meor*) barrow, *T.*; the rock (*carag*) on the sea (*mor*), *Nord.*

C. MURION, the ants' (*murrian*) barrow, *Pr.*

C. PELLOE, *i.q.* CREBILLIOW.

C. SILLICK, the barrow in open view, *T.* (*syll*, a view, prospect).

C. TOL, = *carey tol*, the holed rock, *Bl.*

C. VOSE, the intrenched barrow, *Pr.*

CREEKEN, ? little (*vean*) barrow or rock; or, *i.q.* CREGAN.

CREEK LUDDRA, ? thieves' (*ladruu*) rock.

CREENS, ? *i.q.* CARN ENYS.

CREEP, ? = *i.q.* PENGREEP.

CREEPER, *n.f.*, ? *i.q.* CREBAR.

CREFFEL, ? = *cyrafol*, service berries, *w.*

CREFTOA, strong hatch or poleaxe, *H.*

CREGA, CREGGO, CREGO, ? = *cregow*, hillocks, mounds, barrows, tumuli.

CREGAN FIELD, ? little hill (*crechen, a.*) field.

CREGARLAND, ? partridge (*gregor*) close (*lan*).

CREGLOW, rocks by the pool (*lo*), *T.C.*

CREGOOSE, ? barrow in the wood (*cuz*).

CREGWORTHGAN, ? high (*warth*) barrow on the downs (*goon*).

CREISWELL, ? middle (*cres*) well.

CRELL-A, -OW, -Y, CREILLY, ? *i.q.* CREGLOW, or CRELLAS.

CRELL-AS, -YS, ? = *crehyllys*, ruined

K

[dwellings]. Green (glas) hillock (creeg), R.E.

CREM-BLE, -ILL, (Car. CRYMELL), the hill (aill, ga.) of Crom, Beal; sharp-edged (crimp) hill, M.

CREN-ICK, -NICK, ? i.q. CARNICK.

CRENVAL, ? i.q. CARN EVALL.

CRENVER, ? i.q. CARRENVER.

CRESKIN, ? i.q. CARSCAIN.

CRESLOW, ? i.q. CARSELLA.

CRESSARS, midway (cres) [rocks], T.C.

CRESTA, ? the scrubby (crestu) [field], M.

CRESTICK, ? Ysteg's (w.) rock (carn).

CREVELLAN, ? i.q. CARWOLLEN.

CREWE, n.f., ? i.q. CAREW.

CREWELL, ? high (uhal) castle or rock.

CREWES, CRUIS, n.f., curled, d., F.

CRIB AN ZAWN, ? the crest (crib) by the ZAWN.

CRIBBAGE, ? lower (iza) crest.

CRIBBA HEAD, the crestlike headland, Bl.

CRIBBAWIDDEN, i.q. CREBAWETHEN.

CRICKAPIT, ? the pit near the barrow (cryg) or rock (carrac).

CRICKEY PARK, ? rocky close.

CRICKLEY, ? rock pasture (lea, t.) or place (le, w.).

CRIDDLE, n.f., ? = gwrdeol, an exile, w.

CRIFF, CRIFFET, CRIFT, = croft.

CRIFFIER, ? long (hir) croft.

CRIFTOE, CRIFTS, ? the crofts.

CRIGANTALLAN, the high (tal) barrow (cryg), Po.

THE CRIGG, the rock or barrow.

CRIGGLES, ? church (eglos) rock.

CRIGGMAJOR, ? rock feeding ground (mager, Pr.).

CRILLA, -EY, ? i.q. CRELLA.

CRIM, CRIMP, sharp-edged [rock], M.

CRINE, = caer rhyn, the castle on the promontory, M'L.

CRINNIS, ? rock near the island (enys).

CRIP-SON, -TON, ? Crapp's town, T.C.

CRIST, ? east (est) rock (carn).

CROAGAN, ? hut on the downs (goon).

CROAN, the cross, Pr.; ? the hut or stye (crow). (crwn, round, w., R.W.).

CROCKADODON, ? the under (dadn = dan) barrow.

CROCKADON, the barrow (cruc) or rock (carrac) on the hill (dun).

CROCKARD, n.f., high (ard) barrow.

CROCKER, CROAKER, n.f., i.q. CROOKER; or = krogour, a hangman, a.

CROCKET, ? barrow gate (yet).

CROCKWOOD, barrow or rock wood.

CROF HER, long (hir), or, higher croft.

CROFT AN BROSE, the great (bras) or thicket (brouse) croft.

C. AN CONS, causeway (coans) croft.

C. AN CREEK, the field with the tumulus (cryc), M'L.

C. AN DARREN, the oak (derwen) croft, R.W.

C. AND CROUSE, the (an) cross croft.

C. & WITH, i.q. CROFT EN GWEETH, the croft with the trees.

C. AN GARRAT, ? the garden or enclosure (gardd) croft.

C. AN HELLOW, croft by the moors (hallow).

C. AN MEERE, ? the great (meor) croft.

C. AN VOUNDER, the lane (bounder) croft.

C. BARTH, -BERTH, ? side (parth), or bush (perth, w.) croft.

C. BIB, ? pipe (pib) croft.

C. BROASE, -BROWSE, i.q. CROFT AN BROSE.

C. CAIRN, the carn croft.

C. CHAIR, ? darnel (jure, Po.) croft.

C. COATH, the wood (coat) croft.

C. CROW, hovel (crow) croft.

C. DEW, -DUE, black (du) croft.

CROFTEDEDOR, d.d., (e.d.d., CROUTEDEDOR), ? great (ethy) croft by the water (dour).

CROFT EN CRANETH, croft with the heap of stones (carnedd, w.).

C. FOLD, croft with the sheep fold.

C. FRIGELS, church-road (for eglos) croft.

C. GARRA, higher (gwartha) croft.

C. GODNA, the neck (codna) croft.

C. GOTHAL, ? Irishman's (godhal) croft.

C. GURDDEN, ? mountain-ash (*cerden*) croft.

CROFTHANDY, convenient croft ; or croft by the house (*an ty*) ; the fire (*tan*) croft, *Francis.*

CROFT HARRY, ? acre (*cru*) croft.

C. KELLIER, ? long grove (*celli hir*) croft.

C. LOGE, calf's (*loch*) croft.

C. MAIN, stone (*maen*) croft.

C. MAINER, long-stone (*menhir*) croft.

C. MARGETT, ? magpie croft.

C. MEDLYN, ? Magdalen's, or battle-field (*midlan, w.*), croft.

C. MILGEY, greyhound (*milgy*) croft.

C. NETHAN, the furze (*an eithen*) croft.

C. NOALS, the cliff (*an als*) croft.

C. OVAL, ? apple (*aval*) croft.

C. PASCOE, Pascoe's croft.

C. PEDAN, ? croft end (*pedn = pen*).

C. PENDREA, town end croft.

C. PILLAS, *pillas* or poor croft.

C. ROSE, heath *or* moor croft.

C. SEA, dry (*sech*) croft.

C. SHENAUL, CHENHALL croft.

C. STUBB-Y, -YS, croft with the cut furze stems.

C. SUGAL, rye (*sygal*) croft.

C. TIDNEY, ? fowler's *or* narrow (*idne*) croft, *T.C.*

C. TOTTAN, ? the lay (*todn*) croft ; ? hill (*dun*) croft, *T.C.*

C. VEAN, little (*bihan*) croft.

C. WEND-JACK, -ZACK, ? lower (*isach*) white (*gwin*) croft.

C. WEST, west croft ; (*gwestu*, to shelter).

C. ZEATH, dry croft, *Gw.*

CROGGAN, ? hovel on the downs (*goon*).

CROG-GET, -ITH, wooden cross, *T.* ; ? heath (*heyth*) barrow (*crug*).

CROGHANS, ? lambs' (*eanes*) barrow.

CROKE, *n.f.*, = *crug*, a barrow, hillock.

CROLL-A, -OW, ? calf's (*loch*) hovel (*crow*).

CRONE, CROON, *i.q.* CROAN.

CRONICK, ? frog (*cronec*) [field].

CROOKEDY, ? Edy's barrow, *T.C.* ; ? crooked piece.

CROOKER, ? long (*hir*) barrow.

CROOK HEEL, ? moor (*hal*) barrow.

CROOKLAND, ? barrow (*crug*) enclosure (*lan*).

CROOK PARK, barrow close.

C. SANS, ? holy rock (*carrac*).

CROOM FIELD, ? crooked (*crom*) field.

CROSCOMBE, the valley at right angles to another.

CROSSICK, ? boggy (*corsic*) field.

CROSSMAN, *n.f.*, ? stone (*maen*) cross.

CROSSOBY, place (*by, d.*) of the cross, *M·L.* ; ? *i.q.* CROUSE HARVEY.

CROUG-ATH, -ARTH, ? high hovel.

CROUS, cross, *or* = *cors*, moor.

CROUSA DOWNS, the cross downs.

CROUSANRASE, the middle (*cres*) cross.

CROUSANVEAN, the little cross.

CROUSANWRAGH, the witch's (*an wrach, w.*) cross, *R.W.* ; cross of the hill (*bre*), *T.C.*

CROUSE HARVEY, ? battle field (*heir-va*) cross.

CROUSLEVAN, ? St. Levan's *or* lamentation cross (*llevain*, to lament, *w.*).

CROUSMENIGGUS, the blessed (*beniges*) cross, *G.L.* ; ? the nun's (*manaches*) cross.

CROW, the stye, hovel, *or* shed.

CROWAN, *from p.s.* St. Crewenna, *O.* ; *crow-an*, the cross, *grouan*, moor-stone gravel, *Pr.*

CROWD-A, -EY, -ER, ? hovel by the water (*dour*), *T.C.* ; ? fiddler's (*crowder*) [field].

CROWDILLION, the owls' (*dylluan*) hovel.

CROW-GEY, -GIE, cross hedge (*ce*), *or* house (*chi*), *or* dog's (*ci*), cross, *Pr.*

CROW HILL, the hill with the camps (*caerau*) on it, *M·L.*

CROWL, CROWLE, *n.f.*, ? the same ; *or*, hovel on the moor (*hal*), *T.C.*

CROWLAS, grey (*glas*) hut, *T.C.*

CROWLEY, *n.f.*, ? hut pasture.

CROWNICK, the dwelling at the cross, *Pr.* ; ? *i.q.* CRONICK.

CROWN PARK, hovel close.

CROWN ZAWN, ? hovel ZAWN.
CROWSADJACK, ? lower (*issach*) cross (*crous*).
CROWSATH, ? high (*arth*) cross.
CRO-WSER, -ZIER, ? long (*hir*) cross.
CROWSWIN, white (*gwin*) cross, *Pr.*
CROWTON, ? *i.q.* CROW HILL.
CROW WEETHS, ? crow trees (*gwedd*); or, uncultivated lands (*gwydd, w.*) with the hovel.
CRUCARESKEN, 11 *cent.*, barrow by the sedgy camp (CRESKIN).
CRUDGE, *n.f.*, ? = *crudzh, crous*, cross.
CRUFF, CRUFFE, *n.f.*, ? = *gariff*, rough.
CRUGIGIZARD, = *crug a giz ard*, tumulus of the woody ridge, *M'L.*
CRUGKERN, *n.f.*, ? barrow in the corner (*corn*), or, of the handmill (*quern*).
CRUG-LASE, -GLASE, green (*glas*) barrow.
CRUGMEER, the great (*meor*) barrow, *Pr.*
CRUGSILLICK, the conspicuous barrow, or, in open view, *Pr.*
CRUGVES, the barrow outside.
CRULLA, CRYLLA, ? *i.q.* CROLLA, or CROWLAS, or CRUGLASE.
CRUMP, *n.f.*, ? = *crom*, crooked.
CRUNDLE, = *crundwell*, a spring or well with a basin, *t.*, *Leo.*
CRUNO, ? = *cernow*, horns, corners.
CRUP-LIGHT, -LITE, *i.q.* CURPLY.
CRU-TER, -TOUR, ? hovel (*crow*) land (*tir, doar*), or by the water (*dour*).
CRUTHERS, *n.f.*, from CARTUTHER.
CUBBERT or CUPBOARD, mine, ? *i.q.* CUBERT.
CUBERT, from *p.s.* St. Cuthbert.
CUBLIDOICE, ? stream (*gover*) pasture (*lea, t.*) with the stack (*disc, B.*).
CUBY, from *p.s.* St. Keby, *O.*
CUCURRIAN, ? basin (*cuwg, w.*) at the boundary (*yrhian*).
CUDDAN BEAK, CUDDEN POINT, the woody promontory, *Pr.*; the promontory with a neck (*codna*), *T.C.*
CUDDIE, -Y, *n.f.*, ? = *coed ty*, house wood.

CUDDLE PARK, ? Irishman's (*gwyddel, w.*) close.
CUDDRA, the wood by the house.
CUDDUCOMBE, ? *i.q.* CATACOMBE.
CUDJORE, CUGAR, ? play (*choary*) wood.
CUDLIP, *n.f.*, ? moist (*leb*) wood.
CUDNO, ? = *codna*, the neck.
CUGURRICK, ? rock (*carrac*) close (*ce*).
CULLION, ? *i.q.* CARLEAN, or CALLEAN.
CULLODEN, steer (*lodn*), bank (*ladn*), or broad (*ledan*) field (*gweal*).
CULLIS, *n.f.*, ? = *goles*, bottom, lowest part.
CULLYNOUGH PARK, ? holly (*celenic*) close.
CULLY PARK ? grove (*celli*) close.
CULOMS, ? from ST. COLUMB.
CULVER-LAND, -PARK, dovecot (*clomiar*) close.
CULVER-Y, -HAY, ? the same.
CUMBERLAND, Welshman's close.
CUNA, CUNNY PARK, ? corner or coney close, *t.*
CUNAIDO, *m.s.* Carnsew, good (*da*) lord (*cuniaid, w.*).
CUND-AY, -Y, *n.f.*, ? *i.q.* CUNAIDO.
CUNICOURT, (*now* PLACE), the king's court, *t.*
CUNMOR, duke, great head or chief.
CUNNACK, *n.f.*, ? *i.q.* CONOCK.
CUNNING, *n.f.*, ? *i.q.* CONAN.
CUNOWAL, *m.s.* Madron, head (*cyn*) of praise (*maul*), *Dr.*
CUNSIE, *w.B.m.*, bold victory (*sige*), *t.*
CUNWORI, *m.s.* Fowey, = CUNMOR.
CURGALLON, *i.q.* CARGALLON.
CURG-EAR, -ARE, ? = *carrag hir*, long rock; or, *grugyer*, a partridge.
CURGENVEN, ? Kenwyn's court (*cur*).
CURGURWEN, *n.f.*, Gerwyn's (*w.*) court.
CURLY-GHON, -ON, *n.f.*, *i.q.* CARLYON.
CURN-O, -OW, *n.f.*, = *Cerniw*, CORNWALL.
CURPLY, = *caer plas*, palace camp, *Po.*; ? BELI's or BLIGHT court.
CURRAN NIEGAN, *i.q.* CARN NIEGAN.
CURRAS, ? = *cors*, a moor.

CURVEAN, little (*bihan*) close (*ce*).

CURVODA, ? court (*cur*) by the wood.

CURVOZA, *i.q.* CARVOSSA.

CURWEN, white (*gwyn*) court.

CURY, *from p.s.* St. Corentinus, *O.*

CURYAN, ? = *curvean*, little court.

CUSBURRIER, ? long (*hir*) barn (*skeber*) wood (*cus*).

CUSECCA, *i.q.* COOSEHECCA.

CUSHING FIELD, ? turf (*cesan*) field.

CUSK-AIN, -EAN, *i.q.* CARSCAIN; *or*, ridge (*cein*) wood (*cus*).

CUSK-AYS, -EASE, ? the enclosed wood.

CUSTENTIN, *w.B.m.*, *i.q.* CONSTANTINE.

CUSTUS LOGGAS, ? = COST IS LOST.

CUS-VARTH, -VEORTH, -WARTH, ? high (*warth*) wood.

CUSVEY, ? little (*bich*) wood (*cus*).

CUSWYN, white (*gwyn*) wood.

CUTBRAWN, = *w.*, *coed bron*, wood on the hill.

CUTCARE, ? camp (*caer*) wood.

CUTCREW, wood with the hut (*crow*) or camps (*caerau*); ? deer (*carow*) wood, *T.C.*

CUTECLIFFE, *n.f.*, ? cliff wood.

CUTHILL, wood on the river (*heyl*), *Pr.*

CUT-KEIVE, -KIVE, ditch (*keif*) wood, *M·L.*; wood of hiding place (*cuddva*, *Ev.*).

CUTLINWITH, ? high (*warth*) lake (*lin*) wood. (*enwydh*, ash trees).

CUTMEAR, great (*meur*) wood.

CUT PARK, wood close (*parc*).

CUTPARROT, ? gate close (*parc yet*) wood.

CUTPIT, ? wood with a grave (*bedh*).

CUTTEN PEAT, ? *cutting peat* [field].

CUTTI-FORD, -VET, wood by the road (*fordh*).

CUTTINE, ? = *coed wyn*, white wood.

CUTTY, ? = *w. coetiey*, a field, *R.W.*

CYGNEY, ? kitchen (*cicne, s.*) [field].

DABB, *n.f.*, ? *dab*, a flat fish; *or*, *i.q.* DOBB.

DACON, *n.f.*, ? = *diacon*, a deacon.

DADDYPORT, the parent (*tad, w.*) port, *W'h.*

DAD-, DOD-DYCROSS, cross of position or mark (*dodi*), *C.*; ? DODO'S, *or*, DAUID'S (*s.B.m.*), marsh (*cors*).

DAD WOOD, ? fox (*tod*) wood, *t.*

DAGGE, *n.f.*, ? *tuch*, a warrior, *i.*

DAG-GEL, -GLE, *n.f.*, ? *from* TINTAGEL.

DALA-WHITTON, -WIDDEN, ? white (*gwidn*) dale; *or*, little DELI.

DALIAS GEW, ? foliaged or leafy ravine (*cew*), *C.*

DALLACK, foremost or front (*tal*) of land, *or*, headland, *C.*; ? the place in the dale.

DALLARD, ? high (*ard*) dale.

DAMASINNAS, ? the look out; (*dam*, round about, *synu*, to observe, *w.*), *N.*

DAMELSA, *i.q.* DEMELZA; ? under (*dan*) cliff (*als*), *T.C.*

DANDY, *n.f.*, under (*dan*) house; *or*, *i.q.* DAWNAY, *Lo.*

DANE CLOSE, fire (*tan*), *or*, under (*dan*) close.

DANESCOMBE, the Danes' valley, *t.*

DANIEL, *n.f.*, ? *i.q.* TINNEL.

DANGER, DAUNGER, *n.f.*, ? under (*dan*) the camp (*caer*).

DANMONII, *from den*, men; *or*, *dun*, a hill; *or*, *dyfn*, deep; and *moina*, mines. ? DAMNONII, from *damn*, *or*, *w. dwrn*, deep, *R.W.*

DANNAR'S CLOSE, ? *i.q.* DINAS.

DANNET, ? below (*dan*) the gate (*yet*).

DANNON CHAPEL, ? under (*dan*) down (*oon*) chapel.

DANNONDOZEL, ? under down low (*isal*) land (*doar*). (*dwzel*, a spout, *w.*).

DAPIFER, *n.f.*, the steward (*lat.*).

DARBY PARK, ? little (*bich*) water (*dour*); *or*, oak (*dar*) close (*parc*).

DARKE, *n.f.*, ? = *darag*, an oak, *i.*

DARKEY, ? = *dourgy*, a low hedge.

DARLEY, = Oakley; *or*, oak (*dar*) place (*le*); Oak green (*lees*), *Pr.*

DARMAN, ? stone (*maen*) field, (*doar*, land).

DARN-ABY, -EY, BAY, ? little (*bich*) oak (*derwen*) [field].

DARNICOMBE, ? the oak (*derwen*) valley.

DARNIGHT, ? *i.q.* DANNET.

DARRACOT, ? oak (*derow*) or dairy cottage.

DARR-APS, -AS, ? = PARK AN DARRAS.

DARRITY HOLE, *dirty* cave, *Woodley*.

DARSELL, low (*isal*) land (*doar*).

DARTHZEY, ? = *doar sech*, dry land or oak, *T.C.*

DARUNDLE, *n.f.*, of (*d',f.*) Arun vale (*dal*).

DAUNAS, ? = *dinas*, a fortification.

DAVEN MEADOW, ? deep (*dyfn*), or trickling (*davn, w., R.W.*) meadow.

DAVIDSTOW, *v.* DEWSTOW, St. David's (*p.s.*) place. (DAUID, *s.B.m.*).

DAW, *n.f.*, ? = Dauid, or, *dehau*, south.

DAWARNE, *n.f.*, ? *i.q.* TREWARN.

DAWN-A, -AH, ? the down, or, down enclosure (*hay*).

DAWNAY, *n.f.*, = D'Aunai (*Normandy*), Lo. (*aune*, an alder, *f.*).

DAWNET, ? = *down gate*.

DAWNS-MYIN, -MEN, the stone dance, or dancing stones, *Bl.*

DAWRACK, ? = *dourick*, watery [field].

DAZARD POINT, ? high (*ard*) stack (*das, w.*) point.

THE DEADMAN, solitary (*man*) horn, end, or point (*deadh*), ga., *Beul.**

DEAN, ? = *den*, a woody pasture, *s.*

DEASON, *n.f.*, ? = *dyson*, noiseless.

DECUM, ? house (*ty*) in the coombe.

DEEBLE, *n.f.*, *i.q.* Theobald, people's (*theod*) prince (*bald*), *t.*

DEGEMBRIS, *i.q.* TREGIMBRIS.

DEGIBNA, ? house on the confines (*cyffiniau, w.*).

DEJEY FIELD, ? house (*tshei*) field.

DELABOLE, ? the clay (*bol*) hole (*tol*),

Pr.; ? DELI pit (*pol*).

DELAHAY, *n.f.*, ? *i.q.* DELI; or, of (*de*) the (*la*) enclosure (*haie*), *f.*

DELAVAL, *n.f.*, ? *i.q.* DELABOLE; or, of the valley (*val*), *f.*

DELAWYDDLE, ? Irishman's (*gwiddal*) dale.

DELBRIDGE, *n.f.*, ? BRIXI's dale.

DELI, DELLE, *d.d.* DELIAV, ? dale (*dal*) enclosure (*hay*).

DELIONUTH, ? new (*nowydh*) DELI.

DELLAS, ? green (*glas*) dale.

DELLYMEER, ? great (*meer*) DELI.

DEMBLE, *n.f.*, ? *i.q.* DENNEBOUL.

DEMELZA, ? eel (*malsai*) house (*ty*).

DENANT, ? = *du nant*, black vale.

DE NARROW ZAWN, ? rough (*harrow*) hill (*din*) ZAWN.

DENBOW, *n.f.*, ? *i.q.* DENNEBOUL.

DENBY, ? little (*bich*) wooded vale (*denu, s.*), or castle (*din*).

DENCH, DINCH, *n.f.*, ? = DENNIS.

DENCREEK, *i.q.* TENCREEK.

DENEMY, ? Amy's wooded vale, *t.*

DENGEL, *s.B.m.*, ? = *dungel*, dungeon.

DENIS-EL, -LY, *n.f.*, ? lower (*isala*) hill (*din*); or, *i.q.* Dinsul.

DENN, *n.f.*, ? *i.q.* DEAN.

DENNA-, DINNY-BROAD, ? castle (*din*) of treachery (*brad*).

DENNEBOUL, clay (*bol*) hill (*din*), Pr.; fortress (*dinas*) on round hill (*bol*), C.; *i.q.* DELABOLE.

DENNICK, the hilly [field].

DENNIS, *i.q.* DINAS.

DENNIS EIA, St. Ive's castle.

DENNITHORNE, *n.f.*, ? the hilly (*dinnick*) place with the thorn.

DENNY, ? *i.q.* DENNICK; or, DENNIS; or, hill (*din*) enclosure (*hay*).

DEN-SIL, -ZELL, hill in open view (*syll*), Pr.; ? *i.q.* DINSUL.

DER BETTYS, DERBY'S CLOSE, ? beet

---

* There is however "a bay of corpses," BAIE DES TREPASSES, in Brittany. Sailors call the Cornish headland The DODMAN (*T.C.*); ? the stone (*maen*) of mark or position (*dodi*), C. Gwavas says, DUBMAN or GUBMAN, a place where much ore (*gubman*, sea weed) is cast. Dudman is given by Bailey as scarecrow, hobgoblin; and is also a personal name.

root (*beatus, w.*) field, (*doar,* land).

DERDEN, ? oak (*dar*) vale (*den, s.*).

DERGAN, *i.q.* DOURGAN.

DERNIFORD, ? the oak (*derwen*) passage.

DERR-AS, -ES, -IES, *i.q.* PARK AN DARAS; *or,* PARK DRIES.

DERRYCOMB, ? oak (*deru*) vale.

DER-VAL, -WELL, ? high (*uhal*) oak.

DEUI, *w.B.m., i.q.* DAVID.

DEVERA, ? hill (*bre*) side (*tu*).

DEVIOCK, ? DEUI's estate.

DEVIS, sheep (*davas*) place, *Pr.*

DEVORAN, ? = *difron,* a bosom.

DEW, *n.f.,* ? = *du,* black; *or, deheu, w.,* south; *or, edhow,* the Jew.

DEWCOME, ? black *or* south vale.

DEW DRY, ? south homeward (*adre*) [close].

DEWEN, *n.f.,* ? of (*de, f.*) St. Wenn; *or,* white (*wen*) house (*ty*).

DEWEY, ? south enclosure (*hay*).

DEYMAN, DIAMOND, *n.f.,* ? the stone (*maen*) house (*ty*).

DIARY, ? dairy [farm].

DICE MEADOW, stack (*dise, B.*) meadow.

DICKEY, DIGGEY, ? the tithe [field] (*dege,* tenth); ? = *ty isa,* lower house, *T.C.*

DIDDIS, ? ? stack (*dise*) house (*ty*).

DIDDY LAKE, ? ? TEHIDDY by the pool (*lacu*).

DIMELIOCK, ? Mailoc house *or* castle (*din*).

DINAH'S HILL, fortification (*dinas*) hill.

DINAKY, ? *i.q.* TANGEY.

DINAN, *n.f.,* ? *i.q.* DENANT; *or,* the valley (*nant*) castle (*din*).

DINAS VEAN, the little (*bean*) fortification (*dinas*).

DINERDAKE, ? Arthog's (*w.*) castle (*din*).

DINGDONG, ? bell [mine].

DINGEREIN, Gerennius's castle, *Wh.*

DINGEY, ? *i.q.* TANGEY.

DINGLE, ? wooded (*gelli*) valley (*den, s.*).

DINHAM, *n.f., i.q.* DINAN.

DINNAB-ELL, -OLE, -OWL, -OLD, *i.q.* DENNEBOUL.

DINNACOMBE, ? castle vale.

DINNARS HEAD, *i.q.* PENDENNIS.

DINNAVAL, *i.q.* DINNABELL.

DINNERS PARK, DINAS close.

DINNEY PIECE, THE DINNICK, ? hilly field, *or,* = DINNIS.

THE DINNIS, *i.q.* DINAS.

DINSUL, hill sacred to the sun (*sul*), *B.*; conspicuous hill, *Wh.*; high (*uhal*) castle (*dinas*), *Po.*; ? hill of view (*syll*).

DINWORTH, high (*warth*) hill.

DIPPER PARK, ? pit (*dippa*) close.

DIRFORD, ? passage over the water (*dour*), *M'L.*

DIRLING, *w.B.m.,* darling, *t.*

DIRMANTLE, field (*doar*) with the holed-stone (*maen tol*).

DIRTY POOL, ? ? water (*dour*) house (*ty*) by the pool.

DIRWYN, *n.f.,* ? = *derwen,* an oak.

DISH, ? *i.q.* PARK AN DISE.

DISTIN, *n.f.,* ? tin (*stean*) house (*ty*).

DITCHEN, ? John's (*Dzhuan*) house.

DITCHI PARK, ? *i.q.* DISH; *or,* DEJEY.

DIZZARD, ? *i.q.* DAZARD; *or* = *dysert,* a wilderness, *w.*

DOBB, *n.f.,* ? *dubh,* black; *or, dobh,* boisterous, *ga.*; *or, i.q.* DABB.

DOBBS, DOBBINS, *n.f.,* = Roberts.

DOBLE, *n.f.,* = Theobald.

DOBNA, ? *i.q.* PARK TUBBAN.

DOBWALLS, = *daub* (*i.e.* cob) *walls, C.*

DOCK, ? sheaf (*attock*) [field].

DODBROOK, ? Dodo's brook.

DODD, *n.f.,* ? *i.q.* DODO, *t.d.d.,* from *theod,* people, *s.*; *or,* Dauid, *s.B.m.*

DODDEN, *i.q.* PARK TODDIN.

DODMAN, *i.q.* DEADMAN.

DODNAL, ? under (*dan*) the moor (*hal*).

DODSON, ? Dodo's down (*oon*).

DOENGAND, *s.B.m.,* ? ? dark (*dun*) fox (*canddo, w.*).

DOFFAL CROFT, ? dock (*tafol*) croft.

DOIDGE, *n.f.,* ? = Dodo's son.

DOLCOATH, wood (*coed*) by the hole

or shaft *(tol)*, *C.*; the old *(coth)* pit, *T.C.*; old valley, dale, *or* meadow *(dal)*, *Pr.*

DOL-EER, -YER, long *(hir)* dale.

DOLGEY, ? *i.q.* DOLLEGY; *or*, hedge *(ce)*, *or* dog *(ci)*, dale.

DOLHUE CROFT, ? high *(uch)* dale croft.

DOLKA PARK, ? DOLGEY close.

DOLL-AH, -AR ROCK, rock of grief *(dolur, w.)*.

DOLLAND, ? dale enclosure *(lan)*.

DOLLARD, ? high *(ard)* dale.

DOLLEGY, dale near the house *(agy)*.

DOLLING, ? little *(vean)* dale.

DOLPHIN, *i.q.* GODOLPHIN; *or*, DOL-VEAN; *or*, little *(vean)* dale.

DOLREE, ? dale field *(eru)*.

DOLRENNY, ? valley REENS.

DOLRUNNY, ? plum *(aeranic)* valley.

DOLSBERRY, ? dark *(dulas)* hill *(bre)*.

DOLLY-WHIDDEN, -WITHEN, ? white *(gwidn)*, *or* tree *(gwedhen)*, dale.

DOLVEAN, *i.q.* DOLPHIN; ? little hole *or* shaft, *C.*

DOM BUCKA, ? ghost *or* scarecrow *(bucca)* hill *(dun)*; *bucha*, a milking fold, *C.*

DOMELLICK, ? Mailoc's down *(dun)*.

DONECHENIF, *d.d.*, ? autumn *(cynaif)* castle; *or*, nut *(cnyf)* hill *(dun)*.

DONEY, *n.f.*, *i.q.* DAWNAY.

DONGEY, *n.f.*, *i.q.* TANGEY.

DONHAVERN, *i.q.* GOONHAVERN.

DONIERT, *m.s.* Redgate, *i.q.* DUN-GERTH, warrior *(gereit)* king *(donn)*, *ga.*, *Beal.*

DONNE-NY, -EGNEY, ? Cennych's *(w.)* castle; *or*, worm *(cynac)* hill *(dun)*; *or*, *i.q.* DONECHENIF.

DOOR DOWNS, ? water *(dour)* downs.

DOPP, ? the summit *(top)*.

DOR, ? = *doar*, land, *i.e.* field; *or*, *dour*, water.

DORANVITHAN, the *(an)* tree *(gwedhen)* field.

DORAS, *i.q.* PARK AN DARAS.

DOR ATTY, ARTHUR'S field, *T.C.*

DORAVAL, apple *(aval)* field.

DORBEAR, ? barley *(bere, s., C.)* field.

DORBERRY, ? rich *(berric)* field.

DOR BOTHICK, ? cottage *(bothoc)* field.

DORCAS, wood *(cus)* land.

DOR CATCHER, ? daisy *(cajah)* field.

DORCLAY, ? grove *(celli)* field.

DOR-COATH, -OOTH, -OTH, *i.q.* DOL-COATH; *or*, DORCAS.

DOR-DEAW, -DEW, -DUE, ? south *(de-hau)*, *or* black *(du)*, *or* David's field.

DORDOWN, ? deep *(down)* water *(dour)*.

DOR EAR, long *(hir)* land.

DOR EYE, ? water *(dour)* field *(hay)*.

DOREY, *n.f.*, ? *the same*; *or*, *i.q.* DOWRICK.

DOR GULVAL, GULVAL land.

DORGWIDEN, white *(gwidn)* land.

DOR-HEERE, -HAIR, *i.q.* DOR EAR.

DORHERVAS, ? outside *(ves)* long field.

DORJOAN, ? down house *(choon)*, *or* John's *(Dzhuan)* field.

DOR LEE, ? flat stone *(lech)* field.

DORLIS, ? broad *(les)* field.

DOR-MAN, -MUN, stone *(maen)* field.

DOR MARTH, ? water plain, *or* meadow *(marth, C.)* land.

DOR-MEAR, -MEER, -MER, great *(meer)*, *or* marsh *(mere, s.)*, field.

DORMINNACK, stony *(maenic)* field *or* land.

DOR MINNIS, ? little *(minys)* field; *or* lambs' *(eanes)* stone *(maen)* field.

DORMULLION, ? clover *(meillion, w.)* land.

DORN, ? = *trone*, a depression between the furrows of a field.

DORNELLA, ? the elm *(an elaw)* field.

DORNEOUTH, new *(newydh)* land.

DORNOLDS, ? the cliff *(an als)* field.

DOROTHEGVA, ? tithe *(degeve)* lands *(doarou)*.

DOR POL, pool *or* pit *(pol)* field.

DOR PONS, bridge *(pons)* field.

DORRACKS, watery *(douric)* fields.

DORRE, ? *i.q.* DOR; *or*, DORHEERE.

DORSEALL, ? low *(isal)* land.

DORSET, seat, *or*, dry *(seth)* field.

DORSPUL, ? = PARK DARAS by the pool *or* pit *(pol)*.

DOR STENOR, tinner *or* waterwagtail (*stenor*) field.

DOR VELHA, ? look out (*wylfa*) field.

DORVOR, ? water (*dour*) lane (*for*), *T.C.* ; *or*, great (*veor*) field.

DORWARD, *n.f.*, ? = *s. duru-weard*, door-keeper ; *i.q.* Porter, *Lo.*

DORWASE, ? outside (*res*) field.

DORWICK, *n.f.*, ? = *dourick*, watery.

DOSMAR-E, -Y, DOZMERE, a drop (*dos*) of the sea (*mere, s.*), *C.**

DOTSON, *i.q.* DODSON.

DOUBLEBOIS, Two woods, *f.*

DOUBLE PARK, ? dock (*tavol*) close.

DOULIN, ? black (*du*) pool (*lyn*).

DOUNE, *n.f.*, = *dun*, a hill, down.

DOUR CONNOR, ? Connor's water.

DOURGAN, white (*can*) water (*dour*) ; *or*, water mouth (*genau*).

DOUROCK, ? watery *or* oak place.

DOVEAR, ? *i.q.* DORVOR.

DOVRIGGER, daisy (*egr*) field, *T.C.*

DOWBER, the short (*ber*) water (*dour*), *Pr.* ; ? *i.q.* DOVEAR.

DOWDLE, south (*dehau*) *or* double (*deau*) dale (*dal*).

DOWERNICK, ? marshy (*wernic*) land (*doar*).

DOWER PARK, water (*dour*) close.

DOWGAS, water in the wood (*cus*), *Pr.* ; ? *i.q.* DORCAS.

DOWGATH, ? south garden (*garth*).

DOWLAND, ? south enclosure (*lan*).

DOWLSDOWN, water dingle, *C.* ; ? devil's (*diaoul*) down.

DOWNANCE, ? south vale (*nance*).

DOWN CHAINEYS, ? *Chenisi's* down.

DOWNDERRY, ? oak (*deru*) down.

DOWN HAY, ? hill (*dun*) close (*hay*).

DOWNING, *n.f.*, ? narrow (*ing, w.*) down.

DOWRAN, ? *i.q.* DOURGAN.

DOWRICK, *n.f.*, = *douric*, watery.

DOWSTALL, ? south (*dehau*) shop (*stal*).

DOZER, ? darnel (*jure*) field (*doar*).

DRAGON PIT, ? king's pit.

DRAINOS, DRAWNS, ? thorn (*draen*) [fields].

DRAISES, ? bramble (*dreis*) [fields].

DRAKE, *n.f.*, = *draig*, a dragon, *w.*

DRAKEWALLS, ? conspicuous (*drych*) walls, *C.*

DRALL, ? moor (*hal*) land (*tir*).

DRANGLING, ? = *draen lan*, thorn close, *T.C.*

DRANGS PARK, ? *i.q.* DRAINOS.

DRANN-ACK, -OCK, ? thorny place (*draenic*). Place of oaks, *Pr.*

DRAWCOMBE, ? oak (*derow*) vale.

DRAWLAS, DRELLOS, ? green (*glas*) oak ; *or*, *i.q.* DREWOLLAS.

DRAY, *n.f.*, ? = *tre*, a dwelling, home-stead ; *or*, *deru*, oaks.

DRAYTON, DREADON, *n.f.*, ? oak hill (*dun*) ; *or*, *i.q.* DRYDEN.

DREAN, ? *i.q.* PARK DREAN.

DREASON BALL, ? ? bramble (*dreis*) down (*oon*) round hill (*boll, C.*).

DREEK KERROW, ? = *doar carow*, stag land.

DRENNICK, ? *i.q.* DRANNACK.

DREURY, *n.f.*, ? oak field (*eru*).

DREW, *n.f.*, = *derow*, oaks.

DREWOLLAS, ? lower (*wolas*) oak.

DREY FIELD, ? oak, *or* home (*adre*), *or*, dry field.

DRIBNA, ? = *dor behenna*, lesser field.

DRIFF, DRIFT, ? = *tref*, a dwelling.

DRIGG, *n.f.*, ? *i.q.* TRIGG.

DRONE PARK, ? *i.q.* PARK TROON.

DROSKIN, ? HOSKEN'S land, *T.C.*

DROWN, *n.f.*, ? = *tir oon*, down land.

DROWNGELLOW, ? down-land groves (*celliow*).

DRUSE, ? *i.q.* DORWASE.

DRUSELLET DOWNS, DRUZEL gate (*yet*) downs.

DRUZEL, ? *i.q.* DORSEALL.

---

* *Or*, sea (*mere*) with small-pebble-beach (*dos*), *C.* Sweet *or* fresh water sea (*douce mer, f.*), *Bond.* *Doz-marc.* the water that ebbs and flows, *Pr.* From *doz*, to come, and *maur*, great, *Car.* The pool (*mere*) in the bush (*dos*), *ga., Beal.* The meeting *or* coming together (*dos*) of the lake (*mer*) water (*uy*), *B.* ? *i.q.* MERRYMEET.

DRYDEN, *n.f.*, ? oaks (*deru*), or dry vale (*den, s.*).

DRYFIELD, home (*adre*) field, *T.C.*

DRYM, ? oak (*dar*) border (*hem*).

DRY-SACK, -SOCK, -SUCK, *i.q.* PARK DRYSACK.

DUBBERS, ? ? = *Two barrows*.

DUBHILL, ? black (*dubh*) hill.

DUBWALLS, *i.q.* DOBWALLS.

DUDNANCE, ? lambs' (*eunes*) lay field (*todn*).

DUDWELL, ? DODD's well.

DUFFNAL, ? moor (*hal*) bank (*tubben*).

DUION, *B.m.*, ? *duon*, grief, sorrow.

DULASTON, *n.f.*, ? dark (*duglas*) hill.

DULEAR, ? *i.q.* DOLEAR.

DULGER, ? camp (*caer*) dale, *T.C.*

DULGOON, ? the down (*goon*) dale.

DULLAN, *n.f.*, ? *i.q.* DOWLAND.

DULMER, ? great (*meer*) dale (*dol*).

DULOE, black (*du*) pool (*lo*), *T.* ; or, God's pool, *Pr.* ; ? south (*deheu*) pool ; (*p.s.* St. Keby, *O.* ; ? *o.* St. Theliau, *Bond*).

DUM-ABOLE, -BLE, *i.q.* DENNEBOUL.

DUMBLEDERRY, ? DENNEBOUL with the oaks (*deru*).

DUNBAR, ? the *bar* below (*dan*).

DUNBLE, *n.f.*, *i.q.* DENNEBOUL.

DUNCAN, ? below the down (*goon*).

DUNDAGELL, *n.f.*, *i.q.* TINTAGEL.

DUNDER PARK, ? oak (*dar*) down close ; or = *the under* close, *T.C.*

DUNDHILL, ? moor (*hal*) lay (*todn*) [field].

DUNGAR, ? castle (*caer*) hill (*dun*).

DUNGEL, the dungeon, *Wh.*

DUNGERTH, *i.q.* DONIERT.

DUNGEY, *n.f.*, below the house (*chy*).

DUNHAY, ? hill or down enclosure.

DUNHEVED, down head (*heafod*) *s.*, *Po.* ; summit of the hill, *O.*

DUN-KEN, -KING, *n.f.*, ? *i.q.* TONKIN ; or, brown head, *donn cean, ga., Lo.*

DUN-MEERE, -MERE, -NAMERE, great (*meor*) hill, *Pr.* ; lake (*mere, s.*) camp (*dun*), *M‘L.*

DUNN, *n.f.*, brown ; a teacher, *ga.*

DUNNEFORD, *n.f.*, ? hill ford.

DUNNICK, hilly [field].

DUNSFORD, *n.f.*, ? castle (*dinas*) ford.

DUNSLEY, green hill, *Pr.* ; ? *i.q.* DENISEL.

DUNSTAN, *w.B.m.*, ? tin (*stean*) hill.

DUNSTANVILLE, Dunstan's town, *f.*

DUNSTONE, ? dark (*dun, s.*) stone, *t.*

DUNSTER, *n.f.*, ? castle land (*tir*).

DUNVETH, the grave's (*bedh*) hill, *Pr.*

DUNY, ? *i.q.* DONEY or DUNHAY.

DUPATH, ? south (*deheu*) side (*parth*).

DUPLIN, *n.f.*, ? black (*dubh, i.*) lake.

DUPORTH, black (*du*) beach, *G.F.*

DURANT, *n.f.*, ? water vale (*nant*).

DUR-FOLD, -VAL, ? = *s. deorfald*, deer park ; or, oak (*dar*) field.

DURGAN, *i.q.* DOURGAN.

DURLAN, ? oak or water close (*lan*).

DUR LEAN, ? flax (*lin*) land (*doar*).

DURLO, oak (*dar*) pool (*lo*).

DURRA, *river*, ? the water (*dour*).

DURRABEANS, ? the little (*bean*) lands or fields (*daourou*).

DURRACOT, ? oak wood (*coat*).

DURRAW, ? = *derow*, oaks.

DURVA, oak or water place (*va*).

DUSTON, *n.f.*, ? *i.q.* DUNSTONE.

DUSTOWE, *n.f.*, *i.q.* DAVIDSTOW.

DUTSON, DODD's down (*oon*).

DUXHAM, ? the duke's, or ducks', border (*hem*) [land], or home.

DUZZARD, DYSART, *i.q.* DAZARD.

DWELLA, ? *i.q.* TREWELLA.

DYER, *n.f.*, ? = *tyor*, a thatcher.

DYMMA, ? Emma's house (*ty*), *T.C.*

DYMYNS, = *f.* demesnes, the land occupied by the lord himself.

DYPPER, ? = *dippa*, a pit, *B.*

EADE, *i.q.* ETHY ; or, EDDY.

EAD-, ED-, EED-LESS, Ethelred's court (*les*), *Po.*

EARISH, *i.q.* ARISH PARK.

EARLING, ? = *hurling*, [field].

EARTH, ERTH, = *arth*, high.

EASEM CROFT, ? lower (*isa*) border (*hem*) croft.

EASTRY, ? east acre or field (*eru*).

EASY PARK, *i.q.* PARKISSEY.

EATHNEVAS, ? Nywys's (*w.*) heath (*heyth*) ; (*neves*, new, *a.* ; *hennaways*, refuse, *m.c.*).

EATHORNE, ? corner (*horn*) gate (*yet*), *T.C.* ; ? thorn enclosure (*hay*).

EAVER CROFT, *eaver*-grass croft.

EBAL ROCKS, ? colt (*ebol*) rocks.

THE EBBER, fishing ground at the *ebb*-tide, *T.C.* ; ? carcase (*abar*, *w.*) [rock].

ECGLOSTUDIC, *e.d.d.*, ST. TUDY church [land].

EDD-EUA, -IDA, *i.q.* EDUUARD, rich (*ead*) guard, *t.*

EDDY, *n.f.*, ? the same ; or = *ethic*, great ; or, *s.* eadig, happy, rich, prosperous.

EDELET, *d.d.*, ? Ethelred's heath, *now* ALLET.

EDENSE, ? *i.q.* ENIS.

EDGECOMBE, *n.f.*, edge of the vale, *t.*

EDMER, *t.d.d.*, rich fame, *t.*

EDNOD, *t.d.d.*, rich threatening, *t.*

EDRICUS, *w.B.m.*, rich rule, *t.*

EDUUI, *t.d.d.*, rich war (*wig*), *t.*

EDYVEAN, *n.f.*, little (*bean*) EDDY.

EFFLINS, ? ? St. *Eval's* island (*enys*).

EFFORD, = EBBINGFORD, the passage (*fordh*) at the *ebb* of the tide.

EGBERE, ? the farm on the edge, *t.*

EGLA-, EGLOS-ROSE ? the heath (*ros*) church (*eglos*), *Wh.*

EGLASDERRY, ? Edric's church [land] ; or, church oaks (*derow*).

EGLOSBERRIE, *d.d.*, St. *Berriona's* church [land].

EGLOSCROC, church of the cross, *Po.* ; ? of the barrow (*crug*).

EGLOSELLIS, ? Ellis's church [land].

EGLOSERUE, ? church field (*eru*).

EGLOSHALLOW, church moors.

EGLOSHAYLE, the church on the river (*Pr.*), or estuary (*M'L.*), or of St. *Helie*, *Wh.* (*p.s. not known*).

EGLOSHELLEN, ? church corner (*elin*) ; or, *i.q.* ELLENGLAZE.

EGLOSKERRY, church of love (*Pr.*), of St. *Keri*, *Wh.* (*p.s.* SS. Ide & Lydy, *O.*)

EGLOSMERTHER, the church of the martyr (St. Coanus).

EGLOSSANT, holy (*sant*) church.

EIULF, *t.d.d.*, ? island wolf, *t.*

EIULPHUS, *t.d.d.*, island wolf, *t.*

ELERCHY, swans' (*elerch*) house (*chy*), *i.e.* the swannery, *T.*

ELFNOD, *w.B.m.*, elf-bold (*noth*), *t.*

ELIOT, *n.f.*, ? *i.q.* ILIUTH, or, ALLET.

ELLA, ? = *elau*, the elms.

ELLBRIDGE, ? bridge moor (*hal*), or, *i.q.* TELBRIDGE.

ELLCOMBE, ? moor, or elm vale.

ELLENGLAZE, green (*glas*) elms, *Pr.*

ELLERY, *n.f.*, ? moor field (*eru*) ; or, from ST. HILARY.

ELLIS, *n.f.*, ? = *els*, a son-in-law ; or, green (*las*), or, broad (*les*) moor ; or, = Elias.

ELMENTOR, *i.q.*, HELMENTOR.

ELMER, *t.d.d.*, ? *i.q.* AYLMER.

ELPHINSTONE, *n.f.*, ? moor stone.

ELRIC, *t.d.d.*, noble (*adel*) power, *t.*

ELSON, *n.f.*, ? *i.q.* HELSTON.

ELUUIN, noble friend (*wine*), *t.*

ELVANS, ? nuns' (*manaes*) moor ; or, from *elvan*, moor stone.

ELWELL, ? high (*uhel*) moor (*hal*).

ELWERDUS, *w.B.m.*, noble guard, *t.*

EMBLA, ? *i.q.* AMBLE.

EMBLANCE, ? ? Hannibal's ENAS.

EMLETS, ? ? little borders (*hem*).

ENAS, ? = *eanes*, lambs ; or, *i.q.* PARK EN EANES ; or, ENYS.

ENDEAN, *n.f.*, ? = *an dean*, the man.

ENDSLEIGHS, pasture (*lea*) end [fields], *T.C.* ; ? lambs' (*eanes*) pastures.

ENGEW, ? = *an ceow*, the closes.

ENGILLY, the (*an*) hazel grove.

ENGOLLAN, the bottom, *Pr.*

ENGOOSE, the wood (*cus*).

EN-IS, -NIS, *i.q.* ENAS or ENYS.

EN-MOR, -MOAR, -NOR, great (*maur*) island, *Po.*

ENNIS-VARTH, -VATH, green (*gwyrdd*, *w.*) island, *T.C.*

ENNISWORGY, ? lambs' (*eanes*) pound (*gwarchae*, *w.*).

ENNYS MORVA, ENIS marsh.

ENTR-AL, -EL, middle *or* half (*hanter*) the moor.

ENYS, an island, *R.IV.* ; *also*, a peninsula made by a river or the sea, *Pr.*

ENYS DODNAN, the island with the soil on it, *Bl.* ¶

EPLETT, *n.f.*, ¶¶ colt (*ebol*) gate (*yet*).

EPPS, EPSE, *n.f.*, *i.q.* APPS.

ERA, ERRA, ERRO, ERROR, ¶ = *eru*, an acre, a field.

ERA GROSIZE, ¶ lower (*isa*) cross (*crous*) field.

ERA LEDAN, broad field.

ERA WIDN, ¶ tree (*gwedhen*) field.

ERCHENBALDUS,*t.d.d.*,sacred prince,*t.*

ERE, ¶ *i.q.* ERA, *or*, PARK HERE.

ERISEY, the dry (*sech*) acre (*eru*) ; *or*, upon (*er*) the bottom (*izy*), *Pr.*

ERMEN, *B.m.*, public, universal, *t.*

ERMENHALDUS, *t.d.d.*, public power, *t.*

ERMENHEU, *d.d.*, ¶ *i.q.* CARMINNOW.

ERNEIS, *t.d.d.*, ¶ earnest, *t.*

ERO FENTON, spring field.

ERO PENHALE, moor's head field.

ERRA DRYSACK, ¶ thorny (*dreisick*) field.

ERRA GEAR, ¶ camp (*caer*) field.

ERRA WARTHA, higher field.

ERW WIDDEN, *i.q.* ERA WIDN.

ESCALLS, ¶ = *esgols*, the holy place ; *or*, *iz goles*, corn valley, *T.C.* ; ¶ the thistles (*ascall-s*).

ESCOTT, *n.f.*, ¶ east (*est*) cottage, *t.*

ESHES, ¶ stubble (*arish*) fields.

ESS, ESSE, *o.n.f.*, ¶ = *esc*, the ash, *s.*

ESSA PARK, lower (*isa*) close.

ESSEL, *n.f.*, ¶ below (*is*) the moor (*hal*).

ESSERY, *n.f.*, ¶ lower field (*eru*).

ESSET PARK, ¶¶ lower (*isa*) gate (*yet*) close (*parc*).

ESSEY, *i.q.* PARK ISSEY.

ESTR-AY, -Y, ¶ east field (*eru*).

ETHNEVAS, *i.q.* EATHNEVAS.

ETHORN, *i.q.* EATHORNE.

ETHY, ¶ the great (*ethic*) [house]. *i.q.* TETHY.

EULCEN, *s.B.m.*, *i.q.* ÆULCEN.

EUSEBI, *B.m.*, = Eusebius.

EVA-, EVAR-, EVER-PARK,*i.q.*EAVER.

EVANS, *n.f.*, son of Evan ; = Johnson.

EVERY, *n.f.*, ¶ *i.q.* Avery.

EWSANNEC,*s.B.m.*, ¶ = *ewnhinsic*, just.

EX, EXE, ¶ = *œces*, oaks, *s.* ; *or*, *hesk*, rushes.

EXWELL, well by the oaks, *t.*

EYLES, *n.f.*, ¶ = *als*, a son-in-law.

EYRE, *n.f.*, ¶ Long (*hir*), *i.q.* ANNEAR.

EYRIE, ¶ eagle's nest.

FAERDON, ¶ *fair* hill (*dun*).

FAGGELFORD, ¶ fowl (*fugel*) ford.

FAIRWASH, ¶ the fair stream.

FAL, the prince's (*fal*, *Pr.*) [river] ; ¶ *foill*, slowly, softly, *ga.*

FALMOUTH, mouth of the Fal (*p.s.* K. Charles the Martyr).

FAWEY, cave (*faw*) river (*gwy*), *Po.* ; ¶ *folhaidh*, quick, nimble, *ga.*

FAWGAN, ¶ cave down (*goon*).

FAWTON, ¶ cave enclosure (*ton*, *s.*).

FEADON, ¶ *i.q.* FENTON *or* FAERDON.

FELT PARK, ? skin close, *t.*

FENDERLEASE, ? *i.q.* FENTALEY.

FENTAFRIDDLE, ? Bartholomew's (*Bertyl*) well (*fenten*).

FENTALEY, the spring on the green (*les*), *Po.*

FENTEN-GLEDER, ? sparkling spring.

F.-HORN, corner (*corn*) spring.

FENTER-GAN,? fountain of the singers, the singing, *or* the white well, *Pr.* ; down (*goon*) spring.

F. LARRICK, ? Aluric's spring.

F. NELLA, ? elm (*elw*) spring.

F. OON, spring on the down (*oon*).

F. VEAN, little (*bean*) spring.

F. WANSON, ? murmuring (*manson*) spring.

FENTON, = *fenten*, the spring, fountain, *or* well, *Pr.*

F. ADDLE, the foul *or* dirty well, *Pr.* ; ? well with a ladle (*huddal*, *B.*).

F.-ARE, -ER, ? battle (*heir*) well.

F. BERRAN, St. Piran's well.

F. EAST, the east (*est*) well.

F. GAY, ¶ spring by the hedge (*ce*).

F.-GOE, -GOV, the smith's (*gof*) well.

FENTONGOLLAN, holy (*glan*) well, *Po.*; hart's well, *Car.* (*colon*, the heart).

F. GOOSE, the wood (*cus*) well.

F. GYMPS, the continual (*gempes*), *i.e.* ever-flowing spring *or* well, *Pr.*

F. LADOCK, St. Ladock's well.

F.-OON, -WOON, *i.q.* FENTEROON.

F. SCAUAN, elder tree spring, *B.*

F. VAL, source of the Fal, *B.*

F. VEASE, the outer (*vez*) well, *R.W.*

F. VEDNA, the high (*ban*) well, *Pr.*; ? lesser (*behennu*) well.

F. WEST, ? shelter (*quest*) spring.

FENTRIGAN, ? *i.q.* FENTERGAN; *or,* Regan's well.

FEOCK, *from p.s.* St. Feoca. *O.*; ? = *fre ick*, hill by the water, *M'L.*

FERN, ? = *forn*, an oven, *T.C.*

FERN ACRE, ? alder (*gwern*) acre.

FERNDON, *n.f.*, ? fern hill, *or* down.

FERN-GO, -IGO, the fern wood (*coed*) *or* brake.

FERN-, FERNY-SPLAT, a spot (*splot, s.*) abounding with *ferns.*

FERRELL, *n.f.*, ? = *Fearghal*, man of strength, *ga.*, *Y.*

FERRETT, *n.f.*, ? = *ferhiat*, a thief.

FERRIS, *n.f.*, *i.q.* FERRERS, *from* Ferriere, *Normandy*; ? the iron mine *or* forge, *Lo.*

FERRYWIDDEN, ? white (*gwidn*) hill (*bre*).

FERSNEWTH, ? *i.q.* FORSNOOTH; *or,* new (*newyth*) thicket (*browse*).

FETCH FIELD, ? = *vetch* field.

FIDDICK, *n.f.*, ? *fithcach*, a vulture, *a.*

FISCAR, ? pixie *or* fairy field (*eru*).

FITCHET, *n.f.*, the polecat, *t.*

FLAMANK, *n.f.*, burning (*flam*) glove (*maneg*), *H.*

FLAMMOCK, *n.f.*, = *flammog*, blazing, *w.*, *R.W.*; blear eyedness, *H.*

FLANKEY CROFT, ? mill (*melin*) hedge (*ce*) croft.

FLATCHES BRIDGE, ? = Fletcher *or* flesher's bridge.

FLEARDON, ? fiddler's (*filwr*) hill.

FLEMMING, *n.f.*, ? = *fleming*, a runaway, *s.*; *or, from* Flanders.

FLEXBURY, ? *Felix's* earthwork.

FLOYD, *n.f.*, *i.q.* Lloyd, *R.W.*

FLUSHET, FLUTCHET FIELD, floodgate field, *t.*

FLUSHING, ? flood meadow (*ing*), *t.*; (*c.d.* St. Peter).

FOGE, FORGE, *i.q.* FOUGE.

FOGHAM, ? cave border (*hem*) [field].

FOGOU, FOGUE, the cave.

FOLAMOOR, ? the foal's moor.

FOLDRESSICK, ? brambly (*dreisick*) [field] with the *fold.*

FOLNEY, ?? the *fold* by the enclosure (*an hay*).

FOODLELOOSE, ? green moor (*hallas*) ford.

FORD, = *fordh*, way, pass, *Pr.*

FORDA, *the same*; *or,* A = *hay*, enclosure, field.

FORDER, ? long (*hir*) passage.

FORDINNIC, ? hilly (*dinnic*) road [field]; ? *i.q.* PRADANACK.

FORDLE, ? = ford hill *or* dale.

FOREBORE, ? = *four barrows.*

FORE BOW, ? [field] *before* cow (*beu*) [field].

FORGE, FORGUE, ? *i.q.* FOGE, *or,* FOGOU.

FORRABURY, ? the *burial* place of St. [Sym]phori[an] (*p.s.*, *O.*), *Mur.*; *far* off, *or,* beautiful (*fair*), hiding *or burying* place, *H.*

FORSNOOTH, ? new (*nowydh*) way *or* road (*fordh*), *Pr.*

FORSWINE, ? white (*gwyn*) road, *Pr.*

FORTESCUE, *n.f.*, *forte escu*, strong shield, *f.*, *Lo.*

FOSS, entrenchment, ditch.

FOSSWIDN, white (*gwidn*) trench.

FOSTER, *n.f.*, ? entrenched land (*tir*).

FOUGE, the hearth *or* blowing house, forge *or* furnace, *Pr.*

FOWEY, *i.q.* FAWEY.*

---

* *o.* BURG DE FOWY; *d.d.* FAWINTONE; *e.d.d.* FAWITONA; "the town on the FAWY," *i.e.*

FOYEFENTON, source (*fenton*) of the Fowey. Walled spring, *H.*

FRAD, *n.f.*, ?=*frath*, noise, objection, *B.*

FRADDON, ? FRAD'S hill (*dun*).

FRA-GGIN, -DJAN, ? *i.q.* PARK JANE.

FRANKET, ? *i.q.* PARK AN YET.

FRATHY, FREATHY, ? *i.q.* FRETH ; or great (*ethic*) hill (*bre*).

FRAUNINUS, ? *t.d.d.* ? Frea's friend (*winc, s.*).

FRAYNE, *o.n.f.*, ? *the same.*

FREETHING, FRETH, ? field with a wattled (*frith*) hedge *or* gate.

FREL, ? moor (*hal*) hill (*bre*).

FREOC, *w.B.m.*, = *fricca*, a preacher, *s., F.* ; *or, i.q.* ST. BREOCK.

FRIGGANS, ? ox (*udgeon*) closes (*parc-s*).

FROAN, ? *i.q.* PARK OWEN.

FROG-COOM, -HAM, ? FREOC'S, *or,* frog valley (*cum*), *or* home (*ham*), *or* border (*hem*), *t.*

FROXTON, ? *d.d.* FORCHETESTAN, front gate (*forgeat*) stone (*stan, s.*).

FROXWATER, ? ? FREOCK'S *or* frog (*frox, s.*) stream.

FRYE, *n.f.*, ? = *w. bry, fry,* high, *R.W.* ; *fri,* free, *s., J.T.*

FUDGE, FUIDGE, FUGE, *n.f., i.q.* FOGE.

FUGLESOME, ? fowl's (*fugel*) border (*hem*), *or* lowland (*holm*), *s.*

FUGOE, ? *i.q.* FOGOU.

FURD-A, -AR, ? *i.q.* FORDA.

FURLEY, *n.f.*, ? far, *or* the fair meadow.

FURMEDGE, *n.f.*, ? = *f. fromage,* cheese.

FURNELL, *n.f.*, ? = *fern hill* ; *or, i.q.* PARNELL.

FURNISS, *n.f.*, wisdom, sagacity, *w.*

FURSNAP, ? furze *knap or* brow.

FURSPARK, furze close.

FURZA PARK, the furze close.

FURZ-DON, -DOWN, -ON, hill (*dun*) with the entrenchment (*fos*), *M'L.* ; ? furze down *or* hill.

FURZE BALL, ? furze field *or* hill.

FURZE HAM, ? furze border (*hem*).

FURZEY GWIN, ? furzy down (*gwon*).

FYNTENGYMPYS VEAR, *and* VEAN *or* BIAN, 15 *cent.*, great *and* little FENTONGYMPS.

GABALLAS, ? arable (*palas,* to dig) enclosure (*ce*) ; *or, pillas* down (*goon*).

GABER LANDS, ? goat (*gavar*), *or* brook (*gover*), closes (*lan-s*).

GABNAS, ? *i.q.* GOBNAS.

GABRIAS, ? hill (*bre*) closes (*cae-s*).

GADDONS, ? lambs' (*eanes*) wood (*coed, w.*), *or,* castle (*dinas*), close (*ce*).

GADERN, ? *i.q.* GUDERN.

GADLES, the moles' (*godh*) green (*les*), *Pr.* ; the battle (*cad*) court (*les*), *i.e.* the camp, *R.W.*

GADYCUMBE, *n f.*, ? goat (*gat, s.*) combe.

GAFFELFORD, *i.q.* CAMELFORD, *Cum.* ; tribute (*gafol, s.*) ford, *Bo.*

GAIRE, *d d.* GAER, *i.q.* CAER.

GAKES GROUND, hemlock (*cegas*) land.

GALANGULLAS, the bottom (*an goles*) field (*gweal*).

GALDS-, GALS-WORTHY, *n.f., i.q.* GOLDSWORTHY.

GALGEATH, field with trees (*gwydh*).

GALLACOMBE, *i.q.* GOLLACOMBE.

GALLAND, ? bottom (*golla*) close (*lan*).

GALI E, GALE, GALY, *n.f., i.q.* GELLY.

GAL-LENA, -ENNA, -IDNA, ? harrow *or* fowler's (*idne*) close (*ce*).

GALLEY MEAD, ? grove (*celli*) meadow.

GALLILOES, ? ? barrow (*low, t.*) grove (*celli*) [field]s.

GALLOWRES, *i.q.* GOLOWRES.

GALLOWS PARK, ? bottom (*goles*) close.

GALVER, ? great (*meer*) field (*gweal*).

GAM, = *cam,* the crooked [place], *Pr.*

GAMBEL, ? distant (*pell*), *or* river (*heyl*) combe.

GAMBE MEADOW, crooked, *or combe* meadow.

GAMBER, GAMPER, ? = *campier,* a champion ; *or,* crooked close (*parc*), *or* bay (*porth*).

"the water (*wy*) of the deep ditch, vault, or den (*fau*)," *B. Carew* has "FOY HAVEN, in Cornish, FOATH." *p.s.* St. Nicholas ; *o.* St. Fimbarrus, *O.*

GAMBRIDGE, *i.q.* CAMBRIDGE.
GAMES, *n.f.*, ? *i.q.* KEAMS.
GAMMEL WOOD, ? *i.q.* CAMEL.
GAMMON PARK, ? foot-path close.
GAMON, *n.f.*, ? = *cammen*, foot-path.
GAMPEN SEEZ, a crooked bay with a rock in it, *Mur.* (?)
GANG, a path, drain, *s.* ; ? meeting-place, *t.*, *L.Sz.*
GANGUMPIS, *t.b.*, *i.q.* GOONGUMPAS.
GANHAFFORNE, ? *i.q.* GOONAVERN.
GAN-HILLY, -ILLY, -NILLY, ? *i.q.* GOONHILLY.
GANNEL, the channel, creek, &c., *Po.* ; ? river's (*heyl*) mouth (*genau*) ; or white (*can*) river.
GANNET, ? down (*goon*) gate (*yet*).
GANNICK, ? *i.q.* CARNICK.
GANT, *n.f.*, ? *i.q.* CANT.
GANVER, ? great (*veor*) down.
GANWHEAL, ? down field (*gweal*).
GAP, ? the breach, or = cape.
GARADOWN, ? *i.q.* CARADON.
GARD, *n.f.*, ? = *ceard*, a refiner, mechanic, *ga.* ; or, *i.q.* GARRET.
GARDEN AND BAGS, ? kite's (*bargus*), or back of the house garden, or enclosure (*garth*).
GARDER WARTHA, *and* WOLLA, higher *and* lower fortification, *T.*
GARDY, ? castle (*caer*) house (*ty*).
GARE, *i q.* GEAR.
GARGALLE, *d.d.*, ? by (*gar*) the grove (*celli*) ; or green (*gear*) grove.
GARGES, GARGUS, the wood (*cus*) afar off (*cer*), *Pr.* ; ? over (*gwar*), or by (*gar*), the wood.
GARGRAVE, *n.f.*, ? enclosure (*garth*) by the grove or grave, *t.*
GARKER MOOR, ? partridge (*grugyer*) moor.
GARLAND, ? *i.q.* GORLAND.
GARLENNA, ? *i.q.* CARLENNOW.
GARL-ENNICK, -INNICK, -YNNICK, ? *i.q.* CARLANICK.
GARLES, on (*gw.r*) the green (*les*), *Pr.* ; herb (*les*) garden (*garth*), *R.W.*
GARMOE, ? pigs' (*mogh*) yard (*garth*).
GARN CLOSE, = *garden* close.

GARNDARNEY, thorny (*draenic*) garden ; or by thorn (*draen*) close (*hay*).
GARNEGGAN, *i.q.* CARNEGGAN.
GARNICK, ? *i.q.* CARNICK.
GARNON, *n.f.*, ? *i.q.* CARNON.
GARRACK = *carrag*, the rock, stone.
G. DOWNS, rock or rocky downs.
G. SANZ, holy (*sans*) rock.
GARRAH, on the top of the hill, *Pr.*
GARRANCE, *n.f.*, ? from ST. GERRANS.
GARRAPARK, ? *i.q.* CARA park.
GARR-AS, -IS, -OWS, -US, *i.q.* GARRAH, *Pr.* ; = *gwarhas*, summit.
GARRATOR, rough (*garow*) tor, *C.*
GARRET, *n.f.*, ? = *gearait*, a warrior, champion, *ga.* ; or, *Gerhard*, firm spear, *t.*
GARRICK, *i.q.* GARNICK or GARRACK.
G. PARK, rock or rocky close.
GARRICKS, rocky [field]s.
GARRIER, ? long (*hir*) leg's (*gar*), or heron's (*cryhyr*) [field].
GARRIGAN, *n.f.*, *i.q.* GAVERRIGAN.
GARROW, ? *i.q.* GARRAH, or CAREW.
GARTHWAITE, *n.f.*, ? *white* enclosure (*garth*).
GARTHWOOD, ? wood enclosure.
GAR-VES, -WES, ? *i.q.* GAVES.
GASKIN, *n.f.*, ? sedge (*hesken*) close (*cae*, *w.*) ; or, *i.q.* GOONHASKEN.
GASS, *n.f.*, ? = *gouz*, a goose, *B.*
GATE, *n.f.*, ? = *geat*, a goat, *s.*
GATE PARK, ? *i.q.* PARK YET.
GATHERS, ? brambles (*dreis*) close (*ce*).
GATLEY, *n.f.*, ? goat (*geat*, *s.*) pasture.
GAT-TY, -Y, gate or goat close (*hay*).
GAUDRETE, *w.B.m.*, ? = *Godrced*, divine council, *t.*
GAVER, ? goat (*gaver*) [field] ; or, great (*veor*) close (*ce*).
GAVER-RIGAN, -IGON, GAURIGAN, the goat's down (*goon*), *II.* ; twenty (*iganz*) goats, *Pr.*
GAVES, outward (*ves*) close (*ce*).
GAWDY, *n.f.*, ? *i.q.* CUTTY, or GATTY.
GAWENS, ? from *c.n.* Gawen = *gavin*, hawk of battle, *Y.*
GAWLAND, ? enclosed (*cau*, *w.*), or manured (*cawch*) land.

GAW MEADOW, ? smith's (*gof*), or, cow meadow.

GAWN, ? = *gwon*, a down.

GAWTON, ? goats' or cows' enclosure (*tun, s.*), or hill (*dun*).

GAY, *n.f.*, ? i.q. GEE.

GAYCHE, GEACH, *n.f.*, ? *cae issa*, lower close.

GAYER, *n.f.*, ? long (*hir*) close (*ce*).

GAYLAND, ? flourishing (*gay, m.c.*) field.

GAYLARD, *n.f.*, ? the dancer (*galliard*, B.); or, i.q. Celert, *w.s.*

GAYLSE, *n.f.*, ? green-moor (*hellas*), or cliff (*als*) close (*ce*).

GAYRICK, ? i.q. GARRICK.

GAYRY, ? i.q. CAREY, or GEARY.

GAYRLAKE, ? willow (*helig*) garth.

GAZA, ? daisy (*egr*) close (*ce*).

GAZELAND, dirty (*gasa*), or deserted (*gasa*, to leave) enclosure (*lan*), *Pr.*

THE GAZERS, ? the daisy closes.

GAZICK COVE, dirty (*gassic*) cove.

GEAHOW, ? = *ceow*, enclosures.

GEAK, GEAKE, GEEK, *n.f.*, to pry, peep, squinny, *m.c.*; or, *giach*, a partridge.

GEAL FIELD, ? a reduplication, *gweal* = field; or, leech (*gel*) field.

GEAR, = *guer*, a green, flourishing, lively, fruitful, pleasant place, *Pr.*; ? i.q. GAIRE.

GEAR PARK, ? camp close (*parc*).

GEARN PARK, ? alder (*gwern*) close.

GEARS, green or camp [field]s.

GEAR VEAN, ? little camp [field].

GEARY, *n.f.*, ? camp close (*hay*).

GEDGE, *n.f.*, ? i.q. GAYCHE.

GEDRICUS, *w.B.m.*, ? song rule, *t.*

GEDY, *n.f.*, ? goat (*geat*) close (*hay*).

GEE, *n.f.*, = *ce*, a hedge, a close.

GELGEE, ? hazels (*cyll*) hedge (*ce*).

GELLANGYS, ? fields (*gweal-s*) by the house (*an chy*).

GELLIES, = *celliow*, the groves.

GELLINGWARTHA, ? = the higher (*an wartha*) field (*gweal*) or grove.

GELLY, = *celli*, a grove, more commonly, a hazel grove, *Pr.*

GELMEARS, the great (*mear*) fields (*gweal-s*).

GELYDNA, i.q. GALLENNA.

GEN-DALL, -TIL, *n.f.*, ? = *cendel*, fine linen; or, *cenedel*, a tribe; or, i.q. KENDALL.

GENEAU, the mouth (*genau*); or troubled (*cen*) water (*eau, f.*), *Pr.*

GENIS, *n.f.*, from St. Gennys.

GENN, *n.f.*, ? = *gwen*, white; or, *cein*, a ridge; or, *gen*, a chin; or, i. *gen*, a sword; or, from ST. KEYNE.

GENNETT, ? huntsman's (*cynydd*) [field]; or, i.q. GUNNETT.

GEN-NING, -YAN, ? = *cenion*, skins or tents; or, *cenin*, a leek; or, *cwningen, w.*, a rabbit.

GENTER CROFT, ? nail (*center*) croft.

GENVOR, ? great (*meor*) ridge (*cein*) or head (*cean, ga.*); or, = Genevour.

GERMOE, from *p.s.* ST. GERMOCH.

GERNICK, ? = CARNICK.

GERRAS, i.q. CAIRO, M‘L.; GARRAS, T.

GERRESH, *n.f.*, ? the same.

GERRIER, i.q. GARRIER.

GERRY CROFT, ? camp (*caerau*) croft.

GERRYS HILL, ? hill or moor (*hal*) top (*gwarhas*).

GERVEYS, *n.f.*, spear eagerness, *t.*; ? = *gervas*, a good word.

GESTIN, *w.B.m.*, ? = *castan*, a chestnut.

GEW, ? = *ceow*, pl. of *ce*, a hedge, enclosure, field.*

GEWANS, ? the valley (*nans*) GEW.

---

* "GEW, the stay, support. On many estates one of the best fields is called THE GEW, from its being the support of the estate," *Pr.* A plain field, *B.* A *plain amidst hills*, which would be the best land in an estate, *Wh.* ?=*w. cau.* hollow, *R.W.* Sometimes it is "a common," as, THE GUEW, touching St. Agnes, Scilly, *S.G.* The GEWS is often found; as also several fields in the same farm, called GEW with a prefix; as Barn Gew, Horse Pool Gew, Lower Hilly Gew, &c., in Pollard, Wendron. In Irish, *cuan* is a bay, a haven, a field; *cuas*, a hollow, *J.B.*

GEWENS, ? island (*enys*), or lambs' (*eanes*) GEW.

GEW-GRAZE, -GREASE, middle (*cres*) hollow or cove, *J.B.*

GEW GYNANCE, hollow or bottom leading from KYNANCE cove, *J.B.*

GEW JANE, ? ox (*udzheon*) GEW.

GEW PEARIS, ? GEW meadow (*pras*).

GIBBEY MEADOW, ? *from* ST. CUBY.

GIDD-EY, -Y, *n.f.*, ? *i.q.* GEDY ; or, = *Ceadda*, war, *Y.*

GILBERIC, ? fallow (*havrec*, a.) or fat (*berric*) field (*gweal*).

GIDGEON, *n.f.*, ?ox (*udzheon*) close (*ce*).

GIDGEY, ? *i.q.* ST. ISSEY.

GIDLEY, *n.f.*, ? *i,q.* GATLEY.

GIGGAS, *i.q.* COGEGOES, *R.B.R.*

GILB-ARD, -ART, -ERT, -URD, *n.f.*, companion or servant (*gele*) of St. Bridget ; or, bright pledge, *t., Y.*

GILCHRIST, *n.f.*, ? servant of Christ.

GILHILLS, ? = *gweal-s*, fields ; or, moor (*hal*) fields.

GILL, *n.f.*, ? = *cil*, a recess ; or, *gele*, a companion ; or, *cell*, a grove.

GILLA, ? = *gwealow*, fields ; or, *celliow*, groves.

GILL-ARD, -ET, ? *i.q.* GAYLARD.

GILLEBON, ? down house (*bo oon*) grove (*celli*).

GILL-EY, -IE, -Y, *i.q.* GELLY.

GILLIES, groves ; or broad (*les*) fields.

GILLIN, ? = *celin*, holly ; or, *i.q.* GLYNN.

GILLINWARTHA, *i.q.* GELLINGWAR-THA.

GILLONS, ? lambs' (*eanes*) field.

GILL PARK, hazel trees (*cyll, w.*) close.

GILLY GABBON, ? foot path (*cammen*) grove.

G.TREGOD, woodhouse (*tregoed*) grove.

GIMBLECOOM, ?? = vale of the CAMEL.

GIMNEN SCREPHA, *Beal, i.q.* GUN-MENSCRYFA.

THE GIN FIELD, ? = *cein*, a ridge.

GINGYNS DOWN, *T.a*, = Jenkin's Down, *T.C.*

GIRLES, ? *i.q.* GARLES.

GIRLS PARK, ? herb garden close.

GIRTLEY, ? = *great lea*, or meadow.

GIRTYMILK STREET, the street of milk and girts, *i.e.* grits or groats.

GISHARD, *n.f.*, ? = *Giselhart*, pledge of firmness, *t., Y.*

GLADNEY, ? *i.q.* GELYDNA.

GLAND PARK, ? river-bank (*glan*) close ; or, *i.q.* CLAM.

GLANVILLE, *n.f.*, ? town (*ville, f.*) on the bank.

GLAS-ENEY, -NEY, green water (*ea, s.*), *Nord.* (? *enys*, island) ; Le. GLAS-NITH, green nest (*nith*) ; green ford, *H.* (*hyth*, a coast, port, haven, s.).

GLASS, *n.f.*, ? = *glas*, blue, grey, green ; the stomach ; or, *i.q.* GOONLASE.

GLASSCOT, *n.f.*, ? green wood (*coat*).

GLASSWORTHY, *n.f.*, ? higher (*wartha*) GOONLASE.

GLASTON, *n.f.*, *i.q.* GLAZDON.

GLAZ-DON, -ON, green hill or down (*dun*).

GLAZELAND, green close (*lan*).

GLEBRIDGE, ? grove (*celli*) bridge.

GLEEST, ? east (*est*) field (*gweal*).

GLEN, *n.f.*, *i.q.* GLYNN.

GLENCROSS, *n.f.*, ? glen moor (*cors*) ; or, cross (*crous*) glen.

GLENDENNING, *n.f.*, ? Dinan's glen.

GLENDORGAL, ? ? Torquell's (*t.*), or noisy glen. (*deragla*, to brawl).

GLENDURGAN, glen of the DOURGAN.

GLEN WITHAN, ? = *gweal an wedhen*, the tree field ; or, tree glen.

GLIDDEN, ? broad (*ledan*) field (*gweal*) ; or, *i.q.* GLYNN.

GLI-, GLU-VIAN, ? little (*bihan*) grove (*celli*) or groves (*celliow*).

GLOOM, ? loam field (*gweal*).

GLOWETH, the down (*goon*) with the barrows (*loweth*), *M'L.*

GLOYNS, ? = *glens* ; or, lambs' (*eanes*) field (*gweal*).

GLUBB, *n.f.*, ? = *glub*, wet, moist, a.

GLUDDENS, ? broad (*ledan*) fields (*gweal-s*).

GLU-IS, -YASS, *n.f.*, from ST. GLUVIAS.

GLUSTONE, *d.d.* for BLISTON, ? church (*eglos*) town ; or, *i.q.* GLAZDON.

GLUTH, ? garden (*lowarth*) close (*ce*).

GLYNFORD, road in the *glen.*

GLYNN, the glen; ?? wooded (*celli*) valley with a river (*avon*).

GOAD, *n.f.*, ? = *coid*, a wood ; or, *godh*, a mole, a goose; or, *god*, *s.*, good.

GOAH, ? = *gover*, a stream.

GOAL GWIDDEN, ? tree (*gwedhen*), or white (*gwidn*), field.

GOAMARTH, ? *i.q.* GONAMARTH.

GOAN NOATH, new (*nowyth*) down.

GOARD, *n.f.*, ? high (*ard*) down (*goon*).

GOATSLAND, ? goats' close (*lan*).

GOBBAS VEAN, ? little GOBNAS.

GOBB-EN, -INN, ? little down (*goon*).

GOBMAN CROFT, ? sea-weed croft.

GOBNAS, ? lesser (*behenna*) down (*goon*) [field]s, *or* closes (*cae-s*).

GOBRIA, ? *i.q.* GOONVREA.

GODA, *w.B.m.,* = Goth, *s.*

GODCOT, ? Goda's cottage, *t.* ; *or*, cottage near a wood (*coed*, *w.*).

GODDARD, *n.f.*, divine firmness, *t.*, *Y.* ; *godard*, a cup, *w.*

GODFREY, *n.f., i.q.* GODEFRIDUS, *t.d.d.* God's peace.

GODGEN, ? ox (*udzheon*) down (*goon*).

GODOLGAN, *o.n.f.*, ?? tin (*alcan*, *w.*) smelting (*goddeithiol*), *C.* ; land of tin, *ph.*, *Po.* ; white eagle, *Cur.*

GODOLPHIN, *the same* ; a little (*go*) valley (*dol*) of springs (*fenten*), *Pr.* (*c.d.* St. John Baptist, *DuB.*).

GODREN, ? thorn (*druen*) down.

GODREVY, little (*go*), or wood (*coed*), town (*tre*) by the water (*wy*). *Pr.* ; *godre*, a border, edge, *w.* ; *godro*, to milk, *w.*

GODRIC, *t.d.d.*, divine king, *t.*, *Y.*

GODVEN, *t.d.d.*, divine friend, *t.*, *Y.*

GOES FIELD, ? blood (*gois*) field.

GOFADDLE, a shop, a workhouse, a smith's shop, *Pr.*

GOGLAS, green (*glas*) down (*goon*).

GOGWELL, the cuckoo's (*goy*) town (*ville*, *f.*) or work (*wheal*), *B.*

GOLANCE, ? lambs' (*eanes*) field (*gweal*).

GOLANT (*or* ST. SAMPSON, *p.s.*), adoration, *C.* ; holy (*gol*) church (*lan*), *Po.* ; the stream (*nant*) from the

down (*goon*) with the tumulus (*lo*, *s.*), (*W.W.* GOLONANT), *M'L.*

GOLBERDON, ? screech-owl (*berthuan*) field (*gweal*).

GOLBORN, holy well (*burne*, *s.*), *Pr.*

GOLD-ARROWS, -ARRISH, ? stubble (*arrish*) field (*gweal*) ; *or*, field by the door (*daras*).

GOLDAWDEN, ? lay (*todn*) field.

GOLDBERRY, ? rich (*berric*) field.

GOL-, GOAL-, GUL-DEN, *i.q.* WOLVEDON ; ? = *col din*, castle hill.

GOLDEN GUMPAS, *i.q.* GOON GUMPAS.

GOLDEN VEAN, little GOLDEN.

GOLDEN VERRIS, ? = *golden furze.*

GOLDEW, ? south (*deheu*, *w.*) field.

GOLD FOLD, ? fold (*fald*, *s.*) field.

G. HILL, ? moor (*hal*) field.

G. HOSKEN, ? rush (*hescen*) field.

GOLD-ING, -NEY, *n.f.*, ? narrow (*idne*) field, *T.C.*

GOLDMELLIN, ? yellow (*melyn*), *or* mill (*melin*) field.

GOLD-, GOOL-MORRISH, Morrish's *or* marsh field.

GOLD PERROW, ? pear trees (*perwydh*) field.

G. RAFTER, ? rough land (*tir*) field.

GOLDRICK, ? watery (*douric*) field.

GOLDSITHNEY, ?? SITHNEY'S field, *or* hill (*col*), *or* hazels (*coll*, *w.*); *v.* GOLSINNY.

GOLD SLIP, ? narrow-strip field.

GOLDSTANNA, ? tinner *or* water wagtail (*stenor*) field.

GOLDSWORTHY, *n.f.*, ? further (*wartha*) bottom (*goles*).

GOLHOSKING, *i.q.* GOLD HOSKEN.

GOLL-A, -AH, ? = *goles*, a bottom ; the bottom *or* lower place, *Pr.*

GOLLACOMBE, ? lower (*gwolla*) valley (*cum*).

GOLLASTREA, bottom near home (*tre*).

GOLLAWATER, stream in the bottom.

GOLLAWEST, ? west, or shelter bottom. (*gwestu*, to shelter).

GOLLOBEN, ? little (*bihan*) bottom.

GOLON, *i.q.* COLON.

GOLONA, ? *glanow*, the banks, *R.W.* ;

water flag (*galunga, f.*), *C.J.*

GOLOURES, at (*go*) the garden (*lowarth*), *Pr.*; tumulus (*low, s.*) down (*goon*), *M·L.*

GOL-OYTHA, -YTHA, obstruction, *C.*; ? dairy (*luitty*) down (*goon*).

GOLPITHY, ? birch (*bedho*) field.

GOLPRONTER, ? preacher's or priest's (*praonter*) field.

GOLSANS, ? lambs' (*eanes*) bottom or valley (*goles*).

GOLSTICK, ? narrow-slip (*stitch*) field, or bottom (*goles*).

GOLVADNECK, ?stony (*maenick*) field; or, *i.q.* COLVANNICK.

GOLVEAN, little field (*gweal*).

GOLVOEL, the bald hill (*moel*) of light (*yolow*), *Beal.*

GOLWARRA, further (*wartha*) field.

GOMAN, *n.f.*, ? stone (*maen*) down.

GOMER, *n.f.*, ? horses' (*merh*) down (*goon*).

GONA-BARREN, -BARN, ?crow (*brahan, bran*), or, barn down.

GONAMARROES, ? MEDROSE down.

GONAMARTH, ?down of the wonder (*marth*), or horse (*march*), or water plain or meadow (*marth, C.*).

GONAMENA, ? stony (*maenic*) downs.

GONEBRAS, ? great (*bras*) down.

GONEVA, ? down place (*ma, va*).

GONEW VISCA, ??high (*uch*) down of the *piskies* or fairies.

GONGEARS, ? green or camp downs.

GONIGHTEN, furze (*eithen*) down.

GONNETS PARK, St. *Conant's* close.

GONNORWARTHA, higher CONNOR.

GONOMAN DOWNS, no man's down (*reduplicated*).

GONORMAEL, ?Gwrmael's (*w.s.*) down.

GONORMAN, ??St. Rumon's downs.

GON PARK, down close (*parc*).

GONPIPER, ? baker's (*peber*) down.

GONREE, *i.q.* GOONREETH.

GONVEAN, little (*bihan*) down.

GONVELLOCK, ? Mailoc's down.

GONVERZETH, ?the dry (*sech*) great (*veer*), or, *furze heath* down.

GONWIN, white (*gwin*) down.

GONZION, Zion or Jews' (*edzhewon*) down, *C.*; down with a defence (*sion, ga.*), *Beal*; ? *i.q.* GODGEN.

GOO, ? *i.q.* GEW.

GOOCH, *n.f.*, ? *i.q.* COUCH.

GOOD, *n.f.*, *i.q.* GOAD.

GOOD-AGRANE, -YGREAN, ? gravel (*grean*) wood (*coed, w.*).

GOODALL, *n.f.*, moor (*hal*) wood.

GOODAMOOR, ? great (*mawr*), or, moor wood.

GOODAVEOR, ? great wood.

GOODERN, ? alder (*gwern*), or oak (*derwen*) wood, *R.W.*

GOOD GRACE, *t.b.*, ?middle (*cres*) wood.

GOODING, *n.f.*, ? little (*rean*) wood.

GOODLAND, *n.f.*, ? wood close (*lan*).

GOODMAN, *n.f.*, the stone (*maen*) wood; *or* = *Godmund*, divine protection, *t.*

GOODMANSLEIGH, Goodman's pasture (*leah, s.*).

GOODMERRY, ? MEORE'S wood.

GOODNESS, ? lambs' (*eanes*) wood; or, castle (*dinas*) down.

GOODWIN, *n.f.*, divine friend, *t.*; ? white (*gwin*) wood.

GOODYERE, ?long (*hir*) wood.

GOODYVOAL, ? blackbirds' (*moelh*) wood, or field (*coetiey, w.*).

GOOLAMANK, ? [fox]glove (*maneg*), or the monk's (*manach*)field (*gweal*).

GOOLD DARRAS, *i.q.* GWEAL DARRAS.

G. HARP, ? harrow (*harv*) field.

G. HERRING, ? oak (*derwen*) field.

G. HINGEY, ? field by the house (*an chy*).

GOOL VELLAN, mill (*melin*) field.

GOONABARN, *i.q.* GONABARREN.

GOONAVERN, alder (*gwern*) downs, *R.W.*

GOON BALLAS, ? *i.q.* GABALLAS.

G. BARROW, ? higher (*warra*) down.

G. BEL, the fair (*bel*), or far off (*pell*), or further down.

G. BREA, hill (*bre*) down, *Po.*

G. BROZE, great (*bras*), or thicket (*browse*), down.

G. CROUZA, the cross (*crows*) downs.

GOON DEAN DOWNS, ? castle (din) down (reduplicated).

G. EVAS, ? the down outside (vez).

G. GALLIS, ? bottom (goles) down.

G. GARTHA, ? higher (gwartha) down.

G. GEATH, ? down of the limit (geyth), or the trees (gweydh).

G. GILLIN, ? holly (celin) down.

G. GIVIN, ? boundary (cyffen, w.), or ridge (cefn, w.), down.

G. GLAZE, ? green (glas) down.

G. GOOSE, the common by the wood (cus), Pr.; hill of blood (gos), Nord.; ? cheese (caus) down.

G. GOOTH, ? goose (godh), or wood (coed, w.) down.

G. GREGOR, partridge down.

G. GUMP, ? combe down. (gump, down hill, Pr.).

G. GUMPAS, v. GOONGUMPY, wrestling or games (campau) down.

G. HASKIN, sedge (hescen) down.

G. HAVERN, i.q. GOONAVERN.

G. HEATH, ? heath (heyth) down.

G. HILLY, " Hilly hethe," Le.; ? hunting down. (hellia, to hunt).

G. HINGEY, ? down by the house (an chy).

G. HOWER, down by the water (dour), Bot.; ? ram's (hor) down.

G. HUSMAN, ? husbandman's (husman, w.), or, huntsman's down.

G. INNIS, ? ENYS'S, or island (enys), or lambs' (eanes) down.

G. LAZE, green (lays) down.

G. LOAF, ? Leof's (t.) down.

G. MELLON, ? clover (meillion) down.

G. MENHEERE, long-stone (menhir) down.

G. MINE, ? stone (maen) down.

G. MINE MELLON, ? yellow (melyn) stone down.

G. NOWETH, new (nowydh) down.

G. OON, -OWN, ? Owen's down.

G. PEDNY VOUNDER, lane (bounder) end (pedn) down.

G. PRAUNTER, PROYNTER, the priest or preacher (praonter) down.

G. PRINCE, Prince's down.

GOON RAW, rough or Ralph's down.

G. REETH, open (rhydd, w.) downs, Pr.

G. RINSEY, ? dry (sech) hill (rhyn) down.

G. SOIL, ? stubble (saul) down.

G. STRESS, ? narrow (strez) down.

G. VEAN, little down.

G. VENA, ? lesser (behenna) down.

G. VREA, hill (bre) downs, R.IV.

G. WALKIN, ? frog (cuilcen) down.

G. WARTHA, ? higher (gwartha) downs.

G. WIDDEN, -WIN, -WYN, ? white (gwyn, gwidn), or tree (gwedhen) down.

G. WINNOWS, marshy (winnoc) down [field]s.

G. YERL, the earl's (yerl) down, Pr.; HEARL'S down.

GOOSEBEAN, i.q. COOSEBEAN.

GOOSEFORD, the way or pass (fordh) by the wood (cus), Pr.

GOOSEGWARRA, higher (gwarthah) wood.

GOOSEHAM, ? wood boundary (hem).

GOOSE PARK, ? wood close (parc).

G. MOOR, ? i.q. GOSSMOOR.

G. NECK ? neck of the wood.

G. WELL, ? the wood well; or, high (uhel) wood.

GOOTH, GOUTH, ? = coed, a wood, w.

GORE-DEN, -DON, ? i.q. CARADON.

GORGUT, o. GORRACOT, on (gwar) the wood, Pr.; ? wood rock (carrag).

GORINGY, ? enclosure (garth) by the house (an chy).

GORLAND, ? a sheepfold or cote (corlan); or, a graveyard (corhlan).

GORLYN, ? = grelin, cattle pond.

GORMEAN, ? by (gar, w.) the stone (maen).

GORMELLICK, on (gor) the mill premises, Pr.; ? i.q. CARMAILOC.

GORRAN, from p.s. St. Goronus, O.

G. GORRAS, ? St. Gorran moor (cors).

G. HOANE, Gorran haven (hauen).

GORRES, ? = garz, a hedge, fence, M·L.; guriz, a girdle, Po.

GORT LANE, ivy or garden (gort, ga.) lane, Beal.

GOSCOTT, ? moor (cors) cottage.

GOSLEY, ? moor place (*le*).

GOSLING, *n.f.*, ? goose pond (*lyn*).

GOSPENHEALE, *i.q.* COISPENHAILE.

GOSS, *n.f.*, moor; or, wood (*cos*).

GOSSMOOR, ? great (*mawr*) moor (*cors*); or, wood (*cos*) moor; or, a *redup.*

GOSSOSE, *i.q.* COSAWES.

GOSTICK, *n.f.*, ? pleasant (*tec*) wood.

GOSWARN, ? alder (*gwern*) wood.

GOTCHA, ? *i.q.* PARK CADJAW.

GOTH-A, -ERS, ? *i.q.* GATHERS.

GOTLEY, *n.f.*, ? goat or great pasture, *t.*

GOUDGE, *n.f.*, ? *i.q.* COUCH.

GOUGH, *n.f.*, ? = *goch*, red, *R.W.*; or *gof*, a smith.

GOULAR ROCKS, coral rocks, *Bl.*

GOULD, *n.f*, ? *golud*, wealth, *w.*

GOURD, *n.f.*, ? *i.q.* GOARD.

GOUTH, ? wood = *coed*, *w.*

GOUTHERS ROCK, ? CARUTHERS rock.

GOV-ARROE, -ERROW, the streams.

GOVER, rivulet, stream.

GOVERIGAN, *i.q.* GAVERIGAN.

GOVETT, *n.f.*, ? smith's (*gof*) gate (*yet*).

GOV-ILE, -ILLY, -EYLEY, ? stream place (*le*); or Beli's down (*goon*); ? *govail*, a smithy, *R.W.*

GOVIS WATER, ?? higher (*gwarthah*) down (*goon*) outside (*ves*).

GOVORRACK, *nickn.*, snubnose, *T.*

GOW, ? *i.q.* GEW.

GOW-ANS, -ENS, ? *i.q.* GEW-ANS, -ENS.

GOWER, *n.f.*, ? *i.q.* GOVER.

GOWEYS, ? lower (*isa*), or outside (*ves*), enclosures (*ccow*).

GOWN PARK, down (*gwon*) close.

GRACK, ? rock (*carrag*) [field].

GRAD-DON, -ON, ? *i.q.* CARADON, or GRADY.

GRADE, *from p.s.*; (*c.d.* Holy Cross and St. *Gradus, O.*).

GRADN-AR, -ER, -EY, ? long (*hir*) GRADDON.

GRADY PARK, ? steps (*gradow*) close.

GRAF-NER, -TNER, *i.q.* GRADNAR.

GRAGON, ? *i.q.* CARICON.

GRAHAM, *n.f.*, ? *i.q.* GRIM.

GRAING PARK, ? grange close.

GRAMAIRE, *o.n.f.*, ? = *gramr*, fierce, *o.n.*

GRAMBL-A, -ER, the scrambling place, *Pr.*, (*grambla*, to scramble).

GRAMMERS PARK, ? grandmother's, or woodlouse (*grammer sow*) close.

GRAMMERY, ? grandmother's *hay* or close.

GRAMPOUND, *o.* GRANPONT, the great (*grond, f.*) bridge (*pons, pont, w.*); (*c.d.* St. Mary).

GRAMPUS, ? grandpapa's [field].

GRANFARS MEADOW, *the same.*

GRANKIN, *n.f.*, ? = *crencyn*, a limpet, *w.*

GRANNICK, ? *i.q.* CARNICK.

GRANNKAM, ? *i.q.* CRANKUM.

GRANT, *n.f.*, ? *i.q.* St. *Geraint*; or = *grand*, great, *f.*

GRANVILLE, *n.f.*, great (*grand*) town, *f.*

GRASKEN, *i.q.* CARSCAIN.

GRATNA, *i.q.* GRADNAR.

GRATT-AN, -EN, -ON, ? *i.q.* GRADDON.

GRAVE, *n.f.*, ? = *gerefa*, a steward, *s.*

GRAVESEND, ? *i.q.* GROVESEND, end of the grove, *t.*, (*craobh*, a tree, *i.*).

GRAWLEY, ? *i.q.* CRAWLE, or CROWLEY.

GRAZELAND, ? middle (*cres*) enclosure (*lun*); ? parched (*cras*), *w.*, *R.W.*

GRAZES, the middle (*cres*) [field]s.

GREADON, ? herd (*gre*) hill (*dun*).

GRE-ADY, -EDY, -DIOUE, ? Edy's or the Jew's (*edhow*) rock (*carn*).

GREATA PARK, ? the *great*, or steps (*gradou*) close.

GREBER, ? long (*hir*) GREEB.

GREBBLE, GRIBBLE, *n.f.*, ? cattle (*gre*) pool (*pol*).

GREBS, rocks like the comb of a cock.

GREEB, = *creeb*, a crest, comb, summit.

GREEB ZAWN, the crest or comb ZAWN.

GREENAGE, ?? lower (*isa*) gravel (*grean*) [field].

GREENAMOOR, ? the green moor.

GREEN-AWAY, -WAY, = *grenaweg*, the green pathway, *s.*

GREEN BARROW, the sun (*grian*) tumulus, *Beal.*

G. GRIPES, ? green ditch filled with brambles, &c., (*grep*, a furrow, *s.*).

G. GWAIL, ? green field (*gweal*).

GREEN SCREEPS, ? green patches or strips.

G. SLADE, n.f., ? green bottom.

G. SPLAT, grass plot.

G. WEETH, ? green borderland; (? gwydd, wild, untilled, w.).

GREEPS, ditches full of thorns, &c.

GREES, n.f., ? i.q. CRAZE.

GREESEY MEADOW, ? cress (cerse, s.) meadow.

GREET, n.f., ? i.q. GARRET.

GREETHURST, n.f., ? great wood, s.

GREGAN GEGAN, ? ? rock (carrag) with the slit (an gagen).

GREGE, GREGG, n.f., ? i.q. GRIGG.

GREGOES, ? barrows (crygow) [field]s.

GREGOR, n.f., heath-poult or black game, C.; partridge, R.W.

GREGORETH, grouse or heath-poult ground, C.

GREGORY, n.f., ? partridge close (hay).

GRELENBESELS, 11 cent., cattle (gre) pool (lyn) by the birches (bezula).

GRELLY FIELD, ? grelin, cattle pond.

GREN-FEL, -VILLE, n.f., ? i.q. GRANVILLE; or Greenfield.

GRESTON, ? = GREYSTONE.

GRETNA, ? i.q. GRATNA.

GREW LAND, ? hovel (crow) field.

GREW'S HILL, ? CAREW'S hill.

GREY LAKE, ? i.q. CARHALLOCK.

GREY MARE, ? great (meer) heath (grug), C.

GRIBBEN HEAD, ? crest- (gryb) like headland (pen) reduplicated.

GRIDDEFOR, ? great (veor) GREEDY.

GRIDGET, ? barrow (cryg) gate (yet).

GRIFFIN, t.d.d., = w. Gruffin, = lat. Rufinus, ruddy, Y.

GRIFFETH, n.f., = GRIFFIUD, w.B.m., the same.

GRIGG, n.f., ? = grig, heath or ling; or, i.q. GARRICK.

GRIGGIN, ? little (vean) rock.

GRIGLAND, ? heath land or close.

GRILLINS, ? cattle pond (grelin) [field]s.

GRILLIS, ? i.q. GARLES.

GRIM, t.d.d., helmeted, t., Y.; grym, strong, mighty, w.

GRIMSBY, Grim's dwelling (by, d.); o. GRYNSEY, ? green sea, B.

GRIMSCOTT, Grim's cottage.

GRIPE, n.f., ? = garv, rough, a.

GRISSLING, n.f., ? hedge (garz) by the lake (lyn).

GRISSON'S POOL, ? = garz an pol, the hedge pool, M'L; ? hedge by the pool.

GRIST CLOSE, ? i.q. CRIST.

GRIZZLE, ? camps (gear-s) hill, M'L.

GROAN, GROWAN, ? granite [field].

GROAT FIELD, ? field with pile of grute, i.e. roots (gwrydh) and rubbish, A.A.V.

GROGATH, GROGOE, limit (geyth) or boundary cross, or cross of the limits, Pr.

GROGLEY, ? rock pasture or place (le).

GROGOE, ? barrows (crugou).

GROSE, GROWSE, the cross (crows) or marsh (cors).

GROSE PARK, ? cross close.

GROSISE, ? lower (isa) cross; or Saxon's (sais) hovel (crow).

GROTENAGE, ? lower GRADDON.

GROUGHS, ? from garv, rough, a.

GROUS CROFT, cross (crows) croft.

GROUSHIE, ? cross close (hay).

GROUSE VEAN, little cross (crows).

GROUSIER, i.q. CROWSER.

GROWDEN, n.f., ? valley (den, s.) with hovel.

GROWER, ? long (hir) hovel.

GROW VINES, ? ? little (bihan) hovel (crow) [field]s.

GRUBB, n.f., ? = garv, rough, a.

GRUDGDRAHENOT, 11 cent., ? EDNOD'S house (tre) cross.

GRUGITH, heath hillock, or barrow heath, Ped.; ? i.q. GROGATH.

GRUGKENNYWOL, 11 cent., ? Cynhafal's (w.s.) barrow (crug) or cross (crous).

GRUMBLER, i.q. GRAMBLA.

GRUZELIER, n.f., ? huntsman's (hellier) cross.

GRYKE, n.f., ? i.q. GARRICK.

GRYLLS, i.q. GRILLIS.

GUA-EDRET, -ITHRIT, *w.B.m.*, ? = Guiderius, wrathful (?), *Y.*

GUEAL GUBBANS, ? GOBNAS field.

G. LEDIA, ? dairy (*laitty*) field.

GUALDRAN, *i.q.* GWEAL DREN.

GUARANDRE, *i.q.* WARTHANTRE, *Sc.*

GUAVIS, *n.f.*, *i.q.* GWAVAS.

GUBBIN, *n.f.*, ? little (*bian*) down (*goon*).

GUBEES MEADOW, ? *from* St. CUBY.

GUDDA, *t.d.d.*, ? the Goth, *t.*

GUDDER, ? *from gudra,* to milk.

GUDERN, brambly (*draen*) wood (*coed*), *Pr.* ; oak (*derwen*) plain (*gun*), *Ped.*

GUE GRAZE, *i.q.* GEW GRAZE.

GUELA, GUELAZ, easily seen, *Mur.*

GUEL CARNE, rock field.

GUENGUIN, *s.B.m.*, ? doubly fair.

GUERD-EVALAN, *d.d.* (*e.d.d.* -AVALAN) ? apple tree (*avallen*) enclosure (*garth*). ? now WORTHYVALE.

GUEST MEADOW, ? shelter (*guest*) meadow.

GUEW, GUGH, a plain, field, *Bor.* ; ? *i.q.* GEW.

GUFFAER, *from gavar,* a goat, *Po.* ; (? now TRESCO).

GUILDFORD, ? *i.q.* GULLIFORD.

GULALLAS, ? green-moor (*hal-las*), or cliff (*als*) field (*gweal*).

GULANCE, ? lambs' (*eanes*) field (*gweal*).

GULAWANA, ? foxes' (*lowernou*) field.

GULBRAWS, great (*bras*) field.

GULCHYE, ? house (*chy*) field.

GULDONNEL, cask (*tonnel*) field.

GULDUSMET, ? bat (*hisomet*) field.

GULEGULLAS, ? the lower (*gullas*) vallum (*gual*), *Po.* ; ? bottom (*goles*) field.

GULF, ? summer (*haf*) field ; *also* = wolf

GULFWELL, = St. GULVAL'S *well.*

GULGUARN, alder (*gwern*) field.

GULGULLAS, *i.q.* GULEGULLAS.

GULGWARRA, higher (*gwarra*) field.

GULLACKAN, ? pond (*lagen*) field.

GULLACKS, ? lower (*gwollach*) [field]s.

GULLACOMBE, ? combe field, *or* lower (*golla*) vale.

GULLA GEAR, the camp (*caer*) field.

GULLA-GUETONS, -QUETONS, ? tree (*gwedhen*) fields.

GULLAMAIN, ? the stone (*maen*) field.

GULLAND, the gull island.

GULL AN GEAR, *i.q.* GULLA GEAR.

GULLANT, *i.q.* GOLANT.

GULLAS, ? green (*glas*) field, *or* = *goles*, bottom.

GULL BEAN, little (*bian*) field.

GULLEN, ? little (*vean*) field.

GULLET, ? gate (*yet*) field.

GULL GARRAS, *i.q.* GWEAL GARRAS.

G. GWEEK, GWEEK field.

G. GWIDDON, ? tree (*gwedhen*) field.

GULL-IES, -YS, ? broad (*les*) field ; *or* = *goles*, a bottom.

GULLI-EWS, -OWA, ? fields in the *loo* or shelter (*hleow, s.*).

GULLIFORD, field by the road (*fordh*).

GULL NORS, ? the ram's (*an hor*) field.

GULLOVELLAN, apple tree (*avallen*) field.

GULLOW, ? = *gwealow*, fields.

GULLS PARK, ? bottom (*goles*) close.

GULL VEAN, little (*bihan*) field.

GULLY, *n.f.*, ? = *celli*, a grove.

GULLY AMBLES, ? Hannibal's field.

G. BOWLS, ? dug up (*balas*) field.

G. FAWN, ? hay (*foen*) field.

G. MEORS, the great (*meer*) fields.

G. PARK, ? grove close.

GUL-MEAN, -MEN, stone (*maen*) field.

GULMOOR, ? great (*mawr*) field.

GULNANCE, valley (*nans*) field.

GULNINNIS, the lambs' (*aneanes*) field.

GULREEVE, ? the steward's (*s.*) field.

GUL ROBIN, Robin's field.

GULTAN, fire (*tan*), *or* under (*dan*) field.

GULTOL, the hole (*tol*) field.

GULVAL, *from p.s.* St. Gudwall, *O.* ; holy (*gol*) vale ; *or*, bottom (*golla*) of the vale, *Lh.* ; *or*, hazel (*coll, w.*) moor (*hal*), *Pr.*

GUL-VES, -VIAS, field outside (*mes*).

GUL-WARRA, -WARTHA, higher (*gwartha, warra*) field.

GULWEST, *i.q.* GWEAL WEST.

GUMB, *n.f.*, ? *i.q.* COMBE.

GUMBLE CLOSE, ? = *combe hill.*

GUMMA-ER, -OW, *n.f.*, ? long (*hir*) combe ; *or* the combes.

GUMMOCK, ? pigs' (*moch*) field (*cae, w.*).

GUMP, down hill, *Pr.* ; a plain, *Bl.*

GUM PARK, ? *combe* close.

GUMPAS, a plain, *B.*

THE GUMS, ? combe [*fields*].

GUN, = *gwon*, a down.

GUNBURGESES, kites' (*barges-es*) down.

GUNDAVEY, Davey's downs.

GUNDRON, the downs hill (*tron*), *Pr.*

GUNDRY, *n.f.*, ? home (*tre*) down ; *or*, *i.q.* GUNDRED, war council, *t.*

GUNETT'S WELL, St. Gundred's well, *H.*

GUNEW, ? high (*uch*), *or* Hugh's down.

GUNHEATH, ? stag (*hydh, w.*) down, *R.W.* ; *or*, downy heath (*heyth*).

GUNLYN, the lake (*lyn*) down.

GUN MANNELS, ? sheaf of corn (*manal yz*) down.

GUNMANN-IN, -ING, butter (*manen*) down.

GUNMAR'R, Mercury's down, *B.*

GUNMENSCRYFA, the down of the inscribed stone (*maen-scryfa*).

GUNNA, ? down enclosure (*hay*).

GUNNAMEER, ? the great (*meer*) downs (*guniow*).

GUNNICKS PARK, ? Caenog's (*w.*) close.

GUNNISLAKE, the rivulet (*lacca*) from the mining cavity (*gunnies, m.c.*) ; *c.d.* St. Anne, *J.H.H.*

GUNNON, ? St. Non's down.

GUNOAKE, ? empty (*wak*) down, *R.W.*

GUN PARK, ? down close (*parc*).

GUN POOL, ? down pool.

GUNROUNSON, ass (*rounsan*) down.

GUNSWORTHY, ? higher (*wartha*) causeway (*counce*), *or* GUNNIS.

GUNTERS FIELD, ? Gundred's field.

GUNVEANS, little' *vean*) down [field]s.

GUNVER, great (*meer*) down.

GUNVERZEATH, *i.q.* GONVERZETH.

GUNWALLO, *from p.s.* St. Wynwallaus, *O.* ; the castle (*gwal*) mount (*lo, s.*) on the downs (*gun*), *M'L.*

GUNWALLO WINTON,? the conquering town of Dunwallo Malmutius, *H.* !

GUNWELL, the gushing well, *Beal* ; *gun*, a breach, a rapid river, *ga.*

GUNWENNAP, Gwennap's down.

GUNWENSE, ? windy down, (*gwyns*, wind) ; *or*, spring (*fiuns, a.*) down.

GUNWIN, white (*gwyn*) down, *Pr.*

GUNWINTON, spring (*fenten*) down.

GURD-EN, -ON, ? on (*gwar*) the hill (*dun*) ; *or*, = *cerden*, the mountain ash ; *or*, *i.q.* CARADON.

GURLAND, ? *i.q.* GORLAND.

GURLEY, ? little (*le*) camp.

GURLYN, the husband's (*gur*) lake (*lyn*) ; *or* moist*or* wet place (*ker, a.*), *Pr.* ; camp (*caer*) by the lake, *M'L.* ; ? = *grelin*, cattle pond.

GURNEAR, ? the long (*an hir*) camp (*caer*), *or* rock (*carn*).

GURNETS HEAD, headland shaped like the fish *gurnard.*

GURNICK, ? *i.q.* CARNICK.

GURTLA, ? *great lea*, *or* pasture.

GURWEN, white (*gwen*) camp (*caer*).

GUSHLAND, *o.* GOSELAND, = *garzlan*, hedge enclosure, *M'L.*

GUSKUS, ? = *guscys*, shelter, cover.

GUSTER PARK, ? wood (*cus*) land (*tir*) close (*parc*).

GUSTE-VEAN, *and* -VEOR, great *and* little wood (*cus*), *Pr.* ; (? –TE– = *ty*, house.)

GUT, ? = *coet*, wood.

GUT GROUND, ? ivy (*gort, i.*) field, *Beal.*

GUY, *n.f.*, ? = *gwy*, water, *w.* ; *or*, *i.q.* Gwion (*w.*) *or* Caius (*lat.*).

GWALDRAN, *i.q.* GWEALDREN.

GWALLON, down (*oon*) field (*gweal*).

GWALYVELLIN, the mill (*melin*) field.

GWANDRA, *i.q.* GWEAL AN DREA.

GWARDER, the summit (*gwartha*) near the water (*dour*), *Pr.*

GWARNICK, hay (*gwair, w.*) river, *T.*, (? *gwern*, a meadow, *w.*, *R.W.*) ; camp (*caer*) by the river (*a'n ick*), *M'L.*

GWATKIN, *n.f.*, *i.q.* WATKIN.

GWAVAS, winterly place, *Pr.* ; ? [farm by the] winter [station] ; the mole, *C.*

GWAVASVEAN, little GWAVAS.

GWEAL, a field ; or, = *wheyl*, a work, *R. IV.* ; *huel*, a work, a mine, *B.*

G. AN ALEDH, field of the hill (*alt*), or key (*alwedh*) field, *T.C.*

G. AN COOZ, the wood (*cuz*) field.

G. AN DREA, town-place field, *T.C.*

G. AN GEAR, the camp (*caer*) field.

G. AN TOP, the *top* field.

G. AN VEZ, the outward (*mes*) field, *B.*

G. BEVILL, field of the mean (*vil*) house (*bo, bod*), *T.C.* ; Beville's field.

G. CARN, rock (*carn*) field.

G. CLOCK PERMJAR, ? prison (*cloch-prednier*) field.

G. COCK, ? red (*coch*) field.

G. CREEG, ? barrow or hillock field.

G. DARRAS, field before the door (*d·ras*).

G. DERRIS, ? bramble (*dreis*) field.

G. DREA, home (*tre*) field.

G. DREN, thorn (*draen*) field.

G. DRISSICK, brambly field.

G. DUBNAS, ? banks (*tuban-s*) field.

G. DUES, ? sheep (*devas*) field.

G. DURANT, DURANT field.

G. EATH, heath (*heyth*) field.

G. EDNACK, ? narrower (*ednach*) field.

G. ELAVELLAN, ? mill (*melin*), or yellow (*melyn*) moor (*hal*) field.

G. FIELD, *a reduplication.*

G. FOLDS, ? fold fields, or folds' field.

G. GARRAS, top (*gwarhas*), or parched (*cras*), or moor (*cors*), field.

G. GOLLIS, bottom (*goles*) field.

G.-GUARE, -GWARRE, ? play (*gware*), or quarry (*cuare, Pr.*) field.

G. GULLAS, lower field, *B.*

G. GWARRA, ? higher (*gwarra*) field.

G. GWARTHAS, higher (*gwartha*) fields ; or, *i.q.* GWELL WARRAS.

G. HAVERECK, fallow (*havrek,a.*) field.

G.-HELLIS, -HILLS, broad-moor (*halles*), or son-in-law's (*els*) field.

G.-HELLOW, -HILLOW, moors (*hallow*) field.

G. IDNEAUX, ? narrower (*ednach*) fields.

GWEAL LANCHY, the house (*an chy*) field.

G. LEDNACK, broader (*ledanach*) field.

G. MAYOW, ? Mayow's or mowhay field.

G. NAYNE, the lamb (*an ean*) field.

G. NOON, the down (*an oon*) field.

G. NORS, ? rams' (*an hor-s*) field.

G.-NOWETH, -NOATH, new field.

G. ON, ash (*on*) field, *R. IV.*

G. PAUL, ? pit (*pol*), or Paul's field.

G. PEAS, peas (*pys, w.*) field.

G.-POR, -PORTH, cove (*porth*) field.

G. SCAWEN, elder-tree (*scawen*) field.

G. SKIBBER, barn (*sceber*) field.

G. SPERNON, thorn (*spernan*) field.

G. VA, ? bean (*fa*) field.

G. VEZA, ? outer (*vezach*) field.

G. WARTHA, higher field.

G. WEST, shelter (*gwest*) field.

G. WIDDEN, ? white (*gwidn*) field.

G. YATE, gate (*yet*) field.

G. ZELMERE, ? great (*meer*) low (*isal*) fields ; or, grass (*gwells*) moor (*hal*).

GWEALS, the fields, *Pr.* ; ? *i.q.* GWILLS.

GWEDNA, *n.f.*, ? white (*wednac*) down (*goon*).

GWEEG, GWEEK, a village, bay, cove, *Pr.* ; = *guyik*, the watery village, or village on the Guy, *B.*

GWEEK WOLLAS, lower GWEEK.

GWEL DUE, ? south (*deheu*) field.

GWELL, ? = *gweal*, a field.

GWELLAN QUARRY, ? the *quarry* field.

GWELLIN GWETHAN, the tree (*gwedhen*) field.

GWELLMELLAN, mill (*melin*), or clover (*meillion*), or yellow (*melyn*) field.

GWELL SOWAN, ? ox (*udzheon*) field.

G. STINK, ? pool (*stanc*) field.

G. TOMAS, Thomas's field.

G. VEZ, out or outward field, *J.B.*

G. WARRAS, ? top (*gwarhas*) field.

GWEN-DRA, -DRAH, white town (*tre*) ; or, *i.q.* GWINDRAITH, white sand ; ? = *goon dreath*, sand down, *J.B.*

GWENNAP, from *p.s.* St. Weneppa, *O.* ; (= white (*gwen*) face (*enap*), or son (*map*), *Pr.*).

Q

GWENT-ER, -OR, ? white water (*dour*).

GWENTON, white lay field (*ton*), *R.W.*

GWERICK, on (*gwar*) the river (*ick*), *T.*

GWERN, the alders, or marsh.

GWEVEL MOOR, ? the *weevil* moor.

GWILLS, GWYLLS, grass [farm].

GWINEAR, *from p.s.* St. Winnierus, *O.*

GWIN-EAS,-GES, *rocks,* = *gwingois,*
awkward, in the way, *f., C.J.*

GWIN PARK, white (*gwin*) close.

GWYNHILL, white (*gwin*) *isle.*

GWYN-HILLVEOR, -HELLEVER, ?great
(*mawr*) white isle.

GWYN ROCK, white rock.

GWYTHIAN, *from p.s.* St. Gothianus, *O.*

GYLLANVAES, William's grave (*bedh*),
Mur.; William's field (*maes*), *C.*

GYLLYNGDUNE, William's height,
Mur.; William's bank (*tuban*) or
grave, *C.*

GYNN, *n.f.*, ? = *gwyn*, white.

GYTHIOCAEL, *B.m.*, = Judical, sportive, *a., Y.*

H ACK, *n.f.*, ? = *ac*, an oak, *s.* ; or,
hæge, a hedge, *s.* ; or, *each*, a horse,
ga.

HACK FIELD, ? oak field, *t.*

HACKMARSH, ? Hack's or oak marsh, *t.*

HACKTHORN, ? = *hagathorn*, hawthorn, *s.*

HACTON, oak enclosure (*tun*), *s.*

HACUMBE, *o.n.f.*, ? oak vale.

HADDY, *n.f.*, *i.q.* EDDY.

HADLE HOLE, ? rubbish (*atal*) hole.

HADMORE, *n.f.*, ? = *Cathmor*, great in
war, *i.* ; or, *Hadumar*, fierce fame,
t., Y.

HAGAR, ? daisy (*egr*) [field].

HAGE, *n.f.*, ? = *hæge*, a hedge, enclosure, *s.* ; *i.q. cae, ce, k.*

HAGGART, *n.f.*, ? = *hay garth*, rick
yard, *t., Lo.*

HAGGEROWEL, ? Howel's land (*acer,*

s.) ; or, ugly (*hager*) field (*gweal*).

HAGLAND, *o.* HALGHLAND, ? willow
(*helig*), or, holy (*halig, s.*) land.

HAILMEN TOR, great (*hail*) stone
(*maen*) hill (*tor*), *B.* ; *i.q.* HELMIN-
TOR.

HAILSHOP FIELD, field by the shop
covered with slate.

HAILY, *n.f.*, ? = *hælig*, holy, *s.*

HAIME, *n.f.*, ? *i.q.* HAM ; or, HEM.

HAINE, *n.f.*, ? = *hen*, old, aged, *w.*

HAINES, *n.f.*, ? *i.q.* ENYS or ENIS.

HAISKE, *n.f.*, ? rushes (*hesk*) enclosure (*hay*).

HAKE, *n.f.*, ? *i.q.* HACK.

HAKEWILL, *n.f.*, ? oak well, *t.*

HALABESICK, birch (*bezo*) moor, or
hill (*hal*), or height (*alt*).

HALAGLOUR, ??earthnut (*clor*) moor.*

HALAMANNA, ? the monks' (*manach*)
moor (*hal*), or moors (*hallow*).

HALAMANNING, ? butter (*amenen*)
moor.

HALANGY, ? moor by the house (*an
chy*) ; salt (*halan*) house, *N.*

HALANGEAR, the camp (*an gaer*) moor.

HALANKEAN, ?sorrow (*ancen*), or the
ridge (*an cein*) moor.

HALBALLOCK MOOR, calves' house
(*bo-loch*) moor.

HALBATHICK, ?cottage (*bothog*) moor.

HALBOAT, boat moor, *Wh.* ; boundary
(*bord, s.*) rock (*ail*), *M'L.*

HAL BROWN, ? hill (*bron*) moor.

HALCOOSE, wood (*cos*) moor.

HALDEEN, ?? bramble (*draen*) moor.

HALDINAS, castle (*dinas*) hill, *Bl.*

HALDRAWTHA, ? higher land (*tir
wartha*) moor.

HALDREATH, sand (*traeth*) moor.

HALE, = *hal*, moor or hill ; or, *heyl*,
a river.

H. AN DREAN, bramble (*draen*) moor.

H. AN OGAN, the white-thorn berry
(*ogfaen, w.*) moor.

---

* HALGALOWER, = *Haul gole lloer*, the sun and moonlight district ; or = *halogwr*, a
profaner, *ga., Beal.* = *hal gol luir*, the down of the holy moon, *Buller.* ? the moor (*hal*)
of the moon's (*loer*) festival (*gol*).

HALE AN WYTH, the trees (*gwydh*) moor.

H. BAL, mine (*bal*) moor.

H. BROWSE, the moor with the short furze thicket, *Bot.*

HAL-EGGY, -EGY, -IGEY, -LEGEY, the near (*agy*), *or* KEA moor.

HALEGARRACK, rocky (*carrag*) moor.

HALEGARRAS, moor near the summit (*ywarhas*), *Pr.*; camps' (*gears*) moor, *M'L.*

HALEGATHA, ?higher (*gwartha*) moor.

HALEGINECK, worm (*cinac*) moor.

HALEGRASE, middle (*cres*) moor.

HALE LUE, the moor pool (*lo*), *Pr.*

HALEP, *n.f.*, ? moist (*leb*) moor.

HALESVA, ? ? cliff (*als*) place (*ma, va*).

HALESVOR, ? great (*mawr*) cliff.

HALEVEAN, little (*bean*) moor.

HALEVENTON, spring (*fenten*) moor.

HALEVOSE, ditch (*fos*) moor.

HALEWHIST, ? shelter (*gwest*) moor.

HALEWIN, white (*gwyn*) moor; the fair of white hill, *H.*

HALEWOON, the downs (*gwon*) moor, *Pr.*

HALEWORTHY, *i.q.* HALWARTHA.

HALEY, *n.f.*, ? = *helig*, willows.

HALEZY, lower (*isa*) moor.

HALGARRAS,?camps' (*caer-s*) hill,*M'L.*

HALGAVER, goat (*gavar*) moor.

HAL-GEDRON, -GABORN,?goats'moor; (? *cen vron*, a hollow in the side of a hill, *w.*, *R.W.*).

HALGHLAND, *i.q.* HAGLAND.

HAL HAGAR, the ugly (*hagar*) moor.

HALIGLEY, *n.f.*, ? willow (*helig*) place (*le*); *or*, holy (*halig*) meadow, *t.*

HALITON, ? willow enclosure (*tun, s.*); *or*, moor by the hill (*dun*).

HALIVEN, ? smooth (*leven*) moor.

HALL, a mansion; *or*, *i.q.* HALE.

HALLABEER, ? moor farm (*bere, t.*).

HALLABEZACK, *i.q.* HALABESICK.

HALLAGATHER, ? milking (*gudra*), or further (*gwartha*) moor.

HALLAGENNA, ? ponds' (*lagennow*) moor; *or* moors' (*hallow*) mouth (*genau*); *or*, *i.q.* HALLEGAN.

HALLAMELLIN, mill (*melin*) moors.

HALLAMORE, ? great (*mawr*) moors; *or*, a reduplication.

HAL-LAN, -LAND, ? moor land, or enclosure (*lan*).

HALLAN PONDS, ? the moor (*hal*) by the (*a'n*) bridge (*pons*).

HALLANVRANE, the crow (*an bran*) moor.

HALL-AT, -ET, -OT, *n.f.*, *i.q.* ALLET; *or* = *haletta*, a hero, *s.*, *Lo.*

HALLAVIDEON, ? = hallow *gwydhion*, *w.*, wild moors.

HALLAZE, green (*las*) moor.

HALL DINNAS, castle (*dinas*) moor or hill (*hal*).

HALL DOWNS, moor downs.

HALLE, ?*i.q.* HALL; *or* moorplace (*le*).

HALLEAST, east (*est*) moor.

HALLEGAN, ? ? *i.q.* HELIGAN; *or* = *haligern*, a holy place, *s.*

HALLEGO, ? smith's (*gof*) moor.

HALLENBEAGLE, shepherd's *or* herdsman's (*bigel*) moor.

HALLENDUE, ? the (*an*) south (*deheu*) moor or hill.

HALLERDUBIN, ? ? little (*bian*) long (*hir*) black (*du*) moor.

HALL GOATH, goose or mole (*godh*), or old (*coth*) moor.

HALLIVEAR, the great (*meer*) moor.

HALLIVIT, ? LEUIUT'S moor.

HALLHISK, ? sedge (*hesc*) moor.

HALLIMORE, ?*i.q.* HALLAMORE.

HALLINGEY,*n.f.*,?moor by the house.

HALLKISK, ? mare's (*casec*) moor. (*Kisky*, the dry hollow stem of a plant, *m.c.*).

HALL MICHELL, Michell's moor.

HALLOON, down (*oon*), *or* Owen's moor.

HALLORICLE, ? ? merchants' (*harokel, ph.*), *or*, Hercules' (*Aercol*) moor.

HALLOVOWS, ? cows' (*beuch-es*) moor.

HALLOW, moors; *or* = *halow*, hills.

HALLOWAY, ? ? Llwy's (*w.*) moor; *or*, holy (*halig*) way (*weg*), *s.*

HALLOWELL, ? moor field (*gweal*), *or* well; *or*, = Holywell, *s.*

HALLOW HILL, ? moors' hill.

HALLREE, ? moor acre (*eru*).

HALLRICK, ? swan (*elerch*) moor.

HALLS, HALS, HALSE, ? = *als*, cliff, sea-shore; or, *alt*, a high place, *M'L.*

HALLTON, ? moor town.

HALLVELLAN, ? mill (*melin*) moor.

HALLWELL, ? *i.q.* HALLOWELL.

HALL-WIDDEN, -WYN, white (*gwyn*) moor.

HALLY VEAR, *i.q.* HALLIVEAR.

H. WOONE, down (*woon*) moor.

HALNOWETH, new (*nowydh*) moor.

HALROOT, red (*rudh*) moor.

HALSEACRE, *o.n.f.*, ? HALSE'S, or the cliff (*als*) field (*œcer, s.*).

HALSETOWN, HALSE'S town, (*c.d.* St. John).

HALSEY, *n.f.*, ? *i.q.* ÆLSIG.

HALSON, ? Halse's down (*oon*).

HALSTENNICK, tinny (*steanic*) moor.

HALTON, moor town, *T.*; hall town, *H.*; a green place (*ton*) near the water (*huel*), *Sc.*

HALTOWRACK, watery (*dourick*) moor (or sand, *M'L.*).

HALUIN, *s.B.m.*, hall friend, *t.*

HALURY, ? further (*gwarra*) moor.

HAL-VARRAS, -VERRAS, -WARRAS, ? top (*gwarhas*) moor.

HALVENNA, old moor, *Pr.*; ? lesser (*behenna*) moor.

HALVEOR, great (*mawr*) hill (*alt*), *M'L.*, or moor.

HALVERRICK, rich (*berric*) moor.

HAL-VOSSO, -VUSSO, the moor ditches (*fossow*), *Pr.*

HALWARTHA, higher moor.

HALWELL, ? *i.q.* HALLOWELL.

HAL-WHIDDEN, -WIDN, -WIN, -WYN, white (*gwyn, gwidn*) moor, *Pr.*; or, = *altwin*, the fair eminence, *M'L.*

HALWINNICK, marshy moor.

HALWOON, the downs moor, *Pr.*

HALWORTHY, ? *i.q.* HALWARTHA.

HALZAPHRON, *i.q.* ALSEPHRAN.

HAM, HAME, a home, a dwelling, *s.*; a town, a village, *Nord.*; a level pasture, or flat ground, *N.H.*, (? = *holm, R.N.W.*); or, ? *i.q.* HEM.

HAMAIL, *i.q.* AMAL.

HAMBALL, ? ? the near (*ham, s.*) round hill (*ball*), or pool (*pol*).

HAM-BLAND, -LAND, -BLEN, ? Hannibal's enclosure (*lan*).

HAM-BLEY, -LEY, ? Hannibal's pasture.

HAMELDON, *n.f.*, ? HAMAIL hill.

HAM-ELIN, -LIN, LYN, *t.d.d.*, ? = *Heimalin*, brought up or kept at home, *o.n., F.*

HAMETETHY, *d.d.* HAMOTEDI, ? ? = great (*ethic*), or EDDY'S HAMMET.

HAMHORN, ? the home or dwelling in the corner (*horn*), *t.*

HAMM-EL, -IL, *n.f.*, ? *i.q.* AMDLE; or Hannibal, grace of Baal, *i.e.* the lord, *ph.*

HAMM-ELL, -ILL, *n.f.*, ? *i.q.* HAMAIL.

HAMMER, *n.f.*, ? = *an meer*, the great.

HAMMET, *d.d.* HAMET, ? home or border gate (*yet*); or, little HAM.

HAMMETFORD, HAMMET passage.

HAMMOND, *n.f.*, ? *i.q.* Almund, hall protection, *t.*; home defender, *A.*

HAMOAZE, ? water (*uisg, ga.*) border (*hem*).*

HAMPT, ? *i.q.* HAMMET.

HAMPTON, ? near or home (*ham*), or border (*hem*), enclosure (*tun*), *t.*

HAMSTOKE, 9 *cent.*, home or border place (*stoc*).

HANBURY, ? old (*hen*) hill (*bre*) or earthwork (*bury, t.*).

HANCANNON, *n.f.*, ? ? the old ravine (*ceunant, w.*).

HANCOCK, *n.f.*, = *an coch*, the red.

---

* "HAMOSE, a safe commodious road for shipping, compounded of the words *ose* and *ham*, according to the nature of the place," *Car.* "The wet, oozy, habitation, circuit, or enclosure," *s., B.* From *amus*, protection, safety, *ga., Beal.* From the hamlets (*hamaux, f.*) that were formerly on its shores, *R.E.* Others have thought it to be of Phœnician origin.

HANCORNE, *n.f.*, one (*an*) horn (*corn*), or unicorn, *M.* ; ? the corner, *J.B.*

HANDALL, *i.q.* HENDOLE.

HANDER, *n.f.*, ? *i.q.* HENDRA.

HAND FIELD, ? dwelling-house (*an-nedh, w.*) field.

HANDS, *n.f.*, ? *i.q.* ENYS or ENIS.

HANGARRACK, *i.q.* ANGARRACK.

HANGER, ? the meadow, *t.* ; or, = *hen gaer*, old castle, *R.W.*

HANJAGUE, ? old (*hen*) James's ; or JAGO'S isle (*enys*).

HANKFORD, *n.f.*, ? narrow (*ænge, s.*), or horse (*hinge, s.*) ford.

HANKINS, *n.f.*, *diminutive of* Hengst.

HANNAFORE, *i.e.* Haven afore, or Forehaven, *Bond* ; = *annedh vawr*, great house, *w.*, *R.W.*

HANNAH'S MEADOW, ? lambs' (*eanes*) meadow.

HANNAM, *n.f.*, Hanne's (*t.*) home.

HANNE, *n.f.*, ? = *hana*, the cock, *s.*, *F.* ; or = Hannibal.

HANNET, ? old (*hen*) gate (*yet*).

HANNEY COOMBE, Hanne's, or, old close (*hay*) valley.

HANNIS HILL, ? lambs' (*eanes*) hill.

HANNON, the (*an*), or old (*hen*) stream (*non*), *M.* ; the valley (*nant*), *J.B.* ; ? old down (*oon*).

HANSON, *n.f.*, ? HANNE'S son.

HANTERGANTICK, half (*hunter*), *i.e.* noontide or midnight, singing (*cant*) place, *Pr.* ; old opening or cleft, *C.* ; half-hundredth, *R.W.*

HANTER-TAVAS, -DAVAS, half a tongue (*davas*), *Car.*

HANTERVATHEN, half the meadow (*bidhen*).

HAPENSTOCK, [field with] stone mounting-steps (*upping stock*), *t.*

HAR-COURT, -KET, ? = higher gate ; or, = *ar goed*, over the wood.

HARDING, *n.f.*, HARDY'S descendant (*ing, t.*).

HARDY, *n.f.*, a hero (*haddr*, a lock, a curl, *o.n.*), *F.*

HARDYCOT, *i.q.* HERDACOT.

HARE, ? = *hir*, long.

HAREWOOD, ? the lord's (*hearra, s.*), or, higher wood.

HARFOOT, *n.f.*, ? long (*hir*) ford.

HARHILL, ? battle (*heir*) hill.

HARLAKE, ? = *Harlech*, high (*hardh*) sloping stone (*llech*), *w.*, *R.W.*

HARLYN, = *ar lyn*, upon the water, or river, or pool, *Pr.*

HARN SCAUAN, ? elder-tree (*scauan*) corner (*horn*).

HARP-ER, -UR, *n.f.*, ? = *hearpere*, a harper, *s.*

HARRA VEAN, little field (*eru*).

HARRO-, HARROW-BEAR, the place of battle (*heirva*), *Pr.* ; ? arable farm (*bere, t.*).

HARROW BALL, ? mine (*bal*) field (*eru*) ; or, rough (*garw*) hill (*ball*).

HARRY, *n.f.*, ? *i.q.* ERA, or HARVEY.

II. FILACK, ? PHILLACK field (*eru*).

HARRY VEOR, great (*meer*) field.

HARSCOTT, ? cottage by the fence (*harz*) ; or, boundary wood (*coat*).

HARSHAGER, ? daisy (*egr*) hedge.

HARTLEY, *n.f.*, the stag pasture, *t.*

HARTSWELL, ? the stag's well, *t.*

HARVENNA, *T.a.*, *i.q.* HALVENNA.

HARVEY, *n.f.*, = *c'houerv*, bitter, *a.*, *Y*. ; or, *heirva*, battle field ; or, *heriwig*, army war, *t.*

HARVOSE, *i.q.* ARVOSE.

HARWARDE, *n.f.*, ? battle guard, *t.*

HARWICH, *T.a.*, arish, *i.e.* stubble (*arsc, s.*) [field].

HASLAM, *n.f.*, ? the *hazel* border (*hem*), or home (*ham*).

HASSELWOOD, *n.f.*, the hazel wood, *t.*

HASSONS MEADOW, ? asses (*asen-s*) meadow.

HATCH, a forest gate, *Lo.* ; or, flood gate ; or, half gate, *m.c.* ; or, *i.q.* HUTCH.

HATCHALL, ? *i.q.* HATCH MOOR (*hal*) ; or, house (*dzhi*) on the moor.

HATCH-ARD, -ED, -ET FIELD, ? *hutch* gate (*yet*) field.

HATCHMAN, *n.f.*, ? ? HATCH stone (*maen*).

HAT-HAM, -TAM, *n.f.*, ? heath home

(*ham*), *or* border (*hem*), *t.*
HATHFIELD, *i.q.* HEATHFIELD.
HATT, ? *i.q.* YATE.
HATWOOD, *i.q.* ATWOOD.
HAUK-EN, -IN, -YN, *n.f.*, ? little hawk.
HAULSEY, *n.f.*, ? dry (*sech*) moor (*hal*).
HAUNCH, ? lambs' (*eanes*) down (*oon*).
HAVARACK, HAVEROCK, HAVRECK,
    = *havrec*, the fallow, *a.*
HAVELAND, *n.f.*, ? summer (*haf*) en-
    closure (*lan*).
HAVELEY, *n.f.*, ? summer place (*le*).
HAVEN, ? *i.q.* HAY VEAN.
HAVET, = *havot*, summer hut, *w.*,
    R.W.
HAW DOWNS, *i.q.* HOW DOWNS.
HAWEIS, *n.f.*, ? *i.q.* HEWIS.
HAWKEN, *n.f.*, *i.q.* HAUKEN.
HAWKEY'S PRAISE, Hawkey's mead-
    ow (*pras*).
HAWORTH, *n.f.*, ? = *Hayward*, hedge
    or enclosure keeper, *t.*
HAWSTON, ? *i.q.* HURSTON; *or*, bramble
    (*hos*) hill (*dun*), *s.*
HAWTEBRIG, *Le.*, " *i.e.* high bridge ";
    now HORSEBRIDGE.
HAWTLYN, ? duck (*hoet*) pool (*lyn*).
HAY, HAYE, *i.q. haie, f., hage, s., cae,
    ce, k.*, a hedge, enclosure.
HAY ARISH, stubble (*ersc, s.*) close.
H. BYEWAY, ? close by the road.
H. CRAFT, ? croft close.
H. DITCH, ? rick (*dise, das, w.*) close.
HAYDON, ? hill (*dun*) close ; *or*, high
    (*heah*) hill, *s.*
HAYES, *n.f.*, ? = *haies*, enclosures, *f.*
HAYGRA, ? old woman's *or* witch's
    (*gwruch*) enclosure.
HAY LAKE PARK, ? ? willows (*helig*)
    close (*parc*).
H. LANE, close lane, *or* lane close.
HAYLE, river, *B.* ; salt water river,
    Pr. ; *or*, estuary, (*rather*, arm (*el*)
    of the sea), *Ped.* ; *or*, cliff *or* shore,
    M'L. ; = *hal*, a salt marsh, *O.*
HAYLE A MAENAU, the stones of the
    shore, rocks, *or* sands, *M'L.*
HAYLEBOATE ROCK, *i.q.* HALBOAT.
HAYLE DOWN, ? moor (*hal*) down.

HAYLED SHOP, shop covered with
    slate.
HAYLE KIMBRA, ? welshman's moor.
HAYLINNEY, shed *or lean-to* close
    (*hay*).
HAYMAN, *n.f.*, ? stone (*maen*) close ;
    or, i.q. HAWORTH, *or* HAMMOND.
HAYME, *n.f.*, house, home, *s.*
HAY MOWHAY, close (*hay*) by the
    rick (*mow*) yard (*hay*).
HAYNE, *n.f.*, ? = *hagen*, a hedge
    meadow ; *or, i.q.* HEAN.
HAYTISK, ? *i.q.* HAY DITCH.
HAY VEAN, little close.
HAYWELL, ? high (*hea*) well, *t.*
HAYWOOD, ? high wood, *t.*
HEA, *pr. and i.q.* HAY.
HEADON, *i.q.* HAYDON.
HEAL, ? *i.q.* HALL, *or* HAYLE.
HEALEZEY, *i.q.* HALEZY.
HEAME, *n.f.*, *i.q.* HAYME.
HEAN, *n.f.*, high ; poor, *s.* ; *or*, = *hen*,
    old, *w.*
HEARD, *n.f.*, hard ; a herd, *s.*
HEARDBURY, army (*here*) camp (*bury*),
    s., *M'L.* (*heord*, treasure, &c., *s.*).
HEARLE, *n.f.*, ? = *heorl*, an earl, *s.* ;
    or heir-le, battle place, *w.*
HEARM, *n.f.*, ? *from* ST. ERME.
HEARNE, *n.f.*, ? = *haiarn*, iron ; *or*,
    = Heron.
HEART, *n.f.*, ? *i.q.* HEARD.
HEAT, ? = *yet*, the gate.
HEATHAM, ? heath border (*hem*).
HEATHY PARK, close with heath.
HEATHY ROSE, ? moor with heath.
HEAVER, *eaver*-grass [field].
HEBB-ARD, -ERD, -ORD, *n.f.*, ? bright
    (*beohrt*) mind (*hige*), *s.*
HECHYNS, HEKENS, *n.f.*, ? *diminutive*
    of Richards.
HEDGEALLACK, ? lower (*wallach*)
    house (*dzhi*) [field].
HEDGER, ? *i.q.* PARK CADJAW.
HEDNESS, ? *i.q.* ENYS, *or* ENIS.
HEEDON, *i.q.* HAYDON.
HEGLOSENUD-ER, *d.d.*, -A, *e.d.d.*, ST.
    ENODER church (*eglos*) [land].
HEGROW, ? hovel (*crow*) close (*hay*).

HEIL, *n.f.*, *i.q.* HEAL.

HEINE, *n.f.*, *i.q.* HEAN.

HEIN-ES, -S, *n.f.*, ? *i.q.* ENYS, *or* ENIS.

HELA, *d.d.*, ? *i.q.* HALL.

HELAKA, ? willow (*helig*) close (*hay*).

HELANCLASE, *v.* THE GREEN HALL; *i.q.* ELLANGLASE.

HELANGOVE, the smith's (*an gof*) river, *Pr.*, *or* moor (*hal*).

HELB-ORN, -REN, *n.f.*, ? *i.q.* HAL BROWN, *or* HALGEBRON.

HELCHLADE ? moor (*hal*) bottom (*slade*, *t.*).

HELCOOSE, river wood (*cus*), *Pr.*; rather woody river, *J.B.*; ? moor (*hal*) by the wood.

HELDRICUS, *t.d.d.*, battle (*hild*, *s.*) rule, *or* power (*rice*, *s.*).

HELE, *n.f.*, ? *i.q.* HAYLE, *or* HALL.

HELEN MOOR, ? the great (*an mawr*) moor (*hal*).

HELFORD, *o.* HAYLEFORD, river passage (*fordh*), *Pr.*; road over the sea-shore (*hayle*), *M'L.*; the concealed (*hel*) arm of the sea (*fjord*), *o.n.*, *C.G.B.R.*

HELI, *d.d.*, ? moor enclosure (*hay*).

HELIGAN, the place of the willows (*helig*), *Pr.*; *or*, holy (*hœlig*, *s.*) place (*ern*, *s.*); *or*, the legate's hall (*hel*), *H.*; hall on the downs (*goon*), *T.*; *or*, *i.q.* HELLAGAN.

HELING, *o.n.f.*, ? hall meadow (*ing*), *t.*

HELLACANOE, ? *i.q.* HALLAGENNA.

HELLADON, ? moors' (*hallow*) hill (*dun*).

HELLAG-AN, -ENNA, -ON, HELLEGAN, ? *i.q.* HELIGAN, *or* HALLAGENNA.

HELLAN, = *ellan*, the elms, *Pr.* (?); judicature, pretorium, tabernacle, *H.*; ? *i.q.* HALLAN.

HELLAND, *d.d.*, HENLAND, ? old (*hen*) enclosure (*lan*); Helen's land, (*p.s.* St. Helena, *O.*), *T.*; hall (*hel*) temple *or* church (*lan*), *H.*; ? *i.q.* HALLAN.

HELLANGEAR, ? moor by the (*a'n*) castle (*caer*).

HELLANOWETH, new (*nowedh*) elms, *Pr.*; ? the (*an*) new hall (*hel*).

HELLAS, green (*laz*) hall, *Car.*, ? *or* moor.

HELLAS CROFT, green moor croft.

HELLER, HELLYER, *n.f.*, a slater, thatcher, *t.*, *Lo.*; a hunter, *Pr.*

HELLESBURY, earthwork (*bury*, *s.*) on the broad (*les*) moor (*hal*), *or* by the old (*hen*) court (*les*); ? *from haul*, *hayl*, the sun, *M'L.*

HELLESET, ? broad moo gate (*yet*).

HELLESLAND, ? broad moor enclosure (*lan*).

HELLESVEAN, ? little broad moor.

HELLET, *n.f.*, moor gate (*yet*).

HELLISVEOR, the great shore *or* cliff (*als*), *M'L.* ? great broad moor.

HELLMOUTH, ? river (*hayl*) mouth.

HELLNOWETH, *i.q.* HELLANOWETH.

HELLON-WARTHA *and* -WOLES, ? higher *and* lower enclosure (*lan*) on the moor (*hal*).

HELLOW, ? the moors (*hallow*).

HELLWIN, ? white moor *or* hall.

HELMAN, stream *or* river stone, *C.*; ? moor by the stone (*maen*).

HELMINTOR, moor stone hill, *Pr.*; the tor on the stone downs, *C.*

HELSCOT, ? broad (*les*) moor (*hal*); *or*, Ella's cottage.

HELSON, *n.f.*, ? *i.q.* HELSTON.

HELSTON, hill (*dun*) by the green (*glas*) moor (*hal*), *Pr.*; town on the marsh, *D.G.*; town on the green river (*hayl*), *B.*; Ella's town, *Po.*; *d.d.* HENLISTONE, old court town, *Ped.*; (*p.s.* St. Michael).

HELW-IDDEN, -YDDEN, *i.q.* HELLWIN.

HELYGRAVE, holy (*hœlig*) grove, *s.*

HEM, ? a border, limit, boundary, *s.*; *or*, *i.q.* HAM.

HEM-BALL, -BLE, ? old (*hen*) pool (*pol*); *or*, round-hill (*bull*) HEM.

HEMGATE, ? border by the gate (*yet*); *or*, wood (*coat*) border.

HEMLET, ? little boundary.

HEMLEY, *n.f.*, *i.q.* HAMLEY.

HEMMICK, ? little (-*ig*) border.

HEM PARK, ? border close.

HEMPEL, *n.f.*, ? *i.q.* Hannibal.

HEMPEY, ? hemp close (*hay*).

HEMPLING, ? old (*hen*) pond (*pullan*).

HENADA, the old (*hen*) good (*da*), or God's (*du*) place, *Beal.*

HENAFRETH, ? the old hedge or thorn (*freth, Pr.*).

HENCENETHEL, *f.s.B.m.* ? encinethel, a giant.

HENCHMAN, ?? *i.q.* ENESMANEN.

HEND-AR, -ER, *n.f.*, old oak (*dar*), *R.W.* ; or, *i.q.* HENDRA.

HEN-DARSIKE, -DERSICK, -DRESICK, the old (*hen*) corn (*izick*) land (*dar*), *T.C.* ; or, old dry (*sech*) oak (*dur*).

HENDEERN, *s.B.m.*, ?old oak (*derwen*).

HENDIN, *n.f.*, ? old castle (*din*), *R.W.*

HENDOLE, ? old valley (*dol*).

HENDORA, ? the old lands (*doarou*).

HENDOWER, *n.f.*, old water (*dour*); or, = hen dwr, old tower, *w., R.W.*

HENDRA, the old town (*tre*), *Pr.*, or homestead.

H. BURNICK, old town well (*burne, s.*), *Pr.* ; ? old homestead in the rushy place (*bruinic*).

H. CHAPLE, Chapel HENDRA.

H. GOTH, HENDRA by the wood (*coet*), *M'L.* ; or, old wood-house.

H. PAUL, -POL, HENDRA by the pool or pit; or Paul's or pool HENDRA.

H. VEAN, little (*bian*) HENDRA.

H. VENNA, ?lesser (*behenna*) HENDRA.

H. VOSSAN, old town entrenchment, *Pr.* ; old house by the ditch or fortification, *T.C.*

H. WETHER, ? higher (*wartha*) HEN-DRA.

H. WINNICK, ? marshy HENDRA.

HENDRAWNA, ? HENDRA on the downs (*oonou*).

HENDR-E, -Y, *i.q.* HENDRA.

HENDRETHEN, bird's (*edhen*), or furze (*eithen*) HENDRA.

HENDROU, ? *i.q.* HENDORA.

HENDY, *n.f.*, old house (*ty*), *C.*

HENEWARR, old fortification (*gwarth, B.*).

HENFORD, the old road (*fordh*) or ford.

HEN-GER, -GOR, the old meadow (*garth*), *C.*, or castle (*caer*), or marsh (*cors*).

HENGIST, *s.* king, a horse, *frisian, F.*

HEN-JAK, -JAGUE, *i.q.* HANJAGUE.

HENKASTEL, the old castle.

HENLAND, ?poor (*hean*) land, *t.* ; or old enclosure (*lan*).

HENLISTONE, *d.d.*, ? *i.q.* HELSTON.

HENNACLEEVE CLIFF, ? the old cliff (*reduplicated*); or, = s. henge-clif, hanging cliff.

HENNAH, old enclosure (*hay*).

HENNAN, old valley (*nance*).

HENNAS VEAN, ? little ENIS.

HENN-ER, -OR, *n.f.*, ? *i.q.* ANNEAR.

HENNESSEYS, ? Enys's [farm].

HENNIES GROUND, ENIS's land.

HENN-OT, -ET, ? old gate (*yet*).

HENPOINT, *i.q.* THE HEN (*henna, s.*) point.

HENRY, ? = hen eru, old field.

HENSBURROW, old (*hen*) barrow, *C.* ; ? Oenus's (*king*) barrow.

HENSCARTH, ? old boat (*scath*).

HENSDON, ? shrovetide (*enes*), or ENIS hill (*dun*).

HENSHA, ? heron's wood (*shaw*), *t.*

HENSLOW, *i.q.* HENSBARROW.

HENTER-GANTICK, *i.q.* HANTER-.

H. VEAN, *i.q.* HENDRAVEAN.

HEN-VAR, -VER, -VOR, the old road (*for*).

HENVOR GELLIE, old road grove (*celli*).

HENWELL, ? the old (*hen*) well.

HENWOOD, ? the old wood.

HEPPENSTONE, *i.q.* HAPENSTOCK.

HEP-PLE, -WELL, ? the old (*hen*) pool (*pol*).

HERDACOT, ? the herdsman's cottage.

HERLAND, ?long (*hir*) enclosure (*lan*) ; or, the earl's (*yerl*), or higher land.

HERLE, *n.f.*, *i.q.* HEARLE.

HERLES, pillar of Hercules, *Sc.*

HERMAN, *n.f.*, a German deity, *Lo.* ; army man, or, public, *t., Y.* ; here-man, a soldier, *s.*

HER-NAN, -NANCE, *n.f.*, ? long (*hir*) vale (*nance*).

HERNE CROFT, ? *heron* croft, *R.W.*
HERNEST, ? east (*est*) corner (*horn*).
HEROD'S FOOT, *foot* or bottom of the higher wood, *Gl.* (*c.d.* All Saints).
HEROD'S HEAD, *i.q.* PENHEROTS.
HERSHAM, HESAM, ? the wood (*hurst*) home (*ham*), *s.*
HERSPOOL, ? horse or wood pool.
HERWOOD, ? *i.q.* HAREWOOD.
HESATOR, ? lower (*isu*) field (*doar*), or, water (*dour*), or, peak (*tor*).
HESK-IN, -YN, = *hescen*, a rush, sedge.
HESSAFORD, ? Essa's, or lower ford or road (*fordh*).
HESSENFORD, ? Isan's (*w.*), or ox (*udzheon*) ford ; (*c.d.* St. Anne).
HEUSCOTT, *n.f.*, ? enclosure (*hay*) below the wood (*is coed*).
HEW, ? upper (*yew*) [field].
HEWAS, owls, *C.* ; ? the outside (*ves*) close (*hay*) ; or, *i.q.* HIWIS.
HEWES EN FENNON, ? hide of land (*hiwisc*) by the spring (*fynnon, w.*).
HEWETT, *n.f.*, *dim.* of Hugh, *Lo.*
HEXT, *n.f.*, = *hexta*, highest, *s.*, *Lo.*
HEXWORTHY, sedge (*hesc*) farm.
HEY, *i.q.* HAY.
HEYDAH, *i.q.* HAYDA.
HEYDON, *i.q.* HAYDON.
HEYES, *n.f.*, ? *i.q.* HEWAS, or HEWES.
HEYLE BAY, ? estuary bay.
HEYLE LANE, water lane, *T.C.*
HEYME, *n.f.*, *i.q.* HAYME.
HEYMOOR, ? great (*mawr*) enclosure (*hay*) ; or, high moor, *t.*
HICK, *n.f.*, = ISAAC, *B.m.*
HICKENS, HIGGENS, *n.f.*, ? = *igans*, twenty ; or, *i.q.* RICHARDS.
HICKS, HIGGS, = *Hick's* son.
HIDDERLEY, *n.f.*, ? hither or nearer pasture, *t.*
HIGHAM, *n.f.*, high home, or border (*hem*).
HIGH-ELL, -HALE, -HALL, high moor (*hal*) ; or, high (*uhel*) close (*hay*).
HIGHGATE, = *Higgeat*, the high gate, *s.*
HIGHWAY, = *Higweg*, the high road, *s.*
HILCOOSE, *i.q.* HELCOOSE.
HILL, ? *i.q.* HALL, or HALE.

HILL BALL, ? ? moor field (*ball*).
HILLHAY, hill or moor close.
HILMAN, *n.f.*, *i.q.* HAILMEN.
HILSTICK, narrow slip (*stycce, s.*) by the moor (*hal*), or on the hill.
HILTON, ? *i.q.* HILLHAY.
HINDRA, *T.a.*, *i.q.* HENDRA.
HINGEY, ? old (*hen*) house (*chy*).
HINGHAM, ? Inge's (*o.n.*) home, *t.*
HINGON, ? old down (*goon*) ; or = *hengen*, a prison, *s.*
HINGSTON DOWN, = *Hengestes dun*, Hengest's down, *s.* ; or, horse (*henges, s.*) hill (*dun*).
HIPPISLEY, *n.f.*, pasture of the heap (*hype, s.*).
HITCHAM, *n.f.*, ? Richard's home.
HITCHIN, *n.f.*, *dim.* of Richard.
HITHER BROW, ? near summit, *t.*
HIWIS, *n.f.*, *hiwisc*, a family property, a hide of land, *s.*
HOAR ROCK, ? the grey rock, *t.*
HOBB-A, -AH, *n.f.*, ? = Robert.
HOBBACOTT, Hobba's cottage.
HOBLEY, ? Bob's pasture.
HOBL-IN, -YN, ? = *O'Belin*, descendant of a king, *i.*
HOCK, *n.f.*, ? = *hoch*, high ; or, *hog*, prudent, *s.* ; or, *i.q.* Hawke.
HOCKADAY, *n.f.*, fifteenth day after Easter, *Lo.*
HOCKBRIDGE, *n.f.*, high bridge.
HOCKER, *n.f.*, ? = *Hawker.*
HOCK-IN, -ING, -EN, *n.f.*, ? = Hoking, descendant of Hoce, *t.* ; or, *i.q.* HAWKEN ; or, *dim.* of HOCK.
HOCKMORE, *n.f.*, ? high or oak moor, *t.*
HODDY, *n.f.*, ? *i.q.* HUDDY ; or EDY ; or, = *odr*, a dart, *o.n.*
HODGE, *n.f.*, ? *i.q.* ODGER, or Roger.
HOE POINT, ? heel-shaped (*ho, s.*), or, high (*hoch*) promontory.
HOGG, *n.f.*, ? = *hog*, a little lad, *w.* ; or, *i.q.* HOCK.
HOISWELL, *n.f.*, ? duck (*haws*) well.
HOIT, *n.f.*, ? = *hoet*, duck.
HOLBOAT, *i.q.* HALBOAT.
HOL-COMBE, -LACOMBE, ? hollow or holy vale, *s.* ; or, *i.q.* GULLACOMBE.

HOLD, HOLT, *n.f.*, a grove, wood, *s.*

HOLD-EN, -IN, *n.f.*, ?= *holthana*, a woodcock, *s.*

HOLDRAN, *i.q.* ALDREN.

HOLE, a hollow; *or*, *i.q.* HALL.

HOLERODE, ? holy rood *or* cross, *t.*

HOLL-ABEER, -OBER, ? the farm (*bere*) in the hollow *or* combe, *t.*

HOLLAMOUR, ? the great (*mawr*) moors (*hallow*).

HOLLAN, ? moor (*hal*) enclosure (*lan*).

HOLLOWAY, ? *i.q.* HALLOWAY.

HOLLOW PARK, ? moors' (*hallow*) close.

HOLMAN, *n.f.*, ? the stone (*maen*) moor (*hal*); *or*, = *alman*, german, *t.*

HOLM-, HOME-BUSH, holly bush.

HOLTON, ? hill (*hal*) enclosure.

HOLVEAR, the great (*meer*) hollow, *N.*

HOLWELL, ? holy *or* moor (*hal*) well.

HOMEGUNLAZE, the near GOONLAZE.

H. MEAD, the near meadow.

H. PARK, the near close (*parc*).

HOMER BUTTS FIELD, nearer archery field.

H. CEGARS, nearer hemlock (*cegas*) [field].

H. CREASE, nearer middle (*cres*) field.

H. DUNGEY, nearer [field] under the house (*dan chy*).

H. *and* YONDER GEW, nearer *and* further GEW.

H. HAM, ? nearer boundary.

H. MENA PARK, nearer stony (*maenic*) close (*parc*).

H. NARE, -NEAR, ? the (*an*) nearer long (*hir*) [field].

H. PARK BOWEN, ? nearer beef *or* ox (*boen*) close.

H. SHOOTE PARK, nearer water-spout (*shoot, m.c.*) close.

H. SLADE, nearer valley.

H. VENTON VARE, nearer great (*meer*) spring (*fenten*).

H. WAY FIELD, nearer path field.

H. WEETH, ? nearer waste (*gwydd, v.*), *or* field (*gwaeth, B.*).

H. WELL, nearer *well or* field (*gweal*).

HOM PARK, *i.q.* HOME PARK.

HONEY, HONY, *n.f.*, ? = Hannibal.

H. BAG, ? Honey's close (*parc*).

H. COOMBE, ? Honey's, *or* the down (*oon*), vale.

H. MAN, *n.f.*, ? = *Hunimund*, Hunu's protection (*mund*), *t.*, *F.*

H. VEIN, ? little (*vean*) down (*oon*).

HONYTON, Hony's enclosure (*tun*).

HOO, *n.f.*, ? = *ho*, a heel, *s.*; *or*, *hou*, a mountain, hill, *s.*

HOOD GROUND, ? woodland, *t.*

HOOECLIFF, ? hollow (*cau, w.*) cliff.

HOOK, *n.f.*, ? = *huc*, a cloak; *or*, *ogo*, a cave.

HOOKER, *n.f.*, ? = *achor*, small, slender; *or*, *achwr*, a herald, *w.*

HOOK PARK, close with crooked hedge; (*hoc*, a hook, *s.*).

HOOPER, *n.f.*, ? = *hoppere*, a dancer, *s.*

THE HOOTH, ? the waste (*gwydd, w.*); *or*, the bare, naked (*hoeth, w.*) place.

HOPKYN, *n.f.*, *dim.* of Robert.

HOP PARK, ? *hop* close (*parc*).

HOPPY, hop close (*hay*).

HOPSLAND, ? Hobbs' land.

HORAPARK, ram's (*hor*), *or*, further (*warra*), close (*parc*).

HORE, *n.f.*, ? = *hor*, a ram; *or*, *hoar*, a sister.

HORESTONE, ? boundary (*harz*) stone.

HORGUE, ? ram's (*hor*) GEW.

HORN, *n.f.*, ? = *corn*, a horn, a trumpet, a corner.

HORNABROOK, *n.f.*, ? corner by the brook.

HORN-ACOT, -INGCOT, *d.d.* -IECOTE, the iron (*haiarn*) cot *or* house, *H.*

HORNAWIG, a poor bit of a place, fit only for plovers (*hornywinks*), *B.M.*

HORNCASTLE, ? corner *or* iron castle.

HORNER, ? long (*hir*) corner.

HORNINGTOPS, prayer (*urnaige, ga.*) summits, *Beal.*

HORNIWINKS, plovers (*in the east*), slugs (*in the west*).

HORN PARK, corner close.

HORRAPOOL, further (*warra*) pool.

HORR-AS, -IS, ? boundary (*harz*), or
horse [field].

HORREL, ? further hill; *or*, ram's
(*hor*) moor (*hal*).

HORSCOTT, ? cottage by the fence
(*harz*).

HORSE BEAN, ? little (*bian*) horse, *or*
boundary [field].

H. BRIDGE, ? Horsa's (*s.*) bridge, *Dr.*

H. HAYES, ? boundary closes.

H. PARK, ? horse *or* boundary close.

H. PEN, ? pinfold at the boundary.

HORSEY, *n.f.*, HORSNA PARK, ? horse
or boundary close (*hay, parc*).

HORSON, ? Horsa's *or* the horse down
(*oon*).

HORTON, *n.f.*, ? ram's (*hor*) hill (*dun*);
or, herb (*ort = wort*) garden (*tun*), *t.*

HOSGET CROFT, ? hogshead *or* horse-
gate croft, *t.*

HOSKIN, -YN, *n.f.*, ? = *hescen*, a sedge,
bulrush; *or, from asc*, the ash, *s.*

HOT POINT, ? *from odd*, a point, *d.*

HOTT-AN, -EN, *n.f.*, ? *i.q.* HOWTON,
or HOLTON, *or* HOLDEN.

HOULSON, *n.f.*, ? Howel's son.

HOUNDAPIT, ? dog's hole, *t.*

HOUSEAL, *n.f.*, ? = *husol*, an attendant
on a priest at the sacrament, *s.*

HOUSE AN GWIDDEN, ? the (*an*) white
(*gwidn*) house, *or*, by the tree
(*gwedhen*),

HOUSE IN CREEG, ? house by the
mound (*creeg*), or rock (*careg*).

HOUSE PARK, house close (*parc*).

HOUSEY, ? *house* close (*hay*).

HOWE, *n.f.*, ? *i.q.* HOO.

HOWEL, *n.f.*, = *Hywel*, conspicuous,
one that doth not hide himself, *T.R.*

HOWSE, *n.f.*, THE HOWES, ? *i.q.*
HUISH; *or*, the house.

HOWTON, ? hill *or* tumulus enclosure (*tun*), *t.*

HUBBER, *n.f.*, ? *i.q.* HEBBARD.

HUDDY, *n.f.*, ? = *hudig*, cautious, *s.*

HUEAL GOOTH, ? old (*coth*) *or* wood
(*coat*) field (*gweal*) *or* mine (*huel*).

HUEL A GUIDDEN, white (*gwidn*), *or*
tree (*gwedhen*) field (*gweal*).

HUEL AN BRUSH, the (*an*) great
(*broaz*) mine (*huel*); *or*, the field
(*gweal*) of judgment (*brys*), *T.C.*

H. AN CREEK, ? the mound (*creeg*),
or rock (*carrag*), field *or* work.

H. AN DREAN, the thorn (*draen*)
field *or* work.

H. AN GROUSE, the cross (*crous*)
field *or* work.

H. ANOUTH, the new (*nowydh*) mine.

H. AN POOL, ? the pit (*pol*) field.

H. AN TEAL, the manure (*teil*) field.

H. AN TEESE, the stack (*dise, B.*)
field.

H. AN TUTMES, ? Thomas's field.

H. AN YET, *i.q.* GWEAL YATE.

H. BAL, ? mine (*bal*) field (*gweal*).

H. BOYS, ? bush (*bos*) mine.

H. BUDNICK, ? bunchy (*bothanic, B.*)
mine *or* work.

H. -BUSSA, -BUSY, ? the *busy* work;
(*bussa*, an earthen pot).

H. CARNE, Carne's *or* CARN mine.

H. CHANE, ? *i.q.* WHEAL JANE; *or*,
jews' (*edzhewon*) mine.

H. CHELLEY, ? lower (*isella*) field.

H. CLEATH, ? trench (*cledh*) field.

H. CRAGE, ? *i.q.* HUEL AN CREEK.

H. CROFTY, ? croft close (*hay*) mine.

H. CULLIACK, ? cock (*celioc*) mine.

H. DANCE, ? DINAS field *or* work.

H. FAT, ? fat *or* rich work.

H. -GALLISH, -GALLOWS, ? clay slate
(*killas*), *or* hard (*cales*) mine; *or*,
i.q. GWEAL GOLLIS.

H. GANICK, ? ? mine full of cracks
(*agenoc*).

H. GEAR, *i.q.* WHEAL GEER.

H. GOAZ, goose (*gouz*), *or* blood
(*gudzh*) field; *or*, wood (*cuz*) mine.

H. -HOWLA, -OWLA, ? elm (*ula*), *or*
lower (*wolla*), field *or* mine.

H. JOULE, ? the devil's (*jowl*) mine.

H. LAITY, ? milk-house (*lait ty*), *i.e.*
dairy, *or* LAITY'S field.

H. LEATH, = *gweal heyth*, heath field.

H. LEENON, ? nettle (*linhaden*) field.

H. MALKIN, ? rag-mop (*malkin*) work
or mine.

HUEL MENOR, ? long-stone (*menhir*) field *or* work.

H. NOWETH, new (*nowydh*), or bare (*noeth*) field *or* work.

H. OAK, ? oak, *or* empty (*gwag*), field.

H. OATH, *i.q.* HUEL ANOUTH.

H. OWLD, the old, *or* cliff (*allt*, *w.*) mine.

H. OWLS, cliff (*als*) mine.

H. PEEVER, *i.q.* WHEAL PEEBER.

H. REETH, red (*rydh*) work *or* field.

H. SEAREG, ? clot-bur (*serchog*) field *or* work.

H. SHUTT, work *or* field by the water-spout (*shoot*, *m.c.*).

H. SPARABLE, ? hob-nail mine.

H. SPEATH, ? work *or* field below (*is*) the draw-well (*peeth*).

H. STEAN, tin mine.

H. STERRAN, star (*steren*) mine.

H. TOWAN, ? sand-hill mine.

H. TYE, work by the house (*ty*).

H. VERRA, ? bragging mine (*guerha*, to brag, *B.*).

H. VLEW, *i.q.* WHEAL VLOW.

H. VOR, great (*maur*) work *or* mine.

H. VOTTLE, ? bottle mine ; *or*, *buddle* work.

H. WIDDEN, white (*gwydn*), or little (*vidn = vean*) work *or* field.

H. ZAUNDERS, Saunders's mine.

H. ZION, ? *i.q.* HUEL JANE.

HUGH PARK, ? ewe, *or* high (*uch*) close.

HUGHTOWN, town near the height.

HUGOE, *n.f.*, from *hugr*, thought, *o.n.*, Y.

HU-GOOSE, -GAS, -GUS, high (*uch*) wood (*cus*), *R.IV.*

HUISH, HYWIS, *n.f.*, *i.q.* HIWIS.

HULKER, ? camp (*caer*) moor (*hal*).

HUMBLEIGH, ? *Hannibal's* pasture, *t.*

HUMPY, field (*hay*) full of hillocks, *Jo.C.*

HUNA, *s.B.m.*, the Hun *or* giant, *t.*, *F.* ; *also = oonou*, the downs.

HUNCH, HUNDS, ? *i.q.* ENIS.

HUNFRIDUS, *t.d.d.*, giant *or* hound of peace, *t.*, *F.* ; *or* = Humfrey, support of peace, Y.

HUNK-IN, -YNG, *n.f.*, *dim. of* Humphrey, Lo.

HUNN, *n.f.*, ? *i.q.* HUNA.

HUNTER, ? *i.q.* HANTER, the half.

HUON, ? = *gwon*, a down.

HUR-DEN, -DON, long (*hir*) hill (*dun*).

HURDLE, ? higher dale.

HURLAND, ? higher land.

HURLERS, *from* ur, fire and light, *and*, lar, the hearth, *ga.*, Beal ; *rather*, *from* the game of hurling, R.H.

HURLEY, ? long (*hir*) pasture.

HURREL, ? higher hill *or* moor (*hal*).

HURRYGUTTER, ? *gutter* field (*eru*).

HURS-, HUS-TON, wood (*hurst*) town, *s.* ; *or*, boundary (*harz*) hill (*dun*).

HURTY FIELD, ? wortleberry field, *t.*

HUSSEY, *n.f.*, = *Houssaie, from houx,* a holly, *f.*

HUSTLE FIELD, ? low (*isal*) field.

HUSTLER, ? *n.f.*, innkeeper (*hosteler*, *o.e.*).

HUSTYN, wood (*hurst*) town (*tun*), *t.*

HUTCHINGS, *n.f.*, ? *i.q.* HITCHINS.

HUTCH MEADOW, the meadow with a HATCH gate, a coop for animals, *or* a trough.

HUTHNANCE, ? the valley (*nance*), or lambs' (*an eanes*) HOOTH.

HUTT, ? = wood ; *or*, *i.q.* HOOTH.

HUXHAM, *n.f.*, ? sedge (*hesk*), or ox pasture (*holm*, *t.*) or border (*hem*).

HYDE, *n.f.*, ? = *hyd*, a family possession, a hide of land, *s.*

HYDE PARK, ? ? skin (*hyd*, *s.*) close.

HYM-AN, -EN, *n.f.*, ? stone (*maen*) close (*hay*).

HYSICOT, ? *i.q.* ISACOT.

HYSTON, the high stone, *H.M.IV.*

HYTHANCER, ? long (*hir*) furze (*eithen*) [field].

HYTHENS, ? furze [field]s.

I AGO, *n.f.*, *i.q.* JAGO.

IARNWALLON, *s.Bm.*, ? iron (*haiarn*) heart (*wholon = colon*).

IBBOTT, *n.f.*, ? *i.q.* HEBBARD.

ICCOMB-WARTHA, & -WOLLAS, ? higher (*wartha*) and lower (*wollas*) oak (*œc, s.*), or Isaac's (*Ike*) vale (*cum*).

ICTIN, *Diodorus Siculus*, tin (*ph.* ?) port, *R.E.* ; bay (*gwic*) hill (*din*), *J.B.* ; little (*in*) [abode] of hospitable (*icht*) and good-natured people, *Beal.*

IDDY, *n.f.,* ? = *hydig,* heedful, cautious, *s.*

IDELESS, EDELES, the narrow (*idn*) breadth (*les*), *H.* ; *d.d.* EDELET.

IESU, *s.B.m.,* ? = Jesus.

ILBERT, *n.f.,* ? = *Hildebert,* battle bright, *t.,* Y.

ILCOMBE, evil vale, *Nord.* ; ? willow (*helig*) vale.

ILIFF, *n.f.,* ? = *Eylif,* eternal, *t.,* F.

ILLAND, ? hill or moor (*hal*) land.

ILLCUM, *f.s.B.m.,* ill favoured, *t.,* F.

ILLMEADOW, ? hill meadow.

ILLMOUTH, ? *i.q.* HALLACANOE, moors' mouth or opening.

ILLOGAN, *from p.s.* St. Illoganus, *O.* ; = *lug gan,* white tower, *or, lug gun,* tower on the downs, *or, lug dun,* tower hill, *Pr.*

ILLWILL, ? well (*wyl, s.*) hill.

ILMSWORTHY, ? elm farm (*weorthig, s.*).

INCE, an island, *Sc.* ; a peninsula, *Pr.* ; *i.q.* ENYS.

INCEWORTH, = *ines wartha,* the island above, *or* the higher island, *Sc.* ; the high (*warth*) peninsula, *Pr.*

INCH, *n.f., i.q.* ENYS.

INCLEDON, *n.f.,* ? angle (*engel, s.*) of the hill (*dun*).

INDEAN, *n.f., i.q.* ENDEAN.

INDES MEADOW, ? HENDY'S meadow.

INGLES, *n.f.,* english.

INGRAM, *n.f.,* Ing's raven, *t.,* Y.

IN-IS, -NES, -NIS, *i.q.* ENIS.

INISCAW, *Le.,* isle (*enys*) of elder trees (*scaw*) ; *now* TRESCO.

INISPRIVEN, *Le.,* rabbit (*priven*) isle, *R.W.* ; *or,* isle of rushes (*brwyn, w.*).

INISVEAN, little (*bihan*) island.

INKPEN, *n.f.,* ? Inge's fold ; *or,* meadow (*ing, s.*) by the pen, *t.*

INNEY, the little river (*avon*), *I.T.*

INNEYFOOT, the lower part of the river Inney.

INNISVOULS, ? sickle (*fowls*)-shaped, *or* deceitful (*fouls*) isle.

INNISVRANK, the french *or* free (*franc*) isle.

INNIS SARWARTH, ? Edward's (*Jorwarth, w.*) isle ; *or, i.q.* INISWORTH.

INOR, *i.q.* ENNOR, ? *from* St. Eneour, *or* Enemour, *a.*

INSIDGEN, ? ox (*udzheon*) isle.

INSWORK, INTS- *or* INIS-WORTH, *i.q.* INCEWORTH.

INTS, *i.q.* ENYS.

IOHANN, *s.B.m., i.q.* John, grace of Jehovah, *h.*

IONS FIELD, ? = John *or* Joan's field.

IOSA, *B.m.,* ? raised, *h.*

IOSEP, *s.B.m.,* he will add, *h.*

IRELAND, *T.a.,* ? = higher land ; *or,* long (*hir*) enclosure (*lan*).

IRISHES, ? arish *or* stubble (*arsc, s.*) [field]s.

IRISHMAN'S HILL, ? HRESMEN'S (*B.m.*) hill.

ISAAC, *messe preost, w.B.m.,* and *n.f.,* laughter, *h.*

ISA-, ISSA-COT, the lower (*isa*) wood (*coat*), *Pr.*

ISBELL, *n.f.,* ? under (*is*) the pool (*pol*).

IUSTUS, *B.m.,* the just, *lat.*

IVY, ? ? small (*bich*), *or* water (*wy*) enclosure (*hay*).

IZZET PARK, ? ? lower (*isa*) gate (*yet*), *or* Z-shaped close (*parc*).

JACK, JACK-A, -ET, *n.f.,* ? *i.q.* JAGO, *or* JACKMAN.

JACKEY DAW, jackdaw [field].

JACKMAN, *n.f.,* ? *from jaeger,* a hunter, *d.,* F.

JACKYS PARK, ? snail (*janjeaks*) close.

JACKYS ROCK, ? jackdaws' rock.

JACOBSTOW, Jacobus, *i.e.* St. James's (*p.s., O.*) place (*stow*).

JAGO, king, *B.C.,* and *n.f.,* strong (*iach*) spear (*gwayw*), *F.W.P.J.* ; *or,*

T

i.q. Jacobus, James, (*w.*, *Iago*).

JAHAN, JANE, JANNE, *n.f.*, ?= *Jean*, John, *f.*

JARVIS, *n.f.*, spear (*ger*) eagerness (*fus*), *t.*, *Y.*

JAUL, JAULF, *t.d.d.*, ? rich (*ead*) wolf (*ulf*), *t.*

JEFFER-Y, -IES, *n.f.*, *from Godfried*, God's peace, *t.*

JENK-IN, -YN, JENNINGS, *n.f.*, *dim.* of John *and* JOHNS.

JERVEYS, *n.f.*, *i.q.* JARVIS.

JET, = gate (*yet*) [close].

JETWELL, the jetting well, *T.C.* ; *or*, ? well by the gate.

JEW, *n.f.*, ?= le *Jeu*, the Jew, *f.*

JEWELANDREA, *i.q.* GWEALAN DREA.

JEWELL, *n.f.*, ? *i.q.* JOLL.

JOEL, *n.f.*, ? strong willed, *h.*

JOHNS, JONES, JONAS (?), *n.f.*, = John's son.

JOICE, JOYCE, *n.f.*, sportive, *lat.*, *Y.*

JOLIFFE, JOLLY, JULIFF, *n.f.*, = *jolif*, fine, trim, gay, jolly, *o.e.*, *Lo.*

JOLL, JOUL, JOWL, JOWELL, *n.f.*, the devil ; *or*, *i.q.* JOEL.

JORDAN, JERDAN, *n.f.*, ? darnel (*jure*, *Po.*), *or* play (*choary*), hill (*dun*).

JORY, JURY, *n.f.*, ? darnel (*jure*) close (*hay*) ; *or* = *choary*, play.

JOSE, *n.f.*, *i.q.* IOSA.

. JOSLIN, JOSCELINE, sportive, *lat.*, *Y.*

JOUINUS JOVIN, *t.d.d.*, belonging to Jupiter, *lat.*, *Y.*

JOULBY, *n.f.*, ? little (*bich*) devil (*joul*) ; *or*, JAOUL's place, *d.*

JUGGER PARK, ? Jago's close.

JULIAN, *n.f.*, ? *from* LUXULYAN.

THE JUMP, *T.a.*, *i.q.* GUMP, *T.C.*

JUSTIN, *n.f.*, ? = Gestin, Augustin, *B.m.*

JUSTING PLACE, ? playing place, *t.*

JUTSWORTH, ? the Jute's farm (*weor-thig*), *s.*

K AER, *n.f.*, *i.q.* CAER.

KAHELLAN, *T.a.*, *i.q.* KELLYHELLAN.

KAN, *n.f.*, ? white, shining (*can*).

KANDLE, *n.f.*, ? = *cantl*, a candle ; *or*, *cendel*, fine linen ; *or*, *i.q.* KENDAL.

KANNEGY, *i.q.* CARNEGGY.

KARAK CLEWS, *i.q.* CARACLOSE.

KARE MOOR, ? mountain ash (*care*) *or* camp (*caer*) moor.

KARENSY-WORTHY CHAPEL, worthy love *or* affection chapel, (?). (*c.d.* St. Mary Magd.), *H.*

KARKEEK, *n.f.*, *i.q.* CARKEEK.

KARKEET, *i.q.* CARKEET.

KARLY, little (*le*) camp (*caer*).

KARRAMORE, *n.f.*, ? *i.q.* KARE MOOR; *or*, great (*maur*) rock (*carrag*).

KARROW, *n.f.*, *i.q.* CAREW.

KARSALAN, *d.d.*, ? *i.q.* CARSELLA.

KASTELL, *n.f.*, *i.q.* KESSEL.

KAY, *n.f.*, = Caius (*lat.*) ; *or*, *ce*, a hedge, enclosure ; *or*, *from* KEA.

KAY-LE, -ELL, *i.q.* CAYLE.

KEA, an enclosure, *Pr.* ; a hedge *or* mound, a quay *or* wharf, *H.* ; ? *from* Pope Caius, *T.* ; *or* St. Cuby, *Wh.* ; *or* St. Tegai, *O.* ; *o.* LAN-DEGE. (*p.s.* not known).

KEAGLE FIELD, dirty (*geagle*) field.

KEALS, *n.f.*, ? ? = *cyllys*, lost.

KEAMS, KEEMS, *n.f.*, outward (*ames*) close (*ce*).

KEARLS, ? *i.q.* GARLES.

KEARN, *n.f.*, ? = *cern*, side of the face, *w.* ; *or*, *i.q.* CARN.

KEASE, *n.f.*, ? lower (*isa*) close.

KEASON, *i.q.* CADSON, *or* KITSON.

KEAST, ? east (*est*) close (*ce*).

KEATE, KEETE, *n.f.*, ? = *caid*, a slave.

KEEN, *n.f.*, ? *i.q.* GENN.

KEENA PARK, ? worm (*cynac*) field.

KEEVE, KEIVE, ? = *cyff*, a vat, *s.*

KEGELL-ACK, -ICK, hazel-grove *or* copse hedge (*ce*), *Pr.* ; ? dividing (*gyllic*, *w.*) hedge, *N.*

KEGERTHEN, *n.f.*, the quickset (*cer-den*) hedge, *Pr.*

KE-, KEI-GWIN, -GWIDDEN, *n.f.*, white (*gwin*, *gwydn*) dog (*ci*), *Pr.* ; *or*, *i.q.* Whitfield, *R.W.*

KEICH, KEYCH, *n.f.*, ? *i.q.* KEASE.

KEIR, *n.f.*, *i.q.* KARE.

KEIROVER, ?? great (*veor*) CAIRO.

KEISILGEY, ? tottering (*siglu*, *w.*) hedge; *or*, *i.q.* CARSILGEY.

KELBROOK, ?? leech (*gel*) brook; *or*, retreat (*cil*) by the brook, *R.IV.*

KELEANKER, *i.q.* KILLIANCAR.

KELHURLE, ? the earl's (*yerl*) retreat (*cil*), *or* grove (*cilli*).

KELINACK, holly field, *R.IV.*; nettle hedge, *Gw.*; flax field, *Pr.*

KELLAH, ? *i.q.* KELLIOW.

KELLAHAM, ? grove (*celli*) dwelling (*ham*, *s.*), *or* meadow (*holm*, *s.*).

KELLAND, ? grove enclosure (*lan*).

KELLAWAY, *n.f.*, ? grove path (*weg*, *s.*); *or*, retreat (*cil*) by the water (*gwy*).

KELLER, ? long (*hir*), *or* high (*ard*) grove, *or* field (*gweal*).

KELLIFRAY, ? hill (*bre*) grove, *or*, grove hill; *or*, *i.q.* KILLYVERTH.

KELLIGOG, cuckoo (*cog*) grove.

KELLIMAR'R, Mercury's grove, *B.*; *or*, horse (*marsh*) grove, *R.IV.*

KELLI-NOON, -OON, grove on the down (*an oon*).

KELL-IO, -IOW, -OW, the groves.

KELLOR PARK, ? earth nuts (*clor*) field (*parc*).

KELLOW PARK, groves' close.

KELLY, = *celli*, a grove.

KELLYBRAY, *i.q.* KELLIFRAY.

KELLYCOFF, the smith's (*gof*) grove.

KELLYERS, ? boundary (*hars*) grove.

KELLYFRETH, *i.q.* KILLYVERTH.

KELLYGAN MOOR, ?? sheath fish (*cillygan*) moor.

KELLYGREEN, ?gravel(*grean*)grove; *or*, grove of the sun (*grian*), *ga.*

K. HELLAN, HELLAN grove.

K. HELLAN PRASE, KELLYHELLAN common *or* meadow.

K. LAND, grove land *or* field.

K. PARK, grove close (*parc*).

K. ROUNDS, KELLY circular entrenchments.

K. VOSE, grove with the ditch (*fos*).

KEL-SEY, -ZEY, ? the dry (*sech*) neck (*cil*), *Pr.*

KELWAY, *n.f.*, *i.q.* KELLAWAY.

KEMEL, *n.f.*, *i.q.* KEMYEL.

KEMP, KEMPE, *n.f.*, ? = *cempa*, a soldier, a champion, *s.*; *kempe*, a giant, *d.*; *cemp*, a circle, *w.*; *cump*, a game, a prize, *w.*; a contest, battle, war, camp, *s.*

KEMPETHORN, ? KEMP hill (*tron*), *or* thorn, *t.*

KEMSON, *n.f.*, ? KEMP'S son.

KEMUE, ? greater (*mua*) hedge (*ce*).

KEMYEL-DREA, -CREIS, *and* -WARTHA, home *or* near (*adre*), middle (*creis*), *and* higher (*wartha*) Michael's, *or* honey (*mel*), *or* iron *or* gain (*mael*) enclosure (*ce*).

KEN, *n.f.*, ? *i.q.* GENN.

KENACOT, ? Keyna's cottage; *or*, ridge (*cein*) of the wood (*coat*).

KENAP, ?? = *cnœp*, the top *or* brow of the hill, *s.*

KENCREEK, barrow (*creeg*) ridge (*cein*), *M'L.*

KENDALL, *n.f.*, ? head (*cean*, *ga.*) of the dale; *or*, *i.q.* KANDLE.

KENEG-IE, -Y, the mossy (*neag* ?) hedge (*ce*) by the water (*gwy*), *B.*; mossy hedge, *or*, house near the bogs, *Pr.*

KENEWAS, ? ridge outside (*ves*).

KENIDJACK, *i.q.* CARNIDJACK.

KENKEE, ? enclosure (*ce*) ridge.

KENN-ACK, -ICK COVE, ? rocky (*carnic*) cove.

KENNACOMBE, ? Keyna's vale.

KENN-AL, -EL, ridge of the moor (*hal*); *or*, above the moor, *T.C.*

KENNA PARK, *T.a.*, ? corner close.

KENNARD, *n f.*, ? high (*ard*) ridge.

KENNAWENNA, ? white (*gwennack*) ridge (*cein*).

KENNEGO, ? *i.q.* CARNEGGO.

KENNER, ? long (*hir*) ridge (*cein*).

KENNICOT, ? *i.q.* KENACOT.

KENNING-, KENI-STOCK, king's (*cuning*, *s.*), *or*, rabbits' (*cyning*, *w.*) place (*stoc*, *s.*).

KENSEY, river, ? dry (*sech*) ridge.

KENT, *n.f.*, ? = *ceneat*, a singer; *or*,

cant, edge, border, headland, *w.*

KENTEBURY, *n.f., from* Kinterbury (*Devon*), ?= earthwork (*bury*) on the headland (*ceann tir, Beal*).

KENVER, *n.f.,* ? *i.q.* GENVOR.

KENWITH, *o.n.f.,* ?? *i.q.* PENWITH.

KENWORTHY, ? higher (*wartha*) ridge; *or*, KEN'S farm (*worthig, s.*).

KENWYN, *from p.s.* St. Kenwyn, *O.* (= Cein, the virgin ; *or*, jewel (*cein*) of a woman, *Y.*) ; the ridge (*cein*), *or*, rising of the hill over the marsh, *Pr.* ; ? = *cein wyn*, white ridge, *R.W.* ; fair ascent, *Po.*

KERBAGLET, *i.q.* CARBIGLETT.

KEREW, ? *i.q.* CAREW.

KERGECK, *n.f., i.q.* CARKEEK.

KERKEM, ? rock (*carag*) border (*hem*).

KERKETH, ? *i.q.* CROUGATH.

KERLEY, ? *i.q.* KARLY.

KERNEY, ? rock close (*hay*) ; *or, i.q.* KERNICK.

KERNICK, the round (*kren*) or compact place ; *also*, = *carnick*, rocky place, *Pr.* ; *or*, horned, *R.W.*

KERNOW, ? the rocks [field].

KER-OW, -RA, -ROW, *i.q.* CARRAW, CARA, *or* CAREW.

KERRIER, ? = *goror*, higher coast, upper region, confine, border, *w.**

KERRINWELL MOOR, ? ? = *caer an uhel*, the high camp.

KERRIS, *i.q.* GERRY ; a lovely place, *Pr.* (?)

K. ROUNDAGO, the round *or* camp at KERRIS.

K. VEAN, little KERRIS.

KERROW AN GELLY, the camp in the hazel-grove (*celli*), *M'L.*

KERR PARK, ? mountain-ash (*care*), *or* camp (*caer*) close (*parc*).

KERRYWERRY, ? the play (*guare*) enclosure (*cae, w.*).

KERS-, KES-BROOK, -LAKE, ? cress (*cerse, s.*) brook (*leak, Pr.*).

KERS-PIT, -WELL, *n.f.,* ?= cress well (*pytt, s.*).

KER-THEN, -TON, ?=*caerton*, castle *or* rock on the hill, *T.C.* ; *or, cerden*, the quicken *or* mountain ash tree, *Lh.*

KESKEYS, *i.q.* GUSCUS.

KES-SEL, -TAL, -TELL, -TLE, = *castel*, a fort, a village ; *pl., cestel, R.W.*

KESTLEMENACK, ? the stone (*maenic*) fortification.

KESTLEWOOD, castle wood.

KETLEIGH, ? *i.q.* GATLEY.

KEVAR, = *ce-varth*, higher hedge *or* close, *T.C.* ; *or, cyvur*, a piece of land.

KEVER-AL, -EL, the place of goats (*cheverel*, a goat, *f.*), *Pr.* ; opposite *or* over against (*cyver, w.*) the brow (*ael*), *C.*

KEVERN, *n.f., from* ST. KEVERNE.

KEY, *n.f.,* ? *i.q.* KEA.

KEYCHE, *n.f., i.q.* GAYCHE.

KEYSHEYS, ?? Key's closes (*haies*).

KIELS HILL, ? nine-pins hill.

KIG-GAN, -ON, ? = *cegin*, a kitchen ; *or, gagen*, a cleft, chink, *w.* ; *or*, the down (*goon*) close (*ce*).

KILBURY, ? retreat (*cil*) on the hill (*bre*) ; *or*, earth-work (*bury*) grove.

KILCOID, the wood (*coid*) retreat.

KIL-CREW, -GREW, ? grove (*celli*) hut (*crow*) ; *or, i.q.* KILLIGREW.

KILDOWN, deep (*down*) recess (*kil*), *R.W.* ; ? church (*cil*) down.

KILFORD, ? ford grove (*celli*).

KILGATHER, *i.q.* KILLIGARTH.

KILGEAR, the pleasant *or* fruitful grove, *Pr.* ; ? camp (*caer*) grove.

KILGOGUE, ? cuckoo (*cog*) grove.

KILGORRAN, St. Gorran's cell.

KILG-OTE, -OAT, *i.q.* KILCOID.

KILHALLAN, ? *i.q.* KILLEHELLAN.

---

* Carew, speaking of this hundred, says, "*Kery* in Cornish signifieth bearing; and yet you must beare with me, if I forbeare to deriue KERIER herefrom until I see some reason for my warrant." Hals says, "=*kerryer*, a lover"; Pryce, "KIRRIER, the coast *or* border of the country (*Kur-Urian*)"; Whitaker, from "*carhar*, a prison."

KILHAM, ? grove *or* cell home (*ham, s.*); *or*, well (*kell*) meadow (*holm*), *t.*

KILKEA, KEA grove *or* cell.

KILKHAMPTON, church (*kirk*) home *or* dwelling (*ham*) town, *t., II.*; *e.d.d.* KILCHETONA; (? *cylch*, a cycle, circle, *w.*); *p.s.* St. James, *O.*

KILKOBBEN, = *Kilcrobben*, crooked refuge, *C.*

KILLAHAN, ? summer (*han, Pr.*) grove (*celli*), *or* field (*gweal*).

KILLANOAN, ? grove on the down (*an oon*).

KILLA PARK, ? ? clay (*clai, w.*), *or* grove close.

THE KILLAS, ? = *gweal las*, green field; *or*, *goles*, bottom; *or*, clay slate (*killas*) [field]; *or, i.q.* GULLAS.

KILLA-TON, -TOWN, ? grove enclosure; *or, i.q.* CULLODEN.

KILLAVARDER, ? grove on (*war*) the water (*dour*); *or, i.q.* GILLIN-WARTHA.

KILLAWORGY, *i.q.* KILLYWORGY.

KILLCOT, *i.q.* KILCOID.

KILLE-FRETH, -VERTH, *i.q.* KILLY-VERTH.

KILLEGORGAN, ? grove on (*gwar*) the down (*goon*); *or*, Gurgwin's (*w.*) grove.

KILLEHELLAN, enclosed (*lan*) grove by the river (*heyl*), *or* grove of elms, *Pr.*; ? HELLAN grove.

KILLENICK, ? *i.q.* CALENICK, *or* KELINACK.

KILLEWERRAS, ? *i.q.* GWEAL GWAR-THAS; *or*, the Virgin's (*gwyrhes*) grove.

KILLIACK MOOR, ? cock (*celioc*) moor.

KILLIANCAR, ? hermit's (*ancur*) grove; *or*, grove of the fort (*caer*), *R.W.*

KILLIARD, ? high (*ard*) grove.

KILLIERS, ? long (*hir*) grove [field]s.

KILLIGANOON, the sanctuary (*cil*) on the moors, *C.*; *or*, the grove by (*gan*) the down (*oon*), *D.G.*

KILLIGARTH, ? high (*gwarth*) grove.

KILLIGNOCK, ? grove of the hill (*cnwc, w.*), *R.W.*; ? Cænog's (*w.*) grove.

KILLIGORICK, the grove on the waters side (*gwar ick*), *Pr.*

KILLIGREW, the rough (*garow*) retreat (*cil*); *or*, herds' (*grew, w.*) refuge, *C.*; eagles' (*eriew*), *or* crane's (*grew*) grove, *Pr.*

KILLIGWITH, ?? ash (*enwydh*) grove.

KIL-LIMENSACK, -MENSAC, -MANJAC, *i.q.* CALAMANSACK *or* KILMANACH.

KILLINACK, ? *i.q.* KELINACK.

KILLI-O, -OW, the groves, *Pr.*; the sheltered *or* secluded place, *C.*; = *celli wg*, overspreading grove (*w.*), *M.*

KILLIS-ALLOW, -ULLOW, ? the lower (*isellach*) grove, *J.B.*; grove of elms (*ulowe*), *Pr.*

KILLISERTH, steep (*serth*) grove, *R.W.*

KILLI-VOAZ, -VOSE, the grove in the entrenchment *or* descent (?), *Pr.*

KILLIVOR, ? the great (*maur*) grove.

KILLIWERRIS, *i.q.* KILLEWERRAS.

KILLOCK, the oak grove, *Pr.* (?)

KILLYCOOSE, ? *i.q.* GWEAL AN COOZ, *or* KILCOID.

KILLY GRAWZY, ? grove by the cross (*crous*) close (*hay*).

KILLYVERTH, white-thorn (*frith* ?) grove, *Pr.*; ? green (*gwerdh, w.*) grove.

KILLYWITHICK, ? meadow grove.

KILLYWOAS, *i.q.* KILLIVOAZ.

KILLYWORGY, grove by the river (*war gy*), *Pr.*; upper-field grove, *J.B.*

KILMANACH, the monks' cell, *B.*

KIL-MAR, -MARK, -MARTH, the great (*maur*), the horse (*march*), *or* the wonderful (*marth*), grove, *Pr.*; the retreat (*cil*) of the chief (*mar, ga.*), *Beal*; hiding place *or* sanctuary in open ground (*marth, w.*), *C.*

KILMENORTH, the retreat on the stone (*maen*) ridge (*arth*), *M'L.*

KILNA, ? the kiln.

KILNEY MEADOW, ? *i.q.* CALENICK.

KILQUITE, *i.q.* KILCOID *or* CHILCOT.

KIL-TER, -TOR, ? grove *or* cell by the water (*dour*); *or*, grove land (*doar*).

KILVARRACK, ? horse (*march*) grove; *or*, St. Baruch's (*w.*) cell.

KILVORRY, ? higher (*warra*) grove.

KILWARNICK, ? grove *or* cell in the marshy (*gwernic*) place.

KIMBERLEY, the champion's (*campier*), *or* welshman's pasture.

KINANCE, dog's (*ci*) valley, *Po.*, *or* brook, *C.*; ? = *ceunant*, a ravine, hollow, *w.*

KINE PARK, ? ridge (*cein*) *or* kine, *i.e.* oxen close (*parc*).

KING-BEAR, -BEER, ? King's farm.

KINGDON, *n.f.*, ? the king's hill; *or*, = KINGSTON.

KING-EY, -HAY, ? King's, *or* rabbits' (*cwning, w.*) close; *or*, ridge (*cein*) hedge (*ce*).

KINGLAYS, ? green (*glas*) ridge.

KINSEY, *n.f.*, ? *i.q.* KENSEY.

KINSMAN, *n.f.*, ? *kine or* cattle tender, *R.B.K.*; *or*, king's man *or* servant.

KIPPISCOMBE, ? St. Cuby's vale.

KIRCUM, rock (*carrag*) vale.

KIRGOE, rock wood (*coad*).

KIRKANOWAN, the rock (*carrag*) on the down (*an oon*).

KIRKETH, ? *i.q.* CARKEET.

KIRKLAND, rocky land.

KIRLAND, castle enclosure, *T.Q.C.*; land *or* place of berries (*caor*), *C.*

KIRSPIT, *i.q.* KERSPIT.

KIR-THEN, -TON, *i.q.* KERTHEN.

KIRWIN, ? *i.q.* CARWEN, *or* CURWEN.

KISSING CLOSE, KITCHEN PARK, ? turf (*cesan*) close (*parc*).

KISTLE MORRIS, ? castle marsh.

KIT-CHEN, -SON, *n.f.*, ? *i.q.* CADSON; *or*, Christopherson; *or* = *ce udzheon*, ox close.

KITE, ? = *coit*, a cromlech; *or*, *coed*, a wood, *w.*

KITIEL, ? manure (*teil*) close (*ce*).

KITSHAM, ? Christopher's meadow (*holm*), *t., T.C.*

KITTO, *n.f.*, ? = *kitter*, a stealer of ore from another man's pile, *m.c.*

KIVELL, *n.f.*, = *cevil*, a horse.

KIVERN, ? *from* ST. KEVERNE.

KLEDH, the trench, *B.*

KLYMIARVEN, *modern*, the little (*vean*) dovecot, *Jo.C.*

KNACKABY, ?? the little (*by*) knoll (*cnwc, w.*).

KNACKERS, ? = *kein acres*, ridge of the acres, *w., R.W.*

KNAP-PARC, ? top (*cnœp*) close, *s.*

KNAVA, *n.f.*, ? = *cnafa*, offspring, son, boy, youth, *s.*

KNAYLE, *n.f.*, ? *i.q.* CARNHALE.

KNEEBONE, *n.f.*, ? *i.q.* CARNEBONE.

KNEIGHTON'S KEIVE, Knighton's basin (*cyf, s.*).

KNEVETT, *o.n.f.*, ? *from* DUNHEVED; *or*, ridge (*cein*) head (*heafod, s.*).

KNIGHT, *n.f.*, ? = St. GONNET.

KNIGHTON, = NETHERTON, *Beal.*

KNILLY PARK, ? GOONHILLY close.

KNIVER, *n.f.*, ? *i.q.* CARN Y VERTH.

KNIVETON, *n.f.*, ? Knava's town.

KNOLL, KNOWL, the promontory hill *or* eminence, a projection of hilly ground, *Pr.*; *cnoll*, a hill, top, summit, *s.*

KNOTT, *n.f.*, ? = St. GONNET.

KNOTWELL, *n.f.*, ? St. Gonnet's well.

KNUCKEY, *n.f.*, ? *i.q.* CARNKIE.

KUGGAR, ? play (*choary*) wood (*cud*).

KUSKARNE NA HUILAN, the lapwing's (*codnahwilan*) rock (*carn*) by the wood (*cus*), *Lh.*

KUSKEASE, *i.q.* GUSCUS.

KYKYSHERE, ? long (*hir*) hemlock (*cegas*) [field].

KYLGAT, *n.f.*, KILCOID.

KYMBER, *n.f.*, ? welshman.

KYMIEL, *i.q.* KEMYEL.

KYNILM, *w.B.m.*, ? chief helmit.

KYVER ANKOU, the place (*cyvar*) of death (*ancow*), *T.*

L AA, *n.f.*, ? = *lla*, light, clear, *M.*

LABTER, ? = *Lampeter*, Peter's church *or* enclosure (*lan*).

LABURNICK, rushy (*bruinick*) enclosure.

LACCA FIELD, ? well *or* pit field.

LACKEY VEAR, ? great swamp, *M.*

LACUDAN, ? wood pigeon (*cudon*) enclosure.

LADANDRE, Andrew's enclosure, *T.C.*; ? fire (*tan*) place (*tre*) enclosure, *M.*

LADDENVEAN, ? little (*bihan*) broad (*ledan*) [field]; *or*, little bank (*ladn*).

LADDIS, ? stack (*dise*) yard (*lan*); *or*, Laity's [field].

LADNOR, *n.f.*, ? *i.q.* LANDER.

LADOCK, *from p.s.* St. Ladoca, *O.*; steep hill (*ladn*?) of oaks, *Pr.*

LADY PARK, the Virgin Mary's close, *Beal*; *or* LAITY close.

LAFEOCK, St. Feock's church *or* enclosure (*lan*).

LAFFAN, *n.f.*, ? *i.q.* LAVIN.

LAFFENHAC, the church of the monks (*menech*); *or*, the stone (*maenic*) church, *B.*

LAFFORD, *n.f.*, ? enclosure (*lan*) by the road (*fordh*); *or* = *hlaford*, a lord, loaf (*hlaf*) originator (*ord*), *s.*

LAFRONE, ? hill (*bron*) enclosure.

LAFROWDA, the church (*lan*) of the good (*da*) cross (*rood*), *Buller*. (??)

LAHE, *n.f.*, *i.q.* LEAH.

LAHERNE, *i.q.* LANHERNE.

LAI-ETY, -TY, milk (*luit*) house (*ty*), *i.e.* the dairy.

LAIN, *river,* = *elaine*, a fawn, *B.*; *lyn*, a deep still pool, *or*, *leven*, smooth, *I.T.*

LAINE, LANE, ? = *llan*, an enclosure, a church; *or*, *llain*, a slip of land, *w.*

LAKE, ? rivulet *or* stream.

LAKKA, a spring of water rising from the earth, *J.P.*

LAM-, LAN-AIL, the enclosure (*lan*) on the estuary (*hayl*), *M'L.*

LAMALKIN, ? rag-mop (*malkin*) close.

LAMANNA, LA MAYNE, ? monk's (*manach*) church (*lan*).

LAMAN-VA, -VER, ? enclosure by the great (*vear*) stone (*maen*).

LAMAR, ? the horse (*march*) enclosure (*lan*), *or* leap (*lam*).

LAMARN, ?? salmon (*maran, w.*) leap.

LAMARTH, ? high (*arth*) leap.

LAM-B, -BE, ? little (*bich*) enclosure.

LAMBADLA, ?? the outlaw's (*adla*) leap; ? *i.q.* LAMBRADLA.

LAMBE-DO, -SSO, the place (*lan*) of birches (*bezo, w. bedw*), *Pr.*

LAMBERT, *n.f.*, country's (*land*) brightness, *t.*, *?.*

LAMBEST, ? cattle (*best*) enclosure.

LAMB LAYERY, ? Llary's (*w.*) leap.

LAMBLEATHER, ? Bledri's (*w.*) enclosure.

LAMBLOCKS, calf's-house (*bo loch*) enclosures.

LAM-DOURN, -BRON, -BURN, the hill (*bron*) enclosure, *T.*; ? St. Perran's enclosure.

LAMBOURN WIGAN, LAMBRIGGAN, little (*bichan*) LAMBOURNE.

LAMBRADLA, ? enclosure of the judgment seat (*brawdle, w.*).

LAMBRENNY, ? king's (*brennin*) enclosure, *M.*; *or*, *bryny*, crows.

LAMBUSWELL, ? enclosure by the high (*uhel*) house (*bos*); *or*, dung (*busl*) enclosure.

LAMEL-AN, -IN, -ION, -YN, -LYN, ? mill (*melin*), *or* clover (*meillion*), *or* yellow (*melyn*), *or* Melin's, *or* Mellion's enclosure.

LAMELWIN, ? Maelgwn's (*w.*) enclosure.

LAMERE, ? great (*mear*) enclosure (*lan*); *or*, long (*hir*) leap.

LAMETTON, stone (*medn* = *maen*), *or* Merddin's (*w.*) enclosure.

LAMIN, ? stone enclosure, *or*, at the edge *or* limit (*min*), *w.*

LAMINSTER (*i.q.* MINSTER), the (*la, f.*) monastery.

LAMORESK, the marsh (*marais, f.*) church; *now* St. Clements.

LAMORICK, *i.q.* LANVORICK.

LAMORIER CLOSE, ?? wall builder's (*muriwr, w.*) close (*lan*).

LAMORNA, ? Morwenna's enclosure; (*morvah*, near the sea, *M.*).

LAMORRAN, = *lan mor ruan*, the church upon the sea *or* salt-water river, *Pr.*; enclosure by the marsh,

C.; church of St. Maruan, *Wh.*, (*p.s.* not known).

LAM-PARRO, -PRA, ? St. Baruch's, *or* bread (*bara*) enclosure.

LAMP-EER, -IER, *n.f.*, church of St. Peter.

LAMPEN, ? = *lamb pen*, or fold.

LAMPETH-A, -O, ? *i.q.* LAMBEDO ; *or*, graves (*beddau, w.*) enclosure.

LAMPRENNY, *i.q.* LAMBRENNY.

LAMPRETHEN, ? enclosure of the Britons (*brethon*), *or*, of the tree (*predn*).

LAMPROBUS, PROBUS manor (*lan*).

LAMPSHIRE, *n.f.*, ? *i.q.* LAMBESSO.

LAMWIDDEN, ?little (*vidn = vean*) leap (*lam*), or enclosure (*lan*).

LANAGAN, ? hawthorn-berry (*hogan*), or Hagan's (*t.*) enclosure.

LANARTH, the high (*arth*) enclosure, *Pr.*

LANATON, ?? the enclosure on the hill (*dun*).

LANBRABOIS, *e.d.d., i.q.* LAMPROBUS.

LANBUSHA, ? resting place (*bowesva*) enclosure.

LAN-CAR, -CARE, rest rock, *or* rock temple, *H.* ; ? camp (*caer*) enclosure; or church of St. Gwawr(*w.*)

LANCARF, ? grave yard (*corf*, a body); *or*, rough (*gariff*) enclosure ; ? *d.d.* LANCHARET.

LANCARROW, ? deer (*carow*) park ; *or*, rough (*garw*) enclosure.

LANCE, LAUNCE, *n.f.*, LANCH, ?ENES enclosure (*lan*).

LANCELWYS, *now* LANSALLOS.

LANCORLA, ? sheepfold (*corlan*) enclosure.

LANCROW, ? hovel (*crow*) enclosure.

LANDABETHIC, ? meadow land.

LANDARE, ? oak (*dar*) enclosure.

LAND-AVALE, -EVAL, ? apple (*aval*) land ; *or*, St. Idwal's enclosure.

LAND-AVEDY, -EVEDDY, Tafyd *or* David's enclosure, *or* farm, *or* dwelling, *T.Q.C.*

LANDAWARNICK,?the marshy (*gwernic*) land.

LANDAZARD, ? high (*ard*) stack (*das*), or wilderness (*diserth, w.*) enclosure.

LAND-EGAY, -EGEA, *d.d.* -IGHE, ?KEA'S land ; *or*, manor of St. Tegai.

LANDELAKE, ? willow (*helig*) field.

LANDENNER, ? long (*hir*) hill (*din*), *or*, the fowler's (*edhanor*) enclosure.

LANDER, ? oak (*dar*) enclosure.

LANDERHTUN, 11 *cent.*, ? oak enclosure on the hill (*dun*); *now* LANDRAKE.

LANDER-RY, -YAH, oak (*deru*) enclosure.

LAN-DEW, -DUE, God's (*du*) enclosure, *or* the churchyard, the sanctuary, *Pr.* ; *or* David's, *or* black (*du*), *or* south (*deheu, w.*), enclosure.

LANDEWEDNACK, the white (*gwednac*) roof (*to*) holy church, *or* church of God, *Pr.* ; church of St. (*da*) Wednack *or* Winnock, *T.* ; (*p.s.* St. Winwolaus, *O.*).

LAND GOODIX, ? rush (*hesk*) wood (*coat*) field (*land, s.*).

L. GREEK, ? mound (*creeg*) field.

L. HASSICK, ? field with the short coarse grass (*hassuc*), *t.*

LANDICLE, *d.d.* ? church of St. Tecla ; ? *now* LANESELEY, *J.Ca.*

LANDITHEY, the place *or* enclosure of piety *or* mercy (*digethic*), *T.C.*, ? of St. Teithi.

LANDIZEAGE,Eadsige's (*t.*) enclosure; *or*, corn (*izick*) field.

LANDJEW, ? *i.q.* LANDEW ; *or*, the jew's (*edzhow*) enclosure.

LANDLEAKE, the church on the rivulet (*lucca*), *Pr.* ; *i.q.* LANDELAKE.

LAND-LOE, -LOO, the land *or* enclosure on the LOOE.

LANDMANUEL, *d.d.*, ? high (*uhel*) stone (*maen*) enclosure ; ? *now* LEMAIN.

LANDNO, the bare (*noadh*), *or* narrower (*ednach*), enclosure.

LANDOHO, *i.q.* LANOW.

LAND-, LAN-RAKE, ? oak (*derric*) enclosure ; *or*, church of St. Rioch ; (*p.s.* St. Peter, *O.*).

LANDRAWNA, ? = w. *Landraw*, a country over a river; (*lan* = *glan*, a bank; *draw*, over; *na*, that), *R.W.*

LANDR-AYTH, -ETH, *i.q.* LANREATH; also, sand (*traith*) enclosure.

LANDREST, ? east (*est*) LANDER.

LANDREY, *n.f.*, ? oak (*deru*), or sand (*traith*), or home (*tre*) close.

LAN-DREYNE, -DRINE, ?thorn (*draen*) close.

LANDRIVIC, ? the dragon (*druic*) enclosure; ? *drigfa*, a dwelling, *M.*

LAND ROWSE, ?Rowse's field (*land,s.*).

L. SEAGUE, *i.q.* LANSEAGE.

L. SEATON, land on the SEATON.

L. SEW, *i.q.* LANDJEW.

L. SUGLE, rye (*sygal*) land.

L. SWORTH, ? high (*warth*) lands.

L. TALLIC, ? high (*tallic*) enclosure, *T.C.*; or, land full of holes (*tollic*).

L. THORNE, ? hill (*tron*) enclosure (*lan*); or, thorn field (*land, s.*).

LANDUE, *i.q.* LANDEW.

LANDULPH, ? Ulph's land; or church of St. (*da*) Ulf or Olaf; (*p.s.* St. Leonard, *J.Ca.*).

LANDVINE, ? the stones (*myin*), or little (*vean*) enclosure or close (*lan*).

LANDWITHAN, the tree (*gwedhen*) enclosure.

LANDZION, ?? jews' (*edzhewon*), or ox (*udzheon*) enclosure.

LANEAST, eastern, or wood (*hurst, s.*) enclosure; or, church of St. Just; (*c.d.* St. Welvela & St. Sativola, *O.*)

LANEER, long (*hir*) enclosure.

LANEFF, ? evet's (*anaf*) close.

LANEGAN, ? Einigan's (*w.*) enclosure.

LANEGATH, ? enclosure of the [wild] cat (*y gath, w.*), *R.W.*

LANEHAM, ? *lane* pasture (*holm*), *t.*

LANEHOC, *d.d.*, ? ANAOC'S (*B.m.*) enclosure.

LANE KIRDS, ? ?carrot (*caretys, Pr.*) field (*llain, w.*).

L. PARK, ? *i.q.* PARK EN VOUNDER.

LANER, the templar, *H.*; *i.q.* LANEER.

LANERGH, 14 *cent.*, = *llanerch*, a glade,

cleared place in a wood, *w.*

LANESCUT, ? enclosure below (*is*) the wood (*coat*).

LANESELY, lower (*isella*) church, *Wh.*; *now* GULVAL.

LANESKIN, sedge (*hescen*) field.

LANESTICK, ? Ysteg's (*w.s.*) enclosure or church.

LANEW, ? the high (*uch*), or yew-tree (*yw, w.*) enclosure.

LANEWA, the enclosure of St. Ewa.

LANFEATHER, ? Peter's (*Pedyr*) enclosure or church.

LANG, *n.f.*, long, *s.*; or, *i.q.* LANK.

LANGARTH, ? long enclosure (*garth*), *t.*; or, garden (*garth*) enclosure (*lan*); or, *i.q.* LANEGATH.

LANGCARRE, *i.q.* LANCAR.

LANGDON, ? long enclosure (*tun, s.*), or hill (*dun*).

LANGENEWIT, *d.d.*, ? Cynwid's (*w.*) enclosure; (*cynwydd*, land ploughed the first time, *w.*).

LANGFORD, the long ford, *t.*

LAN-GHARNE, -GHAIRON, *n.f.*, holy or sacred laws, *H.*; ? Geirion's (*w.*), or, rock (*carn*) enclosure.

LANGID, *n.f.*, ?*i.q.* LANGUIT.

LANGISAL, *i.q.* NANJISAL, *T.C.*

LANGOROCH, *d.d.*, CRANTOCK manor (*lan*).

LANGOURD, *i.q.* LANGURTHA.

LANGREEK, ? the church of St. Cyric; or, the mound (*creeg*) enclosure.

LANGRIDGE, long ridge, *t.*

LANGSTONE, *t.*, *i.q.* MENHEIR.

LANGUIHENOC, *e.d.d.*, *i.q.* LANWENEHOC.

LANGUIT, the wood (*cuit*) enclosure.

LANGUNNET, ?*i.q.* LANGENEWIT.

LANGURRA, the bay (*gorra*) church, *H.*; *i.q.* LANGOROCH.

LANGURTH-A, -OU, -OW, the higher (*gwartha*) enclosure.

LANGVITETONE, *d.d.*,*i.q.*LAWHITTON.

LANGW-EATH, -ITH, *i.q.* LANGUIT; or, the *long* wilderness (*gwydd*) [piece].

LANGWORTHY, *n.f.*, ? long farm or

field (*weorthig, s.*), *t.* ; or, *i.q.* LAN-GURTHA.

LANHADRON, the enclosure of the mighty (*cadurn*), *Wh.* ; a den of thieves (*ladron*), *Nord.* ; *i.q.* NANS-LADRON, *Pr.*

LANHARGY, ? the forest glade (*lan-herch*) enclosure (*hay*).

LANHASSICK, *i.q.* LANDHASSICK.

LANHAY, the church-yard (*hay*), *Po.*

LANHEAVERNE, *i.q.* LAN KEVERNE.

LAN-HENGY, -HINZY, the church or temple of sentence, judgment, or deliberation, *H.* ; ? the enclosure by the old (*hen*) house (*chy*).

LANHER, *d.d.*, *i.q.* LANNER.

LANHERNE, the sanctuary or church built with iron- (*hriarn*) or hard-stone, *Pr.* ; the church at the angle (*horn*), *Wh.* ; *i.q.* LANG-HARNE ; *d.d.* LANHERWEU, a place of refuge (*herwa*, to flee, *w.*), *T.*

LANHERRIOT, ? Hwroad's (*w.*), or long (*hir*) wood (*cuit*) enclosure.

LANHEYL, *i.q.* LAMAIL.

LANHOOSE, ? temple (*lan*) of Hoesus; or wood (*cus*) enclosure.

LANHUDNOW, ?St. Idno's (*w.*) church.

LANHYDROCK, ?watery (*douric*) bank (*glan*), or, church (*lan*) under a watery hill, *Pr.* ; ? Ydroc's (*w.*) church, or, church of repentance (*edrec*) ; *v.* LANHETHERICK, ? Heth-erick's farm, *T.Q.C.*

LANIESCHI, lower (*isa*) church ; *i.q.* LANESELY.

LANI-LEY, -LLEY, ?St. Hely's church or enclosure.

LANINE, *n.f.*, ? cold (*iein*), or furze (*eithen*) enclosure; or, *i.q.* LANYON.

LANIVET, ? church by the grave (*beth*), or of St. Ivo (*p.s., M.*).

LANJEATH, ? ? dry (*zeth, Gw.*) en-closure.

LANJEW, *i.q.* LANDUE.

LANJORE, the enclosure of the lord (*ior*) or ruler, *Beul* ; ?play (*choari, a.*) enclosure.

LANK, young (*llanc, w.*), or new

[river], *C.* ; ?= *lanherch*, a clearance in a wood.

LANKAIRE, ? camp (*caer*), or moun-tain-ash (*care*), enclosure ; or, oat (*cerh*) field.

LANKEAST, ? east LANK.

LANKELLY, the church grove (*celli*), *Pr.* ; ? Gelhi's (*w.*) enclosure.

LANKEVERNE, St. Keverne manor.

LANKIDDEN, ? ? Icdin's (*m.s.*), or the wood pigeon's (*cudon*) enclosure.

LAN-LAKE, -LEAKE, the lake (*lacca*) enclosure, *Pr.*

LANLARON, *d.d.*, ? St. Lawrence's manor (*lan*).

LANLAVERY, ? Leuric's (*t.*) enclosure.

LAN-LAWRNE, *d.d.* -LAWARNEC, ? fox (*lowern*) enclosure.

LANLEDRA, ? cliff (*ledra*) enclosure ; or, = *lam ledra*, robber's leap, *w.*, *R.W.*

LANLIVERY, church of books (*livrou*) ; or, = *Lan le Vorch*, St. Vorch's church place, *T.* ; ?*i.q.* LANLAVERY. (*p.s.* St. Manaccus & St. Dunstan).

LANLOOE, *i.q.* LANDLOE.

LANLOOME, ? bare (*llom*) enclosure.

LANLOVEY, ? LOVEY's enclosure.

LANMIEL, *o.n.f.*, St. Michael's en-closure.

LANNACHEBRAN, *d.d.*, manor of (*a, B.*) St. KEVERNE.

LANNAR, a forest, a grove, a lawn or bare place in a wood, *Pr.*

LANNARNE, ?marsh (*gwern*)enclosure.

LANNARTH, *i.q.* LANNAR, or LAN-ARTH ; (*c.d.* Christ Church).

LANNAUGH, ?*i.q.* LANOW.

LANN-EAR, -EER, -ER, *i.q.* LANEER.

LANNERVEAN, little (*bihan*) LANEER.

LANNICK, the water (*ick*) enclosure, *M'L.* ; ?*i.q.* LARNICK.

LANNIN, *n.f.*, ?*i.q.* LANINE.

LANNINGLE, ? ? cabbage (*ungle*) field.

LANNOWETH, new (*nowydh*)enclosure

LANOROW, rough (*harow* = *garow*) enclosure.

LANOW, my (*ow*), or egg (*oyow*), church or temple, *H.* ; ?St. Kew's enclosure; *d.d.* LANEHOC; *(lanw,* influx of the tide, *w.*, *M.*).

LAN PARK, ? church close *(parc).*

LANPIRAN, *d.d.*, St. Perran's manor.

LANRAKE, *i.q.* LANDRAKE.

LANREATH, church of merit *(reth), Pr.;* o. LANRETHEU, church of laws *(rhaithow, w.), T.,* or near the forts, *M'L.; e.d.d.* LANREDOCH, ? St. Rheidiog's church; *(p.s.* St. Sancredus, *or* St. Manaccus and St. Dunstan, *O.*).

LANSAGEY, *i.q.* LANDEGEA, *H.*

LAN-SALLOS, *o.* -SALUX, -SALEWYS, *d.d.* -SALHUS, ? Sulleisoc's *(s.B.m.)* enclosure; enclosure of the altars, *C.; p.s.* St. Ildierna, *O.*

LANSANT, *now* LEZANT.

LANSCAVETONE, *d.d.,* ? ? elder-tree *(scaw)* enclosure town.

LAN-SEAGE, -SEAGUE, ? dry *(sech),* or corn *(issic),* enclosure.

LANSEATON, *i.q.* LANDSEATON.

LANSIDWELL, ? Sidwell's enclosure; *v.* NANSUGWELL.

LANSLADRON, ? ? St. Elldeyrn's *(w.)* enclosure.

LANSOWNICK, ? ISNIOC'S *(m.s.)* enclosure.

LANSUGLE, *i.q.* LANDSUGLE.

LANSULHAS, ? *i.q.* LANSALLOS; *or* Julius's enclosure.

LANSULIEN, ? St. Sulien's *(w.)* enclosure *or* chapel.

LANTABETHICK, *i.q.* LANTYBETHICK.

LANTALL-ACK, -ICK, ? Tallwch's, *or* high *(tallic)* enclosure.

LANTALLAN, ? Talan's *(B.m.)* enclosure.

LANTAVYS, ? ? outside *(dy veas)* enclosure.

LANTEGLOS, ? = *Laniliz,* church *or* temple land, *a., Leg.**

LANT-ENDLE, -ERNDALL, ? ? the *(an)* dale *(dol)* land.

LANTENNY, ? St. Anthony's place *(le) or* enclosure.

LANTERRICK, ? Edric's *(t.)* enclosure; *or, i.q.* LANDRAKE.

LANTEWELL, ? the devil's *(dioul)* enclosure; *or,* high *(uhel)* land.

LANTEWEY, ? David's *(Deui, w.)* enclosure.

LANTHORNE, *i.q.* LANDTHORNE, ? hill *(tron),* or thorn *(druen)* enclosure.

LANTIC, sons *(ic)* of the Lann, *ga., Beul;* ? pleasant *(teg),* or the husbandman's *(tyac)* enclosure.

LAN-TINE, *d.d.* -THIEN, -TIEN, cold *(iein),* or furze *(eithen),* enclosure *or* land.

LANTIVIT, ? *i.q.* LANIVET.

LANTMATIN, *d.d.* ? the manor of St. Martin.

LANTOOM, ? the warm *(tom)* enclosure.

LANTORME, ? ? heavy *(trom)* land.

LANT-REASE, -RISE, ? yonder *(treas),* or middle *(cres)* enclosure.

LANTRESWORTH, ? high *(warth)* LANTREASE.

LANTUEY, ? *i.q.* LANTEWEY.

LANTUNDLE, *i.q.* LANTENDLE.

LANTYAN, *i.q.* LANTINE.

LANTYBETHICK, *i.q.* LANDABETHICK, (? bushy, *perthic, w., M.*).

LANUAH, *i.q.* LANEWA.

LAN-UDNO, -UTHNO, *o.* -UTHINOCH, ? church of St. Wedenoc; *or,* the narrower *(idnach)* enclosure. *(udd,* one in authority, a chieftain, *w., M.*).

LAN-VARNICK, -WARNICK, ? *i.q.* LANLAWARNEC.

LANVEAN, little enclosure.

LANVORCH, *i.q.* LANLIVERY, *T.*

LANVORNICK, the church on the way *(for)* to the creek *(an ick), Pr.*

LANWAFFER, ? goat *(gafr, w.)* field, *M.*

---

* Dr. Pryce makes LANTEGLOS "church *(eglos)* of truth" *(laute)*; Whitaker, "the church of some unknown St. *Lanty*"; Maclauchlan, "the church *or* place on the beautiful *(teg)* spot of green *(glas).*" LANTEGLOS by Camelford is dedicated to St. Julitta; the *p.s.* of LANTEGLOS by Fowey is not known.

LANWAMAELL, ? ? enclosure place (*ma, va*) of trade (*mael*).

LAN-WENEOC, *d.d.* (*e.d.d.* -GUIENHOC) ? St. Winnow manor.

LANWHITTON, *i.q.* LAWHITTON.

LANWITHAN, ? the tree (*gwedhen*) enclosure.

LANX-ON, -TON, ? long stone, *t.*

LANYEIN, *i q.* LANYON.

LANYEW, ? high (*uch*) enclosure; (*yw*, a yew tree, *w.*, *M.*).

LANYON, ? the church of St. Jona, *Wh.*; enclosure on the down (*oon*), *B.*, or, of the ash trees (*on*), *C.*; or, *i.q.* LANINE.

LANYHORN, church at the angle (*horn*), *Wh.*; *see* RUAN.

LANZEAGUE, *i.q.* LANSEAGE.

LANZION, *i.q.* LANDZION.

LAPEAN, ? little (*bihan*) enclosure (*lan*).

LAPP-AR, -ER, ? pear (*per*) enclosure.

LAPSTONE, ? boundary (*lappa, s.*) stone, *t.*

LAPTHORN, ? boundary thorn, *t.*

LARAN BRIDGE, the (*an*) floor (*lar, i.*) bridge, *H.*; ? *i.q.* LERRIN.

LARCUM, ? the *lark's* vale.

LARE CLOSE, *T.a.*, ? lower close. (*llar*, overspreading, *w.*, *M.*).

LARDYNER, *o.n.f.* ? *i.q.* LANDENNER.

LAR-GAN, -GEN, -GIN, -RIGAN, ? Regan's enclosure.

LARK, *n.f.*, ? *i.q.* LARRACK.

LARKY, 15 *cent.*, ? *i.q.* ELERCHY.

LARNICK, ? = *louernic*, fox place.

LAROCHE, *n.f.*, ? [of] the (*la*) rock (*roche*), *f.*

LARR-ACK, -AKE, a place of content,

Sc.; ? = LARRICK, *i.q.* LANDRAKE.

LASANT, *i.q.* LANSANT.

LASHBROOKE, *n.f.*, ? salmon (*leix*) brook, *t.*

LASULLIAN, ? Sulcen's (*s.B.m*), or Julian's enclosure; *now* LUXULIAN.

LATCHET, ? = latch gate (*yet*) [field].

LATCHLEY, ? latch [gate] meadow.

LATE PARK, ? dairy (*lait ty*) close.

LATIMER, *n.f.*, interpreter.

LATTY, milk (*lait*) house (*ty*).

LAUGHER, *n.f.*, *i.q.* LAWYER, or LOWER.

LAUGHERNE, *n.f.*, ? *i.q.* LANHERNE.

LAUNCE, ? ENES enclosure (*lan*).

LAUNCELLS, the *cells'* church (*lan*), *T.*; enclosure *or* holy cells, *C.*; grove retreat *or* cells, *M.*; ?? church of St. Julius. (*p.s.* St. Andrew, *O.*).

LAUNCESTON, *v.* LANSON, *i.q.* Llanstephan, St. Stephen's church, *w.*, *M.**

LAUN-DER, -DRY, *n.f.*, ? oak (*dar, deru*) grove (*llwyn*, *w.*), *R.W.*

LAVABE, LAVAPPER, *now* MABE, ? St. Mabe's church (*lan*).

LA VAL, *now* HOLY VALE, ? the vale, *f.* (? = *lavalu*, apples, *M.*).

LAVALSEA, ? Walsige's (*s.*) enclosure.

LAVELIS, *n.f.*, the calves, *f.*

LAVETHEN, enclosure of graves, *C.*; ? the meadow (*bidhen*), or tree (*wedhen*), enclosure (*lan*) or place (*le*).

LAVORACK, *i.q.* LANVORNICK.

LAVREAN, ? Urien's (*w.*) enclosure.

LAWARRAN, *o.n.f.*, ? *i.q.* LEWARN.

LAWELLIN, the mill (*melin*), *or* Melyn's enclosure.

---

* Carew says, " Those buildings commonly knowne by the name of LAUNSTON, and written LANCESTON, are by the Cornishmen called LESTEEUAN (*Lez* in Cornish signifieth "broad," and these are scatteringly erected), and were anciently termed LANSTAPHADON, by interpretation, S. STEPHEN'S CHURCH "; Camden, " LANSTUPHADON, *i.e.* the church of Stephen "; Scawen, " =LEOSTOFEN, which is a place of large extent, *or* a broad end," others say, " Lancelot's town "; Leland, " LAUNSTONE, otherwys cawlled LOSTEPHAN, yn old tyme cawlled DUNEVET "; Borlase, " town of the church (*lan*) by the castle; or, long (*lang*) castle (*ceaster*) town, *s.*," agreeing in sense with " the old Celtic name DUN-HEVED, long hill." *d.d.* LANSCAVETONE. The church is dedicated to St. Mary Magdalene; but the mother church is St. Stephens by Launceston.

LAWENNICK, ? marshy (*winnic*) enclosure; or, i.q. LANWENEOC.

LAWHARN, ? alder or marsh (*gwern*) enclosure; or, i.q. LEWARNE.

LAWH-IBBET, -IPPET, ? = *law y beth*, hill of sepulchre, *M'L.*

LAWHIDDEN, ? white (*gwydn*) enclosure; or, i.q. LAVETHEN.

LAWHIRE, ? Gwyar's (*w.*), or, sister's (*huir*) enclosure.

LAWHITTON, white or fair (*gwidn*) church (*lan*), *T.*; town (*tun, s.*) of St. Iltut's church, *Sc.*; enclosed (*lan*) white town, *C.* (*p.s.* St Michael, *C.S.G.*). *d.d.* LANGVITETONE.

LAWNEY, *n.f.*, = *llawn*, full, complete, *w., M.*; ? i.q. TRELAWNY.

LAWRY, *n.f.*, = i.q. LAWRENCE.

LAWTON, *n.f.*, ? i.q. LAWHITTON.

LAWYER, *n.f.*, = *law hir*, long hand.

LAYLAND, ? unploughed land, *t.*

LAYOWEN, ? Owen's pasture.

LAY PARK, unploughed close.

LAYS, ? green (*las* = *glas*) [field].

LAYTY, i.q. LAITY.

LAZARUS FIELD, ? the leper's (*lizar*) field.

LAZON, ? i.q. GLAZDON.

LAZZICK, i.q. LADOCK.

LEA, LEAH, meadow, pasture, *t.*

LEADER PARK, ? cliff (*leder*) close (*parc*).

LEAFERN, ? marshy (*gwern*) place (*le*); or, ferny lea or meadow.

LEAN, ? the *lane*; or, i.q. LAN or LANE.

LEAN AN KINE, ? the (*an*) ridge (*cein*) close.

L. AN KROW, the hovel (*crow*) close.

L. AN STILLEN, the plank close, *R. IV.*

L. BEAN, little (*bihan*) close.

L. DOURACK, close by the water (*dour*), *T.C.*

L.-DRAIN, -DREAN, ? homestead (*tre*), or thorn (*draen*) close.

L. GUERNEN, alder-tree close.

L. GURNELL, ? corner (*cornel*) close.

L. HEERE, ? long (*hir*) close.

L. HILL, chapel (*lan*) hill, *Beal.*

LEANSKATH, ? boat (*scath*) close.

LEAN TIE, ? house (*ty*) close.

LEAPER PARK, ? leper close, *t.*

LEAR, *n.f.*, the sea; or, i.q. HELLIER.

LEASE, LEAZ, the green open place, *Pr.*; ? = *hal lez*, broad moor.

LEAT, a small stream, *m.c.*; (= *lad*, a way, journey; passage for water, *s.*).

LEATHER, *n.f.*, ? = *leththir*, sea-board land; or, *ledr*, a cliff.

LEATHERGWEARNE, ? dairy (*lait ty*) by the alder trees (*gwern*).

LEATHLEAN, *n.f.*, ? milk (*leath*) close (*lan*).

LEDDEN, ? broad (*ledan*) [field].

LEDDI-COAT, -COTE, *n.f.*, ? dairy (*lait ty*) cot.

LED-DRA, -RAH, ? = *ledra*, a cliff.

LEDDYGOON, dairy down (*gwon*).

LE DEMMYNS, 16 *cent.*, the *demesne*, or land kept in the hands of the lord, *f.*; also called DYMYNS.

LEDGET, ? i.q. LEDDICOAT.

LEE, i.q. PARK AN LEE, *Pr.*, or, LEA.

LEE-DY, -TY, i.q. LAIETY.

LEEK PARK, ? flat stone (*lech*) close.

LE FEOCK, i.q. LAFEOCK.

LEFFRA, ? hill (*bre*) meadow, or enclosure (*lan*).

LEGAR, ? camp (*caer*) place (*le*).

LEGARD, *n.f.*, ? i.q. LETCHER.

LEGARIKE, ? rock (*carrag*) place (*le*).

LE-GASSICK, -GOSSICK, *n.f.*, ? dirty (*gassic*) or woody (*cassic*) place.

LEG-E, -EA, *d.d.*, i.q. LEA.

LEGEFFERY, Jeffry's lodge, *t.*

LEGG, *n.f.*, ? = *clegr*, a rock.

LEGG-O, -OE, *n.f.*, the same.

LEGONNA, ? place on the downs (*gonnou*).

LE-GRICE, -GREICE, *n.f.*, ? the (*le*) grey (*gris, f.*); *i.e.* the boar, *W.N.*

LEHA, a place for calves (*leauh*), or, = *leiha*, a small place, *Pr.*

THE LEHAN, ? i.q. LEAN.

LEIGH, LEIGHA, ? i.q. LEA; or, = *le*, a place.

LEISON, ? broad (*les*), or green (*lus*) down (*oon*).

LEJEARN, ? garden (*dzharn*) place.

LELAND, unploughed land, *t.*

LELANT, *o.* LANANT, *from p.s.* *

LELIZ-ICK, -IKE, the heifer (*ledzhek, Pr.*), *or* bushy (*lessick, Gw.*) place.

LEMAILE, ? Michael's (*Miel*), *or,* trade (*mael*) place.

LE-MAIN, -MAYNE, ? ? stone (*maen*) place; *i.q.* LAMANNA.

LEMALLA, ? Mehalla's place, *T.C.* ; *or,* place (*le*) of trade (*maelva*).

LEMAR, the place of horses, horse (*march*) place *or* green, *Pr.*

LEMARNE, ? Maruan's (*w.*) place.

LEMBRAY, *n.f.,* ? *i.q.* LENABRAY.

LEMELLION, ? *i.q.* LAMELLION.

LEMETTON, *i.q.* LAMETTON.

LEMON, *n.f.,* ? *i.q.* LEMAIN.

LEMSWORTHY, ? *i.q.* Elmsworthy, the elm farm (*weorthig, s.*)

LENABRAY, ? enclosure (*lan*) on the hill (*bre*).

LENAS, LENNAS, ? = *lenez,* nettles.

LENDER, *i.q.* LANDER.

LENDERYON, *n.f.,* oak (*derwen*) close (*lan*).

LENDON, the enclosure on the hill *or* down (*dun*).

LEN-DRA, -DERYOU, *i.q.* LANDERYAH.

LENHORGY, *n.f., i.q.* LANHARGY.

LEN-GIA, -IDGA, ? ivy (*idzhio*), *or* house (*chy*) close (*lan*).

LENIERS, ? long (*hir*) closes.

LENN, *n.f.,* ? = *len,* faithful, true; full; a ling fish; a cloak, blanket.

LENON, ? Non's place.

LENOY, the nephew's (*noi*), *or* Noe's (*B.m.*) place.

LENT PARK, ? linden, *or* linnet close,*t.*

LENTY MEADOW, ? shed (*lean-to, m.c.*) meadow.

LENYER, ? *i.q.* LANHER.

LEOFRIC *prespiter, w.B.m.,* Bishop, *t.d.d.,* beloved rule, *t.*

LEOFSIE, *w.B.m.,* beloved victory (*sige*), *t.*

LEOW FIELD, ? sheltered (*hleo, s.*) field.

LERCEDEKNE, LERCHDEACON, *o.n.f.,* the (*le*) archdeacon, *f.*

LERGAN, *i.q.* LARGAN.

LER-RIN, -RING, -YN, river *or* channel (*ryn*) place (*le*), *M'L.* ; little (*in*) sea (*lear*), *ga., Beal.*

LERRY, ? = *leary,* hungry, empty, *m.c., M.* ; ? moor (*hal*) field (*eru*).

LESALSON, ? ALSTAN'S court (*lis*).

LESCADDOCK, ? Cadwg's court, *H.*

LESCARNICK, ? rocky court.

LESCAWNE, ? elder-tree (*scauen*) place (*le*) ; *or,* down (*goon*) court (*lis*).

LESCHELL, *d.d.,* ? *i.q.* LESKEEL.

LESCLISTON, ? scarlet oak (*glastanen*) border (*lez, a.*).

LESCROW, ? hovel (*crow*) field.

LESCUDJECK, bloody (*gudzhic*) field (*les*), *B.* ; *i.q.* LESCADDOCK, Cara-doc's court, *Bl.*

LESENGY, ? ? court by the river (*angy*).

LESEW, ? dry field (*le*), *W.B.*

LESHOWTT, 15 *cent.,* the (*le, f.*) water spout (*shoot, m.c.*).

LESKEEL, ? rye (*sygal*) field.

LESKERNICK HILL, *i.q.* LESCARNICK.

LESKEYS, ? the burnt (*leskys*) [field].

LESKINNICK, Cennych's (*w.*) court.

LESMANAEK, (13 *cent.*) the monk's (*manach*), *or* Meneage court.

LESNEWTH, new (*newydh*) width (*les*), *Car.* ; new, *or* ash-trees (*enwith*) court. (*p.s.* St. Michael, *O.*).

LE SORE *or* SOOR, *n.f.,* the stag, *f.*

LESPERROW, ? pear trees (*peruith*) court. (*berw,* a boiling, *w., M.*).

LESQUITE, the *quoit, or* cromlech place, *T.Q.C.* ; = *Llys coed,* wood court, *w., R.W.* ; ? place (*le*) under (*is*) the wood (*cuit*).

---

* Whitaker makes the old patron saint to be Lananta, *al.* Kananc, a daughter of K. Brechan; the present patron saint is St. Ewinus or Uny. Tonkin makes LELANT = *le lan,* the church place; Pryce says, = *lan nant,* the church on the plain, *or,* by the river. *R.E.* compares the name of this sandy parish with Les Landes, on the Bay of Biscay. In legal documents the parish is called UNI LELANT, *T.C.*

LES-TEADER, -TOWDER, ?Tudor's court

LESTINNES, ? castle (*dinas*) court.

LEST-OON, -WEN, -UNE, ?? hill (*dun*), or white (*gwin*), or Deon's (*w.*) court.

LESTORMELL, *Car.*, ? king's (*mael*) hill (*tor*) court ; (*now* RESTORMEL).

LESTOU, ? the (*le, f.*) place (*stow, s.*).

LEST-WIDDEN, -WYN, ? white (*gwin, gwydn*) court.

LETCHA, LECHA, ? ivy (*idzhio*) place (*le*).

LETCHER, *n.f.,* ? people's (*leod, s.*) spear (*ger, s.*), *t.* ; *or, i q.* LETCHA ; (*letshar,* a frying pan).

LETCOT, ? *i.q.* LEDDICOAT.

LETHANNECK, a place of much sand, *Sc.* (?) ; *now* Little PETHERICK.

LETHARBY, *n.f.,* Lethar's dwelling (*by, d.*), *t.*

LETHBRIDGE, *n.f.,* ? ? the *bridge* in the broad open plain, (*lledd, w.*), *or* over the *leat or* small stream, *t.*

LETHLEAN, *i.q.* LEATHLEAN.

LETHNEAN, ? the (*an*) lamb's (*ean*) side (*leth, B.*), *or* leat.

LETHOWSOW, (*i.q.* LIONESSE), the shore, *Wh.* (?).

LEU-BELEC, -HELEC, *s.B.m.* ; ?? hairy (*blewac*) lion (*leu*).

LEUCUM, *w.B.m.,* ? the sheltered (*hleo, s.*) vale, *t.*

LEUDON, ? *i.q.* LEWDON.

LEUENOT, *t.d.d.,* ? beloved (*leof*) compulsion (*not*), *t.*

LEUERON, *t.d.d.,* ? beloved shield (*rond*), *t.*

LEUIUT, *m.s. Camborne,* the pilot *or* master of a ship (*leuiut*).

LEUMARH, *w.B.m.,* lion (*leu*) horse (*march*) ; *or,* beloved (*leof, s.*) fame (*mar*), *t.*

LEURIC, *Bishop, d.d., i.q.* LEOFRIC.

LEUTY, *n.f.,* ? = *llety,* house, room, lodging, *w., M.* ; *or, i.q.* LAITY.

LEUUINUS, *t.d.d.,* ? beloved (*leof*) friend (*win*), *t.*

LEVAPPER, *i.q.* LAVABE.

LEVARDER, ?higher (*wartha*)place (*le*).

LEV-ARRICK, -ORRICK, ? church (*lan*) road (*for*) place, *C.J.*

LEVEALE, LEVELES, *n.f.,* the calf, the calves, *f.* ; ? = *laf fel,* a cunning *or* sly hand, *W.N.*

LEVELLAN, ? mill (*melin*) place.

LEV-ENNA, -NA, ? smooth *or* level (*leven*) [field].

LEVERMORE, *n.f.,* ?green (*verth*) moor (*hal*), *reduplicated.*

LEVERS, *n.f.,* ? = Oliver's son.

LEVERTON, *n.f.,* ? *i.q.* ALVERTON.

LEVINWELL, ? smooth (*leven*) field (*gweal*).

LEVREAN, *i.q.* LAVREAN.

LEVREAR, ? = *lle vear,* great place, *w., M.*

LEWANNICK, the church (*lan*) upon *or* near the marsh (*winic*), *Pr.* ; monk's (*manach*) church, *Wh.* ; St. Wednach's church, *T.* ; (*p.s.* St. Martin, *O.*).

LEWARNE, fox (*loarn*) place (*le*), *Pr.* ; ? swampy *or* alder (*gwernic*) place.

LEWCOMBE, ? sheltered (*hleo, s.*) vale, *t.*

LEWCOTT, old (*coth*) place (*le*), *M.* ; ? sheltered cot *or* wood, *t.*

LEWDON, ? sheltered hill (*dun*), *or* down, *t., A.A.V.*

LEWELL-EN, -AND, the horizon (*llyweli, w.*), *M.*

LEWHAM, ? the sheltered (*hleo, s.*) meadow (*holm*), *t.*

LEWIRES, ?the virgin's (*wyrhes*) place.

LEW PARK, sheltered close, *t.*

LEWRATH, ? = *luwarth,* a garden, *R.W.*

LEY, *i.q.* LEA.

LEYLAND, *i.q.* LELAND.

LEY PARK, unploughed close, *t.*

LEYROS, ? heath (*ros*) pasture land ; *or,* the (*le, f.*) heath.

LEZANT, *o.* LANSANT, Holy church, All hallows, *Pr.* ; (*p.s.* St. Briocus, *O.*).

LEZEREA, *i.q.* LIZEREA.

LIBBY, *n.f.,* ? *from llibid,* soft, *w., M.* ; *i.q.* Mary, *Y.*

LICKHAM, ? the flat stone (*lech*) enclosure (*ham*), M.

LIDCOT, ? *i.q.* LEDDICOAT.

LIDDA PARK, ? dairy (*lait ty*) close.

LIDDEL, *n.f.*, = LITTLE, *s.*

LIDDEN, ? broad (*ledan*) [field].

LIDDER CROFT, ? dairy croft.

LIDG, *f.m.*, ? = the *ledge*.

LIDGA, ? *i.q.* LETCHA.

LIDGATE, ? = *hlidgeat*, a postern gate, a back door, *s.*

LIDGEY, *n.f.*, ? *i.q.* HALLINGEY ; *or*, ivy (*idzhio*) place (*le*).

LIDWELL, Our Lady's well, *t.*, M.

LIFTCOT, ? old (*coth*) flood (*llif*, *w.*), M. ; ? cottage on the summit, *t.*

LIGG-AR, -ER, ? = *clegar*, a rock.

LIGWRATH, place (*le*) near the shore (*gwarth*), M. ; ? root (*gwredh*) place.

LILLECRAP, LILLICARP, *n.f.*, ? lily or little croft, *t.*

LIM-ITS, -ICKS, *from limax*, the sea snail, *lat.*, Jo.C.

LIMPIT, *T.a.*, ? = *lime pit.*

LIMSWORTHY, *i.q.* LEMSWORTHY.

LINDERS, ? oak (*dar*) closes (*lan-s*).

LINE, *n.f.*, ? *lyn*, a pool.

LIN-GER, -GEY, ? flax (*lin*) close (*ce*).

LINHAY PARK, shed close, *t.*

LINKAN VOUNDER, ? the moist place (*lynnic*) in the (*a'n*) lane (*bounder*), T.C.

LINKANDALE, ? the moist place in the dale, T.C.

LINKINGHORNE, ? the church (*lan*) on the rising of the iron (*haiarn*) hill, Pr., church in the corner (*horn*) ; (*p.s.* St. Milorus, O.).

LINNER, ? long (*hir*) lake (*lyn*), or

enclosure (*lan*).

LINNEY, shed (*lean-to*, *m.c.*) [field].

LINNICK, ? flax (*lin*) field, R.W. ; *or*, moist place (*lynnic*).

LINYON, *n.f.*, *i.q.* LANYON.

LIPSON, *n.f.*, ? = Philip's son.

LISART, *d.d.*, *i.q.* LIZARD.

LISCONE, *i.q.* LESCAWNE.

LISEADREN, ? Sadwrn's (*w.*) court.

LISKEARD, ? Carwyd's (*w.*) court ; *or* court by the castle (*caer*) in the wood (*cuit*).*

LISKERNICK, rocky (*carnic*) court.

LISK-ERS, -ES, -IS, ? = *lescys*, burnt.

LISKOMBE, *n.f.*, ? Luke's, *or* bushy (*lesic*) vale ; *or*, *i.q.* LOSCOMBE.

LISKROW, ? heifer (*ledzhec*) shelter *or* hovel (*crow*).

LISKY, ? bushy (*lesic*) close (*hay*).

LISLE, *n.f.*, the (*l'*) isle, *f.*

LISNIWEN, *d.d.*, *i.q.* LESNEWTH.

LISQUITE, *i.q.* LESQUITE.

LISTER, *n.f.*, ? = *lwythter*, fine land, *w.*, R.W. ; *or*, *lesler*, a ship.

LISTETHA, ? Teithi's (*w.*) court.

LISTOO, ? = *lluestou*, cottages, *w.*

LITHIOCK, ? = *llaethog*, yielding much milk, *w.*

LITHTON, *n.f.*, ? ? hill (*dun*) side (*leth*).

LITH-ONEY, -NEY, *v.* LUNY, ? Theony's (*w.*) place (*le*).

LITTENS, ? broad (*ledan*) [field]s.

LITTLE GOOD GRACE, *t.b.*, ? little middle (*cres*) wood (*coed*) ; *or*, = *little good-grass* [field].

LIVELOE, cliff (*clive*) castle *or* tumulus (*low*), *t.*, M'L. (?)

LIVERS, ? Oliver's [field].

LIZARD, ? high (*ard*) court (*lis*), or

---

* B.m. LYSCERRUYT ; *d.d.* LISCARRET ; *old seal of the borough*, LESKERRT ; *official name*, LISKERRET, *alias* LISKEARD. These latter forms have been rendered "fortified *or* castle (*caered*, pl. of *caer*, *w.*) court or palace (*lis*), *or*, refiner's (*ceard*, *e.*) court or green (*les*)," Pr. ; "the court (*cuird*, *e.*) at the castle or earthwork (*lios*, *e.*)," Wh. ; "square (*carret*=*quadrata*, *lat.*) camp," W.S. ; "some say 'a place affected' ; others take it from the Cornish word *Leskeveres* (?), 'like length, like breadth, *i.e.* a square' ; and so it anciently was, and so fortified, as the castle walls, yet in part remaining, shew," Sc. ; "widenesse (*les*, broad) gone (*ker*)," Car. ; "LIS- *or* LIOS-CEART, the court (*lios*) of the old (*ette*) fortified (*caer*) town, *and*, of workers in metal (*ceard*), ga. ; *otherwise*, LYS-KERRET, the lesser (*et*, *s.*) law court," Beal.

cliff (*als*) ; *or*, steep (*serth*) place (*le*).*

LIZAREA WARTHA & WOLLAS, ?higher *and* lower leper's (*lizar*) enclosure (*hay*).

LIZZON *or* CLUSION, ? green (*glas*) down (*oon*).

LLOYD, *n.f.*, = *w.* llwyd, grey, hoary, brown, *R.W.*

LOBB, *n.f.*, ? = *leof*, beloved, *s.* ; *or*, *lob*, a spider, *s.*

LOCKE, the calf's (*loch*) place, *T.C.*

LOCKETT, *n.f.*, = *lokket*, curled, *i.e.* a hero, *d.*, *F.*

LOCKHAM, ? Lucco's home, *t.*

LOCK PARK, ? calf's close.

LOCKSTICH, ? calf's intake *or* narrow strip (*sticce*, *s.*).

LODDECOOMBE, ? heifer (*lodn*), *or* muddy (*lleidiog*, *w.*), *or* prince's (*leod*, *s.*) vale.

LODEN, ? = *ludn* = *glan*, a bank.

LODENEK, *Leland*, brim *or* bank (*ladn*) of the water (*ick*), *Wh.* ; LODERICK, robber's (*lader*) creek (*gwic*), *Po.* ; *now* PADSTOW.

LOE, = *lo*, a lake, pool, pond, *or* inlet of water, *R.W.* ; LOE POOL, *a re-duplication*.

LOENTER, *n.f.*, ? = *lowender*, joy, mirth ; *or*, *i.q.* LAUNDER.

LOEVAN, little (*bihan*) mound (*low*, *s.*), *M'L.*

LOGAN ROCK, LOGGON STONE, rock-ing (*loging*, *m.c.*) stone.

LOGGAN, *n.f.*, ? Luke's down (*goon*) ; *or*, *from* ILLOGAN.

LOGG-AS, -US, -ATS CLOSE, ? calf's (*loch*) house (*hws*, *w.*), *or* wood (*cus*) close.

LONGABEAK, the *long* promontory *or* point (*pyg*, *w.*).

LONGA PARK, long close (*parc*).

LONG CARNE, ? carn enclosure (*lan*).

LONG CHEPYNGE, 15 *cent.*, ?market (*ceaping*, *s.*) enclosure (*lan*).

LONGCOE, ? wood (*coed*) close (*lan*).

LONG GRASE, = *long grass*, *R.B.K.* ; ? middle (*cres*) enclosure (*lan*).

LONGLEAN, = *lawan lan*, field of birds, *T.C.* ; ? *long lane.*

LONGORE, ? the moor (*cors*) enclosure (*lan*).

LONGUNNET, ? Cunedda's (*w.*) enclos-ure ; *or* enclosure of the downs (*goon*) with a gate (*yet*).

LONG VILLAN, ? mill (*melin*) enclos-ure ; *or*, long mill [field].

LONKAMOOR, ? = *long moor.*

LONKELLY, ?grove (*celli*) enclosure (*lan*).

LOOE, *i.q.* LOE.†

LOOM HILL, ? naked *or* bare (*llwm*, *w.*) hill.

LOOSE-LORAN, ? ? fox (*lowern*) bottom (*goles*).

LOOSEMORE, *n.f.*, ? = *Luke's moor.*

LOPS CLOSE, ? Lobb's Close.

LOPTHORNE, ? the *lopped or* cut thorn.

LOSCOMBE, ? burning (*losc*), *or* camp (*lost*) vale (*comb*, *s.*).

LOSTWITHIEL, ? WITHIEL, *or* the Irishman's (*gwyddel*) encampment (*lluest*, *w.*).‡

---

* Borlase says, "LYSHERD, much (*liaz*) thrust out (*herdya*, thrust forward, promi-nent) ; a chief place thrust forth, *or* headland jutting forth" ; Gough, "something thrown forward and high" ; Baxter, "high cape" ; Hals, "lofty (*ard*) *or* dangerous gulph between two lands, &c., (*liz*)" ; Norris (speaking of LIZARD POINT, *Scilly*) says, it im-plies a gate *or* passage = *w.* llidiart, *or* lidiard ; Jephson refers it to *lazar*, a leper ; others to the reptile lizard, from its resemblance ; the Rev. W. Beal asks, "Was it in early days the high (*ard*) [beacon] light (*les*), *ga.*"?

† St. Mary is the patron saint of West Looe, *O.* ; East Looe is otherwise called "St. Martin juxta Looe," *O.* ; Scawen renders LOOE and LOE a low *or* watery place ; M'Lauchlan prefers referring both LOOE and LOE to the tumuli near, (*low*, a mound, tumulus, *s.*), rather than to *llwch*, a lake *or* pool, *w.*, in Cornish, *lo.*

‡ The UXELA *or* UZELLA of Ptolemy, *Cam.* ; = *Les uthiel or uhal*, the high palace (referring to its old site (?) at Restormel), *Po.* ; the palace (*lis*) of [earl] Withiel, *Wh.* ;

Z

LOTHON, *n.f.*, ? *i.q.* LODEN.

LOUCHLANDS, ? fields by the water-side (*louc'h*, *a.*).

LOUCUM, *cleric, w.B.m.*, pool (*lo*) in the valley (*cum*), *M.*

LOUMARCH, *w.B.m.*, *i.q.* LEUMARH.

LOV-AGE, -IS FIELD, ?? = *Lovey's field.*

LOVE, *n.f.*, = *loup*, wolf, *f.*, *Lo.* ; or, *leof*, beloved, *s.*

LOVELL, *n.f.*, *dim. of* LOVE ; or, *i.q.* LEVEALE.

LOVEY, *n.f.*, ? = *w.* Llywy.

LOVICE, *n.f.*, ? son of Llywy.

LOWARTH COOSE, *t.b.*, ? wood (*cus*) garden (*lowarth*).

LOWBRYGGE, *IV. Worc.*, = *Loe bridge.*

LOWDON, ? mound (*loe*, *s.*) hill.

LOWENAN, *w.B.m.*, ? = *lovennan*, a weasel.

LOWER, *n.f.*, ? = *law hir*, of the long hand, *w.* ; or, *lower*, a lord, *Pr.*, a leper, *Po.*

LOWLEY, river, ? flowing (*lli*) pool (*lo*), *M.*

LOWRES HOSPITAL, leper's hospital.

LOYS CAVE, St. Eloy's cave.

LUAR DREN, ? home (*dre*), or thorn (*draen*) garden.

LUBY, *n.f.*, ? *i.q.* LOVEY.

LUCCO, *s.B.m* , unexpected, one who was got by luck, *t.*, *F.* (?).

LUCKETT, ? = *lock gate.*

LUCKHAM, ? LUCCO's home (*ham*), *t.*

LUC-, LU-COMBE, ? Luke *or* LUCCO's vale (*comb*, *s.*).

LUCOT, ? LUCCO's cot, *t.* ; *or* sheltered (*hleo*, *s.*) wood (*coat*).

LUCY, *n.f.*, ? = *Lucius*, light, *lat.*

LUDCOT, *o.* LUTCOT, ? = *w.* llwydcoet, grey wood, *R.W.* ; ? Lutta's cottage, *t.*

LUDDENGARTH, ? bank (*ladn = glan*) enclosure (*garth*).

LUDDRA, ? the cliffs *or* steep hills (*ledrou*) ; or, oak (*deru*) enclosure (*lan*).

LUDGVAN, *from p.s.* St. Ludowanus, *O.* ; = *lud*, or *lug uan*, high tower, *B.* ; ? = *Llwydvan*, grey stone, *w.*, *R.W.* ; ? ox (*udzheon*) enclosure (*lan*), *T.C.*

L.-LAZE, -LEES, ? LUDGVAN meadows (*lea-s*, *t.*), *T.C.* ; (*les*, broad, *Dr.*, court, *Po.*).

LUDGY, ? *i.q.* LIDGEY.

LUDON, ? sheltered (*hleo*, *s.*) down.

LUFF, *n.f.*, ? *i.q.* LOVE.

LUFFCOTT, ? *o.* LUFFING COTTE, ? Leof's cottage, *t.*

LUGG, *n.f.*, ? the undergrowth of weeds, clover, &c., among corn, *m.c.*

LUGGAN, *n.f.*, *i.q.* LOGGAN.

LUGGER, *n.f.*, ? *i.q.* LONGORE.

LUKEY, *n.f.*, ? *i.q.* LUKE.

LUMBERT, ? Beort's (*t.*) enclosure (*lan*).

LUN-A, -EY, -NA, -Y, ? *i.q.* LITHONY.

LUNCEN, *s.B.m.*, ? *from w.* llyngcu, to swallow ; *m.c.*, clunk.

LUXON, = *Llwyn on*, ash grove, *w.*, *R.W.*

LUNSTONE, ? puffin (*lundi*, *o.n.*) rock.

LURE, *n.f.*, ? = *luior*, a painter ; or, *i.q.* LOWER.

LUSCOMBE, ? Luke's *or* LYWCI's vale ; or, *i.q.* LOSCOMBE.

LUSKEYS TOR, ? the burnt (*leskys*) hill, *or* tor of burning.

LUSON, *n.f.*, ? *i.q.* GLAZON.

LUTMAN, *n.f.*, a man who stoops (*lutan*, *s.*) in his gait, *t.*, *Lo.*

LUTTRELL, *n.f.*, *dimin. of loutre*, an otter, *f.*, *Lo.*

LUX CROSS, St. Luke's cross.

L. MOORE, *n.f.*, ? Luke's moor.

L. STREET, St. Luke's street.

LUX-TON, -ON, *n.f.*, ? Luke's town.

LUXULYAN, *o.* LASULLIAN, = *lan Julian*, church of St. Julian, *T.* ; (*p.s.* St. Cyrus and St. Julitta, *O.*).

LYD-COTT, -CUTT, *i.q.* LUDCOT ; *or* = *llydiart*, a country gate, *w.*

the tented encampment (*lluest*, *w.*) of the stranger (*gwyddel*, an Irishman), *Fenton* ; the lion's (*guitfil*, *B.*) tail (*lost*), *Le.*, *Car.* (!) ; *vulgo*, "Lost i' (=*in*) the hill," from its very low situation, (! !) ; *p.s.* St. Bartholomew.

LYDE ROCK, ? *from* St. Elidius.

LYLE, *n.f.*, *i.q.* LISLE.

LYNAM, *n.f.*, ? dwelling (*ham*, *s.*) on the lake (*lyn*).

LYNE, *n.f.*, ? = *lyn*, a lake.

LYNHER, *river*, long (*hir*) lake, *B.*

LYTHE, *n.f.*, ?? = *lyth*, a limb, the back, *Pr.*

LYWCI, *s.B.m.*, ? lion (*leu*) dog (*ci*).

LYZON, ? *i.q.* GLAZON.

MABBOT, *n.f.*, *dim.* of Mabb = Abraham, *Lo.*

MABE, *from p.s.* St. Mabe, *C.S.G.*, or St. Mabon or Mabyn, *M.* ; son (*mab*) [of God], *H.* ; *o.* LAVABE, *v.* LAVAPPER, ? church (*lan*) of the son of Mary (*mabmair*).

MABELBURROW, ? maple tree, or Mabil's mound, *t.*, *Jo.C.*

MABIN, *n.f.*, from St. MABYN.

MACEY, *n.f.*, *from* Macei (*Normandy*), *Lo.*

MACHUS, *t.d.d.*, MACCOS, *w.B.m.*, ? ? = *maximus*, greatest, *lat.* ; or, *makarios*, blessed, *gr.*

MACKWORTH, *n.f.*, ? *i.q.* MACURTH, *w.B.m.*, ? *i.q.* Machraith (*w.s.*).

MAD-DEN, -DERN, -ERN, -RON, *n.f.*, *from* St. MADRON.

MADDERHAY, mugwort (*madere*, *s.*) enclosure (*hay*), *t.*

MADDOX, *n.f.*, son of MADOC (*w.*), *i.e.* the beneficent.

MAD-ERS, -US, ? Madern's [place].

MADFORD, ? the place (*mod*, *w.*) at the ford ; or = *mulford*, *t.*

MADLY, ? good (*mad*, *w.*), *i.e.* fertile place (*le*), or pasture (*lea*, *t.*).

MADVERN, ?? alder (*gwern*) meadow (*maes*, *maed*).

MAEN ADDICK, ? the great (*uthic*) rock or stone (*maen*).

M. DOWER, the stone near the water (*dour*), *Bl.*

M. DU, the black (*du*) stone.

M. HEERE, the long (*hir*) stone.

M. TALLACK, the high (*tallic*) rock.

MAENTOL, the holed (*tol*) stone.

MAEN Y GRIB, the comb-like rock.

MAES PARK, ? meadow (*maes*), or May's close.

MAGARUS, *m.s. Worthyvale*, ? = *makarios*, blessed, *gr.*

MAGER, the feeding place (*maga*, to feed) ; MAGOR, *n.f.*, *the same*, *Pr.*

MAGMAIN, ? a brood (*mag*) of stones (*myin*), *i.e.* many stones, *M.*

MAIDEN BOWER, = *men vor*, the great stone or rock, *N.*

M. HAYS, stone closes.

MAIL PARK, ?? Michael's (*Mihal*) close (*parc*).

MAINADEW, *i.q.* MAENDU.

MAINA-, MAIN-PARK, stone (*maen*) close (*parc*).

MAINLAY, ? *i.q.* MANELEY.

MAINPORTH, ? stone cove (*porth*) ; or stone of the cove.

MAINWARING, *n.f.*, = *Mesnil Warin*, the manor of Warin, *f.*, *Lo.*

MAIOWE, *n.f.*, *i.q.* MAYOW.

MAKER, *d.d.* MACRETONE, ? Macurth's (*B.m.*), or Magarus's (*m.s.*) town ; (*p.s.* St. Julien, *O.*).

MALE, *n.f.*, ? = *Mehal*, Michael.

MAL-EDDEN, -IDDEN, ? broad (*ledan*) field (*maes*).

MAL-ET, -LET, *n.f.*, a mace, *t.*

MALPAS, *pr.* MOPAS, bad passage, *f.*, *Pr.* ; ? traffic (*mael*) passage, *C.*

MANABURLA, ? place (*man*), or stone (*maen*) of embracing (*byrla*), or of roses (*breilu*).

MANACCAN, *o.* MINSTRE, MONATHON, monk (*manach*) town (*tun*, *s.*), *Wh.* ; the stony (*maenic*) haven (*an = haun*), or, haven (*ack*) of white (*can*) stones (*myin*), *Pr.* ; (*p.s.* St. Antoninus, *O.*).

MANACK POINT, monk's point.

MANACLES, church (*eglos*) rock or stone (*maen*), *Po.*

MANALLACK, ? lower (*wollach*) stone.

MANATON, stony hill (*dun*), *T.* ; monk (*manach*) town, *Wh.*

MANAULOE, tumulus (*low*, *s.*) of stone ;

or, the monk's (*manach*) tumulus, M'L.

MANE, = *maen*, a stone.

MANEHAY, stone enclosure (*hay*).

MANELEY, the stone pasture (*lea, s.*), *or* place (*le*) ; *or, i.q.* MINGELI.

MANELS, ?? sheaf of corn (*manal yz*), *or* MANNEL'S [field].

MANGITHA, ? St. Ceitho's (*w.*) stone ; *or*, great (*ithic*)stony (*maenic*) piece.

MANIIAN-ICK, -IOT, *n.f., from* MENHENIOT.

MANHIRE, *n.f., i.q.* MENHEIR.

MANKEY, stone hedge (*ce*) ; *or* St. Cai's stone.

MANLEY, *n.f., i.q.* MANELEY.

MANN, *n.f.,* ? *i.q.* MANE, *or* MOHUN.

MANNA, *n.f., i.q.* MANEHAY.

MANNEL, *n.f., i.q.* MANUEL.

THE MANNICK, the stony (*maenic*) [field].

MANNING, ? *i.q.* MANNERING.

MAN OF WAR, *i.q.* MENAVORE.

MANNERING, *n.f., i.q.* MAINWARING.

MANOR-GWIDDEN, -WIDDEN, white (*gwidn*) mountain (*mener*), *Fr.* ; ? white long (*hir*) stone (*maen*).

MANUEL, *n.f.,* ? high (*uhel*) stone (*maen*) ; *or* = Emmanuel.

MANUEL SCUD, Manuel's low ledge of rocks (*scud, m.c.*), *T.C.*

MANUTE, *n.f., i.q.* MENHENIOT.

MANY GULLAS, ? = *maen y goles*, the bottom stone.

M. PARK, *i.q.* MAINAPARK.

M. WITHIN, ? white (*gwydn*) stone.

MAR-ADON, -RADON, ? horse (*marh*), *or* market (*marchad*), *or* boundary (*mearc, s.*) hill (*dun*).

MARAZION, Jews' (*edzhuon*) market (*marhas*), *B.**

MARBLE FIELD, ? = *maple field*.

MARBURY, *n.f.,* ? *from* MARRABOROUGH.

MARCAIEW, *Car., i.q.* MARKET JEW.

MARCH, MARH, *w.B.m.,* ? horse.

MARCRADDEN, ?fern (*reden*)boundary (*mearc, s.*).

MAR-DEN, -DON, *n.f.,* ? *i.q.* MARADON.

MARGATE, *i.q.* St. MARGARET'S.

MARGHAS-BIGAN, -BEAN, little market ; *i.q.* MARAZION.

MARHAM, the dwelling (*ham*) on the frontier, *I.T.* ; ? MARH'S dwelling.

MARHAM-, *o.* MARWYN-CHURCH, the church of St. Morwenna, *p.s. O.*

MARHASANVOSE, the (*an*) maid's (*mos*), *or* trench (*fos*) market (*marhas*).

MARK, *king*, and *n.f., i.q.* MARCH.

MARKET JEW, Jew (*ezow*) market (*marchad*).*

MARKWELL, the knight's (*marheg*), *or* boundary (*mearc, s.*) well.

MAROONEY, *i.q.* MERTHER UNY.

MAROW, *n.f.,* ?? dead (*marow*).

MARRABOROUGH, ? knight's barrow.

MARRACK, *n.f.,* ? = *marheg*, a horseman, knight, cavalier, soldier.

MARR-AIS, -YES, = *marais*, marsh, *f.*

MARSHALL, ? *marsh* moor *or* hill (*hal*), *or* hall (*hel*).

MARSH PARK, ? marshy close.

MARSLAND, = *marshy land.*

MARTHA, ? *i.q.* MATHA.

MARTH MEADOW, ? flat, low, *or* sea sedge (*merydd, w.*) meadow.

MASHGATE, *i.q.* MARSHGATE.

MASS PARK, ? *i.q.* MARSH PARK.

MATELE, *d.d., now* METHLEIGH.

MATHA, a flattening down (*mathr, w.*), a flat place, *M.*

---

* Professor Max Müller says, MARAZION may be "little (-*en*) market " (*i.q.* MARGHASBIGAN, -BEAN), but, with friend and correspondent, *J.B.*, prefers considering both MARAZION and its *alias* MARKET JEW simple plurals of *marhas*, a market (*pl. marhasion*), and its more ancient form *marchad* (*pl. marchadyou*). *See* " Macmillan's Magazine," April, 1867, p. 486 ; and "Journal of the Royal Institution of Cornwall," 1867, p. 333. Leland, Camden, Carew, Norden, Oliver, &c., make both "Thursday (*dieu*) market," the *n* being regarded as a mistake for *u*. Halliwell makes Marazion " market on the strand (*zian*)"; Pryce, " market on the sea coast "; Hingston, " market of the island (*ia-n, s.*)"; Isaac Taylor, " hill by the sea" (*ph.*) ; and others, " bitter ZION " (*h.*) !!

MATTOCK, *n.f.*, ? *i.q.* MADOC, *w.*

MAUDL-EY, -IN, -ING, ? = St. Mary Magdalene; ? *i.q.* MADLY, *R.W.*

MAULS MEADOW, ? mules' (*moyls*, *m.c.*), or wether-sheep (*mols*) meadow.

MAUNDER, *n.f.*, a beggar, *t.*; ? = *mawndir*, peatland, *w.*, *R.W.*

MAWGAN, *from p.s.* St. Mauganus, *O.*; ? = *mor gan*, by the sea, *Pr.*

M. PORTH, MAWGAN cove.

MAWLA, *i.q.* MOLA.

MAWNAN, *from p.s.* St. Maunanus [and St. Stephen], *O.*; boy's (*maw*) plain or valley (*nans*), *perhaps* MOR-NAN, valley or plain by the sea, *Pr.*

M. SMITH, Mawnan smithy, *W.R.*

MAXWORTHY, ? Maccus's (*B.m.*) farm (*worthig*), *t.*

MAY, *n.f.*, ? = *me*, May, the month; (*mæg*, a man, a maiden, *s.*, *F.*).

THE MAY, ? the *may*-[pole place].

MAYNARD, *n.f.*, mighty (*mein* = *megin*) firmness, *t.*, *Y.*; ? high (*ard*) stone (*maen*).

MAYNDY, *n.f.*, *i.q.* MENDY.

MAYNE, *n.f.*, ? *i.q.* MEAN.

M. PORT, *i.q.* MAINPORTH.

MAYO, *o.* MAYHEW, *n.f.*, ? the yew (*eo*) plain (*mach*), *i.*

MAYON, *i.q.* MEAN.

MAY PARK, ? hawthorn close.

MAY ROSE, ? hawthorn moor (*ros*); or, *i.q.* MEDROSE.

THE MAZE, ? = *maes*, a field.

MAZEDIPPER, ? ? May's pit (*dippa*, *B.*); or, pit field (*maes*).

MEADENWELL, ? *i.q.* MANUEL.

MEAD PARK, ? meadow close.

MEAD ROSE, *i.q.* MEDROSE.

MEALHERN, ? Michael's (*Mihal*), or trade (*mael*) corner (*horn*). (*haiarn*, iron).

MEAL PARK, ? Michael's close.

MEAN, = *maen*, the stone.

M.-A, -HAY, stone close.

M. GEAR, ? camp (*caer*) stone.

M. HEER, long (*hir*) stone.

MEAN LAND, rock of the sacred enclosure (*llan*, *w.*), *M.*

M. MELLIN, ? the yellow (*melyn*) stone.

M. PARK, stone close (*parc*).

M. SCREEFIS, the inscribed (*scrifys*) stone.

M. TOLL, the hole (*tol*) stone.

M. VOSE, ? the maid's (*mos*) stone.

MEAR, ? the lake (*mere*, *s.*).

MEARS PARK, ? close with the boundary (*gemere*, *s.*) stones.

MEASHAM, ? ? meadow (*maes*) island (*holm*, *t.*), or home (*ham*, *s.*).

MEASMEER, great (*mear*) field (*maes*).

MEAT PARK, ? *i.q.* MEAD PARK.

MEAVER, ? great (*vear*) field.

MEDDESCHOLE, 13 *cent.*, *now* MICHELL.

MEDGUISTYL, *f.s.B.m.*, ? ? mead or bashfulness (*meth*) pledge (*guistel*).

MEDHUIL, *f.s.B.m.*, ? the same.

MEDLAND, ? mead or meadow-land; or, *middle* field, *t.*

MEDL-ANE, -YN, ? = *meddal lyn*, soft swamp or pond, *T.C.*; or, *midlan*, a field of battle, *w.*

MED-RES, -ROSE, *i.q.* MODROSE.

MEER, *i.q.* MEAR.

MEHAL MILL, ? Michael's mill.

MEIN, *n.f.*, *i.q.* MAYNE.

MEIN AN DANS, *t.b.*, *i.q.* DAWNSMEN.

MEINEK, rock, strong, *Bl.*; ? stony.

M. POINT, stony (*maenic*) point, *Bl.*

MELANCOOSE, mill (*melin*) by the wood (*cuz*).

MELANDREWS, *i.q.* MELLANDRUCHA.

MEL-ANGYE, -INGY, water-mill, *Wh.*; or, mill by the water (*gy*).

MELGESS, the mill woods, *Po.*

MELHUISH, *n.f.*, the mill estate (*huisc*), *t.*

MELINDRAFT, yellow (*melyn*) sands (*trait*), *C.*; mill scour (*traf*, *w.*), *M.*

MELINGISSEY, the mill woods, *Pr.*

MELLAN-DRUCHA, -DRUCHIA, the mill with the solid wheel (*drucha*), *W.B.*

M. GOOSE, *i.q.* MELANCOOSE.

M. EAR, long (*hir*) mill.

M. HAYLE, mill on the river (*heyl*), or moor (*hal*).

MELLANOWETH, new (*nowydh*) mill.

MELLENGETH, ? wood (*coed*) mill; or, *i.q.* MELLINSETH.

MELL-EWARNE, -WARNE, alder *or* marsh (*gwern*) mill.

MELLIDEN, ? mill vale (*denu, s.*).

MELLIDOR, ? mill by the *tor*, or water (*dour*).

MELLINIKE, mill, lake, leat, *or* bosom of waters (*ike*), H.

MELLINSETH, the dry mill, *Pr.*

MELLON, *n.f.*, ? = *melin*, a mill; or, *meillion*, clover, *w.*; or, *melyn*, tawny.

M. COOSE, *i.q.* MELANCOOSE.

MELLOW PARK, ? *mullow* close.

MELLUCKHORN, 16 *cent.*, ? Mæiloc's (*s.B.m.*) corner (*horn*).

MELLYNCARNE, the yellow (*melyn*) rock, *Bl.*; mill of the rock, *R.IV.*

MELLYS, ? lower (*isa*) or corn (*iz*) mill.

MELORN, ? mill corner.

MELROSE, honey (*mel*) moor, C.

MEN, o. MAEN.

MENABILLY, the colts' (*ebilli*) hill (*menedh*), *Pr.*; stone of the wolf (*bleit*), C.

MENACHURCH POINT, ? monks' (*manach*) church point.

MENACRIN, ? stone of wailing (*creen*?).

MENACUDDLE, hawk (*cudyll,w.*) stone (*maen*), C.; ? Irish (*gwyddel*) monk (*manach*).

MENADARVA, rock by the running water, *T.C.*; the watery hill, *or* by the water, or, the hill of oaks, *Pr.*; rock of the oak place, *R.IV.*

MENADEWS, ? stones outside (*dyves*); or, black-stone [field]s.

MENADODDA, ? Dudda's (*t.*) stone.

MENADRUM, ? ridge (*trum, w.*) stone.

MENADU, the black (*du*) mountain (*menedh*), *Pr.*, or stone (*maen*).

MENAFIELD, ? the stone field.

MENAGISSEY, *i.q.* MELINGISSEY.

MENAGUE, the stone of lying (*gue*), or of the smith (*gow*), or of the chief (*cu, ga.*).

MENAGULLAS, *i.q.* MANYGULLAS.

MENALIDA, 12 *cent.*, ? stone of wrath (*llid, w.*), M.; ? ? Ida's manor (*mesnil, f.*); ? now TEHIDY.

MENALLACK, *i.q.* MANALLACK.

MENALU, ? *i.q.* MANAULOE.

MENAMBER, Ambrose's rock, *Car.*; rounded (*ambol*) stone, C.; stone of crookedness (*camder, w.*), M.; *i.q.* MENANBAR, the top (*an bar*) stone, B.

MEN AN TOL, the stone with the hole (*tol*), or holed stone.

MENARIDDEN, ? *i.q.* MANORGWIDDEN.

MENAR-VORTH, -WARTH, ? the high (*arwarth*) stone.

MENAULS, ? *i.q.* MENAGULLAS.

MENAVEAN, little MEANHAY.

MENAVORE, the great (*maur*) stone or rock.

MENAW, ? ? = *maenau*, the stones.

MENAWETHAN, the rock of the tree (*gwedhen*), N.

MENDY, the black (*du*) stone, *J.B.*; or, house (*ty*) by the stone; *or* stone house.

MENEAGE, = *maenic*, stony, B.; the deaf (*aege*?) stone, *Pr.*; a peninsula (*ph.*), *Dr.*; = *meneague*, stony clefts, C.

MENEBURL, ? rock of peril (*peryl*); or, *i.q.* MANABURLA.

MENEDEGLOS, ? church (*eglos*) hill (*menedh*), *R.IV.*

MENEFES, ? outside (*ves*) MANEHAY.

MENE-GISSEY, -GUISSEY, *i.q.* MELIN GISSY, the mill woods, *Pr.*

MENEGLASE, ? the blue (*glas*) stone; or, *i.q.* MANYGULLAS.

MENEGWINS, the white (*gwyn*) hills, H.; wind (*gwyns*) rock (*maen*), *J.B.*

MENE-HY, -HEY, *i.q.* MANEHAY.

MENELY, ? *i.q.* MANELEY.

MENERDUE, *i.q.* MENADU.

MENERLUE, *i.q.* MENALU.

MENESSA, ? lower (*isa*) MEANHAY.

MENEWETHEN, *i.q.* MANY WITHIN.

MENEWINK, *i.q.* MENWINNICK.

MEN FLEMING, the Fleming's Rock, N.

M. GEARN, ? the stone on the face

(*cern*) of the hill, *R. IV.*

MENGLOW, the coal (*glo, w.*) rock.

MENGREES, ? the middle (*cres*), or hedge (*garz*) stone.

MENHEIR, battle (*heir*), or long (*hir*) stone.

MENHEN-ICK, -ITT, *n.f.*, *from*

MENHENIOT, the old (*hen*) stone (*maen*) gate (*yet*), *H.*; the mountain (*menedh*) of the elder (*heneth*), *Wh.*, *or*, ? of St. Neot, (? *o. p.s.*, now St. Antoninus, *O.*); a hill on a high-way (?), *Sc.*

MENHERRIAN, ? the boundary (*ur-rian*) stone.

MENIES, ? stone fields (*haies, f.*).

MEN-KE, -KEE, *i q.* MANKEY.

MENNA, MENNAH, *i.q.* MEANHAY.

M. BROOM, ? broomy MEANHAY; or stone of offering (*offrwn, w.*).

M. CLUE, ? stone of light (*golcu*).

M. DOWN, ? stony (*maenic*) down.

M. GLAZE, *i.q.* MENEGLASE.

M. WARTHA, higher stone (*maen*), or MEANHAY.

MENN-EAR, -EER, -ER, -OR, ? *i.q.* MEN-HEIR; (*mener*, a mountain, *Lh.*).

MENNEREES, ? long-stone (*maen hir*) closes (*haies*).

MEN-PENGRIN, -PERKIN, the pilgrim or stranger's (*pirgirin*) rock, *N.*; (*pengarn*, a gurnard).

MENPERHEN, ? the king's (*bren*), or proprietor's (*berhen*) stone.

MENSHAM, ? ? nuns' (*manaches*) enclosure (*ham, w.*).

MENWI-DDEN, -NNION, the windy place (*man*), *B.*, (*gwyns*, wind).

MENWINNI-CK, -ON, head (*men* = *pen*) of the marshes, *Pr.*; marshy (*win-nic*) place (*man*), *J.B.*

MEREDITH, *n.f.*, sea protector, *Y.*

MERKIU, *Cum.*, *i.q.* MARKET JEW.

MERLINS CAR, Merlin's rock, *Bl.*

MERLYN, the great lake, *Pr.*; or, = *w. merchlyn*, the horse-pond, *R. IV.*

MERR-ET, -ITT, *n.f.*, ? *i.q.* MEREDITH.

MERRI-, MERRY-FIELD, = Mary's field

MERRICK, [the rock of the sea bird] *merrick.*

MERRIOTT, *n.f.*, ? Rhyod's (*w.*) place (*ma*), or field (*maes*).

MERR-IS, -OSE, -OWS, *i.q.* MEDROSE.

MERRYMAIDENS, ? the dancing and therefore *merry* stones, (*maidens* = *maen-s*).

MERRY-MEETING, -MIT, ? *the same*; *or*, place where the hounds meet.

MERTHA, ? *i.q.* MARTHA *or* MERTHER.

MERTHEN, hill (*din*) by the sea (*mor*); *or*, *i.q.* MERLIN, *Ped.*

MERTHER, *from p.s.* St. Conanus (*O.*) the martyr (*merthyr, w.*); or, the martyrium over his grave, *J.Ca.*; = *mor dor*, sea water, *Pr.* (!).

MERTHER DER-UA, -VA, the martyrium in the oak (*deru*) place (*ma, va*).

M. UNY, the martyrium of St. Ewinus.

MESACK, the field, *Pr.*; dry (*sech*) field (*maes*), *T.C.*

MESKALL, *n.f.*, ? = *mareschal*, a mareschal, *f.*; or, hazel (*coll, w.*) field (*maes*).

MESMEAR, *i.q.* MEASMEAR.

MESSENGER, ? ? field (*maes*) of the (*a'n*) camp (*caer*); or, *from n.f.*

MESSENGROSE, ? the (*an*) cross (*crous*), or marsh (*cors*) field.

MESSER, *n.f.*, ? long (*hir*) field.

METFORD, *n.f.*, ? *i.q.* MADFORD.

METHER-ALL, -ELL, -ILL, ? ? the meadow (*mead*) on (*ar*) the river (*heyl*).

METH-ERES, -ROSE, *i.q.* MEDROSE.

METH-ERIN, -ERN, ? the corner (*horn*) meadow.

METHERS COLLING, ? ? the martyr chapel of St. *Colan.*

METHERUISTEL, *w.B.m.*, ? martyr (*merthyr*) pledge (*guistel*).

METHERUNY, *i.q.* MERTHER UNY.

METHLEY, *d.d.* METHELE, ? feeding place (*le*); (*methia*, to feed).

METTERS, *n.f.*, ? *i.q.* MEDROSE.

MEULE, *n.f.*, *i.q.* MUEL.

MEVAGISSEY, *from p.s.* St. Mewa and St. Ida (*O.*), or Issey, *Car.* ; *al.* MENAGISSEY, mill (*melin*) woods, *Pr.* ; a hill (*menedh*) to keep mares (*cassegy*) in, *Sc.*

MEWDON, the great hill (*dun*), *Pr.*

MEWSTONE, ? greater (*mui*), or gull (*mæw, s.*) rock.

MICHAELSTOW, the place (*stow, s.*) of St. Michael, (*p.s., O.*).

MICHELL, *n.f., i.q.* Michael ; or, *from* MICHELL, *o.* MODISHOLE, MEDDES-CHOLE, ? the low (*isal*) place (*mod*).

MICHELL MORTON, ? great (*mycel, s.*) MORTON.

MICHELSTOW, *n.f., i.q.* MICHAELSTOW

MIDDLECOAT, *n.f.,* ? middle cottage (*cote, s.*), or wood (*coat*).

MID-DLING, -LEN, *i.q.* MEDLANE ; *or,* middle meadow (*ing, s.*).

MID GARGUS, ? the meadow (*mead*) near (*gar*) the wood (*cus*).

MIGEL, *t.d., i.q.* MITCHELL.

MIGHSTOW, *i.q.* MICHAELSTOW.

MILCENOC, *s.B.m.,* servant or disciple (*mael, i.*) of St. Cynoc.

MILCOMBE, the mill vale, *t.*

MIL-DERN, -DREN, *n.f.,* ? servant or disciple of St. Edeyrn.

MILE, *n.f.,* ? = *Mihal,* Michael.

MILET, *n.f.,* ? *i.q.* MALET.

MILHAM, ? the dwelling at the mill, *t.* ; *d.d.* MELLEDHAM.

MILIAN, *w.B.m.,* ? = *meilion,* clover,*w.*

MILLA-DON, -TON, the mill enclosure (*tun, s.*), *t.*

MILLAN, *n.f.,* ? *i.q.* MILLAND, the mill field (*land, s.*), or enclosure (*lan*).

MILLENCOOSE, *i.q.* MELANCOOSE.

MILLENDRAFT,*f.m., i.q.* MELINDRAFT

MILLET, *n.f.,* ? mill gate (*yet*) ; *or, i.q.* MALET.

MILLINDRETH, mill on the sand (*traith*) ; *o.* MELYNTRAIT.

MILLINGTON, *n.f., i.q.* MILLATON.

MILLINOWAL, cliff (*hal* = *als*), or high (*uhal*), *or* Howel's mill.

MILLINOWITH, *i.q.* MELINOWETH.

MILLINSE, ? dry (*sech*) mill.

MILLROSE CROFT, ? mill valley (*ros*) croft, *J.B.* ; ? *ros,* a wheel.

MILLS, *n.f.,* Michael's [son].

MILROY, *n.f.,* ? the king's (*roue, a.*) soldier (*mael, a.*).

MILTON, ? the mill, *or* middle, *or* Michael's enclosure (*tun, s.*).

MILWAIN, *n.f.,* ? *i.q.* Merlesuain, *t.d.d.*

MIN-ACK, -NACK, ? *i.q.* MANNICK.

MINALTO, the cliff (*allt, w.*) rock (*maen*), *N.*

MIN-AMEER, -NIMEAR, ? the great (*mear*) stones (*myin*).

MIN-ARS, -ORS, *n.f.,* ? boundary (*harz*) stone (*maen*), *or* stones (*myin*).

MINAS COVE, ? little (*minys*) cove, *M.*

MINCAMBER, *Sc.,* Welshman's rock ; *i.q.* MENAMBER.

MINCARLO, the martin (*carlo, o.n.*) rock, *N.*

MINERD, ? high (*ard*) stone.

MINE-Y, -HAY, *i.q.* MANEHAY.

MINGELI, *d.d.,* ? stone (*maen*) by the grove (*celli*) ; *or,* Gelhi's (*w.*) stone.

MINGEYS, *n.f.,* ? *i.q.* MELINGISSEY.

MINGOOSE, the kids' (*min*) wood (*cus*), *R.W.* ; ? wood mine.

MINICHESLAKE, *O.,* the nuns' (*manaches*) lake.

MINIT, = *mynydd,* a mountain, *w., Wh.*

MINMANUETH, ? scrubby isle *or* rock; (*numwydd,* brushwood, *w.*), *N.*

THE MINNACK, the stony piece.

MINNER, ? = *menhir,* long stone.

MINNEY, ? *i.q.* MINACK, *or* MANEHAY.

MINSES DOWN, ? the nuns' (*manaches*) down.

MINSTER, the monastery, (*p.s.* St. Mertheriana, *O.*).

MINWONNET, ? ? the stone on the down (*gwon*) with a gate (*yet*).

MIRRIL, *n.f.,* ? = *moor hill, t.*

MISERY, ? ? acre (*eru*) field (*maes*).

MISSLE PARK, ? moor (*hal*) meadow (*maes*), *or* blackbird close (*parc*).

MITCHELL, *n.f.,* = Michael, *or, migel,* great, *s.* ; *or, i.q.* MICHELL.

MITCHINSON, *n.f., i.q.* MITCHELLSON.

MITHIAN, the feeding place, *Pr.*, (*methia*, to feed) ; *c.d.* St. Peter.

MITTER, *n.f.*, ? = *meder*, a reaper.

MIXTOW, *i.q.* MICHAELSTOW.

MOASE, *n.f.*, ? = Moses.

MOCHIL TREWINT, great (*mucel, s.*) TREWINT.

MOCK, *n.f.*, ? = *mach*, a surety, bail, *w.*

MOCKARD, *n.f.*, ? a mocker ; or, *i.q.* MACURTH, *s.B.m.*

MODDERN, *n.f.*, *from* MADRON.

MODESHOLE, 14 *cent.*, now MICHELL.

MODITON, ? the meeting (*mot*) enclosure (*tun*), *t.*

MODITONHAM, the meeting *or* court dwelling, *H.* ; *or*, MODITON home.

MODROSE, place (*mod*) in the valley (*ros*), *Pr.*, *or* heath.

MOFFATT, *n.f.*, ? *i.q.* MUFFORD.

MOHUN, *n.f.*, *from* Moyon (*Brittany*), *Lo.* (*moun*, lame, maimed, *a.*).

MOLA, ? the bare (*moel*) place ; *or*, = *mola*, a mill, *lat.*, a blackbird, *c.*

MOLE, *n.f.*, ? *i.q.* MOYLE.

MOLESWORTH, *n.f.*, ? Mole's estate (*weorthig, s.*) ; *or*, sheep (*mols*) farm.

MOLEYNS, *o.n.f.*, ? *i.q.* MOLINESS.

MOLINGEY, *i.q.* MELANGEY.

MOLINICK, the place of goldfinches (*molinek*), *Pr.*; the mill place, *Wh.*

MOLIN-ESS, -NISS, ? lower (*isa*), *or* island (*enys*) mill.

MOLINSEY, *i.q.* MELLINSETH.

MOLLARD, *n.f.*, ? miller.

MONGLEATH, = *w.* Mwnglawdh, *from mwn*, ore, *clawdh*, a quarry, *R.W.*

MOON, *n.f.*, *i.q.* MOHUN.

MOPAS, sea (*mor*) passage (*pas, f.*), *M'L.* ; *i.q.* MALPAS.

MOR, *B.m.*, the sea ; *or*, = *maur*, great.

MORAH, ? *i.q.* MORVAH.

MORCANT, *w.B.m.*, ? sea margin (*cant*).

MOR-COM, -COMBE, *n.f.*, a bend (*cam*) of the sea (*mor*), *R.W.* ; ? sea vale.

MOR-DAN, -DEN, ? moor hollow (*denu, s.*), *t.*

MORELL, *n.f.*, ? moor hill, *t.*

MOR-EPS, -EBS, -RABS, -ROPS, ? ? [field]s

by (*ryp*) the sea side, *Pr.* ; ? = *moreb*, the ebb-tide, *w.*, *M.*

MOR-ES, -IS, *i.q.* MARRAIS.

MORESK, = *moresc*, sedge, *w.*, *R.W.* ; sea (*mor*), estuary or creek (*esk*), *M'L.*

MORGAN, *duke*, by the sea, *Pr.* ; sea born (*geni, w.*).

MOR-ICE, -RISS, *n.f.*, *i.q.* MORES.

MORKHAM, *n.f.*, *i.q.* MORCOM.

MORLAH, ? sea enclosure (*lan*).

MORLAND, moorland, *t.*

MORLEY, *n.f.*, ? moor pasture, *t.*

MOR-RAB, -RAP, by the sea-side, *Pr.*

MORSHEAD, *n.f.*, *i.q.* PENHALLOW.

MORTH, = *murth*, a foundation ; *or*, *marth*, flat, open, plain, *w.*, *M.*

MORTHA, *i.q.* MARTHA.

MORTON, *d.d.* MORTUNE, ? MOR'S, *or* the moor enclosure (*tun*), *t.*

MORVAH, the place (*va*) near the sea, *Pr.*, *or* a fenny place (*morfa*, a marsh), *Po.* ; (*p.s.* not known).

MORVAL, *the same*, *Pr.* ; sea valley, *T.* ; brink (*ael, w.*) of the marsh, *C.* (*p.s.* St. Wenna, *O.*).

MORVILLE, *n.f.*, ? the town (*ville, f.*) by the sea (*mor*) ; *or* MOR'S town.

MORWEL, ? MOR'S, *or* the moor well.

MORWINSTOW, the place (*stow, s.*) of St. Morwenna, (*p.s.*, *O.*) ; place of St. Wenna by the sea (*mor*), *R.S.H.*

MOSAL, *i.q.* MODESHOLE.

MOSSE, ? the marshy piece, *t.*

MOTELAND, ? the land where the assembly (*mot*) was held ; *or*, field with a stump (*mot, m.c.*) in it, *t.*

MOTTRAM, *n.f.*, strong (*ram*) courage (*mod*), *s.*, *F.*

MOUDLINWELL, Magdalene's well, *t.*

MOULD, *n.f.*, ? = *mont alt*, high hill, *f.*, *Lo.* ; *or* = *mollt*, a wether sheep, *w.*

MOULS ROCK ? wether sheep rock.

MOUNE, *n.f.*, *i.q.* MOHUN.

MOUNT CARLESS, ? castle (*caer*) court (*lis*) hill, *M.*

M. COLDWIND, ? cold wind, *or* white hazels (*coll win*) hill.

M. HAWKE, ? Hawke's, *or* high (*hawk*, *Pr.*) hill.

MOUNT HERMON, ?? long (*hir*) stone (*maen*) hill.

M. HAY, ? hill field, *t.*

M. HOLMAN, ? holed stone (*tolmen*) hill, *M.*

M. PISKEY, fairy hill.

MOUSAL, maid's (*mos*), or sheep (*mols*) moor (*hal*), or river (*hayl*).

MOUSE CLOSE, ? wether sheep (*mols*) close.

MOUSEHOLE, *from a large* cavern near, *Bp. Stafford*; maid's (*mos*) river (*heyl*), *R.E.* ; or, *i.q.* MOUSAL, *or* MODESHOLE. (? = *mousheol*, the bone of the cuttle-fish, *Jo.C.*).

MOWHAY, the stack (*mow*) enclosure (*hay*), *t.*

MOW PLOT, stack piece, *t.*

MOX FIELD, ? MACCOS's field.

MOXLEY, *n.f.*, ? MACCOS's pasture.

MOYES, MOYSE, *n.f.*, ? Moses.

MOYLE, *n.f.*, a mule, *m.c.* ; bald-headed (*moel*), *R.W.*; or = *moelh*, a blackbird.

M. PARK, mule close.

MOZENS, ? maid's (*mos*) island (*enys*).

MOZRANG, the maid's (*mos*) pool, *Bl.*

MUCH LARNICK, great LARNICK.

MUCHMORE, *n.f.*, ? great moor, *t.*

MUCKFORD, ? dirty (*muck*) ford, *t.*, *T.C*

MUDDY PARK, ? *muddy* close (*parc*).

MUDG-AN, -EON, -IAN, = *muchan*, a short chimney, *H.* ; ox (*udzheon*) field (*maes*), *T.C.*

MUDGE, *n.f.*, ? = *much*, great, *s.*

MUDLEY PARK, muddy pasture close, *t.* ; or, *i.q.* MADLY.

MUEL, *s.B.m.*, ? *i.q.* MOYLE.

MUG-AUN, -EON, *n.f.*, *i.q.* MUDGAN ; or, = *mogyon*, the vulgar, *B.*

MUFFORD, *n.f.*, ? mud, or swine (*moch*), or dirty (*muck*, *t.*) ford.

MUGBERRY, the great (*much*) hill (*burg*), *t.*

MUL-BERRY, -FRA, -VERA, -VRA, the bare (*moel*) hill (*bre*), *Pr.*

MULLION, *from p.s.* St. Melanus, *O.* ; St. Meliana, *M.*; the cold (*iein*) bare (*moel*) place *or* exposure, *Pr.*

MULLION PARK, *o.* clover (*meillion*) close (*parc*).

MULLIS, *n.f.*, = *moel-lys*, bare court, or *moellas*, green bare place, *w.*, *R.W.* ; a she mule *or* ass (*mules*, *w.*), *M.*

MUM-, MUN-FORD, *n.f.*, ? St. Mawan's (*w.*) ford.

MUN-DAY, -DY, *n.f.*, ? ore (*mwyn*) or mine house (*ty*).

MUNGEON, *n.f.*, ? *i.q.* MUDGAN.

MUNGLOR, ? musician's (*cler*) stone (*maen*), or place (*man*).

MUNSELL, *n.f.*, ? seal (*sel*) stone (*maen*) ; or, lower (*isal*) bog (*moin*, *i.*).

MURDON, great (*mur*) hill (*dun*).

MURLEY, *n.f.*, ? moor pasture, *t.*

MURTH, *i.q.* MORTH, *M.*

MURTON, *n.f.*, moor enclosure, *t.*

MUSH-, MUS-TON, ? moss *or* marsh enclosure, (*tun*), *t.*

MUTTENHAM, *i.q.* MODITONHAM.

MUN BEACON, ? stone (*maen*) observatory.

MUTTON, *n.f.*, *from* MODITON.

MUTFORD, ? *i.q.* MADFORD.

MYDHOPE, *n.f.*, ? middle opening (*ope*, *m.c.*).

MYENDU, *Lel.*, black (*du*) stones (*myin*).

MYLOR, *from p.s.* St. Meilyr, *M.*, (*Meilorus*, *O.*)

MYN, MYNNE, *n.f.* ? = *myn*, a kid ; or, *mayn*, a friend, intimate.

MYRMEN, *w.B.m.*, ? great (*mur*) stone (*maen*), *M.*

N

NABINE, ? *i.q.* NAPEAN.

NACKERS, ? *i.q.* NANCARRAS.

NACOTHAN, *n.f.*, *i.q.* NANCOTHAN.

NADDERWELL, adder (*nædre, s.*) well.

NAFFEAN, *i.q.* NAPEAN.

NAFFETON, ? NAVA'S enclosure (*tun*, *s.*) ; or, *i.q.* NANCEVENTON.

NAG PARK, ? horse close, *t.*

NAGLE, *n.f.*, *from* *nægel*, a nail, *s.* ; or, *i.q.* NIGELLUS.

NAILBOROUGH, ? NIGELS barrow, *t.*
NAILE, *n.f., i.q.* NAGLE.
NAIRN, *n.f.,* ? = *an haiarn,* the iron.
NAJARROW, *i.q.* NANCHARROW.
NAKERRIS, *i.q.* NANCARRAS.
NAMAIL (13 *cent.*), Michael's (*Mial*)
  valley (*nance*) ; *now* AMBLE.
NAM-BELL, -BOL ? distant (*pel*), or
  pit (*pol*) valley.
NAMPARA, ? hand-mill (*brow*), or
  higher (*warra* = *wartha*) valley.
NAMPEAN, *i.q.* NANCEPEAN.
NAM-PETHA, -PITTY, *i.q.* NANPITHO.
NAMPL-OE, -OUGH, -OW, ? further
  (*pella*) valley.
NAMPRATHICK, ? meadowy vale.
NANCADDEN, ? wood-pigeon (*cudon*)
  vale ; battle (*cad*) vale, *Beal.*
NANCALLAN, ? *i.q.* NANSAGOLLAN.
NANCAR, the valley rock (*carn*), or
  rock in the valley, *H.* ; ? rock vale.
NANCARRAS ? fen (*cors*) vale.
NANCARROW, the stag (*carow*) valley,
  Pr. ; brook (*carrog*) vale, *T.*
NANCASSICK, ? woody (*cussic*), or the
  mare's (*caseg*) vale.
NANCATHA, ? higher (*gwartha*) vale.
NANCE, a plain, valley, dale, ravine ;
  = *nant,* a ravine, a brook, *w.*
N. ALVERN, ALVERTON valley.
N. CROSSA, ? valley of the crosses
  (*crowsow*), or marshes (*corsow*).
N. FYNTON, *i.q.* NANCEVENTON.
N. GLOS, *i.q.* NANSEGLOS.
N. GOLLEN, *i.q.* NANSAGOLLAN.
N. JEVAL, *i.q.* NANKIVEL.
N.-KEAGE, -KUGE, -KUTE, the village
  (*gwic*) on the plain *or* near the
  valley, *Pr.*
N. LOE-GREAZ, -WARTHA & WOLLAS,
  the middle (*cres*) higher (*wartha*)
  & lower (*wollas*) valley with the
  tumulus (*low, t.*), or pool (*lo*).
N. LONE, grove (*llwyn, w.*), or fox
  (*lowern*) vale.
N. MABYN, ? St. Mabyn's vale.
N. MARROW, ? ? the vale of the dead
  (*marow*) [man].
N. MEER, great (*mear*) valley.

NANCEMELLIN, mill (*melin*) vale.
N. MOLKIN, dirty valley, *Pr.*
N. NOY, nephew's (*noi*), or Noye's, or
  Noe's valley.
N. NT, *i.q.* NANSANT.
N. NTURIES, ? ? the valley of the
  SANCTUARIES.
N.-PEAN, -VEAN, little vale.
N. VENTON, spring (*fenten*) vale.
N. WALLON, *i.q.* NANSAVALLAN.
N. WIDDEN, white (*gwydn*) tree
  (*gwedhen*), or little (*veun*) vale.
N. WRATH, ? giant's (*wrath*) vale.
NANCH-ARROW, -ERROW, ? higher
  (*warra* = *wartha*) valley.
NANCHERT, *d.d.,* ? ? heron (*cerhidh*)
  vale.
NANCHOLLAS, *n.f.,* ? *i.q.* NANCOLLAS.
NANCKIVEL, *i.q.* NANKIVEL.
NANCLASSONS, vale of the green
  (*glas*) island (*enys*).
NANC-LEDRY, -LEDRA, valley of cliffs
  (*ledrow*), *T.C.*; *or, i.q.* NANSLADRON.
NANCOLLA, ? lower (*gwollach*), or
  Colo's (*t.d.d.*) vale.
NANCOLLAS, ? bottom (*goles*) vale.
NANCOLLETH, ? hazel-grove (*colluith*)
  valley.
NANCOR, ? *i.q.* NANCAR.
NANCORRAS, ? *i.q.* NANCARRAS.
NANCOTHA, *i.q.* NANCATHA.
NANCOTHAN, the old (*coth*) valley,
  Pr. ; the wood (*coat*) valley *or*
  river (*nant, w.*), *Gw.* ; valley of the
  wood, *T.C.* ; ? *i.q.* NANCADDEN.
NANCROBUS, ? valley of the hut
  (*crow*) by the bush (*bos*), or of
  Rufus.
NANCROSSA, *i.q.* NANCECROSSA.
NANF-AN, -ON, *n.f., i.q.* NANCEVEAN.
NANFELLOW, ? *i.q.* NAMPLOE.
NANFISICK, Fisick's (*t.*) valley.
NANFONS, ? bridge (*pons*) valley.
NANGARTH-AN, -IAN, *n.f.,* ? valley of
  the mountain ash (*cerden*).
NANGES, cheese (*ces*) valley.
NANGIDNAL, ? ? narrow (*idn*) vale by
  the moor (*hal*).
NANGILES, ? the valley of Julius,

Silus (*m.s.*), or Giles.

NANGITHA, ? hide away (*cudhe*, to conceal), or Ceitho's (*w.*) valley.

NANGOLLAN, *i.q.* NANSAGOLLAN.

NANGOTHAN, *i.q.* NANCOTHAN.

NANGUAN, owl's (*cuan, w.*) valley, *M.*

NANGUITHNEA, ? woody (*gwithenic*) valley.

NANGUITHO, ? ? the widow's (*gwedhow*) vale.

NANHELLON, ? fir-tree (*aidhlen*) vale.

NANHETHAL, high (*uthal*), Irishman's (*gwydhel*), or hawk (*cudyll, w.*) vale.

NANJARROW, *i.q.* NANCHARROW.

NANJENKIN, Jenkin's valley.

NANJETH, ? vale of the arrow (*zeth*).

NANJEVAL, *i.q.* NANKIVEL.

NANJEWICK, ? village (*gwic*) vale.

NANJIZEL COVE, the cove beneath the valley, *Bl.*; (*isal*, low).

NANJULEAN, valley of hazels (*coll*), *Pr.*; ? king-fishers' (*guilan*) vale.

NANKEG, ? snipe (*giach, w.*) vale.

NANKELLY, hazel-grove (*celli*) vale.

NANKERSEY, the winding vale, *T.*; (*ceirsio*, to wind, *B.*).

NANKERVIS, ? ? Gervis's (*t.*) valley.

NANKIVEL, horse (*cevil*) valley, *Pr.*

NANPE-AN, -DN, *i.q.* NAMPEAN.

NAN-PETHO, -PITHO, the rich valley (*pethou*, riches), *Pr.*; ? valley of the graves (*bedhow*), or birches (*bedho, Pr.*).

NANPHYSICK, *i.q.* NANFISICK.

NANPLOE, *i.q.* NAMPLOE.

NANPOUUS, ? bush (*bagas*) vale.

NANPUS-CAR, -KER, four (*pesguar*) (*piscadur*) valleys, *T.C.*

NANQUIDNO, Gwyddno's (*w.*) vale.

NANS, NANSE, *i.q.* NANCE.

NANSACRE, ugly (*hagar*), or daisy (*egr*) valley.

NANSALVERN, *i.q.* NANCEALVERN.

NANSADURN, the valley of Saturn, *B.*; ? Sadwrn's (*w.*) vale.

NANSAGOLLAN, the hazel-tree (*collen*) valley, *R.W.*; ? valley of the holy (*gol*) enclosure (*lan*), *T.C.*; the

hart's valley, *Pr.*; (*colon*, the heart ! !).

NANSALSA, ? SULLEISOC'S vale.

NANSALTER, ? the valley of the altar, or of Aldar (*w*), or of Aladur.

NANSANT, holy (*sant*) vale.

NANSANTON, the town (*tun, s.*) or hill (*dun*) of the holy vale, *T.*

NANSARTH, high (*arth*), or steep (*serth*), or hedgehog (*sarth*) vale.

NAN-SAUGH, -SOUGH, the fat, *i.e.* fertile vale, (*soath, soa*, fat, tallow), *T.*; ? *i.q.* NANSOG.

NANSAVALLAN, apple-tree (*avallen*) valley, *Pr.*; ? *from* ALBALANDA.

NANSAWHAN, ? ZAWN valley, *T.C.*

NANSAWSAN, the Saxon's valley.

NANSCARRA, *i.q.* NANCARROW.

NAN-SCAUAN, -SCAWN, ⅄ -SCOVEN, -SCOWEN, the valley of the elder-tree (*scawen*).

NANSCOWE, vale of elders (*scaw*).

NANS-EDDON, -IDON, ? furze (*eithen*), or bird (*edhen*) valley.

NANSEDERN, ? *i.q.* NANSADARN.

NANSEFRINK, French valley, *Pr.*

NANSEGLOS, church (*eglos*) vale.

NANSEVEN, ? little (*bihan*), or Evan's, *i.e.* John's valley.

NANSHEAR, long (*hir*) vale.

NANSHUTAL, ? sorceress's (*hudol*) vale; or, *i.q.* NANHETHAL.

NANSIAS, ? barley (*haiz*) vale.

NANSIDWELL, Sidwell's valley.

NANSILGANS, ? ? SULCAN's valley.

NANSISICKE, ? corn (*izic*) vale.

NANSKERVIS, *n.f., i.q.* NANKERVIS.

NANSKUKE, *i.q.* NANCEKUGE.

NANSKYLLY, *i.q.* NANKELLY.

NANSLADRON, the thieves' (*ladron*) valley, (or bottom, *J.B.*).

NANSLOE, *i.q.* NANCE LOE, the vale leading to the lake or pool, *D.G.*

NANSLOWEN, *n.f.,* ? *i.q.* NANCELONE.

NANSME-AR, -OR, *i.q.* NANCEMEER.

NANSMELLYN, *i.q.* NANCEMELLIN.

NANSOG, moist (*sog*) valley, *Wh.*

NANS-PERIAN, -PIAN, *n.f.,* the valley

of thorns (*spern*).

NANSTALLON, ? Talan's (*w.B.m.*) vale.

NANSTANCE, *n.f.*, ? castle (*dinas*) vale.

NANS-, NAN-TRISSACK, ? brambly (*dreisic*) bottom or ravine.

NANSUG-ALL, -WELL, ? rye (*sygal*), or bench (*scarel*) valley.

NANS-WHYDEN, -WIDDEN, the white (*gwydn*) valley, *Pr.*; or, tree (*gwedhen*) vale.

NANTALLAN, the miry (*teil*, dirt, mire) valley, *Pr.*; the valley of the church or chapel (*lan*), *M'L.*; ? vale of the ALAN river.

NANTALLIS, ? echo (*adlais*, *w.*) valley.

NANTARNAN, ? Aronan's (*w.*) vale.

NANTEG, fair (*teg*) valley, *R.IV.*

NANTEGLAN, ? enclosure (*lan*) in the fair valley.

NANTELLAN, ? elm-tree (*elan*) vale; or, *i.q.* NANTALLAN.

NANTEREN, ? prince's (*teyrn*) vale.

NANTERROW, ? bulls' (*terrow*) vale.

NANTHEN, ? bird (*edhen*) vale.

NANTIAN, ? furze (*eithen*) dale; or, *i.q.* NANTVEN.

NANTIRRAT, ? trout (*trut*) dale.

NANT-ORYAN, -URRIAN, ? boundary (*yrhian*), or Urien's (*w.*) vale.

NANTOWAS, sheep (*dauas*) bottom (*nant*); or, vale outside (*aves*), *W.B.*

NANT-RELLOW, -ILLO, ? Trillo's (*w.*), or brewer's (*darllawydd*, *w.*) vale.

NANTS, *i.q.* NANCE.

N. MELLYN, the mill river valley, *Pr.*; *i.q.* NANCEMELLYN.

N. WELL, ? valley spring.

NANTURRAS, ? bramble (*dreis*) dale.

NANTVEN, *n.f.*, little (*vean*) dale.

NANTYRACK, ? golden (*oirech*), or dung (*orrach*), or water (*douric*) valley.

NAP, ? turnip (*neap*, *Po.*) [field].

NAPH-AN, -EAN, *i.q.* NAMPEAN; or, = an vean, the little.

NAPHANT, *n.f.*, *i.q.* NAFFETON.

NAPPER, *n.f.*, ? great (*vear*) vale (*nans*); or, = an vear, the great.

NARABOE, ? Riabach's (*k.*) valley.

NARAMORE, *n.f.*, ? narrow-moor.

NARE POINT, ? the long (*an hir*), or battle (*an heir*), or Ner's (*w.*) point.

NAR-IN, -RAN, *n.f.*, ? *i.q.* NAIRN.

NARKURS, ? *i.q.* NANKERVIS.

NARROW HALE, ? PARK AN ARROW taken from, or by the moor (*hal*).

N. WIDDEN, ? tree (*gwedhen*) PARK AN ARROW.

NASH, *n.f.*, ? = atten ash, by the ash, *t.*, *Lo.*; or = *næs*, a cape, *s.*

NASSINGTON, *n.f.*, *i.q.* NANCEFYNTON.

NATASIAS, *i.q.* NEGOSIAS.

NATHANS CAVE, *i.q.* St. Nectan's or KNEIGHTON'S KEIVE.

NATH DOWN, *T.a.*, ? north downs.

NATT, *n.f.*, ? from ST. NEOT.

NATTER BRIDGE, *i.q.* NODDETOR.

NATTLE, *n.f.*, ? *i.q.* NETTLE.

NAUTRISICK, *n.f.*, *i.q.* NANTRISSICK.

NAV-A, -AS, *n.f.*, *i.q.* KNAVA.

NAWKERVIS, *n.f.*, *i.q.* NANKERVIS.

NAWNS CROFT, ? valley (*nance*) croft, *H.M.W.*

NAW-VOZ, -WHOORS, -WHAWRS, nine maids or sisters.

NEAGELLE, ? grove (*celli*) down (*oon*).

NEAM, ? *i.q.* NEWHAM.

NEATFORD, ? St. Neot's, or the cattle (*neat*) ford, *t.*

NEEDS, *n.f.*, ? Neot's son.

NEGOSIAS, *v.* NICKIES EASE, Nicholas's resting place; or, *i.q.* NANKERVIS.

NELLS, ? *i.q.* PARKNELLS.

NEMEA SYLVA, *Le.*, the wood (*silva*, *lat.*) of the bright (*naimh,e.*) [fountain], *Wh.*

NEMETOTACIO, *Ravennas*, = *nemetomagus*, *i.q.* DUNHEVED, the citadel (*magus*?) in the groves (*nemet*, *a.*, *Z.*), *Bax.* (*magus* = *mach*, a plain, *e.*, *Z.*).

NE-, NI-OTESTOV, *d.d.*, the stow or place of ST. NEOT.

NEPEAN, *n.f.*, *i.q.* NAMPEAN.

NETHERCOMBE, lower vale, *t.*

NETHERFORD, lower ford, *t.*

NETHER-TON, -TOWN, lower town,

farm place *or* enclosure (*tun, s*).

NETTLE, *n.f., dim. of knecht,* a servant, knight, *s.*

NETTI EBED ? bed of *nettles, t.*

NE-VILLE, -VOLL, *n.f.,* new town, *f.*

NEWALL. *n.f.,* ? *from* BURNUHALL.

NEW BERRY, new castle [field].

NEW-COMBE, ? the new, *or* yew (*an yw*) vale.

NEWER PARK, ? *i.q.* PARKEN OWER.

NEWETT, *n.f.,* ? new gate (*yet*), *t.*

NEW-HALE, -HALL, *n.f., i.q.* NEWALL.

NEWHAM, the new home, *t.*

NEWHAY, the new enclosure, *t.*

NEWINGTON, = *Niwantun,* the new town *or* enclosure, *t.*

NEWIS, *Nord.,* ? *i.q.* PARK AN USE.

NEWKAY, *now* NEWQUAY, *t.*

NEWLAND, ? recently acquired land, *or* the yew (*an yw*) land, *t.*

NEWLEIGH, new pasture, *t.*

NEWLICOMBE, ? new pasture (*leu*) vale, *t.*

NEWLYN, new pool; *or,* = *niul-in,* in a fog *or* mist, *Gw.**

NEWNHAM, ? = *Niwanham,* the new home, *s.*

NEW NOI, = *noon noi,* the (*an*) nephew's moor *or* down (*oon*) *T.C.*

NEW PARK, new close (*parc*).

NEWPORT, *nova porta,* new-gate, *lat.*

NEWS ROCK, ?? the (*an*) *rock* outside (*aues*).

NEW-TON, -TOWN, *d.d.* NIEWTONE, the new enclosure, farm, *or* town.

NICKELL, NICKS, NILE, NILES, *n.f., from* NIGELLUS, *t.d.d., from nigellus,* darkish, *lat., or nœgel,* a nail, *s.*

NIGH PARK, ? the near close, *t.*

NINCE, NINNES, NINNIS, NISS MEADOW, = *an ynys,* the island; *or,* PARK AN EANES.

NIZZLE CLOSE, ? the (*an*) lower (*isella*) close.

NOAL, NOALE, NOEL, *n.f.,* christmas, *f.; or, i.q.* PARK NOWEL.

NODDE-R, -TOR, snake (*nœder, s.*) tor.†

NOE, *messe preoste, w.B.m., i.q. Noah,* consolation, *h.; or,* Naoi, (*i.*); *noi,* a nephew.

NOLLAS, ? *i.q.* PARK NOLLAS.

NOMANSLAND, waste piece, *t.*

THE NOOKEY FIELD, ? the field full of corners, *t.*

NOON AN GROAS, the (*an*) down (*oon*) of the (*a'n*) cross (*crous*).

N. ANTRON, ANTRON down.

N. BELL, the (*an*) far (*pell*) down.

N.-BELLAS, -BILLOSE, -BILLOWS, the works *or* diggings (*ballas*) downs, *J.B.;* ? *i.q.* PILLAS downs.

N. COUTH, the old (*coth*), *or* wood (*co:t*) down.

N.-CREEK, -CREEG, the barrow (*creeg*), *or* rock (*carrug*), *or* heath (*grig*) down.

N. CROFT, the down croft.

N. GALAS, ? the bottom (*goles*) down.

N. GAY, ? the hedge (*ce*) down.

N. GLASSON, ? GLAZDON, *or,* scarlet-oak (*glastanen*) down.

N. GOOSE, the wood (*cus*), *or* moor (*cors*), *or* goose (*goaz, B.*), *or* mole (*gwdh*) down.

N. GRAZE, -GREASE, the middle (*cres*), *or* cherries (*ceiroes, w.*) down.

N. GREAN, gravel (*grean*) down.

N. GUMPAS, *i.q.* NUNGUMPAS.

N. NOWETH, the new (*nowedh*) down.

N. REETH, the circling (*reath, ga.*) heavens (*nion*) *ga., Beal;* ? red (*rydh*) down; *or, i.q.* GOON REETH.

N. TERRAS, ? the cross (*tres*), *or* tillage (*trevas*) down; *or,* the down by the door (*daras*).

N. VARES, ? summit (*gwarhas*) of the down, *or* down by the roads (*varas, Pr.*).

---

* The open *or* naked (*noath*) lake (*lyn*), *Pr.*; near (*nes*) the lake, *R.E.* The church of NEWLYN EAST was dedicated, 1259, to *St. Newelina.*; that of NEWLYN WEST, 1865, to S. Peter.

† Or the *tor or* hill with a mark (*nod, w.*). The *tor* land (*tir*) *or* high place of the congregation (*noit, ga.*) for prayer (*not, ga.*), worship, &c., *Beal.*

NOON VEAN, the little down.

N. VEOR, the great down.

N. WARTHA, the higher down.

N. ZERRAS, the down of the heath cocks (*zar-es*, *B.*) *or* turkeys (*Pr.*).

NOOTH, ? *i.q.* PARK NOATH.

NO PARK, ? *i.q.* PARK NOW.

NOP HILL, ? hill knap *or* top, *t.*

NORCOTT, *i.q.*, NORTHCOTT, *t.*; *or*, NORTHWOOD.

NORRINGTON, *n.f.*, ? north meadow (*ing*, *s.*), *or* the Norwegian's (*norna*, *s.*) town, *t.*

NORRIS, *n.f.*, = *le Noreis*, the Norwegian, *f.*, *Lo.*; *or*, *norice*, a nurse, *s.*

NORS, ? the (*an*) boundary (*hars*), *or* stubble (*ersc*, *s.*) [field].

NORTHEY, *n.f.*, the northern enclosure (*hay*, *or* island (*ig*, *s.*), *t.*

NORTH HILL, *t.* (*p.s.* not known, *O.*, St. Torney, *C.S.G.*).

NORTHPER JACKA, ? JACKA'S north close (*parc*).

NORTON, *d.d.*, NORTONE, the north town *or* enclosure (*tun*, *s.*).

NOR WENN, ?? = *an* or *wen*, the white land *or* field (*or* = *dor*).

NOSWORTHY, *n.f.*, ? NOE'S farm (*weorthig*, *s.*).

NOTT, *n.f.*, ? *from* St. Neot.

NOTTER, *i.q.* NODDETOR.

NOT-TLE, -WELL, *n.f.*, ? St. Neot's well.

NOWAN, *i.q.* PARK NOWAN.

N. VROSE, ? great (*bras*) down close, *or* by the thicket (*brouse*).

NOWELL, *n.f.*, ? *i.q.* NOAL.

NOYE, *n.f.*, ? *i.q.* NOE.

NUBBY FIELD, ? field full of knobs *or* hillocks, *t.*

NULING, *n.f.*, from NEWLYN.

NUM-PHRA, -PHERA, ? the down (*an oon*) by the hill (*bre*).

NUNGUMPAS, the (*an*) plain (*gumpas*) downs, *B.*; ? playing.

NYTHAN, *i.q.* PARK NETHAN.

O AKANGWEALS, ? oaken (*aacen*, *s.*) fields (*gweal-s*).

OAKENHAYS, ? oaken closes, *t.*

OAK-EY, -HAY, -PARK, oak close (*haege*, *s.*; *parc*, *c.*).

OAT-, OATEN-ARISH, oat stubble (*ersc*, *s.*) [field].

OATEN, *n.f.*, ? *i.q.* HOTTEN.

OATEN-HAY, -PARK, ? oat close.

OATEN STITCH, ? oat slip (*sticce*, *s.*).

OATEY, oat close (*hay*), *t.*

OATS, *n.f.*, ? = *Otto's* son, *t.*

OBY, *n.f.*, ? = Obadiah, *or* Hoby = Robert, *or* Offy = Theophilus.

OCRINUM, *Ptolemy*, high (*och*) promontory (*rhin*), *w.*, *Bax.*; *now* the LIZARD.

ODDIHAM, ? ODO's home (*ham*, *s.*).

ODD MILL, ODO'S, *or* wood (*ood*) mill.

ODDIE, *n.f.*, ? *i.q.* ODO.

ODGER, *n.f.*, *o.* OGER, rich (*ead*, *s.*) spear (*ger*, *s.*), *Y.*

ODO, *t.d.d.*, ? = *oddr*, a dart, *o.n.*

ODYCROFT, ? *i.q.* ADDICROFT.

OFFER & HOMER HALL WYN, further & nearer white (*gwyn*) moor (*hal*).

OFFERS, *i.q.* OSFERD.

OFFIL, *n.f.*, ? ? = Theofilus.

OGBERE, ? oak farm, *t.*

OGO, the cave *or* cavern.

OGOF HAYLE, the cliff (*hal* = *als*) cave, *M‘L.*

OKE, *n.f.*, ? *i.q.* OAK, *t.*

OLD, OLDE, OULD, *n.f.*, ? = *allt*, a wooded cliff, a steep ascent, *w.*

OLECLIMS, ? Climsland old [town], *t.*

OLDER PARK, ? alder close, *t.*

OLDHAM, *n.f.*, old home, *t.*

OLDHAY, old enclosure (*hay*), *t.*

OLD-, OLDA-PARK, ? cliff (*allt*, *w.*), *or*, old (*eald*, *s.*) close.

OLDS, *n.f.*, ? = *als*, a cliff.

OLDSTOWE (16 *cent.*), old place *or* station, *t.*; *now* Padstow.

OLLAS, ? bottom (*goles*) [field].

OLVER, *n.f.*, *i.q.* HALVEOR, *or* ALUUARD.

ONCENDL, ONGENETHEL, *s.B.m.*, ? the giant (*enchinethel*).

ONE AND ALL, ? = *gwon an hal*, moor down; *or*, river (*hayl*) moor, *J.B.*

ONE FIELD, down (*gwon*) field.

ONEVEAN, little (*bian*) down.

ONEWIDDENS, ? the little, *or* white (*gwydn*) downs (*gwon-s.*).

ONGLE, *n.f.*, ? *i.q.* ONCENEDL.

ONNCUM, *s.B.m.*, ash (*on*) combe (*cum*), *w.*, *R.W.*; uncomely *or* unexpected, *t.*, *F.*

ONURION, *O.*, ? boundary (*yrhian*) down (*oon*), *or* ash (*on*).

ON-WEN, -WUEN, -WEAN, *s.B.m.*, white (*gwen*) ash, *R.W.*; joyless, *t.*, *F.*

ONYPOKIS, *T.a.*, down (*oon*) of the hollows (*vooqou*), *T.C.*

ONYREEN, ? hill-side (*reen*) down.

OPIE, OPPY, *n.f.*, *i.q.* OBY.

ORCHARD, *o.* ORCERT. *d.d.* ORCET, ? = *ortgeard*, a garden, orchard, *s.*; *or*, *i.q.* HARCOURT.

ORD, *n.f.*, origin, chief, *s.*

ORDGAR, earl, chief, *or* rich (*ead*) spear (*ger*), *or* defence (*gurd*), *t.*

ORDULF, *B.m.*, chief wolf, *t.*

ORESTONE, ? *i.q.* HORESTONE.

ORFAL, ? over (*ar*) the Fal.

ORGAN, ? penny-royal [field], *J.S.*

ORLAND, ? *i.q.* HARLAND.

ORNERSEY, ? long (*hir*) dry (*sech*) corner (*horn = corn*).

ORVES VEAN, ? little (*bihan*) outside (*ves*) land *or* field (*ar*).

OSBORNE, *n.f.*, divine bear, *t.*

OSFORD, *t.d.d.*, divine peace, *t.*

OSOLF, *w.B.m.*, divine wolf, *t.*

OTCER, *s.B.m.*, ? *i.q.* ORDGAR.

OTFORD, *n.f.*, ? at *or* by the ford, *t.*

OTTEN, *n.f.*, ? *i.q.* OATTEN.

OTTER, *n.f.*, ? *i.q.* OTCER.

OTTERHAM, ? OTCER's home, *t.*

OULD, *n.f.*, *i.q.* OLD.

OURDYLYC, *f.s.B.m.*, gold (*our*) necklace (*delc*).

OUT & OUTER Park, distant and further close (*parc*), *t.*

OUTH, ? *i.q.* PARK NOWETH.

OVERCOMBE, upper vale, *t.*

OVERHAYS, ? upper fields, *t.*

OVERLAND, upper land *or* field, *t.*

OVERLEIGH, upper pasture, *t.*

OVERWOOD, *t.*, ? *i.q.* BARGUS.

OWANPROSE, ? the down (*gwon*) meadow (*pras*).

OWELS, OWLES FIELD, ? cliff (*als*) field.

OWENVEAR, great (*mear*) down.

OWLA, ? = *ula*, an elm; an owl.

O. COMBE, ? elm vale.

O. PARK, ? elm close.

OWLEY, ? elm *or* owl pasture.

OWN PARK, ? *i.q.* PARK-OON.

OXENH-, OXN-AM, *n.f.*, ? ox watermeadow (*holm*), *t.*

OXMAN, *n.f.*, ? the same.

OZENTON, ? oxen enclosure, *t.*

PACKEN TYE, *i.q.* PARK AN TYE.

PACK JER, *i.q.* PARK CADJAW.

P. SUNDRY, ? Saunder's close.

PA-CORRA,-GORA,*i.q.* PORTHGUARRA, higher cove, *J.Ca.*

PACURNO, *i.q.* PORTHCURNOW, *J.Ca.*

PADAM, ? Adam's close (*parc*).

PADDEN, *n.f.*, ? castle (*din*) close.

PADDICOT, ? Paddy's cottage, *t.*

PADDY, *n.f.*, ? *i.q.* PACKEN TYE.

PADER-, PADRE-DA, prayers (*pader*) good (*da*), *Pr.*

PADERBURY TOP, ? prayer hill (*bra*) reduplicated.

PADGIGER, four (*padzhar*) acre (*acer*, *s.*) [piece]; empty (*posigr*) [field], *T.C.*

PADSTOW, St. Patrick's, *or* St. Petrock's (*p.s.*) place or station (*stow*, *s.*); *o.* ALDESTOW.

PADZHUERA, ? = *paswera*, the fourth.

PAINDAIN, *i.q.* PENDEEN.

PAINDRAN, *d.d.*, ? bramble (*draen*) hill (*pen*), now PENDRIM.

PAINE, *n.f.*, = *paganus*, heathen, *lat.*

P. ROCK, ? rock at the point (*pen*).

PAINTER *n.f.*, *i.q.* PENTIRE.

PALACE, a fish cellar, *A.S.*; a courtyard, *J.S.*; ? *i.q.* PLAS.

PALASTINE, *i.q.* PELASTINE.

PALES PARK, PILLAS close.

PAL-LAMOUNTER, -MAUNTER, -MANT-
ER, *i.q.* POLMANTER.

PALLAS CROFT, *i.q.* PILLAS.

PALLEPHANT, *i.q.* POLLAPHANT.

PALREDEN, *n.f.*, ? ? fern (*reden*) pool
(*pool*).

PALZUM, ? step mother's (*lesvam*)
close (*parc*).

PANGVOL, *d.d.*, ? *i.q.* PENKIVEL.

PANHALLYN, ? = *Pant y llyn*, hollow
of the pool, *w.*, *R.W.*

PAPALLS, ? *i.q.* PARK BELLAS.

PAR, PARR, ? [sand] *bar* ; or = *porth*,
a cove ; or, *bar*, a summit ; or, *i.q.*
PARK.

PARA-DICE, -DISE, *i.q.* PARK AN DISE.

PARAT, *n.f.*, *i.q.* BARRETT.

PARBROOK, ? badger (*broch*) close.

PARC-ABIN, -BEHAN, *i.q.* PARK BEAN.

PARDABERRY,? wild-gooseberry (*day-
berry*) close (*parc*) ; or, *i.q.* PADER-
BURY.

PARDENICK, ? hilly (*dinnic*) close.

PARDON, *n.f.*, ? *i.q.* PADDEN.

PARK, = *parc*, enclosure, close, field,
park.

P.-ABEY, -ABIA, ? *i.q.* PARK AN AB-
BYER ; or, Abraham's close, *E.II.*

P. A DOOR, ? water (*dour*) close.

P. A DORY, ? watery (*douric*) close.

P. ALMACK, ? ? footstep (*ol-mych*),
i.e. pathway close, *T.C.*

P. AMBER, ? the summit (*an bar*), or
Ambrose's close.

P. AN ABBYER, the young-birds'
(*mabyer*) close.

P. AN ALS, the cliff (*als*) field, *Gw.*

P. AN ANNS, *i.q.* PARK AN EANES.

P. AN BEAR, ? the great (*vear*) close.

P. AN BELL, the far (*pell*) close.

P. AN-BEW, -BUE, the cow (*beuch*)
close. *pl.* PARK AN BEWS.

P. AN BICKEN, the *beacon*, or the
little (*bichan*) close.

P. AN BONY, ? the *pony* close.

P. AN-BOOR, -BORE, ? the way (*fordh*)
close ; or, *i.q.* PARK AN MEOR.

P. AN BOUNDS, ? close with the
boundary stones, or bridge (*pons*).

PARK AN BOWAN, *i.q.* PARK BOUAN.

P. AN BOWGEY, *i.q.* PARK BOUDGIE.

P. AN-BRAKE, -BRICK, ? fallow (*havrec*), or the *brake* close.

P. AN BROWSE, *i.q.* PARK BROAS.

P. AN BURLYS, the barley (*barlys*)
field.

P. AN BUSH, ? the *bush*, or post (*pos*),
or cow-house (*boudzhi*) close.

P. AN BUTCHER, the cow-house close.

P. AN BUTTS, ? the archery close ; or,
i.q. PARK AN BUSH.

P. AN CALLE, ? the hazels' (*coll*) close;
or, cabbage (*caol*) field.

P. AN CAMPS, ? the games' (*camp-s,
w.*) or *camps*' close.

P. AN CANS, ? the pavement (*caunse*),
or nuns' (*caines*) close.

P. AN-CARNE, -CAIRNE, the close of
the rock or heap of rocks (*carn*).

P. AN CARRACK, the rock (*carrag*)
close.

P. AN CHAMBER, ? *i.q.* P. AN SKEBER.

P. AN CHERRY, ? the play (*choury*)
close.

P. AN CHY, the house (*chy*) close.

P. AN CLAIES, *i.q.* PARK CLIES.

P. AN COCKING, ? *i.q.* P. KIGGAN.

P. AN-CRANE, -CREAN, the gravel
(*grean*), or hide (*crehan*) close.

P. AN-CREAGUE, -CRIG, ? the rock
(*carrag*) or mound (*crig*) close.

P. AN-CROWN, *i.q.* P. AN GROWAN.

P. AN DANACK, ? the hilly (*denick,
Pr.*) close ; or, *i.q.* P. DRANNACK.

P. AN DANGER, ? the close below the
house (*dan chy*).

P. AN DANOR, ? *the same* ; or, the
fowlers' (*edhanor*) close.

P. AN DARRAS, close by the door
(*daras*) ; or, *i.q.* PARK AN DREAS.

P. AN DAVAS, the sheep (*davas*) close.

P. AND DOE, ? the south (*dehou*) close.

P. AN DEVONS, ? ? the Devonshire
cows' close.

P. AND HALL, ? *i.q.* PARK AN TOL.

P. AND HILL, ? *i.q.* PARK AN HAL.

P. AN DIGGY, ? the tithe (*dege*) close.

P. AN-DISE, -DIX, the rick (*dise, B.*),

or grandfather's (*hendas*) close.

PARK AN DOWLS, ? the hag's (*diowles*) close.

P. AND-PONS, -POND, -POUND, ? *i.q.* PARK AN-PONS, -POND.

P. AN-DRAIN, -DREAN, the thorn (*draen*) close.

P.-AN DREA, -ANDREA, the home (*tre*) close; the town field, *J.B.*

P. AN DREAS, the brambles' (*dreis*), *or* cross (*dres*) close.

P. AND SPIDER, *i.q.* P. AN SKEBER.

P. AND STUFFLE, ? dock (*tafol, w.*) lambs' (*eanes*) close.

P. AND TOWER, the water (*dour*) close.

P. AND TREES, *i.q.* P. AN DREAS.

P. AN DUEL, *i.q.* PARK AN HUEL; *or*, the devil's (*diowl*) close.

P. AND VENTON, *i.q.* P. AN VENTON.

P. AN EAN, the lamb (*ean*) close.

P. AN-EANES, -EANS, the lambs' (*eanes*) close.

P. AN EAST, the east (*est*) close.

P. AN EBBYER, *i.q.* P. AN ABBYER.

P. AN FAT, ? the dormouse (*bat*), *or* rich *or* fat close.

P. AN-FOLD, -FLOOD, ? ? the fold (*ffald, w.*) close.

P. AN FORYER, the thief's (*forrior, L.*) *or*, blacksmith's (*ferror*) close.

P. AN FOWL, the blackbird's (*moelh*) close; *or, i.q.* PARK AN POLL.

P. AN FOX, ? the bush (*bagas*) close.

P. AN GARNE, the *garden*, *or* heap of rocks (*carn*) close.

P. AN GARRACK, *i.q.* P. AN CARRACK.

P. AN GARRATT, ? the *carrot* close.

P. AN GATE, the *gate* close.

P. AN GAYAN, ? the ridge (*cein*) c.

P. AN GEAR, green (*gear*) field, *T.C.*; *or*, the camp (*caer*) close.

P. AN-GEW, -GUE, the GEW close.

P. AN-GILLIE, -GILLY, the grove *or* hazel grove (*celli*) close.

P. AN GLOW, ? the fuel (*glow*, dried droppings of cattle) close, *W.B.*

P. AN GOOSE, ? the wood (*cuz*), *or* goose (*goaz, B.*), *or* cheese (*caus*) c.

P. AN-GORE, -GOVER, the brook (*gover*),

or goat (*gavar, gauar*) close.

PARK ANGOT, ? the short (*cot*) close.

P. AN-GRAIN, -GREEN, *i.q.* PARK AN CRANE.

P. AN GROUSE, the cross (*crows*) c.

P. AN GROWAN, the *growan*, *i.e.* granite-gravel (*T.C.*), *or* granite soil (*W.B.*) close.

P. AN GUEN, the wasp (*guhien*), *or* down (*guen*) close; *or*, the vine-yard (*guin*): the GEWS close, *J.B.*; the white *or* fair (*gwen*) field, *M.*

P. AN GWITH, the trees (*guryth*) c.

P. AN-HAL, -HALE, -HALL, the moor (*hal*), *or* river (*hayl*) close.

P. AN HALS, *i.q.* PARK AN ALS.

P. AN HEAN, *i.q.* PARK AN EAN.

P. AN HERBS, ? ? the ripe (*arvez*) c.

P. AN HOAR, *i.q.* PARKEN HOAR.

P. AN HOWAN, *i.q.* P. AN NOON.

P. AN HUEL, the mine (*huel*) close.

P. AN-ITHAN, -ITHEN, the furze (*eithen*), *or* bird (*edhen*) close.

P. AN JANE, ? *the same*; ox (*udzheon*), *or* the chaff (*ision*) close.

P. AN JARNE, the garden (*dzharn*) c.

P. AN JAVIS, *i.q.* PARK AN DAVAS.

P. AN JEDNAS, ? the lambs' (*eanes*), *or* near (*nes*) gate (*yet*) close.

P. AN JETS, ? the gate closes.

P. AN JETT, the gate (*yet*) close.

P. AN JORA, *i.q.* PARK AN CHERRY.

P. AN JOSE, ? outside (*aues*) house (*chy*) close.

P. AN-JOY, -JY, *i.q.* PARK AN CHY.

P. AN-LAY, -LEA, ? the pasture (*lea, l.*) close.

P. AN LEAR, ? the hunter's (*hellier*) c.

P. AN LEE, the calves (*lee*) close, *B.*

P. AN LENIES, the nettle (*linaz*) close.

P. AN LORN, the fox (*lowern*) close.

P. AN-LOR, -LOUR, -LOWER, -LOWR, ? the garden (*luar*) close.

P. AN LOT, the mire (*lued*), *or* slaughter (*lladd*, to kill, *w.*) close.

P. AN LUAZ, ? ? the outside (*ves*) sheltered (*lew = hleo, s.*) close.

P. AN MANNER, ? the long-stone (*maen hir*) close.

PARK AN MENAS, ?? the little (minys), or corn-sheaf (manal yz) close.

P. AN MEOR, the great (meur) close.

P. AN MEW, ? ? the greater (mui) c.

P. AN-MOE, -MOW, the pigs' (moch), or rick (mow) close.

P. AN MOWHAY, the stackyard c.

P. ANNA, ? = parc genau, close at the mouth or entrance.

P. AN NARROW, ? = parc an warra, the further close.

P. ANNAS, i.q. PARK EANES.

P. AN NEAN, i.q. PARK AN EAN.

P. AN-NEWETH, -NOWETH, the new (newydh, nowydh) close.

P. AN NICHOLAS, Nicholas's close.

P. AN-NOON, -NOWAN, -OUNE, the down (gwon) close.

P. AN-NOWLES,-OLDS,-OWLES,-OWLS, i.q. PARK AN ALS.

P. AN ORBER, herbs-garden (erber) close.

P. A NOWER, i.q. PARK AN HOAR.

P. AN-PEAS, PEASE, the pease (pes) close.

P. AN PEATH, draw-well (peeth, W.B.) close.

P. AN PINK, ? the wry-neck (pinnick), or bench (benc) close.

P. AN PIT, ? the pit close.

P. AN POLL, the pool (pol) close.

P. AN POLLARD, ? the lopped-tree close.

P. AN-POND, -POUND, ? the cider-mill, or pond, or pound close; or, i.q.

P. AN PONS, the bridge (pons) c.

P. AN-POSS, -POST, the post close.

P. AN PRAPP, ? the worm (pref) c.

P. AN QUAKER, ? the mother-in-law's (hweger), or merchant's (gwicgur) c.

P. AN REES, ? the middle (cres) c.

P. AN ROPER, rope-walk close, W.B.

P. AN ROSE, the heath (ros) close.

P. AN ROUND, ? the round close.

P. AN SCREBO, ? the barns' (sciberiow) close.

P. AN SEAYER, ? the artizan's or carpenter's (saer) close.

P. AN SHOP, ? the shop close.

PARK AN SHUTTER, ? the shoot or waterspout close; or, i.q.

P. AN-SKEDER, -SKEBA, -SKEBO, the barn (sciber) close.

P. AN SHAFTS, ? the mine shafts c.

P. AN SPARES, ? the ghost (speris) c.

P. AN SPRING, i.q. P. AN VENTON.

P. AN STABLE, ? i.q. P. AND STUFFLE.

P. AN STAGAN, ? the pool (stagen) c.

P. AN STALLEN, ? ? the hedge (stillen) close.

P. AN STARVE US, ? ? = oak-field (dar res) lambs' (eanes) close.

P. AN STEP, ? ? the gridiron-stile c.

P. AN STRIFE, ? ? the dispute close.

P. AN-TIDNA, -TIDNO, ? ? the close below (tadn).

P. AN TOL, the hole (tol) close.

P. AN TOP, the top close.

P. AN TRAP, ? the trap, or bull (tarb, ga.) close.

P. AN TREATH, the sand (traith) c.

P. AN TROAN, ANTRON, ? close by the turning (torn), or of the depression between the furrows (tronc); or, down-house (tre-oon) c.

P. AN TROUBLE, ? ? the close by DOR POL; or, mole-hill (turumel) close.

P. AN TULE, i.q. PARK AN DUEL.

P. AN TURK, the watery (douric) c.

P. AN TWIST, ? the crooked c., W.B.

P. AN TYE, the house (ti) close.

P. AN UN, i.q. PARK AN NOON.

P. AN USE, ? ? the nightingale's (eus, B.) or outside (aues) close.

P. AN VAU, ? the cave (fow) close.

P. AN VEAR, the great (mear) close.

P. AN VEL, the honey (mel), or ball (pel), or distant (pell) close.

P. AN-VELLAN, -VELLIN, the mill (melin), or clover (meillion, w.) close.

P. AN VELVAS, the lark's (melhues) c.

P. AN-VENTON, -VENTUM, the spring (fenten) close.

P. AN VETHAN, the tree (gwedhen) c.

P. AN VICTER. ? i.q. P. AN QUAKER.

P. AN-VIEW, -VUE, the cow (beu) c.

P. AN-VOGUE, -VOGE, the cave or hollow (vug), or forge (foc) close.

PARK AN VOME, ? the balm (*bawm, w.*) close.

P. AN-VORN, -VORNE, the oven or furnace (*forn*), or alder (*gwern*) c.

P. AN VOUNDER, field of pasture, *B.* ; or, the lane (*bounder*) close.

P. AN VOUSA, ? the ditches', entrenchments', or walls' (*fossow*) close.

P. AN VOWNE, *i.q.* P. AN BOWAN.

P. AN VRANE, the crow (*bran*) close.

P. AN WATCH, ? the *watching*, or outside (*aues*) close.

P. AN WHALYER, the workman's (*wayler*) close.

P. AN WHEAL, *i.q.* PARK AN HUEL.

P. AN WHENS, the wind (*gwens*) close.

P. AN WRAHAN, ? *i.q.* P. AN VRAHAN.

P. AN WRECK, ? the woman's (*gwrec*) close.

P. AN YALE, *i.q.* PARK AN HAL.

P. APPLE, ? apple's close (*aval*) or orchard ; or, colt's (*ebol*) close.

P. ARTER, ? *Arthur's*, or long (*hir*) hill (*ard*) close.

P. A VARCA, ? prison or cattle-pound (*gwarchae, w.*) close.

P. AVON, ? *i.q.* PARK AN BOWAN.

P. BACON, ? *i.q.* P. AN BICKEN.

P. BANNEL, broom (*banal*) close.

P. BANS, ? close with the circular-entrenchments (*bans*), *W.B.*

P. BANT, ? close in the hollow, bottom, or valley (*pant, w.*).

P. BARROWS, barrows' close.

P. BASTARD, ? base-child's close.

P. BAUKER, ? *i.q.* PARK BUCKA.

P.-BEAN, -BEHAN, -BEN, little (*bihan*) close.

P. BELLAS, *i.q.* PARK PELLAS.

P.-BENGY, -BINGEY, ? *i.q.* PARK BOUNGAY.

P. BENNET, Bennet's or beneath c.

P. BETTY, ? cow-house (*beuty*) close.

P. BEW, *i.q.* PARK AN BEW.

P. BILLIER, water-cress (*beler*), or hogshead (*baliar*) close.

P. BLASE, *i.q.* PARK BELLAS.

P. BLOOD, ? blossom (*blodh*) close.

P. BOAZ, ? bush (*bagas*) close.

PARK BODA, ? the cow-house (*beu ti*) close.

P. BOLLEN, pool (*polan*) close.

P.-BORN, -BORUN, ? hill (*bron*), or oven (*forn*) close.

P. BOTTOM, *bottom* or lowest close.

P.-BOUAN, -BOWEN, -BOWIN, ? beef (*bowin*) close.

P. BOU-DGEY, -DGIE, -DJIE, -DZHI, fold-close, *T.C.* ; or, cow-(*beuch*) house (*chy*) close.

P. BOUND-EA, -ER, *i.q.* PARK AN VOUNDER or BOUNDS.

P. BOUNGAY, ? *i.q.* P. BOUDGIE ; or, boundary fence (*ce*) close.

P. BOUNDS, *i.q.* PARK AN BOUNDS.

P. BOUR, ? *i.q.* PARK AN BOOR.

P. BOWDEN, ? BAWDEN's close.

P. BRACKET, ? *brake* gate (*yet*) close.

P. BRAKE, ? *i.q.* PARK AN BRAKE.

P. BRAMBLE, bramble close.

P.-BRANS, -BRONS, crow (*bran*) closes.

P. BRAURE, ? brother's (*broder*) close.

P. BREENY, BRINEY, crows' (*bryny*) c.

P. BRENT, ? *burnt*, or Briant's close.

P. BRITON, ? ? southernwood (*bryttwn, w.*) close.

P.-BROAS, -BROASE, -BROAZ, -BROZ, -BRAWS, big (*bras*), or thicket (*brouse*) close.

P. BRONGY, ? breast of the house (*bron gy*) close, *R.W.*

P. BRONSE, ? lambs' (*eanes*), or dry (*sech*) hill close.

P. BROOK, ? badger (*broch*) close.

P. BROOM, *i.q.* PARK BANNEL.

P. BROW, ? hand-mill (*brou*) close.

P. BROWN, ? hill (*bron*) close.

P. BUCK-A, -ER, scarecrow (*bucca*) c.

P. BUDGA, ? *i.q.* PARK BOUDGIE.

P. BULLA, the bull (*bwla, w.*) close.

P. BULLAS, ? *i.q.* PARK BULVIS.

P. BULVIS, ? outside (*ves*) pool (*pol*) close ; or, *i.q.* PARK AN VELVAS.

P. BU-NNY, -RNEY ? *i.q.* P. BREENY.

P. BURGAN, ? bulrush (*brychan, B.*).

P. BUSSA, ? close of the earthen pot (*bussa*), or birches (*bezo*) ; or, *i.q.* P. BUDGA.

PARK BUTTS, *i.q.* PARK AN BUTTS.

P. BYVYAN, ? little (*bihan*) cow (*beu*), or Vivian's close.

P. CAB, close with the mess (*cab*) in it; *or*, crooked (*cabm*) close.

P. CADJAW, daisy (*gajah, B.*) close; ? = *parc egr.*

P. CALIGER, ? *i.q.* PARK CLODGEY.

P. CALLON, ? hazel-tree (*collen, w.*) c.

P. CANDY, ? white-house (*candy, w., R.W.*) close; *or, i.q.* PARK AN TYE.

P. CARN, CARN close.

P. CARNAL, ? moor (*hal*) rock (*carn*), *or* corner (*cornel*), *or* crundle close.

P. CARREETH, ? red (*rydh*) fort (*caer, R.W.*) *or* rock (*carn, J.B.*) close; *or*, root (*gwredh*) close.

P. CARR-EG, -IG, rock (*carrag*) close.

P. CARRY, ? rough (*garow*) close.

P. CASER, *i.q.* PARK CADJAW.

P. CASTLE, round *or* castle close.

P. CAUL, ? *i.q.* PARK HALL.

P. CHAPEL, ? *chapel* close.

P.-CHAY, -CHIE, -CHUY, -CHY, house (*chy*) close.

P. CHEGROUSE, ? cross (*crows*) house-close; *or*, CHYGROUS close.

P. CHERRY, *i.q.* PARK AN CHERRY.

P. CHIVERTON, CHIVERTON close.

P. CHYWOOLAS, lower- (*wolas*) house close; *or*, lower PARK CHY.

P. CLEBURA, ? KELLYBRAY close.

P. CLEMOE, ? CLEMOWE'S close.

P. CLI-ES, -ZE, wattled-hedge close, *W.B.*

P. CLIFT, ? *cliff* close.

P.-CLOGEY,-CLUDGIE,-CLERGY,sticky (*clidgy, m.c.*), *i.e.* muddy c.

P.-CLOSE, -CLUSE, ? green (*glas*), *or* church (*eglos*), *or* bottom (*goles*) c.

P. COBBER, ? *i.q.* PARK AN GOVER.

P.-COCK, -COOK, ? red (*coch*), *or* cook *or* cuckoo's (*cog*) close.

P. COCKEN, ? [hay]cock (*coccyn*) close, *R.W.*; *or, i.q.* PARK HOCKING.

P. COLAS, ? *i.q.* PARK CLOSE.

P.-COLDERN, -COLDRAN, ? ? thorn (*draen*) hill (*col*) *or* moor (*hal*) c.

P. COLLEY, ? lower (*golla*) close.

P. CONNIN, ? rabbit (*cynnin*) close.

P. COORE, ? goat (*ganar*) close.

P. COOSE, wood (*cuz*) close.

P. COOTHA, ? mustard (*caddw, w.*), *or* privy (*gaudy*), *or* husks' (*kutho*) c.

P. CORNER, ? corner, *or* long (*hir*) corner (*corn*) close.

P. COUSIN, ? turf (*cesan*), *or* ox (*aulzheon*) close.

P. COUTH, ? old (*coth*) close.

P. COWING, ? *i.q.* PARK OWEN.

P. COWL, ? *i.q.* PARK HALL.

P. COWLS, ? = *parc als*, cliff close; *or, i.q.* PARK-GULLAS *or* -CLOSE.

P. CRAB, ? *crab*-tree close.

P.-CRANE, -CREAN, gravel (*grean*), *or* crane (*garan*), close.

P. CRANK, frog (*cronec*), *or* toad (*cronec du*) close.

P.-CRASE, -CRAISE, -CREES, -CREIS, -CRESS, -CRIES, -CRIZE, middle (*cres*) close.

P.-CRAZIE, ? crooked (*ceirsio*, to wind) close; *or, i.q.* PARKERISEY.

P. CREA, ? cattle (*gre*) close.

P.-CREAD, -CREED, ? *i.q.* P. CARREETH.

P.-CREAGE, -CREEG, ? mound (*creeg*), *or* rock (*carrag*) close.

P.-CRIGAR, -CROCKER, ? partridge (*grugyer*), *or* long-mound (*crug-hir*) close.

P. CRIGKET, ? heron (*crychyild, w.*) c.

P. CROSS, cross, *or* bog (*cors*) close.

P. CROW, hovel (*crow*) close.

P. CROW-AN, -N, ? round (*crwnn, w.*) close.

P.-CUDDLE, -CUTTAL, ? Irishman's (*godhal*), *or* wilderness (*gwyddwal, w.*) close.

P. CULLAN, ? holly (*celyn*) close.

P. CULL-AS, -IS, ? bottom (*goles*) c.

P. CUTCHUY, *i.q.* PARK AN CHY.

P.-DANGY, -DUNGEY, ? close below (*tan*) the house (*chy*).

P. DANIEL, ? close below the moor (*hal*); *or*, Daniel's close.

P.-DARAS, -DARRASS, -DARROWS, close by the door (*daras*).

P. DARROW, ? oaks' (*derow*) close.

2E

PARK-DARY, -DAIRY, ? *i.q.* P.-DREA, or -DOWRICK, *or* -CHERRY.

P. DAVERS, *i.q.* P. DEVAS.

P. DAVEY, ? David's (*Deui*) close.

P. DAY, ? day, *or* house (*ti*) close.

P. DEAN, ? cream (*dehen*) close.

P. DEANS, ? castle (*dinas*) close.

P. DEES, ? rick (*dise, B.*) close.

P. DEGLIS, ? church (*eglos*) house (*ti*), *or* pleasant (*tig*) green (*glas*) close.

P. DE-JAM, -ZHAM, ? ? poor (*ezom*, poverty, *w.*) house (*ti*) close.

P.-DEVAS, -DEVERS, sheep (*davas*, pl., *deves*) close ; *or*, tongue c., *H.M.W.*

P. DEWERRA, ? ? further (*warra* = *wartha*) side (*tu*) close.

P. DINNY, ? narrow *or* fowler's (*idns*) close.

P. DONAL, cask (*tonnel*) close.

P. DOWER, water (*dour*) close.

P. DOWN, ? deep (*down*), *or* hill (*dun*) close.

P. DOWRICK, watery (*douric*) close.

P.-DRAEN, -DRAIN, -DREAN, thorn (*draen*) close ; home close, *T.C.*

P. DRANNACK, thorny (*draenic*) close.

P.-DRAY, -DREA, -DREE, -DRY, house (*tre*), *or* homeward (*adre*) close.

P. DREA AN WARTHA, the (*an*) higher (*gwartha*) home close.

P. DREER, ? long (*hir*) home (*tre*) c.

P. DRIES, brambles' (*dreis*) close.

P. DRUID, ? oak-wood (*deru-with*) c.

P. DRUM, ? ridge (*drum, w.*) close.

P. DRY-SACK, -SACK, -SOCK, -SUCK, brambly (*dreisic* close.

P. DUCHY, ? *i.q.* PARK DANGY.

P. DZAIN, ? chaff (*ision*) close.

P. EADER, ? ? common (*cyttir, w.*) c.

P. EALIN, ? ? lamb's (*ean*) moor (*hal*) close.

P.-EANES, -EANS, *i.q.* PARK INNIS.

P. EAR, long (*hir*) close.

P. EAST, east (*est*) close.

P. EAVES, ? close outside (*aves*).

P. EITH-AN, -ON, furze (*eithin*) close.

P. EMMET, ? ant's close.

P. EN ABLE, ? the (*an*) colt's (*ebol*) c.

P.-EN BALL, -ENBALL, ? *the same* ;

or, the mine (*bal*) *or* pool (*pol*) c.

P. ENBANK, ? the bench (*benc*) close.

P. EN BAYS, ? ? boar (*baez*) close.

P. ENBEAR, ? *i.q.* PARK AN ABBYER.

P. ENBEWS, *i.q.* PARK AN BEWS.

P. EN-BLOWER, -BLUBBER, ? the *plover* close.

P. EN BODZHI, *i.q.* P. AN BOWGEY.

P. ENBONE, *i.q.* PARK AN BOWAN.

P. EN BOORE, *i.q.* PARK AN BOOR.

P. EN BOUNDS, ? the tin *bounds* croft, *T.C.*

P. EN BROSE, *i.q.* PARK AN BROWSE.

P. EN BULLS, ? *i.q.* P. AN BURLYS.

P. EN CADY, ? *i.q.* PARK CANDY.

P. EN ENTRY, the SANCTUARY c.

P. EN CHAPEL, the *chapel* close.

P. EN-CHEWEY, -CHU, -CHUY, ? south (*dehou*) close ; *or*, *i.q.* P. AN CHY.

P. EN CLAYS, *i.q.* PARK AN CLAIES.

P. EN COWLS, ? the bottom (*goles*) c.

P. EN CRAIG, *i.q.* P. AN CREAGUE.

P. EN CREASE, ? PARK CRASE.

P. EN CREET, ? *i.q.* PARK CREAD.

P. EN CROWS, the cross (*crows*) close.

P. EN DALLS, ? the hag's (*diowlez*) c.

P. EN DANES, *i.q.* PARK DEANS.

P. EN-DARIS, -DORS, *i.q.* PARK AN DARRAS.

P. EN DARRA, the oaks' (*derow*) close.

P.-ENDEAVOUR, -ENDEVER, ? the water (*dour*) close.

P.-EN DEUS, -ENDEAVOURS, *i.q.* PARK AN DAVAS.

P. EN DORREL, ? the close in the middle (*hanter*) of the moor (*hal*).

P. EN DOWDRY, ? the homeward (*adre*) water (*dour*) close.

P.-ENDRAY, -EN DRY, *i.q.* PARK AN DREA.

P. EN DREAN, *i.q.* PARK AN DRAIN.

P. EN DYAS, *i.q.* PARK AN DISE.

P. EN ELL, the moor (*hal*) close.

P. ENELLICK, the (*an*) willows' (*helec*) close.

P. EN GAIN, ? *i.q.* P. AN GAYAN.

P. EN-GARDEN, -GARN, *i.q.* PARK AN GARNE.

P. EN GARRAS, *i.q.* PARK GARRAS.

PARK EN GEER, *i.q.* PARK AN GEAR.

P. EN GRAMP, *? grandfather's* close.

P. EN GRANNAS, *? grandmother's* c.

P. ENGREGOR, *i.q.* PARK CROCKER.

P. EN GROWSE, *i.q.* P. AN GROUSE.

P. EN GUES, the GEWS close.

P. EN GULLAS, *i.q.* PARK GULLAS.

P. ENGWARRAS *i.q.* P. EN GARRAS.

P. EN HALLAN, *?? the* salt (*halan*) c.

P. EN HARBOR, *? the* herbs'-garden (*erber*) close.

P. ENHELL, *i.q.* PARK AN HAL.

P. EN HOAR, the ram's (*hor*), or sister's (*hoer*), or boundary (*or*) c.

P. EN JEAN, *? the* cold (*yen*) close, *T.C.* ; *? i.q.* PARK AN JANE.

P. EN-JEAT, -JET, *i.q.* P. AN JETT.

P. EN KINE, *? i.q.* PARK EN GAIN.

P. EN LANE, the *lane*, or patch (*llain, w.*) close ; *or, i.q.* P. EN HALLAN.

P. LETA, *? the* dairy (*lait-ty*) close.

P. EN LOARNE, *i.q.* PARK AN LORN.

P. EN LOCKS, *?? the* calves' (*leauch-s*) c.

P. EN-MARROW, -MORROW, *? the* corpse (*marow*) close.

P. EN MORRISH, *? field* of the sea-rushes (*morhesg, w.*), *R.W.* ; *or,* Morrish's close.

P. ENNOWETH, *i.q.* P. AN NOWETH.

P. ENNOWER, *i.q.* PARK EN HOAR.

P. EN NOWLS, *i.q.* P. AN NOWLES.

P. ENOORN, *? the* corner (*corn*) close.

P. EN PENS, *? the* parsnip (*panez*) c.

P. EN PENTON *alias* SPRING (*fenten*) FIELD, *T.a.*

P. EN PLUD, *? the* pool (*pludn*) c.

P.-EN PONDS, -ENPONS, *? i.q.* PARK AN PONS.

P. EN PROCTOR, Proctor's field, *W.B.* ; *? the* maltster's (*bragwr*) c.

P. EN QUARRA, the higher (*gwarra*) close ; *or, quarry* field.

P. ENRISE, *? i.q.* PARK AN REES.

P. ENROWS, *? i.q.* PARK AN ROSE.

P. EN RUFFLER, *? the* fidler's (*harfelor*) close.

P. EN SACKS, *? the* parched (*seghes*) c.

P. ENSCAWEN, the (*an*) elder-tree (*scauen*) close.

P. EN SHAFTY, *?? lambs'* (*eanes*) close by the summer hovel (*hafdy*) ; *or, i.q.* PARK AN SHAFTS.

P. EN SKIBBER, *i.q.* P. AN SKEBER.

P. EN SKIBBON, the barns (*sciberion*) close.

P. EN SQUARE, *? i.q.* P. AN SKEBER.

P. ENTHORN, the thorn (*draen*) c.

P. EN TIDNOE, *i.q.* PARK AN TIDNA.

P. ENTODDEN, *? the same; or,* the lay (*todn*) close.

P. ENTOWER, the water (*dour*) close.

P. EN TREASE, *? i.q.* P. AN DARRAS.

P. ENTRUCKLE, *? ? the* (*an*) small-ragwort (*teircaill, w.*) close.

P. ENVAUGHAN, *? i.q.* P. AN VORN.

P. EN-VANE, -VEAN, the little (*bihan, bean, vean*) close.

P. EN VELLIM, *? i.q.* P. AN VELLYN, the mill (*melin*) close, *W.B.*

P. ENVEOR, *i.q.* PARK AN VEAR.

P. EN VOARN, *i.q.* PARK AN VORN.

P. EN VOR, the close by the road (*fordh*) ; *or,* great (*maur*) close.

P. EN VRA-HAN, -N, crows' field, *Pr.*

P. ENWICKER, *i.q.* P. AN VICTER.

PARKER. *n.f.*, *? long* (*hir*) close.

PARK ERA, *?* acre (*eru*) close.

P. ERISEY, field (*parc*) upon (*er*) the bottom (*izy*), *Pr.* ; *or,* dry (*sech*) acre (*eru*) close.

P. FAMOUS, *? fifth* (*pemfas*) close.

P. FAT, *? i.q.* PARK AN FAT.

P. FAVEN, *? brick* (*pobfaen*) close.

P. FAWN, *? i.q.* PARK AN BOUAN.

P. FILLEY, *? colts'* (*ebilli*) close.

P. FITCHER, *? badger's* field, *W.B.* ; *or,* four (*padzhar*) [acre] close.

P. FLY, *? colts'* (*ebilli*) close.

P. FODDEN, *? little* (*vadn*) close.

P. FOGE, forge (*fog*) close.

P. FREATH, *? wattled-hedge* close.

P. FRIG-GLES, -GLEYS, -GLUS, -LES, *? church-road* (*for-eglos*) close.

P. GABBIN, *? i.q.* PARCABIN.

P. GABBY, *? i.q.* PARK ABEY.

P. GADGER, *i.q.* PARK CADJAW.

P. GALOWAS, *? i.q.* PARK GULLAS.

P. GARDAND, *? garden* close.

PARK GARNE, *i.q.* PARK AN GARN.

P. GARR-ACK, -ICK, rock (*carrag*) c.

P. GARRAS, top (*gwarhas*) close.

P. GARRET, ? root (*gwredh*) close.

P. GE-AR, -ER, *i.q.* PARK AN GEAR.

P. GELLAS, ? bee-swarm (*glez*) close.

P. GERNICK, rocky (*cernic*) close.

P. GEUGLE, ? sheep-dung (*cagal*) c.

P. GIDEON, ? ox (*udzheon*) close.

P. GIGLESS, church (*eglos*) close.

P. GILLY, grove (*celli*) close.

P. GLA-SE, -ZE, ? *i.q.* PARK CLOSE.

P.-GLIDDEN, -GLUTTON, -GOLDEN, ? broad (*ledan*) close.

P. GO, ? wood (*coat*) close; or, = *parcow*, closes; or, *i.q.* PARK GOVE.

P. GOAR, ? *i.q.* PARK AN GOAR, or PARKEN HOAR.

P. GOODNAS, ? *i.q.* PARK EANES.

P. GOON, down (*gwon*) close.

P. GORLAND, ? sheepfold (*corlan*) c.

P. GOVE, smith's (*gof*) close.

P. GOWTHER, ? mole (*gudhar*) close.

P. GRAIN, ? *i.q.* PARK CRANE.

P. GRIGLAN, heath (*griglan*) close.

P. GROSISE, GROSISE close.

P.-GROUCE, -GROUS, -GROWSE, cross (*crows*), or heath or moor (*ros*) c.

P. GROWN, *i.q.* PARK AN GROWAN.

P. GUARYS, ? *i.q.* PARK GARRAS.

P. GUERNEN, alder-tree close.

P. GULLET, ? QUILLET close.

P.-GULLAS, -GOLLAS, -GULLES, -GUL-LIES, ? bottom (*goles*), or green-down (*goon-las*) close.

P. GUMPAS, *i.q.* PARK AN CAMPS.

P.-GURRA, ? hay (*gorha*); or, *i.q.* PARK-GWARRA, -GWARRATH, ? higher (*gwarra*) close.

P. GUTHAL, Irishman's (*godhal*) c.

P. GWAIL, ? mine (*wheal*) close.

P. GWANETH, wheat field.

P. GWARROW, ? cattle (*gwarrhog*) c.

P. GWEALDER, ? mastiff (*guilter*) c.

P. GWENNAP, Gwennap's close.

P. GWILIAS, ? grass (*gwells*) close.

P. GWIN, white (*gwyn*) close; or, the VINE-(*gwin*) YARD.

P. HAGEL, ? sheep dung (*cagel*) c.

P.-HAIR, -HARE, -HEAR, -HERE, long (*hir*), or battle (*heir*) close.

P.-HAL, -HALE, -HALL, moor (*hal*), or river (*hayl*), or cabbage (*caol*) c.

P.-HALES, -HALLS, ? cliff (*als*), or broad-moor (*hal les*) close.

P. HAM, ? HAM's close.

P. HAMBLY, Hambly's close.

P. HARBOUR, ? *i.q.* PARKEN HARBOR.

P. HARRY, ? *i.q.* P. HARVEY, ? Harvey's, or battle-field (*heirva*) close.

P. HATCH, ? *i.q.* PARK CADJAW.

P. HAY, ? ? hedge (*ce*) close.

P. HAYS, ? barley (*haiz*) close, *R.W.*

P. HEARNE, ? alder (*gwern*) close.

P. HEBYE, *i.q.* PARK ABEY.

P. HEC-CA, -KA, Dickie's close.

P. HEDRAS, ? *i.q.* PARK AN DARRAS.

P.-HELLAS, -HILLAS, -HILLS, ? green-moor (*hal las*), or son-in-law's (*els*) close; or, *i.q.* PARK HALES.

P. HENDRA, old-town close.

P. HENVER, old (*hen*) road (*fordh*) close; or, *i.q.* PARKEN VOR.

P. HERRET, ? long (*hir*) gate (*yet*), or higher wood close.

P. HETCHA, *i.q.* PARKCADJAW.

P. HEWAS, ? *i.q.* PARK AN USE.

P. HITHER, ? ? PARK COOTHA.

P. HOCK-IN, -ING, Hockin's close; or, *i.q.* PARK COCKIN.

P.-HOE, -HOW, ? *i.q.* PARK GO.

P. HOLDRAN, ? *i.q.* PARK COLDRAN.

P. HOLLAND, ? Holland's close.

P. HOLLY, ? *i.q.* PARK COLLEY.

P. HOMER, homeward or nearer c.

P. HORN, ? corner (*corn*) close.

P. HOSK-EN, -IN, -ING, the field of rushes, *Pr.* ; ? Hosken's, or sedge (*hescen*) close.

P. HUMPHREY, Humphrey's, or the hill close (*parc an vre*).

P. HURGLE, ? ? heap (*grachel*) close.

P. IN, *n.f.*, ? = *parc ean*, lamb close.

P. INARROW, ? *i.q.* P. AN NARROW.

P. IN BEAN, *i.q.* PARK BEAN.

P. IN-BELLOWS, -BELLS, the *pillas*, or peeled-oats close.

P. IN BOO, *i.q.* PARK AN BEW.

P. IN BOTH, ? the hut (*bwth, w.*) c.

P. IN BOUNDER, *i.q.* P. AN VOUNDER.

P. IN BURRAWS, ? the *barrows'* close; or, *i.q.* PARK AN BROWSE.

P. IN-CALLS, -CLOSE, ? *i.q.* PARK EN COWLS.

P. IN CLIFF, the (*an*) cliff close.

P. IN CLUE, ? the groves (*kelliow*) close; or, *i.q.* PARK AN GLOW.

P. IN CLYSE, *i.q.* P. AN CLAIES.

P. IN DAVIS, *i.q.* PARK AN DAVAS.

P. IN DRANE, *i.q.* PARK AN DRAEN.

P. INDUKY, ? *i.q.* PARK DUTCHY.

P.-IN-DU-RY, ? *i.q.* PARK A DORY.

P. IN GARRIS, *i.q.* P. EN GARRAS.

P. IN GREEN, *i.q.* P. AN GRANE.

P. ING VENTON, *i.q.* P. AN VENTON.

P. IN HELL, *i.q.* PARK AN HAL.

P. IN KIND, ? *i.q.* PARK KINE.

P. IN LEASE, ? the (*an*) broad moor (*hal-les*), or church (*eglos*) close.

P. IN LOWER, ? the garden (*luar*), or *lower* close.

P. INNIS, island (*enys*), or lambs' (*eanes*) close.

P. IN OVER, ? *i.q.* PARK AN ORBER.

P. INRREAN, ? ? the (*an*) hill (*ryn*) c.

P. IN WALLACE, the (*an*) lower or bottom (*wollas = gollas*) close.

P. IN ZETH, the dry (*sech*) close, *Pr.* ; field of the arrow (*zeth*), *R. W.*

P. ISAAC, ? corn (*izic*) field.

P. ISAU, ? lowest (*isa, w.*) close, *R. W.*

P. ISSEY, ? corn (*izic*) field ; or, *i.q.* PARKERISEY.

P. ITH-AN, -EN, furze (*eithin*) close.

P. IVAY, ? *i.q.* PARK ABEY.

P.-JACKA, -JACKFY, -JACKET, -JAGO, Jacka's, Jago's, or Jacket's close.

P. JANE, *i.q.* PARK AN JANE.

P.-JARNE, -JEARNE, *i.q.* PARK AN JARNE.

P. JENNY, ? fowler's (*idne*) close.

P. JET, gate (*yet*) close.

P. JEWS, ? south (*dehou*) closes.

P.-JOAN, -JONE, ? Joan's, or John's, or down (*oon*) house (*chy*) close.

P. JOPPA, ? barn (*sciber*) close.

P. JOY, *i.q.* PARK CHY.

P. KEEN, = *parc ean*, lamb close.

P. KENNIN, ? wild leek (*kennin, w.*) field, *R. W.* ; or, rabbit (*cynin*)close.

P. KERRIS, ? *i.q.* PARK CRASE.

P. KEW, ? ewe, or GEW close.

P. KIGGAN, ? kitchen (*cegin*) close.

P. KINE, ? ridge (*cein*) close.

P. KISTALL, ? *i.q.* PARK WHISTLE.

P. KITCHEN, ? = *parc udzheon*, ox c.

P. KNELL, *i.q.* PARK IN HELL.

P. KNOLLS, *i.q.* PARK AN ALS.

P. KNOWAN, *i.q.* PARK AN OUNE.

P. KNOWETH, *i.q.* PARK NOWETH.

P. KRUGE, ? *i.q.* PARK CREAGE.

P.-LAITA, -LEETA, -LETA, ? dairy (*lait-ty*) close.

P. LANCE, ? nettle (*linaz*) close.

P. LANE, ? *i.q.* PARK EN LANE.

P. LANYER, ? glade (*lanherch*) close.

P. LATCH, ? grey (*ludzh*) close.

P.-LAY, -LEA, -LEE, -LEAH, -LEHA, -LEY, ? the *lay*, or pasture close ; or, *i.q.* PARK AN LEE.

P. LEAN, *lean* or poor field, *W.B.* ; ? = *parc celyn*, holly close.

P. LEAR, ? *i.q.* PARK AN LEAR.

P. LECK, ? = *parc helec*, willows' close.

P.-LEDDAN, -LEDDON,-LIDDEN, broad (*ledan*) close.

P. LEGAN, ? pond (*lagen*) close.

P. LEHANS, ? nettle (*linaz*) close.

P. LESS, ? broad moor (*hal les*) close.

P. LEVEN, smooth (*leven*) close.

P. LEW, ? sheltered (*hleow, s.*) close.

P. LIBBA, ? sticky (*clibby, m.c.*) c.

P. LIDGET, ? muddy (*luedic*) gate (*yet*), or LIDGATE close.

P. LIDGEY, ? *i.q.* PARK CLODGEY.

P. LOAN, ? bush (*loin*) close, *R. W.*

P.-LOAR, -LOUR, -LOWER, -LOWETH, -LUAR, -LURE, ? garden (*lowarth, luar*) close.

P. LOOSE, ? grey (*ludzh*) close.

P. LUDRA, ? grey (*llwyd, w.*) oaks (*derow*), or LUDDRA close.

P. LUGG, ? field with much undergrowth of weeds, &c. (*lug, m.c*).

P. MAB-ER, -IER, -YAR, ? young-hen or pullet (*mabyer*) close.

P. MAGE, ? discovery (myc) close.

P.-MAIN, -MAYNE, stone (maen) c.

P.-MAISE, -MAIZE, -MAZE, ? close outside (ames) or outer close.

P. MAN-EN, -NEN, -NING, ? = Butter-field (manen, butter).

P. MAR-IA,-Y, ?=dairyman's (maerwr), or wall-builder's (muriwr) close.

P.-MARTH, -MATH, ? MARTH close.

P. MARTHA, ? flat (mathr, w.) close.

P. MART-IN, -ON, -YN, ? Martin's, or MURDON close.

P. MAYHAZ, field of much seed (haz), T.C. ; ? i.q. PARK MAISE.

P. MEAG, discovery (myc) close.

P. MEAN, stones (myin) close.

P.-MEANNA,-MENA, ? stony (maenic), or long-stone (maen hir) close.

P.-MEAR, -MEER, -MEOR, -MERE, ? great (mear), or the mere or lake c.

P. MENAS, ? i.q. PARK AN MENAS.

P. MEN-EERE, -ER, -HER, -HOR, -NER, -NOR, -OR, ? long (hir), or boundary (or, w.) stone (maen) close.

P. MINNICK, ? stony (maenic) close.

P. MINNUS, ? ? little (minys) close.

P. MIRE, ? [black]berry (moyar) c.

P. MOH, pigs' (moch) close.

P. MOOR, ? moor field, or big (maur) close.

P. MOWHAY, stackyard close.

P. MUTTON, ? ? morning (mytin) c.

P. NANCE, ? valley (nans), or the lambs' (an canes) close.

P. NAPP, ? close on the brow (knap) of the hill ; or, turnip (neap, Po.) c.

P. NAVA, ? KNAVA'S, or old road (henvor) close.

P. NEAGUE, ? ? moss (neay, B.) close.

P. NEAR, the near, or long (an hir) close.

P. NEBIL, the colt's (an ebol) close.

P. NEEN, the lamb (an can) close.

P. NEES, ? near or next (nes) close.

P. NELLANS, ? the nettle (an linaz), or lambs'-moor (an hel canes) close.

P. NELLS, ? the son-in-law's (an els), or cliff (als) close.

P. NEST, ? the east (an est) close.

P. NETHAN, i.q. PARK NITHAN.

P.-NEWAN,-NOWEN,-NOWAN,-NOON, new, or the down (an won) close.

P. NEWEL, ? the high (an uhel) c.

P. NEWETH, new (newedh) close.

P. NICHOLL, Nicholl's close.

P. NIEVAN, the yew (an hivin) close.

P. -NITHAN, -NITHON, -NOTHING, -NYON, the furze (an eithin) close.

P.-NOATH, -NORTH, ? north, or bare (noath), or new (nowydh) close.

P.-NOLLAS, -NOWLES, i.q. PARK AN NOWLES.

P. NO-R, -WER, i.q. PARK AN HOAR.

P.-NOW, -NOWAH, ? = parc genau, close at the mouth or opening ; or, bare, or new close.

P. NOW-ATH, -ETH, i.q. P. NOATH.

P. NOWEL, ? i.q. PARK AN HUEL.

P. O'DOURICK, i.q. PARK DOWRICK.

P.-OLDS, -OWELS, -OWLES, ? PARK GULLAS ; or cliff (als) close.

P. OLVIN, ? white (gwin), or stone (maen), or little (bihan) moor (hal) close (? elvan, trap rock, W.B.).

P.-OON, -OWIN, down (gwon) close.

P. OUSE, ? outside (aues) close.

P. OW, ? i.q. PARK GO.

P. O PLUD, i.q. PARK PLUD.

P. PARISH, ? i.q. PARK BROAS.

P. PARNALL, PARNALL close.

P. PARNALS, ? close by the top (bar) of the cliff (als).

P. PARROW, ? barrow close.

P. PARRUCK, ? ? badger's (broch), or fallow (havrec, a.) close.

P. PASCOE, PASCOE'S close.

P. PATE, ? peat, or BATE'S close.

P. PAW, ? foot (paw) close.

P. PEAL, ? herdsman's (biyel) close.

P. PE-ARN,-RRIN, ? purchase (perhen), or tree (pren) close.

P.-PEAS, -PEASE, ? peas (pes) close.

P.-PEATH, -PEETH, draw-well close, W.B.

P. PELEW, ? parish (plu) close.

P. PELL, distant (pell) close.

P. PELL-A, -OW, ? more distant (pellach) close.

P. PELL-AS, -OWS, oat-grass, or poor close.

P. PENDAR, ? water (dour), or oak (dar) head (pen) close.

P. PENROSE, PENROSE close.

P. PENTON, ? spring (fenten) close.

P. PENVER, ? close at the head (pen) of the road (for).

P. PENWITH, ? ash (enwith) head c.

P. PERES, ? meadow (pras) close.

P. PERROW, Perrow's close.

P. PILLAS, i.q. PARK PELLAS.

P. PILLEN, ? ball (pellen), or pool (pullan), or mill (melin) close.

P. PILLION, ? pebble (bilien) close.

P. PINK, ? i.q. PARK AN PINK.

P. PLACE, ? i.q. PARK PELLAS.

P. PLEASANT, ? principal-house (plas an), or weedy (plos an) field, T.C.

P. PLETA, ? BOLITHO close.

P. PLUD, ? pond (pludn, B.), or muddy (plud, mire, m.c., W.B.) close.

P. PODEN, ? cloth (padn) close.

P. PON-DS, -S, ? bridge (pons) close.

P. POOL, ? pool close.

P.-POOR, -POR, ? ? poor, or fat (bor), or meadow (pawr, w., M.) close.

P. PORA, ? morning (bora) close.

P. PORN, ? hill or heap or stack (bern), or rush (broen) close.

P. POS-EN, -T, ? the post close.

P. POT-CHER, -TS, ? i.q. P. BOUDGEY.

P. POUNDER, i.q. PARK BOUNDER.

P. POVERTY, ? ? baker's-house (peber ti), or very poor close.

P. PRATTLE, ? Bartholomew's close.

P. PRAZE, meadow (pras) close.

P. PREA, ? hill (bre) close.

P. PRICKERS, ? kite's (barges) close.

P. PRIDD-EN, -ON, ? tree (predn) c.

P. PRILL, ? rose (breilu) close.

P. PROCTOR, ? maltster's (bragwr) c.

P. PROWSA, ? thicket (browse) close.

P. PRY, ? clay (pri) close.

P. PUCK, ? he-goat's (boch) close.

P. PUNCH, ? i.q. PARK BOUDGEY.

P. PUR, ? bush (berth, w.) close.

P. PYAS, ? Tobias's close.

P. PYE, ? magpie (pi, pia) close, R.IV.

P. QUEST, ? west, or waste, or shelter lodging or inn (guest) close.

P. QUETT-A, -AR, ? mole (godhar) c.

P. QUILLA, ? lower (gwollach) close.

P. RAMBLE, ? GRAMBLA close.

P. RANK, i.q. PARK CRANK.

P. REDDICK, ? radish (redic) close.

P. REENS, ? hill (rhyn) closes.

P. REES, i.q. PARK CREES.

P.-REGULUS, -RG-GLOS, ? i.q. PARK WRIGGLES; or, heaps' (grachel-s), or green-acre (eru glas) close.

P. RINSEY, ? dry-hill (rhyn sech) c.

P. ROD, ? red (rud, m.c.) close.

P. RO-SE, -ASE, -USE, ? heath or moor or wheel (ros), or cross (crows) c.

P. ROUND, camp, or castle close.

P. ROW, rough (row, m.c.) close; or, i.q. PARK CROW.

P. RUMER, ? i.q. GRAMMER'S PARK.

P. SAFFRAN, ? crocus (saffrwm, w.) c.

P. SAUNDRY, ? ash house close, W.B.

P.-SAY, -SEA, ? dry (sech) close.

P. SCADDEN, ? ? wood-pigeon (ysguthan, w.) close; or, i.q. P. SCAUAN.

P. SCATH, boat (scath) close.

P. SCA-UAN, -WEN, -WN, elder-tree (scawen) close.

P.-SCHEBA, -SHEEPER, -SHIVER, i.q. PARK SKEBA.

P. SCUE, ? privet (skeow, m.c., S.G.), or elders' (scow) close.

P. SHAFT-ER, -Y, -IES, -OES, ? i.q. PARK AN SHAFT.

P.-SHEETA, -SHUTTER, ? water-shoot close.

P. SKE-DA, -DER, -BO, -BOR, -BOW, -PPER, -VER, barn (sciber) close; also, SKIBBER, SKIVER.

P.-SKEATH, -SKITT, ? underwood (is cuit) close.

P. SKILLY, under-grove (is gelli) c.

P. SKINNER, ? SKINNER'S, or long (hir) rush (hescen) close.

P. SLAD, valley (slad) close, N.H.

P. SLEETE, ? under stream (is leat) c.

P. SLEDDON, ? ? little (vean) valley (slad) close.

P.-SOLE, -SOWELL, ⁈ stubble (*soul*), or under-moor (*is hal*) close.

P. SOON, ⁈ ⁈ under-down (*is oon*) c.

P.-SOOTH, -SOATH, ⁈ *south*, or rich fat (*soath*) close.

P. SPAR, *spar*-stone field, *W.B.*; or, ⁈ barn (*sciber*) close.

P. SPARNELL, ⁈ thorn (*spern*) moor (*hal*), or below (*is*) PARNALL close.

P. SPARNON, ⁈ thorn down (*oon*) c.

P. SPEARN, field of thorns.

P. SPELLER, ⁈ tinner's (*spallier, Po.*) close.

P. SPERM, ⁈ crocus (*saffrum, w.*) c.

P. SPRY, ⁈ Spry's close.

P.-STAIL, -STALL, -STEEL, ⁈ ⁈ plank or board (*astel*) close.

P.ˊ STAMP-IS, -S, ⁈ mine *stamping*-mill close.

P. STARVEN, ⁈ ⁈ close below (*is*) the oak (*derwen, w.*) ; or, *starving* c.

P. STARVER, ⁈ close below (*is*) the great oak (*dar ver*), *R.W.*

P. STERRES, close below the door (*daras*), or the brambles (*dreis*).

P. STRAY, ⁈ under-town (*is dre*) c.

P.-TABLE, -TAMLYN, ⁈ ⁈ dock (*tafol, tavolyn*) close.

P.-TAN, -TANNA, ⁈ under (*tan*) close.

P. TEM, ⁈ thyme (*tim*) close.

P. TINKER, ⁈ close under (*tan*) the castle (*caer*).

P.-TODDEN, -TODN, ⁈ lay (*todn*) c.

P. TOLL, ⁈ high (*tal*), or hole (*tol*), or dale (*dol*) close.

P. TOLVAN, ⁈ the holed-stone (*tol vaen*), or little (*bihan*) high (*tal*) c.

P. TOWAN, ⁈ the strand or sand-hill (*towan*) close.

P.-TRAY, -TREA, home (*tre*) close.

P. TRE-ATH, -ETH, sand (*traith*) c.

P. TREBOR, ⁈ three roads' (*tri vor*) c.

P. TREENS, ⁈ three lambs' (*canes*) c.

P. TREES, ⁈ *i.q.* P. DARAS or DRIES.

P. TREMAN, ⁈ passage (*tremyn*) close.

P.-TRESSOCK, -TRISACK, brambly (*dreisic*) close.

P. TREWS, ⁈ outland (*tir aues*) close.

P. TRIGLEY, ⁈ three-grove (*tri gelli*) c.

P.-TRISSEN, -TRUDGEON, ⁈ mole-hill (*dorossen, B.*), or starling (*trodzhen, Lh.*), or Trudgeon's close.

P. TRO-NE, -ON, close with the depression between the furrows (*tronc, T.Q.C.*) ; down-house (*tr-oon*) c., *W.B.* ; tron, a nose of land, *R.W.*

P. TROT, ⁈ oak (*dar*) wood (*cuit*) c.

P. TRUST, ⁈ east (*est*) oaks' (*derow*) close.

P. TUBBAN, ⁈ dam or bank (*tuban*) close; (*tubban*, a hard clod, *W.B.*).

P. TURTLE, ⁈ close at the foot (*troed*) of the moor (*hal*).

P. URLIN, ⁈ the *hurling* field.

P. VAIN, ⁈ narrow (*main, vain, w., R.W.*), or stone (*maen*) close.

P. VALLEN, ⁈ apple-tree (*avallen*) c.

P. VARNE, ⁈ alder (*warn, gwern*) c.

P. VARRAS, ⁈ meadow (*pras*) close.

P. VEAN, little (*bian*) close.

P. VEAN GLAS, ⁈ the green (*glas*), or church (*eglos*) little close.

P. VEASE, ⁈ close outside (*aves*).

P. VEDRAS, ⁈ wether-sheep (*gwedhar-s, B.*) close.

P. VELL-AM, -UM, ⁈ William's, or, *i.q.*

P. VELL-AN, -IN, ⁈ mill (*melin*) close.

P. VENT-AN, -ON, -UM, spring (*fenten*) close.

P. VENTON SAH, ⁈ dry (*sech*) spring close.

P. VERN, alder (*gwern*) close.

P. VERTH, ⁈ green (*gwyrdd, w.*) close.

P. VERYAN, ⁈ ants' (*murrian*) close.

P. VETHAN, ⁈ meadow (*bidhen*) close.

P. VIEW, ⁈ cow (*beu*) close.

P. VINE, *i.q.* PARK VAIN, *R.W.*

P. VINGLE, ⁈ fennel (*fennochel*) close.

P. VINTAL, ⁈ winnowing (*gwyntyllio*, to winnow) close.

P. VISTA, beast's (*besta*) close.

P. VIZ, close outside (*aves*).

P. VOAN, ⁈ *i.q.* PARK BOUAN.

P. VOGUE, ⁈ forge (*fog*) close.

P. VOIN, ⁈ sainfoin field, *W.B.*

P. VOLE, ⁈ blackbird (*moelh*) close.

P. VOR, *i.q.* PARK EN VOR.

P. VORRAN, ⁈ crow (*bran*) close.

P. VORRIAN, ants' (*murrian*) close.
P. VORTH, ? road (*fordh*) close.
P. VOUNDER, *i.q.* PARK BOUNDER.
P.-VOURNE, -VOWRN, oven (*forn*) field, *T.C.* ; ? *i.q.* PARK VARNE.
P. VREGLES, *i.q.* PARK FRIGGLES.
P. VRO, ? handmill (*brou*) close.
P. VULLEN, ? pond (*pullan*) close.
P. WALL, the walled field, *T.C.*
P. WALLER, ? workman's (*wayler*) c.
P. WAR-NE. -REN, *warren*, or alder, or marsh (*gwern*) close.
P.-WARRA, -WARRAH, -WARTHA, -WARROW, ? *i.q.* PARK GWARRA or GWARROW.
P. WARTHA HALE, higher close by the moor (*hal*).
P.-WARVELL,-WAVEL, ? kid's (*ceverel*, *Pr.*) close.
P.-WASTE, -WEST, ? *i.q.* P. QUEST.
P. WATER, *i.q.* PARK WARTHA ; or, *water* close or field, PARK DOWER.
P. WATTY, ? WALTER'S or hare c.
P. WAYN, ? wain or waggon, or white (*gwyn*) close.
P.-WEAL,-WHEEL, ? mine (*wheal*) c.
P. WELL, ? *well*, or high (*uhel*) close.
P. WELLS, ? grass (*gwells*) close.
P. WHENNON, ? bees' (*gwenyn*) close.
P. WHERRY, wheel-dray close, *IV.B.*
P. WHISTLE, ? lodging (*gwestle, w.*) close ; or, *i.q.* HUSTLE FIELD.
P.-WIDDEN, -WITHAN, meadow (*bidhen*), tree (*gwedhen*), or little (*vidn*) close.
P. WITHEY, willow (*t.*) close.
P. WOLLAS. bottom (*goles*) close.
P. WOON, down (*gwon*) close.
P. WRECK, wife's (*gwrec*) close.
P. WRIGGLES, *i.q.* PARK FRIGGLES.
P. YAWM, ? home, *i.e.* near close.
P. YET, gate (*yet*) close.
P.-ZEATH, -ZETH, dry (*zeh*) field, *Gw.* ; *i.q.* PARK IN ZETH.
P. ZIGGAN, ? close with the standing-pool (*sagen, B.*) ; or, elder-tree (*scauen*), or sedge (*hescen*) close.
P. ZOM, ? poverty (*ezom, a.*) close.
P. ZOUL, *i.q.* PARK SOLE.

PARLEBEN, *n.f.*, ? *i.q.* PORTHLEVEN.
PARLEYS, ? *i.q.* PARKLESS.
PARLIAN GARRICK, ? PARK LEE by the rock (*carrag*).
PARLOUR, ? *i.q.* PARK LOUR.
PARLYVOSSO, ? PARK LEE by or with the intrenchments (*fossow*).
PARMENTER, *n.f.*, tailor, *f.*, *Lo.* ; ? *i.q.* POLMANTER.
PARN-ALL, -ELL, ? top (*bar*) of the moor (*anhal*) ; or, *i.q.* PARK AN HAL.
PARN GOVER, *i.q.* PARK AN GOVER.
PARNVOSE, ? the (*an*) fortified or intrenchment (*fos*) cove (*porth*).
PARQUEST, *i.q.* PARK QUEST.
PARQUIN, *i.q.* PARK GWIN.
PARRAMOOR, ? *i.q.* PARK MOOR.
PARRET, *n.f.*, ? *i.q.* BARRET.
PARRY, *n.f.*, = *ApHarry*, *i.q.* Harrison.
PARSLEY, ? lower (*isella*) close.
PARTEY TOWN, PARK DAY near the farm place (*town, m.c.*).
PARTON CARNE, *v.* PAIRTING CAIRNE, the rock dividing the farms, *A.S.*
PARVENTON, *i.q.* PARK VENTON.
PARVIS, *i.q.* PARK VEASE.
PASCOE, *n.f.*, ? *i.q.* PADSTOW ; or, = *parc scaw*, elder-trees close ; or, = *pasche*, easter, *f.*
PAT-ERDA, -REDA, -UDA, -HADA, ? *i.q.* PADERDA.
PATREC, *s.B.m.*, *i.q.* Patricius, *lat.*
PATTACOT, ? Patrec's cottage.
PATTEN, *n.f.*, ? *i.q.* PADDEN.
THE PATTER, ? *i.q.* PARK DOUR.
PAUL, *from* St. Paulinus, *p.s.*, *O.* ; ? St. Paul de Leon, *D.G.*
PAUL PRY, *i.q.* POL- or PARK-PRY.
PAWN, ? = *parc on*, ash close.
PAW-TEN, -TON, *d.d.* PAUTONE, ? *i.q.* POLTON or POULTON.
PAYNE, *n.f.*, *i.q.* PAINE.
PAYNTER, *n.f.*, ? *i.q.* PENTIRE.
PEACH, *o.* PEO, PECH, *n.f.*, ? = *bich*, little.
PEALE, a spire, *Sc.*
PEAN-PROSE, -VROSE, ? little (*bihan*) meadow (*pras*) ; or, *i.q.* PARK AN BROWSE.

PEA PARK, ? *pea* or cow (*beuch*) close.
PEAR-CE, -SE, *n.f.*, ? = *Ap Rhys, w.* ; or, PERCY, *f.*
PEARLS, *i.q.* PORLES.
PEARNE, *n.f.*, ? *from* PERRAN.
PEAS ARISH, pea stubble [field].
PEASEN CLOSE, the pea close, *t.*
PEATH FIELD, *i.q.* PEETH.
PECOBBEN, *i.q.* PENCOBBEN.
PEDAN PONDS, *i.q.* PENPONS.
PEDDANGWARRY, PEDNANGWARY, ? ? *quarry* end (*pen*) ; or, *i.q.* PLAIN AN GWARY.
PEDDANRIDEN, ? *i.q.* PENRITHEN.
PEDELEFORD, *d.d.*, ? the ford over the narrow stream (*pedele, s.*), *t.*
PEDENEGAR, ? *i.q.* PENGAER.
PEDENPOLL, *i.q.* PENPOLL.
PEDENVARDEN, *i.q.* PEDNVADN.
PEDENVOUND-E, -ER, *i.q.* PENFOUND.
PEDNA CARNE, ? rock end (*pen*) ; or, head of the CARN.
PEDNAMORE, the great (*maur*) headland (*pedn* = *pen*).
PEDNAN-, PEDN-DREA, top (*pen*) of the town, or = Townsend.
PEDN-ANKREN, -CREN, head of the spring, *Po.* ; (*cren*, round).
PEDNAN-LAAS, -LASE, the (*an*) green (*glas*) head or promontory (*pen*), *H.* ; (*now* the LAND'S END).
PEDN BE JUFFIN, ? BEJOWAN point.
PEDN BOAR POINT, ? the great (*maur*) point or head.
P. CARN, ? *i.q.* PEDNA CARNE.
P. CONDURROW, CONDURROW head.
P. CREW, ? hovel (*crow*) end ; or, head of the camps (*caerau*).
P. CRIFTON, ? ? TENCRIFF point.
P. ERVOUNDER, *i.q.* PENFOUNDER.
P. EY CROUSHA, ? end or top (*pen*) of cross (*crows*) close (*hay*).
P. GARRICK, ? rock (*carrag*) end.
P. GELLIER, ? long grove (*celli hir*) end, or top, or point (*pen*).
P. GWAY, ? *i.q.* PEDDANGWARRY.
P. GWINION, ? head of the marshes (*gwinnion, Pr.*).
P. MEAN-DU, -DUE, black (*du*) stone

(*maen*) head.
PEDN MENAN MERE, the (*an*) great (*mear*) stone head.
P. OLV-A, -ER, head of the breach (*dolva*), *Bl.*, or of lamentation (*olva*), *R.W.* ; or, OLVER head.
P. POL, *i.q.* PENPOL.
P. PONS, *i.q.* PENPONS.
P. PRAZE, *i.q.* PENPRAZE.
P. SAWANACK, headland with the caverns, *Bl.* (*sawan*, a hole).
P. VADN, the little (*vean*) headland, *Wh.* ; ? *i.q.* PENMEAN.
P. VENTON, *i.q.* PENVENTON.
P. VOUNDER, headland with a road, *Bl.* ; ? *i.q.* PENFOUNDER.
P. WARROW, ? *i.q.* PENWARTHA.
P. Y COANSE, the causeway (*coance, m.c.*) head or end.
P. YET, gate (*yet*) head or end.
PEE-PER, -VER, ? great (*vear*) close (*parc*). *Peber*, a baker.
PEEPOW, cow (*beuch*) close.
PEETH, draw-well [field], *W.B.*
PEGUARRA, ? *i.q.* PARK WARRA.
PEL, afar off (*pell*), *T.*
PELAMELLIN, *i.q.* POLMELLIN.
PELASTINE, ? ? scarlet-oak (*glastan, Lh.*), or Austin's pool (*pol*).
PEL-AYNE, -EAN, -LEAN, -LYN, ? lamb (*ean*) pool (*pol*) ; or, *i.q.* PENLENE, or PELLYN.
PELLA, ? *i.q.* PARK PELLA or PELLAS.
PELLAR CROFT, ? wise-man's croft.
PELL-ARS, -AS, -IS, ? peeled oats' (*pellas*) [field].
PELLESCOURT, ? from "*pel isca*," distant water, *Bond.*
PELLEW, *n.f.*, ? head (*pen*) of the pool (*lo*).
PELLITRAS POINT, gymnasium point, *Woodley* ; (*from the greek* ! !) ; ? head (*pen*) of the slope (*lledrod, w.*), *R.W.*
PELLOW ZAWN, ? more distant (*pella*) hole in the rock (*sawan*).
PELLYN, the distant pool (*lin*), or pool afar off (*pell*), *Pr.*
PELLY POINT, ? more distant (*pella*) headland.

PELSUE, *i.q.* POLSUE, *T.*

PELUE-VEAN, -WARTHA, *&* -WOLLAS, ? little-(*bian*), higher-(*wartha*), *&* bottom (*goles*) calves' (*leauh*) field (*parc*).

PELVELLAN, *i.q.* POLVELLAN.

PELYNT, *v.* PLYNT, ? = *pen-lyne*, or *-llwyn*, head of the streams *or* wood, *M'L.* ; ? head (*pen*), or bulwark (*pil*) of the grove (*lhyn*), *Bond* ; *d.d.* PLUNENT, ? parish (*plu*) of St. Nonnita *or* Non, *p.s.*, *Wh.* ; (*p.s.* St. Mary, *O.*).

PEMBERNOSE, head (*pen*) of the night (*nos*), or midnight (*hanter nos*), *Sc.*

PEM-BOLE, -PWELL, ? *i.q.* PENPOL.

PEMBR-E, -O, *Le.*, = *pen bre*, mountain height, *Wh.* ; ? *now* BREAGE.

PEMBROKE, ? *i.q.* PARK AN BRAKE.

PENADL-AKE, -ICK, ? *i.q.* BENALLOCK.

PENAIR, ? long (*hir*) point or head.

PENA-LAWEY, -LEWY, -LUEY, = *pen a loeau*, hill of the tumuli, *M'L.* (?).

PENAL-GAY, -GUY, -GWAY, *i.q.* PEN-ALGUY.

PENALL, *n.f.*, *i.q.* PENHALL.

PENALL-ECK, -Y, ? *i.q.* PENELLICK.

PENALL-OME, -UM, *i.q.* PENHALHAM, ? moor-head (*penhal*) HAM.

PENALLUND, ? moor-head *land.*

PENALS, head cliff, *Pr.* ; ? head (*pen*) of the cliff *or* shore (*als*), *M'L.*

PENALUNA, ? moor *or* hill head (*pen hal*) of the downs (*oonou*), *H.M.W.*

PENALVERNE, ? ALVERNE (*i.q.* AL-VERTON) top *or* summit (*pen*), *T.C.*

PENAN, ? *parc an on*, the ash close ; *or*, *i.q.*

PENAN-CE, -T, *i.q.* PENNANCE.

PENAPONDS, *i.q.* PENPONS.

PEN-AR, -ARE, ? *i.q.* PEN-AIR, *or* -ARTH.

PENARE-WARTHA *&* -WOLLAS, higher *&* lower PENARE.

PENARTH, high (*arth*) top *or* hill, *Pr.*

PENASKEN, reed (*hescen*), or ascent (*ascenna*, to ascend) point, *N.*

PENATILLY, *i.q.* PENTILLIE.

PENAUGER, *d.d.*, ? = *pen an gaer*, head of the camp, *R.W.* ; tumulus

(*haugr*, *t.*) hill, *Beal* ; ? *i.q.* PEN-HALGAR.

PENAVAR-RA, -THA, the higher *or* further head *or* top (*warra* = *wartha*)

PENA-WEN, -WIN, head of the down (*guen*) ; *or*, white (*gwyn*) hill, *J.B.*

PENB-ALL, -OLE, ? *i.q.* PENPOL.

PENBEAGLE, *i.q.* PENBUGELL.

PENBEATH, ? head of the grave (*bedh*); *or*, boar's (*baedh*) head.

PENBERTH, the green (*verth*) top, *Pr.* ; ? bush (*perth*) top, *R.W.* ; ? head of the cove (*porth*).

PENBERTHY, top of the bushes, *R.W.*

PENBETHA, head of the graves (*bedhou*), *Pr.*

PEN BLUE, ? = *parc an plu*, the parish close. (*pelu*, to play at ball).

PENBOTHIDN-A, -OW, ? ? smaller (*bohatn*, *B.*) end *or* top.

PENBRAHA-M, -N, the crows' (*bran*) head ; *or*, ? *i.q.* PARK EN VRANE.

PENBRAWS, *i.q.* PARK AN BROWSE.

PENBRAZE, *i.q.* PENPRAZE ; *or*, PEN-BROSE, *a nickname*, great (*bras*) or dolt head, *Car.*

PENBRO, *i.q.* PEMBRO.

PENBROTH, ? *i.q.* PENBERTH.

PENBU-ALE, -GELL, -GLE, the herdsman's (*bugel*) head, *or* superior herdsman, *Pr.* ; ? hound's-tongue (*pigel*, *w.*) close (*parc an*).

PENBU-RTHEN, -THEN, -THON, ? thorn bush (*perthen*) end, *M.*

PENCAIR, headland of the mountain-ash (*cure*), *C.* ; ? head of the camp (*caer*) ; *or*, camp hill.

PENCALLINICK, head place of the holly trees (*celynnec*), *or* head of the hollies, *Pr.* ; head of the flax (*linec*) field (*gweal*), *R.W.*

PEN-CARANOW, -KARANOW, hill of rocks (*carnow*), *T.*

PENCAR-N, -NE, *i.q.* PEDNA CARNE, *or* PARK AN CARNE.

PENCARNS, ? head of the rocks.

PENCARRA HEAD, rock (*carrag*), *or* further (*gwarra*) head, *reduplicated.*

PENCARR-OE, -OW, the head place of

the deer (*carow*), *or* the stag's head, *Pr.* ; headland of the stag, *C.* ; head *or* height of the camps (*caerau*), *M'L.* ; head Roman (*row*) castle, *Po.*

PENCAST-EL, -LE, castle head.

PENCAVEAN, ? ? ridge (*cefn*) head.

PENCISE, ? ? = *parc en syhys*, the dry close.

PENCLIFFS, ? head of the *cliffs*.

PENCOBBEN, ? GOBBEN head.

PEN-COID, -COIT, -COLL (?), -COOTH, head wood (*coit*), *H.* ; ? *i.q.*

PEN-COOSE, -COOZ, -COWSE, head of the wood (*cus*), *Pr.* ; or, wood hill, *J.B.* ; or, *i.q.* PARK AN GOOSE, *or*, PENCORSE, head of the moor, bog, *or* fen (*cors*).

PENC-OY, -OYSE, *i.q.* PENCOOSE.

PENCRAFT, ? head of the *croft*.

PENCREB-AR, -OR, ? GREBER head.

PENCREEK ? *i.q.* PARK AN CREAGUE.

PENCRENNOW, *i.q.* PENCARANOWE.

PENCY GULLAS, ? = *park en sech goles*, the dry bottom close.

PENDANVADAN, *i.q.* PEDNVADAN.

PENDAR, *n.f.*, oak (*dar*) head, *Pr.*

PENDARGY, ? otter (*dourgi*), *or* turf-hedge *or* water-dike (*durgy*) head.

PENDARVES, head of the oak (*dar*) field (*maes*), *Pr.* ; or, *i.q.* PARK AN DAVAS.

PENDA-VEY, -VY, the projection (*pedn* ?) on the river (*gwy*), *Pr.*

PENDAVI-S, (*d.d.* -D), sheep's head, *Pr.* ; ? *i.q.* PARK AN DAVAS.

PENDEEN, head man's (*den*) [place], *Pr.* ; castled (*din*) headland, *Bl.* ; (*c.d.* St. John).

P. VOWE, PENDEEN cave (*fow*).

PENDENHAR, now RAME- (*hor*, a ram) HEAD (*pedn*), *Sc.* (?).

PENDEN-ICK, -OCK, ? furzy (*eithenig*), *or* lonely (*idnac*) headland.

PENDENNANT, 12 *cent.*, head of the deep (*down*) valley (*nant*), *R.W.*

PENDENNIS, headland of the fort (*dinas*), *C.* ; the peninsula or forti-fied headland, *Pr.* ; also, *i.q.* PARK AN EANES.

PENDER, *n.f.*, *i.q.* PEN-DAR *or* -DREA.

PENDERLEIGH, ? Pender's pasture.

PENDERMOOR, ? head of the great (*maur*) oak (*der*), *R.W.* ; or, PEN-DREA moor.

PEN-DEW, -DIU, black (*du*) head.

PENDE-WEY, (*o.* -VE, -VY), ? David's (*Dewi*) head *or* end.

PENDILLY, ? close of the (*parc an*) cart (*dilly*, *m.c.*), *or* house-site (*tyle*).

PENDINANT, *Le.*, ? head of the black valley (*du nant*), *R.W.*

PENDIN-AS, -NIS, castle (*dinas*) point; *or*, principal *or* head fortification, *B.* ; or, island (*enys*) head (*pedn*), *Ped.* ; *i.q.* PENDENNIS.

PENDIREN, ? *i.q.* PARK AN DRAIN.

PEN-DOUR, -DOWAR, -DOWER, the land's (*doar*) end, *or* head of the water (*dour*), *Pr.* ; water-head, *J.C.* ; or, *i.q.* PARKENTOWER.

PENDOURVOSE, the head of a small (?) river *or* open water, *Pr.*, *or* head of the good (*vaz*) land, *Gw.* ; (*fos*, a trench, wall).

PENDOWN, ? ? down head *or* end.

PENDRATHEN, head of the sand-bank (*traith*), *N.*

PEN-DRAY, (*n.f.*), -DRE, -DREA, the principal town (*tre*), *Pr.* ; head house, *T.C.* ; head of the town, *or* Townsend ; *or* = PARK AN DREA.

PEN-DREAN, -DRINE, the brambly head, *Pr.* ; or, *i.q.* PARK AN DREAN.

PENDR-EFFY, -IFFY, ? PENDREA by the water (*gwy*) ; or, *i.q.*

PEN-DRIEF, -DRIFT, ? = *pentref*, a village, *w.* ; or, *i.q.* PENDRAY.

PENDR-IFFEL, -UFFEL, ? chief place (*pentref*, *w.*) on the moor (*hal*).

PENDR-IM, -YM, head of the ridge (*trum*) ; or, *i.q.* PARK DRUM.

PENDRISSICK, ? *i.q.* PARK DRYSACK.

PENDRUSCOT, PENDREA below (*is*) *or* outside (*aues*) the wood (*coat*) ; DRWS COET, door of the wood, *w.*, *R.W.*

PENDULOW, ? head of the two (*dew*) pools (*low*), *or* tumuli (*t.*).

PENEARTH, ? high (*earth*) summit.
PENEGOU, ? *i.q.* PARK AN GEW.
PENELEWEY, *i.q.* PENALAWEY.
PENELIGGON, *i.q.* PENHALIGON.
PENELLARRICK, *n.f.*, *i.q.* PENHAL-
LURICK.
PENELLICK, head of the willows
(*helic*) ; or, *i.q.* PARKENELLICK.
PEN ENYS, island (*enys*) point.
PENERA, ? higher (*warra*) point.
PENES-KYN, -SKEN, [at] the head of
the rushes, *Pr.* ; or, the sedge (*un
hescen*) close (*parc*).
PENESTA, ? ? wortleberry (*iz diu, B.*)
head, or close.
PENEVARRA, *i.q.* PENAVARRA.
PENFENT-EINON (*Cur.*),-ENIO,-IDNOE,
(*d.d.* -INIO), -INOW, head of the
springs (*fentiniow*).
PENF-ON, -OUN, head well or spring
(*fynnon,w.*), *H.*; or, *i.q.* PENFOUND.
PENFORD, head of the road (*fordh*).
PENFOUN-D, -DER, head of the lane
(*bounder*), or, lane end, *Pr.* ; or, *i.q.*
PARK AN VOUNDER.
PENFRA-N, -NE, *i.q.* PENBRAHAN.
PENGA-ER, -RE, head of the camp
(*caer*) ; camp end or close.
PENGARR-ACK, -ICK, -OCK, the head
rock (*carrag*), *Pr.*; ? rock end ;
or = *parc un garrag*, the rock field.
PENGARWICK, *i.q.* PENGERSWICK.
PEN-GELLY, -GILLY, o. -GHELLY, *d.d.*
-GELLE, head of the grove (*celli*), or
of the hazel-grove, *Pr.*
PENGELLYS, Pengelly's (*n.f.*) [farm].
PEN-GERICK, -JERICK, ? *i.q.* PENGAR-
RACK, *R.W.* ; watery head, *T.C.* ;
or, *i.q.* PARK O'DOURICK.
PENGERSICK, ? moorish or fenny
(*corsig*) head, *R.W.**
PENGIRT, ? *i.q.* PARK AN GARRATT.
PENGLA-SE, -ZE, the green (*glas*)
head, *Pr.* ; or, *i.q.* PARK GLASE.
PENGLEE, *i.q.* PARK AN GILLIE.

PENGOULD, ? ? the end of the region
or territory (*gulat*), or = *parc en
gould*, the marigold field.
PENGOVER, the head of the rivulet
(*gover*), *Pr.*; or, *i.q.* PARK AN GORE.
PENGREEP, ? ridge (*crib*) end.
PENGRON, ? round (*cron*) head, *R.W.*
PENGROUSE, ? cross (*crows*) head or
end ; or, *i.q.* PARK EN GROUSE.
PENGRUGL-A, -ER, heath (*griglan*)
hill or headland, *C.* ; ? head of the
heath place (*crug le*), *R.W.*
PENGUARE, *d.d.*, play (*gware*) hill,
J.B. ; ? quarry (*cuare*) top.
PENG-UARNE, -WERNE, head of the
alder-trees (*gwern*), or mast-head,
Gw. ; or, head of the marsh.
PENGULLAS, ? bottom (*goles*) end.
PENGWARRAS, ? top (*gwarhas*) end.
PENGWARROW,*i.q.* PARK GWARROW.
PENGWEDNA, ? ? downs' (*guenou* ?)
end ; or, white (*gwednac*) head.
PENGWIN, *i.q.* PARK AN GUEN.
PENH-AILE, -ALE, -AL, -ALL, head of
the moor (*hal*), *Pr.*, or river (*hayl*)
T., or strand, *M'L.* ; or, *i.q.* PARK
AN HAL.
PENHALE AN DREA, home (*tre*) P.
PENHAL-ES, -LLS, -LS, ? broad-moor
(*hal les*) end ; or, *i.q.* PARK AN ALS.
PENHALGUY, head of the Hele river,
Po. ; water (*gwy*) from the head
(*pen*) of the hill (*hal*), *B.*
PENHAL-HAM, -LAM, *i.q.* PENALLUM.
PENHALIGON, *n.f.*, *i.q.* PENLIGGEN.
PENHALLACK, ? *i.q.* BENALLOCK.
PENHALL-ERICK, -URICK, head of the
rich (*berric*) moors, *B.* ; ? end of
LEURIC's moor (*hal*).
PENHALLINYK, *n.f.*, ? *i.q.* PENCAL-
LINICK.
PENHALLOW, moors' (*hallow*) head ;
hill (*hal*) top (*pen*) with the tu-
mulus (*low, M'L.*).
PENHALT, ? cliff (*alt*), or wooded hill

---

* The green headland, *Pr.*, *Po.*; the head (*pen*) ward (*gwercs*) of the cove (*ike*),
Mur.; *from Pen gueraz*, a head to help, *Car.*; the head word or command (*gar*) fenced
or fortified place (*wick*) ; or, the creek, cove, or bosom of waters (*ike*) head help, *H.* !

(*gallt, w.*) head, end, *or* field.

PENHALUN, *d.d.*, head of the ash (*on*), *or* little (*vean*) moor (*hal*).

PENHALVEAN, little PENHAL.

PENHALVEOR, great PENHAL.

PENHALWARD, ? head of the high-moor (*hal warth*); *or*, garden (*low-arth*) end.

PENHANGER, ? head of the camp (*an gaer*).

PEN-HARGARD, -HERGARD, = *pen ar gear*, head of the camp, *M'L.*

PENHARG-ATE, -ETT, ? *the same*; *or*, Argwedd's (*w.*) summit.

PENHASGAR, ? Osgar's (*t.*) summit.

PENHAWG-AR, -ER, *i.q.* PENHANGER, *M'L.*, *or* PENAUGER.

PENHAYES, ? *i.q.* PARK HAYS.

PENH-AYLE, -EALE, -EL, -ELE, -ELL, -ILL, *i.q.* PENHAILE; *or*, the chief hall (*hel*), *T.*

PEN-HEDDRA, -HENDRA, -HEDRA, ? *i.q.* PENDREA, *or* PARK HENDRA.

PEN-HELLICK, -HILLICK, the head of the willows (*helic*), *Pr.*

PENHER-IOTS, -ODS, ? ? *higher woods* end *or* head.

PENHERRET, ? *i.q.* PENHARGATE.

PENHESK-EN, -IN, *i.q.* PENESKYN.

PENHOLE, *i.q.* PENHAL, *or*,

PENHOLT, *i.q.* PENHALT.

PENHORN, ? ? corner (*corn*) end.

PENHURDEN, ? HURDEN top.

PENIMBLE, ? *i.q.* PEDENPOL.

PENINNIS, head of the island (*enys*), *N.*; *also*, *i.q.* PARK AN INNIS.

PENISCA, ? elders' (*scaw*) end.

PENKELLY, *i.q.* PENGELLY.

PEN-KENNER, -KINNA, ? point *or* head-land of the whelp (*cenaw, w.*).

PENKESTLE, *i.q.* PENCASTLE.

PEN-KEVEL, -KIVEL, the horse (*cevil*) head, *Pr.*; *d.d.* PANGVOL.

PENKEY, ? hedge (*ce*) end.

PEN-KNEK, -KNETH, -KNIGHT, hill of the king (*konig, t.*), *Wh.*

PENKUKE, the head village (*guic*), *Pr.*; ? end of the village, *J.B.*

PENKYLL, *o.n.f.*, *i.q.* PENKEUEL.

PENLAND, ? = *pen lan*, end of the village, *R.W.*; ? sheep *pen* field, *t.*

PEN-LEAN, -LEN, -LENE, -LYN, -LYNE, ? head of the grove (*loin, w. llwyn*), *or* pool (*lin*).

PENLEE, the lesser (*le*) head *or* point of land, *Pr.*; end of the place (*le*), *or* rock (*lech*), *N.*; headland to the *leeward*, *Sc.*

PENLEESE, ? ELLIS end *or* top.

PENLIGGEN, ? HELIGAN end.

PEN-LITA, -LITHA, ? *i.q.* PARK EN LETA, *or* BOLITHO.

PENLU, ? sheltered (*hleo, s.*) end.

PENLYER, ? *i.q.* PARK AN LEAR.

PENLYKY, *n.f.*, ? *i.q.* PENHALGUY.

PENLYM, *i.q.* PENNALIM.

PEN-MAN (*n.f.*), -MAINE, -MAYNE, -MEAN, stone (*maen*) end.

PENMARTH, ? *i.q.* PARK MARTH.

PENMEDEL, ? reapers' (*medel, w.*) end.

PENMENETH, hill (*menedh*) end *or* top.

PENMELLEN, ? mill (*melin*) end.

PENMEN-ER, -NER, -OR, -NOR, the principal mountain (*mener*), *Pr.*; ? MENHEIR end *or* top.

PENMENNA, ? MANEHAY end.

PEN-MONT, -MOUNT, *m*, hill top.

PENMOYLE, mule's (*moyle, m.c.*), *or* bare (*moel*), *or* blackbird's (*moelh*) head.

PENN, *n.f.*, = *pen*, an end, point, top, summit, promontory, the chief *or* principal, *R.W.*; *also* a height, upland, hill, *Po.*

PENNA, *n.f.*, ? = *pennou, plural of pen*, *R.W.*; *or*, *i.q.* PENNECK.

PENNA-IR, -RE, *i.q.* PENAR.

PENNALERICK, *n.f.*, *i.q.* PENHALU-RICK.

PENNAL-IM, -YM, *i.q.* PENHALLAM.

PENNALT, *i.q.* PENHALT.

PENNAN-CE, -S, -T, head of the valley *or* plain (*nans*), *Pr.*; *nant*, a ravine, brook, *w.*

PENNAR-D, -TH, ? high (*ard*) summit.

PENNA-TILLY, -NTILLY, ? ? head of the toft, *or* of the enclosure (*hay*) with the house-site (*tyle, w*).

PENN-ECK, -ICK, -OCK, *n.f.*, the head creek, brook, rivulet, *or* place ; *or*, head oak, *Pr.* ; ? one with a great head (*pen*); *or, from* ST. PINNOCK.

PENNEDARN, ? oak (*derwen*) head.

PENNEHALGAR, *d.d.*, ? head of Algar's enclosure (*hay, t.*).

PENNEHEL, *d.d., i.q.* PENHAYLE.

PENNELICK, *i.q.* PENHELLICK.

PENN-EY, -Y, *n.f., i.q.* PENNA.

PENN-IES, -YS, ? *i.q.* PARK HAYS.

PENNIGHT, *i.q.* PENKNIGHT.

PENNINGTON, *n.f.*, ? the enclosure (*tun*) of PENNA's descendants, *t.*

PENNISCEN, ? rush (*hescen*) head.

PENNISCOT, ? under-wood (*is goat*) end, head, *or* close.

PENN-O, -OW, *n.f.*, ? *i.q.* PENNA.

PENNORE, ? *i.q.* PENAR ; (*nore*, a promontory, *t.*).

PENNURRA, ? *i.q.* PENAVARRA.

PENNY BALL, the BALL end.

P. BRIDGE, ? ? *i.q.* PENPONS.

P. COMEQUICK, head of the creek (*gwic*) valley (*cum*), *J.B.* ; of the contracted (*cuch* ?) valley *or* dingle, *D.G.* ; *or*, of the cuckoo (*cog, ga. cuach*) vale.

P. CLOSE, ? *i.q.* PENGULLAS.

P. CRADOCK, ? Caradog's, *or* Cradock's head enclosure (*hay, t.*).

P. CROCKER, ? partridge (*grugyer*) top.

P. CROFT, croft end.

P. CROSS, headland of the cross, *C.*, *or* fen (*cors*) ; *or, penny* ferry.

P. DEARN, *i.q.* PENNEDARN.

P. GASKIS, ? covert (*guscys*) end.

P. GILLA-M, -N, ? William's head.

P. GONEAR, long down (*gwonhir*) end *or* top.

P. KEY, ? *i.q.* PENKEY.

P. LANE, ? *i.q.* PENVOUNDER.

P. LEDGE, ? head of the *ledge* of rocks.

P. LIGON, *i.q.* PENLIGEN.

P. MEADOW, ? ? head of the meadow.

P. PARK, ? head of the close (*parc*).

P. POOL, ? *i.q.* PENPOL.

P. QUICK, ? *i.q.* PENKUKE.

PENNY-TINNY, beacon hill, *J.B.* ; ? fire (*tan*) enclosure (*hay*) summit.

P. VEER, ? ? *i.q.* PARKENVEOR.

P. VOUNDER, *i.q.* PENVOUNDER.

P. WILLOWS, ? *i.q.* PENHELLICK.

P. WIN, white (*gwin*) head.

P. WRINKLE, ? *periwinkle* head.

PENOAK, ? head oak, *Pr.*

PENOLV-A, -ER, ? *i.q.* PEDNOLVA.

PENONACK, ? = *parc an unack*, the solitary *or* lonely field.

PENOWELL, ? *i.q.* PARK NOWEL.

PENPALL, ? *i.q.* PENNY BALL.

PEN PARK, ? ? sheep *pen* close (*parc*).

PEN-PELL, *d.d.*, -PEL, far off *or* remote (*pell*) top *or* head, *H.*

PENPELLOW, top of the round (*pel*) tumulus (*low, s.*), *M'L.*

PENPERRY, ? ? hill (*bre*) top.

PENPERSES, ? Byrhisiys's (*B.m.*) top.

PENP-ERTH, -ETH, -ITH, ? *i.q.* PENBERTH *or* PENBEATH.

PENPETH-EY, -Y, ? *i.q.* PENBERTHY ; *or*, head of the graves (*bedhou*).

PENPETHICK, ? PETHICK end.

PEN-PILL, -PILLICK, head of the creek *or* little harbour, *Pr.*

PENPINE, ? *i.q.* PARK VINE.

PENPOD, ? ? the house (*an bod*) close (*parc*).

PENPO-L, -LE, -LL, -UL, head of the pool, well, pit, *or* lake (*pol*), *Pr.*

PENPON-DS, -S, -T, the head bridge (*pons*) *or* head of the bridge, *Pr.* ; *or*, bridge foot *or* end.

PENPONSKEENS, ? bridge foot rush (*hescen*) [field]s.

PENPRA-SE, -ZE, top of the meadow (*pras*) ; *or*, *i.q.* PARK PRAZE.

PENPRETHY, ? ? meadowy (*prathec*) summit *or* end.

PENQU-AIN, -EAN, *i.q.* PENNYWIN.

PENQUARO, *e.d.d., i.q.* PENGUARE.

PENQU-ET, -IT, -ITE, -ITT, -OIT, top of the wood (*cuit*), *Pr.*

PENQUINDLE, ? *i.q.* PARK VINTAL.

PENREST, ? ? top of the wood (*hurst, t.*) ; *or*, Grwst's (*w.*) summit.

PEN-RICE, -REES, head of the fleeting

ground, (*reese*, to flit *or* slide away), *Pr.* ; ? *i.q.* PARKANRISE.

PENRITHEN, ? fern (*reden*) end *or* top ; *or, i.q.* PENDRATHEN.

PEN-ROOSE, -ROUSE, red (*rooz*) head, *or* top, *or* field ; *or, i.q.*

PEN-ROSE, *o.* -ROS, head (*pen*) of the moor, *R.W.*, of the valley *or* moss, *Pr.*, of the heath, *T.* ; hill of the heath, *Wh.*

P. BURDEN, BURDON'S PENROSE.

P. SOPHIA, SOAPER'S PENROSE.

P. UD-D, -DA, ? UDY'S PENROSE.

PENRUKE, ?? Rieuk's (*a.*) summit.

PENRYN, a curled head, *Car.* ; head of the river channel (*ryne*), *or* promontory (*rhyn*), *Pr.* ; ? hill (*rhyn*) end.

P.-E BRYN, -FOREIGN, *or* -FORRYN, the court of Penryn, *Wh.*

PENSAGOLLAN, ? NANSAGOLLAN head, summit, end, *or* field.

PENSCAWN, ? elder-tree (*scauen*) end.

PEN-SCOMBE, -SECCOMBE, ? head of the dry (*sech*) valley (*comb, t.*).

PENSHANDY, ?? the springs (*fenten-s*) near the house (*an dy*).

PENSI-GILLIS, -QUILLIS, head of the dry copse (*celli*), *or* dry hill of wood, *T.* ; ? *goles*, a bottom *or* vale.

PENSIGNANCE, head of the dry valley (*nans*), *R.W.*

PENSILVA, ? look-out (*sulva, w.*) summit *or* height.

PENSIPPLE, chapel (*seipeal, ga.*) hill, *Beal* ; ? head of the dry pool (*pol*).

PENSIZE, ? parched (*syhys*) end.

PENS-KEN, -SKIN, *i.q.* PENESKYN.

PENSTR-ASE, -AYS, -AZE, ? *i.q.* PARK STERRES, *or*,

PENSTRASS-A, -OW, head of the springs (*stret*, a fresh spring), *T.*

PENSTRA-W, -Y, ?? the field (*parc en*) below (*is*) the oaks (*derow*) *or* house (*tre*).

PEN-STROAD, -STRODE, -STRODD, ?? springs head.

PENSTRUTHAL, ?? the end below (*is*) the foot (*troed*) of the moor (*hal*).

PENTAFRIDDLE, *i.q.* FENTAFRIDDLE.

PENTANE, ? *i.q.* FENTON.

PENT-ANGO, -ENGOE, ? the smith's (*gof*), *or* wood (*coat*) well (*fenten*).

PENTARGAIN, ? DURGAN point.

PENTARGEN HILL, ? the head-dragon (*pendragon*) *or* supreme ruler's hill ; *or*, silver (*archans*) well hill.

PENT-AVALE, -AVALL, -ENVALL, the head *or* chief (*pen*) good *or* consecrated (*da*) spring *or* well, *H.* ; the source (*fenten*) of the FAL.

PENTEARTH, ? bear's (*arth, B.*) well.

PEN-TELLA, -TILLY, ? = *parc en teile*, the manure close ; *or*, elms' (*elau*) well (*fenten*).

PENTELVADDEN, ? the spring on the little (*vadn* = *vean*) moor (*hal*).

PENTENHALE, ? moor spring.

PENTER, *n.f., i.q.* PEN-DER, *or* -TIRE.

PENTESCOOMBE, ? Penter's, *or* the well (*fenten*) below (*is*) vale.

PENTIOGA, ?? cave (*ogo*) spring.

PENTILLIE, = *penteilu*, the master's, *or* head of the family, *Pr.*

PENTINNEY, camp (*dinas*) of the head, *or* principal camp, *M'L.*

PENTINNICK, ? *i.q.* PARK AN DANACK.

PENTIRE, the head-land (*tir*), *Pr.*

P.-GLAZ, -GLAZE, the green (*glas*) headland *or* promontory.

PENT-ELL, -LE, ? hole (*tol*) point.

PENTON CROSS, ? the [village of the] spring at the *cross* roads.

PENTONWARRA, the higher (*wartha*) spring (*fenten*).

PEN-TOWAN, -TUAN, -TEWAN, -TEWYN, head of the sand-banks (*Pr.*), *or* hillocks (*Po.*), *or* heaps (*C.*).

PENTREA, *i.q.* PEN-DREA, *or*,

PENTREATH, head of the sands (*traith*), *R.W.*

PEN UCHEL COIT, the lofty hill in the wood ; (*now* LOSTWITHIEL), *Cam.*

PENVE-ARN, -RN, ? alder *or* mast (*gwern*) head ; *or, i.q.* PARK WARNE.

PENVENT-ENNEW, -INUE, -YNYOWE, *i.q.* PENFENTINOW.

PENVENTON, spring (*fenten*) head, *Pr.*; or, *i.q.* PARK AN VENTON.

PENVER, *i.q.* PARK AN VEAR.

PENVERANCE, ? crows' (*bran-s*) top.

PENVERE, great (*mear*) headland.

PENVERGATE, ? the *gate*, or wood (*coat*) by the great field (*parc an vear*).

PENVETH, *i.q.* PENBEATH.

PENVETHAS, *i.q.* PENWETHAS.

PENVIVIAN, ? VIVIAN's head or end.

PENVOARN, ? *i.q.* PENVEARN.

PENVOR, ? great (*maur*) headland.

PENVORDER, ? higher (*wartha*) head.

PENVORES, ? *i.q.* PARKENGWARRAS.

PENVOSE, head of the intrenchment or ditch (*fos*), *Pr.*

PENVOUNDER, *i.q.* PENFOUND.

PENVRANE, head of the rookery, *Po.* ; ? *i.q.* PARK AN VRANE.

PENWAR-DEN, -REN, ? *i.q.* PENVOARN.

PENWARNE, ? *the same* ; head of the alder-trees (*gwern*), *Pr.**

PENWARTHA, the higher (*wartha*) head or hill, *T.*

PENWATER, ? ? head of the *water*.

PENWELL, ? ? high (*uhel*) head.

PENWEN-ACK, -NICK, ? ? white or marshy (*winnic*) head.

PEN-WENHAM, -WINNAM, ? PENWINE meadow (*ham*).

PENWERRIS, the green or flourishing (*gwer*) head, *Pr.*; ? *i.q.* PENGWARRAS.

PEN-WETHAS, -WITHERS, ? = *parc en guedhar-s*, close of the wether-sheep.

PENW-IN, -YN, ? *i.q.* PENAWIN.†

PENWINDLE, ? *i.q.* PARK VINTAL.

PENWITH, ? the promontory of blood (*guit*).‡

PENWITHEN, ? *i.q.* PARK AN VETHAN.

PENWITHICK, woody (*withic, R.W.*) end.

PENWORTHA, *i.q.* PENWARTHA.

PENWORVAL, ? whale's (*morvil*) head.

PENWYTH, ? head of the wood (*gwyth*), *R.W.* ; or, *i.q.* PENWITH.

PENYGADER, a chair (*cadar*) form of hill, a terrace, *w., R.W.* ; ? pirate's (*ancredour*) point.

PENYMAEN, *i.q.* PENMAIN.

PENYOKE, ? ? upper (*uch, w.*) end.

PENYQUINDLE, ? *i.q.* PENWINDLE.

PENZANCE, holy (*sans*) headland.||

PENZ-ER, -OUR, gull (*zethar*) head-land, *T.C.* ; or, water (*dour*) head.

PEPPER, *n.f.*, ? = *piber*, baker.

PERBULLAR, ? *i.q.* PARK BILLIER.

PERCAMLYN, ? Hamlyn's close.

PERCENT, *i.q.* BOSANT, *C.*

PERCOCK, ? cuckoo's (*cog*) close.

PERCONGER, *conger*-eel cove (*porth*).

---

* — *Pen warn nan*, head of the alder-tree valley, *T.* ; head notice or summons (*gwarnya*, to warn), *H.* ; a head beloved, *Sc.* ! !

† "PENWYN is the beloved (*t.*) head or promontory ; but properly, *pen gwynsa* (?) is head or chief wine," *H.* ! ! ? white or fair end.

‡ This hundred is named after its most prominent feature the LAND'S END, "called by the British bards or poets PENRHINGUAED, *i.e.* the promontory of blood ; by their historians, PENWITH, *i.e.* the promontory to the left (*chwith, w.*); by the Saxons, PENWITH-STEORT, *steort* with them signifying ground stretched into the sea ; and by the inhabitants in their language, PEN VON (?) LAZ, *i.e.* the end of the earth," *Cam.*, or "headland of slaughter (*las=ladh*)," *Wh.*; this is given by *Leland* "PENWOLASE, *id est*, infimum caput," the last head or promontory ; and by *Carew* PEDN AN LAAZ.—Other renderings of PENWITH : "head of the Ashen-trees (*enwith*)," *Car.* ; "head of the breach or separation" (*gwyth*), *Gw., Pr., Po.* ; "head of the island" (*uiet*), *Bax.* ; "high or conspicuous (*guydh*) promontory," *B.* ; "? *i.q. fenwith*, the end," *Po.*

|| The saint's head, *Car.*; "that this is the right name appears from the arms of the town, which are S. John Baptist's head in a charger," *Bp. Gibson*, ! ! head of the Belra or sacred (*sans*) district, *Beal*; head of the bay (*sans*), *T., Pr.*; bay of the head, *Wh.*; head of the sands, *Cam.*; head of the channel (*savas*), *Gw.* ! *c.d.* St. Mary ; *o.* St. Nicholas.

PERCOSE, ? cheese (*caus*) close.

PERCOTHEN, *i.q.* PORTHCOTHAN.

PERCOTHY, ? *i.q.* PARK GOOTHA.

PERCRESSA, *i.q.* PORCRASSA.

PERCUL-A, -LAS, *i.q.* PARK GULLAS.

PERCURTIS, ? Curtis's close (*parc*).

PERDREDDA, ? the traitor's (*trayta, Pr.*) field (*parc*); or, *i.q.* PADERDA.

PEREAVE, ? summer (*haf*) field.

PERELMAN, ? HELMAN close.

PEREM, *B.m.*, ? *i.q.* Abraham.

PERGAL, ? *i.q.* PARK HAL.

PERGUARRA, ? *i.q.* PARK WARRA.

PERGWINS, ? *i.q.* PARK AN GWENS.

PERHILLICK, ? withy (*helic*) close.

PERICLES BAY, = *porth eglos*, church cove, *N.*

PERIL PARK, ? *i.q.* PARK PRILL.

PER-IN, -YN, *i.q.* PENRYN.

PERIOCK, ? pig (*yoch, B.*) close.

PERKIBET, ? newt (*ebbet*) close.

PERKILLA, the hidden (*celes*, to conceal) cove (*porth*), *N.*

PERKIN, *n.f.*, ? ? lamb (*ean*) close.

PERLEDAN, *i.q.* PARK LEDDAN.

PER-LEEZE, -LESE, -LEZE, ? *i.q.* PARKLESS, *or* BORLASE.

PERLINE, ? = *perlan*, an orchard, *R.W.*; or, *i.q.* PELLEAN.

PERLINNEY, *i.q.* LINHAY PARK.

PERLINYER, ? *i.q.* PARK LANYER.

PERLO, ? *i.q.* PORTLOE.

PERLUTES, ? midwife's (*lavethas*) close (*parc*).

PERMAYNE, *i.q.* PARK MAINE.

PERMELLIN, mill (*melin*) port; *or*, yellow (*melyn*) cove, *N.*

PERMEWAN, *n.f.*, ? St. Mewan's cove.

PERMIZ-EN, -ZEN, ? = *Porth Moesen*, Moses's cove, *N.*

PERNAGGIE, the broken port (*agenu*, to break; *agenoc*, fall of cracks), *N.*

PERNANCE, valley (*nans*) close.

PER-OSE, -ROSE, -ROWS, ? *i.q.* PENROSE, *or* PARK EN ROWS.

PERPITCH, ? little (*bich*) cove.

PERPOL, ? pit *or* pool (*pol*) close.

PERRAN ARWORTHAL, Perran parish of the manor of ARWOTHEL.*

P. PORTH, Perran bay (*porth*).

P. UTHNO, Perran parish of the manor of UTHNO.*

P. VOSE, ? cove (*porth*) of the (*an*) intrenchment (*fos*).

P. ZABULO, Perran in the sand.*

PERROW, ? = *perwith*, pear trees, *w.*

PERRUP-A, -ER, *i.q.* BAREPPA.

PERRY, *n.f.*, ? = *bre*, a hill.

PERR-YMAN, -IEM, *n.f.*, ? *i.q.* PEREM.

PERSGUIDDLE, ? close (*parc*) under (*is*) the wilderness-piece (*gwyddwal, w.*).

PERT, *n.f.*, ? = *perth*, bush.

PERTHCOLUMB, *i.q.* PORTHCULLUM.

PERTHILLICK, ? willow (*helic*) bush.

PERTHSASNAC, Saxon's cove (*porth*).

PERVELLIN, ? mill (*melin*) close.

PER-WENNACK, -WINNICK, marshy (*winnic*) close (*parc*).

PETATSON, ? Petite's down (*oon*).

PETHER-, PETHY-BRIDGE, *n.f.*, ? St. Petrock's *bridge*.

PETHERICK, *from* St. Petrock, *p.s.*

PETHERNION, ? the boundary (*eirionyn, w.*) bush (*perth*).

PETHERWIN, *from* St. Paternus (*p.s., T.*) the little (*vean*).

PETHICK, *n.f.*, *from* PETHERICK.

PETT, PETTET, PETTY, *n.f.*, *o.* PETITE = *le petite*, the little, *f.*

---

* The patron saint of the three PERRAN parishes is St. Pieran (*O.*), the Irishman (*Cornice, gwidhal, godhal, wodhal*), from whence, possibly, ARWORTHAL, in the 14 *cent.* ARWOTHEL; others say this is "upon (*ar*) the noted (*woth*) cliff *or* height (*hal*)," Pr.; "upon the noted river (*heyl*)," *Wh.*; upon (*arwarth*) the salt-water-river (*heyl*), *or* estuary (*el*, an arm of the sea), *Ped.* The chief village in this parish is " PERRANWELL, so called from a chalybeate spring," *D.G.*—UTHNO is " the high bare place, *or* naked exposure," Pr.; *or* " =*edn*, narrow," *T.C.*—ZABULO is from the middle latin *sabulum*, sand. *Leland* who speaks of " RYVIER absorptum a *sabulo*," calls the parish ST. PIRANES IN THE SANDES; *Cornice*, PIERAN IN TRETH, *Wh.*

PETTIGREW, ?crane's (*grew, Pr.*) bush (*perth*).

PETVIN, *n.f.*, ? *from* PETHERWIN.

PEVERELL, *o.n.f.*, *pevr*, fair, *w.*, *R. IV.*; -ELL, *diminutive*.

PEZZACK, *n.f.*, ? *i.q.* BEZACK.

PHARNISSICK, ?? lower (*isach*) furnace (*foru*), or alders (*fearn, i.*).

PHILLACK, *from p.s.* St. Felicitas, *O.**

PHILLEIGH, *from p.s.* St. Filius, *O.**

PHILLPOTTS, PHILPS, *n.f.*, the son of Philip (a lover of horses, *gr.*).

PHIPPEN, little (*en = vean*) PHILIP.

PHYSICK, *n.f.*, ? *from* TREVISICK.

PICCE, ? little (*bich*) enclosure (*hay*).

PICKEN PARK, ? beacon, or little (*bichen*) close (*parc*).

PICKENS, ? little [close]s; or = *park eanes*, lambs' close.

PICKLAND, ? shepherd's (*bigel*) land.

PIECE A DIECE, ? rick (*dise*) piece.

PIGGY NELL, ? *i.q.* PARK EN HELL.

PIG LOOSE, ? *i.q.* PARK CLOSE.

PIGSCOMBE, ? bush (*bagas*) vale.

PIGSDON, *d.d.* PIGESDONE, ? bush (*bagas*) hill (*dun*).

PIKES PARK, ? bush close (*parc*).

PILL, the salt-water trench, or little harbour, *Pr.*; the creek, *Wh.*; or = *pil*, a hillock, mound; or, *pol*, a pit, pool.

PILLANCE, ? lambs' (*eanes*) PILL.

PILL-AS, -ARS, -ERS, -OWS, -OWES, -S, *i.q.* PELLARS.

PILLATON, *d.d.* PILETONE, ? the PILL enclosure (*tun*); *p.s.* St. Odulphus, *O.*

PILLER PARK, ? *i.q.* PARK BILLIER.

PILLIANATH, ?? wormwood (*fuelein*), or pebble (*bilien*) heath.

PILLORY, *i.q.* PULLERY.

PILSEY, ? dry (*sech*) PILL.

PILVER, ? great (*mear*) PILL.

PINARD, *n.f.*, ? *i.q.* PENNARD.

PINCEY, ? dry (*sech*) end (*pen*).

PINCH, ? *i.q.* PARK EANES.

PINE, *n.f.*, ? = *bihan*, little.

PINGAR, ? *i.q.* PARK AN GEAR.

PINGLES, ? PENGELLY'S [field].

PINGLESTONE, ? P. enclosure (*tun, s.*).

PINK CARNE, ? the wry-neck (*pinnick, Po.*) rock *or* rocks (*carn*).

PINKEY, ? wry-neck close (*hay*).

PINKSKIN, ? *i.q.* PARK HOSKEN.

PINNACOMBE, ? Pinnock's vale.

PINNA PARK, ? Penna's close.

PINNATON, ? Penna's farm (*tun, s.*).

PINNECK, ? pine (*pin*) [grove].

PINNIONS, ? *Ap Enion's* (*w.*) [field].

PINSDON, ? Penna's hill (*dun*).

PINSEY, ? Penna's enclosure (*hay*)

PINSKIN, ? *i.q.* PENHESKIN.

PISKEY-, PISCAY-, PIXEY-PARK, fairy close.

PISTAIL COVE, waterfall (*pistyll, w.*) cove, *Po.*

PITCHER, *n.f.*, ?? *i.q.* BOWGEHEER.

PITCH PARK, ? little (*bich*) close.

PITHEM, ? pit *or* hole HAM.

PITNEY, ? the pit close (*hay*).

PIT PRAZE, pit meadow (*pras*).

PITPRY, clay (*pri*) pit.

PITSLEW-ERN, -REN, ? fox (*luern*) holes.

PITTEN PARK, the *pit* close.

PITT-ICE, -IES, ? pit closes (*haies, f.*).

PITTON, pit farm (*tun, s.*).

PITTY, pit close (*hay*).

PITTYME, ?? *Amy's* grave (*bedh*).

PLACE, *o.* PLAS, the palace, mansion, place (*plas*).

PLAIN AN GUARY, PLANENGWARY, PLENGWARY, the level place *or plain* of sport and pastime, *B.*; the plain floor *or* stage for the play (*guare*), *Ped.*

PLAIN PARK, ? *playing* close (*parc*).

PLAIN PLACE, ? = *playing place.*

PLAINS, ? = *pol eanes*, lambs' pool.

PLAIN SANCTUARY, the playing[field] near *or* belonging to the church.

PLAIN STREET, ? smooth road ; *or* = *pol an stret*, the spring pool.

PLAMING, *n.f.*, ? *i.q.* FLEMMING.

PLANE, ? *i.q.* PELAYNE.

PLASH, puddle, pool, swamp, bog, marsh ; *also, i.q.* PILLAS.

PLASH CROFT, swampy croft, *T.C.*

PLASHFORD, ? ford at the swamp.

PLASH TOWN, muddy town-place [field], *W.B.*

PLAS NOUN, the palace (*plas*) of the monk (*nonnus, lat.*), *Wh.*

PLAUNDER, ? = *plann-dir*, planted field, *R.W.* ; *or*, launder field (*parc*).

PLAYDY, = *plaidey*, partitions, *w.*, *R.W.*

PLAYER, *n.f.*, ? = *pol heir*, battle pool.

PLEA-, PLE-TON, ? *i.q.* PILLATON.

PLINT, PLYNT, *i.q.* PELYNT.

PLISHAY, PILLAS close (*hay*).

PLOD MEADOW, miry meadow.

PLOSH, PLOSHET, PLUSH PARK, PLUSHA, PLASH close.

PLOT, ? = *pol hoet*, duck pool.

PLOWDEN, *n.f.*, ? *i.q.* PLUDN, the pool, *Bl.* ; ? = *pol vean*, little pool.

PLOWSDON, PILLAS *or* PLOSH hill.

PLUM-B, -P, *pump* [field].

PLUMIER, ? dove-cot (*clomiar*) close (*parc*).

PLUSSIN, ? little (*vean*) PLOSH.

POAD, POAT, PODE, *n.f.*, ? = *bod*, a kite, *w.*, a messenger, *s.*

PODBRANE, ? *i.q.* BODBRANE.

PODESTOC, *d.d.*, ? PODES place (*stoc, s.*) ; *now* POUNDSTOCK.

POFFALAND, ? people's (*pobyl*) enclosure (*lan*) ; *or*, pebble (*pabol, s.*) land.

POKE TOR, ? ? Puck's peak.

POLAGENNA, ? the pool *or* pit (*pol*) at the mouth *or* opening (*genau*).

POLAND, *n.f.*, ? pool field (*land, s.*).

POLANNES, ? lambs' (*eanes*) pool.

POLARVAN, ? St. Rumon's pool, *W.H.*

POLATH-A, -ER, ? Uthr's (*w.*) pool.

POLAUGHAN, *i.q.* POLLAWGHAN.

POLBARROW, tumulus pool.

POLBATHICK, pool of the coins (*bath*, a coin), *C.*

POLBITHEN, head (*pol*) of the meadow (*bidhen*), *Gw.* (?).

POLBEROCK, ? *i.q.* POLBROCK.

POLBERR-O, -OW, ? *i.q.* POLPERROW.

POLBORDER, ?? traitors' (*bradwr*) p.

POLBRAGES, ? kites' (*barges*) pool.

POLBRE-AN, -EN, ? hill (*bryn*), *or* tree (*pren*) pit *or* pool.

POLBRIDGE, ? ? pool of counsel (*brys*).

POLBRO-CK, -KE, -OK, ? hoar-frost (*barrug, w.*), *or* badger (*broch*), *or* St. Breock's pool.

POLCA-IRN, -RNE, rock pool.

POLCAN, ? white *or* song (*can*) pool.

POLCARNICK, rocky (*carnic*) pool.

POLCATT, ? battle (*cad*) pool.

POLCOAT, forest (*coat*) pool.

POLCOCKS, ? red (*coch*) pools.

POLCONLA, ? ? the pool *or* pit (*pol*) with the rail (*canllaw, w.*).

POLCOVERACK, COVERACK pool.

POLCREBO, ? GREBAR pool.

POLCREEK, ? mound (*creeg*) pool.

POLDAWS, ? sheep (*daues*) pool.

POLDEN, ? *i.q.* PLOWDEN.

POL-DEW, -DUE, *d.d.* -DUH, *c.d.* -DU, black (*du*) *or* God's, *or* David's (*Du*), *or* south (*dehou*) pool.

POLDICE, ? stack (*dise*) pool.

POLDISTRA, ? home (*tre*) POLDICE.

POLDORY, ? watery (*douric*) pit.

POL-DOSE, -DOWSE, *i.q.* POLDAWS.

POLDOURIAN, ? pool of the shield (*tarian, w.*).

POL-DOWER, -DOWR, water (*dour*) pit *or* pool.

POLDREA, homeward (*adre*) pool ; *or*, pool by the house (*tre*).

POLDRISSICK, briery (*dreisic*) pool.

POLDROAS, pool by the door (*daras*).

POLEADRICK, ? Ydroc's (*w.*) pool.

POLEAN, ? lamb (*ean*) pool.

POLECACK, ? dung (*cac*) pit.

POLEGRASS, ? ? dry (*cras*) pit.

POLEMARTIN, ? Martin's, or lake (*mer-thyn, a.*) pool or pit.

POLENDRA, HENDRA pool.

POLENNICK, ? ? moist or wet (*lynnic*) close (*parc*).

POLEO, *i.q.* POLLOE.

POLERRY, ? pool field (*eru*).

POLESCAT, *d.d.,* ? the pit or pool below (*is*) the wood (*coat*).

POLESKAN, ? sedge (*hescen*) pool.

POLEYS PARK, ? ? broad (*les*) pool close (*parc*).

POLGA, ? smith's (*gof*) pool or pit; or, *i.q.* POLECACK.

POLGANOGO, *i.q.* POLKANOGOU.

POLGARTH, ? pool of the enclosure (*garth*), *R.W.*

POLGARVIS, ? outer (*arves*) castle (*caer*), or rock (*carn*) pool.

POLGA-SICK, -SSICK, -ZZICK, ? dirty (*gassic*) pool ; or, mare's (*caseg*) p.

POLGAVER, goat's (*gavar*) pool.

POLGEAR, castle (*caer*), or green (*gear*) pool.

POLGEEL, ? leech (*gel*), or horse (*cefil*), or retreat (*cil*) pool.

POLGIGGA, ? the fools' (*guccy*) pool.

POLGIGGAN, ? kitchen (*cegin*) pool.

POLGLA-CE, -S, -SE, -ZE, the green (*glas*) top or pool, *Pr.*

POLGLEESE, ? ? church (*eglos*) pool.

POL-GOADA, -GODA, ? wood (*coat*) pit or pool close (*hay*).

POL-GOODH, -GOOTH, -GOTH, the old (*coth*) pits, *Pr.* ; old pit, *J.B.* ; ? goose (*godh*) or wood (*coat*) pool.

POLGOON, down (*gwon*) pool.

POLGORRON, St. Guron's pool.

POLGOVER, a rivulet (*gover*) pool, or head of the rivulet, *B.*

POLGR-AIN, -EAN, -EEN, -ENE, gravel (*grean*) pits, *Pr.,* ? pit (*pol*).

POLGRAY, ? cattle (*gre, w.*) pool.

POLGREER, ? shoemaker's (*cereor*) p.

POLGRIGGONS, ? pool of the gins (*croccan-s*) pool.

POLGRINNA, ? cranes' (*garanou*) pool.

POLGUIN, white (*gwyn*) pool.

POL-GUM, -GUMB, ? pool COMBE.

POLGURTAS, ? camps' (*caer-s*) head, *M'L.* ; ? castle (*curtis, m. lat.*) pool.

POLGUTTER, cess pool, *m.c., W.B.*

POLGWANA, ? *i.q.* PORGWANA.

POLGWARRA, ? higher (*gwartha*) pool.

POLGWINS, ? windy (*gwens*) pool.

POLHAL, *d.d.,* moor or hill (*hal*) pit or pool ; or, *i.q.* POLWHELE.

POL-HARMAN, -HERMON, -HORMON, ? long (*hir*) stone (*maen*), or St. German's pool.

POLHAY, ? pool close (*hay*).

POLHEATH, ? pool heath, or heath p.

POLHENDRA, HENDRA'S pool, *B.*

POLHERN, iron (*hern*) pool, *R.W.*

POLHERNOU, ? ? pool corners (*cornou*).

POIHIBBET, newt (*ebbet*) pool.

POLHILL, ? ugly (*hyll, w.*) pool, *R.W.*

POLHILSA, ? Elisau's (*w.*) pool.

POLHOLME, ? holly (*holm, m.c.*) pool.

POLHUEVERAL, ? kid's (*cererel*) pool.

POLICY, ? St. Issey pool.

POL-IGEY, -INGEY, ? *i.q.* BOLINGY.

POLINGARROW, ? cattle (*gwarhog*), or stag's (*carow*) pool (*polan.*)

POLISCOURT, ? underwood (*is goat*) p.

POLJEW, jew's pool, *C.* ; black (*zu = du*) pool, *J.B.* ; *zew,* a bream, *Pr.*

POLKANOGOU, ? ? close (*parc*) of the (*an*) cave (*ogo*).

POLKEA, ? hedge (*ce*) pool.

POLKEATH, ? captive's (*caeth*) pool.

POLKEEVES, the drinking pool, *Po.* ; (? *kieve,* a basin, *m.c.*)

POLKERE, ? *i.q.* POLGEAR.

POLKERNICK, rocky (*cernic*) pool.

POLKERRIS, ? Kirys or Cirusius's (*m.s.*) pool, *Lh.* ; or = *pul kerriss,* lowest stream, (*R.*), *B.*

POLKERTH, ? quaking (*creth*) pool.

POLKIL, the pit in the slip or neck (*cil*) of land, *B.* ; ? cell pool.

POLKILLICK, ? ? cock (*celioc*) pit.

POLKIN-GHORNE, -HORN, pool with (*gan*) iron (*hoern*), *H.* ; chalybeate or medicinal pool, *Pr.* ; ? = *parc an gwarn,* the alder close.

POLKIRT, ? tinker's (*ceard*) pool.

POLKYTH, ? *i.q.* POLKEATH.

POLLADRAS, ? bramble (*dreis*) pool.

POLLAMOUNTER, the pool *or* mire under the hill, *Po.* ; ? *Maunder or* beggar's pool ; *mawn dir*, peat land, *w.* ; PILLAMOUNTAYNE, *Nord.*

POLLANDS, ? lambs' (*eanes*) pool.

POLLANGHAM, pond (*polan*) meadow (*ham, l.*) ; *or*, crooked (*cam*) pond.

POLLANNY, ??little-ewe-lambs' (*ornig, w.*) pool; *or* pond (*polan*) close (*hay*).

POLLANVEOR, ? great (*mear*) pond.

POLLAPHANT, the top (*pol*) spring *or* fountain (*fenten*), *H.* ; ? spring pools *or* pits.

POLLARD, ? high (*ard*) pool.

POLLARIAN, ? *i.q.* POLURRIAN.

POLLAVAS, the pool outside (*aves*).

POLLAWGHAN, ? *i.q.* POLYOGAN.

POLLAWYN, joyful (*lowen*) pool, *R. IV.*

POLLBRANDY, ? crow (*bran*) house (*ty*), *i.e.* rookery pool.

POLL BROWN, rush (*bruin*) pool.

POLLEAN, full (*len*) pool, *Pr.* ; river (*lin*) pool, *M'L.* ; ? *i.q.* POLEAN.

POLLEDAN, broad (*ledan*) pool.

POLLEOWE, *n.f., i.q.* POLLOE.

POLLESCAN, *i.q.* POLESKAN.

POLLFRY, ? *i.q.* POLPRY.

POLLGLESE, *i.q.* POLEGLEESE.

POLLGREASE, ? middle (*cres*) pool.

POLLGREEN, *i.q.* POLGRAIN.

POLLICK, ? flat-stone (*lech, B.*) pool.

POLLINDRA, *i.q.* POLHENDRA.

POLLINGSHIRE, ?artizan's (*sair*) pond.

POLLINNY, ? LINNEY close (*parc*).

POLLIVEDEN, ? *i.q.* POLBITHEN.

POLLIWIDDEN, little (*widden, m.c.*) pit *or* pool, *W.B.* ; *or*, *i.q.* POLWIN.

POLLOCK, *n.f.,* ? calf 's (*loch*) pool.

POLLOE, ? *the same* ; the pools (*pl.*), *J.B.* ; *or*, sheltered (*hleo, s.*) pool.

POLL PARK, ? pool close (*parc*).

POLL STACK, ? *stuck* pool.

POLLVA, ? pool place (*ma*).

POLLY JOKE, ? heifer (*ledzhek*) pool.

POLLYNE, ? linen (*lien*) pool ; *or, i.q.* PELAYNE.

POLLY VELLYN, *i.q.* POLMELLIN.

POLMANTER, *i.q.* POLLAMOUNTER.

POLMARH, horse (*marh*) pool, *Pr.*

POLMARKIN, ? Merkin's (*d.d.*) pool.

POLMARTH, the wonderful (*marth*) pool, *Pr.* ; ? open (*mathr, w.*) pool.

POLMARY, ? Meore's (*f.s.B.m.*) pool.

POLMASE, ? field (*maes*) pool.

POLM-ASICK, -ASK, -ESK, the top (*pol*) *or* upper field, *Pr.* ; ? stinking (*musac*) pool.

POLMAUGAN, -MAWGAN, great (*mogan*) pool, *Pr.* ; ?St. Mawgan's pool.

POLMEAR, -MEARE, -MEER, great (*mear*) pool *or* pit, *Pr.*

POLMELLIN, mill (*melin*) pool.

POLME-NA, -NNA, -NNOW, ? monk's (*manach*), *or* monks' (*menech*, *or* stony (*maenic*), *or* little (*menou*) p.

POLMENAS, ? nun's (*nunaes*) pool.

POLMENN-ER, -OR, ? long (*hir*), *or* battle (*heir*), *or* boundary (*or*) stone (*maen*) pool.

POLMORGY, ? dogfish (*morgi*) pool.

POLMOR-LA, -LAR, -LE, ? sea place (*mor-le, R. IV.*), *or* sea calf (*morlo, w.*) pool.

POLMORLAND, ? moorland pool.

POLMORVA, marsh (*morva*) pool.

POLNEY, ? pond (*polan*) close (*hay*).

POLNICK, ?? mossy (*neag, B.*) pool.

POLOSTOC, cap-like headland, *Bl.* ; ? = *pen losteg*, fox head.

POLPARROW, ? *i.q.* POLBARROW.

POLPATES, ? lunatic's (*budus*) pool.

POLP-EA, -Y, *i.q.* POULPEA.

POLPE-AR, -OR, ? great (*mear*) pool.

POLPENGY, the pool at the head (*pen*) of the field (*ce*), *J.B.*, *or* end of the house (*chy*), *R. IV.*

POLPENN-ICK, -Y, ? PENNICK'S, *or* nipple (*pennig, w.*) pool.

POLPENWITH, the pool at the head of the breach *or* separation, *Pr.*

POLPERR-O, -OW, sandy (*pura, T.* ?) *or* mud (*pri, Bond*) port (*porth*) ; *Le.* POUL PIRRHE, Paul's pier *or* quay, *Wh.* ; ? *i.q.* POLPARROW.

POLPEVER, ?? beaver (*befer*) pool.

POLPI-DNICK, -NK, ? *i.q.* POLPENNICK.

POLPRY, clay (*pri*) pit, *Pr.*, or pool, *Bl.* ; miry pool,*W.B.* ; pool-clay,*B.*

POLPUCKY, ? scarecrow (*bucca*) pool.

POLPYZE, fish (*pisc*) pool, (*now* POL-PERROW), *Jo.C.*

POLQUEST, ? shelter (*guest*) pool.

POLQUICK, ? head of the village (*gwic*), *H.M.W.* ; ? village pool.

POLREAG, the woman's (*gwrec*) pool.

POLRIDMOTH, ? Rhydmarch's (*w.*) p.

POLRO-AD, -DE, ? messenger's (*herod, w.*), or wheel (*rhod, w.*) pool or pit.

POLROSE, wheel (*ros*) pit.

POLROZZER, warrior's (*rhyswr, w.*) p.

POLRUAN, ? St. Rumon's pool, *C.**

POLRUDDON, head (*pol*) of the ford (*ryd*), *T.* ; ? fern (*reden*) pool.

POLRUNNY, ? the pool of charms or enchantment (*rhiniau, w.*)

POLSCAD, ? underwood (*is goat*) pool.

POLSC-ATH, -OATH, -OOTH, -OTH, ? boat (*scath*) pool.

POLSCATHA, boats' (*scatha*) pool.

POLSCOE, pool of the elders (*scaw*).

POLSCO-PP, -VE, ? bishop's (*escop*) pool.

POLSETHOW, southern (*didhiou*) pool, *J.B.* ; ? pool of the arrows (*sethow*).

POLSEW, pool [sometimes] dry, or a tidal pool, *W.B.* ; ? *i.q.* POLJEW.

POLSHEA, ? dry (*sech*) pool.

POL-SHEAS, -SKEASE, ? the dried up (*syhys, sychys*) pool.

POLSKEWES, ? elder-trees' (*scow-s*) p.

POLS-ON, -TON, ? Paul's town.

POLS PARNICK, ? thorny (*spernic*) pool (*pol*), or close (*parc*).

POLSTAIRS, ?? narrow (*striz, a.*) pool.

POLSTANGY, muddy, sticky, stoggy pool, *W.B.* ; (*stanc, B.*).

POLSTEAN, the tin (*stean*) pit, or miry pit, *Pr.* ; miry head, *Car.* ; tin pool or pit, *B.*

POLSTOGGAN, muddy pool (*stogged*, stuck in the mud), *Jo.C.*

POLSTREATH, ?? pool or cove (*porth*) of the fresh spring (*stret*).

POLSTRONG, ? Sadwrn's (*w.*) pool.

POLSUE, black (*zu = du*) pool, *Pr.*

POL-TAIR, -TARE, -TER, ? the back (*der*), or oak (*dar*) pool.

POLTARROW, ? bull (*tarow*) pit.

POLTEGGAN, ? Digain's (*w.*) pool.

POLTER-, POLTRE-WORGIE, ? POLTAIR on (*war*) the river (*gy*), or cattle pound (*gwarchae, w.*)

POLTESCA, = *pull is goed*, pool below the wood, *C.*, ? *ti*, house.

POLTICK, ? clear (*tec*) pool.

POLTON, ? Paul's or pool town.

POLTRAY, ? home (*adre*) pool.

POLTREASE, ? bramble (*dreis*) pit.

POLURRIAN, ? Urien's (*w.*), or boundary (*yrhian*), or silver (*arian, w.*) p.

POLVADDEN, ? stone (*mae[d]n*) pool.

POLVARTH, ? high or laughing (*gwarth*) pool ; or, *i.q.* POLMARTH.

POLVATHICK, *i.q.* POLBATHICK.

POLVELLAN, mill (*melin*) pool, *C.*

POLVENNA, ? lesser (*behenna*) pool.

POLVENTON, spring (*fenten*) head or pool, *Pr.* ; ? *i.q.* PENVENTON.

POLVETHAN, meadow (*bidhen*) pool.

POLVIL-AN, -ION, ? snail (*melyen*), or pebble (*bilien*) pool.

POLVORTH, ? road (*fordh*) pit.

POLWAIN, ? white (*gwyn*) pool.

POLWARTHA, higher (*gwartha*) pool.

POLWH-ARVEL, -EVEREL, ? kid's (*ceverel*) pool, *Pr.*

POL-WHEEL, -WHELE, the pool work (*wheyl*), or top of the field (*gweal*), *Pr.* ; miry (*pol*) work, *Car.* ; head of the manor (*guel*), *M'L.* ; ? field p.

POLWILLOWS, ? pool of the *willows.*

POLW-IN, -YN, white (*gwyn*) pool.

POLWINK, ? marshy (*winnic*) pool.

POL-WORTH, -WROTH, -WRATH, ? giant's (*wrath*) pool.

---

* Roman (*Ruan*) pool or port, *Po.*, *Wh.* ; the river (*ruan*) head or pool (*pol*), or the pool of the river, *Pr.* ; the head (*pol*) of the steep or sloping (*rhiw, w.*) haven (*haun*), *M'L.* ; a frosty (*rhew*, frost, *w.*) bottom or pool, *Sc.*! ? *i.q.* POLRUMAN (Lysnewth), *t.*, Henry IV, *Car.*

POLYBLANK, *n.f.*, ? colts' (*blanc*) pool.

POLYGLAIZE, ? *i.q.* POLGLEESE.

POLYMELLIN, *i.q.* POLMELLIN.

POLYPHUNT, *i.q.* POLLAPHANT.

POLYN, ? little (*vean*) pool.

POLYOGAN, ? p. of the cleft (*agen, w.*).

POLYWEN, ? the white (*gwen*) pool.

POL-ZATH, -ZEATH, -ZETH, dry pit, *Pr.*; ? pool of the arrow (*seth*), or by the seat (*asedh*).

POLZ-EA, -A, ? dry (*sech*), or lower (*isa*) pit *or* pool.

POLZEAL, low (*isal*) pool.

POMEER, *i.q.* PARK- *or* POL-MEAR.

POME PARK, ? ? causeway (*bom, a., B.*), or sledge (*bom*) close (*parc*).

POMER-OY, -Y, *n.f.*, = *pommeraye*, an orchard, *f., Lo.*; *or, i.q.* POMBRE, *o.n.f.*, ? hill (*bre*) bridge (*pont*); *or*, POLMEROIA, *i.q.* POLMARY; *or*, PEMBR-E, -O, *Le.*

POND, *n.f.*, ? = *pant*, a hollow, bottom, valley, *w.*; *or, i.q.* PONT.

PONDHU, ? black (*du*) valley.

PONJARAVAH, ? bridge by the oak place (*darva*), *J.B.*

PONJIO, black (*du, zu*) bridge, *J.B.*; ? ivy (*idzhio*) bridge (*pont, w.*) or vale.

PONS, bridge (*pons*).

PONSANBERTH, ? the bridge by the grove (*an berth*), *R.IV.*

PONSANDANE, the man's (*den*) bridge, *Bl.*; *i.e.* foot bridge, *T.C.*

PONS AN MAIN OAR, the boundary (*or*) stone (*maen*) bridge.

PONSANMEDDA, ? the *meadow* bridge.

PONS-ANNOWTH, -ANOOTH, the (*an*) new (*nowydh*) bridge, *T.*; *or*, bridge by the naked (*noath*) place.

PONS-ARDEN, -HARDYN, -HARDY, bridge of the steep (*ard*) hill (*din*), *S.G.*; ? forest hill bridge, *J.B.*; *or* = *pont ardent*, burning bridge, *f.*

PONS-AVERRAN, -EVARREN, ? bridge by the alders (*gwern, gwarn*), *J.B.*

PONS-BRITAL, -PRITAL, ? Brithail's *or* Bartholomew's bridge.

PONSMAYNE, stone (*maen*) bridge.

PONSM-EOR, -UR, great (*mear*) bridge.

PONSONGATH, *or* PONT ST. GARTH, ? bridge of the cat (*an gath*), *R.IV.*

PONT, bridge (*pont, w.*); *or, i.q.* POND.

PONT-ABOYES, -BOY, -EBOY, ? = *pont de bois*, bridge by the wood, *f.*

PONT BALDWIN, Baldwin's bridge.

POOLE = *pol*, a pool, pond, a miry place; mire, mud; a well, pit.

POOLER, ? long (*hir*) pool, *R.IV.*

POOL-EY, -HAY, pool close (*hay*).

POOL HALL, ? pool moor (*hal*).

POOL PARK, pool close (*parc*).

POOL VENTON, spring (*fenten*) pool.

POOR GAMES, ? games' *i.e.* playing, or outer (*ames*) close (*parc*).

POPE, *n.f.*, ? = *pab*, pope.

POPHAM, ? Pope's dwelling (*ham, s.*).

PORBUAN, *i.q.* PORTHPEAN.

PORCOLLAS, *i.q.* PARK GULLAS.

PORCRASA, *i.q.* PORTHCRASSOU.

PORCULLUM, *i.q.* PORTHCULLUMB.

PORDENACK, ? hilly (*dinnic*) cove.

PORE, *n.f.*, ? = *peochaer*, peacemaker, *a.*

PORFELL, ? pasture (*porfa, w.*) field.

PORGUARNON, cove of the amphitheatre, *Bl.*; (*guare*, a play).

PORGWANA, *i.q.* PARK GWANETH.

PORKAN HILL, the hill of the port *or* haven, *Dr.*; ? *i.q.* PARKENHELL.

PORK-ELLIS, -ILLIES -LES, gate (*porth*) of the grove (*celli*), *Po.*; ? ELLIS close (*parc*).

PORKIDNICK, ? pullet (*idnic*) close.

PORK-LEDAN, -LIDDEN, *i.q.* PARK LEDDAN.

PORLOE, the inlet *or* cove (*porh*) of the tumulus (*low, t.*), *M'L.*

PORMEER, *i.q.* PARK MEAR.

PORMENNA, ? *i.q.* PARK MEANA.

PORMORRAN, ? woman's (*morwyn, w.*), or whale (*moran, w.*) port, *N.*

PORNANVEN, the port of the stony (*maen*) or rocky valley (*nant*), *Buller*

PORREPTER, *i.q.* PERRUPA.

PORSELLI, conger-eel (*selli*) cove.

PORSKENTLE, ? *i.q.* BOSCUNDLE.

PORT-ALLAND, -ALLOW, TALLAND bay.

PORT BULLA, ? *i.q.* PARK BULLA.

PORT CORNICK, ? rocky close (*parc*).

P. CUEL, ? work (*wheal*) cove.

P. EAST, ? *east*, or St. Just cove.

P. EATH, ? noisy (*aedd, w.*) cove.

P. EITHEN, *i.q.* PARK EITHAN.

P. ELIOT, [Lord] Eliot's cove.

PORTEOUS, *n.f.*, ? *i.q.* PARK DEES.

PORTERS, ? *i.q.* PARK DARAS.

PORTEUR, ? *i.q.* PARK DOWER.

PORTGAVERN, ? *cavern*, or little goat (*gavar vean*) cove.

PORT-GUIN, -QUIN, white (*gwyn*), or wine (*gwin*) cove.

PORTH, a gate, cove, bay, port, harbour (*porth, porh*).

P. ALL-A, -AS, ? lower or bottom (*gollach, goles*) cove.

P. ALLOW, TALLAND cove, *J.H.*

P. ASKEL, ?? thistles' (*ascall*) cove.

P. BARN, ? Bran's cove.

P. BEAN, little (*bichan*) cove.

P. BEER, great (*mear, vear*) cove.

P. CAUL, ? the cove where the wild-cabbage (*caul*) grows, *R.W.*

P. CHAPEL, *chapel* cove.

P. COR, ? giant's (*caur*) cove.

P.-COTHAN, -CUTHAN, Cathan's (*w.*), or wood-pigeon (*cudhan, w.*) cove.

P. COTHERN, ? the hero's (*cadarn*) c.

P. CRASSA, ? winding or crooked (*ceirsio*, to wind, *B.*) cove.

P.-CULLUMB, -COLLUM, ?? bare or naked (*llwm,w.*) hill or summit (*bar*).

P. ELLICK, herring (*allec, B.*) cove.

P. EN-NIS, -YS, island (*enys*) haven, *D.G.* ; now MOUSEHOLE.

P. ENTHAN, ? St. Nectan's cove.

P. ER-AS, -RAS, ? *i.q.* PARK DARAS.

P. ERROW, ? *i.q.* PORTHGURRA.

P. EUE, ? David's (*Dewi*) cove.

P. GLA-S, -ZE, ? green (*glass*) cove.

P.-GUARRA, -GWARTHA, higher cove.

P.-GWIDEN,-GWIDDEN,-GWYDN,white (*gwydn*) cove.

P. HOLLAND, *i.q.* PORTHOLLAN.

P. HORN, iron (*haiarn*) gate (*porth*), *Car.* ; haven (*haun*) gate, *M'L.*

P. HOSKEN, ? *i.q.* PARK HOSKEN.

P.-IA, -IA, -EA, St. Ive's (*Ia*) port,

T. ; PORTHIA PRIOR, the *prior's* manor of PORTHIA.

PORTH-ILLY, -ILLA, Church (*eglos*) cove, *Dr.* ; ? St. Helie's cove.

P. JOKE, ? the *shag* or cormorant cove ; or, *i.q.* PORT ISAAC.

P. KEA, ST. KEA'S cove.

P. KERNICK, rocky (*cernic*) cove.

P. KERNOW, *v.* PORCURNOW, the cove surrounded by horn- (*corn*) like hills, *Bl.* ; *Kernow*, Cornwall ; *curnow*, rocks.

P. KERRIS, ?? cherry (*ceiroes, w.*) cove.

P. KIDNEY, ? dinner (*cidnio*) cove.

P. KILLIER, *i.q.* PERKILLA.

P. LEA, ? flat-stone (*lech*) cove.

P. LED-AN, -DAN, ? wide (*ledan*) cove.

P. LEVAN, *i.q.* PORTLEVAN.

P. LISPIN, ? little (*bian*) PORTLEASE.

P-LOE, -LOO, port of the pond (*lo*), or of dust (*llwch, w.*), *N.* ; *i.q.* PORLOE.

P. LUN-EY, -Y, ? LAWNEY cove.

P. MEL-LIN, -LYN, -ON, ? mill (*melin*), or yellow (*melyn*), or MULLION cove.

P.-MERE, -MEAR, ? great (*mear*), or lake (*mere, l.*) cove.

P. MEW, ?? great (*mu?*) cove.

P. MINNICK, ? stony (*maenic*), or monks' (*menych*) cove.

P. MINSTER, ? *monastery* cove.

P. MOINA, monk's (*manach*) port, *Bl.*

P. NANVEN, port of the high (*ban*) valley (*nant*), *Bl.*

P. NAVAS, ? Nywys's (*w.*) cove.

P. OLLAN, HOLLAN cove.

P. OUSTOCK, ? Ysteg's (*w.s.*) cove.

P. PEAN, *i.q.* PORTH BEAN.

P. ROW, ? rough (*row, m.c.*) cove.

P. TOLLICK, cove with the noted hole (*tol*) ; or, Tallwch's (*w.*) cove.

P. TOWAN, TOWAN cove.

P. VYAN, *i.q.* PORTH BEAN.

P. ZENNOR, ZENNOR cove.

PORT-ISAAC, -ISSIC, the corn (*izic*) port, *Pr.* ; ? ISAAC'S cove.

P. KERNE, crane port, *Nord.* ; ? rock (*carn*) cove.

P. KISKEY, the blessed (*kesky*, to bless, *Pr.*, sleep, *R.W.*) haven, *Pr.* !

PORTH LEASE, ? slaughter (*lleas, w.*) cove.

P. LEVAN, open bay, *Pr.* ; smooth port, *B.* ; *c.d.* St. Bartholomew.

P. LOOE, *i.q.* PORTHLOE.

P. MISSEN, ? Moses' (*Moesen, w.*) cove.

P. PIGHAM, *i.q.* PORT BEAN.

P. PRIOR, the *prior's* cove.

P. QUIN, *i.q.* PORTGUIN.

P. REATH, sandy (*treath*) cove, *Pr.* ; *or,* red (*rydh*) cove.

P. SAUSSEN, Saxons' (*sowsen*) cove.

P. SCATH-A, -O, boats' (*scatha*) cove.

P. UAN, tumulus (*tuyn, Lh.*) cove, *M'L.* ; ? *i.q.* PORTH VYAN.

P. WRINKLE, *periwinkle* cove.

P. YLLYGLOS, ? PORTHILLY by the church (*eglos*).

P. YLLYGRES, ? middle (*cres*) P.

POSEY, ? post (*pos*) close (*hay*).

POTBRANE, *i.q.* BODBRANE, *C.*

POTENESS, ? *i.q.* PARK DEANS.

POTRAM, ? Potter's meadow (*ham*), *t.*

POTT, *n.f.,* ? *i.q.* PODE.

POTTER, *n.f.,* ? = *bodhar*, deaf.

POUGHILL, *v.* POFFIL, ? = *pou guil*, the country frequented by gulls, *or pou gulla*, the low country, *Pr.* ; ? *i.q.* POLWHELE; *d.d.* POCHEHELLA; *p.s.* St. Olave, *O.*

POULGARRAH, *i.q.* POLGWARRA.

POULPEA, ? magpie (*pi, w.*) pool.

POULTERS, ? *i.q.* POLDROAS.

POULTON, *i.q.* POLTON.

POULZA, *i.q.* POLZA.

POUND, ? the pinfold ; *or*, cider-mill (*m.c.*) ; *or, i.q.* POND.

POUNDA, ? POUND close (*hay*).

POUNDSCOANSE, the causeway (*coans*) by *or* between the ponds, *J.M.* ; *or,* POUND's (*o.n.f.*) causeway.

POUNDSCROSS,?POUND's marsh(*cors*), *or cross* roads.

POUNDSTOCK, *d.d.* POND-, POD-ESTOCH, ? POUND *or* POUND's place (*stoc, s.*) ; *p.s.* St. Neot, *O.*

POU-, POW-TON, *i.q.* POLTON.

POWDER, the hundred, country, *or* province (*pow*) of oaks (*dar,* an oak), *Pr.* ; house (*tre*) of the province, *Po.*

POWELL, *n.f.,* = *Ap-Howel,* Howel's son ; *or,* Paul ; *or, from* POUGHILL.

POWER, *n.f., i.q.* PORE.

POWLELIS, ? ELLIS pool.

POWLES, *n.f.,* ? POWELL's son.

P. COMBE, *n.f.,* Powell's valley.

POWLEY, *n.f.,* the pool (*pol*), *or* Powell's close (*hay*).

POWN-A, -ALL, *n.f.,* ? *i.q.* PARNAL.

POYLE, *n.f.,* ? *i.q.* POWELL.

PRADANNACK, ? ferny (*redanic*) country (*pou*), *or* close (*parc*).

PRADE,*n.f.,*PRAED,PRATT, a meadow, *prad, a.* ; *i.q.* PRAS.

PRADOE, ? = *w. paradwys,* paradise, *R.W.* ; *or, parc aradow,* plow close.

PRAES MEADOW, a *reduplication.*

PRAIRE, ? = *parc hir,* long close.

PRAKE, *n.f.,* ? = BRE-AGE, *or* -OCK.

PRALA, *i.q.* PORTHALLA.

THE PRAN, ? *i.q.* PREAN.

PRAS, PRAZE, PRAISE, PRAYERS, = *pras,* a meadow, common.

PRAZE AN BEEBLE, ? the (*an* people's (*pybl, w.*), *i.e.* common meadow, (*pebyll,* tents, pavilions, *w.*).

P. BEAN, little (*bichan*) meadow.

P. GOOTH, ? old (*coth*), *or* wood (*coat*) meadow.

P. LOAR, ? garden (*luar*) meadow.

P. RUTH, ? red (*rudh*) meadow.

PREAD, PEARD, *n.f.,* ? *i.q.* PRAED.

PRE-AN, -DDEN, -DEN, ? = *pren, predn,* tree, *Pr.*

PREGUE, ? *i.q.* PARK AN GEW.

PRE MEADOW, a *reduplication* ; *or, i.q.* BRAY.

PRESINGOL, ? ? cabbage (*ungol*) meadow ; *v.* SKALL, ? = *ascall,* thistles.

PRESKIN, ? *i.q.* PARK HOSKEN.

PRESLEA, ? Prest's pasture (*t.*).

PRESTIS, ? close (*parc*) below (*is*) the stack (*dise, B., das, w.*).

PREST, *n.f.,* ? = *prest,* ready, *w., R.W.*

PRESTACOTT, ? priest's *or* Prest's cottage (*t.*).

PRICE, = *ap Rhys,* son of Rhys, *w.*

PRIDACOMBE, ? Pread's vale, *t.*

PRIDEANCE, *n.f.*, ? *i.q.* PRUDENS; *or,*

PRID-EAUX, -YAS, *n.f.*, clay (*pri, prid*) cliff *or* shore (*als, aus*), *T.*; = *près d' eaux,* near the waters, *f.,* *Pr.*; ? stack (*dise*) meadow (*prad*).

PRIDHAM, ? PREAD'S meadow (*ham*).

PRIGLIS BAY, *i.q.* PERICLES BAY.

PRILEY, ? primrose (*briallu, w.*) [field].

PRINDLE, *n.f.*, a croft, *Cam.*

PRINKWELL, ? Brenci's (*s.B.m.*) well.

PRINN, *n.f.*, Rhun's son (*ap, w.*).

PRINSEY, ? Prinn's enclosure (*hay*), *t.*

PRISCAN, ? *i.q.* PARK SCAUAN.

PRISK, ? = *prysc,* underwood, *w.*

PRISLOW, near (*pres, f.*) the water (*l'eau, f.*), *Pr.*

PROBERT, *n.f.*, Robert's son (*ap*), *w.*

PROBUS, *from p.s.* Probus [& Grace].

PROCTOR, ? = *bragudwr,* brewer.

PROCLAIM, ? foot-bridge (*clam, m.c.*) close (*parc*).

PRO-FFIT, -PHET, *n.f.*, ? *from* TREBAR-FOOT.

PROGE, ? cave (*ogo*) cove (*porh*).

PROGAN, ? = *bruchen,* a spring, *w.*

PROSCEN, *s.B.m.*, ? great (*bras*) head (*ceun, ga.,* = *pen*).

PROSPIDNICK, ? ? little (*ig*) magpie (*pioden*), *or* wry-neck's (*pinnick*) meadow (*pras*).

PROUSTOCK, *i.q.* PORTHOUSTOCK.

PROUT, *n.f.*, ? Rhaawd's son (*ap*), *w.*

PROVIS, *n.f.*, ? *from* PROBUS.

PROWSE, *n.f.*, Rowse's son (*ap*), *w.*

PRUDENS, *w.B.m.*, discreet, *lat.*

PRUELLS, ? *i.q.* PARK GWILLAS.

PRUST, *n.f.*, ? ? Grwsts' son (*ap*), *w.*

PRY-CE, -SE, *n.f.*, *i.q.* PRICE.

PRYNN, *n.f.*, *i.q.* PRINN.

PUCKEY HORN, ? *i.q.* PARK HORN.

PUCKLEY, ? cow (*buch*) pasture (*t.*).

PUCKWALLS, ? *i.q.* PARK WOLLAS.

PUDDICOMBE, *n.f.*, ? Bywdeg's (*w.*) vale.

PUDDIFORD, *n.f.*, ? Bywdeg's ford.

PUDDLE, ? dale (*dol*) close (*parc*).

PULEDOWN, ? deep (*down*) pit (*pol*).

PULE-GURRA, -KERROW, ? camps'

(*caerau*) pool; *or, i.q.* POLGWARRA.

PULEJON, ? ox (*udzheon*) pool.

PULGOOTH, *i.q.* POLGOODH.

PULL-A, -ER, ? the pool (*pol*).

PULLANS, ponds *or* pools, *W.B.*

PULLCALLNICK, CALENICK pool.

PULLERY, ? pool field (*eru*).

PULLEYS, ? green (*glas*) pool.

PULLINGTON, ? pond (*polan*) farm *or* town-place (*tun*).

PULL MAIN, ? stone (*maen*) pool.

PULL PARK, pool close (*parc*).

PULPIT, ? *i.q.* POLPRY.

PULROSE, *i.q.* POLROSE.

PULSACK, ? dry (*sech*) pit.

PULSTRONG, *i.q.* POLSTRONG.

PULTEGGAN, ? ? Digain's (*w.*) pool.

PULYNE, *n.f.*, ? *i.q.* PELAYNE.

PULZA, *i.q.* POLZEA.

PUMP-LE, -WELL, ? five (*pymp*) wells.

PUMRIES, POMEROY'S [place].

PUNCHARDUN, *n.f.*, *i.q.* PONSARDEN.

PUNGIES, ? *i.q.* PARK AN GOOSE.

PUNJO, ? *i.q.* PONJIO.

PUNK PARK, ? bench (*benc*) close.

PURCHASE, *n.f.*, ? = *berges,* a citizen, *B.*; *or, i.q.* BURGESS.

PUR-CULLAS, -GALLAS, *i.q.* PARK GUL-LAS.

PURGATORY, *i.q.* PARK A DORY.

PURLAS, *i.q.* PARK GLASE *or* GULLAS.

PURLAWN, ? fox (*lowern*) close.

PURRAW, ? *i.q.* PARK ROW.

PURSE HILL, PUZZLE [PARK], ? = *parc isal,* low close.

PURUPPA, ? *i.q.* BAREPPA.

PUSKUS, ? close (*parc*) below (*is*) the wood (*cus*).

PUSSEY, ? post (*pos*) close (*hay*).

PUZLINCH, ? lambs' (*eanes*), *or* island (*ynys*) low (*isal*) close (*parc*).

PYATT, *n.f.*, ? = *piod,* a magpie, *w.*

PYCLE, ? *i.q.* PARK GILLY.

PYDDERLEY, *n.f.*, ? Peter's pasture, *t.*

PYDER, the fourth (*pedar,* four) [hundred], *Pr.*; *from* St. Peter, *H.*

PYNE, *n.f.*, ? = *bichan,* little.

PYNTAR, *o.n.f.*, ? *i.q.* PENTER.

PYWELL, ? magpie well, *t.*

Q̲UANCE, ? *i.q.* COANSE.

QUANNA PARK, *i.q.* PARK GWANETH.

QUARDALE, ? = *war dol*, on the dale, or high (*warth*) dale.

QUAR-AM, -M, -ME, ?? = *worm*, a serpent, *t.*

QUARL, QUERLE, ? quarry (*cuare*), or camp (*caer*), or play (*guare*) place (*le*).

QUEEN-, QUEENA-, QUEENER-, QUIN-NY-, QUEENY-, QUENA-, QUINN-PARK, white (*gwyn*) or marsh (*winnic*), or red-wing (*winnard*) close.

QUETHIOCK, the weaver's place (*gwia*, to weave), *Pr.*; *p.s.* St. Hugh, *O.*

QUICK, *n.f.*, ? *i.q.* GWEEK.

QUIL-LER, -TER, *n.f.*, long (*hir*), or water (*dour*) field (*gweal*).

QUIL-LET, -LOT, -T, ? little (-*et*), or gate (*yet*) field (*gweal*).

QUILLYS, ? *i.q.* GOONLAZE, or GULVES, or GULLIES, or WILLY'S.

QUININ, 14 *cent.*, ? *i.q.* Uny.

QUINT-REL, -EREL, ? Trywyl's (*w.*), or Terrel's down (*guen*).

QUITE COOMBE, wood (*cuit*) vale.

QUODRI, 14 *cent.*, ? *i.q.* CUBERT.

QUOIT, = *w. coed*, a wood; a cromlech or coit-like flat-stone.

QUOYKIN, 14 *cent.*, ? *i.q.* HOCKIN, *F.H.*

R̲ABBITS, *n.f.*, *i.q.* ROBERTS.

RABEY, *n.f.*, ?? *i.q.* Trebigh.

RABNAN FIELD, ? field with sub-soil of decomposed or unformed granite, *W.B.*

RACE, ? = *cres*, middle; or, *reece*, a heap of turnips; (a row, *w.*, *R.W.*).

RACK PARK, front (*rag*) close.

RAD-DALL, -DLE, *n.f.*, ? *i.q.* RANDALL.

RADDON, *n.f.*, = *radn*, a share, *Ch.*

RADFORD, ? red ford, *t.*

RADDOW, *n.f.*, *i.q.* TRESREDDOW.

RADICK PARK, *i.q.* PARK REDDICK, ? race (*rhedec*, to run, *w.*) field.

RADLAND, ? fern (*reden*) enclosure (*lan*), *Po.*; or = red land, *t.*

RADMORE, ? = red moor, *t.*

RADNOR, *n.f.*, fern (*reden*) land (*nuor* = *an uor* = *an daor*), *Pr.*

RAFFELL, the ready or quick well, *T.C.*; ? *Ralph's*, or rough hill, *t.*

RAF-TON, -TRA, ? Ralph's town.

RAG, before, in front of.

RAGENNIS, opposite or in front of (*rag*) the island (*enys*), *T.C.*

RAGINALDUS, *t.d.d.*, RAINALDUS, power (*wald*) of judgment (*regen*), *t.*

RAIL, RAINS, *n.f.*, ? *the same.*

THE RAKE, ? *i.q.* RAG.

RAINFORTH, *n.f.*, ? Reginald's ford, *t.*

RALEGH, *n.f.*, ? Ralph's pasture, *t.*

RALPH, *i.q.* RADULPHUS, *W. Worc.*; *i.q.* RANDOLPH.

RAME (*c.d.* St. Germanus, *O.*), from RAME HEAD, the ram's head, *t.*; the great, high, steep, or projecting (?!) headland, *Ch.*

RAMSACOMBE, Ram's vale, *t.*

RAMS-AY, -PARK, Ram's, or the rams' close (*huy*, *t.*, *parc*, *k.*).

RAND-ALL, -ILL, -YLL, -OLPH, *n.f.*, ? shield (*rand*, *s.*) help (*ulph*, *s.*).

RANNEYS, ? *i.q.* RAGENNIS.

RAPHEL, *i.q.* RAFFEL.

RAPSON, *n.f.*, RALPH'S son.

RASCASSA, *i.q.* ROSECOSSA.

RASCOW, *Le.*, now TRESCO.

RASHLEIGH, *n.f.*, rush (*resce*, *s.*) pasture, *t.*

RATH, RATHA, hill fort (*rath. i.*), *Beal.*

RATH-WELL, *o.* -WIL, ? fort-well.

RATTENBURY, ? fern (*raden*) hill (*bre*), or barrow or castle (*t.*).

RATTLING FIELD, ? = *w. rhydhlan*, an open area, level field.

RAUFF, *o.n.f.*, now RALPH.

RAUGHTRA, *i.q.* RAFTRA.

RAVEL, ? *i.q.* RAFFELL.

RAVEN, ?? = *ar avon*, on the river.

RAWDON, *n.f.*, Ralph's or rough hill.

RAWE, RAWLE, *n.f.*, *i.q.* RALPH.

RAWLIN-GS, -S, -SON, *n.f.*, son of little RAWLE.

RAYLE, ? = *ar hal*, on the moor.

RAYMOND, *n.f.*, wise (*regin*, judg-

ment) protection (*mund*), *t.*, *Y.*
RAYNSFORD, Reginald's ford.
RE-AD, -ED, -ID, -ATH, *n.f.*, ? = *rid*,
free ; *or*, *ryd*, a ford ; *or*, *rydh*, red.
READER, *n.f.*, ? = *ryd hir*, long-ford.
RECHAREDOC, *d.d.*, REKARADOC,
e.d.d., *now* ROSCRADDOCK, *J.Ca.*
REDANAN, a fern brake, *Pr.*
REDANNACK, ferny [piece].
REDDON, *n.f.*, ? = *redan*, fern.
REDDYFORD, ? red or reedy ford, *t.* ;
or, ford, *reduplicated* (*ryd*, *c.*).
REDEVALLEN, = red valley, *R.B.K.* ;
? apple-tree (*avallen*) ford.
REDGATE, = *rhie-gat*, river's course,
Bond ; open (*gaith*?) ford, *C.*
REDIVER, ? darnel (*efer*) ford.
REDLAKE, ? willow (*helic*) ford.
REDMAN, *n.f.*, ? stone (*maen*) ford.
REDMORE, ?? great (*maur*) ford.
REDRUTH, druids' (*druith*) ford, *B.* ;
or, red (*rudh*) ford, *or* druids' town
(*tre*), *Pr.* ; = *tre trot*, the dwelling
in the bed *or* channel of the river,
W'h. ; *p.s.* St. Euinus (*v.* Uny), or
Erminus, *O.*
RED TYE, ford house (*ti*), *Pr.*
REE, *i.q.* RHI.
REECE, REESE, *n.f.*, ? = *w.* Rhys, *i.q.*
gr. Ares, Mars.
REEDA-, REEDY-MILL, ? ford mill.
REEN, REIN, = *ryn*, hill ; *pl.* REENS,
REINS, RHEENS, RUINS, RUNS.
REEN-WARTHA & -WOLLA, *or* -WOL-
LAS, higher and lower hill.
REES-E, -H, ?*i.q.* RACE *or* REECE.
REEVE, *n.f.*, ? = *gerefa*, steward, *s.*
REFRAWELL, *o.n.f.*, ? *i.q.* TREFRAUL.
REFRY, *o.n.f.*, ? *i.q.* REM- *or* TRE-FRY.
REGINNIS, *i.q.* RAGENNIS.
REGULAR PARK,?*i.q.* PARK GRIGLAN.
REJAINE, ? ox (*udzheon*) ford (*ryd*).
REJARNE, ? garden (*dzharn*) ford.
REJOURRA, ?*i.q.* RESURRA.
RELISTIAN, ? Elystan's (*w.*) dwelling.
RELUBBUS, ? Lupus's (*w.s.*) dwelling
(*tre*).
RELYTHON, ? on (*ar*) furze (*eithin*)
moor (*hal*) ; *or*, RE- = TRE-.

REMFRY, REN-FREE, -FREY, *n.f.*, =
Ragnfrid, ? judgment of peace *or*
freedom, *t.*, *Y.*
REN-AUDIN, -OWDEN, -ORDEN, *n.f.*,
power of judgment,*t.*, *Y.*
RENUEL HILL, ? high (*uhel*) hill (*ryn*),
reduplicated.
REPRIN, *i.q.* RESPRIN.
RESAIR, ? *i.q.* TRESARE.
RESCADDOCK, *i.q.* ROSCARROCK.
RESCARN-AN, -ON, *i.q.* ROSKARNON.
RESCARRETUNUS,14*cent.*,?CARADON
heath *or* moor (*res* = *ros*).
RESCAS-A, -SA, *i.q.* ROSECOSSA.
RESCHER, 14 *cent.*, *i.q.* ROSKEAR.
RES-COLLA, -CORLA, -CORLAR, *n.f.*
ROSCORLIA, *i.q.* ROSCORLA.
RESCRADECK, 14 *cent.*, *i.q.* ROSCAR-
ROCK.
RESCROWA, *i.q.* ROSCROW.
RESCUDGIAN, ? ? turf (*cesan*) heath.
RESEIGH, *n.f.*, ?dry (*sech*) heath.
RESEVEN, = *roseyhan*, the plentiful
vale, *Pr.* ; ? Evan's heath.
RESINGY, ? the heath by the house
(*an chy*).
RESKADINICK,?Cadanoc's (*w.*)heath.
RESK-AGEAGE, -EAGE, ? privet (*scudg-
with*) heath *or* moor.
RESKEAN, *i.q.* ROSKEEN.
RESKEIF, *i.q.* ROSKEIF.
RESKENNAL, *i.q.* ROSKENNAL.
RESKER, *n.f.*, *i.q.* ROSKEAR.
RESKILLEY, *n.f.*, *i.q.* ROSKELLY.
RESKIVE-AS, -RS, ? SKEWES, *or* barns'
(*sciber-s*) heath *or* moor.
RESK-YMER,-IMER,great dog(*ci mear*)
race, *Car.* ; great dog marsh *or*
fen, *H.*, heath *or* moor.
RESOGAN, *i.q.* ROSAGAN.
RES-OGOE, -UGGA, *i.q.* ROSUGGA.
RESOLLA, ? *i.q.* ROSCOLLA.
RESOON, slippery (*rees*) moor (*gwon*),
T.C. ; ? down (*gwon*) heath.
RESORES, ??*i.q.* RESURRANS.
RESPARVA, *i.q.* ROSEPARVA.
RESPERWITH, 16 *cent.*, ? pear-trees'
(*perwith*) heath *or* moor.
RESPR-IN, -YN, ? king's (*brenin*, *w.*) h.

2M

RESTA, *i.q.* TREREST, *Jo.C.*

RESTALL-ICK, -OCK, ? TALLICK heath.

RESTIGAN, ? Digain's (*w.*) heath.

RESTINEAS, ? ? deer (*danas, w.*) heath.

RESTORMEL, = *res tor meal,* the king's tower hill, *Wh.*; a bellyful of money, a place of honey, *Sc.* ! ! ? mole-hill (*turumel, B.*) heath.

RESTOWRICK, *i.q.* ROSTOWRACK.

RESTRONG-ET, -ETH, -UETH, *o.* -AS, valley with the deep (*gwys, w.*) promontory (*tron*), *T.*; valley of the wood (*cuit*) promontory, *Dr.*

RESUDGIAN, *i.q.* ROSOGGAN, *Pr.*; ? ox (*udzheon*) heath.

RESUGGAN, *i.q.* ROSOGAN.

RESURRA, ? *i.q.* ROSEWORTHY.

RESURRANS, *i.q.* ROSURRANCE.

RESVINE, *i.q.* ROSEVINE.

RET, *w.B.m.*, ? *i.q.* READ.

RET-ALLACK, -ALLICK, -ILLOCK (*n.f.*), -OLLOCK, a very (*re-*) high place (*tallic*), *or* with many pits (*tollic*), *Pr.*; *or, i.q.* RESTALLICK, &c.

RETER-GH, -TH, the exceeding (*re*) strict charge *or* command; *or,* the exceeding *or* too much nipple, teat, *or* udder, *H.* !

RETHOGGA, the bearing (*doga,* to bear) *or* fruitful town (*tre*), *Po.*; ? *i.q.* TRYTHOGGA.

REVELL,*o.n.f.*,? = *yr evel,*the smithy,*w.*

REW, ? = *rhiw,* the slope, *w.*

REYN-ALDS, -OLDS, *n.f., i.q.* REGIN-ALDUS, powerful judgment, *t., Y.*

REZARE, *i.q.* RESAIR.

RHEEN CROFT, ? hill (*ryn*) croft.

RHI, RI, chief, prince, king (*ri, ga.*), *Beal.*

RIALOBRAN, *m.s. Madron,* royal (*rial*) prince (*bren*), *B.*

RIBBERY, *n.f.*, ? = *ripere,* a reaper, *s.*

RICE, *n.f., i.q.* REECE.

RIC-HARDS, -KARDS, *n.f., i.q.* RICK-ARDUS, stern (*hard*) king (*ryce*),*s.,Y.*

RICKET PARK, ? Rickard's close.

RIDGOVEAN, ? little (*bean*) ridge.

RIDULPHUS, *t.d.d.,* red (*reid, s.*) wolf (*ulf, s.*), *t.*

RILLATON, royal (*riol*) town.

RINGBURY, round earthwork, *t.*

RINGFORD, ? ford by the round, *t.*

RINGLE, ? grove (*celli*) hill (*ryn*).

RINGS, ? rounds, *or* hills (*ryn-s*).

RINSEY, ? dry (*sech*) hill.

RIOL, *s.B.m.,* ? *i.q.* RIOVAL, = king Howel, *A. Butler.*

RIPPER, *n.f.*, ? *i.q.* RIBBERY.

RIT, ? *s.B.m.,* ? *i.q.* RET.

RIVIERE, great (*mear*) slope (*rhiw, w.*), *M'L.,* or hill (*ryn*); = *rywier,* river, *a., B.*

ROACH, *from* St. Roche, *T.*; *o.* LA ROCHE, the rock, *f.*; *p.s.* St. Goemandus *or* Conandus, *O.*

ROAD-A, -Y, ? road close (*hay*), *t.*

ROAS AN GEAN, ? the giant's (*ghean, B.*), *or* ox (*udzheon*) heath.

ROB-ARTES,-ERTS,*n.f., o.* ROTBERTUS, bright (*beort*) fame (*hrod*), *t.*

ROCK-HAY, rock close (*hay*).

ROCKSEY, rocks' close (*hay*).

ROD PARK, *road* close (*parc*).

ROGERS, *n.f., i.q.* ROGERUS, *t.d.d.,* spear (*ger*) of fame (*hrod*), *t., Y.*

ROMANE, *n.f.*, ? *from* ST. RUAN.

ROOSE, *i.q.* ROS.

ROPE HAWN, = *rope haven, t.*

ROS, a heath, *Wh.*; peatland, moor, common, mountain meadow,*R. IV.*; a valley, *or* dale between hills, *Pr.*; *also,* a wheel.

ROSAGAN, *n.f.,* white (*can*) valley, *Gibson*; *i.q.* ROSOGAN.

ROSAMUNDI, *i.q.* ROSEMUNDY.

ROSANE, ? little (*vean*) heath.

ROS AN HALE, ? the (*an*) moor (*hal*) *or* river (*heyl*) heath, &c.

ROSA PARK, heath close (*parc*).

ROSARRICK, ? *i.q.* ROSCARR-EK,-ICK, -OCK, valley of the brook (*carrog*), *Pr.*; ? rock (*carrag*) heath; *d.d.* ROSCARRETT.

ROSCARREK BIGAN, little (*bichan*) R.

ROSAWEN, ? heath of the hole (*sawan*).

ROSCAS-OWE, -SA, ROSCASSA, *i.q.* ROSECASSA.

ROSCOLL-A, -AS, lower or bottom (*golla, goles*) heath ; or, *i.q.*

ROSCOR-LA, -LAN, ? grave-yard (*corhlan*), or sheep-fold (*corlan*) heath.

ROSCORFLE, ? corpse-place (*corfle*) h.

ROSCORWELL, ? sheep (*caor*) field (*gweal*), or *well* heath ; or, Gurhavel's (*w.*) heath or moor.

ROSCOW, *n.f.*, ? *i.q* ROSCROW, *Ch.*

ROSCRADDOCK, CRADOCK'S heath.

ROSCREEGE, the valley cross, *Pr.* ; barrow (*creeg*) vale, *Po.*, or heath.

ROSCROGG-AN, -EN, the valley of shells (*cregyn*), *Pr.*

ROSCR-OW, -OWA, valley cross (*crows*), *T.* ; valley of the cross, *Pr.* ; ? hovel (*crow*) heath or moor.

ROSCR-UGE, -OUGE, *n.f.*, *i.q.* ROSCROWGEY, CROWGIE heath.

ROSCROWAN, valley or moor of the cross, *T.C.* ; ? gravel (*growan*) h.

ROSCULLION, ? *i.q.* ROSCELYN.

ROSE, *i.q.* ROS.

R. A BARGUS, the kite's (*barges*) h.

R. ANBEAGLE, the (*an*) shepherd or herdsman's (*bygel*) heath.

R. AN DOUR, the water (*dour*) heath.

R. AN-DRANACK, -DRENNICK, the thorny (*draenic*) heath.

R. AN GROUZ, the cross (*crows*) heath.

R. AN HALE, *i.q.* ROS AN HAL.

R. AN PARS, ? the thicket (*brows*) h.

R.-ARTH, -ATH, ? high (*arth*) heath.

R. BROASE, *i.q.* ROSE AN PARS.

R. CADG-ELL, -HILL, -WELL, moor camp hill, *C.* ; *i.q.* ROSKESTAL, *T.C.*

R.-CASSA, -COSSA, the woody (*cosic*) valley, *T.* ; ? dirty (*gasa*) heath.

R.-CREEG, *n.f.*, -CREGG, *i.q.* ROSCREEG.

R. EGL-ESS, -OS, church (*eglos*) heath.

R. EN HALE, ? *i.q.* ROS AN HAL.

R. ETH, = *rhosydh*, heathy ground (*R.*), *B.* ; or, a reduplication.

ROSE-HILL, *i.q.* ROSKESTAL, *T.C.*

R. JANE, ? ox (*udzheon*) heath.

R. KILL-EY, -Y, *i.q.* ROSKELLY.

R. LADDE-RN, -NN, robbers' (*laddron*) heath ; or, *i.q.*

R. LADN, bank (*gladn*), or broad (*ledan*) heath or moor.

R. LAND, heath land.*

R. LATH, ? slaughter (*ladh*) heath.

R. LATHENS, ? heath banks (*ladn-s*).

R.-LIAN, -LYON, vale in open view (*sull*) ; ? SULIENN'S heath.

R. LVUY, ? Ailvyw's (*w.*) heath.

R. LYN, ? lake (*lyn*), or grove (*llwyn, w.*) heath ; or, *i.q.* ROSELIAN.

R. MA-IN, -YN, stone (*maen*), or narrow (*main, w.*) heath or moor.

R. MANNON, ? butter (*menen*) heath.

R. MARROW, dead-man's (*marow*) h.

R. MEL-IN, -LAN, -LAND, -LEN, -LYN, ? mill (*melin*), or violets' (*meillion*), or clover (*meillion, w.*) heath.

R. MENEW-AS, -ES, ? outside (*aves*) or outer stone (*maen*) heath.

R. MENOWETH, new (*nowydh*) stone h.

R.-MERGY, -MORGY, -MURGY, valley near the sea, *T.C.* ; ? dog-fish (*morgi*) heath or moor.

R. MERRIN, blackberry (*moran dhiu*) vale, *Pr.* ; ? Mervyn's (*w.*) heath.

R. MINE, ? stone (*maen*) heath.

R. MOD-ERISS, -RIS, -ERETH, -REUY, the heath with the circle (*moderuy*, a bracelet).

R. MOON, ? peat (*mawn*) heath.

R. MORAN, *i.q.* ROSEMERRIN.

R. MORDER, valley near the sea-water (*mor dour*), *Pr.* ; ? water land (*mor dir*), *R.IV.*

R. MORE, great (*maur*) moor, *R.IV.*

R. MORRIN, vale of blackberries, *Bl.*

R. MULLION, violet moor, *C.*

R. MUNDY, ? black-stones' (*myen du*),

---

* Heath, mountain-land, or sheep walk, *Wh.*; district or land of the moor, *C.*; from *rhos*, a well watered plain, *Gough*; "though the original of the name came as master Camden noted from his former *thickets*, yet his present estate resembleth a *flowrie* effect (*rhos*, roses, *w.*)," *Car.* Besides the district thus called, there are many fields bearing the name of ROSE LAND, *i.e.* heath or moor field; as also ROSE-FIELD, -DOWN, -DALE, -GARDEN, -MARSH, -MOOR, -MEADOW, -CROFT, -PARK, -HAM, &c., &c.

or peat-house (*mawndy*), *or* Mundy's heath *or* moor *or* valley.

ROSE-NANNON, ? heath of the ash-tree (*an onnan*).

R. NEA, ? Ane's (*w.*) heath ; *or*, heath by the enclosure (*an hay*).

R. NITH-AN, -EN, -ON, the furze (*an eithin*) heath *or* moor.

R. NNICK, ? summer (*hanic*) heath.

R. NOWETH, new (*nowydh*) heath.

R. NUN, ? heath of the down (*an oon*) ; *or*, Nonna's heath.

R. NURDEN, ? heath of the furze-brake (*an redanan*).

R. NVALE, ? the *valley* heath.

R. NVEAR, the great (*mear*) heath.

R. PANNEL, broom (*banal*) heath.

R. PARVA, ? pasture (*porfa, w.* heath.

R. PEATH, draw-well (*peeth*) heath.

R. PLETHA, the moor of the house of the tribes (*bod leithow*), *T.C.* ; *or*, heath of cursing (*molytha*).

R. RRAN-CE, -S, ? ? lambs' (*eanes*) long (*hir*) heath *or* moor.

R.-RROW, -SERROW, ? higher (*urra* = *wartha*) heath *or* moor.

R. SILIAN, *i.q.* ROSELIAN.

R. SU-E, -EA, ? black (*zu* = *du*) heath.

R. TAIL, ? manure (*teil*) heath.

R. TEAGUE, fair (*teg*) heath.

R. UNDLE, ? the *dale* heath.

R. VALLAN, apple-tree (*avallen*) h.

R. VANNION, ? ? the heath with the caves *or* hollows (*guagion, Pr.*).

R. VANNOCK, ? turbary (*mawnoy, w.*) moor ; *or*, *i.q.* ROSEWARRICK.

R. VEAL, *n.f.*, calves' valley, *Ch.*

R. VEAN, little (*bean*) heath.

R. VE-ARE, -ERE, -OR, -RE, great h.

R. VELLAN, *i.q.* ROSEMELIN.

R. VETH, grave (*bedh*) heath.

R. VI-DNEY, -THNEY, ? lesser (*behedna* = *behenna*) heath *or* moor.

R.-VIN, -VINE, ? white (*gwyn*), *or* little (*bihan*), *or* stone (*maen*) heath.

R. VINNICK, stony (*maenic*) heath.

R. WALL, ? high (*uhal*) heath.

R. WAR-N, -NE, spreading *or* extensive moor, *C.* ; ? alder (*gwarn*) heath.

ROSE WAR-RICK, -WICK, the marshy (*gwarnic*) vale, *J.B.*

R. WEDDEN, ? tree (*gwedhen*) heath.

R. WELL, ? field (*gweal*) heath.

R. WEN, ? down (*guen*) heath.

R.-WICK, -WEEK, *i.q.* ROSUICK.

R.-WIDN, -WIN, -WYN, ? white (*gwyn*), *or* little (*widden, m.c.*) heath.

R. WOON, down (*gwon*) heath.

R. WORTH, green (*gwyrdh*) valley, *T.* ; ? high (*warth*) heath *or* moor.

R. WORTHY, ? higher (*wartha*) heath.

ROSILLIAN, *i.q.* ROSELLIAN.

ROSKADINNACK, *i.q.* RESKADINNICK.

ROSKARNON, valley of the high rock, *Pr.* ; ? CARNON heath.

ROSKEAR, the lovely (*care*, to love) vale, *Pr.* ; ? castle (*caer*) heath.

ROSKEARN, ? alder (*gwern*) heath.

ROSKE-EN, -N, ? ridge (*cein*) heath.

ROSKEIF, ? ditch (*keif, M'L.*) heath.

ROSK-ELLY, -ILLY, -ILLEY, the grove (*celli*) in the valley, *Pr.* ; ? grove heath *or* moor *or* vale.

ROSKENNAL, ? Cynwal's (*w.*) heath.

ROSKENNING, ? Cennyn's (*w.*) heath.

ROSKERROW, ? camps' (*caerau*) h.

ROSKESTAL, valley of the castle, *Po.* ; ? castle heath *or* moor.

ROS-KILLIN, *o.* -CELYN, -CHELYN, -QUELIN, ? holly (*celin*) heath.

ROSKORLA, *i.q.* ROSCORLA.

ROSKORWELL, *i.q.* ROSCORWELL.

ROSKROW, *n.f., i.q.* ROSCROW.

ROSKR-OWGIE, -UGE, *i.q.* ROSCROUGE.

ROSKURO-H, -K, hag's (*gwrach, w.*) moor, *R.W.* ; *or, i.q.* ROSCROW.

ROSKYMER, *i.q.* RESKYMER.

ROSM-ERAN, -ORAN, *i.q.* ROSEMERRIN.

ROSMINVET, *d.d.*, ? brushwood (*man-wydd, w.*) heath *or* moor.

ROSMODREVY, *i.q.* ROSEMODERISS.

ROSNITHON, *i.q.* ROSENITHAN.

ROSOGAN, the moist (*sog-an*) valley, *Pr.* ; (*agen*, a cleft, chink, *w.*).

ROSOMON, *n.f., i.q.* ROSEMOON.

ROSPREEVE, *n.f.*, ? *i.q.* ROSEPARVA.

ROSRAGE, ? *i.q.* ROSKUROK.

ROSS, *n.f., i.q.* ROS.

ROSSWICK, *i.q.* ROSUICK.
ROSTARLOCK, ? Tallwch's (*w.*) heath.
ROSTEAGE, fair (*teg*) valley, *Pr.*
ROS-TER, -SITER, *n.f.*, = *ros tir*, moor land, *R. W.* ; *or*, Uther's (*w.*) heath.
ROSTIDGEON, ? DITCHEN heath.
ROSTOCRACK, ? watery (*douric*) h.
ROSTOWDA, ? Tudur's (*w.*) heath.
ROSUGGA, *i.q.* ROSOGAN. *Pr.*
ROS-UICK, -WICK, valley of the village, port, or haven (*gwic*), *Pr.*
ROSURRAN-CE, -S, ? ? lambs' (*eanes*) higher (*urra* = *wartha*) heath.
ROSURROW, ? higher heath.
ROSVEAN, *i.q.* ROSEVEAN.
ROSVE-AR, -ER, -OR, great heath.
ROSWARNE, *i.q.* ROSEWARN.
ROSWARTHICK, *n.f.*, ? cows' (*gwarthec*, *w.*) heath ; *or*, *i.q.* ROSEWORTHY.
ROSWARVA, *n.f.*, ? *i.q.* ROSEWORTHY.
ROSY, *n.f.*, ? = *rhosydh*, moors, *w.*, *R. W.*
ROTHER, *n.f.*, ? *i.q.* RUTH DOWER.
ROTHERON, ? = *rhiw derwen*, the slope of the oak.
ROUGH, *n.f.*, ? *i.q.* RALPH.
ROUN-CEVALL, -SEVALE, ? the vale of the horse (*ronse, a.*), *or* of the bramble-thicket (*raunse, f., W.B.*); *or*, = *n.f.* ROUNS-AVILLE, -EVELL, -WELL (*ville*, town), *f.*
ROUNDAGO, ? the round *or* camp, *t.*
ROUNDA PARK, round close, *t.*
ROUND BALL, ? round hill, *t.*
R.-BURY, -ABERRY, the round earthwork (*bury*), *t.*
R. CROFT, ? hill (*ryn*) croft, *T.C.*
R. HAM, ? castle meadow (*ham, s.*).
R. OUTH, ? = *run nowydh*, new hill.
ROUNDY PARK, *i.q.* ROUNDA PARK.
ROUNSLEY ? Rumon's pasture, *t.*
ROUSE, *i.q.* ROS *or* ROWSE.
R. ROSE, ? red (*rooz*) moor (*ros*).
ROUTH MOOR, red (*rudh*) moor.

ROVIER, *i.q.* RIVIER.
ROWAN COVE, ? St. Rumon's cove.
ROW-DEN, -DON, -DOWN, ? rough (*row, m.c.*) down *or* hill (*dun*).
ROWDY, ? = *rhiw dy*, house slope.
ROWE, *n.f.*, *i.q.* RALPH.
ROW-ELL, -LE, *n.f.*, = Raoul, house wolf, *t., Y.* ; ? *i.q.* RIDULPHUS.
ROWLAND, rough land *or* field, *t.*
ROWLING, *n.f.*, *dim. of* ROWELL.
ROWLY, rough pasture (*lea, t.*).
ROW-PARK, -POCK, rough close, *t.*
ROWSE, *n.f.*, ? = *rooz*, red.
ROW-, ROUGH-TOR, rough (*huero*) hill, *B.* ; = *riogh-tor*, king tor, *ga., Beal* ; red (*rudh*) tor, *R.S.H.*
ROYDON, ? king's (*ruy*) hill (*dun*).
RUALLEN, = *rhiw a llyn*, the declivity *or* slope by the lake *or* stream, *M'L.*
RUAN, *from p.s.* St. Rumon, *O.**
RUBERRY, ? slope (*rhiw, w.*) of the hill (*bre*).
RUD-ALL, -DLE, -HALL, *n.f.*, ? red (*rudh*) moor *or* hill (*hal*) ; *or*, *i.q.* RIDULPHUS, *t.*
RUDHERS, ? ROTHER'S [farm].
RUDLEY, ? ford (*ryd*) place (*le*).
RUDLIFF, *n.f.*, ? red cliff, *t.*
RUDMOOR, red moor, *t.*
RUFFY, ? rough enclosure (*hay*), *t.*
RU-IN, -N, -NE, ? *i.q.* REEN.
RULE, *n.f.*, ? *i.q.* ROWELL.
RUM, *s.B.m.*, a giant, *t., F.*
RUMFORD, RUM'S ford, *t.*
RUMUN, *B.m.*, ? the Roman.
RUND-AL, -LE, ? *i.q.* Arundel.
RUNE BRAWS, ? big (*bras*) hill (*run*).
RUNG, *i.q.* REEN.
RUN GUAY, hill by the water (*gwy*).
RUNNALLS, *n.f.*, *i.q.* REYNOLDS.
RUSCARROCK, *i.q.* ROSCARROCK.
RUSDEN, *n.f.*, ? rush vale (*denu, s.*), *t.*
RUSE, (RUSH, *n.f.*), *i.q.* ROSE.

---

* RUAN LANIHORNE, the church (*lan*) of St. Rumon in the angle (*corn*), *Wh.* ; the iron (*haiarn*) church of St. Rumon, *Po.* ; the iron church near the river (*ruan*), *Pr.* ; St. Rumon's by the horn-shaped enclosure (*lan*), *C.* ; RUAN MAJOR & MINOR, St. Rumon's the greater and the less (*lat.*), *Po.* ; RUAN MAJOR, the great river, RUAN MINOR, the less river, *Pr.* ! ! RUANI is found on the *maen scryfa*, Michell = royal, *Po.*

RUSHLADE, *rushy* water-course (*leat*), *t.*
RUSHY, *rush* close (*hay*), *t.*
RUSSELYN, *i.q.* ROSKILLIN.
RUTH DOWER, red (*rudh*) water (*dour*)
RUTHERN, *i.q.* ROTHERN.
RUXMOORE, ? rush (*risc, s.*) moor, *t.*
RUZZ-A, -AH, red (*rooz*) close (*hay*).
RYALTON, royal (*riol,* town, *Pr.*
RYE-ARISH, -EARRISH, rye stubble (*ersc, s.*) field.
RYE PARK, rye close (*parc*).
RYES HILL, ? middle (*cres*) hill.
RYLAND, rye land *or* field.
RYNE HILL, *a reduplication.*
RYT, *B.m., i.q.* READ.
RYVIER, *i.q.* RIVIER.

SADGELL, SAGELL, SADGEWELL, ? sedge hill *or* well, *t.*
SADGE-, SAGE-MOOR, *n.f.,* sedge moor, *t.*
SAFFRON PARK, *i.q.* PARK SAFFRAN.
SAINGUILANT, *e.d.d.,* SANGUILAND, *d.d.,* ? *i.q.* ST. GLUVIAS *or* ST. GENNYS.
SAINT-ADWEN, -ATHAWYN, -ANDE-WIN, ? = *Athelwine,* noble friend, *s., Y.; now* ADVENT, *v.* S. ANNE.
S. AGNES, *from p.s.* (pure, *gr.*).
S. ALDHELM (*chapel*), noble (*adel*) helmet (*helm*), *s.*
S. ALLEN, *from p.s.* S. ALUNUS *or* Elwinus, *O.,* = elf friend, *s., Y.; or,* S. Alun (*a.s.*); the (*an*) moor (*hal*) saint, *Hi.; or,* church (*lan*) moor.
S. AMBRUSCA (*ch.*), ? *i.q.* Ambrose, immortal, *gr.*
S. ANDREW, *Andreas,* a stout *or* strong man, *gr.; see* CALSTOCK.
S. ANIANUS (*ch.*), ? = *uniawn.* just, *w.*
S. ANIETUS, *e.d.d., i.q.* S. NEOTUS.
S. ANTHONY, *from p.s.* S. ANTONI-US *or* -NUS, inestimable, *lat., Y.*
S. AUBYN, *n.f., o.* SANTALBIN, SENT-ABYN, ? = *albinus,* white, *lat.*
S. AUS-TELL, -TLE, *from p.s.* S. Aus-tolus, *O.;* ? *i.q.* Hawystl, *w.s.;*

holy hostelry, *H.;* holy altar, *Po.*
SAINT BARRE, *i.q.* S. FIM-, FIN-BAR-RUS.
S. BARTHOLOMEW, son of furrows, *h.* *See* WARLEGGON, LOSTWITHIEL, &c.
S. BENNETT'S (*ch.*), *i.q.* S. *Benedictus,* blessed, *lat.*
S. BERINUS, *W.W.,* ? = *Bertwine,* bright friend, *t.; or, i.q.* S. Ber-wyn, *w.*
S. BLAZEY, *from p.s.* S. Blazius, lisper, *lat.*
S. BREACA, *see* BREAGE.
S. BREWARD, *from p.s.* S. Brueredus, *O.,* Bp. Brewer, *H.; from bruyere,* heath, *f., T.*
S. BRIDGET (*ch*), = *Brighid,* strength, *i., Y.*
S. BRIOCUS, ? = *breach,* spotted, *i.;* *see* BREOCK.
S. BUDOCUS, *see* BUDOCK.
S. BURYAN, *from p.s.* S. BURIANA, *O.*
S. CAD-IX, -OX, *i.q.* S. CYRICUS, *Ly.*
S. CARANTOCUS, ? = *coronedig,* crown-ed, *w.; see* CRANTOCK.
S. CHRISTINA (*ch.*), christian, *lat.*
S. CHYGWIDDEN, holy white (*gwydn*) Thursday (*de Jeu*), *Dr.*
S. CLEA-, CLE-THER, *from p.s.* S. Cle-derus, *O.,* = *clydwr,* a defence, *R.W.; cledher,* fencer *or* gladiator, *T.*
S. CLEER, *from p.s.* S. Clarus, *O.,* bright, renowned, *lat.*
S. CLEMENT'S, *from p.s.* S. Clement, *O.,* gentle, merciful, *lat.*
S. COANUS, *p.s.* of MERTHER, *O.*
S. COLAN, *from p.s.* S. Colanus, *O.,* ? little (*vean*) dove (*colom*).
S. COLUMB, *from p.s.* S. Columba, the dove, *lat.*
S. CON-AN, -ANDUS, *see* ROACH.
S. CONGAR (*ch.*), ? *i.q.* Concar (*w.s.*).
S. CONOGLASIUS, (*Bishop*), grey (*glas*) [haired] lord (*con*), *Wh.*
S. CONSTANTINUS, firm, *lat.; see* CONSTANTINE.
S. COO-SE, -Z, holy wood (*cus*), *Pr.*
S. CORENTINUS, *see* CURY.
S. CORNELIUS, *see* CORNELLY.

SAINT CRADOC (*ch.*), *i.q. Caradawg,* beloved, *w.*

S. CREWENA, *see* CROWAN.

S. CRIDA, *see* CREED.

S. CUBY, *i.q.* S. KEBY.

S. CUTHBERT, noted splendour, *t.*, *Y.* ; *see* CUBERT.

S. CYR-ICUS, -US (*ch.*), ? *cyriacos,* Lord's-day born, *gr.*

S.-DACHUN,-DACUNUS, ?deacon, *gr.* ; *or, i.q.* S. *Decumanus,* farmer of tithes, *lat.*

S. DAVID, beloved, darling, *h.* ; *see* DAVIDSTOWE.

S.-DAY, *o.* -DAYE, -DYE, *from p.s.* S. Dye, Bp. of Nievre, *Ly.* ; *from* [Holy Trini]*tye, c.d., O.*

S. DENNIS, *from p.s.* S. Dionysius; *or,* camp (*dinas*) saint, *Hi.*

S. DERWE (*ch.*), ? = *deru wy,* the oak by the water.

S. DOGMAEL (*ch.*), ? = *w.* S. Dogfael.

S. DOMINICK, *from p.s.* S. Dominica, *O.,* Lord's-day born, *lat.*

S. DUNSTAN, *see* LANLIVERY.

S.-EAST, -EWST, *i.q.* S. JUST.

S. EDE, 14 *cent., i.q.* S. ISSEY.

S. EDMUND'S, rich (*ead*) protection (*mund*), *t., Y.*

S. ELECTA (*ch.*), elect lady, *lat.*

S. ENDELLION, *from p.s.* S. Endellienta, *O.,* Delian *or* Telian, *T.*

S. ENODER, *from p.s.* S. Ennodorus, *O., i.q.* S. Athenadorus, *T.,* ? = Winheder (*w.s.*) ; holy soul(*ene*) water (*dour*), *or* town (*tre*), *H.* !

S. ENODOCK, *from p.s.* S. Gwinodec, ? *i.q.* CONETOCUS *or* CUNAIDO.

S. ERME, *from p.s.* S. Hermes.

S. ERN-EY, -A, -E, holy (*san*) hour (*urna* !) *or* eagle (*erne, t.*), *T.* ; *p.s.* not known.

S. ERTH *or* ERCY, *B., v.* E-ARTH, *from p.s.* S. Ercus, *O.* ; holy *earth, i.e.* ground, *H.*

S. ERVAN, ? *from* S. Erbin (*w.*) ; a litany, *H.* ; *p.s.* S. Hermes, *O.*

S. ETHELRED (*ch.*), noble (*adel, s.*) threat (*thrydh, s.*), *t.*

SAINT EVAL, *from p.s.* S. Uvelus, *O.* ; ? *i.q.* S. Ewall, = *Ethelwald,* noble power, *t.* ; *aval,* an apple, *Dr.*

S. EVE, *i.q.* S. IVE.

S. EWE, *from p.s.* S. Ewa *or* Eustachius, *O.,* happy in harvest, *gr., Y.*

S. EW-INUS, -NY, ? = *Unchi,* contentious, *i.* ; *see* CROWAN, REDRUTH.

S. EYE, 14 *cent., i.q.* S. IVES.

S. FELICITAS, happiness, *lat.* ; *see* PHILLACK.

S. FEOCA, *see* FEOCK.

S. FIDES (*lat.*), *or* S. FAITH (*ch.*).

S. FILIUS, *see* PHILLEIGH.

S.-FIM-, -FIN-BARRUS, fine hair, *i.* ; *p.s.* of FOWEY, *O.*

S. FINGAR (*i.*), *i.q.* GWINEAR, *Wh.*

S. FRANCIS (*ch.*), free, *t., Y.*

S. GABRIEL (*ch.*), God's hero, *h.*

S. GENNYS, *from p.s.* S. Geniscius, *O.* ; *d.d.* SANGUINAS.

S. GEORGE, tiller of the ground, *gr.* ; *see* TRENEGLOS.

S. GERRANS, *from p.s.* S. GERRENDUS.

S. GERMANS, *from p.s.* S. Germanus.

S. GERMOCHUS, *see* GERMOE.

S. GI-DGEY, -GGY, *i.q.* ZANZIDGIE.

S. GINOKES, *Le., i.q.* S. WINNOW.

S. GLUVIAS, *from p.s.* S. Gluviacus, *O.,* ? *i.q.* Gluwys Cerniw, *w.* ; *from glewas,* to hear, *H.*

S. GOEMANDUS,' *see* ROACH.

S. GORAN, *i.q.* GORRAN.

S. GOTHIANUS, *see* GWITHIAN.

S. GRACE, *see* PROBUS.

S.-GRADE, -GRADUS, *see* GRADE.

S. GREGORY, watchman, *gr.* ; *see* TRENEGLOS.

S. GUDWAL, *see* GULVAL.

S. GUERYR, physician, *Cam.*

S. GUNNET, *i.q.* S. GUNDRED, war council, *t., Y.* ; *or, i.q.* CUNAIDO.

S. GUNGER, ? *i.q.* Cengor, *w.s.*

S. GWINEDOC, *i.q. Gweinidoc,* a minister, *w., R.IV.* ; *see* S. ENODOCK.

S. HELENA, light, bright, *gr., Y.* ; *see* HELLAND.

S. HELIE, *see* EGLOSHEYLE.

S. HENRY (*ch.*) home rule, *t.*

SAINT HERMES, *see* S. ERME; S. ERVAN.

S. HERYGH, *i.q.* S. ERTH, *Wh.*

S. HILARY, *from p.s.* S. Ilarius, *O.*, cheerful, *lat.*

S.-HUGH, -HUGO, mind, *t.*, *Y.*, *p.s.* of QUETHIOCK, *O.*

S.-HYA, -IA, *see* S. IVES.

S. IDA, thirsty, *k.*, rich, happy, *t.*, *Y.*; *see* MEVAGISSEY; S. ISSEY.

S. ILDIERNA, *see* LANSALLOS.

S. ILDUICTUS (*ch.*), *i.q.* ILLTUT, *w.*

S. ILLICK (*ch.*) *same*; or, = Alexander.

S. ILLOGANUS, *see* ILLOGAN.

S. ING-ANGER,-UNGER, *i.q.* S. GUNGER or Gangel = Wingel, *Wh.*

S. ISSEY, *from* S. Yse. *w.*, *Wh.*; *p.s.* SS. Ida & Lyda, *J.Ca.*

S. IVE, *from p.s.* S. Ivo, pers., *O.*

S. IVES, *from p.s.* S. Hya, Ia, or Ya, *O.*

S. JACOBUS (*lat.*), a supplanter (*h.*); *see* TREGONY; *i.q.*

S. JAMES, *see* JACOBSTOW.

S. JANUARIUS [*with* S. KEBY], *p.s.* of Cuby, *Po.*; ? door keeper, *lat.*; or, = *Gwenhwyfar*, white wave, *w.*

S. JOHN (Baptist), *from p.s.*, *O.*

S. JULIAN, *see* MAKER.

S. JULIOT, *v.* JILT, *from p.s.* S. JULITTA, *O.*

S. JUST, *from p.s.* S. Justus, *O.*

S. KANANC, *i.q.* LELANT, *Wh.*

S. KEA, *i.q.* KEA.

S. KEBY *or* KEBIUS, ? ? *i.q.* [Ja]*cobus*; *see* CUBY.

S. KENWYN, *see* KENWYN.

S. KERI, *see* EGLOSKERRY.

S. KEVERNE, *from p.s.* S. Keveran or Kieran, *O.*, black, *i.*; ? *i.q.* S. PIERANUS, *Le.*; *e.d.d.* SANCTI ACHEBRANNI.

S. KEW (*p.s.* unknown), ? S. Keby, *T.*; or, *i.q. w.* S. Kiwa.

S. KEYNE, *from p.s.* S. Keyna, a jewel, *Y.*

S. LADOCA, *see* LADOCK.

S. LALANT, *W.W.*, *i.q.* LELANT, *Wh.*

S. LAUDUS (*ch.*), ? *i.q.* S. *Laudatus*, praised, *lat.*

SAINT LAWRENCE, (*ch.*) laurel, *lat.*

S. LEOFSTAN, *B.m.*, beloved stone, *s.*

S. LEONARD'S (*ch.*) lion strong, *t.*

S. LEVAN, *from p.s.* S. Livinus, *O.*

S. LUDOWANUS, *see* LUDGVAN.

S. MABE, *see* MABE.

S. MABYN, *from p.s.* St. Mabena, *O.*

S. MACHUTUS, *see* S. MAWES.

S. MADERNUS, *see* MADRON.

S. MAGDALEN (*ch.*), *from* S. MARY.

S. MANACCUS, ? = *manach*, a monk; *see* LANREATH.

S. MARCELLIANA, *see* TINTAGEL.

S. MARGETS, *i.q.* S. MARGARET'S.

S. MARTIN, *from p.s.* (= Mars, *Y.*).

S. MARUAN, ? = *morwyn*, a maid, virgin, *w.*; *see* LAMORRAN; ? *i.q.*

S. MARY, *alias* S. MAWES, *Car.*

S. MATERIANA, *see* TINTAGEL.

S. MAUGANUS, ? = MORGAN; or, *i.q.* Meugan *or* Meigan, *w.s.*; *see* MAWGAN.

S. MAUNANUS, *see* MAWNAN.

S. MAWES (or MAUDITUS, *O.*, or MARY, *Car.*), ? *from p.s.* S. Machutus, Machu, Maclovius, *or* Malo, *Wh.*; *from maw*, a boy, *A. Butler.*

S. MELLION, *from p.s.* S. Mellanus, *O.*; Mellyan, *Wh.*

S. MERIADOCUS, ? = *Meireadwg*, sea protector, *w.*; *see* CAMBORN.

S. MERRYN, *from p.s.* S. Marina, *O.*; ? *i.q.* S. Merin *or* Merini, *w.*

S. MERTHIANA, *see* MINSTER.

S. MEUBREDUS, *see* CARDINHAM.

S. MEWA, *see* MEVAGISSEY.

S. MEWAN, *from p.s.* S. Mewanus, *O.*

S. MICHAEL-CARHAYES, -PENKIVEL, -'S MOUNT, &c., *from p.s.*

S. MILORUS, (*Meilyr, w.*), *see* MYLOR.

S. MINVER, *from p.s.* S. MENEFRIDA, *O.*, ? *Maginfred*, powerful peace, *t.*, *Y.*

S. MORWENNA, *see* MORWINSTOW.

S. MYDBARD, *i.q.* S. MEUBREDUS, *Wh.*

S. NEDDIE, *i.q.* S. ENODER, *Nord.*

S. NEOT'S, *from p.s.* S. Neotus, *O.*, compulsion, *t.*, *Y.*

S. NEWELINA, *see* NEWLYN.

SAINT NICHOLAS, *see* FOWEY, &c.

S. NIGHTON'S KIEVE, ? the retreat (*cuddva, w.*) of S. Nectan.

S.-NONN,-NONNA,-NONNITA,-NUNN, nun; *or,* ninth, *lat., Y.; p.s.* ALTARNUN.

S. OLAVE, = *Aulaf or* Olaf, ancestor's relic, *t., Y.; see* POUGHILL.

S. PANCRAS, ? all powerful, *gr.*; ? *now* S. Mary's, Truro, *Wh.*

S. PATERNUS, fatherly, *lat.*; ? *i.q.* S. Padarn, *w.; see* PETHERWIN.

S. PAULINUS, *see* PAUL.

S. PETER, rock, *gr.; see* SHEVIOCK.

S. PETROCK, ? little (*-oc*) Peter; *see* PADSTOW, BODMIN, PETHERICK.

S. PHILLACK, PHILLEIGH, PIALA, &c.; *see* PHILLACK, *note.*

S. PICR-AS, -OUS, ?*.i.q.* S. PIRANUS, *Max M.; or,* S. PANCRAS.

S. PINNOCK, *from p.s.* S. PYNOCUS,*O.*

S. PIRANUS, *see* PERRAN.

S. PROBUS, just, *lat.; see* PROBUS.

S. PROT-US, -ASIUS, *v.* PRATT, *see* BLISLAND.

S. QUODRUS, 14 *cent.,* ? *i.q.* CUBERT.

S. RUAN, *see* RUAN.

S. SAMPSON, *from shemesh,* sun, *h.*; *see* GOLANT.

S. SANCREDUS, *see* SANCREED.

S. SATIVOLA, *see* LANEAST.

S. SAVIERY, ? St. Saviour's (*ch.*) enclosure (*hay*).

S. SENNARA, *see* ZENNOR.

S. SENNINUS, *see* SENNEN.

S. SID-, SITH-UINUS, *see* SITHNEY, *O.*; ? *i.q. Swithun,* strong (*swith*) friend, *t., Y.*

S. SILVANUS (*ch.*), living in a wood, *lat., Y.*

S. SIRUS, *i.q.* S. CYRIACUS.

S. STEDIAN-A, -US, *see* STITHIANS.

S. STEPHENS, *from p.s.*; crowned, *gr.*

S. SYMPHORIAN, *see* VERYAN.

S. TALLANUS, *see* TALLAND.

S.-TANE, -TEEN, *i.q.* ADVENT.

S. TANS, *i.q.* S. AGNES.

S. TEATH, *from p.s.* S. Tetha, *O.,* Tedda, *Wh.,* Tathius, *T.,* Eatha, *H.*

SAINT TATHEN, 17 *cent., i.q.* S. ADWEN.

S. TENNOCUS, TWENNOCUS, 14 *cent., i.q.* TOWEDNACK.

S. TERBYN, *IV.IV., i.q.* S. ERBYN.

THE SAINT TERRY, *i.q.* SANTRY.

S.-TEW, -TUE, *i.q.* S. EWE.

S. TISSIE, *Nord., i.q.* S. ISSEY.

S. TORNEY, *see* NORTHILL.

S. TUDY, *from p.s.* S. Uda *or* Tudius, *O.*

S. UL-ETTE, -IANE, *Le., i.q.* S. JULIANA.

S. UNY, *i.q.* S. EWINUS.

S. UVELUS *or* VUELUS, ? *i.q.* S. EVAL, ?=*hurel,* humble; *see* WITHIEL.

S. VEEP, *from o.p.s.* S. Vepus *or* Vepa, (? = *Gwymp, w.s.*), *now* SS. Cyrus and Julitta, *O.*

S. VORCH, *see* LANLIVERY.

S. WEDNOCK, ? *see* LANDEWEDNACK *and* TOWEDNACK.

S. WELVELA, *see* LANEAST.

S. WENDRONA, *see* WENDRON.

S. WENEPPA, *see* GWENNAP.

S. WENN, *from p.s.* S. Wenna (the fair), *O.*; ? *i.q.* S. Gwennan, *w.*

S. WERBURGHA, powerful protection, *t., Y.; see* WARBSTOW.

S. WILLOWS, *from* S. WILLOCUS.

S. WINNIERIUS, *see* GWINEAR.

S. WINNOW, *from p.s.* S. Winnocus,*O.*

S. WIN-WALOC, -WALOE, -WALLO, -WOLAUS, *see* LANDEWEDNACK.

S. WITHEL, ? = *gwyddel,* Irishman.

S. YDROC, *see* LANHYDROCK.

SALLAKEE, SALLY KEY,? = *sul lechau,* sun stones.

SALMON, ? *i.q.* SALAMAN, *w.B.m., i.q.* SOLOMON (*shalom,* peace, *h.*).

SALTASH, "Esse, his towne by the [salt] sea," *Car.; p.s.* S. Stephen, *O.,* S. Nicholas, *C.S.G.*

SALTER, *n.f.,* = *saltere,* a maker of salt, *s.; or, i.q.* SALTERN, salt pit, *s.*

SAM-BELL, -BLE, -BALLS, -MELL, *n.f., i.q.* SAMWELL, *w.B.m.,* = SAMUEL, asked of God, *h.*

SAMPY'S PARK, Sampson's close.

SANCHO'S MEADOW, *i.q.* SANCOOSE, *i.q.* ST. COOSE.
SANCREED, *from p.s.* St. Sancredus, *O.*; = St. Faith, *C.*; holy belief, *Pr.*
SANCTUARY, *i.q.* SANTRY.
SAND-ER, -OE, -OW, -OWE, -REY, -RY, -Y, *n.f.*, = S. Andrew; *also* SAND-ERS, -OZ, -YS, -S.
SANDERCOCK, *n.f.*, ? red (*coch*) S.
SANGUINAS, *d.d.*, *i.q.* ST. GENNYS.
SANGVILAND, *d.d.*, ? *i.q.* ST. GLUVIAS.
SANGWIN, *n.f.*, ? = SANGUINAS.
SANKEY, *n.f.*, ? *i.q.* ST. KEY.
SANNS, *n.f.*, ? *i.q.* ST. AGNES.
SANSOM, *n.f.*, ? *i.q.* ST. SAMPSON.
SANSBURY, SAUUIN'S earthwork (*bury, t.*).
SANTASPERRY NECK, ? isthmus of the Holy Ghost (*saint esprit, f.*), *O.*
SANTO, *n.f.*, ? *i.q.* SANDOE.
SANTRY, glebe *or* church land, = *sant eru*, holy acre *or* field.
SANWINNEC, *d.d.*, *i.q.* S. WINNOW.
SAPLYN, *n.f.*, ? = S. PAULIN[US] *or* ST. AUBYN.
SAR-A, -AH, *n.f.*, ? *i.q.* SAYER.
SARTIN, *n.f.*, ? = Sadwrn, *w.*
SATAN'S PARK. SARTIN'S close.
SAULF, *t.d.d.*, ? sea wolf, *d.*, *F.*; ? *i.q. w. Selif*, = SOLOMON.
SAUN-, SAWN-TON, ? Sauuin's town.
SAUUIN, *t.d.d.*, a youth, *d.*
SAW-ANNAH, -NAH, ? *i.q.* SEWANNAH.
SAWLE, ? = *suwell*, healthful; *or, i.q.* Sawyl (*w.s.*).
SAWN VEAN, little ZAWN.
SAXON, the Englishman.
SAY-ER, -HAR, *n.f.*, = *sair*, artizan, workman; *i.q.* WRIGHT.
SBERN, *t.d.d.*, = *Asbjorn*, divine bear, *t.*
SCABERIAS, the barns, *or* a sweeper, *Pr.*; sweepers *or* sweeping (*scaberia*, to sweep), *Sc.*
SCADD-EN, -IN, ? *i.q.* SCAWEN.
SCADG-ELL, -HILL, ? *i.q.* BOSCADGELL; *or,* ? under (*is*) the *castle.*
SCAITH, ? boat (*scath*) [field].
SCANTLEBURY, ? under (*is*) Gundulf's, *or* BOSCUNDLE earthwork (*bury, t.*).

SCARBERIO, *i.q.* SKYBURRIOWE.
SCARCE WATER, SCARSWATER, ? higher (*wartha*) [place] under the moor (*is cors*).
SCAR-DON, -SDUN, *i.q.* SCROSDON.
SCARNE, ? under (*is*) CARN.
SCAW-AN, -EN, -N, elder-tree.
SCAWES WATER, ? higher (*wartha*) elders (*scaw-s*).
SCAWN PARK, elder-tree close.
SCHOOL CLOSE, ? thistles' (*ascall*) c.
SCILLY, *o.* SULLEY, flat rocks (*lehau*) of the sun (*sul*), *B.*; conger-eel (*selli*) [isles], *A.S.*; cut off (*scilly*), *Pr.*
SCOB-ELL, -LE, the broom plant, *H.* a bench (*scavel*), *Gw.*; *n.f.*, ? the town (*ville, f.*) of elders (*skuo, a.*).
SCOFFERN, *n.f.*, ? = *scovarn*, ear; *or, scovarnog*, hare.
THE SCOONS, ? the elders (*scawen-s*).
SCORRIER, *from* the tin *scoria* (*lat.*), *W.W.*; ? long (*hir*) ridge (*esgur, w.*); *or, i.q.* SKYBURRIO.
SCOSE, *n.f.*, ? = *is cors,* under marsh.
SCOT, *n.f.*, ? *i.q.* ESCOTT; *or,* = *is goed*, under-wood, *w.*; *or,* Scotchman.
SCOTLAND, underwood field.
SCOWEN, *n.f.*, *i.q.* SCAWAN.
SCOW PARK, elder-trees' close.
SCROS-, SCRAWS-DON, hill (*dun*) of fracture (*sgaradh, ga.*), *Beal.*
SCROUSE, ? under (*is*) cross (*crous*).
SCUDJECK, ? *i.q.* LESCUDJECK.
SCUTTLE, ? under wood (*is cotele*).
SEAGE-, SEDGE-MOOR, = *secgesmœre*, sedge moor, *s.*
SEAFORTH, ? ? = *sea*-port (*porth*).
SEATON, town on the sea, *t.*, *B.*; hill (*dun*) stream (*sa, ga.*), *Beal.*
SEC-COMBE, -CUMB, -OMBE, *n.f.*, dry (*sech*) valley.
SECCOUCH, ? COUCH'S seat (*se*).
SECHELL, *n.f.*, ? sedge hill.
SEDG-, SED-MAN, *n f.*, ? = Sigmund, conquering protection, *t.*
SEDGWICK, *n.f.*, ? sedge cove (*guic*), *t.*
SEGAR, *n.f.*, idle, *w.*; victorious, *s.*
SEGHS-, SEGHYS-ROCK, the *shag or* cormorant's (*shagga*) rock.

SEIBERTUS, *t.d.d.*, = *Sigbert*, conquering brightness, *t.*, *Y.*

SELDON, *n.f.*, ? prospect (*sell*) hill (*dun*) ; or, hill of the sun (*sul*).

SELEVEN, 16 *cent.*, *i.q.* S. LEVAN, *O.*

SELLAN VEAN & VEOR, little *and* great dry (*sech*), or low (*isel*), or sun (*sul*) enclosure (*lan*).

SELLY, *n.f.*, ?= *selic*, conspicuous.

SEMERS-, SEMES-DON, ?SEYMOUR'S hill.

SEMMONS, *n.f.*, Simon's [son].

SEMSWORTHY, ?SIMS'S farm, *t.*

SENDROW, *n.f.*, *i.q.* SANDOE.

SENNEN, *from p.s.* S. Senana ; the saint's *or* holy (*sans*) vale (*nans*), *Pr.*

SENTRY, *i.q.* SANTRY.

SERPELL, *n.f.*, = *sarf pol*, serpent's pool, *Ch.* ; ? service-tree *hill.*

SESCOMBE, *n.f.*, ? *sedge* vale.

SESSION, *n.f.*, ?= *saesyn*, a Saxon, *w.*

SETH-NEY, -NOE, ? = St. Idno ; *or*, Idno's seat (*se*).

SEVARTH, high (*warth*) seat, *Pr.*

SE-VEAK, -VEOCK, the seat in the hollow (*veage*), *Pr.*

SEWANNA, the seat by (? on) the downs (*gwonnow*), *Pr.*

SEWINUS, *w.B.m.*, = *sweyn*, a youth, *d.*

SEWORGAN, ? seat (*se*) on (*war*) the down (*goon*).

SEWRAH, ?old-woman's (*gwrach*) seat.

SEWULF, *w.B.m.*, sea wolf, *t.*

SEXTON, *o.n.f.*, the Saxon.

SEYM-ER, -OUR, *n.f.*, = St. Maur, *Lo.* ; *or, seamere*, a tailor, a packhorse, *s.*

SHAB-BER, -BRA, ? = *scaber*, barn.

SHAKES MOOR, shag *or* cormorant moor ; (*jan jeak*, a snail, *m.c.*).

SHALLBROOK, *n.f.*, shallow-brook. *t.*

SHALLOW CREASE, ? middle *cres* [field] under the moors (*is hallow*).

S. PARK, under-moor close (*parc*).

S. POOL, jawbone (*challa*) pool, *J.Ca.*

SHARPITOR, SHARPY-TOR, -TORRY, = *sharp* point *Tor*, *B.* ; *n.f.*, SHAPTER.

SHARPNOSE, ? sharp point, *t.*

SHAWL, ? = *is hall*, under moor.

SHEEP-AN, -EN, -ING, = *scipen*, a cow-house, stall, stable, *s.*

SHEKEL HILL, ? rye (*sygal*) field (*gweal*), *or* hill.

SHEPNA-, SHEPTON-PARK, SHIPPEN close (*parc*).

SHERRY. *n.f.*, = Jerry, Jeremiah ; *also* SHERR-IES, -YS.

SHERSTON, *shire* boundary *stone*, *t.*

SHEVIOCK, the dwelling (? *chy*) by the *oak* river (*gwy, Pr.*) ; *or, i.q.* SEVEAK.

SHILLINGHAM, the dwelling (*ham*) covered with slates, *t., H.* ; ?Julian's home.

SHILSON, *n.f.*, ?Julian's son.

SHIPLEY, *n.f.*, sheep pasture, *t.*

SHIPPEN PARK, SHIPPING PORT, cow-house (*scipen, s.*) close (*parc*).

SHIPWAY, *n.f.*, ? sheep walk, *t.*

SHIVER PARK, *i.q.* PARK SCHEBA.

SHO-AL, (*n.f.* SHOLL), *i.q.* SHAWL.

SHOE-, SHOOT-, SHOOTA-, SHOOTER-, SHOT-, SHOTA-, SHUT-, SHUTE-, SHUTTER-PARK, *i.q.* PARK SHUTTER.

SHORESTON, *i.q.* SHERSTONE.

SHORLEY, *n.f.*, ? *i.q.* CHORLEY.

SHOVER PARK, *i.q.* PARK SKEBA.

SIBBETT ROCK, SIBELLA'S rock, *Bl.*

SIBLY, *n.f.*, = *Sibella*, an old wise woman, *lat.*, *Y.* ; Jove's council, *gr.*, *Moody.*

SILVA, prospect (*sell*) place (*va*).

SIM-COE, -MONS, -S, *n.f.*, *from* Simon, *Lo.*

SIMON WARD, ? ? Sigismund's guard, *t.* ; *alias* ST. BREWARD.

SINNS, the saints' [abode], *Pr.*

SIREUUOLD, *t.d.d.*, conquering (*sigor, s.*) power (*wald, s.*), *t.*

SITHNEY, the bishop's land, *Pr.* ; *from p.s.* St. Siduinus, *O.*

SITWELL, *n.f.*, *i.q.* ST. SATIVOLA.

SIUUARD, *t.d.d.*, = *Sige-ward*, conquering guard, *t.*

SIZE, *n.f.*, ? = *sais*, a Saxon.

SKABBAR, the barn (*scebar*).

SKAWN, *n.f.*, = *scawen*, an elder tree.

SKEER, ? *i.q.* ROSKEAR.

SKELL-OW, -Y, ? *i.q.* ROSKELLY.

SKENE, *n.f.*, = *ysgien*, a knife, *w.*, *R.W.*

SKEN-NOCK, -OCK, *n.f.*, ? sedgy.

SKENOWETH, ? new (*nowedh*) sedge [field].

SKENTLEBURY, *n.f.*, *i.q.* SCANTLEBURY.

SKERWETHERS, ? ? cliff (*sgeir, i.*) sheep.

SKEW-ES, -IS, -ISH, -S, a shady place (*sces, scod*, a shade), *Pr.*

SKEWJACK, ? shady (*scezack*) [place].

SKIBBER, the barn (*sciber*).

S. WIDDEN, ? white (*gwydn*) barn.

SKIDMORE, *n.f.*, = *escud' amour*, shield of love, *i.*, *Lo.*; ? great (*maur*) shade (*scod*).

SKIN FIELD, ? sedge (*hescen*) field.

SKINHAM, ? sedge border (*hem*).

SKINNARD, *n.f.*, ? feltmonger; or, = SKINNER, *n.f.*, long (*hir*) sedge.

SKINN-ISH, -Y, ? sedgy.

SKIPPER PARK, *i.q.* PARK SKEBA.

SKISDON, ? shady (*sces*) hill (*dun*).

SKITTER PARK, SKITTY, ? privet (*scedgwith*) close (*parc*).

SKYBURRIOWE, the barns.

SLAD, SLADE, valley, *N.H.*

SLADDY PARK, valley close.

SLADDYVEAN, little valley.

SLADESFOOT, ? valley end.

SLATER, *n.f.*, ? *i.q.* SALTER; or SLAUGHTER, *n.f.*, ? = *slagter*, a butcher, *d.*

SL-AY, -EA, -EIGH, *n.f.*, *i.q.* TRESLEA.

SLEE-, SLO-, SLU-, SLY-MAN, *n.f.*, ? *i.q.* SALMON.

SLIMEFORD. muddy passage, *t.*

SLIPPER-, SLIPPY-HILL, ? slippery hill, *t.*

SLOVEN'S BRIDGE, *from is loe vaen*, under the stone tumulus, *M'L.*; *alias* SLAUGHTER BRIDGE.

SLUSHAY, ? sloppy close (*hay*), *t.*

SLUTSCOOMB, ? St. Illtut's vale.

SLUTSWELL, ? St. Illtut's well.

SMALLACOMBE, ? little vale.

SMALLA PARK, ? little close.

SME-ATH, -ATHE, -ETH, *n.f.*, ? = *smoethe*, a smooth plain, a field, *s.*; or = SMITH.

SMEATON, ? SMEATH enclosure, *t.*

SMETHAM, ? SMEATH border (*hem*).

SMITHICK, SMYTHIKE, SMYTHWEEK, ? ? SMEATH'S village (*guic*); or, smithy; or, smooth haven; now FALMOUTH.

SNAIL, SNELL, *n.f.*, ? = *snel*, bold, active, *s.*; or, *i.q.* CHYNALE.

SOADY, SODDY, SODY, *n.f.*, ? ? south, or moist (*sog*) house.

SOARN, SORN, corner (*sorn*), *Pr.*; or, = *sarn*, a causeway, pavement, *B.*

SOCKEMOOR, *n.f.*, ? moist moor.

SODEN, *n.f.*, ? south vale (*denu, s.*).

SOLDIERS' CROFT, *from Sul*, the sun, *jor*, lord or governor, *Buller.*

SOLOM-A, -ON, *n.f.*, *i.q.* SALMON.

SOMERLES, ? SOMER'S, or summer *leas* or pastures, *t.*

SOMERTON, ? *summer, or south* lake (*mere*) enclosure *or* town, *t.*

SOOR, SORE, LE SOR, SOWER, *n.f.*, ? = *zar*, heathcock, grouse, *Pr.*

SOPER, *n.f.*, ? south close (*parc*).

SOUTHERLAND, ? southward field, *t.*

SOUTHEY, *n.f.*, south close (*luy*).

SOUTH HILL (*t.*); *p.s.* St. Samson.

SOWDEN, *n.f.*, *i.q.* SODEN.

SOWDER, ? south, *or* moist (*sog*) land (*tir*).

SOWELL, *n.f.*, south hill; or, *i.q.* SAWLE

SOWETH, *n.f.*, ? south heath, *t.*

SOWKER, ? = *zigyr*, sluggish.

SPAR CROFT, ? barn (*sciber*) croft.

SPARGO, ? barn wood (*coat*).

SPARK, *n.f.*, ? *i.q.* SPERRACK.

SPARN-A, -ECK, -ICK, -OCK, thorny (*spernic*) [place].

SPARNELL, ? thorn moor (*hal*).

SPARNON, ? thorn (*spern*) down (*oon*).

SPARROT, ? = lower (*isa*) PARK YET.

SPEAR HAY, ? barn (*sciber*) close (*hay*).

SPEARIES PARK, spirit (*speris*) close.

SPEARN, = *spern*, thorns.

SPEC-COT, -OT, *n.f.*, Speke's cottage.

SPECKHAM, ? Speke's meadow.
SPEKE, *n.f.*, ?=*esbog*, bishop, *w.*
SPENCER, butler, steward.
SPERNON, a thorn, *Pr.*
SPERRACK, SPERK, *n.f.*, ? = *sperhafoc*, sparrow-hawk, *s.*
SPETTIGUE, ? hospital (*yspytty, w.*) GUE.
SPIGURNELL, *n.f.*, sealer of writs, *f.*
SPILLER, *n.f.*, ? = *spullier*, a pickman.
SPINK PARK, ? Finch's (*s.*) close.
SPITT-AL, -EL, ? the *hospital.*
SPITTLE PARK, *hospital* close.
SPLAT, SPLOT, small piece of land.
SPLATTENRIDDEN, fern (*reden*) splat.
SPOUR, SPURR, *n.f.*, ? *i.q.* BUTSBER.
SPRATT, *n.f.*, ? *i.q.* SPARROT.
SPRAY, SPRY, *n.f.*, ? = *is bre*, under-hill.
SPURNOCK FIELD, *i.q.* SPARNA.
SPURWAY, *n.f.*, ? barn (*sciber*) way.
SQUARE, SQUIRE, SQUIER, *n.f.*, ? = *scebar*, a barn, *or i.q.* esquire; *or*, square.
STABB, *n.f.*, ? = *stub*, tree stump, *s.*
STABB-A, -ACK, field grubbed up (*stub*, to grub up).
STACEY, *n.f.*, = Eustachius, *see* St. EWE.
STAGGY MOOR, sticky moor, *t.*
STAMFORD HILL, *from* Lord STAMFORD = Stoneford, *t.*
STANAWAY, *n.f.*, stony path.
STANBURY, stone castle, *s.*
STANIFORD, stony ford, *t.*
STAN-IX, -NACK, -NICK, -NOCK, tinny (*stean-ic*), *or* stony (*s.*) places.
STANL-EY, -LICK, STANLAKE, *n.f.*, stone pasture (*leag*).
STANNAR FIELD, ? *tinner or* water-wagtail (*stenor*) field.
STAN-ON, -TON, stone town, *t.*
START POINT, *from steort*, a tail, ex-tremity, *point*, promontory, *s.*
STE-ENS, -INS, = Stephen's [place].
STEN-COOSE, -GOOSE, tin (*stean*) wood (*cus*), *Pr.*
STENHILL, tin hill, *R.W.*
STENNACK, *i.q.* STANNACK.

STENNALE-ES, -AS, stone meadows, *s.*
STEP, *n.f., i.q.* STEPHENS.
STEPHEN GELLY, Stephen's grove (*celli*).
STEPHENSDON, Stephen's hill (*dun*).
STEPH-, STEP-NEY, Stephen's close (*hay*).
STERT, *i.q.* START.
STICKEN BRIDGE, ? *from stickedn*, a pale, post, stake.
STICKLE HILL, ? stile (*stigel, s.*), *or* steep (*sticele, s.*) hill, *t.*
STIDIFORD, *n.f.*, ? St. TUDY'S ford.
STITCH, narrow strip of land, *m.c.*
STITIIIANS, *from p.s.* St. STEDIAN-A, *or* -US, *O.*, Bp. Stidio, *Wh.*
STOCK, *n.f.*, = *stoc*, tree trunk *or* stock; *or*, a place, *s.*
STOCK-ADON, -ATON, -ETON, ? stock hill (*dun*), *or* enclosure (*tun, s.*).
STOCKE-, STOKE-LEY, ? stockaded *or* stock pasture, *t.*
STOCKWELL, ? stockaded well, *t.*
STODDEN, *n.f.*, ? = *ystoden*, a swathe of corn, *w.*, *R.W.*; *or*, = *isa todn*, under lay.
STOGGY MOOR, sticky moor, *t.*
STOKE CLIMSLAND, the chief place (*stoc, s.*) on *Clement's* land; *p.s.* not known.
STOKE-MEADOW, *i.q.* STOCK-.
STOKETON, ? stock *or* stockaded enclosure (*tun*), *t.*
STONEMAN, ? stone (*maen*), redup.
STOTTEN, *n.f., i.q.* STODDEN.
STOWE, the place, *s.*
STRANG, ? under (*is*) DRANNACK.
STRANG-WAGE, -WICH, STRANGE-WAYS, *i.q.* RESTRONGUET.
STRATHILL, ? spring (*stret*) hill.
STRATTON, street (*strat, s.*), highway, *or* valley (*ystrad, w.*) town, *B.*; hill of springs, *Pr.*; *p.s.* St. Andrew
STR-AUL, -OUL, -OWL, ? couch-grass (*stroil, T.Q.C.*) [field].
STRAY PARK, ? ? under-town (*-is dre*) close.
STREET AN GARROW, ? the (*an*) rough (*garow*) street.

STREET AN NOWAN, the new street.
S. MEHALE, Michael's street.
STR-ODE, -OOTE, *n.f.*, ? = *w.* ystrad, a
valley ; a street, paved-way.
STROILLY MOOR, ? couch-grass moor.
STRONGET, *i.q.* RESTRONGUET.
STURSDON, ? *steers'* hill (*dun*).
SUD-, SUT-COT, ? *south cot, t.*
SUFFENTON, ? *south* spring (*fenten*).
SUFFREE, ? *south* hill (*bre*).
SULJOR CROFT, *i.q.* SOLDIERS' CROFT
SUTTLE PARK, ? *south-hill* close, *t.*
SUTTON TOWN, south-town farm *or*
town-place, *t.*
SWA-INE, -N, *n.f.*, ? = *yswain*, a squire,
w., R.W. ; *or, i.q.* SAUUIN, *t.*
SWALLOCK, *from* St. Wallocus (*Bp.*).
SWANNACOT, SAUUIN'S cottage, *t.*
SWIFTAFORD, ? rapid ford, *t.*
SWIMMER, SWYNNAR, *n.f.*, ? *from*
St. GWINEAR.

TABB, *n.f.*, ? *i.q.* DABB.
TABBIN'S HOLE, St. AUBYN'S cave, *t.*
TABLE, *n.f.*, ? *i.q.* TEBBOT.
TACA-, TAC-BERE, ? Tago's farm, *t.*
TA-COYSE, -GOS, -GUS, -GGS, ? wood
(*cus*) house (*ti*), or side (*tu*).
TADDIPORT, parent (*tad*) haven, *Wh.*
TAERBYN, *n.f., O.,* ? *i.q.* St. ERBYN.
TAFFY'S CLOSE, *i.q.* Davie's close.
TAGGET, *n.f.*, ? = *tu* goat, wood-side.
TAIL-, TALA-PARK, ? manure (*teil*)
close (*parc*).
TALAN, *w.B.m.*, ? = *talon*, belly.
TALBOT, ? HALBOAT house (*ti*) ; *n.f.*,
a hunting dog, hound, *t., Lo.*
TAL-CARNE, -KARNE, *d.d.* -CAR, -GAR,
high rock, *Pr.*, *or* heap of rocks ;
or, i.q. TOLCARN.
TALGOLLE, *d.d.*, ? top *or* front (*tal*)
of the grove (*celli*); *now* TOLGULLA
TALGOOSE, ? top of wood (*cus*).
TALGROGAN, ? high rock (*carrag*) on
the down (*gwon, goon, oon*).
TALLACK, *n.f.*, ? = *talawg*, one having
a large forehead, *w.* ; *or, talhac*, a
roach *or* rock fish.

TALLAND, high church (*lan*), *Pr.* ;
highland, *H.* ; headland, *C.* ; *from*
p.s. St. Tallanus, *O.*
TALLANGOVE, ? ANGOVE hill (*tal*).
TALLAWARREN, *i.q* TRELOWARREN.
TALLERVEY, *n.f.*, ? = *tal erveu*, end
of the fields, *w., R.W.* ; *or, tall*
HARVEY.
TALLHAY, ? ? high enclosure (*hay*).
TALLING, *n.f.*, ? *i.q.* TALAN.
TALLOW PARK, ? TALLACK's close.
TALMENETH, *Le.*, ? mountain (*men-
edh*) height *or* top; *now* TALMENOR
TALSKI-DDY, -THY, ? privet (*sciddy* =
scedgwith, B.) hill.
TALVAN, ? = *talva*, a projection, *w.,*
R.W. ; *or,* little (*bean*) hill.
TALV-AR, -OR, ? great (*maur*) hill.
TAL-VARN, -VERN, ? alder *or* marsh
(*gwarn, gwern*) hill *or* summit.
TALVRAN, ? crow (*bran*) hill.
TAL Y MEAN, top of the stone, *J.B.* ;
the tall rock (*maen*), *Bl.*
TAMAR, great (*maur*) water (*tau,*
B. ; *ta, ga., F.* ; ? *dour*).
T. HAM, ? Tamar meadow (*ham, s.*).
TAMBL-YN, -INSON, *n.f.*, ? *from* THOM-
AS, = Tomlin, Tomlinson.
TAMELLIN, ? *i.q.* TAMILL, TA MILL,
or TAME MILL ; ? ? the mill (*melin*)
on the gentle (*tam, s.*) [stream].
TAMERTON, the enclosure (*tun, s.*)
on the river TAMAR ; *p.s.* not
known.
TAMLEY PARK, ? *i.q.* TAMLIN (*i.e.*
TAMBLYN'S *or* TAMELLIN) FIELD.
TAMZEN CLOSE, ? Thomasine's c.
TANCREEG, ? fire (*tan*) barrow (*creeg*),
Pr.; i.q. TRENCREEK *or* TENCREEG
TANGEY, *n.f.*, ? under (*tan*) hedge (*ce*).
TAN-HAY, -PARK, ? under *or* fire
(*tan*) close.
TANKARD, *n.f.*, grateful (*thanc*) guard
(*weard*), *or* council (*red*), *s.*
TANKINS, ? Tonkin's [tenement].
TAPSON, *n.f.*, ? *i.q.* Thomasine.
TARAVEOR, *alias* BULL- (*tarow*) LANE
(*fordh, for, vor*).
TARBEAN, ? little (*bean*) field (*tir*).

TAR BOX, ? oak (*dar*) bush (*bagas*).

TARE WASTE, ? waste *or* west land (*tir*) *or* field.

TAR PARK, ? water (*dour*) close.

TARNONDAIN, ?? = *tarn an din*, pool on the hill, *J.B.*

TARR, *n.f.*, ? = *tardh*, issue, *w.*, *R.W.*

TARRET, ? oak gate (*yet*).

TARRY FIELD, ? watery (*douric*) field.

TARTANE, ? under (*tan*) oak.

TAS-COTT, -KIS, -KUS, ? the house (*ti*) outside (*aves*) the wood (*cout*, *cus*).

TAWAY, ? at *or* by the way, *t.*

TAWELL, *o.* ATTE WELL, [the house] by the well, *t.*

TAY-, TEA-COMBE, ? vale (*comb*, *t.*) house (*ti*); *or*, house vale.

TAYLDER, *n.f.*, = TAILOR.

TEAGUE, *n.f.*, = *teg*, fair.

TEAN, *from* St. Theon-a, *or* -us.

TEAR BEAN, *i.q.* TARBEAN.

TEBBOT, *n.f.*, = Theobald, people's (*theod*) prince (*bald*).

TEDDER, *n.f.*, = *Tudwr*, *w.*, Theodore, God's gift, *gr.*

TEGLASTON, *d.d.*, ? *i.q.* TREGLASTON.

TEHIDY, = *ty-hedy*, an extended town, *B.*; the fowler's (*idne*) dwelling (*ti*), *or* single *or* narrow (*edn*) house, *Pr.*; ? Eadig's *or* Ida's house; ? *d.d.* TEDINTONE.

TELVIN, ? = Elwen's house.

TEMPELLOWE, temples, *Pr.*, *pl. of*

TEMPLE, (*tempel*); *o.* Capella de TEMPLO, *O.*; *p.s.* not known.

TENBY, *n.f.*, ? *i.q.* DENBY.

TENCREEG, = *ti an creeg*, house by the barrow, *M'L.*; *i.q.* TANCREEG.

TENDRINE, *i.q.* TRENDRINE.

TENEDRIS, *i.q.* TRENEDRIS.

TENKER'S FIELD, ? TANKARD'S field.

TENNEY, *n.f.*, ? *i.q.* TAN HAY.

TEPPET, *n.f.*, *i.q.* TEBBOT.

TERE BEAN, *i.q.* TARBEAN.

TERENGORES, = *tre an gors*, the dwelling in the marsh, *N.*

TERNEWAN, ? = *tarn ewan*, sheep pool, *J.B.*; *or*, new land (*tir*).

TERNOOTH, new (*nowedh*) land.

TERRORS PARK, ? *i.q.* PARK DARAS.

TERROSE, ? *i.q.* ROSTER.

TERWINCE, ? *i.q.* TREVINCE.

TETHEN HALL, ? furze (*eithen*) house (*ti*) moor (*hal*).

TEUTHEY, Le., ? great (*ethuc*) house.

TEWAN, *i.q.* TOWAN.

TEWARDEVI, *d.d.* *i.q.* TREWARDREVA

TEWEATH, wood-house (*gwydh*, trees), *R.W.*; *or*, watch (*gwith*) house.

TEWINGTON, hillock, barrow, *or* tumulus (*tuyn*) hill (*dun*), *M'L.*

THANKS, *o.* THANCEANS, = *ti ungosu*, house of view, *Po.* (?).

THICK, *n.f.*, ? *i.q.* TEAGUE.

THIRT GROUND, *i.q.* THROAT.

THOMS, *n.f.*, *i.q.* THOMAS.

THORL-ETON, -IBEARE, ? Thorold's enclosure (*tun*) *or* farm (*bere*), *t.*

THRISCUTT, *n.f.*, *i.q.* TRESCOTT.

THE THROAT, ? *i.q.* THWART-LAND, the thwart *or* cross piece of land, *t.*

TIBBOT, *n.f.*, *i.q.* TEBBOT.

TICOITH, *d.d.*, ? *i.q.* TUCOIS.

TIDDY, *n.f.*, ? = *tidi*, a breast, pap; *or*, *i.q.* TEHIDY, *or* TIDI (*river*).

TIDICOMBE, vale of the TIDI river.

TIDIFORD, passage over the TIDI.

TIDWELL, ? = tide well, *t.*

TIENGILLY, ? house (*ti*) by the grove (*an gelli*).

TILLY, *n.f.*, ? = *teilu*, a family, household; *or*, *from* BODILLY.

TIMBERL-, TIMBERLIMB-, TIMBRELHAM, ? timber-hill meadow (*ham*, *t.*) *or* boundary (*hem*), *t.*

TIN-, TING-COMBE, ? bottom of (*tin*), *or* house in (*ti en*), the coomb, *R.W.*; *or*, TINK'S *or* the chaffinch (*tinc*, *s.*) vale.

TINCROFT, sharp-pointed (*tyn*) croft, *T.C.*; ? bottom (*tin*) of the croft.

TINDERN, under oak-tree (*tanderwen*), *R.W.*

TINDEROW, hill of the druids, *Po.*; ? oak (*derow*) hill (*din*).

TINES, ? = *dinas*, castle, city.

TING-TANG, *i.q.* DING-DONG.

TINKERSLAKE, fire (*tan*) castle (*caer*) lake, *Beal.*

TINKLAND, ? TINK'S (*n.f.*) field, *t.*

TINNY, *n.f.*, ? *i.q.* DENNY.

TIN PARK, ? castle (*din*) close.

TINTAGEL, the secure *or* impregnable (*diogel*) castle, *H.* ; castle of deceit (*dixelth* ?), *T.* ; ? ?Toghel's (*i.*) castle.

TINTEN, THINTON, ? bottom (*tin*) of the hill; *or*, fire (*tan*) hill.

TIPPET, *n.f.*, *i.q.* TEBBOT.

TIPPITON, Tippet's farm (*tun, s.*).

TIRRGRISS, *n.f.*, ?mid (*cres*) land (*tir*).

TIVERNHAIL, *d.d.* TIWARTH-EL, -AL, *i.q.* TYWARNHALE.

TOBER TOR, *two barrows'* hill, *Mur.*

TOBY, *n.f.*, = Tobias (*c.n.*).

TODDEN, = *todn*, lay *or* grass land.

TODDY WELL, ? *tad*pole well, *t.*

TODPOOL, *tad*pole pool, *t.*

TODSCAD, *or* TOLLSCAD, the shady (*scod*, a shade) hole *or* pit, *H.*

TODSWORTHY, ? TODD'S (*n.f.*, ? = fox, *t.*) farm (*weorthig, s.*).

TOKER, *n.f.*, ? fuller, *t.* ; *or*, *twciwr*, a clipper, *w.* ; *or*, *i.q.* TALCAER

TOL-CARN, -CAIRNE, the stone *or* rock (*carn*) with a hole (*tol*) in it, *or i.q.* TALCARN, *Pr.* ; T. WARTHA & WOLLAS, higher & lower T.

TOLDAVAS, sheep (*davas*) hole, *or* hill (*tal*), *W.B.*; ?*i.q.* TRELODAVAS.

TOLDOWER, ? water (*dour*) hole.

TOLESCAN, ? elder-tree (*scawen*) hill; *or*, sedge (*hescen*) hole.

TOLFRANK GREEN, [fair-]*green* free (*franc, f.*) of toll.

TOLGARR-ACK, -ECK, rock *or* rocky hill (*tal*) or hole (*tol*).

TOLGATE, hole *or* cell in the wood (*coat*), *J.M.*, ? *i.q.*

TOLGOATH, wood hole *or* hill.

TOL-GOOSE, -GUS, the hole in the wood (*cus*), *or* the quaking hole; *or*, *i.q.* TALGUS, *Pr.*

TOLGROGAN, *i.q.* TALGROGAN.

TOLGULL-A, -O, the bottom *or* lower (*gwollach*)hole, *Pr.*; *o.* TALGOLLEN; *d.d.* TALGOLLE.

TOLKERNE, ? *i.q.* TOLCARNE.

TOLL, a hole, perforation ; *or*, = *tal*, a forehead, a hill, high [place].

TOLLER, *n.f.*, inspector of holes made for tin-bounds, *Pr.* ; ? a toll gatherer (*tollor*).

TOLL WIDDEN, ? little (*m.c.*) hole.

TOLMAN, *n.f.*, hole stone (*maen*); *or*, high (*tal*) place (*man*).

TOLMEN, hole of stone, *B.*

TOLMENOR, ? the hole of the boundary (*or*) stone.

TOLMIE, *n.f.*, ? *i.q.* TOLMEN.

TOL PEDEN PENWITH, ? the holed headland (*pen, pedn*) of PENWITH.

TOLR-OY, -Y, ? king's (*ruy*) hill.

TOLSCATHEN, ? ? washbrew (*sugaethan, w.*) hole.

TOLSK-ADY, -EDY, -ITHEY, ? *i.q.* TALSKIDDY *or* TODSCAD.

TOLVA-N, -DDEN, high (*ban*) hole, *T.C.* ; *or*, little (*vean*) hole ; *or*, *i.q.* TOLMAN.

TOLVEDDEN, little (*vedn, vean*) hole.

TOLVER, great (*mear*), *or* short (*ber*) dale (*dol*), *H.M.W.*

TOLV-ERN, -ORN, the *foreigner's* hole *or* high place, *or* oven's (*forn*) mouth, *Pr.* ; ? = *toll-lowern*, fox hole ; *or*, *i.q.* TALVARN.

TOL Y DAVAS, *i.q.* TOLDAVAS.

TOM, *n.f.*, hot, warm, *S.T.*

TOMALAND, ? the warm land.

TOM-S, -MYS, *n.f.*, *from* THOMAS.

TON-, TONN-ACOMBE, ? ? the farm *or* town-place in the vale ; *or*, TONY's vale ; (*ton*, leyland, a green).

TONARROW, ? = *w.* *tonn arw*, rough ley, *R.W.*

TONKIN, *n.f.*, dim. of TONY, *Lo.*

TONSEN, *n.f.*, ? TONY's son.

TONY, *n.f.*, ? *from* ANTONY.

TOP AN DRY CARN, top of the three carns, *R.W.* ; ? = *tuban druy cann*, the druid's full moon bank, *T.C.*

TOPP-A, -ARK, top close (*hay, parc*).

TOPVOUNDER, top of lane (*bounder*).

TOR CROBM, crooked (*crom*) hill, *B.*

TORDRAIT, *O.*, *i.q.* TYWARDREATH.

TORLEVAN, ? *i.q.* TRELEVAN.

TORLODAVAS, *i.q.* TRELODAVAS.

TORNANVOR, the turning (*torn*) of the (*an*) way (*fordh*), *Pr.*

TORNAWOLLOCK, the turning of one side (*wolock*), *Pr.*; (*woloc = goloc*, sight, a face, *R.W.*).

TORN-COATH, -COTH, ? = *tor an coed*, the wooded hill, *J.B.*

TORNEWIDDEN, ? little (*widden = vean*), or white (*gwydn*) turning, or by the tree (*gwedhen*).

TORNOON, ? = *tor an goon*, the moorland hill, *J.B.*; or, *tornewan*, a side.

TOR PARK, ? *i.q.* PARK DOWER.

TORR, prominence *or* hill (*tor*, a belly); a peak (*tour*, tower); water (*dour*).

TORY, ? watery (*douric*) [place].

TOTTENBIGGAN, ? little (*bichan*) lay (*todn = ton*).

TOTTERTON, *o.* TOTTYSDONE, ? the hill (*dun*) of Teutates, *t.*

TOUCH MY PIPES, = smoke [and rest awhile], *i.e.* resting-place, *t.*

TOUR-, TOWER-PARK, ? *i.q.* PARK DOWER.

TOWAN, a round hill, a tumulus, a sand hill, a sandy coast, *M'L.*; *also* = down ; *and, i.q.* TOWN.

TOWN-PARK, -FIELD, field near the TOWN *or* TOWN PLACE, *i.e.* farmstead and yard, *t.*

TOWSON, *n.f.*, ? = Davison.

TOW'S WELL, David's (*Deui*) well.

TOY, *n.f.*, ? = *Deui*, David.

TOZER, *n.f.*, ? = *touzer*, a shearer, *a.*

TRABISS, ? outer (*aves*) land (*tir*), or dwelling (*tre*).

TRABOC, *i.q.* TRERABOC.

TRABOE VEAN, little TRABOC.

TRABOR, ? pasture (*pawr, w.*) lands (*tiryow*), or dwelling (*treva*).

THE TRACES, *i.q.* DRAISES.

TRAC-EY, -Y, *n.f.*, ?? bramble *or* briery (*drais*) enclosure (*hay*).

TRAD-, TRAF-FORD, ?? = *druid's ford*; or, the dwelling (*tre*) at the *ford, t.*

TRA-ER, -HEIR, *n.f.*, *i.q.* TREHEER.

TRAFALGAR, ?? Algar's dwelling (*tref*).

TRAFFEL, ? smithy (*govail*), *or* field (*gweal*) house (*tre*).

TRAGARADOC, *i.q.* TREGARADOC.

TRAGEAR, *n.f.*, *i.q.* TREGEAR.

TRAGILGUS, *n.f.*, *i.q.* TREGILGAS.

TRAGOL, *d.d.*, ? *i.q.* TREGOLL.

TRAHERNE, *n.f.*, ? *i.q.* TREHERON.

TRAIL, *n.f.*, ? *i.q.* TREAL.

TRAINOR, *n.f.*, ? = *dyrnwr*, a thrasher, *w.*; or, *i.q.* TREVENNER.

TRAMAGENNOW, *i.q.* TREMAGENNOW.

TRAMBLE, *i.q.* TREAMBLE.

TRANE, ? = *truian*, a third [of a parish], *w., R.W.*; or, lamb (*ean*) land.

TRAN-KS, -KUS, ? land (*tir*) by the wood (*an gus*) or marsh (*cors*).

TRANN-ACK, -ICK, -OCK, -O, *i.q.* DRANNACK *or* TREGRANNICK.

TRAP PARK, ? *i.q.* PARK DRAY.

TRASE-, TRASS-PARK, ? *i.q.* PARK-DARAS *or* DRIES.

TRATHA-M, -N, *n.f.*, ? *i.q.* TRUTHAM, or = *tir eithin*, furze land.

TRAVENER, *n.f.*, ? *i.q.* TREVENNOR.

TRAVERN, *i.q.* TREHAVERN.

TRAVIDER, *d.d.*, *i.q.* TREVIDER.

TRAV-IS, -YS, *n.f.*, ? *i.q.* TRABYSS.

TRAVITHOE, *i.q.* TREVITHOE.

TRAVVINT, *d.d.*, *i.q.* TREWINT.

TRA-UZA, -WZA, ? lower (*iza*) lands (*tiryou*) ; or, *i.q.* TREVISA.

TRAWISCOIT, *d.d.*, ? the dwelling (*tre*), or land (*tir*) outside (*aues*) the wood (*coid*).

TRAYNOR, *n.f.*, *i.q.* TRAINOR.

TRAY PARK, *i.q.* PARK DRAY.

TRAYS PARK, *i.q.* TRASE PARK.

TRAYS TOWN, bramble (*dreis*) [close] near the town *or* farm place.

TREADDLE, *v.* RADDLE, ? *i.q.*

TREADWELL, ? Edwal's (*w.*) dwelling.

TREAGE, *n.f.*, ?? *i.q.* TRIGG, *or*

TREAG-A, -HOE, the towns of the barbed iron or fishing spear, *H.*; ? IAGO's town *or* dwelling.

TRE-AL, -ALE, ? *i.q.* TREHAL.

TREALEASE, ? HALLAZE dwelling.

TREAMBLE, Hannibal's dwelling.

TREANMEAN, ? the dwelling (tre) by the stone (an mean).

TREAR, ? i.q. TRAER.

TREARDDLE, ? Ardal's (i.) dwelling.

TREARDRENE, ? Aerdeyrn's (w.) d.

TREARICK, i.q. TREHARICK.

TREA-SE, -ZE, the third, H. ; ? lower (isa) town ; or, i.q. TREISE.

TREASEIL, ? Hawystl's (w.) dwelling.

TREASMILL, ? lower-town mill.

TREASON, ? TREASE on the down (on = gwon) ; or, Isan's (w.) town.

TREATH, sand beach (treath) ; or, i.q. TREVETH, Po., or TREETH.

TREATOR, ? seedsman's (hadwr, w.) d.

TREAVE, = tref, a dwelling, w., R.W.; or, i.q. TREREIFE.

TREAVEAN, little (vean) TREAVE.

TREAVES, ? i.q. TRABISS.

TREAWSET, 15 cent., ? i.q. TRAWIS-COIT.

TREBAH, the boar's (baedh) town, Pr. ; ? = treva, dwelling place ; T. WARTHA, higher TREBAH.

TREBANT, bridge (pont, w.) place, M'L.

TREBARBER, ? i.q. TREBARVAH.

TREBAR-ET, -RET, ? BARRETT's d.

TREBARF-OOT, -UT, the town over (ar) the vault or grave (bedh), Pr. ; ? Barfot's (t.) dwelling.

TREBARN, ? Bran's (w.) dwelling.

TREBARROW, dwelling by the barrow.

TREBAR-THA, -VA, -VAH, -WAH, the high (warth), or wonderful (marth) place, Pr. ; town of baths or washing fountains, H. ; place of the bard (bardh), C₁; ? i.q. TREWARTHA

TREBAR-VATH, -VETH, -WITH, ? i.q. TREBAHWARTHA.

TREBARVAWOON, ? higher (wartha) dwelling (treva) on the down (gwon).

TREBASIL, ? BASIL's dwelling.

TREBATH, ? boar (baedh) town.

TREBATHA, i.q. TREBARTHA.

TREBATHEVY, David's (Deui) dwelling place (treva).

TREBBY, ? i.q. TREBIGH.

TREBEAN, = Little- (bian) ton.

TREBEAR, ? great (mear) town.

TREBE-ATH, -ITH, i.q. TREBATH.

TREBEDICK, ? Bywdeg's (w.) town.

TREBEFFIN, ? little (bian, vian) dwelling place (treva).

TREBEGEAN, town of the giant's (ghean) grave (bedh), Car. ; ? i.q. TREBICEN.

TREBEH-A, -OR, ? i.q. TREBEAR.

TREBEIGH, i.q. TREBIGH.

TREBEIGHAN, i.q. TREBICEN.

TREBE-JEW, -LJEW, -LZEW, -LZOW, black moor (hal zu) dwelling (trev).

TREBELL, the fair or fine (bel) place, Pr.; ? distant (pell) dwelling, R.W.

TREBELLACK, ? priest's (belec, a.) t.

TREBELL-AN, -EN, i.q. TREMELIN, Pr.; ? Belin's town or dwelling.

TREBELLANCE, i.q. TREBOLLANCE.

TREBENNEN, ? woman's (benen) t. ; or, ash-tree (onnen) house (tref).

TREBENNY, ? BENNY's dwelling.

TREBER-ICK, -RICK, fat (berric) or fruitful place, Pr.; ? Berach's (i.) d.

TREBERS-EY, -ICK, i.q. TREBURSEY.

TREBERTHES, ? ferryman's (porthwys, w.) dwelling.

TREBETHERICK, ? PETHERICK's d.

TREBETHIC, ? PETHICK's dwelling.

TREBETTYS, ? i.q. DER BETTYS.

TREBEVERAS, ? i.q. TREHAVERAS.

TREBI-CEN, -CHEN, -GH, -HAN, little (bichan) town.

TREBIFFIN, i.q. TREBEFFIN.

TREBIL-A, -OW, -LOW, ? elm-tree (elaw) house (trev).

TREBIL-COCK, (-LIOCK, n.f.), ? red (coch) moor (hal) or pool (pol) ; or, Bilcock's (Billecog, f.) house.

TREBILE, ? BELI's dwelling.

TREBILJEW, i.q. TREBEJEW.

TREBINE, i.q. TREBICEN.

TREBINNICK, ? i.q. TREFENICK.

TREBISKEN, ? Ysgin's (w.) dwelling.

TREBISKEY, n.f., ? i.q. TREVISKEY.

TREBISQUITE, i.q. TRAWISCOIT.

TREBISSICK, BISSICK town.

TREBISTA, ? east field (est hay) house.

TREBL-ARY, d.d. -ERI, ? Wallaheri's (t.) dwelling (treva).

TREBLE, *n.f.*, ? *i.q.* TREBELL.
TREBLECOCK, *n.f.*, *i.q.* TREBILCOCK.
TREBLETHICK, *i.q.* TREMBLETHICK.
TREBLY, ? BELI's dwelling.
TREBLYAN, *n.f.*, *i.q.* TREMBLYAN.
TREBNET, *n.f.*, ? *i.q.* TREWANNET.
TREBUDANNON, ? DANNON dwelling place (*treva*).
TREBOER, ? pasture (*paur, w.*) house.
TREBOLLAN, the clayey pit, pool (*polan*), *or* miry town, *Pr.*
TREBOLLANCE, ? lambs' (*eanes*) pool (*pol*), *or* moor (*hal*) house (*trev*).
TREBOLLET, ? BOLEIT house.
TREBOST, house by the pillar (*post*).
TREBOTHACK, ? DAGGE's dwelling.
TREBOTHEVY, *i.q.* TREBATHEVY.
TRE-BOWL, -BOUL, ? Paul's dwelling.
TREBOWL-IN, -ING, *i.q.* TREBOLLAN, *Pr.*; the dwelling by the round (*buelin* ?), *Francis*; *or*, bowling green house.
TREBOYS, ? BOAYS's dwelling.
TREBRABO, *i.q.* TREBABOE.
TREBR-AKE, -EAK, *i.q.* TREBERICK.
TREBRASE, ? meadow (*pras*) house.
TREBRAY, ? = HIL- (*bre*) TON.
TREBROWN, *i.q.* TREGABROWN.
TREBUDANNON, *i.q.* TREBODANNON.
TREBULL-AM, -OM, ? ? William's d.
TREBULLEN, ? pool (*polan*) town.
TREBULLET, *i.q.* TREBOLLET.
TREBURGET, ? Argwedd's (*w.*) d.
TREBURG-IE, -Y, *i.q.* TREWORGY.
TREBURLAND, ? BURLAND town.
TREBURLEY, ? rose (*breilu*) house.
TREBURRICK, ? *i.q.* TREBERICK.
TREBURROW, *i.q.* TREBARROW.
TREBURS-EY, -YE, *o.* -US, ? BERSEY's *or* BIRHSI's dwelling (*tre*).
TREBURTHA, *i.q.* TREWARTHA.
TREBURTHES, *i.q.* TREBERTHES.
TREBU-RTHICK, -THICK, ? PETHERICK's *or* PETHICK's dwelling (*tre*).
TREBURTLE, ? Bartholomew's (*Bertyl*) dwelling.
TREB-Y, -YAN, -YNE, *i.q.* TREBICEN.
TREBY JEW, *i.q.* TREBEJEW.
TREC-AGE, -CAGE, ? *i.q.* TREGEAGE.

TREC-AIN, -CAIN, ? KEN town.
TRECALOW, *n.f.*, ? *i.q.* TREGOLLA.
TRECAN, the white (*can*), *or* singer's (*can*, a song) town, *Pr.*; ? *i.q.* TRECARN, *J.B.*; moon (*can*) town, *Beal.*
TRECAREP, *i.q.* TREDARRUP.
TRECAR-N, -NE, -REN, ? hill (*carn*) house, *J.B.*; *or*, CARNE's dwelling.
TRECARREL, ? = CHARLESTOWN.
TRECAZORAN, *i.q.* TREGAZORAN.
TRECHICVELL, *o.n.f.*, ? ANKEVAL d.
TRECHUNSEY, ? CUNSIE's dwelling.
TRECKENDALE, *i.q.* TREGONDALE.
TRECL-AGO, -EGGA, -EGO, -IGOE, ? ? rock *or* cliff (*clegar*) dwelling.
TRE CLOSE, ? *i.q.* PARK TREA.
TRECLYSTEN, 15 *cent.*, ? Glystian's (*w.*) *or* scarlet oak (*glastan*) town.
TRECOLLAS, *i.q.* TREGOLLAS.
TREC-OMBE, -UME, vale (*cum*) house.
TRECONNER, ? *i.q.* CONNERTON.
TRECOOGO, ? cave (*ogo*) dwelling.
TRECOOSE, wood (*cus*) house.
TRECORM, ? ? QUARM's dwelling.
TRECORN, ? corner (*corn*), *or* rock (*carn*) dwelling.
TRECORNER, ? Garanhir's (*w.*) d.
TRECORNICK, ? KERNICK town.
TRECOTHICK, *i.q.* TREGOTHICK.
TRECRABEN, *i.q.* TRECROBBEN.
TRECRAGEN, the ragged rock town, *H.*; ? Grwgawn's (*w.*) town.
TRECREEGE, ? barrow (*creeg*) town.
TRECROB-BEN, -IN, the place on the crooked hill (*tre crom ben*), *Mur.*
TRECRO-GA, -OGO, the shelly town, *Pr.*; ? Rhagaw's (*w.*) dwelling.
TRECROMBE, round (*crom*) town, *R.E.*
TRECUGAR, ? CUDJORE town.
TRECULLIACK, ? Cwyllog's (*w.*) t.
TRECURDEN, *n.f.*, *i.q.* TREGERTEN.
TRECURNEL, ? corner (*cornel*) house.
TRECUT, *d.d.*, ? wood (*coit*) town.
TREDALLET, ? ? Tallard's (*w.*) d.
TREDAN-ECK, -ICK, -NACK, ? Tanwg's dwelling; *or*, *i.q.* TREDENNACK.
TREDAR-AP, -RAP, -ROP, -RUP, *i.q.* TRETHARAP, &c.
TREDAVOE, sheep (*davas*) town, *Pr.*;

David's town, *R. W.*

TRED-AWL, -AULE, *o.* -WEL, *d.d.* -VAL, ? ? Idwal's (*w.*) town.

TRED-EAGE, *o.* -AEK, -EK, *d.d.* -HAC, *i.q.* TRETHEAGE.

TREDEATHY, ? Teithi's (*w.*) dwelling.

TREDEN-DALE, -DLE, ? ? the dale (*an dol*) land (*tireth*), *or* dwelling (*tre*[d])

TREDENEN, ? DINAN's dwelling.

TREDENHAM, DINHAM's town.

TREDEN-ICK, -NACK, -NECK, -NEY, -Y, *i.q.* TREDINICK.

TREDEOWORCH, *e.d.d.*, *i.q.* TRETDE-WORD, *d.d.*, ? *now* TRATFORD.

TREDERR-AP, -IP, *i.q.* TRETHARRUP.

TREDEW-AY, -Y, -I, ? *i.q.* TRETHEWY.

TREDH-EUERGY, -UERGY, *O.*, ? *i.q.* TREWORGY.

TRE-DHU, -DU, black (*du*) town.

TRED-IDON, -ITHEN, -YDAN, ? furze (*eithin*) land (*tireth*), *or* house.

TREDINE, *Le.*, ? = Castle- (*din*) ton.

TREDINHAM, DINHAM's town.

TREDIN-ICK, -NICK, -NY, fortified town, *or* town on the hill, *Pr.*; ? furzy (*eithenic*) land (*tireth*).

TRED-IS, -ICE, -IX, ? stack- (*das, w.*) h.

TREDISECK, 13 *cent.*, ? *i.q.* TREDRIS-SICK, *or*

TREDITHICK, ? Tudwyg's (*w.*) house.

TREDIVETT, ? David's dwelling.

TREDNOW, ? bare (*noth*), *or* new land (*tireth*).

TREDO-LE, -LL, -WELL, ? dale (*dol*) dwelling *or* farm.

TREDO-ER, -ORE, -WER, the town by the water (*dour*) side, *Pr.*

TREDONNELL, ? Domhnal's (*i.*) d.

TREDORN, ? oak (*derwen*) town.

TREDOWN, ? the dwelling on the *down*; *or*, *i.q.* TRETHOWAN.

TREDR-E, -EA, -EE, the town on the thoroughfare (*dre*, through), *D.G.*; ? = *tir-adre*, homer-land; *or*, *i.q.*

TREDREATH, TREATH dwelling.

TREDREN-EN, -NEN, *i.q.* TRENDRENAN

TREDR-ESSICK, -ISICK, ? brambly (*dreisic*) land (*tireth*), *or* dwelling (*tre*).

TREDROSSEL, ? Drwsgl's (*w.*) dwelling.

TREDRUS-SON, -STAN, -STON, ? mole-hill (*torosen*) land (*tir*).

TREDRYNE, ? = THORN- (*draen*) TON.

TREDUAN, ? John's (*Dzhuan*) town.

TREDUDWELL, ? Tudwal's (*w.*) town.

TREDUNDLE, *i.q.* TREDENDALE.

TREDWEN, ? St. Adwen's town.

TREE ACRES, ? *three acre* field, *t.*

TREEGOODWILL, *i.q.* TREGOODWILL.

TREE HAM, meadow (*ham, t.*), *or* boundary (*hem*) with a *tree* on it; *also* TREE-PARK, -CLOSE, -FIELD, -MEADOW, -MOOR, &c., *t.* (?).

TREEMAN, *n.f.*, ? *i.q.* TREMAINE.

TREEN, *i.q.* TREREEN.

TREE-SA, -ZA, ? lower (*isa*) town.

TREETH, ? heath (*heyth*) dwelling; *or*, *i.q.* TREATH.

TREEVE, *i.q.* TREREIFE.

TREEVESA, *i.q.* TREVISA.

TREE YEW, *T.a.*, *i.q.* TREYEW.

TREFAN, little *or* stone (*man*) town.

TREFAUL, *i.q.* TREFRAUL.

TREFDEWIG, 10 *cent.*, ? Dwyvach's (*w.*) town.

TREFECHION, *n.f.*, ? *i.q.* TREBEGEAN.

TREFEDOW, *n.f.*, ? *i.q.* TREVIDO.

TREFELLANS, *n.f.*, *i.q.* TREVELLANS.

TREFEN, ? *i.q.* TREVEAN.

TREFENICK, *i.q.* TREVENEAGE.

TREFEW, ? yew-tree (*yw*) house.

TREFEWHA, higher (*ewha*) h., *R. W.*

TREFFR-EY, -EYE, -Y, dwelling on the hill (*bre*); = HILTON.

TREFGURED, 10 *cent.*, ? Cowryd's (*w.*) d.

TREFILIES, *d.d.*, *i.q.* TREVILLIS.

TREFILL, ? ? rustic's (*fyll*) dwelling.

TREFOIL, ? clover [field].

TREFOR-D, -DA, ? ford (*s.*) dwelling.

TREFORNOC, *d.d.*, *i.q.* TREVORNOCK.

TREFRAN-K, -CK, the French, liberty, *or* Frank's town, *Pr.*

TREFRAUL, ? Rioval's dwelling.

TREFR-EAKE, -EOCK, -EOKE, *d.d.* -IOCK, fruitful (*frech*) town, *Pr.*; wife's (*freg*) town, *H.*; ? FREOCK's farm.

TREFRESA, ? lower (*isa*) TREFRY.

TREFREW, ? dwelling (*tref*) on the slope (*rhiw, w.*).

TREFREWS, ? Trefrew's (*n.f.*) [farm].
TREFRID-A, -AY, *i.q.* TREVRIDA.
TREFRINK, *i.q.* TREFRANK.
TREFR-IZE, -OYSE, -YSE, -YZ, ? Rhys's (*w.*) d., *R.W.*; or, *i.q.* TREFRESA.
TREFROAN, ? hill (*bron*) house.
TREFRONICK, dwelling on the way-to-the-rivulet (*for an ick*), T.; town of frogs or lizards (*cronec*), *Pr.*
TREFRUFF, *i.q.* TRERUFF.
TREFRY, hill (*fry*) town, *Pr.*
TREFRYETHE, 14 *cent.*, ? TREFRY heath (*heyth*).
TREFULA, the owl's (*ula*) town; or, town of elms (*ulau*), *Pr.*
TREF-ULICK, -ULLOCK, 14 *cent.* -UAL-LOC, *the same*, *Pr.*; ? Uallach's (*i.*) d.
TREFUNDRYN, 13 *cent.*, ? HENDEERN'S dwelling; or, *i.q.* TRENDRAIN.
TREFURSDON, *i.q.* TREVORSDEN.
TREFURTHER, ? *i.q.* TREWARTHA.
TREFUS-ES, -IS, -US, walled (*fozes*) habitation, *Pr.*; place of threshing, *C.*; three spindles, *Beal.*
TREFYNESKIN, 14 *cent.*, rush-spring (*fenten hescen*) dwelling.
TREFYNS, *i.q.* TREVINCE.
TREGABEGELLA, ? herdsmens' (*bugel-low*) dwelling place (*tregva*).
TREGABROWN, hill (*bron*), or rush (*bruin*) dwelling (*tregva*).
TREGAD-A, -ICK, -DOCK, ? *i.q.* TRE-GODICK, *or* TREGADIACK.
TREGAD-DRA,-DERETH,*i.q.* TREGODRA
TREGADGER, ? CUDJORE dwelling.
TREGADGWALL, ? castle- (*cadzhel*) ton.
TREGA-DGWITH, -GEWITH, ? CADG-WITH dwelling.
TREGA-DIACK, -DJACK, -GECK, -GA, -JA, ? bloody (*gudzhic*) dwelling.
TREGADIL-ACK, *n.f.* -LOCK, ? TAL-LOCK'S dwelling.
TREGADILLET, ? *i.q.* TREDALLET.
TREGAER, place of the camp (*caer*), *M'L.*; war house or castle, *Wh.*
TREGA-GLE, *o.* -GILL, dirty (*geagle*) town, *Pr.*; ? grove (*gelli*) town.
TREGA-GO, -GE, ? Jago's dwelling.
TREGAIDOW, ? Ceidio's (*w.*) d.

TREGAIN, fair (*cain*) town, *R.W.*
TREGAIR, *i.q.* TREGA-ER, -RE.
TREGAIROON, ? TREGAIR down (*gwon*)
TREGAISE, ? tax-gatherer's (*cais, w.*) d.
TREGAJORRAN, *i.q.* TREGAZORAN.
TREGAKES, *n.f.*, ? TREGEAK'S (*n.f.*) farm.
TREGA-LE, *d.d.* -L, ? moor (*hal*) d.
TREGALLARD, ? Gellard's (*n.f.*) d.
TREGA-LLAS, -LLES, *i.q.* TREGULLAS.
TREGA-LLEN, -LLON, -ALTON, ? ? hazel (*collen, w.*) town.
TREGALLER, ? town of grief (*galar*).
TREGALLY, ? *i.q.* TREGELLY.
TREGALRAVEAN, small (*bian*) miry (*caillar*, mire) town, T.
TREGAMEDON, *i.q.* TREGAVETHAN.
TREGA-MEER, -MERE, -MORE, the great (*mear, maur*) dwelling.
TREGAMELL-IN, -ING, -ON, mill (*melin*) dwelling (*tregva*), *Pr.*; ? MELLION'S
TREGAMEN-A,-NA,? MENNA dwelling.
TREGAMINNI-AN, -ON, the stone dwellings, *Pr.*; ? John's TREGAMENA.
TREGANDEAN, the (*an*) man's (*den*) dwelling, *Pr.*; ? ENDEAN'S d.; or, d. by the fortification (*an din*); or, *i.q.* TREGANIAN.
TREGANELL, *n.f.*, *i.q.* TREGONELL.
TREGANETHA, the spinster's (?) town, *H.*; the great (*an etha*) dwelling, *Pr.*; ? CUNAIDA'S dwelling.
TREGAN-GEEVS, -JEEVS, *o.* TRECON-CHIEVES, ? ? sheep (*deves*) down (*goon*) house; or, house of the drink (*an dewes*); or, the *jews'* h.
TREGANGY, ? *i.q.* TRECHUNSEY.
TREGANH-AWKE, -OE, -OWE, the (*an*) pig (*hoch, hoh*) town, *T.C.*; ? Caenog's (*w.*) town.
TREGANHORN, the iron (*horn*) dwelling, *Pr.*; the dwelling in the corner (*corn*), *Wh.*
TREGANHOSE, ? Cwnws's (*w.*) d.
TREGAN-IAN, -JAN, -JOHN, the cold (*iein*) dwelling, or on the sea-shore (*ian* ?), *Pr.*; furze (*eithin*) town (*tre*) on the down (*goon*), T.
TREGA-NMEDAN, *d.d.*, 14 *cent.* -MEDAN,

now TRE-, TRI-GAVETHAN.

TREGANN-A, -ACK, ? Caenog's (*w.*) d.

TREGANNANE, ?ash-tree (*onen*) house.

TREGANO-AN, -ON, -N, -WAN, -WEN, dwelling on the down (*an oon*) ; *or*, CONAN'S dwelling.

TREGANOER, ? CUNWOR's dwelling.

TREGANSE, 15 *cent.*, ? CHENISI'S d.

TREGANT-ALLAN, -ELLAN, ? ? NANT-ALLAN, *or* Cyndelyn's (*w.*) d.

TREGAN-TEL, -TLE, d. of danger (*antell*), *Pr.* ; place of containing, *i.e.* a depot ; (*cuntell*, a collection), *C.*

TREGANYAN, *i.q.* TREGANIAN.

TREGAR-DEN, -DIN, -THEN, -THYN, -N, a dwelling on (*or*) a high place (*din*), *Pr.*; place of encampment, *C.*

TREGARDER, ?*i.q.* CHE-, CHY-GARDER.

TREGAR-DOCK, *d.d.* -ADUC, ? CRA-DOCK'S dwelling.

TREGARE, town of love *or* friendship, (*care*, to love), *H.* ; *i.q.* TREGEAR.

TREGARG-ET,-OT,?*i.q.*TREBURGET; *or*, TREGARGUS, over-wood (*ar gus*) h.

TREGAR-ICK, -RICK, -RECK, -RACK, dwelling by the rock (*carrag*), *T.*

TREGARLA, ? Crallo's (*w.*) town.

TREGARLAND, ? GORLAND dwelling.

TREGARLICK, ? HARLAKE dwelling.

TREGAR-N, -NE, *i.q.* TRECARN. T. CONDURROW, *i.q.* CONDURROW T.

TREGAR-ON,-N, dwelling on the down (*ar oon*) ; *or*, Caron's (*w.*) dwelling.

TREGARRAS, ? GARRAS dwelling.

TREGARRAST, ? the dwelling in the waste open ground (*gorest, w.*).

TREGART-AN, -ON, -HEN, -YN, ? *i.q.* TREGARDAN.

TREGARTH, ? high (*gwarth*) dwelling.

TREGARTHA, ? *i.q.* TREWARTHA.

TREGARTH-EN, -IAN, -YN, ? *i.q.* TRE-GARDEN, *or* Gorddyfyn's (*w.*) dwelling (*tre*).

TREGARTHERAL, ? TREWARTHA on the moor (*ar hal*).

TREGARTHICK, ? Grathack's (*w.*) d.

TREGARTHY, ? *i.q.* TREGURTHY.

TREGARV-EAN, -IN, little (*bean*) TRE-GEAR.

TREGARVON, ? *i.q.* TREGARON.

TREGASA, *i.q.* TREGASICK.

TREGASCOE, elder-trees' (*scaw*) h.

TREGASEAL, ? council (*cusul*) house.

TREGAS-ICK, -SACK, -SA, -SAH, -SOW, dirty (*gassic*) place, *Pr.* ; wood (*cus-ic*) town, *H.* ; (*cesow*, turfs).

TREGASK-ASS, -ES, -IS, -US, -Y, *n.f.*, ? dwelling in the covert (*guskys*).

TREGASKING, *n.f.*, ? HOŚKIN's d.

TREGASTICK, *i.q.* TREGUSTICK.

TREGASWITH, ? CUSWARTH d.

TREGATH, ? *i.q.* TREGARTH.

TREGATHE-ENAN, -NAN, ? DINAN's dwelling place (*tregva*).

TREGATHER-ALL, -EL, *i.q.* TREGART-.

TREGATILLION, ? owl (*dylluan*) town.

TREGAT-TA, -HA, ? *i.q.* TREGARTHA.

TREGAUR, 14 *cent.*, ? goat (*gavar*) t.

TREGAVARR-A,-AH, bread (*bara*) town, *B.* ; ? higher (*warra* = *wartha*) d.

TREGAVARRAS, *i.q.* TREGARRAS.

TREGAV-ERN, -ORN, ? marsh *or* alder (*gwern, gwarn*) house (*tregva*).

TREGAVETHA, ? graves' (*bedhou*) d.

TREGAVETHAN, grave town, *H.* ; d. in the meadow (*meddon, Lh.*), *Pr.*

TREGAV-ETHICK, -ITHICK, ? Byddig's (*w.*), *or* great (*ithic*) dwelling.

TREGA-VONE, -WNE, the dwelling (*tregva*) on the down (*gwon*).

TREGAVRAN, *d.d.*, ? Gafran's (*w.*) d.

TREGAWEN, ? Gawen's (*w.*) d., *R.W.*

TREGAY, place enclosed by a hedge (*ce*), *Pr.* ; ? Cai's (*w.*) dwelling.

TREGAYES, ? Tregay's (*n.f.*) [place].

TREGAZA, *i.q.* TREGASICK.

TREGAZORAN, dwelling of anger (*sor*), *or* in the corner (*sorn*), *Pr.*

TREGDA, 17 *cent.*, ? *i.q.* TREGADA.

TREGEA, *i.q.* TREGAY.

TREGEAGE, ? Ciwg's (*w.*) d. ; *or*, *i.q.*

TREGEAGLE, *i.q.* TREGAGLE.

TREGEAN, giant's (*ghean*) town, *Car.* ; ? Cian's (*w.*) d., *R.W.*; *or*, John's d.

TREGEA-R, -RE, the green (*gear*) *or* flourishing place, fair *or* pretty town *or* goodly dwelling, *Pr.* ; camp *or* castle (*caer*) town.

TREGEAR VEAN, little TREGEAR.

T. WOON, Tregear on the down (*gwon*)

TREGEDA, ? Cadw's (*w.*) dwelling.

TREGEDICK, *n.f.*, ? *i.q.* TREGADICK.

TREGEDNA, ? Idno's (*w.*) dwelling.

TREGEDON, *n.f.*, ? *i.q.* TREGIDDEN.

TREGEDRA, *i.q.* TREGODDREATH.

TREGEEN, ? *i.q.* TREGEAN.

TREGEETH, ? heath (*heydh*) dwelling.

TREGEGON, ? KIGGAN dwelling.

TREGEL, *d.d.*, ? *i.q.* TREGELLY.

TREGELLA, ? elm (*elau*) house.

TREGELLAN, ? fir-tree (*aidhlan*) h.

TREGELL-AS, -ES, -US, decayed, lost, or destroyed (*cellys*) town, *Gw.*; grove (*kelvez*, hazel grove, *a.*) town, *Pr.*; ? = HELSTON.

TREGELL-AST, -EST, -IST, ? east TREGEL; (*gellast*, a bitch, *w.*).

TREGELLY, grove (*celli*) town.

TREGEMB-ER, -O, ? Welshman's d.

TREGEMBRIS, ? Ambrose's dwelling.

TREGEMELIN, *d.d.*, mill (*melin*) d.

TREGEN-A, -NA, -NAH, -NO, -NOW, dwelling at mouth (*genau*) or entrance of a place, *Pr.*

TREGEND-AR, -ER, ? Enoder's (*c.n.*) d.

TREGENNON, ? Cynan's (*w.*) d., *R.W.*

TREGENOR, *n.f.*, *i.q.* TREGANOER.

TREGENTLE, *i.q.* TREGANTLE.

TREGENVEAN, ? Cynvyn's (*w.*) d.

TREGENVER, ?Cynvor's (*w.*) dwelling.

TREGENYN, ? Cennyn's (*w.*) dwelling.

TREGENZ-A,-ER,?CHENISI'S,CUNSIE'S, or the first (*censa*) dwelling.

TREGEO, ? ? yew (*yw*, *w.*) house.

TREGERE, *n.f.*, *i.q.* TREGEAR.

TREGER-ICK, -RICK, -Y, green (*gear*) or fruitful place, or dwelling of love (*care*, to love), *Pr.*; ? Herygh's (*i.*) dwelling (*tregva*).

TREGERR-IN, -YN, ? Egryn's (*w.*) d.

TREGERTHEN, village (*tre*) of the hill (*din*) fortification (*garth*), *Beal.*

TREGERTHY, *n.f.*, ? *i.q.* TREGURTHA.

TREGERVIAN, ?little (*bian*)TREGEAR; or, *i.q.* TREGIFFIAN.

TREGESEAL, *i.q.* TREGASEAL.

TREGESTICK, *i.q.* TREGUSTICK.

TREGETH-AS, -US, ? father's (*das*), or judgment (*cuhudhas*) house.

TREGETHEN, ? *i.q.* TREGERTHEN.

TREGETH-EW, -OW, ? Iddew's (*w.*) d.

TREGEURAN, *n.f.*, ? UREN'S d.

TREGEV-AS, -IS, ? ? outer (*aves*) d.

TREGEW, the flourishing or place of support, or of spears, *Pr.*; ? yew (*yw*), or GEW or high (*uch*) d.

TREGEWELL, ? JEWELL'S town.

TREGEZA, ? lower (*isa*) dwelling.

TREGGASS-AN, -ON, ? ? COSWIN town.

TREGG-IAN, -ON, *n.f.*, ? *i.q.* TREGEAN.

TREGIDDEN, ? fowler's (*idne*) town.

TREGIDD-ERIS, -RIS, Idris's (*w.*) d.

TREGIDDLE, ?Cadfael's (*w.*) dwelling.

TREGID-EAN, *n.f.*, -EON, -IAN, -IDON, = *treg-i-gian*, giant's dwelling, *Pr.*

TREGIDG-A, -O, *n.f.*, ? *i.q.* TREGEZA.

TREGIDO, *n.f.*,?*i.q.*TREGID-GIA,-IDEO, ? ivy (*idhio*) house.

TREGIE, ? ? *i.q.* TREGVA.

TREGIFFIAN, ? little (*bian*) TREGIE; or, *i.q.* TREVEGEAN; *o.* TREGERVIAN, ? = *treg uar vyen*, the town on the stone wall, *B.*

TREGIGA, *n.f.*, *i.q.* TREGIDGA.

TREGILD-ERN, -REN, ? Elldeyrn's (*w.*) dwelling (*tregva*).

TREGILG-AS, -US, ? moor or hill (*hal*) wood (*cus*) dwelling or town-place.

TREGILLA, ? *i.q.* TREGELLA.

TREGILL-AS, -IES, -IS, *n.f.*, *i.q.* TREGELLAS, or TREGILGAS.

TREGILLI-O, -ON, the dwelling (*tre*) in the groves (*kelliow*), *Pr.*

TREGILVIN, ? ELUUIN'S dwelling.

TREGINGALE, *d.d.*, (TREGHINGALA, *e.d.d.*), the grove (*an gelli*) dwelling (*tregva*).

TREGIN-GY, -NY, ? ? the dwelling by the water (*an gy*); or, CHENISI'S d.

TREGINNAY, ? *i.q.* TREGENNA.

TREGINNEGAR, ? CENGAR'S dwelling.

TREGION, ? *i.q.* TREGEAN.

TREGIRL-ES, -S, *i.q.* TREGURLES.

TREGISEAL, *i.q.* TREGASEAL.

TREGISKEY, the blessed town, *Pr.* ! ! ? *i.q.* TREVISKEY.

TREGISSW-AN, -YN, ⸮ SWAIN's d.

TREGIT, *n.f.*, ⸮ wood (*coit*) house.

TREGITH-A, -EW, *i.q.* TREGETHEW.

TREGLARICK, ⸮⸮ parson's (*cloirec*) h.

TREGLAST-A,-AN, scarlet-oak (*glastan*) town, *Pr.*; ⸮ GLASDON dwelling.

TREGLAWN, wool (*glawn*) town, *Pr.*; the town of caves, *or* near the cave (*clone*), *B.* ; ⸮ fox (*lowern*) h.

TREGLEAH, law (*laha*) town *or* dwelling, *H.*; north (*cledh*) place, *J.B.*

TREGL-EATH, -ITH, the place of the ditch (*cledh*) *or* entrenchment, *M'L.*

TREGLES, ⸮ church (*eglos*) town.

TREGL-IDGWITH, -IGWITH, ⸮⸮⸮ privet grove (*celli yswith*), *or* Elisaued (*s.B.m.*) *or* Elizabeth's dwelling.

TREGLIGH, ⸮⸮ Gelhig's (*w.*) dwelling.

TREGLINES, ⸮⸮ nun's (*laines*) d.

TREGL-INICK, ⸮ *o.* -ENNICHE, ⸮ CALEN-ICK town *or* dwelling.

TREGLINWITH, ⸮ ash grove (*celli en-with*) moor (*hal*).

TREGLIS-SON, -TIAN, ⸮ *i.q.* TREGLAS-TAN, *or* TRECLYSTEN.

TREGLISTIAN WARTHA & WALLAS, higher *and* lower TREGLISTIAN.

TREGLI-TH, -ATH, ⸮ *i.q.* TREGLEATH.

TREGLO-HAN, -WN, -WAN, ⸮ *i.q.* TRE-GLAWN, *or* TRELAWN.

TREGLO-SACK, -SSICK, -JACK, ⸮ *i.q.* TRELASK ; *or*, grey (*ludzhic*) d.

TREGL-OME, -UM, ⸮ bare (*llwm, w.*), naked, *or* barren place; *or*, ST. COLUMB's dwelling.

TREGLY-N, -NN, -NE, ⸮ holly (*celin*), *or* glen (*glyn*) town.

TREGNEDEWID, ⸮ David's TREGNY, *or* TREGONY.

TREGO, *n.f.*, *i.q.* TREAGO, *or*

TREGOA-D, -TH, ⸮ wood (*coat*), *or* old (*coth*) house.

TREGOAN, ⸮ down (*gwon*) house.

TREGO-ASE, -ISE, ⸮ blood (*gois*), *or* wood (*cus*) house.

TREGODDR-A, *o.* -EATH, h. (*tregva*) on the strand (*treath*) ; *or*, Cadrod's (*w.*) dwelling.

TREGODDREATH VEAN & VEOR, little *and* great TREGODDRA.

TREGOD-ICK, -DICK, -DECK, ⸮ ÆDOC's *or* CADOCK's town ; (*coed-ic*, woody).

TREGO-E, -F, -IF, smith's (*gof*) dwelling, *R.W.*

TREGOGIAN, *i.q.* TREGEAN.

TREGOIN, *d.d.*, ⸮ *i.q.* TREGONY.

TREGOL-DS, -LAS, -LS, holy (*gol*), *or* bushy (*gols*), *or* lower (*gullas*) town.

TREGO-LE, -LL, *the same* ; *or*, dwelling by the hazels (*coll, w.*).

TREGOMELLING, *i.q.* TREGAMELLIN.

TREGOMINI-AN, -ON, ⸮⸮ MENWIN-NION dwelling (*tregva*).

TREGON, *d.d.*, ⸮ *i.q.* TREGOON.

TREGONA, downs (*gwonau*) town, *Pr.*; ⸮ *i.q.* TREGONY.

TREGON-AN, -EN, -HAIN, ⸮ CONAN's d.

TREGONCE, ⸮ *i.q.* TREGANCE.

TREGOND-ALE, -ELL, ⸮ *i.q.* BOSCUNDLE

TREGONDEAN, ⸮ *i.q.* TREGANDEAN.

TREGONE, *i.q.* TREGOON.

TREGONEBR-AS, -IS, ⸮⸮ CARN-BRAS *or* -VRES, *or* GONEBRAS dwelling.

TREGONEGGIE, ⸮CARNEGGY dwelling.

TREGONELL, dwelling on the GAN-NEL ; *or*, *i.q.* TREGWINDLE.

TREGONG-AN, -ON, ⸮ dwelling on the down (*an goon*).

TREGONGER, CONGIER dwelling.

TREGONH-ANSA, -OSE, ⸮⸮ CHENISI's d.

TREGON-HAY, -ICK, -IN, dwelling en-closed (*hay*) on the common, *Pr.*

TREGON-ICK, -NICK, -OCK, dwelling on the common (*gwon*) by the water (*ick*), *M'L.* ; ⸮ CONNOCK's d.

TREGON-IN, -ING, -NAN, -NEN, -NIN, -NING, -NON, downs' town, *Po.* ; ⸮ CONAN's dwelling.

TREGONIN-NY, -IA, ⸮⸮ d. on the down by the water (*an ick, M'L.*).

T. VEAR, great (*mear*) TREGONINNY.

T. VENTON, T. by the well (*fenten*).

TREGON-ION, -JOHN, ⸮⸮ John's TRE-GONE ; *or*, *i.q.* TREGANIAN.

TREGON-ISSY, -NIS, ⸮ CHENISI's d.

TREGONITHA, *i.q.* TREGANETHA.

TREGONNA, *i.q.* TREGONA.

TREGONNET, ⸮ Conaid's (*w.*) d.

TREGONN-ICK, -OCK, downy town, *Po.* ; ? CONNOCK's dwelling.

TREGON-WELL,-NELL, ? CYNOWAL's d.

TREGONY, dwellings on the common (*gwon*) near the river (*gwy*), *Pr.* ; castle on the [river] Cenia, *Wh.* ; little-town at the mouth (*genau*), *Cam.* ; *p.s.* St. Jacobus, *O.*

T. HAYN, TREGONY *haven*.

T.-JOHN, -AN, ?? John's (*n.f.*) T.

TREGOODEN, tree (*gwydden*) t., *R.W.*

TREGOODWELL, ? Cadfael's (*w.*) d.

TREGOOLAS, *i.q.* TREGULLAS.

TREGOON, d. on the down (*gwon*).

TREGOONEBRIS, *i.q.* TREGONEBRAS.

TREGOOSE, *i.q.* TREGOASE.

TREGORDEN, *i.q.* TREGARDEN.

TREGORDOCK, *i.q.* TREGARDOCK.

TREGORETH, ? Gwryd's (*w.*) d.

TREGOR-IA, -ROW, *i.q.* TREGURROW.

TREGOR-ICK, -RICK, -RIK, town on the river (*gwar ick*), *Pr.* ; ? *i.q.* TREGARICK.

TREGORLA-N, -ND, *i.q.* TREGARLAND.

TREGORLOE, ? Crallo's (*w.*) dwelling.

TREGOR-RIN, -YAN, ? Carawn's d.

TREGORS, ? moor (*cors*) town.

TREGORTHA, *i.q.* TREGARTHA.

TREGOS-E, -S, -SE, *i.q.* TREGOASE.

TREGOSS-A, -AGH, *n.f.* -OW, -ICK, *i.q.* TREGASICK. (*cossow*, woods).

TREGOTHA, old (*coth*) t., *J.B.* ; hay (*gorha*) town, *Pr.* ; ? *i.q.* TREGORTHA

TREGOTHICK, *i.q.* TRECOTHICK.

TREGOTHNAN, old (*coth*) town on the plain, or in the valley (*nans*), *Pr.* ; place of the twisting (*goth*) brook (*nant, w.*), *C.* ; ? wood (*coed*) valley d.

TREGOULS, *i.q.* TREGOLDS.

TREGOUN, *n.f.*, *i.q.* TREGOON.

TREGOW, smith's (*gov*) dwelling.

TREGOWETH, ? wood (*cuit*) house.

TREGOWNE, *i.q.* TREGOON.

TREGO-WRAS,-URIS, ? *i.q.* TREGARRAS, or TREGARRAST.

TREGO-YD, -YE, -YES, -YS, -ZE, wood (*coed, coz*), or blood (*gois*) town.

TREGRADECK, *i.q.* TREGARDOCK.

TREGRA-GEN, -GON, -N, *n.f.* -HAN,

? *i.q.* TRECRAGAN.

TREGR-AY, -EA, ? Gwrhai's (*w.*) d.

TREGR-EEN,-EN, *o.* -EHAN,-IAN, green town or d., *B.*; ? *i.q.* TREGRAGEN.

TREGR-ELL,*d.d.*-L, -ILL,-YLL, Gwrill's (*w.*) dwelling.

TREGUALL, the walled (*gwal,* a wall) town, *Pr.* ; ? high (*uhal*) dwelling.

TREGUARMOND, ? Wermund's (*t.*) d. ; or, *i.q.* TREWARVENETH.

TREGUD-DICK, -ICK, -DOCK, *i.q.* TREGODICK.

TREGUE, *i.q.* TREGEW.

TREGU-FFIT, -ITH, ? *i.q.* TREGOWETH.

TREGUGIAN, *i.q.* TREGOGIAN.

TREGUIN, *e.d.d.*, *i.q.* TREWIN.

TREGULE, ? field (*gweal*) house.

TREGULL-AN, -AND, -ON, -EN, ? hazel-tree (*collen*) house; or, Collen's (*w.*).

TREGULLAS, lower (*gullas*) town, *R.W.*

TREGULLOW, *the same, Pr.*; d. of light (*golow*), or in the groves (*killiow*).

TREGUNE, *i.q.* TREGOWN.

TREGUNGER, *i.q.* TREGONGER.

TREGUN-ICK, -NICK, *i.q.* TREGONNICK

TREGUNN-A, -O, -OWE, ? *i.q.* TREGONA.

TREGUNN-AN, -ON, *i.q.* TREGONAN.

TREGUNNEL, *i.q.* TREGONWELL.

TREGUNNET, *i.q.* TREGONNET.

TREGUNNUS, ? *i.q.* TREGONNISSY.

TREGURLES, ? crushed (*crehyllys*) d.

TREGURN, ? *i.q.* TRECARN.

TREGURN-O, -W, ? CURNO's dwelling.

TREGURR-A,-O,-OW,-Y, ? camp (*caerau*) town ; or, *i.q.*

TREGURTH-A, -Y, ? *i.q.* TREWARTHA.

TREGURRI-N, -AN, *i.q.* TREGORRIN.

TREGURTHEN, ? *i.q.* TREGERTHEN.

TREGURY, ? goldsmith's (*eure*) d. ; or, *i.q.* TREGUR-RA, or -THA.

TREGUSKING, *n.f.*, HOSKIN's d.

TREGUSTICK, USTICK's dwelling.

TREGUTH, ? *i.q.* TREGOAD.

TREGVA, ? dwelling (*trege*, to dwell) place (*va* = *ma*), abode, house.

TREGVIS, ? field (*maes*) house.

TREGWALL, *i.q.* TREGUALL.

TREGWALLANS, *i.q.* TREVALLANCE.

TREGWERYS, *i.q.* TREWEERES.

TREGWIDE, wood (*cuit*) house.

TREGW-INDLE, -YNNEL, ? Gwynodle's (*w.*) dwelling.

TREGWIN-ES, -YS, GENIS'S dwelling.

TREGWITHEN, *i.q.* TREWITHEN.

TREGY-N, -ON, *i.q.* TREGEAN.

TREHADDLE, *i.q.* TREADDLE.

TREHA-L, -IL, -LE, moor (*hal*) town.

TRE-HALWEN, -HALLWIN, dwelling on the white-moor (*hal win*).

TREHA-N, -NE, summer (*han*) t., *Pr.*; old *or* ancient (*hen*) town, *Po.*

TREHANEVEAN, little TREHANE.

TREHAN-ICK,-NICK, *o.*-ECK, ? *i.q.* TREHAN, *or* TREKENNEIK.

TREHA-RICK, -RRICK, -RROCK, -VARIKE, -VEROCK, ?? *i.q.* TREGORICK.

TREHAVERN, ??? *i.q.* TREGAVERN.

TREH-AVRAS, -EVERES, ? *i.q.* TREGAVARRAS; *or,* Ambrose's dwelling.

TREHA-WKE, *d.d.* -UOC, upper (*uch,* above) town, *Pr.*; hawk t., *H.*

TREHAWLE, ? moor (*hal*) town.

TREHEALE, ? same; *or,* river (*hayl*) d.

TREHEATH, ? heath (*heyth*) dwelling.

TREH-EDDY, -IDY, *i.q.* TEHIDY.

TREHE-ER, -IR, -RE, long (*hir*) town; *or,* place of battle (*heir*).

TREHERON, *n.f.,* ? iron (*haiarn*) h.

TREHIDICK, ? Cedig's (*w.*) dwelling.

TREHILL, ?? = HIL-TON (*tre*).

TREHIMBRIS, ? *i.q.* TREGEMBRIS.

TREHIN-ICK, *d.d.* -OCH, *i.q.* TREHANICK.

TREHIRE, *i.q.* TREHEER.

TREHOME, ?? HAM dwelling.

TREHOWEL, ? Howel's (*w.*) dwelling.

TREHUDRETH, high land (*yu tireth*) d., *J.Ca.*; ? Huathrit's (*w.B.m.*) d.

TREHUIST, ?? = *west* town (*tre*).

TREHUNNEST, ? Unnust's (*w.*) d.

TREHUNSEY, ? *i.q.* TRECHUNSEY.

TREHU-RST, -ST, ? *i.q.* HURSTON.

TREIAGU, *n.f., i.q.* TREJAGO.

TRE-ICE, -IS, -ISE, -ISA, ? lower (*isa*), *or* corn (*is*) town.

TREIGAER, 13 *cent.,* castle town.

TREIRE, *i.q.* TREHEER.

TREI-SAAC, -ZACK, corn (*iz-ack*) town,

Pr.; ? Isaac's (*B.m.*) dwelling.

TREISLOE, the place under (*is*) the tumulus (*loe*), *M'L.*

TREIWAL, *d.d., now* TREUHAL.

TREJAG-O, *n.f.* -U, Jago's dwelling.

TREJEWAS, Jews' village, *A.E.*; ?? beer (*deues,* drink) house, *J.B.*; *i.q.*

TREJOHJEEVES, *i.q.* TREGANGEEVS.

TREKARL, *n.f., i.q.* TRECARREL.

TREKAVUR, ? goat (*gavar*) town; *or,* great (*veor*) dwelling (*tregva*).

TREKE-AN, -EN, -IN, town on the ridge (*cein*), *Pr.*

TREKEE, *i.q.* TREGEA.

TREKEEK, ? Ciwg's (*w.*) dwelling.

TREKEL-AND, -LAND, ? HELLAND d.

TREKELLEARN, ? Aelhaiarn's (*w.*) d.

TREKEN-ING, -NING, *i.q.* TREKYNING.

TREKENNA, ? *i.q.* TREGENA.

TREKENN-AR, -ER, ? *i.q.* TREKINNER.

TREKENNICK, ? Cennych's (*w.*) d.

TREKERN-A, -ER, ? *i.q.* TRECORNER.

TREKERN-AL, -ELL, ? CARNHALE d.

TREKIEVE, ? ST. IVE's dwelling.

TREKILLICK, grove (*celli-ick*) town, *Pr.*; ? Gelhig's (*w.*) dwelling.

TREKIN-NER, -WARD, ? Cynfeirdd's (*w.*) dwelling.

TREKLAD, *o.n.f.,* ? *i.q.* TREGLEATH.

TRE-KNOW, -NOW, ?? *new* dwelling.

TREKYN-ING, -NEN, -NIN, king's t., *Wh.*; town of rabbits (*cwning, w.*), *or* leeks (*kinen*), *or* strife (?), *Pr.*

TRELABE, ?? moist (*gleb*) town.

TRELAGOE, *i.q.* TRECLAGO.

TRELAGOSSICK, *i.q.* TRELOGOSSICK.

TRELAKE, ?? *i.q.* TRELAGOE.

TRELAKES, ?? *i.q.* TRELOGGAS.

TRELA-N, -NE, *d.d.* -ND, church t., *Pr.*; (*lan,* a church, a village, *R.W.*); ? broad (*ledan*), or bank (*glan, ladn*) d.

TRELANDER, ? LANDER dwelling.

TRELANOWTH, ? new (*nowydh*) TRELAN, TREAL, *or* TRELAY.

TRELARGUS, ? over-wood (*ar gus*) TREAL *or* TRELEIGH.

TRELASE, green (*glas*) town, *Pr.*

TRELAS-H, -K, -KE, town of burning (*losc*), *or* burnt town, *Pr.*

TRELASK-A, -ER, ? long (*hir*) TRELASK

TRELASSICK, ? *i.q.* TRELOSICK.

TRELA-UDER, -WDER, thieves' (*ladron*) t., *Pr.*; thief's (*lader*) house.

TRELAV-ER,-OUR, ? Llywarch's (*w.*)d.

TRELAWARREN, *i.q.* TRELOWARREN.

TRELAWGAN, ?? ILLOGAN town.

TRELA-WN, *o.* -UN, wool (*glawn*), or open *or* clear (*lawn*) town, *Pr.*; wool h., *J.B.*; grove (*loin, w. llwyn*) h., *Beal*; *i.q.* TRELOWARREN, *C.*

TRELAWNY, TRELAWN by the water (-Y = *ick*), *Pr.*

TRELAWRY, ? LAWRY's dwelling.

TREL-AY, -EA, lesser (*le*) t.; *or*, town place (*le*); *or*, *i.q.* TRELEASE, *Pr.*

TRELE-AGE, -AGUE, -EK, law (*lacha*) town, *H.*; ? flat-stone (*lech*) d.

TRELEAN, ? Lleyn's (*w.*) dwelling.

TRELEASE, green (*glaz*) town, *Pr.*

TRELEATHICK, ?? LITHIOCK town.

TRELEAV-AN, -EN, *i.q.* TRELEVAN.

TRELEBBICK, *o.n.f.,* ? ? little (*bich*) TRELABE.

TRELECT,*o.n.f.,* ?? Elect's (*w.B.m.*) d.; *or*, moor wood (*hal coed*) house.

TRELEDDAN, ? *i.q.* TRELAND.

TRELEDDRA, cliff (*ledra*) town; *or*, place for stockings (*lydrow*), *Pr.*; ? *i.q.* TRELUDDERO.

TRELE-EVER, -IVER, -AVER, -VER, book (*liver*) town, *Pr.*; ? Lliver's (*w.*) d.

TRELEG-AN, -EN, -GAN, -GARN, ? HELIGAN dwelling.

TRELEGOE, *i.q.* TRECLEGO.

TRELEIGH,*i.q.* TRELAY; *c.d.* S. Stephen

TRELESSICK, *i.q.* TRELISSICK.

TRELETHICK, *i.q.* TRELEATHICK.

TRELE-VAN, -AVAN, -VEN, *n.f.* -VANT, -VING, open (*levan*) or bare place, *or* dwelling-place (*tre le*) above *or* high (*ban*), *Pr.*; flat *or* level place, *C.*; ? LEUENOT's dwelling.

TRELEV-ERA, -RA, ? ? house with chimneys (*llwferau, w.*).

TRELEW, d. by the pool (*lo*); *or*, town place (*lu*), *Pr.*; ? sheltered (*hleow, s.*), *or* Ellyw's (*w.*) dwelling.

TRELEW-ACK, -ICK, ? *the same.*

TRELEWARN, ? *i.q.* TRELOWARREN.

TRELEWITH, ? *i.q.* TRELOWETH.

TRELIDDEN, ? *i.q.* TRELEDDAN.

TRELIDG-AN,-ON, TRELIGGON, ? LUDGVAN dwelling; *or*, *i.q.*

TRELIG-AN, -ON, legate's town, *H.*; ? *i.q.* TRELEGAN.

TRELIG-GO, -O, *i.q.* TRECLEGO.

TRELIGHT, ? *i.q.* TRELECT; *or*, milk (*lait*) town place (*tre-le*).

TRELI-L, -LE, -LL, goat's (*lill*) t., *Pr.*; town of wantonness,*B.*; loyal (*leal*)t.

TRELIN, place of flax *or* linen (*lin*), *Pr.*; ? pool (*lin*) town (*tre*).

TRELINN-O,-OE,-ow, same, *Pr.*; ? dwelling by the ponds (*linnow*).

TRE-LISICK, -LISSICK, -LISK, -LIZIKE, bushy (*lesic*) t.; *or*, heifer (*ledzhek*), *or* calf's place, *Pr.*; d. on the broad (*les*) creek (*guic*), *T.*; d. in the dry (*sech*) place (*le*), *W.B.*; lower (*isach*) d., *C.*; ? Eliseg's (*w.*) dwelling.

TRELISPEN, ? t. of burning (*lostvan*).

TRELISPIC, ? ? bishop's (*ispac*) town (*tre*) on the moor (*hal*).

TRELISTICK, ? Ysteg's (*w.*) moor-town

TRELIVEL, *e.d.d.,* high (*ewhel*) moor t. *or* town place (*trele*); *d.d.* TREWEL

TRELIVER, *i.q.* TRELEEVER.

TRELIZZA, ? lower (*isa*) TREAL.

TRELLISSICK, *i.q.* TRELISICK.

TRELOAN, ? *i.q.* TRELAWN.

TRELO-AR, -OR, moon (*loer*) t., *Pr.*; ? leper's (*lower*), *or* Llawr's (*w.*) d.

TRELOARN, ? *i.q.* TRELOWARREN.

TRELOD-AVAS, -EVAS, ?? sheep (*davas*) lower (*ulla = wallach*) ground (*tir*).

TRELOEN, *d.d., i.q.* TRELAWN.

TRELOFF, *o.n.f.,* ? smith's (*gof*) TREAL

TRELOGGAN, ? *i.q.* TRELAWGAN.

TRELOGGAS, mice (*logos*) town, *Pr.*; ? d. by the lurking-place (*lloches*).

TRELOGGET, ? Lluched's (*w.*) dwelling

TRELOGOSSICK, *i.q.* TRELOGGAS, *Pr.*

TRELONK, long house, *Wh.*; buttery h., *H.*; ? ecclesiastic's (*lanec*) h.

TRELORGAN, ?? moonlight (*lloergan, w.*), *or* woodpecker's (*llorcan,w.*) d.

TRELO-S, -SICK, -SK, *d.d.* -SCH, ? *i.q.*

TRELASK.

TRELOTHER, ? OTCER's moor town.

TRELOTHYK, o.n.f., ?? i.q. TRELUDICK

TRELOW, lousy (low, lice) town, Pr.; calf (leauh) t., R.W.; ? LOOE t.

TRELOW-AH, -EY, -IA, ? dwelling by the lows or barrows (M'L.); ? Llywi's (w.) dwelling.

TRELOWARREN, fox (lowern) t., Pr.; fortification (warren, t.) barrow t., M'L.; ? = a. toul lern, fox-hole.

TRELOWER, i.q. TRELOAR.

TRELOW-ETH, -ITH, garden (lowarth) t., Pr.; town place (lu) of trees (gwith), T.; ? barrow town, M'L.

TRELOWIN, ? i.q. TRELOIN.

TRELOWRIE, i.q. TRELAWRY.

TRELOWTHA, ? higher (wartha) TRELOW.

TRELOWSA, hoary or musty (?) t., Pr.

TRELOWTHAS VOER & VYGHAN, great (maur) and little (bichan) barrow town, M'L.

TREL-OY, d.d.-LOI, i.q. TRELOWSA, Pr.; flowing or abounding town, H.; place for calves, C.

TRELOYAN, i.q. TRELIN, W.W.K.

TRELOYR, ? i.q. TRELOAR.

TRELUCKEY, Lleucu's (w.) dwelling.

TRELUDDERIN, n.f., ? grey oak (ludh derwen) dwelling.

TRELUDD-ERO, -RA, -OW, miry (lued) town of oaks (derow), Pr.; ? grey oaks' town.

TRELUDICK, miry (luedic) town, Pr.

TRELUDWELL, ? grey wall (ludh gual, w.) town, R.W.

TRELUG-AN, -GAN, ? LUDGVAN d.

TRELUGE, d.d., ? i.q. TRELEWICK.

TRELUI-CK, -GE, lake (loe) or river of water (ick) town, H.; i.q. TRELEWICK.

TRELUKING, ? i.q. TRELOGAN.

TRELUL-L, -LA, ?? lower (ulla = wolla) TREAL, or TRELAY.

TRELUSTICK, ? USTICK's moor town.

TRELUSWELL, miry wall town, Pr.; ? i.q. TRELUDWELL.

TRELWEREN, e.d.d., i.q. TRELOWARREN.

TRELWI, d.d., town-place (trele) by the water (gwy); or, Llywy's (w.) d.

TRELYAN, i.q. TRELOYAN.

TRELYBEY, ? LUBY's dwelling.

TRELYN, i.q. TRELIN.

TRELYNIKE, town of the lake, leat, or bosom of waters, H.; ? LINNICK, or CALENICK house.

TRELYON, linen (lin) town, Pr.

TREMAB-E, -YN, boys' or childrens' (meibion pl. of mab) place, Pr.; ? MABE's dwelling.

TREMAD-A, -AH, -ART, ring (moderuy), i.e. circle place, M'L.; extasy, transport, or dart, &c. town, H. !

TREM-ADOCK, -MADOCK, MADOC'S d.

TREMA-GANNA, -GENNA, -GENNOW, dwelling (tre) place (ma) at the entrance; i.q. TREGENNA.

TREMAGWON, 14 cent., down (gwon) dwelling place.

TREMA-IL, -LE, ? Mael's (w.) dwelling

TREMA-INE, -NE, -N, i.q. TREMAYNE.

TREMALL, ? moor (hal) dwelling p.

TREMAN-AN, ? butter (menen) town.

TREMANHEER, n.f., i.q. TREMENHEER

TREMANT, ? hill (menedh) town.

TREMAR, town of Mars, Po.; chief's abode, Beal; Marh's (B.m.) d.

TREMARKYN, ? Merken's (t.d.d.) d.

TREMARLAND, i.q. TREMEARLAND.

TREMARUSTEL, d.d., market (marhas) hole or cell (tol) town, or market town of the chapel (tol), H.; ? = AUSTELL TREMAR.

TREMATON, = Kings- (matern) ton.*

TREMAYLE, ? Mael's (w.) dwelling.

TREMAYNE, town (trema) on the shore or sea coast (ian); or, = tremyn, a passage, Pr.; i.q. TREMEAN.

---

* Kingston or the royal town, Pr.; three (tri) hills on a green top, Sc.; the great (maur) town (tre) on the hill (dun), Po.; dwelling (tre) place (ma) by the wave (ton), Tr.; town (tre) and castle (dun) of the chief (mar), Beal; o. TREMATERN; d.d. TREMBTONE.

TREMB-ATH, -ETH, the (M = *an*) boar's (*baedh*) town, *Po.*; ? burial (*an bedh*, the grave) place, *J.B.*

TREM-BEAR, -BEARE, -BEER, the great (*mear, vear, bear*) dwelling.

TREMB-EL, -LE, ? *i.q.* TREAMBLE; or, HEMPEL'S or HEMBALL dwelling.

TREMBETH-A, -OW, burial (*an bedhow*, the graves) place (*tre*), *J.B.*

TREMBL-EATH, -ETH, -EIGH, -ETT, -OT, the wolf's (*bleidh*) town, *Pr.*

TREMBL-ETHICK, *o.* -ITHEK, ? Bleiddig's (*w.*) dwelling place (*tre ma*).

TREMBLEYON, ? the pool (*polan*) d.

TREMBOTHICK, ? Bywdeg's (*w.*) d.

TREMBR-ASE, -AZE, -OSE, the great (*bras*), or meadow (*pras*) dwelling; *d.d.* TRENBRAS.

TREMBR-EATH, -OTH, *i.q.* TREMBATH, *Po.*; (*brith*, streaked, *R.W.*).

TREMEADAR, oak (*dar*) town-place (*trema*); or, mower's (*meder*) t., *T.C.*

TREMEAL, sweet or honey (*mel*) t., *Pr.*; ? Mael's (*w.*), or Michal's (*Mihal*) d.

TREMEA-N, -NE, stone (*maen*) town.

TREMEANER, ? *i.q.* TREMENHEER.

TREME-AR, -ER, great (*mear*) t., *Pr.* T. LAND, ? TREMEAR enclosure (*lan*).

TREMEARN, ? Merin's (*w.*) dwelling.

TREMEDDEN, ? *i.q.* TREGAMEDON.

TREME-DDU, -ATHO, town of the possession; or, meadows' t., *T.C.*

TREMELETHEN, ?? Bleddyn's (*w.*) d.

TREMELLICK, ? Mailoc's (*s.B.m.*) d.

TREMELLI-N, -NG, *i.q.* TREGAMELLIN.

TREMENHAY, MANEHAY dwelling.

TREMENHE-RE, -ER, MENHEIR dwelling; or, long (*hir*) passage (*tremyn*)

TREMENKEVERNE, place of St. Kevern's stones (*myin*), *R.H.*

TREMER, t. of Mars (*Merh*), *B.*; or, *i.q.*

TREMERE, *i.q.* TREMEAR.

TREMETH-ACK, -ECK, -ICK, physician's (*methic*) t., *Pr.*; ? doctor's house.

TREMHOR, *d.d., i.q.* TREMORE.

TREMOANE, ? turf (*mawn, w.*) house.

TREMODER-ET, -ATE, *i.q.* TREMADART.*

TREMODGE, ?? HODGE'S dwelling.

TREMO-GH, -UGH, -W, -WE, hogs' (*moch*) place, *Pr.*; = *w. Mochdre*, pigs' town, *R.W.*; smoky (*moc*) h., *Ch.*

TREMOLL-A, -ET, -ETH, ? battle (*ymladd, w.*), or wrestler's (*ymaelydd, w.*) town; ?? *moel*, bare [hill].

TREMO-ORE, -OR, -R, great (*maur*) d.

TREMOR-ELL, -LE, -VILLE, ? MORVAL dwelling or town.

TREMOUTHA, ? dwelling at the *mouth.*

TREMP-ER, -ORTH, *i.q.* TREVEMPER.

TREMULITHEN, *i.q.* TREMELETHEN.

TRENA-CK, -GUE, -IG, -KE, ? *o.* -GA, *i.q.* DRANNACK or TREVENEAGE.

TRENADLYN, ? dwelling by the fir-tree (*adlen*), or palace (*adlan, w.*).

TRENA-ILE, -LE, -LL, the (*an*), or old (*hen*) dwelling on the moor (*hal*), or river (*heyl*); *i.q.* TRENHAILE.

TRENAIRN, ? NAIRN'S, or the iron (*an haiarn*), or border (*yr'hian*) h.

TRENALT, ? dwelling on the steep place (*gallt, w.*).

TRENAMAN, *n.f.*, TREHANE, or dwelling (*trefan, w.*) by the stone (*a maen*)

TRENANCE, town in a valley or on a plain (*nans*), *Pr.*; or, *i.q.*

TRENAN-T, *d.d.* -D, d. near a river, *Pr.*, or torrent (*nant, w.*); valley t., *Bond.*

TRENANICK, ? *i.q.* TREHINICK.

TRENARLET, ? Harallt's (*w.*) or Harold's homestead or dwelling (*trefan, w.*)

TRENAR-REN, -RAN, ? d. on (*ar*) the point (*rhyn*); or, Aron's (*w.*) d.

TRENARTH, the high (*an arth*) d., *Pr.*

TRENATHA, ? the higher (*artha*) d.

TRENATHAN, ? *i.q.* TRENITHAN.

TRENA-VIN, -WIN, ? Henwin's (*B.m.*) d.

TRENAVIS-ICK, -SICK, ? TREHANE, or dwelling (*trefan*) by the birches (*bezo-ick*); or, outer (*avesach*) d.

TRENAWETH, ? *i.q.* TRENOWETH.

---

* *o.* TRE-MODERETH, *d.d.* -MODRET & -METERET, *e.d.d.* -METHERET, ? Modret's or Medraut's (*w.*, ? *i.q.* Mordred) dwelling (*tre*), *W.S.*; or, Wuathrit's (*w.B.m.*) dwelling place (*tre ma*). TREMODERET IN HELL, aunt's (*modereb*) hall (*hel*) town (*tre*), *H.*

TRENAWICK, ? dwelling (*trefan*) on the bay (*gwic*); or, little (*bich*) TREHANE.

TRENAWLE, ? *i.q.* TRENAILE.

TRENAY, ? ANHAY dwelling.

TRENB-ATH, *o.* -EITH, *i.q.* TREMBATH.

TRENBRAS, *d.d.*, large (*lren,w.*) meadow (*pras*), *W.S.*; *i.q.* TREMBRASE.

TRENCARN, the CARN dwelling.

TRENCHER PARK, ? TRENCHARD'S (*n.f.* = carver, *f.*, *Lo.*) close.

TRENCR-EEK, -ICK, = *tre an crug*, dwelling by the barrow, *M'L.*

TRENCRO-BBEN, -VEN, -OOM, *i.q.* TRECROBBEN *or* TRECROOME.

TRENDAWAY, = *tre an tir a way*, place on the land by the way, *M'L.*; ? David's (*Dewi*) house (*trefan*).

TRENDEAL, ? ? house (*tre*) of the (*an*) deluge (*dial*), or revenge (*diol*).

TREN-DER, *n.f.*, ?dwelling (*tre*) by the oak (*an dar*), or water (*dour*).

TRENDERA, d. by the oaks (*derow*).

TREN-DRAIN, -DRINE, = THORN-(*draen*) TON *or* -HILL (*trein*, a nose).

TRENDREN-AN, -EN, dwelling (*tre*) by the (*an*) thornbush (*draenen*).

TRENEAG-E, -UE, the mossy (*neag*), or thatched (*eage*) dwelling; or, deaf (?) town, *Pr.*; ? *i.q.* TRENACK.

TRENEAN, ? Anian's (*w.*) dwelling.

TRENE-AR, -ER, -ERE, -R, ANNEAR d.

TRENEARN, ? *i.q.* TRENAIRN.

TRENEARTH, ? *i.q.* TRENARTH.

TRENEATH, ? dingle (*nedh*) h., *R.W.*

TRENEAUTH, new (*nowydh*) house.

TRENED-DON, -AN, ? ? *i.q.* TRENITHAN

TRENEFFLE, ?Neville's(*n.f.*) dwelling

TRENEGLOS, the church (*an eglos*) town, *Pr.*; a stout, strong, robust (!) church, *H.*; *p.s.* St. Gregory *or* St. George, *O.*

TRENEL, *i.q.* TRENHAILE.

TRENELGOE, dwelling (*trefan*) by the moor-wood (*hal goat*); or, *i.q.* TRECLAGO.

TRENEME-AN,-N,-NE, headland(*trwyn, w.*) of rock (*maen*), *N.*; or, dwelling (*trefan, w.*) by the stone.

TRENERRY, ? ? the goldsmith's (*an eure*), or field (*cru*) house.

TRENESQUIT, ? under-wood (*is goed, w.*) house (*trefan, w.*).

TRENESSEN, ? Enisian's (*w.*) d.

TRENETHI-C, -CK, the great (*an ethic*) dwelling; the large town or dwelling. *Pr.*; ? big hill (*trein*).

TRENE-VAS, -AVAS, ? Nywys's (*w.*) d.

TRENEWAN, the cold (*eyn*) dwelling, *Pr.*; ? famine (*newyn, w.*) t., *R.W.*

TRENEW-ET, -ETH, -ITH, -TH, new (*newydh*) town or dwelling.

TRENEY, *i.q.* TRENAY.

TRENGALE, dwelling in the grove (*celli*); or, field(*gweal*) h. (*trefan,w.*)

TRENG-EAR, -AER, *n.f.* -ORE, the (*an*) camp or castle (*caer*) dwelling.

TRENGILLY, the grove (*an gelli*) d.

TRENGOFF, the smith's (*an gof*) d.

TRENGOTHAL, the (*an*) Irishman's (*godhal*), or moor wood(*goat hal*) h.; t. on the noted (*goth*) cliff(*als*),*R.H.*

TRENGOVE,the smythe's towne,*Nord.*; stout, strong, robust, *or* courageous smith, *H.* !

TRENG-REEN, *alias* -ORYON, ?Geirion's (*w.*) dwelling.

TRENGRO-USE,-WSE, dwelling (*tre*) by the cross (*an grows*), or marsh (*cors*)

TRENGROVE, ? *i.q.* TRENGILLY.

TRENGUNE, the down (*gwon*) d.

TRENGWAINTON, d. near the spring (*fenten*) or rivulet, *Pr.*; (*gwaintoin*, spring time); ? GUNWINTON h.

TRENGWEATH, ? ash (*enwydh*) house.

TRENH-AILE, -ALE, -AYLE, -AL, -EAL, -EALE, stout, strong, *or* rapid river, *H.*; *i.q.* TRENHAL, *d.d.*, large (*tren, w.*) salt-marsh (*hal*), *W.S.*; *i.q.* TRENAILE.

TRENHORN, *i.q.* TREGANHORN.

TRENIER, *n.f.*, ANNEAR dwelling.

TRENIFFEL, *i.q.* TRENEFFLE.

TRENINNICK, ? dwelling (*trefan*) on the creek (*an guic*).

TRENINNOW, ?Nynio's (*w.*) dwelling.

TRENIOW, ? the yew-tree (*yw*) h.

TRENITH-AN, -EN, -ON, the furzy

(*eithin,* furze) dwelling, *Pr.*

TRENITHICK, town of the ford (*ath, i.*), bridge, leat, *or* lake of waters (*ick*), *II.*; *i.q.* TRENETHICK.

TRENI-ZICK, -SSICK,-ZACK, same,*J.B.*; the (*un*) corn (*iz-ic*) town, *Pr.*

TRENN-EAGE, -ECK, -ICK, ? *i.q.* TRE-NEAGE.

TRENO-ADEN, -DDEN, ? Nwython's (*w.*) dwelling.

TRENOCK, ? *i.q.* TRENACK.

TREN-ODE, -OAD, ? d. in the wood (*ood, m.c.*); or, *i.q.* TRENOWETH.

TRENOGAN, ? dwelling (*trefan*) by the cleft *or* chasm (*agen*).

TRENOLDS, the cliff (*als*) dwelling.

TRENONNA, ? Nona's dwelling.

TRENOON, the down (*oon*) house.

TRENO-RN, -URAN, *i.q.* TRENHORN.

TRENORREN, = *tre nore en*, town of the point, *T.*; *i.q.* TRENARREN.

TRENOUTH, new (*nowedh*) town.

TRENOVIS, ? Nywis's (*w.*) d.; or, *i.q.* TRENOVISICK, *i.q.* TRENAVISICK.

TRENOW, noisy (*now,* noise) t., *Pr.*; ? NOE's dwelling; *i.q.* TREKNOW.

TRENOWAH, ? bare (*noth*) land (*tir*).

TRENOW-AR, -ER, ? the (*an*) sister's (*hoer*), or ram (*hor*) town; or, *i.q.*

TRENOW-ATH, -ETH, -ITH, -TH, new (*nowydh*), or ash-trees (*enwydh*), or bare (*noth*) land (*tir*), or house.

TRENOWI-DN,-N, ?ash-tree (*enwedhan*) house; or, white (*gwy-n, -dn*) hill (*trein*); or, *i.q.* TORNEWIDDEN.

TRENOWLS, the cliff (*als*) dwelling.

TRENTINNY, d. by the castle (*an dinas*); or, castle hill (*trein*).

TRENUAN, ? *i.q.* TRENEWAN.

TRENUGG-O, -OE, ? *tre an ogo*, dwelling by the cave.

TRENUSSON, *i.q.* TRENISSEN.

TRENUTE, ? the wood (*cuit*) house.

TRENUTH, ? the new (*newydh*) h.

TRENVAN, ? the high (*ban*) dwelling.

TRENVUSE, ? dwelling by the wall *or* entrenchment (*an vos*).

TRENW-ALL, -ELL, ? the high (*uhal*) t.

TRENWARTHA, the higher *or* further

(*an wartha*) dwelling (*trefan*).

TRENWHEAL, dwelling by the mine (*un wheal*); or, field (*gweal*) house.

TRENWI-TH, *d.d.* -T, dwelling among the ash trees (*enwydh*), *Pr.*; *i.q.* TRENUTE, *II.*; large (*tren, w.*) wood (*guith*), *W.S.*

TRENYAN, the cold (*an ein*) dwelling

TRENYLICK, *o.n.f.,* ? dwelling by the willows (*un helic*).

TRENYTH-AN, -YN, *i.q.* TRENITHAN.

TREOLVIS, ? = *tir hal ves,* outer moor land; or, Alvis's (*t.*) dwelling.

TREON, down (*on* = *gwon*) house, *T.*

TREONIKE, ? *i.q.* TREGONICK.

TREOVIS, ? = *tirou aves,* outer lands.

TREPADANNON, *i.q.* TREBODANNON.

TREPELLIN, mill (*belin, melin*) place, *Po.*; (*pellyn,* extreme, *R.W.*).

TREPELLURE, ? Eliver's (*w.*), or paint-er's (*liour*) house (*tref, tregfa*).

TREPILLES, ? *i.q.* TREVELLIS.

TREPISSICK, ? fish (*pisc*) t.; or, *i.q.* TREBISSICK or TREVISSICK.

TREPOILE, ? elecampane (*baiol*) h.

TREPOLL, pool (*pol*) town, *H.M.W.*

TREQUE-AN, -EN, ? white (*gwyn*) h.

TREQUITE, wood (*cuit*) house.

TRERABO-C, -E, ? Riabach's (grey, swarthy, *e.*), or the abbot's (*yr abot, w., R.W.*) dwelling.

TRERAIR, ? eagle (*eryr, w.*) town.

TRERALLET, ? *i.q.* TRENARLET.

TRERAMMET, ? ? Rambert's (*t.*) d.

TRERAN, ? = *tir aeran,* land of plums.

TRERANK, ? *i.q.* TREFRANK.

TRERASSOW, town of graces *or* ex-cellencies (*rasow, grasow*), or of rats (*razow*), *B.*; ? Orso's (*t.*) dwelling.

TRERATHICK, ? ? Arthwg's (*w.*) d.

TRERAVEL, ? ? Rabel's (*d.d.*) d.

TRERAV-EN, -ON, town on (*ar*) the river (*avon*), *Pr.*

TRE-REE, -REEV, ? *i.q.* TREREIFE.

TREREED, ? ford (*ryd*) house.

TREREEN, a fortified *or* fighting (?) place, *Pr.*; ? dwelling on the head-land (*rhym*), *T.*; T. DINAS, castle (*dinas*) TREREEN.

TRER-EIFE, -EIVE, *v.* TREEVE, d. of the *reire (ycrefa, s.),* or steward's h.

TREREGE, ⸮ Rioch's *(w.)* dwelling.

TRERENGORES, dwelling on *(ar)* the marsh *(an gors).*

TREREST, *v.* RESTA, dwelling in the waste-open ground *(gorest, w.);* or, Grwst's *(w.)* dwelling *(tre).*

TREREW, ⸮ *i.q.* TREFREW or BOREW.

TRERIBE, *n.f.,* ⸮ *i.q.* TREREIF.

TRE-RICE, -RISE, -REESE, -REYS, -RIZE, town on the fleeting ground, *or* on the decline of the hill, *Pr., (see* PENRICE); a town of fleeting ground, *Car.;* town in the valley *(ros), B.* ; ⸮ RICE's dwelling.

TRERIDERN, ⸮ Aerdeyrn's *(w.)* d.

TRERIE-F, -VE, *i.q.* TREREIFE.

TRERIHIOC, *d.d.,* ⸮ Rioch's *(w.)* d.

TRERITHICK, ⸮ Ruydac's *(Bp.)* d.

TRERIVEN, *n.f.,* ⸮ Rhufon's *(w.)* d.

TRERO-ACH, -CHE, *alias* TREGARRACK, ROACH town.

TRERONACK, *tre r ownek,* the coward's dwelling, *B.* ; ⸮ *i.q.* TREFRONICK.

TRERO-OSEL, -SAL, ⸮ Arwystli's *(w. =* Aristobulus) dwelling.

TREROOST, ⸮ Grwst's *(w.)* dwelling.

TRERO-S, -SE, -ASE, valley town, *Pr.* ; ROSE dwelling.

TRE-ROUFE, -RUFF, ⸮ RALPH's dwelling ; *or, i.q.* TREREIFE.

TRERULE, ⸮ RIOWAL's dwelling.

TRERUMMER, ⸮ Rumr's *(t.)* dwelling.

TRERUST, ⸮ *i.q.* TREROOST.

TRERUTH-AN, -EN, ⸮ Rheiddun's *(w.)* d.

TRERYN, *i.q.* TREREEN.

TRERYS, *i.q.* TRERICE.

TRESAD-ARN, -DARN, -DERN, -ERN, -DRON, t. of Saturn, *B.* ; strong *(cadarn)* t., *Pr.* ; ⸮ Sadwrn's *(w.)* d.

TRESAHAR, *n.f., i.q.* TRESARE.

TRESAHORVEAN, little *(bian)* T.

TRESALL-ACK, -ICK, ⸮⸮ Seolce's *(t.)* d.

TRESAMBLE, house on the burdensome *(sam,* a burden) big belly *(bol)* hill *(bol), Francis* ! ⸮ SAMBLE's, *or sampling* house.

TRESANCE, saint's *or* holy *(sans)* d.

TRESAR-A, -E, woodman *or* carpenter's town, *Pr.* ; *(sair,* an artizan ; *sair pren,* a carpenter).

TRESARR-AT, -ET, hedge-hog *(sart)* t., *Pr.* ; ⸮ Essart's *(t.)* dwelling.

TRESASTER, *n.f.,* ⸮ *i.q.* CHYSAUSTER.

TRESA-ULE, -WLE, -WELL, healthy *(sawell),* or exposed t., *Pr.* ; ⸮ SAWLE's d. ; T. WARTHA, higher T.

TRESAV-ARAN, -ERN, -REN, ⸮ Osvran's *(w.)* dwelling ; *or, i.q.*

TRESAVEAN, third *(tressa)* little *(vean)* [town], *Francis* ; ⸮ *i.q.* TRESAHORVEAN ; *v.* TRIDGYVEAN, ⸮ ⸮ little TREGIE.

TRESAVIS, *n.f.,* ⸮⸮ outer *(avis)* TREGIE.

TRESAWAY, ⸮ *i.q.* TREDEWAY.

TRESAWNA, charm *(sona,* to charm) town, *H.* ; place of a fence *or* hemming-in, *C.*

TRESAW-SAN, -SON, -ZAN, Saxon's place, *M'L.* ; English t., *T.* ; place of mounds *or* heaps, *C.*

TRESAYES, ⸮ Saxon's *(sais, w.)* d.

TRESCADICK, ⸮ ST. CADIC's h., *P.*

TRESCAR, ⸮ cliff *(sgeir, i.)* dwelling.

TRESC-AW, -O, -OW, *d.d.* -AV, d. of elder-trees *(scaw), A.S.;* ⸮ a sheltering *(scovva,* a tent) home *(tre), N.*

TRESCO-BEAS, -VEAS, threefold kisses, *H.* !! ⸮ outer *(aves)* TRESCO ; *or,* TRESCO field *(maes).*

TRESCO-LL, -WL, ⸮ school *(scol)* h.

TRESCOTT, ⸮ *i.q.* TRAWISCOIT.

TRESCOWTH-IACK, -ICK, -RICK, ⸮ great *(ethic),* or EDRICK's TRESCOW.

TRESCOWVEAN, little *(bian)* TRESCO.

TRESE, the third *(tressa), H.* ; ⸮ *i.q.* TREISE *or* TREGIE.

TRESEAN, ⸮ John's TREASE.

TRESEARE, *i.q.* TRESARE.

TRESEASE, *i.q.* TRESAYES.

TRESED-DER, -ER, ⸮ archer's *(sethar)* d.

TRESELLAN, ⸮ Salenn's *(s.B.m.)* d.

TRESELLER-EN, -N, ⸮ Aelhaiarn's *(w.)* TRESE.

TRESEMPER, ⸮ Sampiere's *(=* S.Peter) d. ; *or,* d. by the cove *(an por).*

TRESEMPUL, *i.q.* TRESAMBLE.

TRESERRICK, ? ? ST. CYRIAC'S d.

TRESEVARRAN, *i.q.* TRESAVARAN.

TRESEVEAN, *i.q.* TRESAVEAN.

TRESHAOR, *i.q.* TRESARE.

TRESIBBLE, ? *i.q.* TRESIMPLE.

TRESICK, ? *i.q.* DRYSACK; *or,* = dry (*sych*) land (*tir*), or house (*tre*).

TRESIDDEN, *n.f.,* ? *i.q.* TRESADERN.

TRESIDOR, *n.f., i.q.* TRESEDDER.

TRESILGEN, *i.q.* TRESULGAN.

TRESILLI-AN, -ON, place for eels (*selli,* an eel), *or* in open view (*sil*), *Pr.*; ? Sulien's, *i.q.* Sulcen's dwelling.

TRESIMPLE, = *tre[s] an pol,* the miry place, *Pr.*; ? *i.q.* TRESAMBLE.

TRESINNEY, ? *i.q.* BOSSINEY; *or,*

TRESITH-ANY, -NEY, -NY, *n.f.* -NOW, weekly (*seithun,* a week) t., *or* t. frequented on the sabbath, *H.* ! ? Seithenyn's (*w.*) dwelling.

TRESIZE, *i.q.* TREZIZE.

TRESKADARN, ? hero's *or* champion's (*cadarn*) TRESE.

TRESKELLAM,? [St.] COLUMB'S TRESE

TRESKELLARD,? Gellard's (*n.f.*) TRESE

TRESKELLOW, ? h. (*tre*) under (*is*), *or* outside (*ves*) the groves (*kelliow*).

TRESKELL-EN, -ING, ? house by the sedge-bed (*hesg lwyn, w.*); *or,* holly (*celin*) house.

TRESKELLY, grove (*celli*) house, *Wh.*; ? under-grove (*is gelli*) house.

TRESKERBY, ? place of the outcry (*scrymba, w.*); *or,* little (*bich*) dwelling (*tre*) on the ridge (*esgeir*).

TRESKEW-ES, -IS, shady (*skes*) town, *Pr.*; ? SKEWES's dwelling.

TRESKIDDY, ? privet (*skiddy, m.c.*) h.

TRESKILL-EN,-ING, *i.q.* TRESKELLING.

TRESKINNICK,? Cennych's (*w.*) TRESE

TRESKOWL, *i.q.* TRESCOLL.

TRESL-AY, -EA, -EIGH, ? lesser (*le*) TRESE; *or, i.q.* TRELAY.

TRESLOG-AT, -GET, *i.q.* TRELOGGET.

TRESLOTHAN, ? Llawdden's (*w.*) TRESE; *c.d.* St. John.

TRESMARROW, town (*tre[s]*) of the dead (*marow*), *or* of graves, *Pr.*

TRESMAYNE, ? d. below the stone (*is maen*) *or* rock; *or, i.q.* TREMAYNE.

TRESMEDON, ? meadow (*meddon*), *or* stone (*maedn* = *maen*) TRESE.

TRESMEER, great (*mear*) town, *or* near the lake, *Pr.*; (? s = *is,* under); *p.s.* St. Winwolaus, *O.*; St. Nicholas, *C.S.G.*

TRESMERE, *alias* TREMERE, same.

TRESO-AKE, -CH, ? *tir sog,* moist land; *or,* ISAAC's dwelling.

TRESODDERN, *i.q.* TRESADERN.

TRESOLE, *i.q.* TRESAWLE.

TRESO-NA, -WNA, *i.q.* TRESAWNA.

TRESONDER, ? SANDERS' dwelling.

TRESONGAR, ? Angar's (*w.*) TRESE.

TRESOOTH, fat (*soath*), *or* fruitful place, *Pr.*; ? = SUTTON, south town.

TRESORO, ? = further (*urra*) TRESE.

TRESOW-ES, -IS, -YS, ? *i.q.* TREZIZE.

TRESOYE, *n.f., i.q.* TRESAWELL, *Ly.*

TRESPADDOCK, ? ? Ædoc's dwelling (*trege,* to dwell) place (*pa = va*).

TRESPARK, ? SPARK'S dwelling (*tre*); *or, i.q.* PARK TREES.

TRESPAR-RET, -ROT, -VET, ? *i.q.* TREBARFOOT, *or* TREBARWITH.

TRESP-EARN, -ARNE, ? = THORN-(*spern,* thorn) TON.

TRES-PEN, -PYN, head (*pen*) town (*tre[s]*), *Pr.*; ? *i.q.* TREVISPAN.

TRESPRISSEN, ? ? haunted h.; (*speris,* a spirit; *pl. spriggian, B.*).

TRESQUARE, ? square (*ysgwar, w.*) h.

TRESQU-ITE, -OIT, *i.q.* TREVISQUITE.

TRESRABO, 15 cent., *i.q.* TRERABO.

TRESREDOW, *n.f.,* ? Rhediw's (*w.*) d.

TRESREYCK, 14 cent., ? *i.q.* TREREGE.

TRESS, *n.f.,* ? *i.q.* TREASE.

TRESSA, *i.q.* TREVESA.

TRESSEL, ? moor (*hal*) TREASE.

TRESS-EW, -UE, ? Jesu's (*B.m.*), *or* black (*du*), *or* Jew's dwelling.

TREST-AIN, -EAN, ? tin (*stean*) house.

TRESTRAIL, mats *or* tapestry (*strail*) town, *Pr.* TRESTREL WOLES, 15 cent., lower (*wollas*) T.

TRESTRAIN, ? thorn (*draen*) TRESE.

TRESUCK, ? *i.q.* TRESOAKE.

TRESUGG-A, -AN, moist (*sug*) *or* boggy

town, *Pr.*; town on the *saggor* bog, *H.*

TRESULGAN, little-village of the sun (*sul*) *or* fire worship, *Beal*; Sulcen's (*s.B.m.*) dwelling.

TRESULIAN, *i.q.* TRESILLIAN.

TRESUNGER, *i.q.* TRESONGAR.

TRESULLA, ? lower (*isella*) house.

TRESUNNY, ? *i.q.* TRESINNEY.

TRESURAN, *n.f.*, ? *i.q.* TRESAVARAN.

TRESURRANCE, ? RESURRANS d.

TRESUTTON, ? *i.q.* TRESADARN ; *or*, dwelling by SUTTON; *syddyn*, a tenement of land, *w.*

TRESVENACK, ? ROSEVANNOCK d.

TRESVINE, ? *i.q.* TRESWAINE.

TRESWALL-AN, -ON, ? apple-tree (*avallen*) house (*trege*, to dwell).

TRESWALLOCK, SWALLOCK dwelling.

TRESWARD, ? Siward's (*t.*) dwelling.

TRESWARROW, ? *i.q.* TREWARRA.

TRESW-AYNE, -EN, -IN, ? *i.q.* SAUNTON

TRESWEETA, ? widow's (*gwedho*) d.

TRESWELL, ? *i.q.* TRES-AULE *or* -IBBLE

TRESWIG-AR, -ER, -GAR, ? *i.q.* TREVEGOR.

TRESWITH-AN, -EN, *v.* TREJETHEN, JETHEN, a town of trees (*gwedh*), *Nord.*, *Pr.*; ? Sidwin's (*t.*) d.

TRESWITHICK, ? *i.q.* TREWITHICK.

TRESYNNY, *i.q.* TRESINNEY.

TRETALLO-CK, -W, ? TALLACK's d.

TRETA-NE, -WN, under (*tan*) town, *Pr.*; (? *tan*, fire).

TRETDENO, *d.d.*, ? Idno's (*w.*) land (*tireth*) ; TRET = *trait*, sands, *W.S.*

TRETHA-KE, *d.d.* -C, *i.q.* TRETHEAGE.

TRETH-ALE, *n.f.* -ALL, moor *or* hill (*hal*) land (*tireth*) *or* farm.

TRETH-AM, -EM, ? *i.q.* TRUTHAM.

TRETHAN-AS, -NAS, -NAY, -NS, ? lamb's (*eanes*) land (*tireth*).

TRETHANICK, ? *i.q.* TRETHENICK.

TRETHAR-AP, -OP, -UP, -RAP, -ROP, -RUP, ? a place (*tre*[*d*]) of tillage (*aru*, to plow, *w.*), *M.* ; *or*, a *redupl.* -THARAP = *thorpe* (*s.*) = *tre*, a vil-

lage, *R.W.* ; ? *i.q.* TRETHURFE.

TRETHA-UKE, -WKE, ? ÆDOC's town.

TRETHA-VEY, -VY, -WE, ? David's t.

TRETHAWLE, ? moor (*hal*) land (*tireth*) ; *or*, dale (*dol*) town (*tre*).

TRETHE-AGE, -AKE, -K, fair *or* pleasant (*teg*) town, *Pr.*, *or* house, *Wh.* ; ? TEAGUE's *or* TYACK's tenement.

TRETHEGEMBER, *i.q.* TREGEMBER, *Ly.*

TRETHEKEL, *o.n.f.*, ? Dichul's (*A.B.*) d.

TRETHELLA, ? back (*delhar*) h., *P.*

TRETHELL-AN, -EN, ? fir-tree (*adhlen*) house; *or*, out (*allan*, *w.*) land (*tireth*) ; *or*, *i.q.* TRETHULLAN.

TRETHEN-AL, -NAL, ? old (*hen*) moor (*hal*) land (*tireth*) ; *or*, *i.q.* TREDENDALE; *or*, Deiniol's (*w.*) dwelling.

TRETHENICK, ? *i.q.* TREDINNICK.

TRETHER-AS, -IS, -RAS, ? d. near the pass (*daras*, a door); *dreis*, brambles

TRETHERGEY, ? land (*tireth*) over (*ar*) the water (*gy*); (*dourgi*, an otter; *durgy*, a turf hedge).

TRETHERN, ? thorn (*drean*) land.

TRETHEV-AN, -EN, John's (*Evan*, *w.*) l.

TRETHEV-AS, -ES, ? sheep (*deves*), *or* outer (*aves*) land.

TRETHEVEREN, ? vale (*dyffryn*, *w.*) house; *v.* TREWETHERN, *J.M.*

TRETHEVY, ? David's (*Deui*) house.*

TRETHEW, ? same; black (*du*) t. ; *or*, God's (*du*, *dew*), *i.e.* holy t., *Pr.*

TRETHEW-AL, -EL, -ELL, high (*ewhal*), *or* ST. EVAL's land (*tireth*) *or* farm.

TRETHEWAR, ? water (*dour*) land (*tir*) *or* house.

TRETHEWEN, ? ? Dwynwen's (*w.*) d.

TRETHEW-Y, -EY, town (*tre*[*the*]) by the water (*wy*); *or*, holy (*dew*, God) t. by the water, *Pr.* ; David's t.

TRETHICK, ? big (*ethic*) town.

TRETHIES, *i.q.* TRETHYAS.

TRETHIGGY, ? Tygwy's (*w.*) house.

TRETHILL, ? Ithel's (*w.*) house.

TRETHILL-ICK, -Y, ? willow (*helic*) l.

TRETHIN, ? Rheiddun's (*w.*) h. (*ty*).

---

* *Nord.*, "TRETHEUIE, called in Latin *casa gigantis*"; *Beal*, dwelling of the god, hero, *or* chief (*de*, *dhe*, *ga.*); *v.* TREVETHY. T. STONE, (a cromlech), *v.* Giant's grave.

TRETHINGEY, ? land (*tireth*) by the water (*an gy*).

TRETHINNICK, *i.q.* TRETHENICK.

TRETHOM, ? poverty (*ethom*) land.

TRETHORN, ? *i.q.* TRETHERN.

TRETHOSA, ? IOSA's land (*tireth*).

TRETHOW-A, -AR, -ER, town by the water (*dour*), *Pr.* ; ? waterland.

TRETHOW-ALL, -ELL, ? Howel's land.

TRETHOWAN, ? Owen's (*w.*) land.

TRETHUGAY, *i.q.* TRETHURGAY.

TRETHULLAN, ? land (*tireth*) belonging to the temple of the sun (*haul lan*) ; *or*, HELLAND house.

TRETHUNE, *Nord.*, ? down (*oon*) l.

TRETHURAS, *i.q.* TRETHERAS.

TRETHUR-FE, *o.* -FF, town of tillage (*trevas*), *Po.* ; ? arable (*aru*, to plow, *w.*), *or* rough (*harow*) land (*tireth*).

TRETHURGAY, *i.q.* TRETHERGEY.

TRETHURRUP, *i.q.* TRETHARRUP.

TRETHWELL, ? *i.q.* TRETHEWALL.

TRETHYAS, ? stack (*dise*) house.

TRETHYN, ? castle (*din*) house.

TRETINNEY, ? castle (*dinas*) house.

TRETIRE, ? third (*teir*) house.

TRETLAN-D, *d.d.*, *e.d.d.*-T, ? = *w.Trellan*, township containing the church, *R.W.* ; *i.q.* TRELAN.

TRETOI-L, -LE, ? *i.q.* TRETHOWALL.

TRETRINNECK, ? thorny (*draenic*) land (*tir*), *or* dwelling (*tre*).

TRETULL, ? *i.q.* TRETHOWALL.

TRETWERET, *d.d.*, ? land (*tireth*) on the descent (*gwaered, w.*).

TREUALGARTHYN, 15 *cent.*, = *w. tre ual garth din*, wall dwelling by the hill fort, *R.W.* ; *or*, TRAFALGAR on the hill.

TREUALUARE, 14 *cent.*, ? Aluard's (*d.d.*) dwelling.

TREUERUEN, 15 *cent.*, *i.q.* TREVERVYN

TREUERY STOWE, *Nord.*, TREFRY'S place (*stow, s.*).

TREUESCOIT, *H.*, *i.q.* TRAWISCOIT.

TREUHALL, high (*uhal*) town, *Pr.*

TREUIST, ?? lodging (*guest*) house.

TREUN, down (*gwon*) house.

TREUNGLE, colewort (*ungl, B.*) t.,

Po. ; ? corner (*ongl, w.*) house.

TREURABO, *Nord.*, *i.q.* TRERABOC.

TREURIS, 13 *cent.*, *i.q.* TREFRYS.

TREURY, *o.n.f.*, *i.q.* TREFRY.

TREUTHA-L, -N, the above (*uthal, uthan*), *or* upper town, *Pr.*

TREV-A, -AH, *i.q.* TREGVA.

TREVAB-ON, -YN, *i.q.* TREMABYN.

TREVAD-DRA, -RA, ? *i.q.* TREWARTHA.

TREVADL-ACK, -OCK, ? Matholoch's (*i.*) dwelling.

TREVA-GAU,-GAV, *d.d.*, *i.q.* TREVALGA, *J.Cu.* ; ? smith's (*gof*) dwelling (*tregva*) ; *or*, *i.q.*

TREVAG-E, -UE, ? *i.q.* TREVEAGE.

TREVAG-EAN,-HEAN, giants' town, *B.* ; *i.q.* TREBEGEAN.

T.-VEAN, little TREVAGEAN.

TREVAGLERS, ?? *i.q.* TREVEGLAS.

TREVAGNION, *i.q.* TREVANION.

TREVAIL, house on the river (*heyl*).

TREVAILER, workman's (*wayler*) t., *Pr.* ; d. of the merchant *or* worker in iron (*maelwr*), *J.W.* ; the shop, *C.* (*maelor*, place of traffic, mart, *w.*)

TREVA-ILS, -LLES, *i.q.* TREVELLAS.

TREVA-L, -LL, ? = *trev hal*, moor h. ; *or*, *tre gwal*, wall t. ; *or*, *tre uhal*, high t.

TREVALADER, Walter's, the lord's (*gwaladr, w.*), *or* Aladur's (*sun, w.*) h.

TREVALFRY, ? Maliewry's (*n.f.*) d.

TREVALGA, town of defence *or* walled (*gwal*, a wall) near the water (*gwy*), *Pr.* ; noble (*alga, i.*) house, *Wh.* ; ? Algar's d. ; *p.s.* St. Petrocus.

TREVALGAN, ? *i.q.* BODVALGAN ; *or*, Maelgwn's (*w.*)d.; *or*, tin(*alcan, w.*) h.

TREVALISSICK WOLLAS, lower TRELISSICK.

TREVALL-ACK, -ICK, -OCK, fenced (*gwal-ic*) town, *Pr.*

TREVALLAN, apple-tree (*avallen*) t., *Po.* ; ? ALAN *or* HALLAN house.

TREVALL-ANCE, -AUNCE, *i.q.* TREVEL-.

TREVALLARD, ? Aluuard's (*d.d.*) d.

TREVALL-ES, -IS, -IES, ? green moor (*hal lays*) d. ; *or*, *i.q.* TREVELLAS.

TREVALLET, ? HALLET's dwelling.

TREVALS-A, -OE, fortified (?) town,

or town on a cliff (*als*), *Pr.*; ? Walsige's (*s.*) town.

TREVALSCUS, ? under-wood (*is cus*) TREVAL.

TREVAN, little town, *w.*, *T.* ; ? = HIL-(*ban*) TON ; *or* = *w.* trefan, a homestead, dwelling, hamlet, village.

TREVANCE, town upon the rising *or* advanced land, *II.*! ? nun's (*manaes*) town ; *or*, *i.q.* TREVINCE.

TREVANGER, ? = *trevan gaer*, dwelling by the camp ; *or*, Angar's (*w.*) d.

TREVAN-IAN, -ION, -NION, town in a hollow (*gwag*) plain (*nans*), *Pr.* ; place of the big *or* covering (*van*) ash (*on*), *C.* ; ? Anian's (*w.*) d.

TREVAN-IN, -NIN, -NING, ? = BUTTER-(*amanen*) TON ; *or*, *i.q.* TREVANIAN

TREVANNAL, ? = broom (*banal*) town.

TREVANSON, ? *i.q.* TREVENSON.

TREVAN-Y, -EY, -NY, ? *i.q.* TREVANEAGE, *or* TREVANIAN.

TREVAPACK FIELD, ? town place (*tre va*) field (*parc*), *reduplicated.*

TREVARBYN, *i.q.* TREVERBYN.

TREVARDER, ? *i.q.* TREWARTHA.

TREVARE, *i.q.* TREVEAR.

TREVARFE, 17 *cent.*, *i.q.* TREVARTH *or* TRETHURFE.

TREVARIAN, ? silver (*arian*) house.

TREVAR-ICK, -RICK, ? d. on the water (*ar ick*) ; *or*, Barrick's (*w.*) d.

TREVARIN, ? hill (*rhyn*) house.

TREVARKEES, ? BARGUS house.

TREVARLE-DGE, -GE, ? WORLEDGE'S *or* lower (*wollas*) dwelling.

TREVARN-EN, -ON, ?alder-tree (*gwarnen*) house ; *or*, house on the down (*war an oon*).

TREVARNER, *i.q.* TREVERNOR.

TREVARNICK, ? marshy (*gwernic*) d.

TREVARR-A, ACK, rocky (*carrag*) t., *W.B.* ; ? *i.q.* TREWARRA.

TREVARR-ON, -EN, ? Aron's (*w.*) d.

TREVARTEA, *n.f.*, ? *i.q.* TREVARTHA.

TREVARTH, high (*arth*) town, *Pr.*

TREVARTHA, higher (*artha*) town.

TREVAR-THEN, -TON, t. on a hill (*war dun*), *Pr.* ; ? Arthen's (*w.*) d.

TREVARTHIAN, ? Arthyen's (*w.*) d.

TREVAS-CUS, -KIS, -KERS, ? d. (*tre, trev*) outside (*aues*) the wood (*cus*).

TREVASHMOND, ? ? CHAUMOND'S d.

TREVASPER, ? VOSPER'S d.

TREVASS-ACK,-ICK, *i.q.* TREVESSACK.

TREVASSACKVEAN, little (*bean*) T.

TREVASTER, ? FOSTER house.

TREVATH-A, -IA, ? *i.q.* TREVARTHA.

TREVATH-AN, -EN, ?*i.q.* TREVARTHEN

TREVATHIAN, *n.f.*, *i.q.* TREVARTHIAN

TREVATHICK, ? *i.q.* TREVETHICK.

TREVAUL, ? Paul's h.; *or*,*i.q.* TREVAL.

TREVAUNANCE, = *trev an nans*, house of the dingle, *R.W.* ; t. in a great (*maur*) valley (*nans*), *Pr.*, in the boy's (*maw*), *or* fanning *or vaunning* valley, *II.*, *or* in the valley of springs (? *fenten*, pl. *fentens*), *T.*

TREVAYLER, *i.q.* TREVAILER.

TREVE, *i.q.* TREAVE.

TREVE-ADER, -DER, ? *i.q.* TREMEDER.

TREVEA-GE, -GUE, town in a hollow (*veag* = *gwag*), *Pr.*; small (*bach*) h., *R.W.* ; ? *i.q.* TREVENEAGE.

TREVEAGO, ? *i.q.* TREAGA.

TREVEAL, ? field (*gweal*) house.

TREVEALA, ? *i.q.* TREVAILER.

TREVEALLY, *n.f.*, ? *i.q.* TREVILLY.

TREVEAN, *i.q.* LITTLE- (*bean*) TON.

TREVEAN-ES, -S, ? ENIS house.

TREVEAR, great (*mear*), *or* long (*hir*), *or* battle (*heir*) house (*tre, trev*).

TREVEASE, ? lower (*isa*), *or* outer (*aves*) dwelling.

TREVEBBYN, boys' (*mebion*) t., *Po.*

TREVECCA, ? Dickie's (*Hecca*), *or* Rebecka's (*Beckie*) dwelling.

TREVEDDAL, ? Irishman's (*gwidhal*) t.

TREVEDD-AN, -EN, -ON, ? *i.q.* TREVETHAN, *or* TREVEAN (*vedn* = *bean*)

TREVEDD-O, -OE, -A, exposed place,*C.*; ? *i.q.* TREVETHEY.

TREVEDDOC, ? Moedhog's (*w.*) d.

TREVEDRA, *i.q.* TREVIDEROW.

TREVED-RAN, -REN, -DERN, t. by the brambly (*draen*, thorns) river (*vy*), *Pr.* ; ? Medron's (*w.*) dwelling.

TREVEEG, *i.q.* TREVEAGE.

TREVEEN, *i.q.* TREVEAN.

TREVEGA, *i.q.* TREVIDGA.

TREVEGAN, ? *i.q.* TREBICEN ; *or*,

TREVEGEAN, ? *i.q.* TREBEGEAN.

TREVEGL-AS,-OS,-OSS, church (*eglos*) h.

TREVEG-O, -A, town upon the top of a stiff hill *or* precipice (?), *H.*

TREVEGOR,?mother-in-law's (*hweger*), *or* merchant's (*guicgur*) house.

TREVEHERET, *d.d.*, ? *i.q.* TRETWERET

TREVEIGHAN, *i.q.* TREBEIGHAN.

TREVELA, ? *i.q.* TREVAILER.

TREVEL-ECII, -ICK, priest's (*belec, a.*) town, *H.*; ? d. by the sloping stone (*lech*), *R. W.*; *or,i.q.* TREMELLICK, *or*

TREVELEDIC, 13 *cent.*, ? = *trev wledic*, prince's dwelling, *R. W.*

TREVELGA, ? sea (*vylgy*) ton, *P.*

TREVELG-AN, -EN, ? EULCEN'S d.

TREVELG-ES, -US, *i.q.* TREGILGAS.

TREVEL-GUE, -JEWE, *i.q.* TREBEJEW.

TREVELL, ? *i.q.* TREV-AIL, -EAL.

TREVELL-A, *o.* -E, apple (*aval*) town, *Pr.*; ? *i.q.* TREVAILOR.

TREVELLACK, *n.f.*, *i.q.* TREVELECH.

TREVELLAN, mill (*melin*) town, *Pr.*

TREVELLAN-CE, -DS, -S, t. in the mill valley (*melin nans*), *T.*; mill h., *Wh.*

TREVELLARD, ? *i.q.* TREVALLARD.

TREVELL-AS, -ES, son-in-law's (*els*) town, *H.*; ? lark (*melhues*) t., *P.*; *or*, HELLAS dwelling.

TREVELLAWAN,15 *cent.,i.q.*TRELAWN

TREVELL-ECK, -ICK, town on the mill river (*ick*), *T.*; *i.q.* TREVELECH

TREVELLISSICK WARTHA, higher (*wartha*) TRE[VEL]LISSICK.

TREVELLO-E, -W, *i.q.* TREVELLA, *T.C.*

TREVELLYN, mill (*melin*) town.

TREVELMOND, ? *i.q.* TREVOLMOND.

TREVELSICK, *i.q.* TREVELLISSICK.

TREVELVA, place near the FAL, *M'L.*; ? Aelfyw's (*w.*) d.; *llifaw*, floods, *w.*

TREVELVER, ? great (*mear*) town on the river (*heyl*) [CAMEL].

TREVELVETH, ? Alviet's (*t.d.d.*) d.

TREVEL-YAN, *d.d.* -IEN, ? -OIEN, d. of the seamen (*vylgyon*), *Gw.*; Elyan's (*w.*) dwelling, *W.S.*

TREVEMEDER, ? mower's (*meder*) d.

TREVEMPER, ? d. near the cove (*an por*) ; *or*, *i.q.* TREGEMBER.

TREVE-N, -NE, -NN, ? = *treven*, dwellings ; *or*, *i.q.* TREVEAN, *or* TREMEAN

TREVEN-A, -NA, bees' (*gwenyn*), *or* old (*hen*), *or* woman's (*benen*) town (*tre, trev*), *Pr.*; high (*ban*) t., *M'L.*; ? lesser (*behenna*) town.

TREVENAN, *n.f.*, ? Gwenan's (*w.*) h.

TREVEN-ARD, -D, *n.f.*, ? MAYNARD h.

TREVEN-ER, -NER, -OR, *i.q.* TREVENA, *Pr.*; TREVENETH, *Ch.*; *or*, TRE-MENHERE.

TREVENEA-GE,-GUE, d. of moss (*neag*), *or* mossy houses (*treren*), *Pr.*; d. in the stony-place (*maenic*), *or* of the stone cleft (*agen, w.*), *C.*; ? spar-thatched (*eage, B.*) houses.

TREVEN-EN,-NEN,-ING,-ION, women's (*benen*), *or* bees' (*gwenyn*) t., *Pr.*; t. of birth (?), *T.*; dwelling by the ash-tree (*onnen*), *R. W.*

TREVEN-ETH, -NETII, -EY, ? = HIL-(*menedh*)TON ; *or*,wheat (*gwaneth*) t.

TREVENETHICK, great (*ethic*) d., *Pr.*

TREVENGENOW, *i.q.* TREMAGANNA.

TREVENGOTHAL, *i.q.* TRENGOTHAL.

TREVEN-IEL, -NEL, ? d. on the hill (*hal*), *H.W.M.*; *or*, *i.q.* WINIELTON

TREVEN-NON, -ON, ? down (*gwon*) h.

TREVENSE, *i.q.* TREVINCE.

TREVENSON, ? well (*fenten*) t., *P.*

TREVENT, ? *i.q.* TREVINT.

TREVENWITH, *i.q.* TRENWITH.

TREVEOR, great (*mear*) d.

TREVER-AS, -ES, -RES, -RYS, -YS, t. on the way *or* roads (*vores* ?), *T.*; ? town of assistance (*gweres*), *P.*

TREVERB-AN, -EN, -YN, *d.d.* -IN, Er-byn's t., *Lh.*; *or*, d. on (*er*) the hill (*ban*), *Ch.*; place against (*er-byn*) [the side of a hill], *C.*

TREVERBET, *d.d.*, t. of recommenda-tion *or* intercession (*erbed* ?), *W.S.*; ? great t. by the grave (*bedh*), *P.*

TREVERDEN, *n.f.*, *i.q.* TREVARTHIAN, *Ly.*; ? d. on (*er*) the hill (*din*).

TREVERDER, ? *i.q.* TREFURTHER.

TREVERGY, *i.q.* TREWORGY.
TREVERGYN, ? Wurcon's (*s.B.m.*) d.
TREVERIM, *d.d.*, hermit's (*eremus,lat.*) d., *W.S.*; ? Perryam's (*n.f.*), or Perem's (*B.m.*) dwelling.
TREVERI-N, -NG, ? Gueren's (*w.*) d.
TREVERLEDGE, *i.q.* TREVARLEDGE.
TREVER-NE, -REN, *i.q.* TREWERNE.
TREVERNEWETH, ? new (*newydh*) TREVERNE, or TREVA.
TREVERN-OR, -ER, ? sister's (*hoer*) T.
TREVERNON, ? alder-tree (*gwernen*) t.; or, d. on the down (*er an con*).
TREVERR-A, -OW, ? *i.q.* TREWARRA.
TREVER-RY, -Y. ? *i.q.* TREFRY.
TREVERTH, *o.n.f.*, ? *i.q.* TREVARTH.
TREVERTON, *n.f.*, *i.q.* TREWERTON.
TREVERV-A, -AH, -OE, ? battle-field (*heirva*) h.; or, *i.q.* TREBARVA.
TREVERV-EN, -IN, *vervain* town, *B.*; ? mermaid's (*morvoren*) town, *P.*
TREVERW-ICK, -YTH, *o.n.f.*, ? *i.q.* TREBARVATH, or TREVARICK.
TREVERYAN, d. on the holme *or* flat land (*marian, w.*), *R.IV.*; ? Urien's (*w.*) dwelling.
TREVES-A, -E, -SA, -SACK, *i.q.* TREVISA, or TREISAAC, or TRABISS.
TREVES-CAN, -KAN, -KIN, ? elder-tree (*scawen*), or sedge (*hescen*), or Ysgwyn's (*w.*) house.
TREVESSIA, *i.q.* TREVIDGIA.
TREVESSON, ? Gwesyn's (*w.*) house.
TREVETH-ACK, -OCK, Iddawg's (*w.*) h.
TREVETH-AN, *n.f.*, -EN, t. among trees (*gwedhen*, a tree); or, meadow (*bidhen*), old (? *hen*), or birds' (*edhen*) town, *Pr.*
TREVETHELECK, ? Alexander's (*Alick*), or willow (*helic*) TREVARTH.
TREVETHENIC, *i.q.* TREWARTHENICK
TREVETH-EY, -O, -OE, -OW, place (town, *Pr.*) of graves (*bedhow*), *T.*
TREVETH-ICK,-OCK, rustic *or* farmer's (*trevedic*) t., *H.*; ? *i.q.* TREMETHACK, *P.*; (*trevidick*, a tilled field, *a.*).
TREVETRAS, blasted (*gueidrys*) t., *P.*
TREV-EVAN, -EWAN, -IBAN, -IBBAN, ? John's (*Evan, w.*) dwelling.

TREVIA, *n.f.*, *i.q.* TREVIE.
TREVI-ADES, -ADOS, -DES, t. by the water (*gwy*) that comes (*dos*, to come), *i.e.* the tide, *Pr.*; ? beautiful (*faidus*) house.
TREVIAN, = LITTLE- (*bighan*) TON.
TREVIC-CA, -KER, ? *i.q.* TREVEGOR, or
TREVICK, ? d. on the creek (*gwic*); or, *i.q.* TREWEEK, or TREVEAGE.
TREVID-A, -O, -OW, ? *i.q.* TREVETHEY.
TREVID-DRON, -ERN, -DER, *i.q.* TREVEDRAN; or, ? oak (*derwen, dar*) h.
TREVIDER, victualler's (*maidor*) h., *P.*
TREVIDEROW, t. upon the river (*wy*) among the oaks (*derow*), *P.*
TREVID-GA, -GIA, -JA, -YER, *i.q.* TREVESA; TREVIDGIA WARRA, higher (*wartha*) TREVIDGIA.
TREVIDOCK, *i.q.* TREVETHICK.
TREVIE, ? little (*bich*) town.
TREVIGIN, ? *i.q.* TREBEGEAN.
TREVIGLAS, church (*eglos*) town.
TREVIG-O, -OE, ? *i.q.* BOSVIGO.
TREVIGOR, *i.q.* TREVEGOR.
TREVIGR-O, -OE, ? hovel (*crow*) h.
TREVIL-AN, -LEN, -LIN, ? = *trev wilan*, Gullston, *w.*, *R.IV.*
TREVILDER, ? *i.q.* TREVALADER.
TREVIL-ES, -LES, -LIS, -LIES, *d.d.* TREFILIES, Feleus's (*Z.*) d., *W.S.*; ? hazel-grove (*gillis*) h., *P.*; ? *i.q.*
TREVILG-AS, -ASS, -ES, ? moor (*hal*) wood (*cus*) h.; or, *i.q.* TREGILGUS.
TREVIL-IAN, -ION, -LIAN, -LION, -LON, *i.q.* TREVELYAN.
TREVI-LL, -LLE, ? *i.q.* TREVEAL.
TREVILL-A, -EY, ? *i.q.* TREVELLA.
TREVILLEDER, ? *i.q.* TREVALADER.
TREVILLET, ? *i.q.* TREVILIUD, *d.d.*, ? Iliuth's (*s.B.m.*) dwelling (*trev*).
TREVILL-ICK, -OCK, ? *i.q.* TREVELECH
TREVILL-IES, -IS, ? *i.q.* TREVILES.
TREVILLINIAN, *n.f.*, ? Einion's (*w.*) house on the moor (*hal*) or river (*heyl*).
TREVILLING, *i.q.* TREVELLAN.
TREVILLIZICK, *i.q.* TRELISICK, *H.*
TREVILLOAD, *n.f.*, ? *i.q.* TREVILLET.
TREVIL-VA, -VAS, mean (*vil*) low (?)

town, *Pr.* ; *i.q.* TREVELVA.
TREVIM-BER, -PER, *i.q.* TREVEMPER.
TREVINA, *i.q.* TREVENA.
TREVINCE, *Nord.* TREUINS, town of springs (? *fenten-s*), *Pr.*
TREVINE, *i.q.* TREVEIGHAN.
TREVING-AY, -Y, dwelling (*trev*) by the river (*an gy*).
TREVIN-ICK,-NICK,*i.q.* TREVENEAGE, *or* TREWINICK.
TREVINIEL, *d.d.*, *i.q.* TREVENIEL.
TREVINT, ? d. by the road (*hynt, w.*) ; (*gwynt*, wind, *w.*).
TREVIO, ? yew (*yw*) house (*trev*).
TREVIRBIN, *i.q.* TREVERBAN.
TREVISA, lower (*isa*) town, *Pr.*
TREVIS-AN, -SAN, *same, Pr.* ; ? Isan's (*w.*) dwelling (*trev*).
TREVIS-CAR, -KAR, -KER, ? d. outside (*arcs*), *or* under (*is*) the camp (*caer*)
TREVISCAUN, slight (*iscaun* ?) d., *B.* ; ? d. outside *or* under the down (*gwon*) ; *or*, *i.q.* TREVESCAN.
TREVISCOE, ? bishop's (*escop*) town ; d. outside *or* under the wood (*coat*) ; *or*, *i.q.* TRESCAW.
TREVISKEY, ? *same* ; *i.q.* TREGISKEY, *Pr.* ; wardrobe (*guiscti*) house, *P.* ; lower (*is*) t. among trees (*celli*, a grove), *Francis* ; ? *i.q.*
TREVISKIS, *i.q.* TREVASCUS.
TREVIS-ICK, -SICK, ? *i.q.* TREVESACK.
TREVISPAN,??primate's (*guesbeuin*) h.; ? lower (*isa*) buttery (*spens*) h., *P.*
TREVISQUITE, *i.q.* TRAWISCOIT.
TREVI-SSA, -SSY, -GA, *i.q.* TREVESA.
TREVISS-AM,-OM,-OME, ?lord's (*somot, Pr.*) lower (*isa*) house, *P.*
TREVIT, 16 *cent.*, wood (*cuit*) house.
TREVITANE, ? *i.q.* TRETANE.
TREVITHALL, *i.q.* TREWHIDDLE.
TREVITHIAN, ? *i.q.* TREWITHIAN.
TREVITHICK, t. in the *meadow* on a creek (*gwic*), *Pr.* ; ? place of a grave (*bedh-ic*), *J.Ca.* ; *i.q.* TREVETHICK.
T. AN HALE, T. on the moor (*hal*).
TREVITH-O -OE, *i.q.* TREVETHEY.
TREVIVI-AN, -ON, d. by the small

water (*gwy vian*), *Pr.*; VIVIAN'S d.
TREVO-AL, -LI, -OOL, ? Paul's d. ; *or*, *i.q.* TREUHAL, *or* TREVAL.
TREVOAN, ? *i.q.* TREWOON.
TREVOET, *d.d.*, ? = *tre-foet*, -*ouet*, district, canton, *W.S.* ; ? wood (*coed*, *w.*) house.
TREVOL-LAN, *o.* -GHAN, ? Eulcen's h.
TREVOLLARD, ? d. by the high (*arth*) entrenchment (*bolla, B.*), *P.*
TREVOLLOCK, *i.q.* TREWOLLACK.
TREVOLMOND, ? Alhmund's (*t.*) d.
TREVOLTER, ? *i.q.* TREVALADER.
TREVOL-VAS, -UAS, ? *i.q.* TREWOLVAS
TREVO-NE, -ON, -ONE, *i.q.* TREVOAN.
TREVONNACK, ? d. near the turbary (*mawneg*); *or*, ANAOC'S dwelling.
TREVOOLE, ? *i.q.* TREVOAL.
TREVOR, *i.q.* TREVORE.
TREVOR-ACK, -RACK, *i.q.* TREVORICK
TREVORDA, ? *i.q.* TREWARTHA, *or* TREFORDA.
T. WOLLAS, lower (*wollas*) T.
TREVORDER, t. by the great (*maur*) water (*dour*), *or* on the road (*fordh*) to the water, *Po.* ; *i.q.* TREWARTHA, *II.*; T. BICKIN, far off *beacon* town, *T.* ! little (*bichan*) TREVORDER.
TREVORE, great (*maur*), sea (*mor*), road (*for*), sister's (*hoer*), ram's (*hor*), *or* boundary (*or*) house.
TREVORG-ANS, -IANS, ? great house of pardon (*gevyans*), *P.*
TREVORG-AY, -Y, *i.q.* TREWORGEY.
TREVORGUS, ? BARGUS, *or* over-wood (*war gus*) house.
TREVOR-IAN, -RIAN, -YAN, *i.q.* TREVERYAN ; *or*, John's TREVORE.
TREVORICK, t. on the creek, brook, *or* rivulet (*war ick*), *Pr.*, *or* bay (*gwic*) ; *or*, Iwrch's (*w.*) dwelling.
TREVORNE, ? *i.q.* TREF-ROAN, -WARN.
TREVORN-ECK, -ICK, -OCK, ? *i.q.* TREFRONICK *or* -VARNICK.
TREVORNON, *i.q.* TREVERNON.
TREVOR-OW, -ROW, -RAH, -Y, ? town on the ways (*voron*), *B.* ; *or*, *i.q.* TREWARRA, *or* TREFRY.
TREVORRICK MORVA, ? TREVARICK

marsh (*morva*).

TREVORSDEN, ? HURSTON dwelling.

TREVORV-A, -OE, t. on the good road (*vor da*), *T.* ! ? marsh (*morva*) t. ; or, *i.q.* TREWARTHA.

TREVOS-A, -E, fortified (*fos*, a trench, wall, *pl. fossow*) t., *Pr.*; maid *or* virgin's (*mos*) t., *H.*; ? IOSA'S h.

TREVOSPER, ? VOSPER house.

TREVOSSEL, ? Hawystl's (*w.*) town.

TREVOST-A, -ER, ? FOSTER house.

TREVOTH-AN, -EN, ? *i.q.* TREVATHAN.

TREVOTTER, ? OTTER'S dwelling.

TREVOUNANCE, deep (*rown* = down) *or* low t. in the valley (*nans*), *Pr.*; *i.q.* TREVAUNANCE.

TREVOW-A, -AH, ? cave (*fow*) town.

TREVOWHAN, low (*down*) t., *T.C.*

TREVOYAN, ? *i.q.* TREVINE.

TREVOZVOWE, 16 *cent.*, TREVOSE cave (*fow*).

TREVRANCE, *n.f.*, ? TREVORIANS.

TREVRANE, *n.f.*, ? crow (*bran*), *or* king's (*brenin, w.*) t.; *or*, *i.q.* TREGAVRAN.

TREVRONE-CK, -K, *i.q.* TREFRONICK.

TREVREA = HIL- (*bre*) TON.

TREVREESA, *i.q.* TREFRESA.

TREVREKE, ? TREBERICK.

TREVRET, *d.d.*, ford (*red*) t., *W.S.*

TREVRGEN, *d.d.*, *i.q.* TREVERGEN.

TREVRIDA, ? Frittag's (*t.*) dwelling.

TREVRNIVET, *d.d.*, dwelling (*trev*) by (*ar*) the palace (*nevat, gaul*), *or* wood (*nemet, o.br.*), *W.S.*

TREVRY, dwelling on the round hill (*fry*), *Pr.* ; high d., *R.W.*

TREVRYS, t. on a small round (*vrys*, breast) hill, *Pr.* ; *i.q.* TREFRIZE.

TREVTHAL. *d.d.*, *i.q.* TREUTHAL.

TREVU, *m.*, prospect place, *or* place of the view (*vu, Lh.*), *G.S.*

TREVURROW, *n.f.*, *i.q.* TREWARRA.

TREVURVAS, ? BARWIS house.

TREVU-SSA, -SE, -ZZA, *i.q.* TREVOSA.

TREVY-ADOS, -AS, *i.q.* TREVIADES.

TREVYDAR, ? *i.q.* TREVIDEROW, *P.*

TREVYDRAN, *i.q.* TREVEDRAN.

TREVYE, ? river- (*wy*) ton, *P.*

TREVYGHAM, *o.*, *i.q.* TREBICEN.

TREVYLYAN, *i.q.* TREVELYAN.

TREVYSYNS, *o.n.f.*, ? *i.q.* TRESANCE.

TREVYRICK, ? *i.q.* TREVORICK.

TREVYVYAN, *i.q.* TREVIVIAN.

TREW, ? high (*uch*), *or* yew (*yw*) t.

TREWA, ? higher (*ucha, w.*) town.

TREWADDRA, ? *i.q.* TREWARTHA.

TREWAFFE, *o.n.f.*, ? *i.q.* TREWOOF.

TREWAGE, *o.n.f.*, ? *i.q.* TREWEEGE.

TREWA-L, -LL, *d.d.* -LE, ? wall (*gwal*) t., *W.S.*; *i.q.* TREUHALL.

TREWALD-AR, -ER, ?*i.q.* TREVALADER

TREWALL-A, -OW, ? lower (*wallach*) t.

TREWALL-AN, -AND, *d.d.* -EN, ? *i.q.* TREVALLAN.

TREWAN, ? *i.q.* TREVAN.

TREWANDRA, oak hill (*ban derow*) h., *P.* ; ? dwelling (*trev*) by the oaks (*an derow*), *or* on oak down (*gwon*).

TREWANE, *i.q.* TREWEN, *P.*

TREWAN-ET, -NET, -TA, *d.d.* -T, ? *i.q.* TREVENETH ; *want*, a mole, *m.c.*

TREWAN-GING, -IAN, -NING, -ION, *i.q.* TREVANIAN.

TREWAR, ? careful (*war, Pr.*) h., *P.*

TREWARAK, *o.n.f.*, *i.q.* TREVORICK.

TREWAR-AS, -RAS, *i.q.* TREGAVARRAS

TREWARD-A, -ER, ? *i.q.* TREWARTHA.

TREWARDALE, ? d. by the high moor (*warth hal*), *P.*, *or* in the dale (*dol*); *or*, *i.q.* TREWOTHALL.

TREWARDREVAH, ? TREWARTH by the oaks (*derow*), *or* water-place (*dourva*).

TREWARLET, ?meadow (*gweirglawdd, w.*) house (*tre*), *or* land (*tir*).

TREWARLETHAN, *i.q.* TREMELETHEN

TREWARMET, ? *i.q.* TREWARVENETH.

TREWARNAYL, *i.q.* TYWARNHAILE.

TREWARNE, ? alder (*gwarn*) town.

TREWARNEVAS, ? upper (*warth*) little (*nebas*) h., *P.*; ? *i.q.* TRENEVAS.

TREWARR-A, -AH, play (*gware, w. chwareu*) t., *P.*; *or,i.q.* TREWARTHA

TREWARRY, ? *i.q.* TREVORR-OW, -Y.

TREWARTH, high (*warth*) town, *Pr.*

TREWARTHA, higher (*wartha*) t., *Pr.*

TREWARTHAN, ? *i.q.* TREWARTHA

VEAN, little (*bean*) TREWARTHA.

TREWARTHENICK, higher town by the (*an*) creek (*gwic*), or rivulet (*ick*), Pr. ; ? *i.q.* TREWITHENICK.

TREWARTHIAN, *n.f.*, *i.q.* TREVARTH-.

TREWARTON, ? d. on the hill (*war dun*) ; or, *i.q.* TREWARTHAN.

TREWARVA, ? marsh (*morva*) town.

TREWARVAL, ? *i.q.* TREMORELL.

TREWAR-VENETH, -NETH, 13 *cent.* -VENE, house upon (*war*) a hill (*menedh*), P. ; ? hill house (*treva*).

TREWARWICK, *i.q.* TREVORICK.

TREWASHFORD, ? ? d. by the *ash*, or sheep *washing ford*.

TREWASHMOND, ? d. by the entrenchment (*fos*) on the hill (*monedh*), P.

TREWASICK, *i.q.* TREVASSACK.

TREWASS-A, -OW, ? *i.q.* TREVOSA.

TREWASTE, ? ? *i.q.* TREVISQUITE.

TREWATERS, ? three (*tri*) streams (*t.*).

TREWATHEN, *i.q.* TREWART-HEN,-ON.

TREWATHERN, ? alder or marsh(*gwern*) TREWARTHA.

TREWATHINOE, ? NOE'S TREWARTHA.

TREWAVAS, winterly (*gwav-as*) or exposed d., Pr. ; ? GWAVAS house.

TREWAY, ? River- (*gwy*) ton.

TREWBODY, *n.f.*, faithful or trusty messenger (*treu bodi*, *o.n.*).

TREWDERET, *d.d.* (*e.d.d.* TREVIDER-ED), *i.q.* TREHUDRETH, *or* TYWARD-REATH.

TREWEATHA, ? widow's (*gwedho*) h.

TREWEATHING, *i.q.* TREVETHAN.

TREWED-ALE, -ELL, *i.q.* TREWHIDDLE

TREWEDNA, ? white (*gwednac*) house.

TREWE-EGE, -EK, -AK, sweet (*whec*) town, Pr.

TREWEEN, ? *i.q.* TREVEAN, P.

TREWEENS, ? ENIS house (*treva*).

TREWEE-R, -RE, ? *i.q.* TREVEAR.

TREWEER-ES, -S, ? maid's (*gwyrhes*) t.

TREWEESE, ? *i.q.* TREVESE.

TREWEET, *o.n.f.*, *i.q.* TREWITH.

TREWEGGA, 14 *cent.*, *i.q.* TREVEGO.

TREWE-LL, *d.d.* -LLE, ? high (*uhel*) t., P. ; or, *i.q.* TREVELL.

TREWELLA, ? *i.q.* TREVELLA.

TREWELLARD, ? *i.q.* TREVALLARD.

TREWELLOGEN, *d.d.*, ? d. on the high (*uhel*) down (*goon*), P. ; or, *i.q.* TREVELYAN.

TREWE-N, -NN, fair (*gwen*) t., or place of innocence, Pr. ; white h., *Wh.* ; ? St. Wenn's t. ; *p.s.* not known.

TREWENCE, *i.q.* TREVINCE.

TREWENETHICK, 14 *cent.*, *i.q.* TRE-VENETHIC, or TREWARTHENICK.

TREWEN-ICK, -NECK, -ACK, *i.q.* TRE-WINEY, TREWEN, or TREWITHENEC

TREWEN-ION, -NAN, *i.q.* TREVANIAN, P. ; ? Gwenan's dwelling.

TREWENT, *d.d.*, windy (*guent*, wind) town, *W.S.* ; *i.q.* TREVINT, or TRE-VENETH.

TREWERNE, marsh or alder (*gwern*) t.

TREWERRY, ? *i.q.* TREVER-OW, -Y.

TREWERTON, *i.q.* CHIVERTON.

TREWETHA, ? widow's (*gwedho*) h.

TREWETHACK, ? *i.q.* TREVETHACK.

TREWETH-AN, -EN, -IN, ? *i.q.* TREV-.

TREWETH-AR, -ER, ? workman's (*gue-idvur*) t., P. ; or, Gwythyr's (*w.*) d.

TREWETH-ARD, -ERT, -ET, ? Guaithrit's (*B.m.*) d. ; or, woodbine (*gwyddfid, w.*) house ; high (*ard*) TREWITH, *P.*

TREWETHERN, ? *i.q.* TREVIDRON.

TREWETHEY, ? *i.q.* TREVETHEY.

TREWETHICK, d. in the woody place (*guithic*) ; or, *i.q.* TREVITHICK.

TREWEY, ? = River- (*gwy*) ton, *P.*

TREWHE-ELA, -LA, -LLA, -LOW, d. by the works or mines (*wheylou*), Pr.

TREWHELE, *i.q.* TRENWHEAL.

TREWHIDDLE, ? *i.q.* TREWARDALE.

TREWIDDEN, white (*gwydn*) place, *C.*; or, *i.q.* TREVETHAN.

TREWIDLAND, ? Gwyddelan's (*w.*) d.

TREWIGGET, a village, little village (*wiccet*) town, Pr. ; ? WICKET'S h.

TREWIGLAS, *i.q.* TREVIGLAS.

TREWIJACK, ? *i.q.* TREVISICK.

TREWILL-A, *n.f.* -E, *d.d. i.q.* TREWHELA

TREWILLEN, *d.d.*, cultured (*gwyllin, w.*) place, *W.S.* ; ? *i.q.* TREVILAN.

TREWILLOW, ? *i.q.* TREVELLOE.

TREWIN, white (*gwyn*) house, *W.S.*;

dwelling on the marsh, *Pr.*

TREWINCE, under-town, *or* town exposed to the weather (?), *H.* ; *i.q.* TREVINCE.

TREWINCY, ? Wunsie's (*B.m.*) d.

TREWINDLE, ? high (*tal*) h. exposed to the wind (*guins*), *P.* ; *or*, Gwynodl's (*w.*) dwelling.

TREWIN-EY, -NEY, -NA, -NECK, -ICK, -NICK,-OCK,marshy(*winnic*)t.,*R.IV.*

TREWINEDOI, *d.d.*, Venetoe's (*Z.*) d., *W.S.* ; ? St. GWINEDOC'S d.

TREWIN-ION, -NION, -NOW, d. on *or* near the marshes (*win-ion, -now*), *T.*

TREWINNARD, *n.f.*, ? Gueneret's (*s.B.m.*) d.; *winnard*, the red-wing.

TREWINNEL, *i.q.* TREWINDLE.

TREWINSICK, windy (*guinsic*) h., *P.*

TREWINT, *i.q.* TREWIN, *Pr.*

TREWINTON, spring (*fenten*) t., *H.*

TREWINVER, 14 *cent.*, Gwenever's d.

TREWIRE, *n.f.*, ? battle (*heir*) h., *P.*

TREWIRG-IE, -Y, *i.q.* TREWORGAY.

TREWISCUS, *i.q.* TREVISKIS.

TREWI-SE, -SH, -TCH, *i.q.* TREWEESE.

TREWITGHI, *d.d.*, *now* TREWITHGY, wild-dog (*gwithgi*) h., *W.S.* ; t. of trees (*gwith*) by the river (*gy*), *T.*; ? *i.q.* TREWORGAY.

TREWI-TH, *o.* -T, ? *i.q.* TREVIT.

TREWITHA, ? *i.q.* TREWETHA.

TREWITHAC, ? *i.q.* BOWIDOC.

TREWITH-AN, -EN, -IN, t. among the trees (*gwedh*) ; *or*, *i.q.* TREVETHAN.

TREWITHENICK, dwelling tree (*gwedhen*) on a river (*en ick*), *T.* ; ? *i.q.* TREWARTHENICK.

TREWITHER, ? Gwythyr's (*w.*) d.

TREWITH-EY, -Y, ? *i.q.* TREVETHEY.

TREWITHIAN, town of peace (?), *T.* ; ? *i.q.* TREWITHAN ; *or*, GWITHIAN h.

TREWITHICK, ? *i.q.* BOWITHICK.

TREWITT, *n.f.*, *i.q.* TREWITH.

TREWITTEN, ? *i.q.* TREWIDDEN.

TREWN, down (*un* = *gwon*) house.

TREWO-DE, *d.d.*, *e.d.d.* -DA, ? fruitful (*voeth*, *Pr.*) farm, *P.* ; *or*, *i.q.* TREVOET.

TREWOLF, *o.n.f.*, *i.q.* TREWOOF.

TREWOLL-A, -AH, -ACK, -OCK, -ICK, -ECK, lower (*wollach*) town, *Pr.*

TREWOLL-AND,-EN, ? dwelling (*tre*) by the lower enclosure (*wolla lun*), *P.*

TREWOLSTA, Wulfstan's (*t.*) d.

TREWOLVAS, ? WULFSIGE'S town.

TREWON-AL,-VAL,-WEL,?CUNOWAL'S *or* MANUEL'S dwelling.

TREWON-ARD, -NARD, WONARD'S t.; *or,i.q.* TREVENARD *or* TREWINNARD

TREWOOD, ? *i.q.* TREVOET.

TREWOODLA, ? Gwodloew's dwelling.

TREWOOF, place frequented by, *or* town of blackbirds (*moelh*), *or* ? the rookery, *Pr.* ; t. of obyarn, *H.*; ?smith's (*gof*) h., *P.*, *or* Wolf's h.

TREWOOL-A, -ICK, *i.q.* TREWOLLA.

TREWOON, down (*gwon*) house.

TREWOOSEL, ? moor wood (*cus hal*) house (*tre*), *P.* ; ? Hawystl's (*w.*) h.

TREWORDER, ? *i.q.* TREVORDER.

TREWORDRA, ? *i.q.* TREWARDREVA.

TREWORELL, 16 *cent.*, ? *i.q.* TREWOTHALL, *or* TREWARDALE.

TREWORG-AN, -EN, ? WURCON'S d.

TREWORG-ANS, -ENS, *i.q.* TREVORG-.

TREWORG-AY, -EY, -Y, d. by the water, *or* just above the water (*wor gy*), *Pr.*; *or*, *i.q.* TREWORTHGY

TREWOR-ICK, -K, -OCK, -ROCK, -RACK, *o.* -EC, -KE, *i.q.* TREVORICK.

TREWOR-L, -LD, ? *i.q.* TREWARLETT.

TREWORL-AS, -IS, town on the high (*warth*) green (*las*), *Pr.*

TREWORN-AN, -ON, *i.q.* TREVERNON.

TREWORR-A, -OW, ? *i.q.* TREWARRA.

TREWORTHA, *i.q.* TREWARTHA.

TREWOR-THAN, -THEN, -TEN, *i.q.* TREWARTHAN.

TREWORTHAT, ? dwelling over (*warth*) a wood (*coat*).

TREWORTHGY, 16 *cent.*, *i.q.* TREWORTHY, house on (*warth*) a hedge (*ce*), *T.* ; ? Gwardogwy's (*w.*) h. ; *or*, *i.q.* TREWORGY.

TREWOR-VACK, -WICK, *i.q.* TREVORICK, *or* TRERABOC.

TREWORVAL, ? *i.q.* TREMORELL.

TREWORVENETH, *i.q.* TREWARVE-.

TREWOSEL, ? Hawystl's (*w.*) d.

TREWOTH-ACK, -ICK, -IKE, noted *or* known (*woth-ic*) t., *Pr.*; t. on the *wood*, *or* known *or* noted (*woth*) creek *or* bosom of waters (*ike*), *H.*; t. on (*warth*) the water *or* creek (*ick*), *D.G.*; ? *i.q.* TREWARTHENICK

TREWO-THALL, *alias* -RTHALL-THELL, ? d. on the river (*warth hayl`*, or moor (*hal*); or, Irishman's (*gwodhal*) dwelling.

TREWOTHER, ? *i.q.* TREWARTHA.

TREWRATH, *alias* TREVARTH.

TREWR-EN, -ING, -ONG, -ON, wren's t., *H.*; place of alder trees (*gwern, gwarn*), *T.C.*; ? UREN's dwelling.

TREWRICKLE, ? d. on the tide (*trig*) river (*hail*), *P.*; ? ARGALL house.

TREWSEN, *n.f.*, *i.q.* TREVISAN.

TREWTHANS, ? *i.q.* TRETHANAS.

TREWULVESES, t. of help, aid, succour (*ulph, s.*), *H.*! = TREVELVA WOLLAS & WARTHA, higher and lower TREVELVA.

TREWY, ? = River- (*gwy*) ton, *P.*

TREWYNIAN, *i.q.* TREWINNION.

TREWYN-S, -T, *i.q.* TREVINT.

TREWYTHE, *o.n.f.*, *i.q.* TREWITH.

TREWYTHENICK, *i.q.* TREWITHENICK

TREYAMON, Hamon's (*t.*) house.

TREYARD, *o.n.f.*, ? *i.q.* TREWETHARD.

TREYDURF, *O.*, *i.q.* TYWARDREATH.

TREYEAN, ? *i.q.* TREVEAN, *P.*; or, TREKEAN ; *or = tir ean*, lamb land.

TREYEO, ? YEO'S h.; or, *i.q.* TREYEW.

TREYE-R, -ERE, ? *i.q.* TREHEER.

TREYEUR, ? gold (*eur*), or goldsmith's (*eure*) h.; or, *i.q.* TREYER.

TREYEW, above (*yuh*) or upper t., *Pr.*

TREYONE, ? *i.q.* TREON.

TREY'S MILL, ? = TRESE mill.

TREZALLI-ON, -NG, ? *i.q.* TRESILLIAN.

TREZAWSAN, *i.q.* TRESAWSAN.

TREZEB-ALL, -EL, colt's (*ebol*) t., *Po.*; ? lower (*isa*) d. by the pool (*pol*); or, = *trusebal*, the herb colt's-foot.

TREZEAN, ? *i.q.* TREGIAN.

TREZ-EBUTT, -IBBET, ? lower (*isa*) dwelling (*tre*) by the grave (*bedh*).

TREZEDA, ? Seidi's (*w.*) house.

TREZE-LA, -ELA, salt (*zal*) town, *Pr.*; ZEALA house.

TREZELL-AND, -IN, -ING, ? Salenn's (*s.B m.*) dwelling.

TREZ-IZE, *n.f.*, -EZE, = *tre yz*, place for corn, *Pr.*; ? Saxon's (*sais*) town.

TREZODDERN, *i.q.* TRESADARN.

TREZOUIAN, ? *i.q.* TRESAVEAN.

TREZOWAN, ? Sauuin's town.

TRIAGO, *n.f.*, *i.q.* TREJAGO.

TRIANGLE FIELD, ? three-corner (*ongl, w.*) field ; or, *i.q.* TREUNGLE.

TRI-BLE, -BBLE, *n.f.*, ? *i.q.* TREBELL.

TRICARN, ? three (*tri*) carns.

TRICK, *n.f.*, ? *i.q.* TRIGG.

TRICKLODEVAS, ? = *tre gweal o devas*, sheep-field house.

TRI-COI, -GOI, *d.d.*, *i.q.* TRECUT.

TRIDDON, *n.f.*, ? *i.q.* TREDIDON.

TRIGANCE, *n.f.*, ? *i.q.* TREGUNNUS.

TRIGANDENON, ? = *tregva an denon*, the dwelling of men, *Po.*

TRIGANIEN, = *tre gan jein*, d. with cold, *Pr.*; ? *i.q.* TREGANIAN.

TRIGANTAN, ? Canotinn's (*w.*) d.

TRIGAVARAS, = *trigou varas*, dwellers in the ways, *Pr.*; ? *i.q.* TREGAVARRAS

TRIGA-VETHAN, *o.* -MEDDON, dwellers in the meadows, *Pr.*; *i.q.* TREGA-

TRIGAVITHICK, *i.q.* TREGAVITHICK.

TRIGG, an inhabitant (*trig*), *Car.*; ebb of the sea, *or* on the seashore, *Pr.*; third [hundred], *C.*

TRIGGJAGO, TRIDJAKA, *i.q.* TRIAGO.

TRIGGS, ? *i.q.* TREGOOSE.

TRIGONDALE, *i.q.* TREGONDALE.

TRILLIAN, ? Lleon's *or* Elian's (*w.*) d.

TRIMBLE, *n.f.*, ? *i.q.* TREMBEL.

TRIMLETT, *n.f.*, ? *i.q.* TREMBLEATH.

TRIMMER, *n.f.*, ? *i.q.* TREMEAR.

TRINDER, *n.f.*, ? *i.q.* TREGENDER.

TRINGY, ? d. by the river (*gy*).

TRIN-ICK, -NICK, -K, ? *i.q.* TRENEAGE

TRINNIMAN, *n.f.*, *i.q.* TRENEMEAN.

TRIPCONY, *n.f.*, ? *i.q.* TREGONY.

TRIPLET, ? *i.q.* TREMBLEATH.

TRIPP, *n.f.*, *from* scaling [a wall] nimbly, *Lo.*; ? = *tregva*, a dwelling.

TRISCOBAYS, *i.q.* TRESCOBEAS.

TRISCOTT, *n.f.*, ⸮ TRAWISCOIT.

TRISKEY, ⸮ *i.q.* TREVISKEY.

TRISPAN, *i.q.* TREVISPAN.

TRISTE, *n.f.*, ? = *trist*, sad, sorrowful ; or, *i.q.* TREWEST.

TRITHA-L, -LL, *i.q.* TREUTHAL.

TRIVET, *o.n.f.*, ⸮ *i.q.* TREVIT.

TRIZACKS, ⸮ *i.q.* DRYSACK-S.

TROAD, *n.f.*, *i.q.* TROOTE.

TROAN, down (*oon, woon, gwon*) t. ; or = *tron*, a nose, promontory, hill.

TROANCE, ⸮ INES lands (*tirou*).

TRODEN, *n.f.*, a starling (*troden*).

TROLENWITH, *o.n.f.*, ⸮ ⸮ = *tre hal enwydh*, d. on the moor of ash-trees.

TROLVIS, ⸮ *i.q.* TREOLVIS.

TR-ON, -OON, -ONE, *i.q.* TROAN.

TRO-OSEL, -SAL, -SEL, -SWELL, ⸮ Hawystl's (*w.*) dwelling.

TRO-OTE, -OUTE, -OTE, -TT, *n.f.*, ⸮ *i.q.* TREWODE; or = *troet*, a turtle dove.

TROTTER, *n.f.*, ⸮ bed (*trot*) of a river (*dour*, water), *P.*; ⸮ = *darador*, door-(*darat*) keeper, *i.q.* Porter.

TROUNCE, *n.f.*, ⸮ *i.q.* TROANCE.

TROUNSON, ⸮ council (*son*, a speech) oaks (*derow*), *P.* ; or = *tre rounsan*, ass town.

TROUTHEL, *d.d.*, ⸮ *i.q.* TREUTHAL.

TROVE, a dent, pit, cave, *or* valley (⸮), *H.* ; *i.q.* TREWOOF.

TROVERROW, *n.f.*, *i.q.* TREVERRA.

TROW-ALL, -ELL, ⸮ = *tirou hal*, moorlands ; or, *i.q.* TREVAL.

TROWSA, ⸮ lower (*isa*) lands (*tirou*).

TR-OWSE, -OYES, -UAS, ? outer (*aues*) lands (*tirou*), *or* oaks (*derow*).

TRUAN, a nose, beak, promontory (*tron*), *H.* ; ⸮ *i.q.* TREVAN.

TRUBODY, *n.f.*, *i.q.* TREWBODY.

TRUBY, ⸮ *i.q.* TREBIGH.

TRUBURROWS, ⸮ three (*tri*) *barrows*.

TRUCK, ⸮ *i.q.* TREGVA, *P.*

TRUCK FIELD, ⸮ manure (*otrach*) field

TRU-DGEON, -GAN, -GEON, -NCHEON, *n.f.*, *i.q.* TREGIAN ; or = *trodzhen*, a starling.

TRUEN, *i.q.* TREWEN, *R.E.*

TRUGO, ⸮ = *trev gof*, smith's h., *R.W.*

TRUMAN, *n.f.*, ⸮ rock (*maen*) of compassion (*trueth*), *P.* ; or, *i.q.* TREMAYNE.

TRUMBALL, *n.f.*, *i.q.* TREMBEL.

TRUMLETT, *n.f.*, ⸮ *i.q.* TREMBLEATH.

TRUMMER, *n.f.*, ⸮ *i.q.* TRERUMMER.

TRUNGLE, ? *i.q.* TREUNGLE.

TRURABO, *i.q.* TRERABOC.

TRURAS, ⸮ *i.q.* TREGAVARRAS.

TRUR-EN, -AN, *n.f.*, ? *i.q.* TREWREN, *or* TREVRANE.

TRURO, ⸮ *i.q.* TREFREW.*

TRUSCOTT, ? *i.q.* TRAWISCOIT ; or, door (*daras*) of the wood (*coat*).

TRUS-EL, -SEL, ⸮ *i.q.* TREROOSEL.

TRUSHAM, *n.f.*, ⸮ *i.q.* TREVISSAM.

TRUSTAR, *n.f.*, ⸮ = *troster*, a beam, rafter, *P.* ; or, *i.q.* TREVOSTER.

TRUTH-AL, -ALL, -WALL, -WELL, barren (*troth*) moor (*hal*), or, entrance (*darat*) of the moor, or, = *tre uhal*, high t., *Pr.* ; ⸮ *i.q.* TRETHALL.

TRUTH-AM, -AN, -ON, the (*an*) trout (*trud*), *H.* ; ⸮ ⸮ trout river (*avon, aun*), or home (*ham, s.*).

TRUTHAN-CE, -S, *from same* ; or, ⸮ foot (*truit*) of the valley (*nans*).

TRUTHURST, ⸮ ⸮ entrance (*darat*, door) of the wood (*hurst, t.*).

TRUY-AN, -EN, ⸮ *i.q.* TREW-AN, -EN.

TRY, ⸮ = *ty ruy*, king's house, *T.C.* ; or, *tre gwy*, dwelling by the river.

TRY CORNER FIELD, ⸮ three- (*tri*) cornered field, *i.q.* TRIANGLE.

---

* *o.* TRIVERV, TRIUERU, TRUUERU, TREURU, TREWREW, TRURU, TRUROW, TRUROE,= *tri ru*, three ways *or* streets, *Cam., Car., T., Pr., Po., Spry, R.W.* ;=*tre vorou* or *norou*, town of *or* on the ways, *B.* ;=*tre uru* or *uro*, town *or* castle upon the river, *Wh.* (*uro*, ? pl. of *ur*, a boundary, *Fenton*) ;=*te river-eu, -ou*, town on the rivers, *Hing.*;=*trev a rhiw*, place *or* village, at the slope *or* declivity, in the road *or* way, *M'L.* ; ? ? ?=*tre u eru*, dwelling above the field ; or, *tirou rhiw*, lands on the slope ; *cf.* TREVORROW, TREWARRA, &c. The manor is TRURO and TREYEW ; *c.d.* St. Mary.—TRURO VEAN, little TRURO.

TRYSACK, *i.q.* DRYSACK.
TRYTHALL, *n.f.*, ? *i.q.* TRUTHAL.
TRYTH-AN, -EN, ? = *w. Treidhyn*, a ridge of high ground running into a vale, *R.W.*; or, furze (*eithin*) land (*tir*), or house (*tre*).
TRYTHOGGA, ? = *w. treidhiog*, penetrating, *R.W.*; vile (*hogen*) harlot (*druth*), *P.*; *see* RETHOGGA.
TUBB, *n.f.*, ? = *tubm*, hot, *P.*
TUBB-AN, -ON, ? *i.q.* PARK TUBBAN.
TUB-BY, -MAS, *n.f.*, = THOMAS, *Cor.*
TUB FIELD, ? dry-dung (*tub*) field.
TUCK, *n.f.*, ? = *tyuc*, Farmer.
TUCKER, *n.f.*, ? *i.q.* TOKER.
TUCK MILL, fulling mill, *t.*
TUCKINGMILL, *same*; *c.d.* All Saints.
TU-COISE, -COYSE, *o.* -CAYS, wood (*cus*) house (*ty*), *W'h.*; wood side (*tu*), *Pr.*; *d.d.* TUCOWIT, *hence* DOGOOD, Toogood, *n.f.*
TUDUDWELL, ? Tudwal's (*w.*) h. (*ty*).
TUKE, *n.f.*, ?? *i.q.* TYACK.
TULA-, TULE-, TULU-MENA, the holed (*tol*, a hole) stone (*maen*), *Pr.*
TULL, *n.f.*, ? *i.q.* TOLL.
TULLA-, TULLI-MAAR, ? great (*mear*) hole (*tol*) or height (*tal*).
TULLOK, *n.f.*, *i.q.* TALLACK.
TUNGAY, *n.f.*, *i.q.* TANGEY, = *tongay*, a break in a field, *w.*, *R.W.*
TURFREY, *n.f.*, *i.q.* TREFRY, *Ch.*
TURGOIL, *d.d.* watch (*goil*) tower (*tur*), *W.S.*; ? *i.q.* TRECARREL, *J.Ca.*
TURKEY PARK, ? otter (*dourgi*), or turf hedge *or* water dike (*durgy*), or turkey close (*parc*).
TURMULLION, ? *i.q.* DORMULLION.
TURN A PENNY, ?? turnip (*turnupan*) field (*hay*).
TURNAVORE, = *tur an vaur*, the great tower, *P.*; or, turn of the road (*fordh, for*), *i.q.* TURNAWAY, *t.*
TURNAWIN, ? = *tur an wyn*, the white tower, *P.*; or, *i.q.* TRENAVIN.
TURNEMERE, ? great (*mear*) turn.
TURNEY, *n.f.*, ?? *i.q.* TREVARNICK.
TURSCOT, short (*cot*) or low tower (*tur*), *Pr.*; ? *i.q.* TRUSCOTT.

TUTTON, ? = *todn*, lay ground, *P.*
TUTWELL, ? *i.q.* DUDWELL.
TWEENA-, TWENE-, TWIN-, TWIN-NEY A-WAYS, [field] between the roads, *t.*, *M'L.*
TWELVEHEADS, [stamping-mill for crushing ore, with] *twelve heads or crushers*, *t.*
TWELVE-, TWIVEL-WOOD, TWELL-, TWILL-HOOD, [near] *two woods*, *t.*, *Beul.*
TWOPENNY FIELD, ? *i.q.* DOBNA.
TYAC-K, -KE, *n.f.*, farmer, husbandman (*tyac*).
TYBE-STA, -ISTER, house (*ty*) for cattle, *Pr.*; h. of good (*da*) prayer (*pysy*, to pray), *H.*; ? = *ty bedhau*, house of graves, *M'L.*
TYDDY, *n.f.*, ? *i.q.* TIDDY; or, = *ty du*, black house.
TYE CLOSE, ? house (*ty*), or adit *or* drain (*tye*, *Pr.*) close.
TYECOMBE, TYE valley; or, vale h.
TYER, *n.f.*, ? = *tyor*, a thatcher, slater, tiler.
TY-ES, -AS, *n.f.*, *o.* TEUTONICUS, *Lo.*, the Teuton; (*tus, ties*, people).
TYETH, *n.f.*, ? *i.q.* TREWITH, *or* TY-WARDREATH.
TYMANNEN CROFT, ? butter (*manen*) house (*ty*) croft.
TYMBRELHAM (*alias* TEMPLE PARK), *i.q.* TIMBERLHAM.
TYNA-L, -LL, ? *i.q.* TYWARNHAILE.
TYNCOMBE, *n.f.*, *i.q.* TINCOMB.
TYNES, *i.q.* TINES.
TYNNEY, *n.f.*, *i.q.* TINNY.
TYNTON, *i.q.* TINTEN.
TYPPET, *n.f.*, *i.q.* TIPPET.
TYRACK, ? *w. tyrwch*, towering, *R.W.*; or, *i.q.* DOUROCK.
TYRRELL, *n.f.*, ? royal (*real*) land.
TYRWHITT, *n.f.*, ? swelling (*chwydh*) land (*tir*), *R.W.*; or, wood (*cuit*) l.
TYSERD, *n.f.*, ? *i.q.* TRESARRET.
TYWARDREATH, dwelling (*ty*) upon [or above] (*war*) the sandy beach (*treath*), *Pr.*; *Car.* TREWARDRETH, sandie t.; *W.W.* TYWOODRETH;

? UCTRED'S, *or* Wuathrit's (*w.B.m.*) dwelling; *p.s.* St. Andrew.

TYWARNHA-ILE, -LE, house on the salt-water-river (*an hayl*), *T.*; h. on the moor (*hal*), *R.W.*; *e.d.d.* TIUUARTHEL.

TYZE-ER, -R, *n.f.*, ? *i.q.* TRESARE.

U CTRED, *t.d.d.*, mind council, *t.*, *Y.*

UDA-LE, -L, *n.f.*, yew dale, *Lo.*

UD-AY, -E, -Y, *n.f.*, ? yew (*yw*) house (*ty*); or, *i.q.* EADE.

UDDER, ? = *y dwr*, the water, *w.*; or, swelling (*ut*) in the water (*dour*), *P.*

UDNOW, *i.q.* UTHNO.

UGBERE, *i.q.* OGBERE, *Pr.*

UGOTHAWR, ? cave (*ugo*) by the water (*dour*).

ULFRIC, *B.m.*, wolf rule, *t.*

ULFRIT, *B.m.*, wolf peace, *t.*

ULNODESTONE, *d.d.*, enclosure of ULNOD, *t.d.d.*, wolf compulsion, *t.*

ULSI, *t.d.d.*, *i.q.* UULFSIE.

ULWARD, *t.d.d.*, wolf guard, *t.*

UNDER DITCH, ? ? half (*hanter*), or *under* DITCHI PARK.

U. GULLIS, half *or* under GULLIES.

U. HAYS, half *or* under HEYES.

U. HILL, ? low on the *hill*, *t.*

U. LAKE, ? below the brook, *t.*

U. LEACH, ? ? below the flat stone (*lech*).

U. PARK, lower close (*parc*), *t.*

U. SHIPPING, ? lower SHIPPEN PARK.

U. TOR, ? below TORR.

U.-TOWN, -TON, ? lower, *or* under, *or* half town-place [field].

U. WAY, under *or* lower road [field].

U. WIDDEN, *under* PARK WIDDEN.

U. WOOD, lower *or* under wood [f.].

UNJEW, ? *i.q.* ANGEW.

UNN GOTH, ? old (*coth*), *or* wood (*coat*) down (*gwon, goon, oon*).

UNY LELANT, *i.q.* LELANT.

UPCOTT, ? higher cottage, *t.*; or, Ubba's (*t.*) wood (*coat*).

UPDOWN, ? higher down, *t.*

UPHAM, ? higher HAM, *t.*

UPHILL, ? higher on the hill, *t.*

UPTON, ? higher, *or* Ubba's (*t.*) enclosure *or* farm (*tun, s.*).

URAGH, ? witch's (*wrach, w.*) [rock].

URBAN, *o.n.f.*, ? *from* TREVERBYN; *or* = *Urbanus*, civil, courteous, *lat.*

UREN, *n.f.*, ? *i.q. w. Urien*, = *ouranios*, heavenly,*gr.*,*Y.*; ? = *eurin*,golden,*w.*

URLICK, *n.f.*, ? *i.q.* HARLAKE.

USPAR, *n.f.*, *i.q.* VOSPER, *Ch.*

USTICK, *n.f.*, ? = *Ewstic*, a St. Juster, *W.C.B.*; = *ystig*, studious, learned, *or yuh sick* (?), a high place, *Pr.*; fair (*teg*) nightingale (*eus, B.*), *H.*

UTARTH, high (*arth*) swelling (*ut, uth*), *Pr.*; *v.* EARTH.

UTFOLD, ? out (*ut, s.*) fold (*fald, s.*).

UTHNANCE, *i.q.* HUTHNANCE, ? high (*huth*) valley, *or* valley of delusion (*huth, Pr.*), affliction, *R.W.*), *or* grief (*cuth*), *Ch.*

UTHNO, high bare (*no* = *noath*) place, *or* naked exposure, *Dr.*; *see* PERRAN UTHNO.

UULFSIE, *w.B.m.* = *Wolfsige*, wolf victory, *s.*

UXELA, *Ptol.*, = *uchel*, high (*uksala, sans.*), *Cam.*; *uisc heli*, salt water, *Bax.*

THE V A, ? *ma, va*, a place, *R.W.*

VAGGA, ? *i.q.* VUGA, or

VAG-HUE, -UE, ? = *vachow*, pl. of *magh*, a field, *R.W.*; or = *bach*, little, *or vug*, a hollow.

VALANBOUNDER, ? = *gwal an bounder*, the lane *or* boundary wall.

VALDO, ? ? = *gweal dour*, waterfield.

VALEAN, ? = *gwal vean*, little wall; *or*, *gweal ean*, lamb field.

VALENOWETH, *n.f.*, *i.q.* VELLANOW-.

VALLACK, *n.f.*, ? = *gwalac*, fenced.

VALLEY TRUCKLE, ? ? *i.q.* GLENDORGAL; *or*, GWEAL- *or* PARK-TRUCKLE

VALLINS, ? = *gweal eanes*, lambs' field.

VALLITORT, *o.n.f.*, = *de valle torta*, of the winding vale, *lat.*, *Cam.*

VALNOWETH, ? new (*nowedh*) field.

VAN, ? = *ban*, height, high.
VANCE LOE, ? barrow (*low, t.*) valley (*nans*), M'L.
VANDERNAIL, ? = [*parc*] *vounder an hayl*, lane close by the river, *P.*
VANDRACK, ? *i.q.* PARK AN TURK.
VANDWELL, ? ? *i.q.* PARK AN TULE.
VANE, ? *i.q.* VEAN, *or* VAN.
VANVEAR, great (*mear*) VAN.
VAREWASH, ? *i.q.* FAIRWASH.
VARF-ELL, -ULL, ? great (*mear*) field.
VARNE GROUND, *f.m.*, ? [sea] *fern* [fishing] ground, *T.Q.C.*
VARTHA, *n.f.*, *i.q.* WARTHA.
VASNOON, *n.f.*, ? = *fos an oon*, wall *or* intrenchment on the down.
VAU, = *fow*, a cave.
VAUGHAN, *n.f.*, = *w. bachan*, little man
VAU LAZ, ? grey *or* green (*glas*) cave (*fow*).
VAUSE, *n.f.*, ? *i.q.* FOS.
VAUTIER, *n.f.*, = Walter, *f.*
VAUX, *o.n.f.*, = *vaulx*, valley, *f., Cam.*
VAWDEN, ? hill (*din*) cave (*fow*) ; *or*, *i.q.* BAWDEN.
VEAB, *n.f.*, ? *from* MABE *or* St. VEEP.
VEALE, *n.f.*, a calf, *f., Lo.* ; = Veli, *t., F.* ; *or*, *i.q.* GWEAL.
VEAN, *n.f.*, = *bean*, little.
V. GARRICK, little rocky [field].
V. PORTH, *i.q.* PORTH BEAN.
VEAR, *n.f.*, ? = *mear, vear*, great.
VEARE MEADOW, ? great meadow.
VEASE, *n.f.*, ? *from* TREVEASE.
VEATONWIND, ? = *fenten wint*, wind, *i.e.*, windy well.
VEDUSCOWAN, ? *i.q.* FENTONSCAUAN.
VEE LANE, ? *i.q.* VALEAN.
VEEN, *n.f.*, = *bean*, little.
VEGAN POOL, ? little (*bechan*) pool.
VEITCH, *n.f.*, ? = *bich*, little.
VEL AN TOWN, ? field (*gweal*) by the (*an*) *town or* farm-place.
VELAN TREMAYNE, Tremayne's mill.
VELHUISH, *n.f.*, *i.q.* MELHUISH.
VELIN-DRUCHA,-DRUCHER,-DRUCTIA, -DROCKYE, *i.q.* MELLANDRUCHA.
VELIN-HAGEN, -NOGEN, mill where loaves *or* pies (? *hogen*) are sold, *B.*

VELLACOT, *n.f.*, ? = *gweal a coet*, wood field ; *or*, cottage *field, t.*
VELLAN ALSA, mill (*melin*) on the cliff (*als*), *Pr.*
V. BRANE, rookery (*bran*, a crow) mill, *Pr.* ; ? crow field.
V. DREATH, ? strand (*treath*) mill.
V. EUSAN, chaff (*usion*) mill.
V. GOOSE, wood (*cus*) mill.
V. GOVE, smith's mill ; *or*, = *gweal an gof*, the smith's field.
V. OWETH, *i.q.* MELLANOWETH.
V. POINT, yellow (*melyn*) point, *C.*
V.-SARGAN,-SERJAN, -SERGA, -SAGER, sieve mill, *W.B.*
V. SAUNDRY, SANDERS' mill.
V. SETH, dry (*sech*) mill, *Pr.* ; *or* = *gweal an seth*, field of the arrow.
V. USAN, chaff (*usion*) mill.
V. VRANE, *i.q.* VELLANBRANE.
V. VROS, great (*bras*) mill, *R.W.*
VELL BRIDGE, ? *bridge* field (*gweal*).
VELLEN CLOSE, ? *i.q.* PARK VELLAN.
VELLENZER, *n.f.*, ? *i.q.* VELLANSARGAN
VELLIES, ? = *gweal haiz*, barley field.
VELLIN ANTRON, ? ANTRON mill.
VELL-INOWETH, -NOWARTH, -OWETH, *n.f.*, *i.q.* MELLANOWETH.
VELLONS, ? lambs' (*eanes*) field.
VELMERS, ? *i.q.* GULLYMEARS.
VELVES, ? lark (*melhues*) [field] ; *or*, *i.q.* GWELLVEZ.
VEN, VENN, ? *i.q.* VEAN, *or* PENN.
VENARD, *n.f.*, ? *i.q.* MAYNARD.
VEN CLOSE, ? *i.q.* PENGULLAS.
VENDELLER, ? back (*delhar*) little (*bean*) [field], *or* well (*fenten*).
VENDEN COCK, cuckoo (*gog*) well, *P.*
VENDER CLOSE, ? bottom (*goles*) well (*fenten*) ; *or*, well *close.*
VENDITH, ? heath (*heyth*) well.
VENDOWN, ? well *down.*
VENEY, stones (pl. of *maen*), *R.W.*
VENHAIL, *alias* PENHAILE.
VENHILL, *same*; *or* = VEN *hill.*
VENLOCK MEADOW, ? BENALLOCK *m.*
VENMAN'S HILL, ? BENIAMIN'S *hill.*
VENNACOMBE, *n.f.*, ? stony (*maenic*), *or* marshy (*winnic*) vale.

VENNARD, *n.f.*, *i.q.* MAYNARD.
VENNE, ? *i.q.* VEN.
VENNER, *n.f.*, ? *i.q.* MENNEAR.
VENNIES, ? *i.q.* MENNIES.
VENNING, *n.f.*, ? *from* TREVENEN.
VEN PARK, VEN close.
VENSCOWAN, ? elder-tree (*scawan*) well (*fenten*).
VENSON, ? same; or, *i.q.* FENTON, *P.*
VENTALUNA, ? ? joyous (*lowannec*) well; or, *i.q.* PENALUNA.
VENTANEGO, ?Jago's, or smith's (*gof*), or wood (*coat*) well.
VENTANGAY, *i.q.* FENTONGAY.
VENT AN LEAGUE, *i.q.* VENTONLEAGE
VENTANVOSE. *i.q.* VENTONVOSE.
VENTERDON, ? spring (*fenten*) on the hill (*er dun*).
VENTERONISICK, 14 *cent.*, ? lower (*isach*) spring or well (*fenten*).
VENT FIELD, spring, or wind (*gwent, a.*), or wheat (*gwaneth*) field.
VENTILEASE, *i.q.* FENDERLEASE.
VENTINE, ? cold (*iein*) well.
VENTOM, *n.f.*, *i.q.*
VENTON, *i.q.* FENTON.
V. ALLEN, ? St. ALLEN'S well.
V. ALLIES, ? HALLAZE well.
V. ARA, ? *i.q.* FENTONARE.
V.-BARREN, -BERREN, ? St. Piran's w.
V. COOSE, *i.q.* VENTONGOOSE.
V. DAVEY, Davey's (*n.f.*) well.
V.-EAGE, -NEAGE, sweet (*whec*) well, *H.T.*; mossy (*neag*, moss, *B.*) w.,*Pr.*
V. EAST, ? St. JUST'S well.
V. ENDS, ? ENAS well.
V. ERRAN, ? silver (*arian, w.*) well.
V. ERTH, ? St. ERTH'S well.
V. FEATHERS, ? martyrs' (*merthyr-s*) w.
V. GEES, ? ? common (*ces*) spring.
V. GHOST, ? haunted well.
V. GILBERT, GILBERT'S well.
V. GIMPS, *i.q.* FENTONGYMPS.
V. GINE, cold (*jein*) well, *T.C.*
V. GLASTER, ? pebbly (*cellester*) well. (*glaster*, greenness or blueness, *R.W.*)
V.-GLIDER, -GLIDOR, -GLEDDOR, -GLIDDOR, -GILDER, *i.q.* FENTENGLEDER.
V. GOLLAN, *i.q.* FENTONGOLLAN.

V. GOOSE, *i.q.* FENTONGOOSE.
V. GOTH, old (*coth*) well.
V. GREAN, ? gravel (*grean*) well.
V. HOME, ? holly (*holm*) or home spring
V. HORN, ? iron (*horn*), or corner s.
V. JEAN, ? ox (*udzheon*), or giant's (*ghean, B.*), or cold (*jein*) well.
V. LADOCK, St. Ladoca's well.
V. LEAGE, ? flat-stone (*lech*) well.
V. LEY, *i.q.* FENTALEY.
V. MOOR, ? ? great (*maur*) well.
V. OOAS, ? outer (*aues*) spring.
V. RASE, ? middle (*cres*) spring.
V. REMFRY, REMFRY'S well.
V. RIGAN, *i.q.* FENTRIGAN.
V. SAW, spring near the *zawan* or cleft with water at the bottom, *E.G.H.*
V. SAWEN, the healing well, *Gw.*; or, *i.q.* FENTONSCAUAN.
V. UNY, St. Uny's well.
V.-VANE, -VEAN, little (*bean*) well.
V. VAUL, ? ? PAUL'S well.
V.-VEASE, -VEZ, *i.q.* F. VEASE.
V. VEDNA, *i.q.* FENTON VEDNA.
V. VEOR, great (*mear*) well.
V. VERTII, green (*gwirdh*) spring, *Pr.*
V. VIDON, ? little (*bedu*) spring.
V. VINE, ? little (*bichan*) spring.
V. VOSE, well of the VOSE.
V. VYVYAN, VIVIAN'S well.
V.-WIN, -WYN, white (*gwyn*) spring.
V. ZEATH, dry (*sech*) well, *Pr.*; ? well of the arrow (*seth*).
VENTUM CROFT, ? well *croft*.
VENVEN, ? *i.q.* VENTONVEAN.
VEOR COVE, *i.q.* PORTHMERE.
VERA, ? ? = *mear hay*, great close.
VERCOE, *n.f.*, ? *from* TREWORGEY.
VERDUN, *n.f.*, ? *from* TREVERDEN.
VERE, *n.f.*, great (*mear, vear*).
VER-, VERR-LAND, ? = *ber lan*, short enclosure, *P.*; or, *far land, t.*
VERMAN, *n.f.*, ? = *ber maen*, short stone, *P.*; *i.q.* BERRIMAN.
VERNEY, *n.f.*, ? = *gwern hay*, alder or marsh enclosure.
VER-RAN, -N, ? *i.q.* GWERN.
VERWELL, ? = *far well*; or, *mear gweal*, great field.

VERYAN, *from p.s.* St. Symphorian, *O., E.S.*; ? *i.q.* St. Urien, *w., C.S.G.*

VESPER, *n.f.*, ? *i.q.* VOSPER.

VI-AL, -EL, -ELL, *n.f.*, ? *i.q.* VEALE.

VIAN, *n.f.*, little (*bean, vian*).

VIBERT, *n.f.*, = *Uibert*, bright sanctity, *t., F.*

VICCA, ? = *gwic hay*, village *or* cove field

VI-CARY, -CTOR, -GOR, -GORS, -GROS, -CARS, *n.f., from gwicgur*, merchant.

VICE, *n.f., i.q.* BICE.

VIDDICKS, *n.f.*, ? BIDICK'S son.

VILES PARK, VILIZ, ? PILLAS *or* skinless-oats' close (*parc*); *or*, = *gweal haiz*, barley field; *or*, lower (*is*), *or* outer (*ves*) field.

VILLARS CROFT, ? *i.q.* CROFT PILLAS

VILVAH, ? = *gilrach*, a recess, *w., R.W.*

VILVOS, ? trench (*fos*) field (*gweal*).

VIL WARLS, ? BORLASE field.

VIN-ACK, -NACK, *i.q.* MINNACK.

VINCE, *n.f.*, ? *from* TREVINCE.

VINCENT, *n.f.*, ? *i.q. Wensent, w.*

VINEGAR PARK, ? close near the hop yard *or* garth (? *vineyard*).

VINE PARK, *i.q.* PARK VEAN *or* VINE

VINER, *n.f.*, ? = *gwinwr*, vintner.

VINEYARD, ? enclosure (*yard, t.*) for the vine (*gwin*), *P.*, *or* hop-*bine.*

VINGOE, *n.f.*, wine taster, *W.B.*; wine (*gwin*) man (*gwr*).

VIN-ICK, -NICK, -OCK, ? wine (*gwin*) [place], *P.*; *or, i.q.* MINNACK.

VINNICOMBE, *n.f.*, ? *i.q.* VENNACOMB.

VINOCKS, ? stony (*maenic*) [field]s.

VINTER VANE, ? *i.q.* VENTONVANE.

VINTON, *n.f., i.q.* FENTON *or* WINTON

VIOL, *n.f.*, ? *i.q.* VEALE.

VIOLENCE, ? = *gweal eanes*, lambs' field; *or, i.q.* GULNANCE.

VIRGA, ? = *wor gy*, above the river, *P.*

VIRLANDS, ? = *far lands or* fields.

VIS-ACK, -ICK, *n.f., i.q.* PHYSICK.

VISCAR, *alias* FISCAR.

VISGAY, ? *pixie or* fairy field (*hay*).

VISSAN, *n.f.*, ? *from* TREVESSAN.

VIVIAN, *n.f.*, = *Vivianus*, lively, *lat., Y.*; = *gwy vian*, small river, *or, from chuyvyan*, to escape, *w., Pr.*

VIXEN PARK, ? fox close, *t.*

VLUINUS, *t.d.d.*, ? = *Ulfwin*, wolf friend, *t.*

VLURIC, *t.d.d., i.q.* ULFRIC.

VOAD-, VOD-EN, ? *i.q.* BAWDEN.

VO-AGE, -UGE, -GUE, = *foc*, a blowing house, furnace, *P.*; *or, gwag*, a hollow.

VO-ASE, -AZ, -CE, *n.f.*, ? *i.q.* VOSE.

VOBEN, ? little (*bean*) cave (*fow*).

VOGAN, *n.f., i.q.* BOGAN.

VOG-LESHAM, -GLESUM, *i.q.* FUGL-.

VOGO, = *fogo*, a cave.

VOGUS, ? = *fog gus*, blowing house by the wood, *P.*; *or, bugas*, a bush; *or, i.q.* BARGUS.

VOICE, *n.f.*, ? *i.q.* VOYCE.

VONY PARK, ? hatchet (*bony*) close.

VOR EGLYX, *i.q.* [PARK] FRIGGLES.

VORG-A, -O, ? = *wartha ge*, higher field, *J.B.*; *or, maur ogo*, great cave ; *or, i.q.* TREVORGAY ; *or*, VIRGA ; *or*

VORGAN, ? = *morgan*, sea-side, *R.W.*

VORLAND, ? front land *or* field, *t.*

VORN, ? *i.q.* PARK VOURNE.

VORNER, ? = *gwarn hir*, long marsh.

VORSE FIELD, ? = *furze field, t.*; *or, i.q.*

VORV-AS, -ES, ? outer (*ves*), *or* good (*mas*) road (*fordh, vor*).

VOSE, *i.q.* FOSS, *or* BOASE.

VOSKELLY, ? grove (*celli*) FOSS.

VOSP-AR, -ER, -UR, *n.f.*, ? pure *or* immaculate (*pur*) virgin (*mos*), *H.*; ? VOSE close (*parc*), *or* cove (*porth*).

VOSSA, *n.f.*, ? *i.q.* BUZZA.

VOSSALL, ? moor (*hal*) trench (*fos*) ; *or*, trench moor.

VOUNDER, = *bounder*, a lane, *or* feeding ground ; ? *also* a boundary.

V. AN TEARE, ? the oak (*dar*) lane.

V. GABMAS, ? crooked (*cabm*), *or* stile (*camfa, w.*) lane [field]s.

V. LEDAN, broad (*ledan*) lane.

V.-PARK, -FIELD, lane field.

V. VEAN, little (*bean*) lane.

V. VEOR, great (*mear*) lane.

V. VOR LANE, lane (*redupl.*) [leading] to the sea (*mor*), *Gw.*

VOW, = *fow*, a cave.

VOWAN GUHAON, ? low (*rown*) down (*gwon*), *P.*; ? cave on the (*on*) down.

VOWELL, *n.f.*, ? = *vuel*, humble, obedient; *or*, cave *hill*; *or*, *i.q.* MOYLE.

VOWLE PARK, ? fool's (*fol*) close, *P.*; *or*, *fowl*, *or foul* c.; *or*, *i.q.* PARK VOLE

VOWLER'S CLOSE, ? Fowler's (*n.f.*) c.

VOYCE, *n.f.*, *i.q.* BICE *or* BOASE.

VRADDEN, VRADON HAY, ? crow (*bradn*, *bran*), *i.e.* rookery close (*hay*), *J.B.*

VRA-HAN, -N, rookery, *Po.*

VRAZE, ? *i.q.* PRAZ.

VROGE, ? = *vrach*, sea-weed, *a.*, *P.*

VROWNS, ? lambs' (*eanes*), *or* lower (*isa*), *or* dry (*sech*) hill (*bron*).

VUG-A, -GA, *i.q.* VOGO.

VUGLASS, ? *i.q.* VAU LAZ.

VUGPARC, cave close (*parc*).

VUINE, *n.f.*, *i.q.* WYNN *or* VIVIAN.

VULLER'S CLOSE, ? snail's (*bulhorn*) close, *P.*; ? BULLER'S close.

VULVERS, ? *i.q.* VELMERS.

VYCE, *n.f.*, ? *i.q.* BICE.

VYCOOSE, river (*wy*) wood (*cus*), *Pr.*

VY-ELL, -OLL. *n.f.*, ? *i.q.* VEALE.

VYEN, *n.f.*, = *bian*, *vyan*, little, *R.W.*

VYNOCK, *i.q.* VINICK.

VYVYAN. *n.f.*, *i.q.* VIVIAN.

WA-AD, -DE, *n.f.*, ? the herb *woad*, *s.*; *or* = *wad*, a ford, *s.*

WACK FIELD, ? empty (*gwag*) *field*.

WADDER, *n.f.*, ? = Walter.

WADDON, *n.f.*, ? ford hill (*dun*).

WADEBRIDGE, ford *bridge*, *t.*

WADE-, WAD-LAND, ? ford field (*land*), *t.*; *or*, *i.q.* WADELTON, *n.f.*, WADHEL'S (? = *gwodhal*, Irishman) enclosure (*ton*, *t.*, = *lan*, *k.*).

WADGE-, WADS-WORTHY, WADGERY, WAAD'S farm (*weorthig*), *t.*

WADHAM, *n.f.*, ? wood home, *t.*

WADLEY, *n.f.*, ? wood pasture, *t.*

WAGER, *n.f.*, ? = *gwicgwr*, merchant.

WAGMUGGLE, ? = *wæg mucel*, great road, *s.*

WAIN PARK, ? waggon close, *t.*

WAINSLADE, ? WYNNE'S bottom, *t.*

WAINSTONE, ? *i.q.* WINSTONE.

WAISTOW, ? = *wælstow*, place of slaughter, *or* battle field, *s.*

WAKE, *n.f.*, ? *i.q.* GWEEK.

WAKE-HAM, -M, *n.f.*, ? Wake's HAM.

WALCOT, *n.f.*, ? = *walla cout*, lower wood; *or*, cottage near the wall, *t.*

WALDON, *n.f.*, ? lower hill (*dun*).

WALES, *n.f.*, ? *i.q.* WALL-AS, *or* -EIS.

WALES-BOROUGH,-BURY, *d.d.* WALES-DRAV, *Wales or* Welsh burying ground, *H.*; ? Welsh *or* foreigners' (*wealas*, *s.*) earthwork *or* hill, *t.*

WALKE, *n.f.*, ? *i.q.* WALLOCHUS.

WALK-OMB,-EM, *n.f.*, *i.q.* WOOLCOMBE

WALL, ? = *uhal*, high; *or*, *gwal*, a wall; *or*, *gweal*, a field.

WALL-A, -OW, ? = *wallach*, lower.

WALLAS, ? *same*; *or*, *i.q.* GOONLAZE, *or* GWELLVEZ, *or*

WALL-EIS, -IS, -EYS, -ACE, *n.f.*; = *wealisc*, Welsh, foreign; *lat.* WAL-ENSIS.

WALLING CLOSE, ? OLD-WALL (*gwal hen*) close.

WALLO, *t.d.d.*, stranger, *t.*, *F.*

WALLOCHUS, *Bp.*, ? = *gwalch*, hawk, *w.*

WALLS PARK, ? *i.q.* PARK WOLLAS.

WALRINGTON, *n.f.*, ? enclosure (*tun*) of the children of Wulfhere, *t.*

WALUR, *n.f.*, ? = *gwalwr*, a waller.

WAMFORD, *n.f.*, ? *i.q.* WANSFORD.

WANDERAWAY, ? home (*tre*) *or* oak (*dar*) down (*gwon*), *or* meadow-land (*gweundir*, *w.*) by the roadside

WANGITHER, ? = *gwon gudhar*, mole down.

WANNA, ? *gwonnow*, downs.

WANNEYS, ? = *gwaneth*, wheat, *P.*

WANSFORD, ? *wains*, *i.e.* wagons' ford, *J.B.*; *or* Woden's *or* Owen's ford, *t.*

WARBOROUGH, ? guard (*weard*, *s.*) fortification (*burh*, *s.*); *or*, *from*

WARBSTOW, the place (*stow*, *s.*) of St. Werburgha (*p.s. O.*).

WARBURTON, *n.f.*, ? Werburgha's town, *t.*

WARD-, WAR-HILL, ? guard hill, *t.*

WARE, ? = *s. wœr*, a weir, dam, fish-pond, *t.* ; = *guare*, a play, *P.*

WARFLETON or WALVERTON, ? Wulfhere's enclosure (*tun, s.*).

WARLANDS, play (*guare*) enclosures (*lan-s*), *P.* ; ? *weir* fields, *t.*

WARLEGG-ON,-AN, high (*warth*) place (*le*) on the common (*gwon*), *Pr.*, or down, *T.* ; upon (*war*) the (*le, f.*) down, *Wh.* ; *p.s.* St. Bartholomew.

WARM, *n.f.*, ? = *wyrm*, a serpent, *s.*

WARMINGTON, *n.f.*, enclosure (*tun, s.*) of the children (*ing*) of WARM, *t.*

WARMWOOD, ? alder (*gwern*) wood, *P.*

WARNE, *n.f.*, ? = *gwern, gwarn*, an alder or marsh ; or = *weardman*, watchman, *s.*

WARN-ICK, -OCK, ? marshy place.

WARNICOAT, *n.f.*, ? = *gwern coat*, alder wood ; or, *i.q.* BARNICOAT.

WARNYSELL, *o.n.f.*, ? low (*isel*) alders.

WARRAH GWEAL, WARTH FIELD, THE WARTHA, *i.q.* GWEAL WARTHA

WARRATON, higher, or play (*guare*) hill (*dun*), or enclosure (*tun, s.*).

WARREN, the fort, *M'L.* ; or, rabbit-warren ; or, *i.q.* GWERN.

WAR-THA, -RA, higher.

WARTHA COOSE, *i.q.* COOZWARRA.

W. HALE, *i.q.* HALWARTHA.

WARTHANTRE, above (*warth*) the (*an*) town (*tre*), or sand (*traith*), *Gw.*

WARTON, ? garrison (*gwarth, B.*) hill (*dun*) ; or, upon (*war*) the hill.

WASHAWAY, entrenchment (*fos*) near the *way* or road, *P.*

WASLEY, *n.f.*, ? mud (*wase, s.*) pasture, *t.*

WASO, *t.d.d.*, = *hwœs*, keen, bold, *o.n., F.* ; ? = *gwas*, a servant (-o, *dimin.*).

WASON, *n.f.*, ? WATT'S or WADE'S son

WASTR-AL,-ELL, piece of waste land, *t.*

WATERFORD, ? higher (*wartha*) ford, *P.* ; ? river passage, *t.*

WATERLEIGH, ? water pasture, *t.*

WATER PARK, *i.q.* PARK WATER.

WATERPIT, [field by the water-pool or spring (*wœterpytt, s.*).

WATER WEETH, ? ? higher WEETH.

WATT, WATTY, WAUTER, WATERS,

WATTS, ? *from* WALTER or WADE.

WAUNFORD, *n.f.*, ? Woden's ford, *t.*

WAVELL, *T.a.*, ? *i.q.* WAY FIELD, *t.*

WAVISH, *n.f.*, ? *i.q.* GWAVAS.

WAYLAND, land enclosed by the [Roman] road, *t., M'L.*

WAYNARD, *n.f.*, ? *i.q.* MAYNARD.

WAYNE, *n.f.*, ? = *waen*, a plain, *R.W.*

WAY PARK, ? road close, *t.*

WAYSEND, ? [Roman] road end, *t.*

WAYTE, *n.f.*, a watchman, *t., Lo.*

WAYTON, enclosure (*tun*) by the *way* or roadside, *t.*

WEAL BARROW, ? barrow field (*gweal*)

WEARE, *n.f.*, ? *i.q.* WARE.

WEARING, *n.f.*, ? = *Warin*, protecting, or protecting friend, *t., Y.* ; or, *i.q.* WERRING or

WEARNE, *i.q.* WARNE.

WEARY LANDS, ? green (*gwir*) fields, *P.*

WEAVER, WEBBE, WEBBER, *n.f.*, ? = *webbe, webbere*, a weaver, *s.*

WEDBERY, ? *i.q.* WEB-WORTHY,-LAND, Webbe's farm (*weorthig, s., lan, c.*).

WEBSTER, a female weaver, *s.*

WEDDON, ? *i.q.* PARK WIDDEN.

WEDGEWORTH, ? *Wadge* or *Wade's* farm

WEDLICK, ? = *wœtleag*, moist pasture, *s.*

WEDLOCK, *n.f.*, ? *wedluc*, a pledge, *s.*

WEEK ST. MARY, sweet (*wheg*) St. Mary, *D.G.* ; village (*gwic*) of St. Mary (*p.s. O.*).

WEEL FAT, ? = *gweal varth*, high field, *P.* ; or, *fat* or rich field.

WEENGS, ? = *guen-s*, downs, *P.*

WE-ETH,-ATH,-ITH, ? = *gwaeth*, a field, *B.* ; or, *w. gwydd*, wild, uncultivated ; trees, shrubs.

W. NOEL, NOEL'S WEETH.

WEIGH CROFT, ? croft by the way-(*wœg, s.*) side, *t.*

WEITLAND, ? *i.q.* LANGUIT, *P.* ; or, = wheat or wet-field, *t.*

WEL-CH, -SH, *n.f.*, *i.q.* WALLEIS.

WELCOM, ? = *gweal cum*, valley field ; or, well or spring valley, *t.*

WELL AN DREA, *i.q.* GWEAL AN DREA

W. BOOT, ? cottage (*bwth, w.*) field.

WELL CARNE, *i.q.* GWEAL CARNE.
W. COCK, *i.q.* GWEAL COCK.
W. DICKEY, ? field with the *diggy*, or pool into which water flows from a shoot, *W.B.*
WELLESLEGH, *n.f.*, ? wells' pasture.
WELL GOOTH, *i.q.* HUEAL GOOTH.
WELL MAN, stone (*maen*), or narrow (*man*) field (*gweal*).
WELL NOR, ? = *gweal an hor*, the ram's or sister's field ; or, *north* field.
WELL PARK, *t.*, ? *i.q.* PARK VENTON
W. VROSA, ? tide (*fros*) well, *P.*
W. WREAN, ? hill-side (*rhyn*) field.
WELWAY, ? field by the way-side ; or, road to the *well* [field].
WENCENETHEL, *f.s.B.m.*, ? white (*gwen*) tribe, or people, or generation (*cenedl*), or linen (*cenedl*).
WENDEERN, *s.B.m.*, ? white hand (*dorn*), *P.*, or oak (*derwen*).
WEND-ON, -YN, *n.f.*, ? *i.q.* WENDRON.
WENDRON, white hill (*tron*), or thorns (*draen*), *Pr.* ; *from p.s.* St. Wendrona, *O.*
WENERIETH, *s.B.m.*, white longing (*hireth*), *P* ; ? *gwen*, a plain, *R.W.*
WENGOR, *s.B.m.*, white dwarf (*cor*), *P.*
WENMOUTH, *n.f.*, ? river's (*avon*) mouth
WENNON, *n.f.*, ? white ash-trees (*on*)
WENOWN, white down (*gwon, won, on*)
WENSON, *n.f.*, ? = Owen's son.
WENTAWAY, ? *i.q.* WANDERAWAY.
WENTON, *n.f.*, *i.q.* VENTON, *P.*
WENWÆNTHLON, *s.B.m.*, ? white besom (*bannolan, w. banadlen*).
WENWIU, *s.B.m.*, ? = *guenuuit*, sagacious, skilful.
WERREN, *i.q.* WARREN, or
WERRING, *n.f.*, ? *wering*, a dam, wall, bank, bulwark, rampart, *s.*
WERRINGTON, (*Dev.*) town of the Varini, *I.T.* ; WERRING town ; *p.s.* St. Martin.
WERRY, *n.f.*, *i.q.* WARREN, *W.B.*, or
WERRY PARK, *i.q.* PARK WHERRY.
WESCOMBE, *west*, or outer (*ves*) vale.
WESTANTON, = *west* STANTON.
WEST-AWAY, -WAY, west road or path

WESTCOT, west wood (*coat*), or *cot.*
WEST DOLE, west or outer dale (*dol*).
WEST-ERLAKE, -LAKE, ? more westerly brook, *t.*
WES-TERLAND, -TRA-PARK, more westerly field, *t.*
WEST-LEE, -LEIGH, west pasture, *t.*
WEST NORTH, ? = *ves an oar*, outer land, *P.* ; ? *north west* [field].
WETHIVEN, ? *i.q.* WITHEYVAN.
WETLEY FIELD, woodplace (*cuit le*) f.
WEV-ELL, -ILL, *n.f.*, ? = *gwefl*, a lip, *w.* ; *or, i.q.* WYVIL.
WEXWORTHY, ? WAKE'S farm, *t.*
WEYDOWNS, ? downs by the way-side, *t.*
WEYERS, *n.f.*, ? = *gweres*, to help, *P.*
WHADDON, *n.f.*, ? *i.q.* WADDON.
WHALE, *n.f.*, ? *i.q.* WHEAL.
W. DRAIN, *i.q.* HUEL AN DREAN.
WHALESBOROUGH, *i.q.* WALESBORO.
WHAR-ATON, -TON, hill (*dun*) of laughter (*wharthe*, to laugh), *P.* ; ? further (*gwarra*) hill.
WHARE, *n.f.*, ? = *guare*, play, *P.*
WHEAL, *n.f.*, a work, a mine ; *or*, = *gweal*, a field, (mostly, arable).
W. AMENA, ? = *gweal an maenor*, field by the boundary stone.
W. AN BOYS, ? *i.q.* GWEAL AN VEZ, or PARK AN BUSH.
W. AN COATS, the work (or mine, *wheal*) in the wood (*coos*), *Pr.*
W. AN CONS, ? field by the causeway (*coans*).
W. AN GOGS, the hemlock (*cegas*) f.
W. AN JETHEWON, the Jews' (*Edhewon, B. Jethewon*) work, *T.*
W. AN KINE, ? mine on the ridge (*cein*)
W. AN VEAN, the little (*bean*) field.
W. AN VOR, work by the way- (*fordh, vor*) side ; or, the great (*maur*) work or mine, *Pr.*
W. AN WENS, ? the wheat (*gwenith*) field, *C.* ; wind (*gwens*) field, *P.*
W. AN WREN, ? the swamp or alder (*gwern*), or hill-side (*rhyn*) field or work.
W. AN YET, *i.q.* GWEAL YATE.

WHEAL BADDON, ? high (*badn*) work, *P.*
W. BARLIS, ? barley (*barlys*) field.
W. BARREN, ? crow (*brahan*) field.
W. BOWEN, ? beef (*bowin*) field.
W. COCK, *i.q.* GWEAL COCK.
W. CORNET, ? corner (*cornal*, *Lh.*) f.
W. CRE-EG, -G. ? *i.q.* HUEL AN CREEK
W. DESGENTLE, *i.q.* WHEAL TEESG-.
W. DOBNA, DOBNA field.
W. DOWER, water (*dour*) field.
W. DREATH, sandy work, *Pr.*; ? mine on *or* near the strand (*treath*).
W. DRUCKIA, ? ? mine *or* field near VELIN DRUCHA.
W. GARRAS, rough (*garow*) works, *C.*; *or, i.q.* GWEAL GARRAS.
W. GEAL, ? narrow (*cul*, *gul*, *w.*), *or* secret (*cel*, *gel*, *w.*) field, *R. W.*
W. GEER, ? camp (*caer*), *or* green (*gear*) field, *or* work *or* mine.
W. GEEVER, goats' (*geur*, *Lh.*) f., *R. W.*
W. GOGUE, cuckoo (*gog*) field, *P.*
W. GRE-AN, -EN, ? gravel (*grean*) f.
W. GROSE, ? cross (*crows*) field.
W. GULLAS, ? bottom (*goles*) field.
W. GWENS, wheat (*gweneth*) field, *J.B.*; ? windy (*gwens*, wind) field.
W. KINE, ? ridge (*cein*) field *or* m.
W. LEAN, ? = *gweal ean*, lamb field.
W. KESSEL, ? castle field *or* work; (? = *w. cessail*, a recess, hollow, arm-pit, *R. W.*).
W. MAGOR VEAN, ? MAGOR's little w.
W. MALKAS, ? cursed (*malegas*) work
W. MEHAL, Michael's work *or* mine.
W. MENAS, ? small (*minys*) field, *P.*
W. NUT, ? ? *i.q.* W. NOWETH, new (*nowedh*) field, mine, *or* work.
W. OWLA, *i.q.* HUEL HOWLA.
W. OWLES, cliff (*als*) mine.
W. PATH, ? money (*bath*) field, *P.*; ? = *paith*, open country, *R. W.*
W. PEE-BER, -VER, ? piper's (*pibor*) f.
W. PRY, clay (*pri*) field *or* work.
W. RAVEN, ? ? buck-thorn (*rhafn*, *w.*) f.
W. REETH, red (*rydh*) work, *or* open (*rhwydd*, *w.*) work *or* mine, *Pr.*
W. ROSE, mine in the vale, *Pr.*
W. SEVEY, ? ? strawberry (*sevi*) field.

W. SHEGES, ? Zaccheus's work *or* mine.
W. SPARNON, ? *i.q.* GWEAL SPERNON
W. SPERRIS, ? spirit *or* haunted m.
W. TEESGENTLE, ? ? field *or* work of the gathering together (*cuntell*) of the people (*tees*).
W.-TERRIC, -TRICK, ? broken-up (*terric*) *or* grave-digger's (*derric*) field.
W. TREATH COATH, ? ? old (*coth*) mine near the strand (*treath*).
W. VELVAS, ? lark (*melhues*) field.
W. VERISACK, ? underwood (*prysg*) f.
W. VLOW, ? boy's (*floh*) work *or* m.
W. WIDDEN, ? white (*gwydn*), *or* little (*bean*, *vidn*) field.
WHEALS, *n.f.*, ? *i.q.* WALLEIS.
WHEEL-ERS, -YARS, ? hens' (*yar-s*) f.
WHEEL PIT, ? *i.q.* POL ROSE.
WHEL AULES, *i.q.* WHEAL OWLES.
WHELE EGLAS, ? church (*eglos*), *or* bottom (*goles*), *or* green down (*goon las*) field.
WHE-LLER, -ELER, *n.f.*, ? long field (*gweal hir*), *or*, = s. *hweolere*, a diviner, *F.*
WHETTER, *n.f.*, ? = *gweader*, weaver.
WHIDDEN, *n.f.*, = *gwydn*, white.
WHIDDON, ? blood (*guit*) hill (*dun*).
WHILANCLEUTH, worke of the ditches, *Car.*; ? ditch field, *P.*
WHIL PARK, ? feast (*gwyl*, *w.*) close.
WHIM MEADOW, meadow with *whim* for winding up from mine shaft.
WHIMPLE, ? pool (*pol*) on the descent (*guimp*, *Pr.*), *P.*; pool among the gorse (*chwynn*, *w.*), *R.E.*
WHINACOT, = *guen coth*, old down, *P.*; ? *cot*, wood, *R. W.*; *or*, cottage, *t.*
WHISTA PARK, ? *i.q.* PARK QUEST.
WHISTLE PARK, *i.q.* PARK WHISTLE
WHITABURROW, ? = white-barrow, *t.*
WHITACROSS, ? blood (*guit*) cross, *P.*
WHITAMORE, ? = white-moor, *t.*
WHITATREE, ? tree of blood (*guit*), *P.*; *or*, white tree, *t.*; *or, i.q.* TREWIN.
WHITSTONE, stone of blood (*guit*), *P.*; *or*, white stone, *t.*; *p.s.* St. Nicholas.
WHITTEN, ? *i.q.* TREWIDDEN.
WHITTINGTON, *n.f.*, *t.*, ? the same.

WHITY BUSH, ? *withy bush* [field], *t.*
WIC-CA, -KA, -KET, little village, *Pr.*
WICH, *d.d.*, ? = *gwic*, a village ; cove.
WIDDA CLOP PARK, ? close (*parc*) of the lame (*clof*) workman (*gweiduur*), *P.*
WIDDACOT, ? wood (*wudu, s.*) cot, *t.*
WIDDECOMBE, *n.f.*, ? *withy* vale, *t.*
WIDDEN, ? little (*bian, vidn*) [field]; W. VOR, great (*maur*), or road-(*fordh, vor*) side W. ; HOMER W. ; homeward *or* nearer WIDDEN.
WIDDOWN, ? ? = *wide down, t.*
WID-ESLADE,-ISLADE, broad bottom,*t.*
WIDIE, *d.d.*, wood enclosure (*hay*),*t.*
WIDLAKE, lake of blood, *P.*; *or*, wide lake, *J.B.* ; *or*, *i.q.* WEDLECH.
WIDLEY, ? = *guit le*, blood-place, *P*
WIDNANCE, blood vale (*nans*),*P.*; tree (*gwedhen*),*or* white(*gwydn*) vale,*J.B*
WIDOW, *n.f.*, ? = *widu*, a wood, *s.*
WIGACOT, little-(*wigan* = *bichan*)wood (*coat*), *P.* ; *or*, wizard's (*wigga, s.*), *or* soldier's (*wiga, s.*) cottage, *t.*
WIGGLE, ? wizard's hill, *t.*
WIGGON, *n.f.*, ? = *bichan, vichan*, little
WIGGY, ? soldier's field (*hay*), *t.*
WILBAR,? = *gweal bar*, upper field,*J.B.*
WILBOT,? = *gweal bod*, field house,*J.B.*
WILCOVE, ? sail- (*goil*) shaped cove, *P.* ; *or*, well (*wyl, s.*) cove.
WILGRESS,? = *gweal gres*, middle field ; *or*, *i.q.* GWEAL GARRAS.
WILLACOMBE, ? *i.q.* WILLOWCOMBE,*t.*
WILLAGE PARK, ? *i.q.* WILLAS FIELD, bottom(*wolas* = *gwollach*)field(*parc*)
WILLA PARK POINT, ? observation (*gwylfa*) close (*parc*) point.
WILL-IAMS, -YAMS, -IAMSON, *n.f.*, son of William = *Wilhelm*, resolute helmet, *or* helmet of resolution,*t.*,*Y.*
WILLOW CRIFF, ? = *willow croft.*
W. GARTH, ? *i.q.* WILLOW GARDEN.
W. HORN, ? ? willow corner (*corn, horn*)
WIL-LS, -S, -LIS, ? *i.q.* WALLAS.
WILLSHEAD, *t.*, ? *i.q.* PENFENTINOW.
WILLSWORTHY, ? WIVEL'S farm, *s.*
WILLY DOWNS, ? = *willow downs.*
WILLYER, ? = *gweal hir*, long field.

WILMER CLOSE, ? sea-rover *or* pirate's (*gwillmer, w.*) *close.*
WILSEY, ? dry (*sech*) field (*gweal*).
WILTON, ? well (*wyl, s.*) enclosure, *t.*
WILVEN, ? = *gwylfaen*, watch stone,*w.*
WINAFORD, ? *i.q.* WINEFORD.
WINARD'S HILL, ? red-wing (*winnard*) hill.
WINCUF, *B.m.*, strenuous (*cuf,s.*) strife (*win, s.*), *F.*; ? wine (*guin*), *or* white (*gwyn*) belly (*gof, a.*).
WINDANCE, ? burnt (*danys*, fired) down, *J.B.*; *or*, castle (*dinas*) *down.*
WINDON, white *or* fair hill (*dun*).
WIN DOWN, ? *a reduplication*, (*guen*, a down) ; *or*, white (*gwyn*) *down.*
WIND RING, ? circle on the downs, *P.*; *or*, thorny (*draenic*) down (*guen*)
WINE, *t.d.d.*, a friend, disciple ; one beloved ; a man, *s.*
WINECOVE, WINE'S cove; *or*, *i.q.* PORTH-GWIDN, -GUIN, *R.W.*
WINEFORD, ? WINE'S ford, *t.* ; *or*, passage over the river (*auon*).
WINEFORK, down (*guen*) over (*war*) the river (-K = *gy, gwy*),*P.*
WIN-ETONE, -ENTON, -NINGTON, WINE'S town, *t.*; *or*, *i.q.* TREWIN, *or* TREWEN.
THE WINGER, ? distant (*cer*) down, *P.*
WINGLE-TON, -TANG, ? St. Wengel's enclosure (*tun*), *or* tongue of land,*t.*
WINICK, marsh (*winnic*) [piece].
WINIELTON, ? Guenhuel's (*w.*) town.
WINKWELL, marshy field (*gweal*), *or* well ; *or*, = *wincel*, a corner, *s.*
WINN, *n.f.*, ? = *gwyn*, white, fair, blessed, *w.* ; *or*, *i.q.* WINE.
WINNEY HAM, ? marshy (*winnic*) HAM
WINNING, ? = WIN-ICK, -NICK.
WINNOW, marshes, *Pr.*
WINPOLE, ? *i.q.* WHIMPLE.
WINS-ER, -OR, turkey, grouse, *or* heath-cock (*sar*) marsh (*win*), *Pr.*
WINSL-ADE, -ETT, ? Winn's bottom,*t.*
WINSLO-E, -W, *n.f.*, ? mound (*hleo, s.*) of battle (*win*), *Ch.* ; ? Winn's m.
WINSTOCK, marsh place (*stoc, s.*), *P.*; *or*, = WINSTOW, place for conflict, *s.*

WINT-ER, -OUR, *n.f.*, ? = *gwyn doar*, fair water.

WINYETT, ? *i.q.* VINEYARD.

WISH, ? *i.q.* WICH, *J.B.* ; or, HIWIS.

WISTOW, ? feast (*wist, s.*) place ; or = *wœlstow*, place of slaughter, *s.*

WITANSTONE, wiseman's (*witan, s.*) stone, *t.*

WITEMOT, *d.d.*, ? = *witenagemot*, meeting [place] of the wise men, *s.*

WITHEL, *n.f.*, = *uthel*, lofty, *P.* ; *from* WITHIEL, ? = *gwydhel*, that is of the woods, a savage, an Irishman.

WITHEN = *gwedhen*, a tree.

WITHER HILL, workman's (*gueiduur*) hill, *P.* ; ? higher (*wartha*) h. field.

WITH-IEL, -YEL, *from* an earl of Cornwall, *Wh.* ; an Irisch sainct, *Le.* (*see* WITHIEL) ; *p.s.* St. Clement.

W. GOOSE, WITHIEL wood (*cus*).

WITHNOE, *from* St. Withinocus, *i.q.* WINNOW.

WITHY AYOT, withy *or* osier plot (*ayot*, a low bushy island, *t.*), *P.*

WITHY-BIND,-VAN,-VIN,-WIN,-WINGS ? [field] where *withies* are cut to *bind* furze-fagots together, *B.M.* ; ? wild convolvulus (*weothebend, s.*) f.

WITHYMOOR, withy *or* sallow-moor, *t.*

WITTON, ? wheat enclosure (*tun, s.*) ; or, *i.q.* TREWIN.

WIVELL, *n.f.*, *i.q.* WYVELL.

WLUUARD, *t.d.d.*, = *Ulfward*, wolf guard, *t.*

WODENOTE, *n.f.*, ? = Woden's wood.

WOLFVEAN, ? *i.q.* GOLVEAN.

WOLLACOMBE, *n.f.*, *i.q.* WOOLCOMBE.

WOLRIDGE, *n.f.*, *i.q.* ULFRIC.

WOLSDON, ? Bp. WOLSI'S (= *Wolfsige*, wolf-victory) hill (*dun*).

WOLSON, *n.f.*, ? = *Wulfstan*, wolf-stone, *t.*

WOLVEDON, *alias* GOLDEN, wolf-hill, *Wh.* ; ? sparrow (*golvan*) hill, *P.*

WOLVE-RSTON, -STON, *n.f.*, ? Wulfhere's (*t.*) town (*tun*), *t.*

WONARD, *n.f.*, ? = *gwon ard*, high down ; or, *i.q.* WINARD.

WOOD-A, -AH, ? the *wood, t.*

WOODALL, ? *wood* moor (*hal*).

WOODAVIS, ? Avis's (*c.n.*) *wood* ; or, the wood outside (*aves*).

WOOD CLAM HAM, ? *wood* foot-bridge (*clam*) low-pasture (*holm*).

WOODHAYS,? wood enclosures(*hays*),*t.*

WOODSAWS, *woods* enclosures (*haws, t.*), *M'L.* ; or, *i.q.*

WOODSAWSEN, *i.q.* COSSAWSIN.

WOOLABURY, lower (*wolla*), *or* Wolf's earthwork (*bury*), *t.*

WOOLAND, ? wood-land *or* field, *t.*

WOOLATON, ? lower enclosure (*tun,s.*)

WOOLCOMBE, *n.f.*, ? lower (*wolla*), or elm, *or* owl (*ula*) vale.

WOOLFREY, *n.f.*, ? = *Ulfred*, wolf peace *or* council, *t.*

WOOLLEY, ? *wood* pasture (*lea, t.*).

WOON = *gwon*, a down.

W. BELLAS, *i.q.* NOON BELLAS.

W. BOCCA, he-goat down, *Pr.* ; ? scarecrow *or* hobgoblin down.

W. CAR-ETH, -REETH, ? red rock (*carn rydh*) down.

W. DREA, homer *or* homeward (*adre*) d.

WOOT-ON, -TON, ? Woden's town, *t.*, *Beal* ; or = *wood* town, *t.*

WORGON, *n.f.*, *i.q.* WURCON, *s.B.m.*

WORLEGAN, *n.f.*, *from* WARLEGGON.

WORLEY, ? = *warth le*, high place, *P.*

WORTH, ? = *warth*, high ; or, *s. worth*, a farm, &c. ; or, *i.q.* WROATH.

WORTHY, *i.q.* PARK WARTHA.

WORTHYVALE, ? higher (*wartha*) vale ; or, *i.q.* GUERDAVALAN, *d.d.*

WORVAS, *i.q.* VORVAS, *Pr.* ; W.CREASE & COLLIS, middle (*cres*) & bottom (*goles*) VORVAS.

WRATH'S HOLE, giant's hole, *B.*

WREN, *n.f.*, ? *i.q.* UREN.

W. FIELD, *i.q.* REEN field.

W. HILL, ? boundary (*urrian*) hill, *P.*

WRIGGLES, *i.q.* PARK FRIGGLES.

WRINGCHEESE, *i.q.* CHEESEWRING.

WRINGFORD, *i.q.* RINGFORD.

WRINGS, *i.q.* RINGS.

WRINGWORTHY, ? castle (*ring*, a round) farm (*weorthig, s.*), *t.*

WRO-ATH,-THE, *n.f.*, ? = *wrath*, a giant ;

or, gwr rudh, red-man ; *or,* Worth.
Wul-fger, -garus, *B.m.,* wolf spear (*gar, s.*), *t.*
Wulvedon, *i.q.* Wolvedon.
Wulston, ? = *Wolf's town.*
Wulfwerd, *w.B.m.,* wolf guard, *t.*
Wur-cant, -gent, -con, *s.B.m.,* man (*gwr*) of song (*ceneat*), *w.*
Wurci, *s.B.m.,* dog (*ci*) man.
Wurgustel, *s.B.m.,* pledge (*gwistl*)m.
Wurlowen, *w.B.m.,* ?joyous (*lawen*), or fox (*lowern*) man.
Wydeslade, Wyde's (*n.f.*) bottom, *t.*
Wyger, ? = *gwicgur,* a merchant.
Wymond, *n.f.,* sacred (*wig*) protection (*mund, s.*); Wymondesham, Wymond's home, *t.*
Wynhall, *n.f., i.q.* Halwin.
Wynne, *n.f., i.q.* Winn.
The Wyth, *i.q.* Weeth, waste, *E.G.II.*
Wythan, the tree (*gwedhen*), *Pr.*
Wyvelcombe, Wyvel's vale, *t.*
Wy-vell, -well, -ppyl, *n.f.,* holy (*wig, s.*) well or manor (*ville, f.*), *H.;* ? = *s. wifel, wibel,* a beetle, a dart.
Wyvelshire, Wyvell's hundred or shire ; *o.* Welleshire, the shire of the Welshmen *or* strangers (*wealas, s.*), *D.*

Yago, ? = *hay gof,* smith's field ; *or, i.q.* Iago.
Yardeley, *n.f.,* enclosed land, *t., F.E.*
Yarn, ? *i.q.* Carn, *F.E.*
Yate, Yeat, = *yet,* gate.
Yearle's, ? Hearle's [place].
Yeilland, ? *i.q.* Illand.
Yendall, *n.f.,* ? *i.q.* Hendole.
Ye-o, -a, *n.f.,* ? = *yw,* yews, *w.*; *or, ea,* water, *s.* (the Yeo, *Devon*).
Yeoman, *n.f.,* a freeholder, *t., Lo.*
Yeo-, Yon-na Park, *i.q.* Yonder P.
Yett, Yetto, *i.q.* Yate.
Yewherns, ? Uren's [place].
Yewmill, ? high (*uch*) mill.
Ynys, *i.q.* Enys.
Yo-, Yeo-lland, Yeo's farm, *t.*
Yonder Coombe, further vale, *t.*

Y. *and* Homer Butts, further and nearer archery field, *or* fold (*boudzhi*)
Y. Park, further close, *t.*
Y. Town, further homestead *or* farmplace [field], *t.*
Youl-don, -down, -ton, -ston, devil's (*dioul*) down, *or* hill (*dun*), *or* town.

Zaggy Park, Zechariah's close.
Zanzidgie, consecrated (*sans*) ivy (*idhio*), *Pr.*; ? = St. Issey.
Zawn, a cove, opening in a cliff, *T.C.*; creek, *B.*; hole, *Pr.*; cave, *J.B.*
Zawn a Bal, mine (*bal*) Zawn.
Z. Brinney, crows' (*bryny*) Zawn.
Z. Buzzengean, ? the giants's house (*bos an gheon*) Zawn.
Z. Gever, ? goats' (*geur, w.*) Zawn.
Z. Groyne, the seal cave, *Bl.*
Z. Innis, island (*enys*) Zawn.
Z. Kellys, fallen (*cellys,* lost) cavern, *B.*; ? lower (*gollas*) Zawn.
Z. Lowarren, fox (*lowern*) Zawn.
Z. Priest, *priest's* Zawn.
Z. Pulbrean, ? = Polbrean Zawn.
Z. Pyg, cave like a bird's beak (*pyg, B.*) ; *Bl.* ? beak Zawn.
Z. Reeth, red (*rydh*) cavern, *Bl.,* or cove.
Z. Stamps an Jowl, the devil's (*an dioul*) stamps Zawn.
Ze-alla, -lah, dry (*sech*) enclosure (*lan*), *Pr.*
Zekiels, Ezekiel's [field].
Zendune, ? = Zennor down.
Zennor, the saint's (*sans*) earth (*or* = *doar*), or holy land, *Pr.*; holy pool *or* lake (?), *or* sea lake *or* creek, *H.*; *from p.s.* St. Sinar-us, -a, *O.*
Ziggal, ? rye (*sygal*) [field].
Zugher, river, ? = *sigyr,* sluggish, trickling (*w. segur, R.IV.*).
Zula, black (*zu* = *du*) enclosure (*lan*), or mowyard, enclosure for straw, reed, *or* stubble (*zoul*), *Pr.*
Zwallock, *i.q.* Swallock.
Zyns, saints' (*syns*) [abode], *or* holy (*sans*) [place], *Pr.*

NAMES UNEXPLAINED *(No. I—IV),*

About which information is solicited.

Aaron and Bushy P. 202, Abbey Ham 187, Above Bars 193, -Ditch 135, Acre-bend *ib.*, -Splat 86, Adder P. 95, Adjustment 75, Agestment 150, Agistment 179, Aglow 95, Airy 35, Aldown 193, Ale P. 110, Amos-M. 75, -moon F. 4, Amys F. 140, Andrew Well 123, Angling Cr. 40, Angle F. 18, The Angles 27, Annas C. 85, Anker-berry 93, Anticose 18, Aply 145, Apple P. 144, The Apson P. 112, Arell M. 72, Arch F. 187, Archindale 166, Argaret 5, Arm 86, Armshouse P. 193, Arrow 29, Arrow Stone 142, Ash-ey 175, -lers M. 50, -Ham 180, -ley H. 153, -P. 139, -walk 203, Asses M. 47, Ass Mr. 35, At Ford 135, Atney M. 160, Aunt Peggs F. 135, Baal Reid 27, Baccas Mr. 83, Backdoor Plot 177, Backes P. 135, Back-house P. 112, -ing F. *ib.*, -leat Plot 177, -side P. 141, -shippen 143, The Baddocks 118, Bad-Bargain 177, -Park *ib.*, -gers P. 144, -War 192, Bag Bury 193, -Lake 184, Baland 103, Bald P. 123, Ball 180, Bales P. 148, Baltic 110, Banspark 123, Bantspark 145, Bapark 160, Barbadoes 203, Barberrys C. 72, Bar-C. *ib.*, -Cr. 51, Bare-Acre H. 180, -F. 167, -Hills 119, -M. 112, -P. 193, Baree 142, Bar F. 192, Barkes 37, Bark P. 159, Bar M. *ib.*, Barls 27, Barnaby F. 1, Barnow 34, Baror C. 35, Barr Cr. 29, Barrow P. 119, Bars 145, Barten 35, Bartin Cr. 29, Barty 103, Base M. 72, -Parks 184, Bases Mr. 86, Basleys 123, Bate P. 125, Batter P. 141, Battle P. 160, Batton 27, Baughan 51, Bayans P. 150, Bayler 1, Bay Park Tongue 177, Bays 142, Beacon P. 114, Beake M. 203, Beakes F. 159, Beaks 115, Bealing F. 118, Beardy 100, The Bears 37, Bears Plot 179, Beaws 12, Beb Shales G. 160, Beckel 175, Beckleys M. *ib.*, Becken P. 135, Beckins Brake 100, Becks P. 144, Becoming C. 78, Bed and Digey 1, Bederla Gardens 32, Bedlam Green 12, Bedmans P. 93, Bedwindle 111, Bedway 156, Bee-G. 21, -Lams 218, Bees lees hill 157, Beeney Bridge 139, Beer C. 35, Beet M. 47, Beglista Mr. 4, Begores 121, Behennat Downs 75, Belbere 29, Belky M. 193, Bellafounder 83, Bellat 111, Bellaw F. 27, Belleisle 22, Bellmans 72, Bellmans P. 94, Bellywinny 72, Belouf 113, Belossack O. 35, Belowly 29, Belowrie 72, Benaney 114, Benney *ib.*, Benaps 180, Benches 123, Bendland P. 177, Bendown 151, Benethick 112, Benewick 93, Benhadren 78, Benies 153, Bennance 86, Benney's Ground 37, Bennies 141, Bennothers 192, Great Bennys 150, Bennys M. 135, Bennywell 159, Bentums 119, Benxykell 111, Berage 177, Berrons 47, Berrys 114, Berthenuse P. 138, Bescone 102, Crooked Besinna 144, Besonthern 153, Besonthers 121, Bess P. 47, Bestangs F. 32, Besta P. 144, Best Grass 183, Bestleys 203, Bet Andrews 95, Bethethlan F. 53, Betony 18, Betreader 37, Betseys F. 10, Betty-Crooks F. 153, -Harters F. 153, -s M. 94, Beudon 175, Bewden 100, Bewder 198, Bias F. 175, Bick Benna 147, Bicking 83, Bigna P. 175, Big P. 148, Bilcocks C. 85, Bilder F. 121, Bilkum 27, Bill Bridge 192, Bill Crook 125, Bing 102, The Bing 105, Binga 134, Bingers 136, Bingleys 140, Binhay 157, Binna 133, Binney 156, Binnies 141, Binny 193, Birch 179, Birchen P. 187, Birch P. 192, Birda D. 119, Birds House 159, Birds Eye 135, Birsa F. 102, Bisemy 177, Bisland 123, Biteys F. 50, Bitha 9, Black-adany 105, -adiness M. 102, -awells 141, -havens 200, -Sticks 148, -Tie 143, -Tor 118, -Wells 135, Bladder P. 187, Blakelet 110, Blankndale 132, Blew-F. 32, -leas 47, Blidhay 184, Blind-Lamb P. 105, -lane F. 150, -well 153, Blood P. 50, Blowing 133, Blown a Hedge *ib.*, Blow the Cold Wind 1, Blue Hatch M. 107, Bluess 112, Boar Arish 133, Boards End 140, Bobbs Plot 118, Bocken F. 100, Bodders M. 27, Bodgura Great F. 148, Body Ground 37, Bohay P. 150, Bold P. 135, Bolorrow 115, Bolsten Piece 184, Bolster-F. 136, -land 135, -P. 156, -Piece 148, Bone-Dust 110, -Fire F. 27, Bongey 37, Bonner P. 184, Bonnet F. 40, Bonneyfords Under Town 160, Bonny 4, -Foot 180, -ventor 32, Booda 184, Boodle H. 186, Boopath O. 160, The Boot 37, Boot-a 108, -C. 51, -field 18, -P. 110, Bor 3, -bas 134, Boring-stock F. 27, Bor M. 150, Bospiller 112, Botany Bay 203, Bounce P. 51, Boundy Down P. 18, Boundy P. 118, Bourage 150, Bousland 196, Bowbrill 46, Bowda 160, 186, Bowla P. 116, Bowlers M. 86, Bowle Cove 13, Bowl P. 114, Bowles H. 112, Bowling P. 41, Boxheater P. 153, Box-H. 157, -well 153, Boys Loye 78, Brackberry 141, Bracket 47, Brack F. 27, Bradland 183, Braes 22, Brains Egg 147, Bramble Eastry 57, Bramlands 111, Branch Coombe 153, Brandies 159, Brandre 102, Brandy-Cr. 44, -P. 94, Brave Way 40, Bray H. 112, Breach Cr. 50, Breack F. 125, The Breage 89, The Break 40, Breakhart H. 148, Bream F. 41, Breckon P. 123, Brecon 18, Brecondrea

---

* Abbreviations here used : C., Close ; Cr., Croft ; D., Down ; F., Field ; G., Garden ; H., Hill ; M., Meadow ; Mr., Moor ; O., Orchard ; P., Park. *For key to figures see* Preface, p. xi.

The Petherwicks 112, Petty C. 44, Phallys Marsh 179, Philadelphia 110, Philpots H.
150, Phillibawdry Mr. 35, Phillies H. 111, Phillys F. 179, Phipes F. 177, Physicis M.
133, Pick Heath 58, Picked Little Steaddon 133, Pickens P. 115, Picket Lane 196,
Pickets Down 134, Pickland 183, Picks 177, Picksy M. 196, Pidney P. 147, Pig -P. 117,
-my-P. 125, Pigna P. 175, Pigney P. 123, Pigs P. 87, Pilaver 181, Pilbrooms 156,
Pilchard F. 42, Pile F. 27, Pilfer Door 105, Pilgers 22, Piles Mr. 69, Piliver 192, Pill-
Pan 123, -Stone 47, Pinch C. 95, Pine F. 110, -Apple 153, Pinkland 144, Pinnocks P.
151, Pinsents F. 122, Pinshare 165, Pinson 94, Pinters 75, Piper 114, Pisgroves 187,
Piskey Pit 169, Piskie F. 8, Pissing Plot 187, Pit-Carn 137, -Lands 18, Piter P. 180,
Pitt P. 135, Yonder Pittice 150, Pitties 144, The Pitts 133, Pitty -C. 86, -Carns 86,
-Down P. 100, Pixter 203, Pixy 100, Pizwell 203, Place M. 148, Plague 10, Plain Sanc-
tuary 177, Planvills 119, Plase M. 156, Plash P. 103, Plashes F. 27, Plat 139, Pleasant
P. 144, Pleasure 75, Plefeet 4, Plinker 37, Plinky P. 159, Plod M. 196, Plot under Great
Run 75, Plota M. 193, Plough -M. 18, -Mangar 78, Ploughed F. 37, Ploughing Match
140, Plovers C. 18, Plow F. 18, Plud F. 8, Plum F. 1, Plumb P. 125, Plump M. 125,
Plushes 145, Pluvers Mr. 177, Pocket O. 123, Point -P. 203, -Cr. 27, -Gilly 58, The
Pointer 18, Pointers H. 105, Foison C. 35, Pokeys M. 100, Poklers Ham 186, Pokles P.
159, Polards P. 135, Pold Garren 90, Pol-dow's M. 112, -gunnick 135, Pollween 147,
Pol-mere 140, -peer 136, -rove 121, -ter 37, Pomeroy P. 144, Pomery P. 116, Pool-and
133, -sEnd 136, -Water Pit 181, Poor Jackey 78.—*Continued Page 201.*

TENEMENTS, ESTATES AND OTHER PLACES.—Alternell 160, Alderbeer 174, Alex's
Torr, 133, All Drunkards 169, Alvinney 145, Ambush Lake 144, Anvoas 31, Apes Head
2, Augillion 1, August or Hogus Rocks 16, Austle 145, Backdon 178, Badash 189, Ba-
diggo 102, Bagga Mills 202, Bag Mill 154, Bales H. 121, Balanimars 192, Balkin H. 3,
Bamham 191, Bangers Whistle 169, Bankadeagle 222, Bany 168, Barcelona 124, Barras
Nose 136, Barris 46, Barva -njack, -jack 33, Bary Court 177, Basowsa 71, Bass or Beast
Point 30, Bastreet 160, Batavellan 13, Bavella 13, The Baw Sand 78, Bawd-ah, -oe,
-ow 119, Bawds Inn or End, or Boards end 140, Bazill 144, Beals 119, Bearah 125,
Beard 125, Beckabins 177, Beckling 42, Bodellah 97, Bedgale, Badgall 163, Bedigga
102, Bedlam 186, Bedr-igga, -iggo, -ugga 85, Beglisti Mr. 4, Belidden *Lizard*, Bellowal
9, Benbollet 135, Bendlowes 22, Benewals 85, Benna- or Bennet-cot 185, Beny 167,
Berwick 77, Bez-awn, -own, or Bezoan 84, Bezzack Rock 23, Besses Tenment 177,
Bessies Cove 17, Bettythorn 171, Bickland 42, Bilkeys 84, Binnies 141, Bisland 123,
Bissaunas 74, Bissom 53, The Bite or Beart 100, Bittams 196, Bittleford 201, Black
-apit 151, -Bottles 153, -Cross 86, -havens 200, -Lane End 143, Bladders 153, Blaken-
ford 160, Blankidnick 52, Blary 143, Blinkers Bed 6, Blue-Carne 1, -Pool 27, -stone 47,
-Top 175, Boardridge 185, Boarrah Tor 159, Bobamere *t.b.* 48, Bocoven 115, Bo Cowloe,
Little Bo *and* Bomear *rocks* 2, Bodervennock 27, Bodraverran 21, Bohilla 57, Bodriggan
160, Bojorrow 35, Bomear or Sharks Fin 2, Bombers Mark 123, Bonaventure *t.b.* 48,
Bondwalls Mill 159, Bony Foot 180, Boquio 27, Borah 5, Bosehan 4, Bosspillers 112,
Boswisnan 15, Boswissack 40, Bottaborough 174, Bovallan 13, Bowda 160. Bowdan 178,
Bowden Rocks, or Boen Marks, or Cow and Calf, or Man and his Man 48, Bowdon 173,
Bowl Cove 13, Box's Shop 169, Bragaton's Cross 174, Brandy Rock 1, Brays H. 175,
Brazil 145, Bredvosy 185, Bree Shute 110, Brickavans 177, Bridals 123, Brim Parks
110, Brimstone H. 1, Brinky Well 115, Broadneck 1, Brogan 31, Broo Mr. 3, Broules
2, Browarth 1, Browda 159, Brownbridge 53, Brudnoe 34, Bruggan 31, Buccabu 1,
Bucclesome 117, Bucka-Mills 125, -pit 151, Buckypit 150, Buckets 46, Buckhill 165,
Buddles 71, Bunkings Bottom 196, Burgham 110, Burgwitha 37, Burney 98, Barnow
34, Burnt-hill 1, -Town 53, Burralda 171, Burrell 202, Burrington *ib.*, Burthallan 13,
Burwood 171, Bush 172, Bushill *ib.*, Buswednack 10, Butter Tor 133, Byngs 102, Ca-
ledno 1, Caffa 104, Cagar 31, Caglinna 126, Caglonnon *ib.*, Cain H. 123, Calloget 201,
Callowden 143, Calls Thorne 171, Callyvardor Rock 103, Calmady 169, Calmanjack 40,
Calmea 35, Calmudu 178, Ca- or Car-lumb 112, Calvanna 187, Calwodley 117, Calyze
23, Canganes 143, Can -or Carn-acannow 100, Canier 166, Canmills 75, Cannnframe
145, Cannap 27, Cannera 154, Cannis Rock 103, Cant 112, Capalloe 82, Cappadocia 184,
Carbittle Burrows 50, Carcurrian 15, Cargoda Zawn 4, Carlauchard 36, Carliquoita
Rocks ?, Carn-Base 1, -Bolenow 24, -Butts 36, -Cobbie 10, -Gwendra 75, -ivs 90, -jewel
100, -Levereth 1, -Sigga or Sugga 21, Carrabone 35, Carratarra 105, Cartmick 59, Car-
vadles 91, Car-Veer 101, -Veor Mr. 101, Casehill 133, Caseleys Mr. 175, Caspard Pool
143, Casterills 27, Castle Coy 28, Caswarth 91, Caswell 169, Catamark *f.m.* 123, Cats-
hole Tor 133, Cawker 177, Challowater 132, Charlicott 192, Cherriton 180, Christalla 9,
Chyngwith 84, Clahar 29, Claun 108, Clicket 161, Clobleats 140, Cloon H. 142, Club-
worth 184, Coal H. 186, Coales 96, Coals 90, Cobelstone 142, Cobthorne 175, Codda
145, Colan 140, Cold-Quag 114, -scent 116, Cole-charton 193, -rose 63, Col-house 145,
-liford 144, -loden 140, -onna Beach 78, -nathes 169, -ross 102, Comes 1, Conternuan
t.b. 48, Conycoombe 194, Coodeys 124.—*For continuation see* End of Preface.

NAMES UNEXPLAINED *(No. V),*

About which the Compiler solicits information.

FIELDS.— Polgarren (*S. Merryn*); Polsdornack (*Constantine*); Polstaggs Ground (*Bodmin*); Ponselena (*S. Just, P.*); Potford (*Lanreath*); Pragra (*S. Just, P.*); Pranglers (*do.*); Pras Ausk (*Gluvias*); Pratlers Meadow (*Quethiock*); Presstis Field (*Launcells*); Pretusence (*Wendron*); Prickley Vine (*Egloshayle*); Pridmouth (*Tywardreath*); Purple Park (*S. Breward*); Put Meadow (*Gorran*); Quail Park (*Bodmin*); Quadrant (*Breage*); Queelsham (*Lanteglos, C.*); Quillaway (*Menheniot*); Radgeland (*Egloshayle*); Radgon Park (*Calstock*); Ragginstone (*Lezant*); Rambleys Meadow (*Landrake*); The Randoms (*S. Keverne*); Range (*Lanreath*); The Rap (*Illogan*); Rascal Vine (*Zennor*); Rattle Back (*S. Wenn*); Rattle Park (*Helland*); Rattle Streets (*Lanreath*); Rattling Field (*Wendron*); Redagins Park (*S. Neots*); Redewan (*Grade*); Reem Moor (*S. Keverne*); Reeps Down (*S. Neots*); Remmick (*Buryan*); Ren-nan, -nance (*S. Columb Ma.*); Rennow (*Madron*); Rennish (*Constantine*); Retha (*Withiel*); Rewan Park (*Padstow*); Rewes Meadow (*S. Thomas*); Rex Meadow (*Northill*); Ribbon (*Kenwyn*); Riddle Park (*Cardinham*); Riels Field (*S. Neots*); Rill (*Pillaton*); Rillaton (*Linkinhorne*); Ring a Bingey (*S. Neots*); Ring and Walbut (*Veryan*); Ring Gales (*S. Germans*); Ring Croft (*Redruth*); Ritbargus (*Perranzabuloe*); Ritchell (*Wendron*); Rittanna (*Constantine*); Rock Avon (*Breage*); Rock Boy (*Ruan Mi.*); Rollers (*S. Breock*); Roll Stone Park (*Helland*); Roman Tee (*Gluvias*); Romsdale (*Lanreath*); Rove and Road (*S. Columb Ma.*); Rowdy (*S. Winnow*); Rubble Close (*Crantock*); Rump Field (*Kenwyn*); Russa Field (*Paul*); Rusta (*Tintagel*); Ruther Embla (*Towednack*); Saddle Park (*Jacobstow*); Safe (*Crantock*); Saggy Park (*Liskeard*); Sam (*S. Austell*); Scalson (*Menheniot*); Sclewes (*Breage*); The Sclewy (*do.*); Scoggans Meadow (*S. Winnow*); Scollagrove (*Werrington*); Scorbargus (*Gorran*); Scorple (*Alternon*); Scrabs Hill (*Calstock*); Scraesdon and Brockhole (*S. Anthony, E.*); Scrasis (*S. Winnow*); Scraps Close (*Veryan*); Scree-, Screet-chets Field (*S. Minver*); Scrub Close (*S. Columb Ma.*); Scurry Close (*do.*); Scuddy Plot (*S. Breock*); Scurrator (*Tintagel*); Scurry Look (*Padstow*); Sead (*Temple*); Searns Meadow (*Tintagel*); Seat Walls (*Minster*); Sent (*Linkinhorne*); Sess Meadow (*Calstock*); Setnett (*N. Petherwin*); Settle Park (*S. Clether*); Shabwell (*Northill*); Shallivill (*Blisland*); Sha-, Shad-daford (*Quethiock*); Shadrick (*Cardinham*); Shaft Pill (*S. Agnes*); Shafty Field (*Breage*); Shambles (*S. Clether*); Sham Hill (*S. Minver*); Sham Park (*Kenwyn*); Sharpland (*Linkinhorne*); Shaving Park (*S. Mabyn*); Sheals (*Northill*); Shearmans Field (*S. Austell*); Sheaver's Clove (*S. Keverne*); Sheepenless (*Morval*); Shebbannoon Park (*Northill*); Sheerall (*Paul*); Shella (*S. Minver*); Shell Gate (*S. Teath*); Shell Stones (*S. Neots*); Sherhill (*Stokeclimsland*); Shilling Meadow (*Anthony, E.*); Shilly Park (*S. Stephens, L.*); Shittle Park (*S. Teath*); Shoe Park (*Bayton*); Shot Close (*Mawgan, P.*); Shuggle Park (*Egloshayle*); Shred Moor (*Temple*); Shroud Moor (*Blisland*); Shubish Hill (*Probus*); Shula Piece (*S. Stephens, S.*); Shurs Beal (*S. Teeth*); Shutters Field (*S. Enoder*); Sibbet Park (*Towednack*); Sicklers Field (*Phillack*); Sidgeons (*Gwennap*); Sieve (*Breage*); Silk Brown Close (*Probus*); Simple Meadow (*Gorran*); Sinews Park (*S. Germans*); Singeroes Park (*S. Austell*); Single New Park (*Liskeard*); Sinks Park (*Endellion*); Sivel Wood (*S. Ive*); Skeusgo (*Davidstow*); Skiddy (*Lesnewth*); Skilla Park (*Treneglos*); Skimming (*S. Kew*); Sklues (*Breage*); Skudley Park (*Davidstow*); Skurry Close (*S. Columb Ma.*); Slapvillan (*Paul*); Slattram (*Kea*); Slave Park (*Kenwyn*); Long Sleave (*S. Neots*); The Sleave (*S. Breward*); Sleves (*S. Clements*); Sliggon (*S. Minver*); Slip go down (*Constantine*); Slodden Field (*Probus*); Sloddy Goonhavern (*do.*); Slowney Well (*S. Winnow*); Slough Park (*S. Breward*); Slow Well (*Mabe*); Slunnows (*S. Austell*); Smelly Barn (*Gluvias*); Smiley Park (*S. Columb Ma.*); Smocks Meadow (*N. Tamerton*); Smoke Ally (*Breage*); Smothy Field (*S. Juliott*); Smutty Croft (*Constantine*); Snap Park (*N. Tamerton*); Snuggo (*Saucreed*); Snuff Box Down (*Linkinhorne*); Soby (*Ruan Mi.*); Solver Anna (*Camborne*); Sounding Pan (*Cury*); Southarrow Nall (*Davidstow*); Sowna (*S. Levan*); Sowder (*Lansallos*); Spacious Park (*Landrake*); Spade Hill (*Cardinham*); Spading Moor (*Lanreath*); Spang (*S. Breock*); Homer Spangs (*Crowan*); Sparable Point (*Liskeard*); Spare and Painful (*S. Austell*); Sparring Down Park (*S. Austell*); Spas Spatten (*Stithians*); Speame (*S. Just, P.*); Speckle Park (*Menheniot*); The Spit (*S. Blazey*); Spin Meadow (*Whitstone*); Spinnage Park (*S. Breward*); Spire Hill (*S. Teath*); Spirs Field (*Whitstone*); Split Field (*Crowan*); Great Sprangs (*Crowan*); Springle Park (*S. Neots*); Springers Field (*S. Winnow*); Sprity Field (*Padstow*); Sprigs Park (*N. Petherwin*); Sprizes Meadow (*Calstock*); Spuckles Meadow (*Linkinhorne*); Spue Field (*S. Columb Ma.*); Spy Glass (*Tywardreath*); Stabilyus (*Phillack*); Stabbage Meadow (*Laneast*); Stades (*Egloshayle*); Stad Close (*S. Martins, M.*); Staddon (*N. Petherwin*); Stadney (*Menheniot*); Staggy Moor (*S. Issey*); Stait Park (*Menheniot*); Stalmack Field (*S. Just, P.*) Standing Park (*Lezant*); Stang Stitch (*Launcells*); Staplins

(*S. Winnow*); Start Field (*S. Erth*); Stara Park (*Egloshayle*); Star Ball (*Luxulyan*); Starch Field (*Kenwyn*); Stare Park (*Lanreath*); Starmack (*Crowan*); Starkes, or Strakes Meadow (*Linkinhorne*); Starra Park (*Lanteglos, C.*); Stars Cross Park (*Linkinhorne*); Start Field (*S. Erth*); Starvey Park (*S. Columb Major*); State Park (*Linkinhorne*; Statty Close (*S. Austell*); The Steer Right Field (*S. Minver*); Steaddon Field (*S. Breward*); Stenlaway (*Egloskerry*); Steel Park (*Whitstone*); Stent Bank (*S. Neots*); Stents Brake (*Liskeard*); Stepna Park (*Stokeclimsland*); Sterling (*S. Columb Ma.*); Sterning Field (*Scilly*); Step an tide (*S. Erth*); Sterra Park (*Davidstow*); Stewert (*Tremaine*); Stick Park (*Probus*); Stids Moor (*Whitstone*); Stiley Close (*Gorran*); Stir Town (*S. Mabyn*); Stonstick (*Constantine*); Store Close (*Probus*); Stove Packs (*Davidstow*); Stotheridge (*Launceston*); Stourpill (*Perranzabuloe*); Stowey Park (*Lesnewth*): Strang (*Launceston*); Strakeshaw Field (*S. Just, P.*); Strain Bridge Field (*Menheniot*); Strap (*Laneast*); Strecks Meadow (*Antony, E.*); Strevor Park (*Cardinham*); Stringham (*Paul*); Stringa-m, or -n (*Buryan*); Striving Moor (*S. Columb Ma.*); Stubba Down (*N. Tamerton*); Stubby Park (*Gluvias*); Stub Croft (*Zennor*); Stunes Meadow (*Menheniot*); Sturt (*Lelant*); Suas Meadow (*Ladock*); The Subban (*Breage*); Sue Meadow (*S. Breock*); Sueys Field (*S Cleer*); Sunery Park (*Talland*); Sumney Croft (*Buryan*); Sush Croft (*Wendron*); Swadland Close (?); Swainer Park (*N. Tamerton*); Swana Park (*Stokeclimsland*); Swart Meadow (*Calstock*); Sweena Park (*Quethiock*); Sweetbone (*S. Breward*); Swiney Park (*Lanreath*); Swinging Head (*Constantine*); Swingey Field (*do.*); Swinster Meadow (*Forrabury*); Swish Close (*S. Enoder*); Sworn or Sorn Field (*Probus*); Sychans Croft (*S. Keverne*); Sydes Meadow (*Crantock*); Sye Meadow (*Blisland*); Symlet Orchard (*S. Minver*); T Field (*Lostwithiel*); Tack-, or Tuck-amean Field (*Gluvias*); Tailan Chuyth (*S. Just, P.*); Tailder (*Wendron*); Talan Vaughan (*Mullion*); Talgleduack (*Sithney*); Tapper Meadow (*Veryan*); Tappy Town (*Blisland*); Tarn Field (*Kenwyn*); Tarton Downs (*Landrake*); Taunton Hays (*S. Blazey*); Tawney Plot (*Breage*); Tays Above Town (*Stokeclimsland*); Teasers Meadow (*S. Issey*); Teddy Hole (*N. Petherwin*); Tee Field (*Sithney*); Teek Field (*Breage*); Telt (*Wendron*); Temaught (*Gorran*); Tempy Park (*S. Cleer*); Tempy's Meadow (*S. Breward*); The Ten (*S. Just, P.*); Tenthrea (*S. Mabyn*); Tenthrill (?); Tentonian (*Lanteglos, C.*); Terngo Brake (*S. Dominick*); Terswain (*S. Cleer*); Teska (*Buryan*); Thafty Field (*S. Just, P.*); Thava (*Lelant*); Therews Close (*S. Columb Mi.*); Throne (*Constantine*); Tidlers (*S. Kew*); Tie Close (*S. Enoder*); Tiger Park (*Bodmin*); Tights Field (*Landrake*); Tiland Field (*Davidstow*); Til Bridge (*S. Kew*); Tiles Field (*Stokeclimsland*); Tillage (*S. Winnow*); Tinager (*Launcells*); Teneward (*Probus*); Tin Hatches (*S. Neots*); Tinivere (*S. Cleer*); Tinner (*S. Neots*); Tithey Field (*Crantock*); Toddagor (*S. Clether*); Todd Park (*S. Neots*); Toddens Steps (*Gerrans*); Tolhorn (*Zennor*); Toll an Jame (*Cury*); Tollyodness (*Lelant*); Tolterry (*S. Austell*); Toltick or Lost Bridge (*Linkinhorne*); Toltreach (*Buryan*); Tom Stone (*Tintagel*); Tong End (*Launceston*); Tungs (*Constantine*); Toodle Hill (*Liskeard*); Tooks Field (*Kenwyn*); Top Bendown (*Morval*); Topnar (*Gluvias*); The Torber (*S. Levan*); Tormentul Field (*S. Keverne*); Torran Hill (*S. Columb Mi.*); Torras (*Probus*); Torreen (*Towednack*); Total Park (*Endellion*); Touch Close (*Lanteglos, F.*); Tour Close (*Veryan*); Tousey Close (*Scilly*); Town Floor (*Landrake*); Town Frow (*Gorran*); Town Roan (*do.*); Town Tanna (*Gluvias*); Transgares (*Lanteglos, C.*); Trap leeket (*S. Just, P.*); Trappa Stitch (*Blisland*); Trap Stile (*S. Columb Ma.*); Traunces Field (*Wendron*); Trebarford (*S. Columb Ma.*); Eastern Trebbus (*S. Columb Mi.*); Treble Park (*S. Teath*); Tree Deane (*Whitstone*); Treen Coth (*Zennor*); Trefountain (*Pillaton*); Trefoy (*Alternon*); Tregenson's Meadow (*S. Wenn*); Tregivinin (*Mullion*); Tregony Jan (*Gluvias*); Tregulleau (*S. Columb Ma.*); Tregusus (*Wendron*); Trench or Trunch Meadow (*S. Kew*); Treloygath (*Stithians*): Trering (*S. Germans*); Treshan Meadow (*S. Mabyn*); Treshot (*do.*); Trestram Downs and Top Trestrams (*Buryan*); Treth-ewys, -uses (*S. Sampson*); Trewerywell (*S. Keverne*); Trewga Field (*Wendron*); Tucka-man or -mean (*S. Gluvias*); Tulan (*S. Just, P.*); Tully Meadow (*Constantine*); Tult Staff (*Budock*); Tump Field (*Stithians*); Turfrey (*Advent*); Turley Meadow (*Stokeclimsland*); Turn Hayle (*S. Kew*); Turney Quins (*S. Columb Ma.*): Tweenas (*N. Petherwin*); Twinatown (*Morval*); Twin End (*Treneglos*); Twinhays (*Pillaton*); Twinna Park (*Treneglos*); Twinnatown (*Werrington*); Twinwell (*S. Dominick*); The Tye (*S. Just, P.*); Udelow (*Lesnewth*); Uglow (*do.*); Ugly Park (*S. Blazey*); Umbrake (*Illogan*); Usty Veale (*Breage*); Vage Park (*Alternon*); Vain Field (*Scilly*); Valentine Field (*Davidstow*); Vanes (*Mawgan*); Vangy Well (*Morval*); Vanstones (*S. Austell*); Varney's Moor (*Ladock*); Varrick Moor (*Gorran*); Vartol Field (*Lizard*); Vassy Close (*Crantock*); Vatta Moor (*Tresmeer*); Veales Park (*S. Issey*); Homer Veals (*S. Columb Ma.*); Veils (*Padstow*); Vernon Hedge (*S. Breock*); Verseans (*S. Austell*); Veryas (*Veryan*); Vespers (*S. Stephens, L.*); Vetan Tellan (*Gerrans*); Veysey Marsh (*N. Petherwin*); Vie Meadow (*S. Gluvias*); Vie Park (*S. Austell*); Vieldses (*S. Columb Ma.*); Villabridge (*Tintagel*); Villey (*Tremayne*); Vil Park (*S. Austell*); Vinegar Hill (*Bodmin*); Vinegar Park (*Egloshayle*); Vine Path (*S. Merryn*); Vingans (*Madron*); Vinis Rillaton (*Linkinhorne*); Vishes Stile (*S. Neots*); Viskins

Columb (*Blisland*); Vithans (*Madron*); Vobins in Rosenithon (*S. Keverne*); Volley (*N. Petherwin*); Vorn Castel (*S. Levan*); Vounder Britain (*S. Keverne*); The Voxen (*Helland*); Voyage Waste (*Grade*); Voylnud (*Morval*); Vung (*Gorran*); Wacker (*Antony, E.*); Waddy Meadow (*Crantock*); Wadge it (*Lanreath*); Wadling Head (*Werrington*); Wads Meadow (*Jacobstow*); Walk Park (*Helland*); Wallows Leys (*Tintagel*); Warelands (*Antony, E.*); Ware Park (*Lezant*); War Gallas (*Grade*); Warmer (*S. Columb Ma.*); Homer and Outer Warps (*Landrake*); Warrick Meadow (*S. Austell*); Wartha Bonds (*S. Keverne*); Warwick hill (*Endellion*); Wash Mendow (*S. Neots*); Wash Moor (*Bodmin*); Wassail Plot (*do.*); Watch Park (*Kenwyn*); Water Tarrow (*Menheniot*); Watty (*Buryan*); The Wavils (*Breage*); Way Vosporth (*Crantock*); Way Dennis (*Gerrans*); Way Kelliers (*S. Erth*); Weal Queal (*S. Levan*); Wedge Close (*Breage*); Wedrack (*Zennor*); Weed Park (*N. Tamerton*); Weed Band (*S. Neots*); Weeder Park (*S. Sampson*); Weedy Park (*Morval*); Week Meadow (*Camborne*); Welcome to Town (*S. Gorran*); Well Breach (*do.*); Well Cur (*Wendron*); Well Cropham (*S. Keverne*); Well Cat Moor (*Probus*); Wellems Close (*Launceston*); Wellis Plot (*Davidstow*); Well Kerrens (*Mullion*); Well Lay (*Liskeard*); Well Lakes (*Cardinham*); Wells Eye (*do.*); Wellsonjones (*Camborne*); Well Stitches (*Lanteglos, C.*); Well Town (*Forrabury*); Well Vosga (*S. Eval*); Welvals (*Wendron*); Wemarland (*Cardinham*); Wenny Wells (*Blisland*); Werris Croft (*Wendron*); Werrys Field (*Breock*); Western Rot (*Kenwyn*); Wetletts (*Egloshayle*); Wheal Lang (*S. Levan*); W. Killahan (*Camborne*); W. Luckly (*S. Teath*); W. Truas (*S. Just, P.*); W. Touchen (*Breage*); Wheat Caney Field (*Wendron*); Wheel Way (*S. Columb Mi.*); Whitclose (*Gerrans*); White Alice or Allis (*Wendron*); White Allies (*Breage*); White Bread Park (*S. Ive*); White Lake (*Linkinkorne*); Whitesheard (*Launcells*); Whitesmock Meadow (*Forrabury*); White Stockings (*S. Thomas*); White Well (*Bodmin*); Whiting (*S. Mabyn*); Whitless (*Lanteglos, C.*); Whitta Park (*Treneglos*); Whittaway Ham (*Werrington*); Whitty (*Helston*); Whole Field (*Wendron*); Wickwater (*S. Blazey*); Widegate (*Morval*); Wild Acre (*S. Keverne*); Wild a Moor (*S. Clether*); Wild Cat (*Endellion*); Wild Dog (*do.*); Wilderness (*Lanreath*); Wild Park (*Whitstone*); Wild Stitch (*S. Breward*); Willy Downs (*S. Enoder*); Windalls (*S. Stephens, S.*); Winda Meadow (*S. Teath*); Wind Stall Field (*Wendron*); Windstock Field (*S. Erth*); Wink hills (*Illogan*); Winnaver Moor (*Helland*); Winnegood (*Probus*); Winnocks (*Breage*); Winnofore (*Minster*); Winnoway (*S. Cleer*); Winshowe Park (*S. Breock*); Winstones Pullery (*do.*); Wish Town (*Lanhydrock*); Witfield (*Kenwyn*); Wooden Arish (*S. Columb Ma.*); Woodrose (*Forrabury*); Woodwell (*Quethiock*); Woody (*Laneast*); Woon-Grey, -Greys (*Luxulyan*); Woonpits (*Towednack*); Woon Summer (*do.*); Work Park (*S. Enoder*); Wormside Hill (*Probus*); Wormy Field (*Wendron*); Worthacre (*Advent*); Woval (*Mawgan, M.*); Wranger Park (*Minster*); Wrah Field (*Buryan*); Wrane (*do.*); Wreath Park (*Quethiock*); Wrenchford (*Werrington*); Wrinkles (*S. Keverne*); Yard Field (*Wendron*); Yarmen Peath (*S. Kew*); Yarn (*Germoe*); Yarn Gooth (*S. Keverne*); Yarner (*Tremaine*); Yarrow Park (*Scilly*); Yawna Park (*Pillaton*); Yealdaman (*S. Just, P.*); Yealings Park (*S. Breward*); Yeana Park Ham (*N. Petherwin*); Yellow Park (*Tresmeer*); Yellowver (*S. Cleer*); Yelloways (*Launcells*); Yellowest (*Menheniot*); Yellow Tor (*Landrake*); Yellion (*Tresmeer*); Yellands Close (*S. Columb Ma.*); Yerru Parc (*S. Eval*); Yogg-Park, -s Park (*Blisland*); Yoke Stitch (*Camborne*); Yolver Meadow (*Calstock*); Yonder Tory (*Gluvias*); Yonder Gustory (*Crantock*); Yonderberry (*Antony, E.*); York Hill (*Zennor*); York Hill Stitch (*do.*); Zackingham (*Tremaine*); Zeekely (*S. Dominick*); Zetons Meadow (*Jacobstow*); Zempern (*S. Merryn*); Zox Moor (*Landrake*).

TENEMENTS, &c.—Polpenenna (*Buryan*); Polstangy Praze (*Grade*); Pomfel (*Stokeclimsland*); Pomish Downs (*Kenwyn*); Ponslego (*Perranzabuloe*); Pontius-, v. Punch-Cross (*Lostwithiel*); Porrown Berry (*Gorran*); Potram (*Bodmin*); Pottleder Bay (*E. Looe*); Powvallet Coyt (*Lostwithiel*); Pra (*Breage*); Praze Zawn (*S. Just, P.*); Prenestin (*S. Michael, Car.*); Puckerell (*t.b., S. Agnes*); Puckwalls (*Advent*); Puddle (*Lanivet*); Pudlins Break (*Morwinstow*); Pudners (*Michaelstow*); Puffeland (*Duloe*); Pugg-ies or -is Mill (*Camborne*); Pughills (*Linkinhorne*); Pullouris (*Lelant*); Pursile Bay (*Scilly*); Quantrel Morvast (?); Quenchwell (*Kea*); Quies (*rock, Trevose Head*); Quies Land (*S. Cleer*); Radjan (*Newlyn*); Radjill Cliff (*S. Just, P.*); Rame (*Stithians*); Ranney (*ledge, Polperro*); Ranneys (*ledge, Scilly*); Ranty Cliff (*S. Keverne*); Raplapit (*f.m., Polperro*); Ray-, or Rye-man (*rock, Ludgvan*); Recevan (*Sancreed*); Reck Gate (*S. Mellion*); Redallan or -ellan (*Breage*); Redding Point (*Maker*); Reeks (*t.b., S. Agnes*); The Reem (*S. Keverne*); Reevers (*Whitstone*); Releath (*Crowan*); Relewes (*Mawgan, M.*); Relly (*S. Germans*); Rennies (*rocks, Looe*); Rentemen (*o.*); Reperry, Resperrie (*Lanivet*); Resparvel (*Boscastle*); Retanna (*mine, Wendron*); Retarriers (*Scilly*); Retew (*S. Enoder*); Retire (*Withiel*); Ribby (*S. Veep*); Riddle (*S. Austell*); Ridga or Rigga (*Ludgvan*); Ridgoe (*Buryan*); Ridhem (*Bodmin*); Riffet Field (*Wendron*); Rigger Field (*Budock*); Riggs (*Luxulyan*); Rilly (*S. Columb Ma.*); Ringing Zawn (*S. Just, P.*); Ringwell (*Feock*); Riskivers (*Veryan*); Rissick (*Buryan*); Robnetts (*Lansallos*); Rockadons (*Morwinstow*); Rock Drall (*S. Keverne*); Rogenun (*Liskeard*); Rombelows (*Quethiock*); Rome (*Kea*);

Rouse (*Pillaton*); Ruddy (*rock, Scilly*); Rude (*Launcells*); Rumps (*rocks, Padstow*); Ruth-oes, -res, or -ves (*S. Columb Ma.*); Ryall (*Scilly*); St. Bodemny (*t. Ed. iii, Kerrier*); S. Carak pillo (*Leland*); S. Bellarmin's Tor (*? S. Kew*); S. Kitts (*S. Gennys*); S. Lavers (*Lezant*); S. Lena (*Buryan*); S. Malves Moor (*Mullion*); S. Nonnio (*Alternon*); S. Sith's Beacon (*? Advent*); S. Syors (*Luxulyan*); S. Winnolds (*S. Germans*); S. Warna Bay (*Scilly*); Salem (*Kenwyn*); Sallock (*Maker*); Salvaddon (*Illogan*); Sandock (*Calstock*); Savath (*Luxulyan*); Sawah (*S. Levan*); Scabuds (*Tuckingmill*); Scad Hill (*S. Neots*); Scagells Hill (*S. Breward*); Scadgick Tor (*Alternon*); Scanreagh (*Stithians*); Scants Garden (*Calstock*); Scar-bine, -ibine (*S. Minver*); Scarret (*Scilly*); Scarrows (*N. Petherwin*); Scar-, Scas-, Scis-sick (*Treneglos*); Scarrows (*N. Petherwin*); Sclerder or Segoulder (*Madron*); Sconhoe (*S. Austell*); Sconner (*Sheviock*); Scope Hill (*Lesnewth*); Scoresham (*Launcells*); Scrapers Park (*Morwinstow*); Screed (*S. Gennys*); Screeda (*S. Austell*); Scribble (*Blisland*); Scuslands (*Quethiock*); Scutchell (*Callington*); Seaurcaugh (*Stithians*); Sell-egan -ogan (*Redruth*); Sensham (*Bridgerule*); Setcott (*Jacobstow*); Sheeralls (*Paul*); Shernicks (*Launcells*); Shilcoom (*Cardinham*); Shilla Mill (*Lanreath*); Shorrish (*Alternon*); Shrubhendra (*Endellion*); Siblyback (*S. Cleer*); Sillaton (*Pillaton*); Sin-a, -ia (*Cardinham*); Sing Moor (*Quethiock*); Skants (*Liskeard*); Skelly Wadden (*Towednack*); Skidden (*S. Ives*); Skirrit Island (*Scilly*); Skonn-er, -or, (*Sheviock*); Sliddon (*N. Petherwin*); Sleeper Rock (*Helland*); Sleeve (*S. Ive*); Slue (*Boyton*); Smourn (*S. Gennys*); Spaddick (*do.*); Spain (*Boyton*); Spare Beau (*t.b., S. Agnes*); Sparnalls Weens (*S. Winnow*); Spar Load Zawn (*S. Just, P.*); Sparna (*Towednack*); Speedwell (*t.b., S. Agnes*); Speddagrew (*Alternon*); North Sperretts (*S. Cleer*); Sperris (*Zennor*); Sprattan Cove (*Illogan*); Stable Hobba (*Paul*); Stalks (*Tresmeer*); Stampers (*S. Stephens, B.*); Standage (*Mawgan, P.*); Stand Cove (*Lanteglos, F.*); Stap Lakes (*Landrake*); Stapland (*S. Winnow*); Staply (*Constantine*); Starabridge (*Linkinhorne*); Starmers (*Bodmin*); Starr (*Landrake*); Starrick (*S. Austell*); Startafold (*Alternon*); Staws (*f.m., Polperro*); Steart (*Davidstow*); Stem Cove (*Mawgan, P.*); Stepper Point (*Padstow*); Steval Rock (*Scilly*); Stevern (*do.*); Stew (*S. Kew*); Steward (*N. Petherwin*); Sterter (*Lanlivery*); Stibb (*Kilkhampton*); Sticker (*S. Ewe*); Stickell (*S. Tudy*); Stick-, or Strick-stinton (*Lanlivery*); Sticklers Corner (*Kenwyn*); Stoney Gwins (*S. Dennis*); Stours-, or Stur-combe (*Lawhitton*); Strand (*S. Petherwin*); Strangator (*Landrake*); Stradeland (*Liskeard*); Strasse Cliff (*Mawgan, P.*); Streigh (*Lanlivery*); Stripple Stones (*Blisland*); Strilands (*Alternon*); Strips Hay (*S. Dominick*); Stuflle (*S. Neots*); Sunney Corner (*Gwennap*); Sunondsham (*Stratton*); Swelcorner (*Poundstock*); Swellscombe (*Lezant*); Swilter (*Whitstone*); The T Zawn (*S. Just, P.*); Talea (*Broadoak*); Tallifrow (*Veryan*); Tall Petherwin (*S. Petherwin*); Talvans (*Landrake*); Talvar (*Pelynt*); Tamer (*S. Neots*); Timitethy (*Trigg H.*); Tam-, or Tomperrowe (*S. Kea*); Tamsquite (*S. Tudy*); Tangist Mill (*Mawgan, M.*); Tankerslake (*S. Thomas*); Tap House (*Broadoak*); Tappara (*Gwinear*); Tarlawn Rock (*S. Neots*); Tawna (*Cardinham*); Teason (*do.*); Tegues (*Towednack*); Tembeath (*Mawgan, P.*); Tembraze (*S. Keverne*); Tencriff (*Mullion*); Teppen (*Tintagel*); Tereardrene (*S. Agnes*); Terladmas (*Sancreed*); Terrars Pill (*Morval*); Tets-on, or -ton (*Marhamchurch*); Tetterdu (*Buryan*); Tettaridge (*Werrington*); Thica Vosa, alias Hack and Cast (*Gorran*); Thongyore (*Scilly*); Thorn (*Warleggon*); Thorne Cobmoor (*Blisland*); Three Stone Oar (*S. Just, P.*); Tibis Hill (*S. Just, P.*); Tiddy (*rock, Mullion*); Tidi (*river*): Tilland (*Quethiock*); Tillacot (*N. Petherwin*); Tinne (*Landulph*); Tinpel Downs (*Budock*); Tinpit (*Mabe*); Tip-hill or -well (*Mullion*); Tipton (*S. Kew*); Titch Beacon (*Lesnewth*); Titch Wihevin (*Jacobstow*); Tit Marsh (*Warbstow*); Titson (*Bridgerule*); Tobban Horse (*rock, S. Agnes*); Tokenbury (*S. Ive*); Toldish (*S. Columb Ma.*); Tolerowan (*Sancreed*); Tolroget or Tollerugget (*Endellion*); Tolskirbit (*Gwennap*); Tolsooth (*rock, Scilly*); Tolteggan (*Illogan*); Tomoutha (*S. Gennys*); Tomrose (*Blisland*); Toplundie Cove (*Padstow*); Torbalk (*Lizard*); Torfrey (*S. Sampson*); Torlidden (*S. Just, P.*); Totens (*S. Keverne*); Touchburrow (*Davidstow*); Touching (*N. Tamerton*); Towan Blistra (*S. Columb Ma.*); Towan Rath (*S. Agnes*); Towan Veals (*S. Merryn*); Transangore (*Cury*); Trean Plat (*rocks, Scilly*); Treases Moor (*S. Stephens, L.*); Trebatches (*do.*); Trebild (*Minster*); Trebost (*Stithians*); Tredellans (*S. Just, R.*); Tredes-or Trees-mill (*Tywardreath*); Trefeefa (*S. Enoder*); Trefrogham (*S. Teath*); Trefunthken (*o.*); Tregarara (*Madron*); Tregas (*Seven Stones*); Trege (*Warbstow*); Tregesdon or Tregenseden (*o. ? Kea*); Tregesteynton (*Lanlivery*); Tregilders (*S. Kew*); Tregigas (*S. Ewe*); Treginges (*S. Keverne*); Tregon-hillion, or -tillion (*Veryan*); Treg-orna, -renna (*Alternon*); Tregothas (*S. Hilary*); Treg-rathes, now -ethes (*S. Erth*); Tregreenwell (*Michaelstow*); Tregunstis (*mine, Wendron*); Trehemb-an, -ourne, -rin, Trembern (*S. Merryn*); Trehingstow (*Stokeclimsland*); Trehorner (*Calstock*); Trehumer (*Tresmeer*); Treises in the Wood (*Menheniot*); Trekemlets (*Lezant*); Trelab-ris, -mas (*Crowan*); Trel-awthas, -owthas (*Probus*); Trelights (*S. Teath*); Trel-obus, -nbbus (*Wendron*); Treloquithack (*do.*); Trelowsa (*Padstow*); Treluga (*Ruan Ma.*); Tremelzer (*S. Wenn*); Tremudlot (*Roach*); Treuant Gert (*S. Breock*); Trenda (*Pelynt*); Trenestreal (*Ruan Lan.*);

Trentgares (*Lanteglos, C.*); Treoigro (*Southill*); Tre-rore, -ore (*Endellion*); Trerafters (*Linkinhorne*); Trera-dgon, -gin (*Calstock*); Trerag-get, -et (*S. Minver*); Treringey (*Crantock*); Trescrowan (*Madron*); Treseat (*Davidstow*); Treshee (*Luxulyan*); Tresithick (*Feock*); Treskey (*ledge, Scilly*); Tresmeak (*Alternon*); Tresmoarn *v.* Smoarn (*S. Gennys*); Trevalstra (*Kea*); Tre-vanta, -wanta (*Lewannick*); Trevanters (*S. Clether*); Trevegro (*Callington*); Trevesham (*S. Eval*); Trevilmick (*Lanlivery*); Trevilsas (*Probus*); Trevilson (*Newlyn E.*); Treviscick (*Poundstock*); Trevoies (*Stokeclimsland*); Trewhitson (*S. Minver*); Treweedland (*Liskeard*); Trysunner (*t.b., S. Agnes*); Tuckenbury (*S. Ive*); Tumple (*Calstock*); Tupton (*S. Neots*); Tyland (*Advent*); Usse or Uske (*Lanteglos, F.*); Valanbounder Bashwasha (*t.b., Gwennap*); Vallancey Bridge (*Forrabury*); Valiton (*Davidstow*); Vandcombe (*Werrington*); Varley Point (*Endellion*); Vaultershome or Voltersholme (*Maker*); Venslo-e, -w, (*Liskeard*); Villaton (*Botusfleming*); Villa Parks (*Minster*); Vinegar Ledge (*Scilly*); Viverdon (*S. Mellion*); Voguebeloth (*Illogan*); Wadfast (*Whitstone*); Walkey Trees (*S. Clements*); Wanga Park (*Minster*); Wanson or Wantsand (*Poundstock*); Wants Mill (*do.*); Warp (*Tresmeer*); Warrow (*Werrington*); Waterstone (*Marhamchurch*); Way (*N. Tamerton*); Wayswandra (*Landrake*); Wearde (*Saltash*); Wee (*rock, Scilly*); Weens (*S. Kew*); Weir Parks (*S. Thomas*); Welemoor (*Warbstow*); Wellencotts (*Northill*); Welloe (*rock, Breage*); Wenfork (*Lezant*); Wenworks (*do.*); Westows (*Ladock*); Wethel (*Scilly*); Wetheram (*S. Tudy*); Wheal an Strepon (*t.b., St. Agnes*); W. Barcla (*do.*); W. Busy (*Kenwyn*); W. Crab (*S. Hilary*); W. Dellinck (*t.b., S. Agnes*); W. Dagger (*do.*); W. Gathue (*do.*); W. Hen (*S. Just, P.*); W. Pink (*Gwennap*); W. Vallue (*t.b., S. Agnes*); Wheatland (*Landulph*); Wheaton (*Broadoak*); Whetleigh (*Week S. Mary*); Whetstone (*S. Gennys*); Whiscan Point (*S. Levan*); Whiston (*Laniret*); Whitehay (*Withiel*); Whitlands (*Duloe*); Whittey Croft (*Kilkhampton*); Whitwell (*Advent*); Wilencots (*Northill*); Wild Duck (*Wendron*); Will (*Poughill*); Wilful (*Illogan*); Wilgarden (*S. Clether*); Willy Allabury (*Northill*); Windon, -sdon (*N. Petherwin*); Windstow (*Lanreath*); Winnacott (*N. Petherwin*); Wish Mushead (*S. Ive*); Wishtown (*Linkinhorne*); Wishworthy (*Lawhitton*); Withyvan (*Warbstow*); Withedon (*Jacobstow*); Witlywell (*S. Teath*); Wolland (*S. Cleer*); Woodbury (*Kea*); Woodcocks Eye (*S. Ive*); Wood in Ham (*Linkinhorne*); Woodknowl (*Marhamchurch*); Wooldown (*do.*); Woolgarden (*S. Clether*); Woolpack (*Scilly*); Woolsome (*S. Cleer*); Woolson (*S. Ive*); Woolston (*Poundstock*); Wooscocks Parks (*Blisland*); Worm (*Stokeclimsland*); Worstland (*Mawgan, P.*); Wra, or Three Stone Oar (*rocks, S. Just, P.*); Wrea (*rocks, S. Keverne*); Wrickle *now* Wrinkle (*W. Looe*); Wrinkle Barrows (*Boconnoc*); Wycoteham (*o.*), Wygenbrys (*o.*), Wythe (*Sithney*); Yeards (*Poundstock*); Yeohn Bridge (*S. Stephens, L.*); Yellow Leigh (*Launcells*); Yeolsdown (*Morwinstow*); Yenard Down (*Alternon*); Yerdbury (*Stratton*); Youngcot (*N. Petherwin*); Zawn Tnrbis (*Land's End*); Zebuscs (*Endellion*); Zichory Island (*S. Columb Ma.*); Zone Point (*S. Antony, R.*).

DOMESDAY.—Polcfund, Raswal-e (*e.d.* -a), Richan (*e.d.* Ricann), Rent-i or -in (*e.d.* Rentis), Rignen, Risleston, Ritwor-e (*e.d.* -i), Schewit (*e.d.* Eschewit), Tedintone (*e.d.* Tedentona), Telbri-g (*e.d.* -cg), Thersent, Thinten, Trefitent, Tregrebri, Tregrenon. Treiswantel, Trelamar, Treli-ngan (*e.d.* -gani), Trel-lewaret (*e.d.* -weren), Trib-ertham (*e.d.* -tan), Trin-nonec (*e.d.* -cnonet), Widewot, Woderon (*e.d.* Uderon), Woreslin.

DOMESDAY TENANTS.—Offels, Rabel, Sistric, Vlniet.

INSCRIBED STONES.—Quenctavus (*Gulval*), Silus or Sejus (*S. Just, P.*), Suani (*Michel*), Ulcagni (*S. Breock*).

BODMIN MANUMISSIONS.—Proscen (*s.*), Proswitel (*s.*), Putrael (*s.*), Rannoeu (*s.*), Rinduran or Sunduran (*s.*), Riol or Siol (*s.*), Saleun (*s.*), Sicreicus (*w.*), Sulcen (*s.*), Sulleisoc (*s.*), Sulmeuth (*s.*), Tancw-oystel, -estel (*s.*), Telent, Terithian (*s.*), Tethion (*w.*), Tidhert, -thert, -tthert (*w.*), Ungust Cilifri (*w.*), Unwalt (?), Walloth (*w.*), Wasso (*w.*), Welet (*s.*), Wuathrit (*w.*), Wudrit (*w.*), Wuencen (*f.s.*), Wunning (*w.*), Wuenumon (*f.s.*), Wunsie Conmonoc, Wunstan, Wurfwothu (*s.*), Wurthicith s.), Wurthylic (*s.*), Ylcerthon(*s.*)

SAINT Beriona,—Colrogus, Mybard, or Mydbard,—Credanus,—Dellyn, Dillo, Dellower *alias* Loy,—Dubslane,—Dydemin,—Eloy or Eligius,—Elvan,—Elwin,—Elidius, —Ergan,—Faugan,—Gelys,—Juncus,—Lydda, Lyddy, or Lyde,—Menna,—Morwetha, Naunton or Nonnio,—Neomena or Nynnina,—Potenciana,—Sanganus,—Senseus,—Servacius,—Thebut,—Theona,—Villoc or Willow,—Wethenya,—Wingel,—Withinocus,— Wynnel; *also*, many other Saint's names unexplained, p. 142, &c.

FAMILY NAMES.—Norcock, Oben, Oldon, Olivey, Oxnap, Pafford, Page, Paige, Palford, Palreden, Parcocks, Pollexfen, Ponton, Powellman, Prater, Prates, Prestin, Quenite, Querquius, Question, Rabley, Rablin, Rance, Rankin, Reddew, Reuth, Ribbery, Ridge, Ridgman, Ridgment, Riley, Rimmick, Rinden, Rowatt, Rutger, Rycheman, Rytches, Sage, Salt, Samblyn, Sarel, Sargeanx, Sarjeant, Saucy, Savery, Sawlay, Scadgell, Scarlet, Schollar, Scior, Scor, Score, Searell, Searle, Selwood, Senhouse, Sennett, Sergeaulx, Serjaux, Serle, Serral, Serscold, Shackelock, Shakerley, Sharrock, Sharrow, Shearm, Shear, Sheere, Sherman, Shilabeer, Short, Shorwell, Shrugg, Siers, Sigdon,

Silly, Silvesdon, Simesdone, Sincock, Sings, Sireston, Sisley, Skerreston, Skeynock,
Skin, Skitch, Skitscoome, Skory, Skryne, Skymes, Skynnard, Skyrne, Slake, Slannen,
Slanning, Slaugh, Sleep, Slegra, Slighton, Slocket, Sloggat, Sloggett, Smale, Smalle,
Snagg, Snow, Sobye, Southeard, Southern, Sower, Sparks, Sprace, Sprague, Sprakelyn,
Spriddle, Spye, Stage, Stallard, Staple, Staples, Stappe, Statt, Statton, Stark, Stead,
Stebbridge, Steed, Steel, Sternhold, Stick, Stickland, Stiles, Still, Stocker, Stockyll,
Stomnour, Storlargh, Stormy, Stoterygge, Stoyle, Stowers, Stracheys, Stradeford, Stran-
gar, Stranger, Street, Stribley, Stribblehill, Stright, Strike, Stripp, Stripling, Stripney,
Strong, Strongman, Stubb, Stuckey, Stuckle, Sturbridge, Sturgen, Sturton, Sturtridge,
Stuttridge, Styles, Sule, Sullard, Sumaster, Swailly, Sweet, Sylly, Symes, Syreston, Tad-
lowe, Tagget, Tallifer, Tapp, Taperell, Tapper, Tatchell, Tanfield, Taw, Taverner,
Temby, Terlin, Terrel, Terril, Tetchell, Thackworth, Thom, Thomye, Thorton, Throwley,
Ties, Tooze, Touche, Touchet, Toupe, Tovey, Transom, Transquillet, Travers, Traxerell,
Treacher, Tredeleberg, Treden, Tregurya, Tregathalosse (14 cent.), Tregesove, Treglow-
naw, Trengthof, Trentheful, Trescullierd, Tresherf (15 cent.), Treuref, Treuroofa, Tre-
use, Trevowyth (14 cent.), Treviho, Trewitch, Trewoef, Trewychosa, Trolewith, Troot,
Trom, Trosse, Trusket, Tuckfield, Tummon, Turgoisel, Turner, Turpin, Turuly, Tuson,
Tussard, Tyler, Vaghere, Valoer, Valler, Vanhouse, Vanar, Vansluys, Varcoe, Varundel,
Vawdrey, Vaynfleet, Venables, Verrant, Vieth, Vinisam, Voysey (Bp.), Wadge, Wadling,
Walkyndon, Wallop, Warham, Warlewast (Bp.), Warr, Wassek, Wassel, Waxfer, Weath-
erall, Wedlake, Weeks, Weimyss, Wellington, Wenlock, Wevin, Wheatley, Wherry,
Whichcott, Whitburn, White, Whitehair, Whitehefd, ? = Whitehead, Whitelock, Whit-
leigh, Whitley, Whitta, Whitter, Whittow, Whitworth, Whylefen, Wibbey, Wichalse,
Wickham, Wicks, Widbury, Wilce, Wilcock, Wilcocks, Willand, Willington, Willoughby,
Willis, Wingfield, Winmouth, Winnacombe, Wise, Wishcombe, Witha, Witherby,
Withers, Withington, Woolcock, Worden, Worledge, Wortley, Wovard, Wray, Wrey,
Wreford, Wrench, Wrentmore, Wroughtson, Wyard, Wybbery, Wycoke, Wyde, Wyet,
Wyot, Wyllington, Wytte, Wyse, o. Wysa, Yandall, Yardeley, Yates, Yeld, Yescombe,
Yorkflete.

 FRESH NAMES from Tithe Apportionment, recently received. Fields in Roman
characters, Tenements, &c., in Italics. See also Page 200.

 S. ANTHONY IN MENEAGE: Bengye Field, Great Calidnum, Little Callidrum, Gui-
dalls, Harterow Meadow, John an goth, Irley Viddon, Kater Close,
Killing Cliffy, Lower Kiltra. Higher Kista, Lane Butts, *Minifters*, Pagigowa, Park Pavis,
Park Maag or Mang, Pencadira, Persens Down, Rose Crees Hill, Tollengith, Victor.—
CROWAN: Adjams Field, Beteta or Botedo, *Binnerton, Bodryoyal*, Crevenor, Croft Mayor,
Deman, Dudlin, Dunning, Elrugar, Flanky Field, Gayer Draft, Gernick, Gold Maggey,
Groats Close, Guel Mala, Hallegan, The Hannack, Hannock, Huddicaff, Inkey Bush,
Ingle Bush, The Lucerne, The Luscombe, Park Gowdon, Park Total, Park Wat, *Releath*,
The Saden, Split Field, Sogers Close, Starmack, *Trelabmas*, Turney Field.—SITHNEY:
Ange Beggan, Carn Clugh, Further Catlas, Little Chy Coulter, Covetous Eye, Croft
Ladu, Foggy Toll, Giggan, Golmas, Guel Street, Guinea Field, Gweald Nors, *Halvanance*,
Linger, London Field, Marer Orchard, Morer Moor, *Minorka*, Park an Creans, *Park
Assow*, P. Clyes, P. Cowas, P. Creave, P. Hingeys, P. Leor, P. Ronne, P. Sutter, P. Tie-
ach Lays, P. Vah, P. Vans, Prickle Point, The Remfry, Tagleduack, Tee Field.—S.
VEEP: Pantletts, *Prinzey*, Promose, Slivers, Treribbey, Tretall-ah, -ow.

ADDENDA, CORRIGENDA, ET DELENDA.

BOSWELLICK, house (*bos*) on the *mill* river (*ick*), T.; ? i.q. TREVELLECH.
CATIN, to be struck out ; the true reading of the inscription is " LATIN," *W. Iago.*
CHENALLS, ? house (*chy*) on the (*an*) cliff (*als*).
CHYNOWETH, new (*nowedh*) house (*chy*).
HALVOSE, ? ditch, trench, or wall (*fos*) moor (*hal*).
MERTHER, *for* " Conanus," *read* " Coanus."
NANPUSCAR, *strike out* "(*piscadur*)."
PARK STRAY, *add* "? enclosure (*parc*) for *stray* cattle, *or* cattle pound."
POLDYS, St. Dye's pit *or* work, *B.*
PORT to be substituted at the head and in the beginning of Page 134 for PORTH.
ROSENURDEN, *for* " furze," *read* " fern."
STRAY PARK, i.q. PARK STRAY.
TOWEDNACK, [the church of] St. (*ta, da*) Wednock *or* Wynnock, T.; the whitish (*wed-
nac*) roof (*to*); *or,* white (*wedn*) dwelling (*ty*) near a port (*ack*), Pr.; whitish (*wid-
nack*) house (*ty*), D.G.
WATERPIT, *for* " [field", *read* " [field]."

See also pp. 194, 198, 199.

AUTHORITIES, REFERENCES, ABBREVIATIONS, &c.

a.—Armoric or Breton, mostly from Le Gonidec.

A.B.—Rev. Alban Butler's "Lives of the Saints."

A.E.—Alphonse Esquiros' "Cornwall and its Coasts."

A.S.—Mr. Augustus Smith, of Tresco Abbey, Isles of Scilly.

a.s.—Armoric saint; many of these saints have names very similar to those who have given names to Cornish parishes, &c., which are commonly found suffixed to LAN, &c.

B.—Dr. Borlase's "Islands of Scilly," "Antiquities," and "Natural History of Cornwall."

Bax —W. Baxter's "Glossarium Antiquitatum Britannicarum."

Beal—Rev. William Beal, author of "Britain and the Gael." His derivations, &c., mostly from the Irish Gaelic. He kindly corrected and annotated most of the proof sheets, and made many suggestions.

Bl.—Blight's "Week at the Land's End," 1861, &c.

B.m.—Names, mostly those of manumitters, found in the manumissions recorded in the Bodmin Gospels (British Museum, select MSS., 9381, A. 1, A.), first printed in Mr. Davies Gilbert's History, v, 3, p. 408; then in Rev. W. Wallis's "Bodmin Register," with a translation; afterwards, more correctly, in Dr. Oliver's "Monasticon," p. 431; Kemble's "Codex Diplomaticus," v. 4, p. 308; and Thorpe's "Diplomatarium Anglicum," p. 623.   The names of these manumitters are for the most part plain Anglo-Saxon, a few appear to be Celtic: nearly all the slaves manumitted bore Celtic names; a few Anglo-Saxon and Bible (mostly Old Testament or Hebrew) names: the witnesses to the manumissions, mostly clerics, bore either Celtic, Anglo-Saxon, or Scripture names.

Bo.—Dr. Bosworth's "Anglo-Saxon and English Dictionary."

Bond's (Thomas) "History of East and West Looe," with MS. notes by the late Mr. Jonathan Couch, of Polperro.

Bp.—Bishop.

Buller's "Statistical Account of St. Just in Penwith," 1842.

C.—Colonel Cocks, of Treverbyn Vean, who not only corrected and annotated several sheets of the Glossary, but also lent his MS. of Cornish Names with meanings.

c.—Old Cornish; the orthography mostly followed is that of Williams's "Lexicon Cornu-Britannicum."   As the chief object of the Glossary is to shew how much of the old Cornish seems to be preserved in the local and family nomenclature of the County, it will be understood, that where a word is found in *Italics (within parenthesis)*, this word, unless otherwise described, is old Cornish, mostly in its primary form, and is to be found thus spelt in "Williams' Lexicon."

c.—Under CAR-, &c., *for* castle, carn, *or* enclosure; *under* PARK, *for* close.

Cam.—Camden's "Britannia" (mostly Bp. Gibson's ed., 1695); and "Remaines concerning Britaine."

Car.—Carew's "Survey of Cornwall," 1602.

c.d.—The church or chapel is dedicated to——.

(ch.).—Chapelry, mostly extinct, from Oliver's "Monasticon," &c.

Ch.—Charnock's "Local Etymology," 1859 ; "Patronymica Cornu-Britannica," 1870, &c.

cent.—Century, showing the date of a document in which the name as spelt is found.

cf.—Confer, compare.   *c.n.*—Christian or fore-name.

C.S.G.—C. S. Gilbert's "Historical Survey," 1817.

d.—Danish; the late Major Bickford referred many Cornish Names to this source.

d.—Under TRE-, *for* dwelling.

d.d.—Name of a manor in the Domesday Survey, 1086.

Dev.—Devonshire The compiler has introduced among the names belonging to Cornwall proper, some that would more properly belong to Devonshire. The river Tamar divides the two counties through the greater part of its course; but Boyton, in Cornwall, and Pancraswyke, in Devonshire, are partly east and partly west of the river; as also is the parish of Bridgerule, but the east part is in Devon, the west in Cornwall. S. Budeaux, though wholly east of the Tamar, is partly in Cornwall; and Maker, though wholly west, is partly in Devonshire, as are also the whole of the parishes of Werrington and North Petherwin, though west of the Tamar But these two parishes and S Giles in the Heath (east of the Tamar and in Devonshire) and the whole of Boyton and Maker are in the Archdeaconry of Cornwall; while the whole of Bridgerule and S. Budeaux are in the Archdeaconry of Totnes; and Pancraswyke is in the Archdeaconry of Barnstaple Thus, almost along the whole course of the river, from its rise in Morwenstow, the most northernly parish in Cornwall, and situated on the shores of the Bristol Channel, to the Hamoaze, where it falls into the English Channel, there is confusion between the ecclesiastical and civil boundary of Cornwall and Devonshire.

D.—Lord De Dunstanville's edition of Carew, with notes from Tonkin's MSS. &c., 1811.

D.G.—Davies Gilbert's " Mount Calvary, 1826 "; " Creation of the World, with Noah's Flood," 1827; " Parochial History of Cornwall," 1838, &c. In consequence of the illness of Mr. Davies Gilbert during the time this history was passing through the press, he was unable to correct the proof sheets; as a consequence, the book is full of typographical errors, especially in the case of topographical and family names, about which the London printer must have been totally ignorant, and therefore it is not strange that these should be sadly mis-spelt.

dim.—Diminutive.

Dr.—Hitchins' and Drew's "History of Cornwall," 1824.

Dyer's " Ancient Mode of bestowing Names on the Rivers, Hills, Valleys, and Plains of Great Britain," 1805.

E.—Right Hon. Lord Eliot, of Port Eliot.

e.—*e.d.*—*e.d.d.*—Exeter Domesday, mostly from Rev. J. Carne.

Ed.—*F.E.*—Flavell Edmunds' " Traces of History in the Names of Places," 1869.

E.G.H.—Rev. Edmund George Harvey, Vicar of Mullion.

E S—Sir Edward Smirke, ex-Vice-Warden of the Stannaries, who furnished Dr. Oliver with particulars as to the Bodmin Manumissions, " Monasticon," p. 431.

F.—Ferguson's "English Surnames," 1858; " River Names," 1862.

f.—French, mostly Norman; to this source Mr. Bottrell would refer many Cornish names.

f.—*Under* WHEAL, &c., *for* field.

f.m.—Fishermen's Marks at sea.

f.s.—*f s.B.m*— Female serf, Bodmin Manumissions; *see B.m.*

Francis' (William) " Gwennap, a poem."

ga.—Gaelic, mostly that of Ireland.   *gr.*—Greek.

Gib.—Gibson's (T A. & G M.) " Etymological Dictionary " of Geographical Names, 1840.

Gibson (Bp.).—His edition of Camden, &c.

Gw.— William Gwavas, of Penzance, who, with Tonkin, prepared a vocabulary, 18th cent.

H.—William Hals's (17—18 cent.) collections for a Parochial History; printed, with omission of scandalous parts, &c., together with Tonkin's collections, in Polwhele's, Davies Gilbert's, and the " New Parochial " History of Cornwall, now publishing by Mr. Lake, of Truro. His derivations and renderings are very frivolous, often absurd, and of little or no value.

h.—Hebrew; many Hebrew names are found in the Bodmin Manumissions.

h.—*Under* Ros-, &c., *for* heath; *under* TRE-, *for* house.

Hal.—Halliwell's " Dictionary of Archaic and Provincial Words."

Heath's " Account of the Scilly Isles." 1570.

Ili.—" Cornish Names," by T. Hingston, Esq., M.D.; Davies Gilbert's History, v. 4, p. 312.

H M.W.—Mr Henry Michell Whitley, of Penarth

Holloway's (William) " Dictionary of Provincialisms," 1833

H.T.—Mr. Henry Trevascus, of Carsawsen, Mylor, who examined several of the latter proof sheets and gave many suggestions, having long paid attention to the meaning of Cornish Names.

i.—Irish Gaelic.   *e.*—erse.

i.q.—idem quod, the same as; where the word following is in ROMAN CAPS, if it requires an explanation, it will generally be found in its proper alphabetical place. Some of these " synonymes " are mere variations in spelling the name of the same place; others are found attached as distinctive names to different places, though really the same name with a different spelling.

I.T.—Rev. Isaac Taylor's " Words and Places."

J.—P. W. Joyce's " Irish Names of Places," 1869.

J.B.—Mr. John Bellows, of Gloucester, to whom the compiler is deeply indebted for most carefully examining and correcting most of his proof sheets, and for many suggestions and hints, as also for some renderings from Gwavas's MSS.

J.Ca.—The late Rev. John Carne, Vicar of Merther, from whose paper, in the Journal of the Royal Institution of Cornwall, No. 4, p. 10, most of the identifications of the Domesday manors are taken.

J.G.—Mr. John George, fisherman, Mousehole; terms in common use among fishermen.

J.M.—Sir John Maclean, author of the " Parochial and Family History of the Deanery of Trigg Minor."

Jo.C.—The late Mr. Jonathan Couch, of Polperro.

J.W.—Archdeacon John Williams' " Gomer," 1854.

k.—Celtic; as well the Gaelic of Ireland, Scotland, and Man, as the Cymric of Wales, Brittany and Cornwall.

L.—Rev. S. Lysons' " Our British Ancestors," 1865; " Our Vulgar Tongue," 1868, &c.

lat—Latin.

l.—*Under* TRE-, TRET-, &c., *for* land.

Le.– Leland's "Itinerary," 16 cent.; printed in Davies Gilbert's History, v. 4. p. 256.

Leg.– Le Gonidec's "Dictionnaire Breton Francaise," &c., edited by Th. Hersart de la Villemarque, 1850.

Leo "On the Local Nomenclature of the Anglo-Saxons," 1852, &c."

Lh.–Edward Lhuyd's "Archæologia Britannica," 1707, &c.

Lo.–Mark Antony Lower's "English Surnames," 1849; "Patronymica Britannica," 1860.

Ly.–Lysons' (Daniel and Samuel) "Magna Britannia," 1814.

m.– *Under* WHEAL, &c., *for* mine.

m –Modern.

Max M.–Max Müller's "Lectures on the Science of Language." 1864; "Chips," &c.

m.c.–Modern Cornish; words now or recently in use; Mr. T. Q. Couch, Journal of the Royal Institution of Cornwall, No. 1, p. 6; the late Mr. T. Garland, ib., No. 3. p. 45; also, No. 2. p. 75, No. 5, p. 39; Mr. W. Sandys' "Specimens of Cornish Provincial Dialect," with Glossary, 1846, &c.

Mc L.–Mr. H. Mac Lauchlan, of the Ordnance Survey, "On the Duchy Manors, Castles, Earthworks, &c., in Cornwall," in the Reports of the Royal Institution of Cornwall.

mi.–mine.

Moody's (Mrs.) "What is your Name," 1863.

m.s.–Names found in the ancient "Inscribed Stones" of Cornwall, mostly Celto-Roman.

M.–J.W.M.–The Rev. J. W. Murray, Vicar of Mylor, who corrected many of the sheets of the Glossary, and made many suggestions, drawn from his intimate knowledge of the kindred Welsh.

Mur.– Murray's "Handbook of Cornwall."

N.–Mr. Edwin Norris's "Names of Places in Scilly," 'Archæologia Cambrensis,' Jan., 1863, p. 41; "Cornish Drama" 1859, &c.

n.f.– Family names, which the compiler has not found as names of places, at least as so spelt, in the County; most of the Cornish names of estates, &c., are found as family names; there are, however, many others from a great variety of sources and languages; very many patronymics, and corruptions of Christian names, and some nicknames.

nickn.–Nickname.

Nord.–Norden's "Speculi Britanniæ Pars," 1728, written 1584.

North's "Week in the Isles of Scilly," 1850.

O.–Dr. Oliver's "Monasticon Diœcesis Exoniensis," 1846; "Lives of the Bishops of Exeter," 1861, &c.

o.–olim, formerly, in olden times, or in old deeds. The compiler would feel obliged to any one having ancient documents, if he would communicate to him archaic modes of spelling.

O.m.–Ordnance Map or Survey.

o.n.–Old Norse.

o.n.f.– Old family name, mostly extinct.

o.w.n.–Old Welsh name; many are marked simply *(w.)*, especially where it is thought a Cornishman, bearing the same or a similar name, has given his name to an estate, &c.

P.–Colonel Peard, of Trenython, who kindly corrected and annotated the latter sheets of the Glossary, and has already given conjectural renderings of most of the Unexplained Names.

Ped.–E. H. Pedler's "Anglo-Saxon Episcopate of Cornwall," 1856; "Names of Places in the Cornish Dramas," 1859, &c.

pers.–Persian.   *ph.*–Phœnician.

Po.–Polwhele's "History of Cornwall" 1806; "Historical Views of Devonshire,"1793,&c.

Pr.–Dr. Pryce's "Mineralogia Cornubiensis," 1778; "Archæologia Cornu-Britannica," 1790, especially the "List of Cornish British Names," believed to be chiefly those explained by E. Lhuyd, and alluded to by him in a letter to Tonkin, May 4, 1703, printed by Dr. Pryce.

pr.–pronounced.

p.s.–Marks most of the ancient parishes in the County (as *c.d.* chiefly does the modern ones), and shews the patron saint, chiefly as determined by Dr. Oliver.

R.B.K.–The Rev. Richard Byrne Kinsman, Vicar of Tintagel.

R.E.–Mr. Richard Edmonds' "Land's End District," &c.

redup.–Reduplication, when the same word is repeated in a name in two languages, &c.

R.H.–Mr. Robert Hunt, author of "Romances and Drolls of the West of England," 1865.

R.S.H.–The Rev. R. S. Hawker's "Footprints," "Echoes," &c.

R.W.–The Rev. Robert Williams, author of "Eminent Welshmen," where most of the Welsh personal names are found; "Lexicon Cornu-Britannicum," the authority mainly followed in the orthography and signification of old Cornish words, &c. Mr. Williams examined the MS. of the Glossary before it was put into the printer's hands, and corrected every sheet as it passed through the press; the number of annotations, suggestions, and corrections made by him on some of these, would shew how carefully he did this, and how much the compiler is indebted to his invaluable aid.

s.—*Under* VENTON &c., *for* spring.   s.—Saxon, mostly Anglo-Saxon; in the lists of Unexplained Names, serf.

sans.—Sanscrit

s.B.m.—Serf. Bodmin Manumission.   *See B.m.*

Sc.—Scawen's " Observations on an Ancient Manuscript, the Passio Christi," &c , and " A Dissertation on the Cornish Tongue "; Davies Gilbert's History, v. 4, p. 190. Mr. Scawen was Vice-Warden of the Stannaries, 17 cent

S.G.—S. Greatheed's (Exeter, 1808) MS. notes, in Mr. Hugh Sims's copy of " Pryce's Archæologia."

T. - Thomas Tonkin (18 cent.).   *See D., Gw.,* and *Hals.*

t. —Teutonic.

t.—*Under* TRE-, &c , *for* town, town-place.

Ta.—Tithe Apportionment. Wanted the loan of those named on the cover of Part IV (p. 200), excepting those of S. Anthony in Meneage. Crowan, Sithney, and S. Veep, received since that part was published, in June, 1870.*

t.b. – Tin bounds.

T.C.—Mr Thomas Cornish, of Penzance, who corrected many of the sheets of the Glossary, and made many suggestions. The compiler is indebted to him also for the loan of " Particulars of the sale by auction " of large estates, with plans, and his renderings of many of the Cornish Names ; as also for provincial words collected by him at the Assizes, sessions, magistrates' meetings, &c.

t.d.d.—Tenants named in the Domesday Survey; most of these names are decidedly. Teutonic ; a very small number can be at all looked at as possibly Celtic.

T.Q.C.—Mr. Thomas Quiller Couch. of Bodmin, who is passing through the press " The History of Polperro." He kindly lent the compiler his interleaved copy of the " Index to Martyn's Maps," with translations of several names by himself and others.

T.R.—Richards' " British or Welsh and English Dictionary."   Tr.—Dr. Tregellas.

v.—Vulgo, vulgarly, commonly.

w.— *Under* VENTON, &c., *for* well ; *under* WHEAL, &c., *for* work.

w.—Welsh ; but in the list of Unexplained Names, witness.

w.B.m.—Witness, Bodmin Manumissions   *See B.m.*

W.B.—Mr. William Bottrell, author of '· Traditions and Hearthside Stories of West Cornwall." 1870, who corrected and annotated several sheets of the Glossary.

W.C.B.--Mr. Borlase, of Castle Horneck, Penzance ; to whom the compiler is indebted for several renderings, marked B., from the manuscripts of Dr. Borlase.

Wh.—Whittaker's " Ancient Cathedral of Cornwall," 1804 ; Supplement to Polwhele, &c.

W.I.—The Rev. W. Iago, of Westheath. Bodmin.

Woodley's " View of the present state of the Scilly Isles," 1822.

W.S.—Mr. Whitley Stokes' " Passion," 1861 ; " Gwreans an Bys," 1863 ; " Cornish Glossary," 1870, &c.

w.s.—Welsh Saints ; the names mostly taken from Rice Rees' " Welsh Saints "; and Williams's " Ecclesiastical Antiquities of the Cymri."

W.W.—Mostly William of Worcester's " Itinerary," Davies Gilbert's History, v. 4, p. 222

W.W.K.—Mr. W. Worth Kempthorne, of St. Ives.

Y.--Miss Yonge's " History of Christian Names," 1863.

Z.—Zeuss's " Grammatica Celtica." 1853.

? marks a purely conjectural rendering, &c. ; ? ? a doubly doubtful one ; confirmation or correction solicited from persons bearing the names, or acquainted with the history, traditions, and peculiarities of the places.

!, !!, point to something more or less extraordinary, out of the way. and apparently unfounded. Such is often the case with Hals's derivations and renderings.

= shews that the name is thought to be equivalent to the word or words following.

ROMAN CAPS used for a personal or family name, supposed to enter into the composition of a local name, shew that that name, if requiring explanation, will be found in its proper alphabetical place.

---

* The compiler begs to thank the many Clergy, and other gentlemen, who have lent or procured for him the loan of Tithe Apportionments. He would especially name the following, on account of the number they procured him : Rev. J. J. Wilkinson, Lanteglos by Camelford ; Rev. C. M. E. Collins, Trewardale; Mr. T. Cornish and Mr. Bottrell, Penzance ; Mr. N. Hare, junr., and Mr. T. A. Glubb, Liskeard; Messrs. Badcock, S Stephens by Launceston ; Mr. Preston Wallis, Bodmin ; Mr. Trewbody Carlyon, Mr. Whitley, and Mr. Symonds, Truro ; Mr. Cunnack, Helston ; Mr. Reginald Rogers, Carwinion.

SUBSCRIBERS' NAMES.

His Royal Highness The Prince of Wales, Duke of Cornwall.
His Imperial Highness Prince Louis Lucien Bonaparte.
The Right Honourable the Earl of Devon.
The Right Honourable the Earl of St. Germans. (2 copies).
The Right Reverend the Lord Bishop of Exeter.
The Right Reverend the Lord Bishop of St. Davids.
The Right Honourable Lord Eliot.
The late Sir Charles Lemon, Bart., *Carclew.*
Sir John Salusbury Trelawny, Bart., M.P., *Trelawne.*
Sir W. C. Trevelyan, Bart., *Wallington, Newcastle-on-Tyne.*
The late Sir William Williams, Bart., *Tregullow.* (4 copies).
Sir Frederick M. Williams, Bart., M.P., *Goonvrea.*
Sir Chas. Trevelyan, K.C.B., *London.*
Sir Edward Smirke, *Brompton, London.*
Sir John Maclean, F.S.A., *Pallingswick Lodge.*

Adams, Rev. J., *Stockcross Vicarage, Berkshire*
Andrew, Mrs. Zaccheus, *St. Day*
Andrew, Henry, M.R.C.S., *Truro*
Andrews, Henry, *Truro Vean Terrace, Truro*
Arthur, Captain W. S., R.N., *Penzance*
Arthur, Samuel Pellew, M.R.C.S., *St. Day*
Badcock, Messrs., *S. Stephens by Launceston*
Baker, Rev. Charles, *Bradninch, Devon*
Barham, Francis, *Bath*
Barnett, John, *St. Day*
Barnicoat, Rev. H. L., *Landrake Vicarage*
Bate, C. Spence, F.R.S., *Plymouth*
Beale, Rev. William, *Liskeard*
Bellows, John, *Gloucester*
Berry, Rev. W. Aubrey, *West Cowes, I. W.*
Bickford, late Major, *Tuckingmill*
Belling, — *Fore Street, Bodmin*
Blamey, Philip, *Cusgarne, Gwennap*
Blight, J. T., F.S.A., *Penzance*
Bloxsome, Rev. W. H., *Mawgan Rectory*
Boase, Rev. Charles William, *Penzance*
Boase, George Clement, *London*
Boger, Deeble, *Wolsdon, Antony*
Bolitho, T. S., *Penalverne.* (2 copies)
Bolitho, William, Junr., *Polwithan*
Borlase, Rev. W., *Zennor Vicarage*
Bosworth, Rev. Professor, *Oxford*
Bosworth, Thomas, *High Holborn*
Bottrell, William, Jun., *Penzance*
Brash, Richard Rolt, M.R.I.A., *Ireland*
Briggs, Arthur, *Bradford, Yorkshire*
Brougham, Rev. M. N., *Gunwalloe Vicarage*
Brune, R. C. Prideaux, *Place, Padstow*
Buller, Rev. Richard, *Lanreath Vicarage*
Carew, W. H. Pole, *Antony*
Carlyon, E. Trewbody, *Trevré, Truro*
Carne, late Rev. John, *Eglos-Merther*
Casey, Rev. E., *Attenborough, Notts*
Chappel, Rev. W. P., *Camborne Rectory*
Chilcott, J. G., *Gwendroc House, Truro*
Chorley, Chas., *Lemon Street,* ,,
Church, Rev. G. L., *Chacewater Vicarage*
Clarke, S. T., *Dowlais House, Merthyr Tydvil*
Clogg, Stephen, M.R.C.S., *Looe*
Cocks, Colonel, *Treverbyn Vean*
Code, Theophilus, *Marazion.* (2 copies)
Coffin, T. W., *Stoke, Devonport*
Coles, Robert, LL.D., *London*
Collins, Rev. C. M. E., *Trewardale*
Collins, J. H., F.G.S., *Falmouth*
Coode, Edward, *Polapit Tamar*
Corfield, T. J. Tressider, *St. Day.* (2 copies)
Cornish, J. H., *Market Street, Penzance*
Cornish, Thomas, *Clarence Place, do.*
Couch, late Jonathan, *Polperro*
Couch, T. Quiller, M.R.C.S., F.S.A., *Bodmin*
Courtney, W. Prideaux, *London*
Curgenven, J. Brendon, F.R.C.S., *London*
Cunnack, James, *Helston*
Dabb, Frederick W., *Perranarworthal*

Danbuz, Rev. J. C., *Killiow, Kea*
Davey, William, *Ninnes, St. Day*
Davies, Miss, *Penmaen Dovey, Wales*
Dix, W. G., *Lemon Street, Truro*
Duckworth, Rev. Robert, *Tiverton*
Edmonds, Richard, *Plymouth*
Edmonds, Rev. Walter, *Exeter*
Edwards, Thomas, *Helston*
Ellacombe, Rev. H. I., *Clyst St. George, Devon*
Enys, John S., *Enys, Penryn.* (3 copies)
Enys, Miss   do.   (2 copies)
Falmouth, The Public Library
Ferguson, Robert, *Morton, Carlisle*
Fisher, Edward J., *Ashby de la Zouch*
Ford, Rev. Prebendary, *Bath*
Fortescue, The Hon. G. M., *Boconnoc.* (2 copies)
Fox, Cornelius B., M.D., *Scarborough*
Freeman, John D., *Falmouth*
Freeth, G., *Duporth, S. Austell*
Garland, Mrs., *Fairfield, Illogan*
Genn, J. H., *Liverpool*
Genn, W. J., *Falmouth*
George, Mrs., *Market Street, St. Day*
Gilbert, The Hon. Mrs. Davies, *Trelissick*
Green, Richard, *Trevarth House*
Green, William, *Fenchurch Street, London*
Grylls, Lieut.-Colonel, *Sewarne, Liskeard*
Grylls, William, *Redruth*
Hamer, Edward, *Talywaen, Monmouthshire*
Harding, Jonathan, *Porthallow, Liskeard*
Hare, N., *Liskeard*
Harris, Peter, *Mellanear, Hayle*
Harrison, Alfred, M.R.C.S., *Walsall, Staffordshire*
Harry, Richard, *Bow, London*
Harvey, Mrs., *Greenway, Devon* (2 copies)
Harvey, Frank, *Foundry, Hayle*
Harvey, William, M.R.C.S., *Penzance*
Hattam, Thomas, *S. Anthony Lighthouse*
Haughton, late Rev. W., *Manaccan Vicarage*
Hawke, Edward Henry, *Tolgulla*
Hawke, late E. H., Junr.,   do.
Hawkesley, Rev. J. H., *Redruth Rectory*
Hawkesley, Rev. J. W., *Lostwithiel*
Heard, Edward, *Truro.* (2 copies)
Henwood, W. Jory, *Penzance*
Herriot, George, *Liskeard*
Hewitt, Mrs., *Westbury, Bristol*
Hext, Rev. George, *S. Veep Vicarage*
Hill, Rev. George, *S. Winnow Vicarage*
Hockin, Rev. Frederick, *Phillack Rectory*
Hocking, John, *Trewirgie, Redruth*
Hodge, Henry, *Bosustow, S. Levan*
Holman, Miss, *Church Street, S. Day*
Hoskin, Capt., 105th Regiment, *Ellenglaze, Cubert*
Hughan, W. J., *High Cross, Truro*
Hunt, Robert, F.R.S., *London*
Hurden, Rev. J. Nott Dyer
Iago, Rev. William, *Westheath, Bodmin*
Jackson, Joseph G., *Belper, Derbyshire*
Jago, Frederick W., M.D., *Plymouth*

James, Rev. T., *Netherthong, Yorkshire*
Jane, Rev. John, *Tavistock*
Jeffery, John, *Perranarworthal*
Jenkin, Silvanus W., *Liskeard*
Joseph, Joseph, F.S.A., *Brecon, Wales*
Karkeek, Paul Q., *Chester*
Kempthorne, W. Worth, *S. Ives*
Kennerley, Joseph Charles, *London*
Kitt, William, *Penzance*
Kneebone, William E., *Pensilva, Liskeard*
Lake, William, *Boscawen Street, Truro*
Latimer, Isaac, *Plymouth*
Laurence, N. H. P., *Launceston*
Lee, Mrs. Chas. H. L., *Matlock Bath, Derbyshire*
Le Grice, D. P, *Trereife, Penzance*
Lemon, General, C B, *Mutley, Plymouth*
Lockwood & Co., Messrs.
Longman, Green & Co., Messrs., *London*
Lower, Mark Antony, *Lewes, Sussex*
Lysons, Rev S, *Hempsted Court, Gloucester*
Mackenzie, John W., F.S.A., Scot., *Edinburgh*
Mann, A. M., H M C., *London*
Marrack, George M., *Newlyn West*
Martin, John, *Trethowell, St. Austell*
Martin, Thomas, *do.*
Mason, Rev R Williams, *Anglesey*
Matthews, Benjamin, *St. Day*
Michell, Edmund, *Tresithney, Carharrack*
Michell, F. W, M R C.S., *Redruth*
Michell, George, M.R.C.S., *St Day*
Michell, Henry, *Wheal Rose, Scorrier*
Michell, late Thomas, M.D, *Redruth*
Michell, William, *Trevethan*
Mitchell, Samuel, *Perran-Coombe Mill*
Morris, E R., F.Eth.S.L., *Gungrog Cottage, Welshpool.*
Morshead, Walter, *Temple, London*
Müller, Professor Max, *Oxford*
Netherton, J. R., *Truro*
Ninness, John, *Chacewater*
Norris, Edwin, *Brompton.* (2 copies)
Noye, William D, *London*
Parry, T. Love D. Jones, M.P., *Madryn Park, Pwllheli, Wales*
Pascoe, J. R. Cartell, *Preston, Lancashire*
Paull, Alexander, F.R.C.S, *Truro*
Pearce, Edward, *Whitehall, Scorrier*
Pearce, Richard, *Swansea*
Peard, Colonel, *Trenython, Par*
Penrose, John F., *Parkhenver, Redruth*
Pentreath, Captain B, *Mousehole*
Pentreath, Richard, H.M C, *London*
Pentreath, Richard, *Blackheath*
Pentreath, Captain W., *Mousehole*
Penzance Public Library
Peter, John Luke, *Trengwreath* (2 copies)
Petherick, T. H. J, *S. John's College, Hurstpierpoint*
Phillips, Capt., *Blackwater*
Phillpotts, Rev Thomas, *Porthgwidden*
Pode, J. D, *Paddington, London*
Polkinghorne, William, *Woodlands, Par*
Polsue, Joseph, *Bodmin*
Rashleigh, Rev Stanhope, *S. Wenn Vicarage*
Remfrey, George F., *Truro*
Richards, William H, *Stepney, London*
Rickards, Rev. R. F B., *Constantine Vicarage*
Roberts, Rev. W Pender, *Trevalga Vicarage*
Robinson, Joseph B, *Derby*
Rodd, Francis, *Trebartha Hall*
Rogers, Miss, *Penrose* (3 copies)
Rogers, Reginald, *Carwinion.*
Rogers, Rev. Saltren, *Gwennap Vicarage*
Rogers, Rev. William, *Mawnan Sanctuary*
Roscorla, John, *Penzance*

Rounsevell, John, *Tregatherall*
Royal Institution of Cornwall
Sanders, W. B., *Wadham House, Liskeard*
Sandys, William, F.S.A., *London*
Saunders, Rev. Cossley Diggle, *Tarrant Hinton*
Scantlebury, William, *Hyde Park* (4 copies)
Scrivener, Rev. Dr., *Gerrans Rectory*
Sharp, Edward, M R.C S., *Truro*
Shelley, John, *Plymouth*
Shuttleworth, Rev. Edward, *Egloshayle Vicarage*
Sims, Hugh, *Scorrier*
Smith, Augustus, *Tresco Abbey* (4 copies)
Smith, J. Russell, *Soho Square, London*
Smythe, Warrington W., *Marazion*
Solomon, Thomas, *Truro*
St. Aubyn, John, M.P., *Pendrea*
St. Aubyn, J. P., *The Temple, London*
St. Aubyn, W. J., *68th Light Infantry*
Stratton, Dr., R.N., *Stoke, Devonport*
Stuart, John, F.S.A., Scot., *Edinburgh*
Symons, John, *Mayon House, Sennen*
Szyrma, Rev. W. S Lach, *Carnmenellis Vicarage*
Tabb, William, *Burwithan, St. Day*
Tatham, Rev. Prebendary, *Bradock Rectory*
Thomas, Henry, *London*
Tom, P. Sandys, *Rosedale, Truro*
Tom, Miss, *Trehaverne*, *do.*
Tombs, Rev. J., *Burton Rectory, Pembroke*
Treby, late H. H., *Goodamore, Devon*
Treffry, Rev. E. J., D.C.L., *Place, Fowey*
Treffry, George, *Exeter* (2 copies)
Tregay, William, *Pednandrea, Redruth*
Tregoning, James, *Tolgullow*
Tregoning, William, *Skyburrier, Gwennap*
Trehayne, John, *Exeter*
Tremayne, Captain, *North Treskerby*
Trengrouse, Henry, *London*
Tresidder, W. Tolmie, *St. Ives*
Tresidder, S. J. N., H.M.C., *Falmouth*
Tripp, C. Upton, *Trent College, Notts*
Tuck, William R., *Truro*
Tucker, E. Beauchamp, *Trevince*
Turnbull, G.W., M.D., *Exmouth*
Tweedy, A. E., *Truro*
Tweedy, H. J, *Lincoln's Inn*
Tweedy, Robert, *Tregolls*
Tyacke, Miss, *Helston*
Tyacke, Rev J. Sydney, *Helston Vicarage*
Vawdrey, Rev. A. A., *St. Agnes Vicarage*
Vivian, Hussey, M.P., *Park Wern, Swansea*
Vosper-Thomas, Samuel, *Eastbrooke, Dorset*
Wallis, Preston J., *Bodmin*
Way, Albert, F.S.A., *Reigate, Surrey*
Wellington, R., *Chyandour, Penzance*
Whitley, H. Michell, *Penarth, Truro*
Wildman, A. C., *Penzance*
Wilkinson, Rev. J. J., *Lanteglos Rectory*
Williams, Miss, *Tregullow*
Williams, George, *Scorrier House* (2 copies)
Williams, John, *Penryn*
Williams, Michael, *Tregullow*
Williams, Richard, M.R.C.S., *Truro*
Williams, Charles H., *Treviskey*
Williams, B., *Truro*
Willyams, E. W. Brydges, M.P., *Nanskeval*
Willyams, Arthur C. P., *Bodrean, Truro.*
Wise, Rev. R Farquhar, *Ladock Rectory*
Wright, Abraham, *London*
Wright, Rev. F. H. A., *Stythians Vicarage*
Wright, J., *Boslandew, St. Paul*
Wright, Martin, *Mousehole*
Wulff, Rev. J. Gee, *Illogan Rectory*

NETHERTON, PRINTER, TRURO.

2990

www.ingramcontent.com/pod-product-compliance
Lightning Source LLC
Chambersburg PA
CBHW030104030726

47498CB00007B/2251